Way and Byway

A

Philip E. Lilienthal

BOOK

The Philip E. Lilienthal imprint
honors special books
in commemoration of a man whose work
at the University of California Press from 1954 to 1979
was marked by dedication to young authors
and to high standards in the field of Asian studies.
Friends, family, authors, and foundations have together
endowed the Lilienthal Fund, which enables the Press
to publish under this imprint selected books
in a way that reflects the taste and judgment
of a great and beloved editor.

The publisher gratefully acknowledges the generous contribution to this book provided by the Philip E. Lilienthal Asian Studies Endowment, which is supported by a major gift from Sally Lilienthal.

WAY AND BYWAY

*Taoism, Local Religion, and Models of Divinity
in Sung and Modern China*

ROBERT HYMES

University of California Press   Berkeley   Los Angeles   London

University of California Press
Berkeley and Los Angeles, California

University of California Press, Ltd.
London, England

© 2002 by the Regents of the University of California

Library of Congress Cataloging-in-Publication Data

Hymes, Robert P.
    Way and byway : Taoism, local religion, and models of divinity in Sung and modern China / Robert Hymes.
       p. cm.
    Includes bibliographical references and index.
    ISBN 0-520-20758-0 (cloth : alk. paper)—ISBN 0-520-20759-9 (pbk. : alk. paper)
    1. Religion and culture—China. 2. China—Religious life and customs. 3. Taoism. 4. Gods, Chinese. I. Title: Taoism, local religion, and models of divinity in Sung and modern China. II. Title.
    BL65.C8 H95 2002
    299'.51—dc21   2001041451

Manufactured in the United States of America
11 10 09 08 07 06 05 04 03 02
10 9 8 7 6 5 4 3 2 1

The paper used in this publication is both acid-free and totally chlorine-free. It meets the minimum requirements of ANSI/NISO Z39.48–1992 (R 1997) (*Permanence of Paper*).♾

*For Dell Hathaway Hymes and Virginia Dosch Hymes
and for Hans Wolff (1920–1967)*

Contents

	List of Illustrations	xi
	List of Abbreviations	xiii
	Acknowledgments	xv
1.	Introduction	1
2.	Celestial Heart Taoism	26
3.	Hua-kai Mountain and Its Immortals	47
4.	The Rise of the Hua-kai Cult	76
5.	Explaining the Rise of the Hua-kai Cult	114
6.	Taoists, Local Gods, and the Transformation of Wang Wen-ch'ing	147
7.	The Bureaucratic Model: A Speculation	171
8.	God Worship and the *Chiao*	206
9.	Conclusion: The Two Models	261
	Appendix. Source Issues	271
	Notes	281
	Bibliography	329
	Glossary of Chinese Characters	339
	Index	349

Illustrations

Map 1. Celestial Heart practitioners active in the Sung / 41

Map 2. Mountains of Fu-chou and its region / 52

Map 3. Places of origin of Northern Sung Taoists active in the capital / 177

Map 4. Places of origin of Northern Sung Taoists not active in the capital / 178

Map 5. Places of origin of Southern Sung Taoists active in the capital / 179

Map 6. Places of origin of Southern Sung Taoists not active in the capital / 180

Map 7. Places of origin of Southern Sung Mt. Mao patriarchs / 182

Map 8. Places of origin of Southern Sung Mt. Lung-hu Taoists / 183

Special altar at West Town / 233

Abbreviations

Chia-hua	*Ch'ung-hsu t'ung-miao Shih-ch'en Wang Hsien-sheng chia-hua.* HY 1240, TT 996.
HKS	Shen T'ing-jui, *Hua-kai shan Fu-ch'iu Wang Kuo san chen-chün shih-shih.* TT 556–57, HY 777.
HY	Harvard-Yenching.
ICC	Hung Mai, *I-chien chih* [Record of the Listener]. Peking: Zhonghua shuju, 1981.
KHCA	Ting Hsiang et al., *(Kuang-hsu) Chi-an fu chih.* 1876.
KHCJ	Ch'en Ch'ien et al., *(K'ang-hsi) Ch'ung-jen hsien chih.* 1673.
KHFC	Hsu Ying-jung, *(Kuang-hsu) Fu-chou fu chih.* 1876.
KHLA	Fang Chan et al., *(K'ang-hsi) Lo-an hsien chih.* 1683.
KHNF	Cheng Yueh et al., *(K'ang-hsi) Nan-feng hsien chih.* 1683.
LWKL	Teng Yu-kung, *Shang-ch'ing ku-sui ling-wen kui-lü.* TT 203, HY 461.
MKNF	Li Kuang-jun et al., *(Min-kuo) Nan-feng hsien chih.* 1923.
SKCSCP	*Ssu-k'u ch'üan-shu chen-pen.*
SPPY	*Ssu-pu pei-yao.*
SPTK	*Ssu-pu ts'ung-k'an.*
TCCJ	Sheng Ch'üan et al., *(T'ung-chih) Ch'ung-jen hsien chih.* 1873.
TCIH	Chang Hsing-yen, *(T'ung-chih) I-huang hsien chih.* 1871.
TCLA	Chu K'uei-chang et al., *(T'ung-chih) Lo-an hsien chih.* 1871.
TCLC	T'ung Fan-yen et al., *(T'ung-chih) Lin-ch'uan hsien chih.* 1870.
TCPY	Yuan Miao-tsung, *T'ai-shang tsung-chen pi-yao.* TT 986–87, HY 1217.
THCF	Teng Yu-kung, *Shang-ch'ing t'ien-hsin cheng-fa.* TT 318–19, HY 566.
TSCC	*Ts'ung-shu chi-ch'eng.*
TT	*Tao tsang.*
WWC	Wu Ch'eng, *Wu Wen-cheng chi.* SKCSCP, second collection.
YCFC	Lo Fu-chin, *(Yung-cheng) Fu-chou fu chih.* 1729.

Acknowledgments

The research that led to this book had its beginnings more than fifteen years ago. There were many stops, restarts, and pauses for other projects along the way, all of which taught me much and helped shape the book. Some of those projects arose out of the initiative of friends and colleagues, and I thank in particular William Theodore de Bary, Patricia Ebrey, Steven Sangren, Pauline Yu and Theodore Huters, Stephen West, and (repeatedly) Peter Bol for leading me in directions that from one point of view were scholarly byways but that ultimately helped me find my way.

While writing my first book on the local history of Fu-chou, and afterward, I often wondered whether useful materials were hiding somewhere in the Taoist canon of scriptures, for whose vast contents there was then not even barely adequate bibliographic control. I owe to the late Michel Strickmann my first awareness of a whole book about Fu-chou in the canon, *Verities of the Three Perfected Lords*, the single most important source for this book. I am not sure I ever got around to telling Michel the eerie sort of joy it gave me to read the miracle stories in the *Verities* and find gentlemen and gentlewomen from my first book among their leading characters. It was the kind of feeling he would have appreciated, I think. To Judith Boltz I owe not only the foundation her pathbreaking work provides to anyone whose work touches on Celestial Heart Taoism, but also the invaluable stimulus that conversation and correspondence with her about Celestial Heart and Mt. Hua-kai offered in the earliest stages of my project. One of our friendly arguments is addressed in the Appendix. For the opportunity to see and climb Mt. Hua-kai, Mt. Hsiang, and other Taoist mountains and to visit active shrines to the Three Immortals, I thank a whole host of hosts in China: in particular, Professor Ouyang Xin of Nanchang University and Fang Jun, then of Nanjing University; Chen Haizi, Dai Fangying, Yu Fangsheng, Xu Bingsi, and Chen

Wei of the Cultural Affairs Bureau and county government in Chongren County; County Head Yang and County Office Director Hu in Lean County; County Office Director Liu Zhixun and Foreign Affairs Office Director Xiu Ganchuan in Jinqi County; and the late Professor Qiu Shusen, then director of the Yuan Dynasty Studies Institute at Nanjing University.

I tried parts of the book out on many helpful people along the way. For comments on an early presentation in 1987 of material that eventually found place in several chapters, I thank the members of the Columbia University Seminar on Oriental Thought and Religion, especially Irene Bloom, Wm. Theodore de Bary, John Hawley, and Alex Wayman. For their remarks on earlier versions of Chapter 5, I am grateful to the participants in a 1990 session of the Oriental Studies Colloquium at the University of Pennsylvania, in particular Jeanne diBernardi, the late Robert Hartwell, Terry Kleeman, Susan Naquin, and Paul Smith; and to Poul Andersen, Katherine Bernhardt, Philip Huang, David Johnson, John Shepard, and Richard von Glahn at the Workshop on Chinese Religious Culture in 1991, sponsored by the Center for Chinese Studies and the Southern California China Colloquium. Chapter 7 benefited from the comments of William Boltz, Hill Gates, Elizabeth Morrison, Stephen West, and others when I presented its argument at Stanford University in 1995. Raoul Birnbaum, Glen Dudbridge, John Lagerwey, William Powell, Kristofer Schipper, Stephen Teiser, and Franciscus Verellen offered important thoughts on Chapter 4 when I presented it at the Conference on Saints and Sites organized by Verellen in Paris in 1995; and a crucial critical remark by Ellen Neskar at that conference was a shaping influence on the Introduction. For comments on versions of Chapter 8, I am grateful to Timothy Brook, Katherine Carlitz, Theodore Huters, Bruce Lincoln, Steven Owen, Kenneth Pomerantz, R. Bin Wong, Pauline Yu, and other participants in the Conference on Culture and State in Late Imperial China at Laguna Beach in 1992, as well as to the participants in a follow-up workshop at Irvine in 1993, especially Michael Fuller, Tom Kierstedt, Dorothy Ko, and Richard Okada; and to the members of the Columbia University Seminar on Traditional China, especially Terry Kleeman, Murray Rubinstein, Conrad Schirokauer, and Angela Zito. Chapter 8 is a greatly expanded version of my article "A Jiao is a Jiao is a ? Thoughts on the Meaning of a Ritual," in *Culture and State in Chinese History: Conventions, Accommodations, and Critiques,* edited by Theodore Huters, P. Bing, and Pauline Yu, published by Stanford University Press in 1997.

Peter Nickerson and Edward Davis were kind enough to send me their dissertations, both of which proved important for my larger picture of the history of practitioners' Taoism and for my view of the place of Taoists and spirit mediums in Sung religious life respectively. David Faure shared unpublished work that was crucial to my final chapter and offered very helpful thoughts. Bettine Birge, Peter Bol, Valerie Hansen, Paul Katz, John

Lagerwey, Ellen McGill, Georgia Mickey, Ellen Neskar, and Christian de Pee read parts or all of the manuscript, and all offered valuable comments and corrections. At the publication stage, reader reports from Donald Sutton and Robert Weller were enormously helpful, and criticisms by an anonymous reader helped me articulate the arguments in my last chapter more precisely.

At Columbia I have had the great good luck to find colleagues of rare breadth of interest and generosity. For reading parts of the manuscript, for conversations about the project, or for offering friendly wisdom drawn from fields far from my own, I am grateful to Caroline Bynum, Katherine Eden, Patricia Grieve, Alan Segal, and Elaine Sisman, as well as Vassiliki Limberis of Temple University. Paul Rouzer kindly read my translations of poems and reassured me that I had not completely misunderstood them. Myron Cohen's work has been a constant influence and example and his colleagueship a gift and pleasure. I have had the privilege of teaching students who have taught me in turn; apart from those already mentioned, Jennifer Carpenter, Lucille Chia, Jesse Dudley, Kang Xiaofei, Ari Levine, Liu Hsiang-kwang, Rebecca Nedostup, Zhihong Liang Oberst, Sarah Schneewind, Sarah Thal, and Jaret Weisfogel all contributed to my thinking as the project progressed. My wife, Debora Worth, read the Introduction and advised me on how to shape it for a nonspecialist reader. The love and support that she and my son, Saul Hymes, have given me helped make the book possible.

Midway through my research, having traveled to Mt. Hua-kai and back, I discovered that a woodcut that had long hung on my office wall, a gift from my wife years earlier, was a portrait of the chief of the Four Lords of Pa Mountain, who were rivals of my Three Immortals and whose shrine I had also visited in China; the woodcut appears on the book's jacket. The coincidence not only startled me but made me reflect on the odd chances that had come together to bring me to this topic. Confucius, we are told, did not speak of spirits. Some years ago I would not have expected to write a book about them. If I have been guided here more by Immortals than by Confucius, I hope I have not been led too far astray.

CHAPTER ONE

Introduction

What were the Chinese gods? Were they heavenly officials, governing the fate and fortunes of their worshippers as China's own bureaucracy governed their worldly lives? Or were they personal beings: patrons, or parents or guardians, offering protection to those who relied on them? This book examines these questions through the lens of two new religious traditions of the Sung dynasty. I argue that gods were both, but for different audiences or at different times. Two models informed how the Chinese saw gods, and whether they were bureaucrats or personal protectors depended and still depends on who worships them or who tells about them, in what context, and to what purpose. The setting for much of the book is the birthplace claimed by both new traditions, a misty three-peaked mountain named Hua-kai. Mt. Hua-kai was the scene of wonders told and retold in South China for more than a thousand years.

One day in a time we call the late third century, in a hilly and rustic southern county, two strangers appeared. They were travelers, searching for their lost teacher and bound for fabled Ma-ku Mountain in Nan-ch'eng County to the east; but on their way they saw, towering in the distance to the south, another mountain. They asked the local elders its name. "That is Hua-kai Mountain," the elders said. The two strangers marveled. "It is an auspicious place," they said; "even its name is extraordinary."[1] They found their way to it, cast divining sticks to find a proper resting place, and there began to refine a heavenly elixir of immortality. For these strangers, it seemed, were Taoist masters and far from ordinary men.

The elders visited the two holy men to pay their respects and ventured to ask their names. "We are cultivating our will for the Void," they replied, "and do not wish to tell about it." A later visitor, a fellow Taoist, was able to learn who had been their teacher: a certain Master Fu-ch'iu, "a great Immortal of the higher regions," whom they had known at Chin-hua Mountain far away.

The two strangers stayed at the mountain and proved themselves a boon to the county. They had remarkable powers: they could make stones fly, use divine talismans to communicate with Heaven, bring clouds and rain, aid the harvest, heal the sick, even return the newly dead to life. But they could not linger very long as mortals. In the second year of the reign period Yuan-k'ang, under the state of Chin (292 in the Western calendar), multicolored clouds appeared over the mountain and remained for several days, accompanied by clamoring winds and "Immortals' music." At the end of this time, the two strangers, escorted by a pair of fabulous *luan*-birds and mounted on cranes, rose from the mountain into the heavens.[2]

This story of Hua-kai Mountain and its Two Perfected Lords circulated at least as early as the end of the sixth century, when a Taoist of the Sui dynasty inscribed it on stone. The T'ang dynasty scholar-official Yen Chen-ch'ing retold it in a freshly carved inscription in the late eighth century. Yen was then holding office in Fu-chou, a prefecture in what is today Jiangxi Province, whose jurisdiction then as now included Ch'ung-jen County, where Hua-kai Mountain stands.[3] By that time the mountain held shrines to the two holy men and to their master Fu-ch'iu. Yen tells us that prayers in time of drought never went unanswered. Over time the Two Perfected Lords had become Three: Master Fu-ch'iu, who in some traditions had met the Two at Hua-kai and joined them in their ascent, was worshipped with them. Thus in later times we still read sometimes of Two Perfected Lords, but more often of Three. In Yen Chen-ch'ing's time, the cult of the Three Lords was only one of what must have been a large number of minor local deity cults. Yen gives us no reason to think it reached beyond the neighborhood of Hua-kai Mountain itself. In the next major dynasty, the Sung (960–1278), and its successor, the Yuan (1279–1368), the cult blossomed and spread across the county, the prefecture, and the surrounding Chiang-hsi region.

To trace the rise of this cult, especially among the Southern Sung and Yuan elite, and see its relation both to other strands of Taoist religion that arose in the Sung and to broader social changes in the same period, is one aim of this book. But such a study must have some wider purpose. Why care about a trio of (perhaps) third-century saints and their rise to twelfth- and thirteenth-century fame, and only regional fame at that? Two larger issues come together here. The first is relatively specific in time and place. My own previous research has been part of a body of work arguing that between the Northern Sung (960–1127) and the Southern Sung (1127–1278), the Chinese elite underwent a major shift of concerns and self-conceptions: broadly, a turn from national to local spheres of interest.[4] It can be argued, but has yet to be fully shown, that the change marked an epoch not only within the Sung but in Chinese history as a whole. In Chapter 5, I argue that the growth of the Three Lords cult among the local elites of Ch'ung-jen County, Fu-chou, and surrounding counties gave this change religious expression.

But the issue that has come to stand foremost as this book grew and changed is the one I raised at the start, an issue that grows out of the broader study of Chinese religion. In much anthropological work one may read that religious Chinese project into the supernatural realm the relations and roles of their own society, and so imagine their gods as divine officials operating within a bureaucratic hierarchy. Stephen Feuchtwang, in an article whose argument he has since moved away from, was the first to state the case simply and forthrightly: "I conclude with the proposal that gods are a metaphor for the system of authority, the state."[5] But Arthur Wolf, in one of the most influential articles in the field, gave the idea its classic formulation, placing the gods in a three-term relation that for him exactly mirrored Chinese social structure:

> The conception of the supernatural found in San-hsia is thus a detailed reflection of the social landscape of traditional China as viewed from a small village. Prominent in this landscape were first the mandarins, representing the emperor and the empire; second, the family and the lineage; and third, the more heterogeneous category of the stranger and the outsider, the bandit and the beggar. The mandarins became the gods; the senior members of the line and lineage, the ancestors; while the stranger was preserved in the form of the dangerous and despised ghosts.[6]

This picture seemed to me to raise more questions than it answered. Treating "the system of authority" as equivalent to "the state," as Feuchtwang did, leaps over central issues. Is there only one "system" of authority (at least beyond kinship) in Chinese society, and is that system everywhere, always, and simply the state? The question is especially acute for the student of the Sung and the Yuan, when sources of authority apart from the state gained force in the thinking of major teachers to the elite. In Wolf's three-member social landscape and its divine reflection, where is the village leader, the powerful landlord, or the local gentleman whose power and influence in his own community and locality do not rest on official position? Where is the religious specialist himself? Are equivalents or "projections" of these salient social types simply missing from Chinese religion? If so, why? There were certainly forms of trans-kin authority in Chinese society that did not belong to the sphere of government. Does their omission here reflect who is doing the believing?

Wolf's article had of course allowed for this: note his important qualification, "as viewed from a small village," which implied that there could be other angles of view; but his own study did not unpack the implication. More recent work in new directions, by Emily Martin, Robert Weller, and Steven Sangren, in particular, has set out to do so: to question or complicate Wolf's model and in particular the idea of gods as bureaucrats. This book offers what I hope is a new solution to the problem these and other scholars have worked on.[7] I argue not only that who does the believing is crucial—a point that has been common property in the discussion since Wolf—but specifically that two contending models of authority, used in different proportions by different social actors, informed alternative or competing strands of religion in the Chiang-hsi region in the Sung and Yuan and continue to do so where Chinese worship gods today. Hua-kai Mountain is particularly apt ground for an argument of this kind because it spawned not one but two traditions in the Sung: the layman's cult of the Three Immortals, as well as a sect of professional Taoist practitioners and exorcists called Celestial Heart. The two differed precisely in the weight they gave to the bureaucratic or official model in their image of the divine. This book seeks to show that when that model appears in Chinese portrayals and conceptions we must ask which religious actors are putting it forward, how they are using it, and what alternatives they are excluding. We must notice also when, where, and with whom the model does not appear, and what other models or images we may find instead. Models of the divine were models of *authority* and so always held at least potential implications for the social world, though people did not always engage the potential. But it was just this potential that made it unlikely that models would always be shared.

The contending models that form the book's problem, again, are two: the bureaucratic model on the one hand, and a *personal* model of divinity and of divine-human relations on the other. Just what these are emerges more clearly in the chapters that follow, but let me set them out here in summary. Each comprises a number of elements, separable but in practice usually traveling together. In the bureaucratic model, these include most obviously the explicit representation of (1) gods as officials; but also the representation of (2) divine hierarchy as multileveled; (3) authority for all but the highest gods as originating from *outside*, in a *delegation* by higher figures; (4) human interactions with divine authority as *mediated*, both by lower levels of gods who mediate to higher levels and by religious professionals who mediate between even the lowest gods and humans; (5) gods' relations to specific places and their particular inhabitants as, in principle, temporary and the result of *appointment* rather than of any inherent connection to, or the god's own choice of, a place and its inhabitants.

In contrast, the personal model represents (1) gods as *extraordinary persons*— a deliberately vague formulation, though the frequent Chinese use, when gods or godlike figures are encountered by humans on earth, of the term *i-jen*, literally, "different person" or "extraordinary person," persuades me it is apt; (2) hierarchy between gods and humans or between gods themselves as usually *dyadic* (one-to-one) instead of multileveled, and as based in a variety of connecting principles, including descent, teacher-student or master-disciple ties, or in such media of *chosen* connection as *exchange* or *promise;* (3) gods' authority or special power as *inherent* in the person of the god, rather than delegated—this is an aspect of the god's character as "extraordinary person"; (4) human interactions with divine authority as *unmediated, direct* (or at least relatively so); (5) gods' relations to places and their inhabitants as either *inherent* or founded in the *god's own choice,* and as *permanent.*

To recognize these two models at work in China is to see that in representing gods, the Chinese drew on all the authoritative human relationships known to them from social life, rather than only on relationships within the state or between the state and its subjects. Indeed, in some cases—such as when they formed a tight patron-client relation with a chosen god, a kind of relation not deeply characteristic of real, earthly Chinese social life since at least the Sung—they forged a tie uncommon in their secular lives, and of which perhaps for that reason they felt need. This makes the relation between Chinese religion and Chinese life both more interesting and more intelligible. In talking of religion in this way, I am of course in large part sharing Wolf's and Feuchtwang's own starting point: I am searching out relations between people's views of society and their views of the cosmos. My point is simply that if one takes the notion of such relations seriously, one must expect the models that religion offers to vary with time, with space, with social setting, and with the point of view, life strategy, or even momentary purpose of the modeler; and one must expect even single persons to draw, as they do in everyday social relations, upon a repertoire that includes more than one model. These comments suggest something of the assumptions that lie behind my work, of which I should say more here.

This is a book about history, but it is partly shaped by and shares concerns with social and cultural anthropology. It is a book about religion *as culture,* as part of cultural processes. It is informed by a particular view of culture, for which I have found more resonance in the work of some cultural anthropologists than in others. I see culture, and thus religion within culture, as a *repertoire*—not a smoothly coherent system but a lumpy and varied historical accumulation of models, systems, rules, and other symbolic *resources,* differing and unevenly distributed, upon which people draw and through which they negotiate life with one another in ways intelligibly related to their own experiences, places in society, and purposes. It is by drawing on and choosing among the cultural resources available to them that human beings show themselves as cultural *actors,* as constant makers and remakers of culture, not simply as middlemen through whom culture somehow does its inexorable work. The central project of this book is to connect the different choices that different actors make from a repertoire of religious models to differences in their places in society, the situations in which they find themselves, and their views of religious and secular authority.

This view of culture, and of religion within it, is hardly original, but it does differ from some influential tendencies among historians and anthropologists. During my years as a historian, cultural anthropology has exerted profound influence on the field of history, first largely through the work of Clifford Geertz, and later in more varied ways, though I think Geertz's impact remains strong. The influence has made itself felt in a number of ways, some rather specific and perhaps now less current—the search for rituals or institutions that could be read as paradigmatic of a society or community in the way Geertz famously read the Balinese cockfight, for example—but one that is much more general: the infusion of historical work with a notion of culture as a shared and unitary *system*, all of its parts somehow dependent on one another or informed by a single principle or ethos, and all of its parts common property.[8] Whether this notion adequately represents Geertz's own evolving views is unclear, but in any case, like many commentators on Geertz and on the theory of culture, I find it inadequate to historical and cultural reality.[9] The more recent and still current Foucauldian tendencies and linguistic turn among historians both seem to me to reproduce the assumption of unitary and all-containing (or all-imprisoning) culture or discourse at least as often as they depart from it. My own view may be more akin to anthropological postmodernists, who give full recognition to cultural variety and flux, though I do not share their allergy to large-scale generalization (or the occasional grandish narrative). Closer to my own approach is this statement of the issues by Fredrik Barth:

> [V]ariation in a traditional civilization is not a surface disturbance, to be covered over by generalization or tidied away by a typology. It is a ubiquitous feature of great civilizations, and we should make it a major component of our description and characterization of these societies rather than a difficulty to be overcome. Variation should emerge as a necessity from our analysis. How might that be achieved? First, we must break loose from our root metaphor of society as a system of integrated parts. The image is too simple, and it misleads: the connections we are trying to conceptualize are linkages without determinate edges, in a body without a surface for a boundary.... In a civilization, there is a surfeit of cultural materials and ideational possibilities available from which to construct reality. The anthropologist has no basis for assuming all these materials are contained in one complete, logically compelling package or structure.... *On the contrary the sense that is being made, the reality that is being created, in any community or circle must be diverse.* (1) There are variations in the level of "expertise" in the population: which level could hold authority for all? (2) There is diversity of received traditions. (3) There is a varied particularism of local history, contention, and context. (4) There are all the differences between people in positioning and experience, besides that of expertise: old and young, male and female, rich and poor, powerful and vulnerable. (5) Finally, there is the pragmatics of purpose and interest: differing representations for different tasks. Which should the anthropologist privilege? Or do we adhere to a belief that, if only it is thoroughly abstracted, it all coheres in its essence? [Emphasis mine.][10]

Barth proceeds to organize his book largely around the idea that differing traditions of knowledge coexist, and treats these both as limits on the views available to actors and as resources on which actors draw in imagining and making reality. In this, he is unusually successful, I think, in integrating the materials and distinct traditions of "high culture" into his picture of ordinary social life, treating them as several resources among others that shape actors' views and that actors shape in turn.

For a supporting argument from quite another corner of the field, one may turn to Roy D'Andrade, a leading promoter of the tendency that calls itself cognitive anthropology.

> One of the things that both structuralism and symbolic/interpretive anthropology had as a basic assumption was the idea that culture is *a* structure, or system—some kind of unified thing. Geertz's defense of this during the *Culture Theory* conference was quite passionate . . . : "As I've said before, the elements of a culture are not like a pile of sand and not like a spider's web. It's more like an octopus, a rather badly integrated creature—what passes for brains keeps it together, more or less, in one ungainly whole."[11] . . . The various definitions of culture across the last hundred years have often stressed that culture is "a complex whole," "integrated," "structured," "patterned," etc. This is an article of faith, since no one ever offered an empirical demonstration of any culture's structure. What could be demonstrated was that any one piece of culture was very likely to be connected in *some* way to some other piece. But a world in which everything is somehow related to something else does not make a *structure* or even a *system*, and certainly not "one ungainly whole." . . . During the early years of cognitive anthropology there was an idea that there might be a *grammar* for each culture. The idea . . . did not last very long; the particularities of any domain quickly led away from anything so grandiose. Work across a wide variety of cultural domains in a number of cultures has found that cultural models are independent of each other. The empirical fact is that culture looks more like the collected denizens of a tide pool than a single octopus. Empirical work on plant taxonomies, color terms, models of the mind, navigation, land tenure schemas, kin terms, etc., reveals a world of independent mental representations. Each cultural model is "thing-like," but all the models together do not form any kind of thing.[12]

Barth and D'Andrade may be taken together as arguing against two distinct but often intimately intertwined assumptions about culture. Both those who argue that culture is "unitary" and those who deny it often elide the distinction, so it is important not to miss it. D'Andrade is attacking the assumption of internal integration: that every part of any group's, or presumably any individual's, culture is coherent with every other part. Barth touches on the same issue but draws it into an attack on a related but different assumption: that culture-bearers agree, and that every member of a society carries the same culture. There are thus two different senses here in which culture is *not* unitary: that it is not the same thing *for everybody*, and that it is not just one, or somehow a unified, thing *for anybody*.

Arguments over just these points, and sometimes the confusion of the two, have a deep history in the China field itself, and came to the fore in the conference volume that included Arthur Wolf's founding article. There Maurice Freedman drew a picture of a single Chinese religion, within which variations were only transformations of underlying likeness; or systematic complementarities, thus interdependent parts of a unified system; or examples of "religious similarity . . . expressed as if it were religious difference."[13] Robert J. Smith, approaching the studies in the volume from the outsider's perspective of a Japan specialist and impressed with the variety he saw, countered that it was as likely that Chinese society "treated religious differences as though they were religious similarities," and cited Victor Turner and Harold Rosenberg for a view of culture much like D'Andrade's or Barth's:

> The culture of a society at any moment is more like the debris, or "fall-out," of past ideological systems than it is itself a system, a coherent whole. Coherent wholes may exist, but human social groups tend to find their openness to the future in the variety of their metaphors for what may be the good life and in the contest of their paradigms.[14]

Smith saw that variation could be important even "within the religious life of the individual worshipper"—the not-one-thing-*for-anybody* half of the anti-unitary argument—and argued for treating variation itself as the central phenomenon to be understood and explained. Wolf's introduction to the volume comes down solidly on Smith's side and against Freedman but neglects a large part of Smith's point by stressing variation among persons—the not-the-same-thing-*for-everybody* half—much more than the other. And his own application of Smith's argument to the case of gods as bureaucrats recognizes the possibility of differing *interpretations* or *views* of a single shared model, but neglects the possibility that quite other or opposing models were available.

> We should begin by reconstructing the beliefs of people who viewed the Chinese social landscape from different perspectives. Surely the imperial bureaucracy did not approach *gods modeled on that bureaucracy* with the same attitude as peasants who were understandably awed by the power of imperial officials. The fact that *an idea was shared by people with such very different perspectives* would suggest to me that it was relatively insignificant or that it was easily invested with very different meanings. [Emphasis mine.][15]

To assume that only the bureaucratic model is available, so that differences of perspective can only work themselves out as different interpretations of that model, does indeed threaten to rob it of significance by making it a superficial shell within which the real work of cultural argument goes on unhindered. But this neglects more fundamental difference. Certainly, the model can be invested with different meanings, and certainly that process is significant. But the model can also be rejected or ignored. When one sees that there is more than one model to choose from, the choice of the bureaucratic model by certain people or in certain contexts fills up with meaning again. We shall see, for example, in Chapter 7, contrary to all expectation, that at least in the Sung dynasty, the imperial bureaucracy itself, precisely when it honored gods with official titles, did *not* treat them as "modeled on that bureaucracy," but according to quite a different model. Thus it rejected or left aside the model of gods used by the very Taoist priests it often employed to worship them. And we shall see in Chapter 8 that, in our own time, Chinese peasants sometimes tell anthropologists that gods are like bureaucrats, sometimes vigorously deny it, and often treat them in quite other ways in their own rituals. There are a variety of perspectives *and* a variety of models; and it is the interaction between the two kinds of variety that we should study.

Barth and D'Andrade are thus taking part in a very old argument among anthropologists, an argument that the anthropology of China has already been having with itself. But the argument is not one for anthropologists only. A historical view akin to Barth's and D'Andrade's, and carrying a parallel critique of rival or predecessors' views, seems to emerge strikingly in the new program for social and cultural history articulated in recent years by the enormously influential French journal *Annales*. The program is well represented in a recent conference volume. The editor, Bernard Lepetit, begins by tracing the history of French historiography, or really the *Annales* movement itself, from World War II to the present day, noting its passage in the 1950s and 1960s through a first stage with a "macro-economic approach, the study of social structures, the concurrent analysis of secular trends and of the short conjuncture," and a second stage beginning in the 1970s, in which "the alteration of the historiographic model was assured chiefly by including new objects in the discipline's field: the body, table manners, love, rites of passage, languages, images, myths . . . the study of material culture and of mentalities. This change of project was accompanied by a modification of temporal frames of reference: the apparent inertia of the fundamental categories of cultures led one to pay less attention to development or variation than to the enduring efficacy of such phenomena as lay within the jurisdiction of a history nearly motionless."[16]

After reviewing what he sees as the problems in this second approach—not only its atemporality, but a tendency to fragment the discipline into fields and methods with no points of mutual contact—Lepetit introduces what he sees as the third, and current, project: a new social history that will make its object "the question of identities and of social ties," but treat these not, like the history of mentalities, as part of "a universe of representations indifferent to the situations in which [people] find themselves active," but rather as things worked out in action and use. Where this echoes Barth especially is in bringing to the fore the *problem* of agreement among social and cultural actors, precisely as a problem and not as something assumed. Lepetit proceeds at length to a discussion of norms and conventions, central topics of the collection:

Norms, values, or conventions seem at every moment to draw their force from their duration and appear as a framework inherited from the past, which hems in and molds individual and collective practices. But how could one imagine norms that had not yet been applied? Conventions are at the same time the transitory product of a system of individual interactions: they fashion local agreements but find themselves fashioned in turn by these. . . . Norms and values are polysemic, indeed unstable, in every case susceptible in context to being endowed with variable meaning and sense. . . . Norms and taxonomies are plural, and so can no longer be analyzed in terms of pure imposition, but constitute for actors a set of reference points to situate oneself in relation to and of *resources to mobilize* under the constraint of situations.[17]

Whether D'Andrade, Barth, and the historians of the new *Annales* tendency would agree to being brought together under a single head, I do not know,[18] but my reading of their work has resonated with and supported the theoretical predispositions that shape this book. The purpose of the book is to identify two such resources, two pieces of culture—the two models of divinity—and to show how these and sometimes other models are drawn upon, used, varied, set against one another, and sometimes combined by various religious actors in ways that make sense in relation to their views of authority, relation to authority, or *claims* to authority in the secular world.

But in looking for resonances between religious views and views of authority in society at all, I risk seeming to ally myself with well-known positions I do not share. The idea of religious notions as "projections" of social relations is an old one, associated especially with the name of Emile Durkheim and extremely influential in anthropology and sociology for some years. In one of its most influential forms, it asserts that religious ideas, rituals, and vocabulary are not about what they purport to be about—not about a supernatural world or divine beings really thought to influence human lives—but are really metaphoric assertions "about" society itself. For some theorists, the virtue of this idea is that it argues out of existence beliefs that seem incredible or irrational and so, in a sense, brings the apparent believers back into a common universe of rational, and thus comprehensible, human beings. But it may also simply recognize complexity of possible meanings. This may be part of its appeal to Clifford Geertz, who argued at a conference some years ago for care in taking apparent "false beliefs" at face value:

> It's often very hard to tell whether it's a belief—whether it's an assertive. . . . [Y]ou're not always sure you're faced with a belief, true or false. When a Javanese tells me that his son fell out of a tree because the spirit of his grandfather pushed him out, if I were to take that as a simple empirical proposition in my terms, I have no doubts about whether it is true or false. But I'm not sure that's what's being said. . . . Suzanne Langer once said . . . that the interpretation of Pueblo rain dances as causing rain is really quite wrong. . . . that what the Pueblos are

doing is to present to themselves a living tableaux [*sic*] in which the rain gods, nature, and people are all having some meaningful interaction—a drama.... [W]hat she's saying is that the whole assumption that the Pueblos are thinking about this mechanistically, that they are thinking about it causally may be wrong. They may be trying to imagine for themselves the relationship between rain, people, and landscape.[19]

Here and in Geertz's ethnographic work, it is clear he is attracted to such interpretations, but in this passage he only proposes them as possible and urges cautious sensitivity to their possibility. At this level one can hardly disagree. Statements of belief, stories about gods, and rituals addressed to them *may* sometimes have metaphoric or dramatizing force, and sometimes that may be their main content. There is no obstacle to accepting this, so long as one is willing also to allow that, say, the Pueblo rain dance *may* also be about causing rain and that whether it is or is not is an empirical question. A more exclusive version of Geertz's position is available, however: in this version, claims to interact with or believe in spirits or gods or nonhuman intelligences, and the rites that act out such claims, are *always* about something else and never mean what they seem to say. Edmund Leach may serve as an example when he proclaims almost plaintively: "I . . . continue to insist that religious behavior cannot be based upon an illusion."[20]

The tempting response is, "Why not?" The evidence that human beings may share and have shared a real, thoroughgoing conviction that beings we would call supernatural exist—at least *some* of whom presumably do not—is abundant, strong, and everywhere around us. We ought not to see such convictions as strange, much less as irrational, for we can easily find them in our own culture.[21] We do not elevate our informants to a higher sphere of rationality when we refuse to take their word about what creatures populate their mental and so their social universe: we only assimilate them to our most flattering view of ourselves. One may certainly go on to argue that what they say also means or accomplishes other things, even perhaps things of which they are not aware. But where evidence abounds that, at least at one level, they mean what they say literally, then as a first step we should take it so too. John Skorupski has, I believe, demonstrated that the "not-gods-but-only-symbols" view is, in any conceivable application, logically inconsistent, empirically ill supported, and in any case analytically unnecessary. For Skorupski, there can be no adequate understanding of religious behavior "until it is clearly understood that to a large extent religious rites *are* social interactions with authoritative or powerful beings within the actor's social field, and that their special characteristics are in large part due to the special characteristics these beings are thought to have."[22] The view Skorupski articulates underlies this book as a fundamental assumption, and it is important to lay my cards on the table. The Chinese, many of them at least, interacted with gods as real beings, and the stories they told about them were often—whatever else they may also have meant—statements of things they believed to have happened, thought to be really so. Their religious activity would be incomprehensible if this were not true.

To use the very word "believe," of course, raises still other issues. Some would argue that the word is inappropriate outside a Western or even specifically Christian context: that it presumes a discourse of faith and doubt that one cannot expect to find elsewhere. Others might claim that "believe" is the wrong term to use when people, as far as they are concerned, simply *know* the things we are calling their "beliefs." To say that Chinese believe that obedience to parents is a primary human duty, this argument would run, is to attribute an attitude to the Chinese that is not theirs, an attitude that recognizes the possibility of believing something else. Or finally one might argue that Chinese religion is not about mental commitment to propositions at all, whether this be called belief or knowledge or something else, but about proper ways of speaking and acting.[23] Now, when I say Chinese "believe" in gods, I am using the word in an entirely rough-and-ready sense: that (some) Chinese would, if asked, affirm that there is or may be such-and-such a god who does such-and-such in the world, that he (or she) hears people's prayers and receives their sacrifices, that he is a figure or a force to be reckoned with in planning one's own conduct. I imply nothing about what degree of certainty any particular "believer" feels, whether he more nearly "believes" or "knows" or simply "hopes" or "wagers." I certainly imply no idea of "faith" in a Christian or European sense.

But these disclaimers are not the whole story, for one can certainly defend "belief" as a category in the Sung Chinese world. From Hung Mai's (1123–1202) collection of occult anecdotes, the *Record of the Listener* (*I-chien chih*) one might gather that gods were everywhere in Sung society. If one reads the stories carefully, however, one will see that doubt was everywhere too: doubt whether a particular god was real or a swindle undertaken by charlatans; doubt, when a god was real, whether the words or dream or vision one had received were in fact the god's communication or simply the deception of an impersonating ghost; doubt, when the words or dream or vision were a real communication, whether one had understood them. Each of these issues is sometimes articulated, in Hung's stories, by the word *hsin*, conventionally translated as "believe." As I have shown elsewhere, *hsin* often functions interchangeably in Hung's stories with *i wei jan*, "take (it) to be so": the truth or falsity of a proposition or utterance, the actuality of a state of affairs, is precisely what is at stake here.[24] Often a character, until some crucial event or juncture in the story, does not *hsin*—take it to be so—that the god exists, or that the vision is really from the god, or that the interpretation of the vision is correct; and afterward he does *hsin*. In other contexts, the word conveys something more akin to our "believe in": not a mere recognition of existence, but acknowledgment of authority and power. Chapter 3 recounts the story of a cook who is hired for a ceremony for the Three Immortals although "he did not believe in them [*hsin chih*] at all." After the Three punish him miraculously for urinating at their shrine, he declares: "Now I know that I had committed an offense against the Two Immortals Wang and Kuo, but that the Immortal Perfected in their gracious compassion let me not fall into great harm, merely making known my transgression and making clear their numinous power." This is a tale of conversion, and "belief in" is one of the things at issue.

There were also some in the Sung, especially among Neo-Confucian would-be classicizers of worship and sacrifice, who denied that any of the gods worshipped by the people were actually gods, or at least denied that the worshippers understood the real character of what they worshipped. Some denied that "gods" or "spirits" were persons and argued that they were mere accumulations of *ch'i*, material force, gathered about a place in a sort of quasi-physical response to the natural features of the place and the tendencies of the larger universe.[25] There was power here, that is, but it was natural power, without personality. In short, many a proposition about gods or about some god was asserted in the Sung, and any such proposition was, under the right circumstances or with the right audience, open to question or to denial. In this context, committing oneself in speech or writing or action to a view of some god meant committing oneself on a real question: their question, not just ours. Nor were action and speech everything and thoughts unimportant: long before the Sung, the Taoist *Precepts of the Three Primes* (*San-yuan p'in*) began: "To those who pursue the highest Way! You must not commit the following sins!" and listed as the first and presumably highest sin "to disregard the scriptures and precepts, *harbor doubts*, or *be in two minds* about the teaching" and added as the fifteenth "to receive the scriptures when you do not have belief [*hsin*] or when you *think lightly* of the Way" (emphasis mine).[26] The notion and problem of *hsin* in Chinese religion needs much more inquiry: we cannot assume it encompasses the same range of notions as our "believe." But there is considerable overlap, and the problem of "belief" in a broad sense is a real and public one in the Sung.

But let us return to my central argument. To deny that gods are *only* symbols of something else—to affirm that they were, for their worshippers, precisely gods, powerful personalities with whom one interacted—is again not to deny that they and their worlds may have symbolic force beyond their immediate context, may be both gods and symbols, or at least models, of something else, the social world. It is precisely because gods are, in Skorupski's words, "authoritative or powerful beings," who act as higher members of society or in some conceptions inhabit a special and more perfect society of their own, that believers' notions of what authority is in human society may easily be extended to them, or that the structure of authority among them may become a model for the proper distribution of authority in human society. This is not unconscious and automatic "projection" but simple, often conscious, and sometimes deliberately controversial analogizing. We may expect it to happen, at least, wherever people see their gods as (on the whole) good and their authority as (on the whole) just and legitimate. We may especially expect it where people argue explicitly that the human and divine worlds, earth and Heaven, are parallel, or alike, or parts of an overarching single cosmic and moral whole. And this the Chinese, like many other people, very often did.

I am arguing, then, not for the "projecting" of social relations and roles into a purely symbolic divine sphere, but for a strong, sometimes unthought but sometimes purposeful tendency to analogize between two spheres treated as equally real: from the human to the divine and back again. Where different people hold different views, different experiences, or different expectations of authority on earth, there—if the question of whom and how to worship is salient in their lives—we may expect to find different pictures of the divine as well. These pictures will sometimes be different interpretations of beings or notions that in some broader sense are shared. But they will sometimes be different choices and combinations made from a cultural repertoire of beings, notions, practices, and models that history has made available in their own day. It is the second sort of process that I argue is at work in the growth of the Three Lords cult and accounts for its differences from other traditions of belief and practice that emerge or thrive in the same region. Different views of authority, as well as different social and religious purposes, resonant with different places in society, shaped the choices of available approaches to the supernatural made by men of Chiang-hsi in the Sung.

Before we can move in the chapters that follow to see how this was so, we must look at the world—or rather worlds—that the worshippers of the Three Immortals lived in. We may imagine three spheres of diminishing cultural radius that surrounded them: first, by way of background, the whole rapidly changing social, economic, and political world of Sung China, and, second, the more specifically religious world and the possibilities, problems, and choices that it offered. But finally, we should consider just what sort of world people built around themselves when they chose these Three Immortals to worship.

Sung China, it is by now a cliché to say, was a society in change, so acutely so that Sung observers almost obsessively said it themselves. Naitō Torajirō, of course, called the Sung the world's first modern society, and more recently William McNeill has built a history of power and technology in the world since A.D. 1000 around essentially the same idea. Francis Bacon lent them unwitting and anticipatory support centuries earlier when he argued that the three inventions most consequential for his own world were gunpowder, the mariner's compass, and the printed book. We now know that all three, in their origin or first widespread application, were inventions or innovations of the Sung.[27] If, to this list of Sung transformations, we add coal and paper money, Marco Polo's marvels; the written civil service examination, which Joseph Needham sees as both a signpost of modern bureaucracy and a Chinese export to the West;[28] and perhaps even Sidney Mintz's two historically strategic fuels of working-class consumption and industrial effort, caffeine (in China, tea) and cane sugar;[29] and if we note also that in this period, rice first became the primary food of the Chinese and the main commercial crop of southern China, and that classical learning and ethical self-discovery in their new "Neo-Confucian" form produced the body of texts and commentaries that would be state orthodoxy for the next seven hundred years, then whether or not we choose to call any of this "modern" we may still conclude that China as the West conceives it even today originated in large part in the Sung.

The arguments over modernity, of course, have grown out of the economic and social transformation of China that has been called the "T'ang-Sung transition," beginning presumably in the middle T'ang dynasty (618–906) but clearly extending well into the Sung itself. Its broad outlines are clear. The development of new staple and commercial crops, rice and tea among them; a vast increase in population, particularly in the rice-growing south, reversing the old demographic and economic dominance of the north and promoting the growth of cities; the collapse of the old T'ang system of government markets under the weight of rapidly increasing trade, which generated new markets in city and countryside and extended the reach of the commercial economy and contractual relations into the daily life of the peasantry; an extraordinary expansion in the use of money, which came to include government-issued paper currency for the first time in world history—these are the directions of change that Japanese scholarship in particular has long since made clear. Technological innovation spawned vast new industries in iron and steel and in porcelain, as well as Bacon's three inventions. Gunpowder was used extensively in warfare by the middle Sung. The compass helped to support the vast south-sea trade of the period, which brought Chinese goods to the Indian Ocean world and even to the east coast of Africa. Printing, in some ways the most consequential of the three, gave new opportunities for education and so, as it became easier to grow rich through trade or commercial agriculture, expanded the educated, office-seeking, and largely wealthy elite who found their way into the system of civil service examinations, new in the T'ang and greatly expanded in the Sung. Within this group, as time went on, southerners came to predominate in a way unprecedented in Chinese history.

The lives of ordinary rural people changed too, as money and the market reached deep into the countryside. Commercial cloth production took root inside the individual rural household, employing largely female labor to supplement agricultural or other family income. Everywhere small kilns and potteries, oil presses, wine-making shops, paper-making firms, and similar small enterprises drew on rural labor largely in the agricultural off-season. In the villages, "peasants" themselves (the term grows less appropriate from this period on) divided their labor and specialized at the household-to-household level: in stories and anecdotes of rural life in the Sung, one meets the broommaker, the fish cook, the innkeeper, the petty diviner, the drug seller, the cloth trader, and indeed the landless day laborer as often as the farmer himself. Sung surveyors of rural welfare assumed in drawing up their forms that households with little or no land—and these were the majority of Sung households in the south—would always engage in some non-farming activity at least as a sideline.[30] The pace and content of Chinese daily life had been transformed.

From the Sung on, China would be the most populous political unit in the world, with producing and consuming capacities that repeatedly affected the commercial patterns and balance of trade of the Indian Ocean, the Islamic world, and even Europe in ways largely favorable to China right through the eighteenth century. But politically the international outlook was problematic. Historians divide the Sung into two periods, lying on either side of a major political and territorial change. From the late tenth century to the 1120s, during what we now call the Northern Sung, the Sung governed almost all of China proper. The Liao state of the Khitan people to the north controlled only a strip of sixteen prefectures at the northern edge of what had traditionally been Chinese territory. The Sung capital was K'ai-feng, lying on the north China plain. But in 1126 a successor state to the Liao, the Chin, founded by the Jurchen people of what is now Manchuria, drove down on the Sung from the north and seized the capital. In the years that immediately followed, the Chin was able to consolidate its control of northern China, and the Sung state was forced into a southern territory only two-thirds its former extent, with its capital at Hang-chou. This situation continued to 1278, when a third northern people, the Mongols, conquered the Sung and reunited China under their Yuan dynasty. Historians call the period of reduced territory the Southern Sung.

The consequences of the loss of the north were considerable. Defense of a long northern frontier continued, as in the Northern Sung, to drain the resources of the state into military expenditures. At the same time, the catastrophe had largely discredited the expansive state-building efforts of the reforming minister Wang An-shih and his successors of the same party in the late Northern Sung. In the new climate, state action from the center to address problems in the localities, whether to strengthen order, to generate wealth, to redress the consequences of economic change, or simply to enrich the state purse (all aims claimed by or attributed to Wang An-shih), no longer commanded the support of the intellectual and political elite, and so was no longer a serious possibility. In fact, from a combination of causes, state power in the localities diminished in the Southern Sung. Local order sometimes became precarious, and outbreaks of banditry and famines more frequent, while despite its weakness, the state may still have satisfied its hunger for revenue well enough to contribute to economic stagnation or even depression in the countryside, though this remains very uncertain. Among intellectuals and the educated generally, the loss of interest in state action or reform on a large scale partly informed the rise of the school of Neo-Confucianism called the Learning of the Way (*tao-hsueh*), which retained the utopian view of a lost classical age and something of the belief in human perfectibility that had been Wang An-shih's, but relocated the route to a moral society in the individual and his learning and cultivation and saw the improving of the social world—still keenly felt as sick and in need of cure—as dependent on individual and private action in local communities. This may have made the doctrine attractive to wealthy and educated gentlemen more and more inclined, or impelled by circumstances, to concern themselves with local and private matters and to define themselves by their position in their communities and counties.

Ch'ung-jen County and Fu-chou, the county and surrounding prefecture in which Hua-kai Mountain stood and where the cult of the Three Immortals had its center, lay well south of the new border with the Chin state and so suffered much less directly from the Chin invasion and the loss of the north than some other regions of southern China, though we shall see in Chapter 5 that the war and its penumbra of marauding soldiers did for a time reach here and may have made a considerable impression on the local elite. Disorder and dearth increased here, as elsewhere. Fu-chou, a hilly, well-watered, relatively prosperous rice-producing region, and in contemporary terms a highly cultured prefecture, had been a leading producer of civil service degree holders and officials of all ranks in the Northern Sung; Wang An-shih himself was a Fu-chou man. Examination success and office-holding continued strongly in the Southern Sung, though not so exceptionally as before, and high officials in particular did not emerge from Fu-chou nearly as often. The prefecture had continued cultural prominence as one of several centers of Neo-Confucian learning in the broader Chiang-hsi–Fu-chien region and as the home of an important teacher, the philosopher and skilled debater Lu Chiu-yuan (1140–1192). But in this period, the wealthy and educated men of Fu-chou blossomed as a *local* elite. Gentlemen (and often gentlewomen too) were founders and sponsors of community institutions—schools, academies, charitable granaries, famine-relief programs; leaders when necessary of local militia and self-defense organizations; poets and members of poetic and scholarly clubs and societies; organizers of lineages and charters of genealogy; and significantly for our purposes here, donors to Buddhist monasteries, Taoist abbeys, and shrines to local gods.[31]

Against this broad background, the devotees of the Three Lords cult offered their prayers and the Taoist practitioners of Celestial Heart performed their rites, how and to what ends we shall see. But I have said almost nothing so far of religion. One may enter the Sung religious world through the stories in the *I-chien chih* of Hung Mai, who collected the tales of gods, ghosts, miracles, unexplained events, and weird apparitions that people told him as true over a period of decades, publishing them in installments to an increasingly eager reading public. What strikes the eye first in Hung's stories is variety: variety of actors, variety of acts, variety of texts, variety of ideas, variety of gods, variety of *religions*. Nonetheless, certain broad notions do seem common ground, especially if we start from the perspective of ordinary laypeople—people neither specialist in religious matters nor unusually wealthy or educated. First: souls migrated. That the spirit of a dead person traveled to a purgatorial underworld governed by a large and frightening, if ultimately just, bureaucracy; that it was there judged, perhaps punished, and in the end assigned a new place, which might be a new life and new body on earth, a position in the underworld administration itself, or even in some cases the status of a god: all this seems to have been common knowledge, accepted or at least acted upon not only by most laypeople but also by both professional clergies, Buddhist and Taoist, if not necessarily by some intellectuals. This knowledge supplied many of the problems to which Sung religion offered solutions. One might want to influence the fate of a soul, whether a parent's or one's own, perhaps to gain a quicker or more satisfactory new placement, perhaps to help it into a paradise from which future ill rebirths would not occur. One might want to placate a soul that had received permission from the underworld to haunt one in revenge for a grievance in life, or a soul who had no descendants to give it sacrifices and wandered the earth in anger. That is, there were ghosts, and they could cause trouble. Sometimes they could even set themselves up as gods without proper authority; or so Taoists would see it. For all these problems religious professionals, Buddhists and Taoists as well as village spirit mediums and the like, could offer their rites as solutions. One might also want to break out of the normal cycle and free oneself from unpredictable and painful rebirths by seeking enlightenment and release in the life of a Buddhist monk or by cultivating one's inner embryo and pursuing immortality as a Taoist. In any case, one could care for one's own ancestors—who were not usually conceived of as especially powerful for good and ill, to be sure—with regular sacrifice and veneration.

Second: there were, or probably were, or might be, gods. Gods came in many forms, some of them adopted into the everyday religion of ordinary people from the pantheons of the professional clergies, some of them moving in the other direction into the clergies' rites, some of them held largely as their own by clerics or by the state and never worshipped by laymen. Many had been living human beings and become gods after their deaths, some through virtue, some by the disturbing or amazing ways they had died. For professional Taoists, the real or most legitimate divinities were the Immortals and the Perfected, who had gained their immortality and their positions in the ruling heavenly bureaucracy through Taoist cultivation. For professional Buddhists, "god" was one level of rebirth like rock or animal or woman or man, but alongside or above these gods, there were also bodhisattvas and Buddhas, the successful pursuers of enlightenment, who regarded the world with grace and benevolence and who had their own godlike powers. Both clergies thus asserted the primacy of their own means to salvation over ordinary people's worship of what in any case might not be real or proper gods, and Taoists in particular represented themselves as the legitimate and only reliable middlemen for dealing with the divine. For ordinary people, however, gods of whatever origin had or might have power, might help, and might answer prayers, though they might hurt or punish as well. All the problems of migrating or nonmigrating souls could be brought to gods as well as to clerics; but one could bring gods virtually any other problem too. Illness, childlessness, madness, possession by a ghost, business difficulties, a bad harvest, one's hopes for a civil-service degree—all might call for a god's consideration and help. Some people devoted themselves to a single god who became their protector and patron. Many people prayed and sacrificed to many different gods and judged them against one another by the adequacy of their responses.

Finally, how one acted and thought mattered, to gods as to people. Good and ill conduct were—often, usually, always? (views may have differed)—rewarded and punished. Hung Mai's stories are filled with occult rewards and punishments, often of very surprising kinds and almost always explicable by the offenses or good deeds of the story's actors. Buddhist and Taoist clerics alike, not to mention the state and Neo-Confucian commentators and teachers, preached and wrote for laymen about what conduct was good. The content might differ in important ways, but again there was also much common ground. Obedience to parents, loyalty to the ruler, care and guidance of one's children, consideration of one's neighbors, honesty in business dealings, moderation in conduct of all kinds: all of these might appear as easily in a Buddhist or Taoist as in a Neo-Confucian tract.

If these were usually commonalities, the variety that sprang up around and between them was extreme and provoked disapproving and even despairing comment from clergy, state, and teacher. We may think of four organized agencies, within but also distinct from ordinary society, that confronted the variety of lay practice and tried to regulate, sort, redefine, or control it: the Buddhist clergy, the Taoist clergy, the state, and—here the word "organized" becomes more problematic—secular intellectual commentators of classicist or Neo-Confucian bent, in the Southern Sung especially the teachers and promoters of the Learning of the Way. Of these four, Buddhists were at least in the Sung probably the least intrusive or authoritarian, offering a variety of religious services to laymen, especially for the dead, but to a great extent leaving lay practice alone. But Buddhist authors did write tracts advising laymen how to remake their lives so as to accumulate the least ill karma and improve their chances of a favorable rebirth; and Pure Land preachers, urging ordinary people to rely on faith in the Buddha Amitabha for salvation and rebirth in the Pure Land paradise, were common figures in the Sung landscape. Taoists, with their heavenly bureaucracy of gods largely distinct from the gods of laymen, were much more likely than Buddhists to act against popular gods or practice in specific cases, and midway through the dynasty, under the emperor Hui-tsung, achieved supreme religious authority at court and attempted to impose one form of the Taoist religion on Buddhists and laymen alike. Yet they too appealed to lay needs with services of all kinds. We shall see a great deal more of them in what follows.

The state on the one hand maintained a set of gods of its own—the nameless gods of the soil and grain and of the mountains and rivers, derived at least in theory from classical models—and in the person of the emperor and of its officials in each locality offered sacrifices to them without popular participation. In principle, *only* the state and its agents could worship these gods. On the other hand, the state "enfeoffed" and thus sanctioned large numbers of local and popular gods and maintained a register of those it recognized. In theory, gods off the register were to be suppressed. In practice, the central government acted against local gods only occasionally and spasmodically, and generally in response to a perceived specific political threat. Much more often, the suppressors of gods, burners of shrines, or defrockers of monks and nuns were zealous local administrators acting within or outside the law but on agendas very much their own, sometimes Taoist and often Neo-Confucian. Finally, for Neo-Confucian intellectuals themselves, especially those of the Learning of the Way movement in the Southern Sung, none of the "commonalities" necessarily held—though they might for some. The Neo-Confucian teacher often acted the part of a sort of Puritan of Chinese rites, seeking to restore an imagined original religion and to sweep away the crudities and corruptions that ordinary lay worship by its very existence must represent. The classical system had been a hierarchy of gods—again the nameless essences of soil, grain, river, mountain—standing alongside the feudal hierarchy of territorial lords, who alone were empowered to worship gods, and only the gods at their respective levels. The modern analogues to the feudal lords of antiquity were the local administrators appointed by the emperor. In principle, then, the Neo-Confucian position could be (though it was not always) that nobody but officials should worship gods at all: ordinary people had ancestors to sacrifice to and ought not to be trucking with gods. Nor, as we have seen, did the Neo-Confucian necessarily assume that gods were real personalities rather than mere emergent concentrations of material energy. When classical purity in local office met the variety and disorder of daily religious life, in which almost everybody prayed to gods, the consequences could sometimes be devastating for lay worship. But more often, Neo-Confucians simply did not have the power to enact their starker classical visions.

Sung religion, then, was the meeting point of a relatively few common assumptions, an extremely wide variety of usages, gods, rituals, and practitioners, and several organized or semi-organized bodies contending to impose order on the variety. It looks very much as if religious activity of all kinds expanded and multiplied and differentiated in the Sung, its mechanisms oiled by new wealth and market penetration, by printing, and by the state sale of religious ordination as a commercial good. Many new religious phenomena emerged in the course of the dynasty, of which I shall mention only two here. Valerie Hansen has shown the spread from local bases of a few gods she calls "regional" (I would call them national), who in the Southern Sung for the first time won the devotion of worshippers from across the empire. She speculates plausibly that traveling merchants were among the main bearers of these gods and their cult from place to place and shows how contemporary educated observers objected that a god was supposed to receive worship only in its own place. The Three Immortals cult represents quite a different tendency: the growth of god cults of merely local or regional scope and their continuous spread across a countryside from a definite center (rather than via waterway from trade node to trade node as with Hansen's gods), promoted by myths and texts that stress the tie between god and place and treat gods' authority as general but territorial rather than either geographically universal or topically specialized. For the cult of the Three Immortals it is clear, and I suspect it would prove true for many other regional and territorial gods, that secular local elites of the gentlemanly sort (*shih-ta-fu* in Chinese terms) rather than merchants or other habitual travelers are the cult's most prominent promoters. The Three Immortals begin and end as gods of a particular place, though the "place" grows from a single mountain to a large section of Chiang-hsi.

But what did it mean—what was it *like*—to be a devotee of the Three Immortals? What sort of world did one enter when one entered their cult? We can read much of this world in miracle tales and poems in the chapters that follow, but there I concentrate on the contrast between Three Immortals worship and Taoist practitioners' religion or seek to explain the rise of this cult rather than others, and much of the rich and striking specific quality of Three Immortals religion will be evident only when I quote the texts themselves. I should try to convey something of it here.

A believer in the Three Immortals entered a world of mountain and mist and half-hidden power. Pilgrims and observers write of mountains that "in their ripe beauty and steep upthrusting are worthy dens for divine Immortals,"[32] of a mountain's "several peaks ringing it about like a screen," of summits "shaped by spirits and sharpened by ghosts." Clouds and mist are everywhere. The official and poet Sun Ti, visiting in 1132, writes, "The misty vines grow thick enough to let one clamber up / ... At the cave's mouth there still remain patches of purple mist." On Mt. Hua-kai itself, "In the cold of winter and in the height of summer the clouds and mist abound ... [when there are many worshippers] a whirling, sweeping fog then rises to the sun." A woodcutter in 1109 meets three men "capped with stars and garbed in mist"; a sick gentlewoman who has received sagely water from the Three Immortals shrine sees "blurrily three Taoists, ... riding on many-colored clouds." When in 1985 I climbed Mt. Hua-kai's neighbor Mt. Pa, home of a different Four Immortals, whom we shall meet in Chapter 5, the upper reaches of the mountain were so shrouded in fog that my guides could hardly find the summit, and the county officials climbing with me joked that the Immortals were hiding from us. But if Immortals clothe their mountain and themselves in cloud, they also produce apparitions well fitted to misty surroundings: great round lights that float in air and in which the Immortals sometimes show themselves.[33] Worshippers see "thick clouds and mist, with a light inside like the sun's corona, as big as a carriage.... Inside the light appear the Three Immortals. Their caps and garments and their bodily forms can be made out dimly." In 1182 "a circular light appeared at night. When people below the mountain looked at it, it seemed attached to the face of Heaven above. When people on the summit looked, it covered the surface of the ground below." At the completion of a shrine "there was a circular apparition with three arch-like lights. The lights illuminated the sky, like a boat, like a bridge." Some years later at the next renovation "they suddenly saw three heavenly lights rise blazing from the mountain," which soon became several hundred. But shows of inexplicable lights, however startling, were only a faint sign of the powers of the Three over nature, weather, and especially water. After an Offering (*chiao*) to the Three, "feather screens of cloud arose on all sides; then thunder and lightning came all at once, covering the sun's charioteer in the east and whipping awake the sleeping dragons in the vast seas." At another site, in 1186, "a numinous spring burst out of the ground; when the sick drank of it they were immediately cured." One poet-pilgrim tells us, "The thunder and lightning come to their beck and call / Cloudy Heaven lends them shelter and shade." Another, granted clear weather for his climb, writes, "Thank the Perfected: wind abates, shadows are screened away / The tops of the myriad peaks gush a clearing brilliance upward."

The power of the Three Immortals was not only mysterious, shielded from normal view, a mixture of all-obscuring mists and all-illuminating light-circles from nowhere; it also emerged from a source remote and hard to attain. Again and again pilgrims or the witnesses of pilgrimages stress the difficulty of the climb: "I only hope my feet are strong and healthy / That year after year I may here renew my covenant." "The mountain is steep and not accessible to carriage or horse; at many points he pulls himself up with his hands." "Pulling ourselves along by the creeping vines, we clambered up and deposited our sincere confession of faults beneath the starry altar." One poet listed the obstacles he met: "At Losing Heart they've placed a forbidding ridge / . . . The mountain is long and like a sword's edge / The path perilous, I've walked nine windings / The terraces tricky, I've taken three rests." Another remembered the weather: "A damp week, a freezing rain, a road turned to mud / At every hour, filling the sky, the snow and sleet flew." The difficulty of the pilgrimage was itself an expression of the worshipper's devotion and sincerity. But it also reenacted the original sincerity of the Two Immortals, who had ignored distance and hardship and in some tellings wandered all the remotest byways of the region, stopping at every mountain in search of their patron and teacher. When the Taoist Pai Yü-ch'an first visited Mt. Pi-chia, where the Two had stopped on their way, "he sighed at how far away Fu-ch'iu had been and marveled that Wang and Kuo [the Two] had gone there." I have climbed Mt. Hua-kai myself and cannot say it was extraordinarily difficult. But the way was steep and winding, and at one point one of my companions slipped and seemed about to fall off the mountain. Hua-kai lay at the southern end of the county, far from town through hilly country. The gentlemen who wrote our texts did not have the jeep that got me as far as the mountain's foot, and they were used to sedan chairs ("Doing without a sedan chair, I've already reached the top") and unaccustomed to hard travel on foot. The effort they felt in a journey to the mountain and a climb to the top was real. Yet the pull of a place where the Immortals had lived or stopped was very strong. The texts love to tell of the crowds of pilgrims and seekers: "Worshippers rush to it as if to market, all year and throughout each month without cease." "The prayers are unceasing; the seekers of good fortune are often unsparing of their wealth." "From this time on, from near and far, all rushed to gather here. . . . Visitors of rank came one after the other, into the hundreds and thousands. . . . And the daily and monthly increase of the gentlemen who have come seeking from the four directions from that day on will surely never end."

What drew so many to a place so far and so difficult was the Three Immortals' reputation for generous and immediate response to prayer. "Whenever the people suffered from flood, drought, or sickness, they would pray there and be answered instantly." "No sincerity went unrequited, no prayer unanswered." "[W]hen we call, they answer; when we want, they grant, turning drought into abundance, changing sighing and sorrow into joy and music, as instantly as shadow copies shape or echo answers sound." Before their ascent the Three Immortals had promised that they would always hear prayers, and according to the miracle tales their worshippers told, they regularly kept the promise. To grant their favor, the Immortals might even come to one directly—in a dream, in a vision, or even in earthly form—rather than require one to come to them. And here they show a face different from the face of cloud and mystery we have already seen: a face of matter-of-fact, even rustic or humble interaction with the human world. A vagrant Taoist comes to a sick household, as in the everyday world of Sung China a vagrant Taoist often might, refuses to be chased away, and enchants water to cure all the family. Only later, after a long journey to repay this unasked kindness, does the householder learn that this was Lord Kuo, one of the Three Immortals. A man who cries out to the Immortals to save him from drowning when his boat is wrecked is rescued by two "old men" with a boat of their own, who pull him from the water, tend to him, and show him the right way home. Three Taoists appear in a dream to a sick woman and give her a pair of chopsticks; she awakens and recovers. The face-to-face contact, but also the appearance of Immortals simply as old men or anonymous Taoists, figures one might meet anywhere in the Sung countryside, mark a shift of tone away from mist-shrouded, hidden, vast power that masters all of nature, toward quotidian encounter and the intimacy of a personal favor, freely given to a single person or family. On direct and unmediated contact with the Three, I have much more to say in Chapters 3–5. But the combination or alternation of these two faces may go to the heart of what the Three Immortals meant to those who prayed to them: it gave access to awesome power, but access that might wear the simple dress of an everyday meeting with a stranger, a stranger who proved surprisingly kind. The Immortals were powerful, dangerous, and perhaps ultimately incomprehensible, and on their mountaintop they could show themselves so. But they could also show themselves as household visitors of unthreatening mien and out to help. It was hard to get to them; but then they might come to you instead. This brought mystery and power home.

In giving shape to this book, I move back and forth between the local, the regional, and the national, and between the Three Lords cult and other forms of religion that shared its world. Chapter 2 examines the ritual texts of Celestial Heart Taoism, a nationally active school of healing and exorcistic ritual, which claimed to originate from the same mountain as the Three Immortals cult, to show that the bureaucratic model in an elaborately worked-out form is central to the sect's conception of its practitioners' place in the world. Chapters 3, 4, and 5 return to the world of the Hua-kai Immortals' cult. In Chapter 3, I examine the texts of the cult and show that, by contrast with the Celestial Heart texts, the bureaucratic model has very little place in them. In Chapter 4, I take up the cult's history, showing that its rapid rise and spread among the local elites of Ch'ung-jen County, Fu-chou, and Chiang-hsi is a phenomenon of the Southern Sung and the Yüan dynasty, with no real precedent in preceding periods. In Chapter 5, I attempt to relate this development to the broader social circumstances of the Southern Sung elite in Fu-chou, specifically the increasing localism of elite life that I have argued for in previous work, and to show how the contending religious choices made by the local elite and by a late Southern Sung administrator can be comprehended by a single explanation, an opposition between authority that is inherent and comes from within the locality and authority that is delegated and comes from outside. In Chapter 6, I return to the world of professional Taoist specialists and refine my picture of their religious conceptions by showing that the bureaucratic model was not the only model even for them—that in specific contexts Taoists too used and elaborated personal, learning-centered, and even descent-based models, especially when they explained their own relations with other Taoists, both living and Immortal. In Chapter 7, I attempt to answer the question: since the bureaucratic model was neither consistently dominant in Sung Chinese ideas of the divine nor even the only model that Sung Taoists themselves used, why is the model nonetheless so central to Sung and post-Sung Taoism? Chapter 8 turns to the modern ethnographic literature about a ritual, the Offering *(chiao)*, that on the one hand is Taoist but on the other hand honors local lay gods, to argue that the tensions between personal and bureaucratic models that I find in the Sung can help explain modern religious phenomena as well.

A broader curve unites these shifts of topic. The book first examines the two models of divinity separately and then moves to explore their interactions. Thus the second chapter explores the bureaucratic model in Celestial Heart Taoism, while Chapters 3, 4, and 5 move to the personal model as it appears in the Three Immortals cult. Chapters 6 and 7 then return to professional Taoists, Chapter 6 to explore the combination or alternation of the two models in Taoists' own self-representations, Chapter 7 to suggest that part of the point of the bureaucratic model for Taoists lies in their interaction with laymen who may not share it. Chapter 8 ends by examining the meeting, though not necessarily the mixing, of the two models in a single ritual, the Offering. By showing where the models occur independently, where they seem to combine or alternate, and where they interact in the competitive collaboration of ritual, I hope to show not only that they are distinguishable by the analyst, but that their Chinese users distinguish them as well. The models, I hope to show, are not simply mine, but theirs.

CHAPTER TWO

Celestial Heart Taoism

Beginning in Northern Sung times, a second tale was told of Hua-kai Mountain. In this tale the Three Perfected Lords played little part; and the story grounded a new textual tradition and a new ritual practice with no relation to the Three Lords cult. The very lack of connection is illuminating.

REVELATION AND TEXTS

In the fifth year of the Ch'un-hua period (994), thirty-four years after the first Sung emperor seized power, and only eighteen years after he annexed the Chiang-hsi region and Hua-kai Mountain to his new state, something extraordinary happened. A former clerk in the criminal court of the prefectural government, Jao Tung-t'ien by name, was at Hua-kai Mountain one night when he saw a gemlike light of five colors on its summit. As he watched, the light rose from the ground and flew upward with a rush to the Milky Way. The next day he searched out the place where the light had taken flight and found it at the Altar of the Three Pure, the highest and most abstract divinities of Taoism. There he dug in the ground and unearthed a book wrapper made of gold. Opening this, he found a set of engraved plates, also of gold, bearing writings under the title *Correct Rites of Celestial Heart* (*T'ien-hsin cheng-fa*). These would form a new school of demon-catching and healing ritual in the Sung, and Jao Tung-t'ien would become its founding patriarch-Immortal. But for the moment he was unable to understand or use what the texts revealed. Some time later, he met an unnamed divinity who told him to seek out a Master T'an Tzu-hsiao and make him his teacher. T'an, a man of nearby Nan-feng County and a practitioner of some fame, helped Jao to master the new revelation and directed him to seek audience with the god of Mt. T'ai, who received him in turn and asked the celestial court on high to place a detachment of spirit troops under Jao's command. Jao became the first master of the Celestial Heart rites and in the end ascended to Heaven, but not before passing on the new knowledge to a favorite disciple.[1]

What did Jao read in his gold plates and hand down to his spiritual descendants? Three books survive in the canon of Taoist scriptures that claim to derive from the original revelation. Though the present canon is a compilation of the Ming dynasty, the books themselves date from the Sung. For one of them we can speak more precisely: it is the work of a compiler named Yuan Miao-tsung, a man who has left no record elsewhere, but who presented his collection of ritual material to the emperor Hui-tsung, patron of the new Taoisms of the late Northern Sung, in 1116. It bears the title *Secret Essentials of the Most High on Assembling the Perfected for Relief of the State and Deliverance of the People* (hereafter *Secret Essentials*). The other two books bear no dates but probably originated in the late Northern Sung: these are *Correct Rites of Celestial Heart from Shang-ch'ing* and *Spirit Code: A Numinous Text from the Marrow of Shang-ch'ing*. Both are the work of a single compiler, Teng Yu-kung, whose prefaces provide the biography of Jao Tung-t'ien I have sketched here.[2] In all essentials, as Judith Boltz has shown, these texts and Yuan Miao-tsung's work represent a single ritual strain.[3] If our main body of liturgical writing thus comes from the Northern Sung, a great deal of later anecdotal writing shows that Celestial Heart practice still thrived in the Southern Sung.[4] From their presentation at Hui-tsung's court through their employment in the Southern Sung countryside, Celestial Heart ritualists consistently claimed to heal sickness and relieve personal or social ills by expelling harmful spirits and communicating with higher divine powers.

The Northern Sung origins of Celestial Heart and its concern with healing and aiding the world unite it with broader developments in religious Taoism. Michel Strickmann was the first to call attention to the "Taoist renaissance" of the Northern Sung. This encompassed the rise of major new sects and teachings, which eventually reached the court; the establishment of a new canon of scriptures; and the promotion of Taoist religion by two emperors, Chen-tsung (r. 998–1023) and especially Hui-tsung (r. 1101–1126).[5] Celestial Heart, despite its presentation to Hui-tsung, never achieved the high place at his court won for a time by another new sect, the Divine Empyrean (*shen-hsiao*), whose practitioner-promoter Lin Ling-su placed Hui-tsung himself at the head of a revised pantheon. For a few years Lin even achieved the official abolition of Buddhism and the absorption of its clergy, if only through a change of names and titles, into a new national Divine Empyrean Taoist institutional structure. In the long run, however, the practitioners of Celestial Heart were as successful as those of the Divine Empyrean in spreading their rites and purveying their services in the provinces in the Southern Sung.

The new teachings had a great deal in common.[6] Neither one, it should be said at once, promoted a new religion in any sense. Both took for granted the major elements of religious Taoism as they had stood since the fourth century: the cosmology of a celestial hierarchy of Immortals and Perfected, and the central promise that the practitioner could by self-perfection escape worldly mortality and reach the status of an Immortal or, still higher, a Perfected, and so join the hierarchy and dwell in Heaven. Within this larger framework, the sects shared a prime concern with healing, with helping people at large, with applying the powers gained in inward self-transformation to benefit the living.

The new sects shared something more: these were teachings for specialists, and usually for professionals. *Correct Rites of Celestial Heart from Shang-ch'ing* (hereafter *Correct Rites*) advises the would-be master that he can achieve the powers he seeks by repeating a fundamental exercise, the imbibing of ether from the Three Radiants, for a thousand days, or nearly three years. In this training period, there is a great deal else he must learn. The manuals offer him a wealth of ritual procedures, with talismans, invocations, and manual signs for each. It is clear that he must learn most of these by heart. The texts place crucial elements of a single rite in widely dispersed sections or chapters, and the practitioner who tried to work "from the book" would look a fool as he thumbed madly from this passage to that. People of the time poked fun at practitioners whose skills were not yet honed:

> Chao Po-an, Tzu-chü's son, followed his father's example and practiced the Correct Rites of Celestial Heart, but he had not yet mastered them fully. Someone gave a carp to his family, and [when it was cooked] the fish leapt out of the dish and rose several feet into the air, where it seemed to dance. At the time Tzu-chü was out on a case, and in haste his family called Po-wu. Po-wu waved his sword and chanted invocations, using the Correct Rites against it. But the fish rose still higher, till it was ten feet up. Po-wu was frightened too and ran away.
>
> Another time he was drinking with his associates at the Paired Streams Pavilion in Yen-chou. A maidservant who was lying next to the railing suddenly let out a loud moan. When questioned she did not answer. Po-wu knew she was possessed by something and again practiced his arts against it. From mid-afternoon to the third watch of the night he continued without stopping; then, utterly worn out, he gave it up and left.[7]

This tale was told on Chao Po-wu by his brother, Po-t'i. The number and profundity of the rites to be learned might also allow a teacher to offer deliberately incomplete instruction to a student he did not quite approve of. This was told of the master of Five Thunders (a ritual practice descended from the Divine Empyrean sect), Wang Wen-ch'ing (1093–1152):

> When Fu Hsuan was assistant director-general of Chiang-hsi, he invited Wang [Wen-ch'ing] of Lin-ch'uan County to Hung-chou, where he studied the

Thunder rites under him. Wang disliked this man greatly, but felt his influence for ill was something much to be feared and so dared not fail to share [his knowledge] with him. But he taught him only a rough outline, which by itself made a great sensation among Fu's friends. As Fu Hsuan's skills matured, it came time for him to give them a test. Looking off [into the distance], he saw a single Buddhist pagoda towering above its surroundings. So he burned a talisman to subdue it. After a moment fire came up from inside; the heat made smoke and cinders, but the pagoda was utterly undamaged.[8]

Celestial Heart practitioners sometimes proclaimed the simplicity of their arts as compared with older forms; but there was much to learn, and to learn it took time and concentration. As Chapter 7 shows, we sometimes read in Southern Sung sources of a serving official who had acquired the arts, but most practitioners look like men who have made Celestial Heart an occupation, indeed their life's work. This was not, for the most part, a job for amateurs.

THE CELESTIAL HEART MASTER AND HIS UNIVERSE

Judith Boltz's work draws a clear picture of Celestial Heart practice, particularly as it dealt with mental disturbance. My plan here is only to call attention to certain broad features so as to set Celestial Heart in relief against other strands of belief and practice that I describe in later chapters. A survey of *Correct Rites*, perhaps the most fundamental of the three surviving texts, will lay a foundation.

The opening two chapters of the *Correct Rites* instruct the practitioner in basic procedures for healing ills and aiding the world. Standing first is the fundamental practice that supplies his special powers: the "requesting" and imbibing of ether from the Three Radiants: sun, moon, and stars. The instructions are typical in specifying precise spoken invocations and bodily postures for each step in appealing for the heavenly ethers. When the practitioner masters this, great things will be his:

> When an official of rites can successfully request the ether of the Three Radiants each day and night without pause for a thousand days, his merit will flourish. This will make his countenance pleasant, strengthen his limbs, lighten his body, and free him from ills. If he is untiring in it all his life, little by little he will enter into [the company of] the Immortals and the Perfected. . . . If he is able to imbibe [the ether] for merely a thousand days, then when he is to treat an illness . . . he need only, while focusing his mind on the dispensing of ether, blow once upon the body of the sick person, and the illness will be healed of itself and a myriad perverse spiritual influences subdued. Does this not deserve reverence?[9]

The passage suggests that the chief field of action for the Celestial Master will be to heal sickness, and the book generally bears this out, though there are other fields as well. The chapter goes on to outline general ritual procedures for treating disease, and here the use of written "talismans" (*fu*), a central feature of the Taoist tradition, comes to the fore. The second chapter presents further techniques, in particular the method of "transformation by refinement," in which the practitioner transforms himself into a god, and that of "pacing the Dipper," in which he envisions himself ascending to the heavens and stepping, according to set patterns, from one star to another in Ursa Major.[10] The last pages of the chapter offer incantations and accompanying talismans for the general aid of the world. Here, under "Rite of the great incantation for assembling the Perfected," we find, within the incantation itself, a list of the benefits that Celestial Heart can provide. The practitioner takes his stand against all ills that may afflict mankind:

> The Correct Rites of Celestial Heart will help what is proper and remove what is perverse; support those in danger and lift up those in distress; save the dead and aid the living; dissolve trouble and relieve affliction for state and for people; pray for grace and confess sin; ask rain, bring thunder, seek clear skies, end floods; control the perverse spirits of the three realms and bring them back to what is proper; reward good and punish evil; record merits and report failings.[11]

The third, fourth, and fifth chapters get specific, supplying a very extensive catalogue of talismans, ritual incantations, and procedures. We find talismans for locking up or tying up dragons (presumably against floods), for bringing rain, and for hastening a birth; rites to cure madness; to heal aches, pains, and swellings; to end intermittent fevers, diarrhea, and insect bites; to recover a soul that has been snatched away from its body; to protect silkworms and drive away rats; and to eliminate harmful hidden ties of enmity extending from the dead to the living.[12] Most common of all are talismans for expelling, incarcerating, or destroying ghosts and evil spirits. For the first assumption of the practice is that spirits cause much of the illness and suffering of humanity. The practitioner heals, first, by exorcising.

The concluding sixth and seventh chapters append a variety of rites, procedures, and forms, such as "lighting the lamps" of the Dipper and divining good and ill from the character of the lamps once lit; setting up a "Platform for Rebirth in Heaven" and carrying out a rite to grant such rebirth to one's ancestors or to resentful ghosts meddling in the living world; sending official communications to the celestial court on high; constructing a "jail" in which to interrogate an offending spirit; and using talismans to summon gods to give aid.[13]

This overview gives some sense of the Celestial Heart master's range but only hints at one of the most striking aspects of his work, its bureaucratic character. To the student of Taoism and its history, the point hardly needs making, and what follows may seem to rehearse the obvious. I dwell on it for two reasons. First, the bureaucratic model, a part of religious Taoism from its origins, is especially strong in Celestial Heart and in its contemporary and rival, Five Thunders. Second, it is in this that Celestial Heart differs most strikingly from the other strand of Sung religion that claims origin from Hua-kai Mountain, the cult of the Three Perfected Lords.

For the Celestial Heart master, society and the cosmos are the domain of a celestial government of divine bureaucrats. Of this hierarchy the master himself is a member, and not the lowest in rank. His title in the *Correct Rites* is symptomatic: "official of rites" or "rite officer" (*fa-kuan*). As an official, he derives his power to act against earthly ills and spiritual evildoers from the agencies and functionaries above him, and in turn oversees subordinates of various kinds—in particular the "spirit officers" (*shen-chiang*) and "spirit troops" (*shen-ping*) he can order into action to arrest ghosts and demons. The texts present his relations with superior and subordinate alike in uniformly bureaucratic terms.

The divine hierarchy itself is not charted in the texts in any thorough or systematic way. At its top, clearly, is the Jade Emperor, or Emperor on High. But the texts mention many other agents and agencies without specifying the lines of authority that order them. A few of these are especially important for the Celestial Heart master. He falls under the authority of the Northern Bourne Bureau for Expelling Perverse Forces (*pei-chi ch'ü-hsieh yuan*), "the principal enforcement agency to which initiates in the [Celestial Heart] rites were affiliated" and "the clearinghouse for their communications with the celestial realm."[14] The authority of the master's primary talismans, however, derived from the Three Radiants, the Dark Warrior, and the Dipper. At the same time he is sometimes represented as reporting to the office of the god of Mt. T'ai (the "Eastern Mount"), a figure that had gained considerably in stature in the Sung through its promotion under the emperor Chen-tsung. Indeed, the Celestial Heart founder, Jao Tung-t'ien, on the one hand entitled commissioner of the Bureau for Expelling Perverse Forces, is, on the other hand, said to have received his complement of spirit troops through the auspices of the Mt. T'ai god.[15] The lines of authority among these various superiors are not, as far as I can tell, made clear. Finally, the master may also address a memorial—like a Sung prefectural administrator or circuit intendant addressing his sovereign—directly to the court of the Emperor on High and "fly" it up to present it in personal audience.[16]

Such crosscutting multiple lines of authority and communication were hardly without parallel in the earthly bureaucracy of the Sung; but their effect here is to make the practitioner's exact relation to the other elements of the hierarchy a bit unclear—and perhaps thus to weaken the limits on his authority and field of action. He is a kind of roving emissary, whose responsibilities lie in the world of men but who ranges easily across the cosmos, from earth to the Dipper to the heavenly court and back to earth again, where too his jurisdiction is unbounded. Yet it is certain that his authority is not his own, that it comes from above.

Like an earthly bureaucrat, the practitioner uses written orders and appeals to perform his duties.[17] His talismans themselves are orders to specific spiritual agents, and the oral invocation that accompanies each talisman's use ends with the words "urgently, urgently, as the Code directs," a phrase taken from Han dynasty legal documents.[18] A "memorial" to the celestial throne was, like its earthly equivalent, a formal written document. In executing his tasks, the practitioner might need to convey instructions to a variety of lower-level supernatural organs; and this communication too he performed in writing, through bureaucratic documents called "dispatches" (*tieh*)—terminology paralleled again in the procedures of the Sung's own earthly bureaucracy.[19]

The Celestial Heart texts supply formats for many of these documents. Only an example can convey their flavor, and the flavor of the Celestial Heart world. Here is part of a form to be filled out and sent to Mt. T'ai to give notice of the transmission of the Celestial Heart rites and techniques to a fledgling master:[20]

> From the Omnicelestial Controller of the Perverse and Demonic for their Return to the Correct (insert ranks, surname, and given name, in full): This bureau,[21] on the (Xth) day of the (present) month, has received the application of the disciple B, of (X) prefecture, county, and ward, offered in heartfelt sincerity, requesting transmission of the Correct Rites of Celestial Heart of the Northern Bourne, in order to assist the proper and remove the perverse, to aid Heaven in its transformations, to relieve the ills and sufferings of the people, and to cut short the ambitions and strivings of evil spirits. The officiant A, above, has already personally drawn up an account of this matter and notified the Emperor on High by memorial, and has further accepted B for appointment to office (X), and further given him talisman-texts, lists of manual signs, and the printed formats of the Bureau for Expelling Perverse Forces; and has, in accordance with regulations, performed the transmission and ordination. This completed, the officiant A carefully inscribes [this] notification to his Humane Sageliness of T'ien-ch'i of the Eastern Mount [the god of Mt. T'ai], begging that his sagely intelligence grant the favor of an order universally notifying the Great Kings of Walls and Moats [i.e., city gods] within the Three Regions ... and all the spiritual intelligences of the Five Mounts, of the Four Rivers, of the mountains of renown and the great streams, of the temples and of the altars of the soil, and of the hills and streams and numinous marshes, and directing them to take notice that B has received the rites and undertaken an office, and that if in the future he may for others' sake treat illness or expel perverse forces, they must assist him in his rites and capture evil spirits without lapsing into laziness or sloth.
>
> The officiant A further requests, in accordance with the precedents, the assignment of two spirit officers and a thousand spirit troops to be dispatched to the office of the new appointee, B, for him to oversee and to assist him in his rites.
>
> Respectfully drawn up on (X) day of month of the year (X), by (insert ranks, surname, and given name).

Alongside this document are forms for the postulant himself to use in applying to his master to receive the transmission and in asking Mt. T'ai to approve his application,[22] and for the master to use in memorializing to the Jade Emperor on High on his behalf;[23] forms for appealing to the same authorities for rain, and for notifying the celestial Board of Rain of the orders issued in response;[24] and forms for requesting aid against plague, possession, and other ills.[25]

The Celestial Heart practitioner was a bureaucrat; but a bureaucrat of a special kind. His prime role was judicial. Boltz has shown how he acted as judge, jailer, and executioner in dealing with the spirits possessing the mad. As a free-ranging enforcer of spirit law, he drew on penal statutes conceived in terms precisely parallel to the codes (*lü*) of the T'ang and earlier dynasties.[26] Teng Yu-kung's *Spirit Code* preserves a version of the Celestial Heart code, which also makes up one chapter of Yuan Miao-tsung's *Secret Essentials*. The code governs not only the ghosts, demons, and spiritual emanations with which the practitioner contends, but also the gods and spirits who aid him and the practitioner himself. Again a sampling may serve better than a description:

> Any spirit [*kui-shen*] who steals men's property, if the amount be a full thousand cash, shall be exiled to a distance of two thousand *li;* or, if the amount be less than a thousand cash, shall receive two years' penal servitude. If it is property donated to a temple, regardless of amount, he shall be destroyed. Where the chief [divinity] of one of the various geographic divisions knowingly indulges [such] perverse spiritual manifestations within his jurisdiction, it is up to the spirit clerks who accompany him daily to report it. Violators shall be beaten one hundred strokes with the heavy rod.[27]
>
> When any spirit secretly shuts off rain and moisture and does not relieve drought and alleviate suffering in time of emergency, and where the chief [divinity] of that water conspires in covering this up and does not expose it, they shall both be given two years' penal servitude.[28]
>
> Any spirit officer, spirit clerk, or spirit soldier who leaves an officiating rite officer without authorization shall be beaten one hundred strokes with the heavy rod. In case of emergency shortage of personnel, [the rite officer] is permitted to borrow spirit troops from the shrine of a neighboring deity, not to exceed five hundred persons. Once their service is done, he is to reward them with special grants and report by memorial to their superiors to record their merit.[29]
>
> All spirit officers, spirit clerks, and spirit troops assigned by the Eastern Mount shall complete one service rotation in three years. (One rotation each year is also permitted.) Record fully all achievements and violations, and report them to the Mount for examination and reward or punishment. Replacements shall be assigned one month in advance of the completion of and departure from a rotation. Failure to rotate or unauthorized rotation shall be punished by one hundred strokes with the heavy rod.[30]
>
> Any deceased person who, bearing a grievance against a living person and

having made a statement of his case through the Office of Hell, prior to its resolution and without authorization causes spiritual monstrosities in the person's home . . . shall be turned over to the Office of Hell to be destroyed.[31]

Similar provisions provide for punishing a spirit who occupies somebody's home without authorization;[32] a master who fails to report a candidate deserving ordination or ordains a candidate without reporting first;[33] and a spirit officer who accepts bribes from ghosts he is supposed to arrest.[34] The classes of punishment and most of the terminology closely copy T'ang and Sung penal law. These and a host of similar provisions were given to the Celestial Heart master to enforce, or to be enforced against him if he was negligent.

These books are manuals. They outline a practice and a view of the cosmos that it is up to a reader to adopt. In other words, they record their authors' views on how one must act to be a Celestial Heart master. Without other evidence, we would not know whether Celestial Heart practitioners out in the world accepted the system the texts set out, or even whether anyone practiced at all. We are lucky then that Hung Mai's vast twelfth-century compendium of occult gossip, the *I-chien chih* (Record of the Listener), includes thirty or so anecdotes that retell the dealings of Celestial Heart masters with possessing ghosts and other spirit-ills during the Sung. We have already seen two. The penal character of the practice is as clear in Hung's stories, retold as true by a man with no special loyalty to Celestial Heart, as it is in the manuals. In one anecdote, the master Liang Kun has come to treat the possession of a servant girl in the household of a county administrator in Hou-kuan County, Fu-chou, Fu-chien. Liang interrogates the possessor, asking whether it has attacked other households in the region. Certainly, replies the spirit through the girl's mouth; but it had skirted Liang's own house when it saw the thousands of spirit troops on guard there.

> In a shout, Liang asked: "What spirit are you? Tell me plainly! If you don't speak, I shall have you fettered in the Eternal Prison of Pei-feng!" Not for some time did it answer. "I am the stone lion outside the South Gate. I hope you will take pity on me and forgive my crime. I shall stay away [from now on]." Liang conferred with [his partner], and they drafted a report of the facts and dispatched it to the Eastern Mount, which took the spirit into custody. The servant girl came to her senses at once.[35]

Another story shows that the minor officers of the Celestial Heart bureaucracy were as susceptible to extralegal influences as their earthly counterparts.

> The Taoist Chao Tsu-chien, a man of Heng-chou, began his career practicing the rites of Celestial Heart. Once he was treating a spirit-ill for a neighbor. After he had stopped it, it arose again. He was infuriated, seized the possessing spirit, and interrogated it. "I would not have dared to come on my own say-so," came its reply; "but you see, the spirit officer of your own rite bureau took my bribe. That's why I dared to act this way. I shall go now."

Chao pondered: "When I subdue demons and spirits with the Correct Rites, by which I make my living, I depend on spirits as my instruments. In this case one of them has openly taken bribes. Where am I to lean my staff now?" He was about to draw up an impeachment and present it to the Eastern Mount when that night he dreamed an armored soldier stood before him, of fearsome mien and very wild, with hands folded on his breast.

"I am a spirit officer under the rite master's jurisdiction," he said. "When I lived I was a soldier, great in strength, and the multitude called me Ch'en of the Iron Whip. When I died I was able to become a god and managed to be assigned to your altar. But I have failed to attend carefully to myself, I have taken bribes from demons, and now I hear that the rite master intends to report me to Mt. T'ai, in which case I must fall into the Eternal Prison of Pei-feng, with no date of release to eternity. I beg your pity and forgiveness and ask to be allowed to cleanse my heart and renew myself."

Chao said: "I have no heart to report your crime. I shall say only that I do not wish to practice these rites any longer and leave you to repent of yourself." The man made obeisances and apologies and withdrew. Chao did send up a memorial renouncing his arts and planned to turn to the study of Five Thunders.[36]

In a third story, no master appears; but a ghost speaks directly to his family of his own experiences with the heavenly bureaus and courts central to Celestial Heart practice:

In Feng-hua County the households of the great surnames usually build small buildings next to their dwellings to worship a god they call "Three Halls." They say that if one sacrifices to it with real sincerity, it can make one prosperous. But after long years, it can also do harm.

A rich man of Hsia-she Village in that county, named Ch'ien Ping, served this god with special diligence. Every third year without fail he would slaughter an ox, a sheep, and a pig and offer rich sacrifices. When the sacrifice was over, he would gather all his kin and neighbors, drink to their good fortune, and share the sacrificial meat, just as if it were a wedding ceremony. Ch'ien Ping died in the prime of his life.

In the last month of mourning, which happened to be the same as the time for sacrifices to the god, [Ch'ien's] concubine, one A-Ch'üan, was suddenly possessed. She spoke to his sons in her master's voice:

"Originally I was not meant to die yet; for Three Halls improperly checked my name off and forced me to become his servant. Every day I shouldered his falcon and went off into the wilderness. At night I passed through the marketplaces causing apparitions and making bizarre mischief. For two years I had not a moment's rest; I could not bear the hardship. Finally, I asked for a leave and so was able to go and bring suit to the Eastern Mount.

"It happened that the Lord of the Mount had gone out on tour. I stopped before a small palace and called to the attendant to invite me in. I told him everything. 'This need not be handled here,' he said; 'the Bureau for Expelling Perverse Forces will do.' Pleading, I bowed my head: 'I am but a lowly ghost. How would I know where the Bureau for Expelling Perverse Forces is?' The attendant sent an azure-shirted guard along to guide me. We rose gradually into the air for a hundred *li* or so, till we reached a grand palace gateway whose golden rays filled Heaven. Two mailed warriors, very grand, stood at the gate. I told them the situation, and they led me into a long corridor that stretched on and on, with no one to be seen, and then we came to the palace, where I made repeated obeisances. I was facing a hanging screen, with a brilliant glow of five colors behind it, too bright to look at straight on; but from time to time I could hear a sound of pendants jingling from a belt.

"Suddenly the screen was rolled up and someone called out: 'On what business does Ch'ien Ping come here?' I then told the whole story of my abuse by Three Halls. In a moment a piece of paper flew out from within, and in the blink of an eye the god was brought before the court. I could not see that he was bound, but he hobbled and held his breath, and his pleading and wailing were most acute. Then another piece of paper flew out, revolved around the god's body several times, and finally turned into searing flames and burned him. In a moment he was ashes. I bowed my thanks and withdrew. You should tell all the local people that from now on they should cease this improper worship."

Little by little his words had grown faint, and A-ch'üan now revived.[37]

Thus a community learned that Heaven had withdrawn the authority that till then had been invested in its local god. Bureaucratic apparatus (the officials, the buck-passing from one agency to the other, the flying paperwork) and judicial function (the lawsuit, the accused in fetters, the judgment and execution) both show up here clearly. But the story also bears on the relation of the Celestial Heart hierarchy and its earthly practitioner to local gods. I turn to this in the section that follows.

CELESTIAL HEART AND LOCAL CULTS

The story of Jao Tung-t'ien, which Teng Yu-kung retells and Yuan Miao-tsung alludes to, placed the first Celestial Heart revelation on Hua-kai Mountain. Since the T'ang dynasty, Hua-kai had been the focus of a local cult: the cult of the Three Immortals. It is natural then to ask what place a cult of local deities could have in Celestial Heart teaching. The question can be framed in two ways. First, what place did Celestial Heart Taoists find for local divinities in general? Second, what place did it give to the Three Lords of Mt. Hua-kai in particular?

On the general question, evidence abounds in both kinds of sources so far treated here. Hung Mai's story of the Three Halls god gives the essential picture. The story assumes the authority of the central bureaucratic organs of the Celestial Heart hierarchy to condemn a god long worshipped by a local populace. The god holds his position on good behavior. A judgment that he has violated his trust may lead to his execution; and his worshippers may be notified that his cult is now "improper worship" (*yin-ssu*) and so must end.

"Improper (excessive, licentious) worship" had long been the standard epithet for local cults, gods, and practices that fell outside the bounds of the tolerable; but different observers applied it to very different things. To claim authority to define the bounds—to decide which gods were proper and which improper—was to claim a great deal. The Celestial Heart master claimed it not only for his heavenly superiors but also, by delegation, for himself.[38] This is clear from several statutes in *Spirit Code:*

> Any spirit whom the state does not record in the *Sacrificial Statutes,* and who in disorderly fashion brings spiritual retribution, or who deceives the people and causes unauthorized good or ill fortune, shall be exiled to a distance of three thousand *li.* Any who does injury to human life shall be destroyed. But for any spirit not recorded in the *Sacrificial Statutes* who is yet able to bring good fortune to the people, one shall investigate its accomplishments and petition for a grant of grace.[39]
>
> If any of the auspicious gods in the *Sacrificial Statutes* should do harm among men, one shall record its violations, submit a memorial to Heaven, and await a decree rendering judgment.[40]

The *Sacrificial Statutes* was the state register of deities and shrines recognized as legitimate or tolerable in each prefecture. *Spirit Code* here claimed for its practitioners an authority that cut across the categories of the state's own authorized index of the divine. The practitioner was to discover and judge ill conduct among the gods the *Statutes* recognized, as well as beneficence among those it did not.[41] Rewards and punishments as well as promotions and demotions were to depend on his inquiry and recommendation. The effect was to subordinate local cults and their gods to the delegated power wielded by the Celestial Heart master.

The same relation is clear elsewhere in the Celestial Heart texts. As we have seen, the official form that notified the god of the Eastern Mount that a new master had been ordained also asked for an order directing all gods of mountains and rivers and at local temples and altars to aid him when he called on them. We have also seen that *Spirit Code* allows a practitioner to borrow spirit troops from any shrine in the neighborhood in an emergency; and the *Secret Essentials* supplies a format for the notice to be sent to the shrine's god when this happened.[42] Other *Spirit Code* articles list punishments for local gods who do not respond speedily enough to the orders they receive through the Celestial Heart master.[43] One of Hung Mai's anecdotes documents a master's official dealings with two local deities:

> When [my brother Hung] Kua became director-general of Huai-tung circuit, he took our little brother Hsun along with him. Hsun's natural mother grew ill, and because there was no good doctor available, they sent her to Ch'ang-chou. At the time, our cousin [Hung] Ching-kao was administrator of Chin-ling County there, and in fear that the illness might be catching, he sent her to the home of the

minor military officer Fan An. There they called in a doctor and a spirit medium to treat her, but in the end she rose no more, and they stored her encoffined remains in a Buddhist temple.

On the first night of the following new year, our cousin's son Yi turned ten years old. With two friends he watched the lights at the local shrine to the god of the Eastern Mount. Fan An's residence was just outside the shrine, and Fan invited them in for a snack. When the boy returned home, he fell ill and spoke wildly and randomly, unaware of the world around him.

A man of that prefecture, a minor official named Yao who had bought his office by contributions of relief grain, was a capable practitioner of the rites of Five Thunders and Celestial Heart, and they summoned him to examine the boy. Yao first ordered a spirit officer to summon the god of the locality for interrogation. Descending into a young boy, the god cried out: "My government office is well and strictly ordered; why would it yield any perverse apparition? It must be one of their maids and concubines' doing. How can you hold me responsible? There is no demon for me to capture." Yao thanked him, left, and sent up talismans and spat talismanic waters in his own home for more than ten days, at last ferreting out [the spirit of] a woman. It was Hsun's mother, who was unwilling to say why she had come. Yao notified the city god and placed her in its custody.[44]

The two deities Master Yao calls upon—the city god, or god of walls and moats (*ch'eng-huang shen*), and the god of the locality (*t'u-ti*)—are the most important local gods in the Celestial Heart bureaucratic scheme. Elsewhere, Hung Mai tells of a master of Lo-p'ing County, Jao-chou, who when hired to find out what spirit is spoiling the religious ceremonies of a nearby family first summons the god of the locality and interrogates him.[45] One of the many talismans provided in the *Correct Rites* will summon only this god. But the city god was even more important. It was prescribed Celestial Heart practice when confronting any of a variety of spiritual depredations—among them madness and plague—to notify the local city god of one's intended course of action.[46] The form for borrowing spirit troops was more precisely entitled "Form to Notify City God or Neighboring Deity Shrine of the Borrowing of Spirit Officers or Troops"; and the two forms preceding it would communicate with the city god alone.[47]

The city god's importance in Celestial Heart practice is symptomatic: as David Johnson has shown, the god's cult was from its first expansion in T'ang closely interwoven with the idea of gods as divine bureaucrats.[48] Apart from the city god, the god of the locality, and less often the classical deity of the soil (*she*), local gods receive little attention in the Celestial Heart texts. When they appear, it is as a vague mass, differentiated only by certain broad categories (as in the order to local gods requested in the application form for ordination), or as objects of control, surveillance, and discipline (as in the *Spirit Code* and Hung Mai's anecdotes). They are accepted on good behavior as actors in the divine hierarchy but find their place firmly and clearly at the bottom—well below the Celestial Heart master himself.

In Sung China, this stance had serious meaning. Local gods were the center of day-to-day religious practice outside the family, not only for ordinary people but often for officials and gentlemen. The state acknowledged this in its grants of titles—"enfeoffments" as they were formally conceived, on a feudal, not a bureaucratic model—to gods local administrators or worshippers recommended.[49] To move from Hung Mai's anecdotes of god worship to the liturgies of Celestial Heart is to see vital figures of common religious life reduced to minor and suspect hangers-on of an enormous celestial superhierarchy, most of whose higher spiritual bureaucrats never appear in the shrines and prayers of ordinary people. Into this structure, and above its minor local functionaries, the Celestial Heart teaching interposed its own practitioners as roving supervisors. This was a claim of practitioner authority over much of ordinary religious life.

What of the Three Perfected Lords themselves? Strictly speaking, of course, these were not "gods" in the same sense that many other local divinities were. They were not called gods, *shen*, but Immortals or Perfected, *hsien* or *chen-jen*, marking them as specifically Taoist figures in contemporary notions and signaling the self-perfection in life that had brought them as living beings into Heaven. Many gods were dead human beings. Immortals or Perfected were people who had transcended death.[50] Yet as we shall see in more detail in later chapters, the Three Perfected Lords—like many other Immortals or Perfected in Chiang-hsi and elsewhere—offered just the same favors that worshippers asked of local *shen:* rain or clear skies, heirs, healing, and so on. Their cult was old, specific to one region, and by Southern Sung times widespread there. In these ways, theirs was a local or regional cult like any other. One may speculate that a Celestial Heart practitioner during the Southern Sung would have fitted them into his bureaucratic hierarchy at roughly the place reserved for the miscellaneous shrines of local gods. Speculate is all one can do, however, since none of the Celestial Heart scriptures makes reference to any role at all for the Three Lords in Celestial Heart practice—despite their long association with Mt. Hua-kai, where the first revelation was supposed to have been given.[51] The only mention of the Three in any of the texts appears in Teng Yu-kung's preface to the *Correct Rites*, and the terms in which Teng treats them are revealing. The Lords, he tells us, were "in reality incarnations of the Three Pure, who in former times showed their traces upon Hua-kai."[52]

To claim the Three Lords as incarnations of the Three Pure would seem to exalt them beyond measure. Its real import, however, was to exalt them right out of existence and make any specific cult to them irrelevant. The Three Pure are divine abstractions—hardly even gods in any very concrete sense—who hold the highest position in Taoist cosmology. Associating them with the Celestial Heart revelations gives those revelations the highest possible authority. This surely is Teng's main intention. But the claim reinterprets the Three Lords out of the picture by depriving them of any longer-term reality. They are not, as they are for their cult, specific beings always present at Mt. Hua-kai (even while partaking of the celestial), but the temporary *and past* garb of god-principles even more distant than the celestial bureaucracy. The reinterpretation thus frees Celestial Heart from ties to a particular local cult, or indeed any particular place, and connects it instead to the transcendent and eternal. Teng places Jao Tung-t'ien's discovery of the texts at the site of the Three Pure's altar, clinching the tie. An altar to the Three Pure was a focus of every Taoist abbey in the empire; the Three Pure could be worshipped anywhere (if in principle only by legitimately constituted practitioners). There is no need then to talk at any length of the Three Lords as such: "Their titles of enfeoffment and their beneficent influences are handed down quite clearly by the various inscriptions on stone; here I shall not recount them superfluously." Though we are told that "the good fortune and auspices they have made for the world are great beyond conceiving," here this seems to refer less to their miracles and benefices than to the revelation itself, whose story follows immediately.

This approach to its relation with the mountain where its scriptures were revealed, and with the cult rooted there, is part of a general lack of concern in Celestial Heart with distinctions among particular places or with places as important in their own right. The sect's writings treat all places as interchangeable abstractions, naming them by letter or number in the forms supplied to practitioners, referring to "the city god"—of whatever place—and so on. This floating free from local connection fits well with Celestial Heart's real earthly career. It was never in any sense a local sect, never maintained a special relation to one place. A map of the places its masters were active, drawn from the prefaces of its scriptures and from Hung Mai's anecdotes, shows this nicely (see Map 1). There is a certain concentration in Chiang-hsi, particularly in Jao-chou, but this surely only reflects Hung Mai's own residence there. Other cases are spread throughout the populous areas of South China, with a scattering in the north as well. There is not the slightest concentration in Fu-chou, despite more than a hundred other stories from Hung Mai that deal with Fu-chou men or events.[53] If we are to take seriously the tradition of Celestial Heart's origin at the mountain, then its transmission quickly took it far from its first home. The sect was an expansive one.

Not only the sect traveled; so did its masters. The evidence is not abundant: Hung Mai's stories especially are like snapshots, showing nothing of the practitioner's life course before or after. But we know that Yuan Miao-tsung practiced both in Teng-chou and in the capital (K'ai-feng) and had "traveled through the famous mountains and numinous peaks of the four directions for over thirty years."[54] Teng Yu-kung had spent time at major

Map 1. Celestial Heart practitioners active in the Sung

abbeys in Hung-chou, Chiang-chou, Nan-k'ang Chün, and Shu-chou, and probably in the capital.[55] Chao Tzu-chü (fl. ca. 1127), who appears in two of Hung Mai's accounts, practiced both in Yang-chou, north of the Yangtse River, and in Yen-chou, well to the south in the Che River valley.[56] Prominent Celestial Heart masters—and as we shall see, the same is true of masters of Five Thunders—showed no tendency to stay at home, but ranged across China to acquire their arts and to practice them. If their scriptures made them roving surveillants spiritually, tied to no single jurisdiction and able to wield authority anywhere, men like Yüan, Teng, and Chao lived the role well in their earthly lives.

CELESTIAL HEART AND TAOISM

That the cosmology of Celestial Heart replicated earthly Chinese government in the spirit world goes without saying. What this meant to those who acted it out and to their clientele is a question best put off until we have seen something of an alternative view. But one should not take leave of Celestial Heart without pointing out how thoroughly it repeated and varied themes long traditional in religious Taoism. The point needs pursuing. Anna Seidel has shown that myths and symbols of imperial authority were central to Taoist religion from its origins near the end of the Han dynasty. The parallel of spiritual to secular government, indeed their unification in a single structure, was a leading motive of the new religion.[57] From Rolf Stein's work it is clear that Taoist antagonism to local "popular" cults, and the role of the practitioner as controller not only of demons and their worshippers but also of gods of uncertain origins or lowly status, were just as old.[58] "Spirit codes" were not wholly a Celestial Heart invention: works of a roughly similar kind had been included in the Ling-pao revelations of the late fourth century.[59]

In its own time, too, the worldview of Celestial Heart was broadly at one with that of Taoist practitioners of all stripes. Consider, for example, at the far end of the political scale from the private cures and exorcisms with which most Celestial Heart masters occupied themselves, the grand list of Taoist divinities in *Ceremonial Forms for the Performance and Completion of the Unsurpassed Grand Retreat of the Yellow Register* (*Wu-shang huang-lu ta chai li-ch'eng i*), compiled by Chiang Shu-yü (ca. 1156–1217). This is a Southern Sung guide to the performance of a Taoist liturgy of the largest scale, such as one might hold at major temples in the capital on weighty occasions; it was addressed to the fullest assemblage of deities, numbering 3,600 in all. The list divides the gods into complements of the right and of the left and, on each side, into three orders of protocol (*pan*) of descending rank. The orders of protocol in turn divide into level upon level of gods: crowds of Imperial Lords, Heavenly Worthies, Primal Lords, Perfected Lords, Star Lords, Perfected Men, each belonging to a defined segment of the cosmos or region of the earth as well as to a particular rank and (though this is often unnamed) a particular function.

Two points in this list are of concern here. A bow at least is taken toward the Celestial Heart and Five Thunders vocations. We find the "Thunder-Master Officer-Lords of the Several Ranks of the Thunderclaps of Celestial Heart"; the "Spirit Officers and Spirit Troops of the Bureau of the Northern Bourne for the Expulsion of Perverse Forces"; and the "Perfected Lord, Commissioner of the Bureau of Five Thunders."[60] But more important is the gulf that with few exceptions separates this vast panoply of deities from the gods we know were worshipped by the populace at large. The surviving records of the local and regional gods whom the state granted enfeoffment—and these are many—overlap only occasionally with those in this Taoist list.[61] Certain Taoist figures who were common objects of lay veneration do appear, though their rank is far from high. But all the innumerable deities of local and regional cults are assigned in a body to two or three of the 3,600 "seats" (*wei*) available. "Gods of the Respective Shrines of the National Registers and Sacrificial Statutes" occupy, with a crowd's anonymity, the fifth place from the last in the complement of the left;[62] in the complement of the right the "Gods of the Shrines within and without the Capital" fall eleventh from the last, immediately after "City Gods of the Prefectures and Counties of the Empire."[63] And while the gods worshipped individually at shrines and temples locally or throughout the empire are almost always personal figures, with definite identities, names, and previous lives as historical or supposedly historical human beings on earth (this is as true for the Immortals and Perfected who emerge from the Taoist tradition as for *shen* at large), most of the gods of the *Ceremonial Forms* pantheon appear as simple positions in a hierarchy or as functionally defined posts.

A student of Sung popular worship who surveyed this list of deities after long exposure to records of other sorts and found hardly any familiar faces could be forgiven for thinking that these Taoist gods were not "real" gods at all, but the elaborate intellectual construct of a tiny elite of practitioners and enthusiasts. Yet rituals calling upon these or similar lists of gods—the Retreat (*chai*) and Offering ceremonies that were chief functions of regular Taoist priests—did take place at all levels of society in the Sung, and often, to judge from Hung Mai's anecdotes. We may assume that these pantheons were real at least for those who performed the rituals; and in Chapter 8, I take up the relation between practitioner and lay devotee in such rites. It remains true, however, that in these lists, and so at least formally in the rituals that assembled and addressed the deities listed, the chief objects of much popular and some elite worship were tucked inconspicuously, with no attention to their particular identities, into the bottom of a hierarchy that rose to unimaginable heights above them.

The *Ceremonial Forms* pantheon is not a Celestial Heart artifact. A Celestial Heart or Five Thunders pantheon might for all we know have been very different in membership or sequence. But with its general picture of the cosmos and of the place of local cults and their deities a Celestial Heart master could not have disagreed. The Yellow Register Retreat and the Celestial Heart rites belonged to the same universe.

Celestial Heart masters also belonged to the same social world as other Taoists. Kristofer Schipper has suggested that the division in modern Taiwan between the "gentleman of the Way" (*tao-shih*)[64] and the "rite master" (*fa-shih*)—orthodox, ordained Taoist priests, masters of the classical Offering ritual on the one hand, and trance-using exorcist officiants of vernacular rituals on the other—existed already in the Sung.[65] The roots of the distinction may indeed lie this deep. Yet from Schipper's own and other evidence it does not seem that in the Sung these terms had quite their modern meaning, or that they defined two distinct or mutually exclusive types or roles. It is certain, though, both that Celestial Heart masters spanned the gap, if gap there was, and that to be a Celestial Heart "rite master" in the Sung was to be something very different from Schipper's modern vernacular ritual master. The issue is worth a brief detour.

The *Secret Essentials* of Yuan Miao-tsung calls the Celestial Heart master a "rite master." In the *Correct Rites* and the *Spirit Code*, Teng Yu-kung generally calls him a "rite officer" (*fa-kuan*) but sometimes uses "rite master" as well.[66] Hung Mai often refers to Celestial Heart or Five Thunders practitioners as "rite master." At the same time the "gentleman of the Way" (*tao-shih*), the officially ordained Taoist priest, is a familiar figure in Sung writings and appears again and again in Hung Mai, often as officiant at a Retreat or Offering or as a resident of one of the abbeys (*kuan*) that dotted the Sung landscape. It is clear, as Schipper points out, that Hung Mai recognizes as gentlemen of the Way only bearers of official ordination certificates. For those who lead a similar life without ordination he uses other terms. Schipper, I think, sees "rite master" as one of these residual terms, applied specifically to exorcists. Since Hung sometimes also uses "rite master" for popular spirit mediums (*wu*), there is some plausibility in this. But at least one Hung Mai anecdote applies both terms to the same man. Chao Tsu-chien in the story of the bribed spirit officer is a gentleman of the Way, Hung tells us; but he is a Celestial Heart specialist, and when his spirit officer appeals to him for mercy, he addresses Chao repeatedly as rite master. (When Chao in disgust abandons Celestial Heart, he moves on to another exorcist tradition, Five Thunders.)

In another place, Hung Mai implies that the conjunction of the two roles in one man might even be normal or expected: "In that locality a certain rite master surnamed T'an was a commoner who could perform the rites of Mt. Mao. He received this appellation [*fa-shih*] even though he was not [ordained] a gentleman of the Way [*tao-shih*.]"⁶⁷ Here "even though" would make no sense unless Hung thought it normal that a man with the title of rite master should also be a gentleman of the Way. Conversely, a Celestial Heart master might perform Offerings and other rites characteristic of ordained Taoists although he was not himself ordained.

> A certain rite master Wang practiced the rites of Celestial Heart daily inside the Yung-chin Gate in Lin-an, conducted Offerings to present memorials [to Heaven] on others' behalf, and wore the ritual vestments; but he was not a gentleman of the Way [*tao-shih*]. He was much employed by the common people because his fees were one-third less than those of a true Taoist.⁶⁸

Ordination is significant, to be sure—here it affects fees—but it does not define a role. This rite master does not look like Schipper's. In another story Jen Tao-yuan, a Celestial Heart master whom Hung never calls a gentleman of the Way, is similarly called upon to perform a Yellow Register Offering.⁶⁹ The *Correct Rites* itself instructs the practitioner, at the end of the "Platform for Rebirth in Heaven" for salvation of souls, to conduct an Offering of thanks.

Roles in some Hung Mai anecdotes look more distinct. When the Taoists (here called *huang-kuan*, "Yellow Caps") holding an Offering for a family in Lo-p'ing County in 1197 discover that their rite has somehow been unpleasing to the gods, they employ their "follower," one Rite Master Wang (but is he a gentleman of the Way too?) to use Celestial Heart rites to identify the spirit responsible.⁷⁰ But on the whole the lines between rite masters (of the Celestial Heart sort at any rate) and ordained Taoists are neither clear nor definite, and it is certain that a Celestial Heart master may be either or both.

Finally, in modern Taiwan it is crucial to the distinction that a rite master is the devotee of one god, and a god of the sort worshipped by the populace,⁷¹ while gentlemen of the Way are the bearers of a vast, impersonal, and abstract bureaucratic pantheon. But as we have already seen, the Celestial Heart rite master of the Sung shared wholly in the larger Taoist view of the celestial realm, with no connection or commitment to any popular god, treating these as potential assistants at best or as malefactors at worst. To view the Celestial Heart master against the modern distinction is to see how thoroughly he belonged, in his theory, his practice, and his associations, to the world that in Taiwan today is the sphere of the ordained Taoist priest.

We find here, in sum, an expansive school of specialist, often peripatetic masters of ritual, holding a free-floating position within a vast celestial hierarchy, but acting within it as bureaucrats above all; committed to the authority of a divine emperor above and to his various subordinate and assisting divine agencies; and wielding a well-delineated and severe code of celestial laws and punishments against the threats and vagaries of spiritual beings below. Within this framework, local gods or saints not only hold no privileged place (with perhaps the sole exception of city gods), but are prime objects of the control and discipline exerted by the ritual specialist himself. The school arises early in the dynasty but maintains itself well into the Southern Sung.

In the chapter that follows, we return to Hua-kai Mountain itself, to examine in another Sung text the very different world of the cult of the Three Perfected Lords.

CHAPTER THREE

Hua-kai Mountain and Its Immortals

The story of Jao Tung-t'ien and his miraculous find has another version. In this telling, when Jao was about to leave the world, he led his disciples to the peak of Mt. Hua-kai. There he spoke for the last time:

> He conferred the highest Way on them and made a vow: "To preserve one's substance, to be of few words, to renounce profit and sensual pleasure, and to establish merit are highest; confessing one's faults is next to these. To rescue people from disease, disaster, famine, flood, or drought is the highest merit. Loyalty, filiality, harmony, submission, humanity, and fidelity are fundamental conduct. On any who accomplishes these, union with the Way will be secretly conferred, and though he has never made obeisances to the Most High [*T'ai-shang*], yet he too will live among the Immortals."[1]

Jao then bade them farewell and made his ascent to Heaven.

Neither this speech nor the last climb of Mt. Hua-kai appears in the texts of Celestial Heart. The version of his life that includes them survives only in a Southern Sung miracle story collection, one section of a larger work called *Verities of the Three Perfected Lords Fu-ch'iu, Wang, and Kuo of Hua-kai Mountain*.[2] Aside from the speech itself, it differs from the Celestial Heart texts in three important ways.[3] First, although the Celestial Heart texts supply no location for Jao Tung-t'ien's ascent to Heaven, the story in *Verities of the Three Perfected Lords* places it at Mt. Hua-kai, where the original revelation took place. Second, the Celestial Heart texts tell us that the marvelous light that drew Jao took off from the Altar of the Three Pure (where he also dug up the texts). *Verities of the Three Perfected Lords* instead places the light at the Altar of the Ascent—that is, at the spot where the Hua-kai Immortals themselves had ascended to Heaven. Third, the Celestial Heart texts and *Verities of the Three Per-*

fected Lords agree that Jao, having gained mastery with T'an Tzu-hsiao's help, paid a visit to the god of Mt. T'ai and received spirit troops. In *Verities,* however, the Mt. T'ai god tells Jao of receiving a "decree from the Three Immortals ordering [me] to confer on you a precious seal [*pao yin*] and shade-troops." In the equivalent passage in the Celestial Heart version, the Three Immortals do not appear at all.

These three differences are important and point in one direction. By placing Jao's ascent as well as his discovery at Mt. Hua-kai—the end as well as the beginning of his mortal Celestial Heart career—the *Verities* tale makes the mountain much more important in the story of Jao's life than do the Celestial Heart texts themselves. By placing the light that leads Jao to the scriptures at the Altar of the Ascent rather than at the Altar of the Three Pure, the story brings the Three Immortals to the fore in the genesis of Celestial Heart, not as transient incarnations of the Three Pure but as specific figures with their own history.[4] And by having the Mt. T'ai god receive an order from the Three Immortals, the *Verities* makes them the superiors of a god of national importance. That is, this version of the Jao Tung-t'ien story magnifies the Three Immortals and Mt. Hua-kai itself at just those points where the Celestial Hearts texts diminish them. The reader learns that Celestial Heart itself owes its place in the world to the Three Immortals and their mountain.

It makes sense to be told this in this book, because *Verities of the Three Perfected Lords* is devoted to showing the greatness and power of the Three Immortals and Mt. Hua-kai. Jao Tung-t'ien's career and the history of Celestial Heart are important to the editors only if they help to show this; they appear only once elsewhere in the book. Jao's discovery and ascent form only one of many miracle stories that show the mountain's importance or the Immortals' power. Indeed, the editors play Jao down a bit, rather than place him front and center; their collection is ordered roughly chronologically, but Jao's story falls later in the series than its early date (ca. 994) would justify. The concerns of these editors are as far as possible from those of the promoters of Celestial Heart. The power and authority represented here, I shall show, are independent and inherent and do not depend on the hierarchical structures of delegation and intermediation that inform practitioners' Taoism. In this light, the reshaping of Jao Tung-t'ien's story along the lines we have just seen is to be expected.

Jao's speech itself is intriguing. Together with other materials in *Verities of the Three Perfected Lords,* it presents an ethical ideal focused neither on specific techniques such as those of Celestial Heart nor even on Taoist cultivation and refinement—though these are always available—but on conventional virtues of a gentlemanly and not specifically Taoist sort. This ideal fits the models of power and authority the book presents and—though this argument must await a later chapter—the concerns of the audience the book and the Hua-kai cult appealed to.

HUA-KAI MOUNTAIN AND ITS IMMORTALS 49

THE AUTHORITY OF THE SPECIAL PLACE

Verities of the Three Perfected Lords is a compilation of the early Ming dynasty, but the materials it assembles are largely of Sung and mainly Southern Sung origin.[5] Its contents are diverse and far from tightly organized. The first chapter, the most miscellaneous, has a prefatory feel: among a variety of documents, we find stories of the earthly career of Lord Fu-ch'iu before his arrival at the mountain, placing him at the courts of the Chou and Han dynasties across several centuries; the text of Yen Chen-ch'ing's eighth-century stone inscription on the Three Immortals; and a second inscription, this of Sung date, composed in honor of the Three by the Chiang-hsi circuit official Li Chung-yuan in 1099.

With the second chapter, we enter the heart of the work and of the Three Lords' story. Most of the chapter reproduces *The Veritable Record of the Two Perfected Lords*, an account of the travels and wonders of the Immortals Wang and Kuo said to be from the hand of a Taoist of the Ten Kingdoms and early Sung period, Shen T'ing-jui, and here enlarged enormously by interwoven commentaries of unspecified but clearly later Sung date. The chapter closes with a series of Sung imperial edicts, ranging in time from 1075 to 1237, "enfeoffing" the Three and granting titles to their temple on Mt. Hua-kai. Chapters 3 and 4 reproduce (with some Yuan-period interpolations) yet another Sung work, *Verities of Hua-kai Mountain* by the Taoist Chang Yuan-shu, who wrote in the early thirteenth century. Here we find long lists of sites, rocks, cliffs, caverns, and shrines connected with the Three, beginning around Mt. Hua-kai but extending to surrounding counties and even neighboring prefectures. The effect is to provide a sacred geography of the Three Immortals cult. The last two chapters, also largely the work of Chang Yuan-shu, add recent sacred history to the sacred geography: they are a collection of miracle stories, set in Sung times and mainly in the twelfth century, demonstrating the extraordinary character of the mountain and the continuing power of the Three Lords to work wonders for humankind.

Let us begin with the story of the Two Lords' lives as it appears in the book. This is the story of a journey—not the ever-ranging travel of a Celestial Heart master, but a journey with a goal, a journey that, however it may wind, finally ends. From our first sight of the Two Lords in historical records, Yen Chen-ch'ing's eighth-century inscription for their shrine (incorporated into the first chapter of *Verities*), they are traveling. We have seen the core of Yen's account already, but as the earliest version of the story it is worth reproducing here:

> Having respectfully received the sagely [emperor's] grace, I serve as inspector in Lin-ch'uan [Fu-chou]. One day, examining geographic charts, I learned that Hua-kai Mountain in the minor county of Ch'ung-jen had an altar to two Perfected, Wang and Kuo, surviving on it. I noted this extraordinary thing with

delight but did not trace its origin. At another time, at leisure from my duties, I took the occasion to order an army commander to the foot of the mountain to search for an inscription, and he did in fact find a record on stone. This had been made by the Taoist caretaker Li Tzu-chen in the fifth year of the K'ai-huang period [585] under the Sui dynasty. When I copied his writing from the broken stela, I learned that the Two Perfected Lords Wang and Kuo, [though] Immortals, are not well known.

Wang was the collateral descendant of [Wang] Fang-p'ing, and Kuo was Wang's younger paternal cousin. They first cultivated the Way at Mt. Chin-hua, with the aim of weightless ascension; then they wandered the cavern-offices. From Mt. Yü-ssu they were heading to the caves of [Mt.] Ma-ku. The way passed by a mountain, and they asked the elders: "What mountain is this?" The answer: "That is Hua-kai Mountain of Pa-ling [County]." The Two Perfected Lords said to each other: "This mountain is an auspicious place. Its very name is extraordinary." And so they found a stopping place by divination and once more refined their divine elixir.

The elders at the foot of the mountain paid a call and bowed down again and again. "Dare we ask the Perfected's names?" they said. "We are cultivating our will for the Void," said the two, "and do not wish to tell about it." Later a Taoist came to visit and ventured to ask [who had been] the Perfected's teacher. "Our teacher was Master Fu-ch'iu," they said. This was a great Immortal of the higher realms, whom they had met at Mt. Chin-hua.

The Two Perfected Lords could make stones fly and "fly amulets," raise clouds and bring rain. When someone was sick or suffering or had died a sudden death, if people came and appealed to them, they would fly an amulet at once to save him. If there was great drought at harvest time, they would bring long rains to relieve it. In the second year of Yuan-k'ang under [Emperor] Hui-ti of Chin [292], on the first day of the second month, there had been clouds of many colors for days on end, Immortals' music and clamorous winds. The Two Perfected Lords, with *luan*-birds as their escorts[6] and riding cranes, slowly made their ascent.

Today the altar of their ascent and an altar to Master Fu-ch'iu survive. Later an abbey was established to care for these. Whenever the counties of this region faced drought, if they visited the altar and prayed to them, clouds and rain responded at once.

... Thus I joined with the officials of the prefecture in planning to honor the abbey so as to provide care for it forever [*ch'ung kuan yü yung lieh fan-hsiu*] and afterward assigned the army commander to go to the mountain with public funds and renovate beams, gates, and verandas. Before long he returned and said the work was done.[7]

There are many journeys here. Even if we leave aside the Immortals' ascent and attend only to the earthly, their own journey to the mountain is paralleled by the journeys that others make after their arrival: the elders who come to ask their names and learn their business; the Taoist who visits and learns the name of their teacher; the appellants who come again and again to beg for help in sickness or drought; the worshippers who have come to pray for aid since the ascent; and the army officer, whose two journeys to the mountain and back frame Yen's own involvement. All movement has the mountain as its focus, ends at it or begins from it; and this holds for the ascent as well.

But there is more to say of the Immortals' own journey, the implicit model for the journeys others make. At the start, the Two set out to "wander the cavern-offices," to travel the empire and visit the famous mountains that house the cavern-heavens of the Taoist religion. This is a journey like those of Celestial Heart and Five Thunders practitioners in the Sung and traditionally common among Taoists—a sort of grand tour, with enlightenment and refinement as its goal, or the practice of one's art and service to others, but with no one destination on earth. They are proceeding from one typical station on such a journey to another—from Mt. Yü-ssu, well to the west of Hua-kai, to Mt. Ma-ku in the east—when their first sight of Hua-kai makes them break off their wandering and find a stopping place. They never continue on. Thus their discovery of Mt. Hua-kai suddenly transforms a peripatetic grand tour into a journey with an end—an end they have now reached—and changes the travelers from free ramblers into resident patrons. From now on all their marvels, before and after their descent, are performed for people in the mountain's region and in response to prayers offered at the mountain. The narrative device of wanderings interrupted and transfigured by an unexpected destination brings the mountain, and travel aiming at the mountain, splendidly to the fore.

Later expansions of Yen's account vary or even abandon this device, but always to the same end. *The Veritable Record of the Two Lords,* incorporated into the second chapter of the *Verities* and presented as the work of Shen T'ing-jui, changes the Lords' original journey from a mere grand tour to a search for a lost teacher.

> At the beginning they left their homes for the Hsuan-yuan Abbey in their own commandery and made Lord Fu-ch'iu their teacher. Afterward they followed him to Mt. Chin-hua to gather pharmacopoeia. He later made transmissions to [his other disciples] Huang and Wu and to the Two Perfected, saying: "You must ponder finely and cultivate diligently. Before long your Way will be achieved and I shall confer your ordination." He also conferred on the Two Perfected the arts of "guiding and nourishing."
>
> The Two Perfected were almost thirty-seven years old. Day and night they performed their rites, always in just the same way from beginning to end. Their teacher delighted in them. One day Fu-ch'iu said to the Two Perfected: "I have somewhere to go. The time of our future meeting is not yet set." When he finished speaking, suddenly he disappeared. The Two Perfected pined after him morning and night and prayed weeping to Heaven, vowing to see their first teacher again and complete the task of their Way. Suddenly one evening

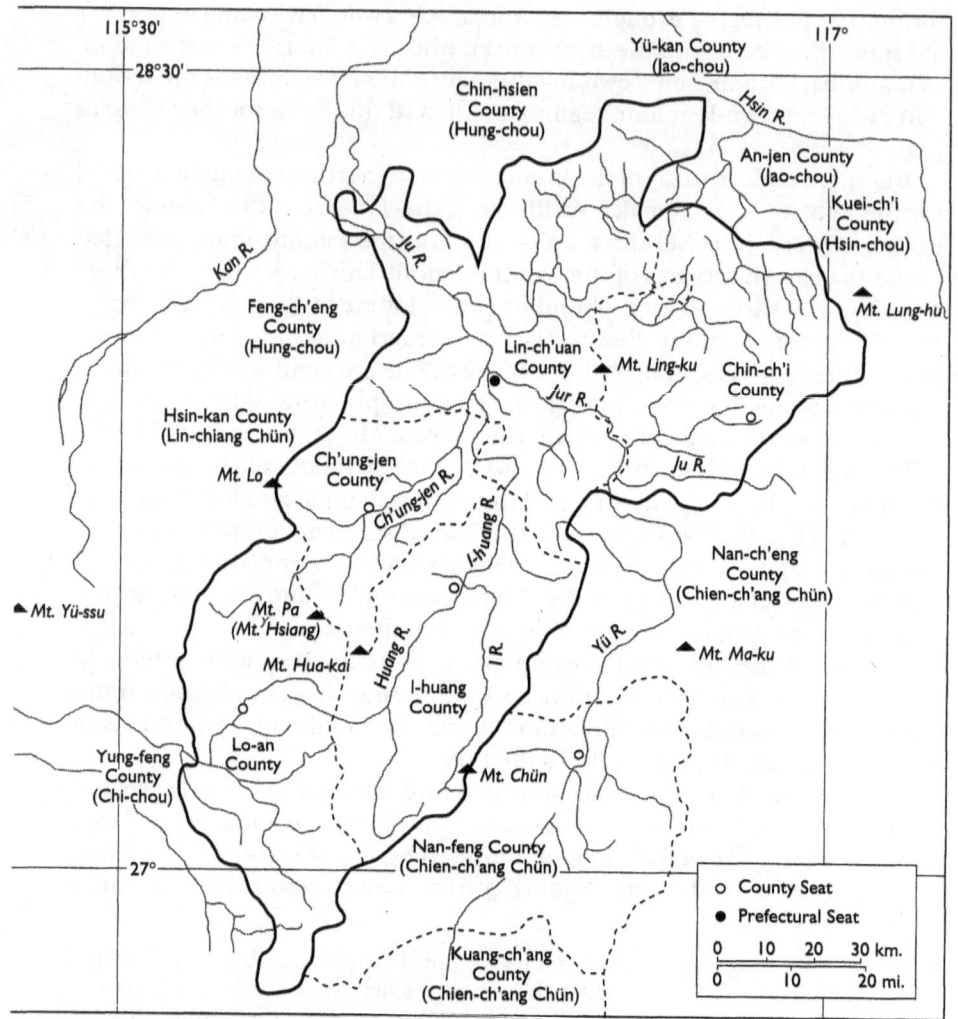

Map 2. Mountains of Fu-chou and its region

they dreamed a god [*shen-jen*] told them: "Just head for the topmost three peaks of Chiang-nan; then he may be seen." Having received this favorable response [to their prayers], the Two Perfected made no excuse of distance, but took up their calabashes, put on bamboo hats, and made straight for Chiang-nan, where they passed through all the cavern-offices.[8]

... From Yü-ssu Mountain they were going to Ma-ku, and on the way they saw a mountain with three peaks thrusting up into the void. They asked the local elders: "What mountain is this?" "That is Hua-kai Mountain of Pa-ling [County]," the elders replied. The Two Perfected said to each other: "This is an auspicious place. Its very name is extraordinary. Our Master left word of a place of three peaks, the loftiest in Chiang-nan; he must surely be there." They made obeisances and offered ceremonies from afar.[9] ... Then they made their way in search to Hua-kai [*yü shih hsun chih Hua-kai*], where they met their master indeed.[10]

Here Fu-ch'iu chooses Mt. Hua-kai as his disciples' destination from the start, and though they still experience the discovery of the mountain and the interruption of their itinerary, it is a discovery for which they and the reader are prepared. The discovery still depends, however, on their recognition of the mountain's special qualities, qualities reinforced when the story brings Fu-ch'iu there too. It will be a fateful place for him as well:

> The master said: "Your will to cultivate Perfection is truly hard to curb." Once again he conferred the Way of cultivating Perfection and refining substance upon them. The Two Perfected performed their refining and carried out their rites without slacking in heat or cold. One day the master said to them: "Your Way is now near achievement. But if you have no means to benefit the people, your merit cannot be complete. You should also study the arts of Three-and-Five-Flying-Paces and the rites of Nine-One-Upper-Clarity, so as to aid your time and complete the enactment of your merit. Then, on your behalf, I will memorialize your names to the Gold Court. When you ascend to the Imperial site [*ti-so*] you will be divine Immortals." The Two Perfected studied these according to his spoken transmission.
>
> In the first year of Yuan-k'ang [291], on the twenty-second day of the eleventh month, Lord Fu-ch'iu was playing the lute west of his lodgings at the Jade Pavilion north of the mountain, when suddenly multicolored clouds and jade mists filled the gorge and joined it to the Void. Immortals' music clamored and crashed. Ceremonial insignia gathered grandly in the clouds. A red-shirt brought an edict: "The Emperor on High decrees it is time for Master Fu-ch'iu's ascent." With subtle words and mysterious gestures he transmitted ordination to the Two Perfected. Master Fu-ch'iu then ascended a dragon-carriage and rose, climbing the clouds. The Two Perfected bowed in farewell.[11]

Again the mountain has gained in importance. In Yen Chen-ch'ing's version, the Two come as fully formed practitioners, ready to take up the role of living Immortals for the community. But here when they arrive, their education is incomplete, and the mountain is where they complete it. Even more, it is now the site not only of their own ascent but of Fu-ch'iu's as well. *The*

Veritable Record goes on to tell of the miracles the Two performed after their master left, culminating, as in Yen's story, in their own ascent. We then learn of the attentions the mountain received afterward:

> The local authorities reported the matter, and it was decreed that all places that the Two Immortals had passed through should be honored with abbeys. East of the mountain they built the Immortals' Woods Abbey, south of the mountain the Southern Immortals Abbey, north of the mountain, at the Jade Pavilion lodging, the Ascend-to-Immortality Abbey, and west of the mountain, where the Two Immortals had spat ethers to make a bridge and walked to the summit to have audience with Heaven and pay respects to the Dipper, the Bridged-the-Immortals Abbey.[12] . . . In front of the abbey was a mountain shaped like a flying dragon climbing to heaven, a place where Master Fu-ch'iu had often dwelt, which they called Fu-ch'iu's Altar. The place where the bow had descended, they called Bow Mount. The place where the Immortals had battled with the mortal troops, they called Battle Plain. The place where Immortal Women had played music while the Two Perfected ascended, they called Immortal Women's Peak. The place where the Two Perfected had audience with Heaven and paid respects to the Dipper, they called Immortals' Altar. All of these are authentic evidences from antiquity. After their ascent, to the places where the Two Perfected had ruled, the Jade Emperor sent thirty-six Immortal officials and eighteen gods of the locality to guard them and allow no violation or offense. Such places as . . . [a list of twelve place-names follows], all of which are sagely traces, and these erected abbeys, were among these.[13]

This catalogue shows the connection of the Perfected to each of a series of places that devotees must have held sacred at the time the author wrote. But it also reinforces the extraordinary character of the mountain by showing just how many special places are to be found on and around it, and how a real history—the acts and movements of the Perfected—has made these special. It magnifies the mountain by listing the marvelous spots that can be visited and recognized there.

With all this, we are still on the mountain itself. For an extension of the last device over a far greater geographic field, we must turn to a still later version of the story, preserved in the long "commentary" (*chu*), which at some stage a Sung editor has interspersed through Shen T'ing-jui's *Veritable Record*.[14] This commentary always begins "another version says,"[15] and when reassembled from its dispersal, it presents in a single almost continuous narrative an alternative account of the Two Perfected's travels, in much greater detail. Here, interestingly, the device of the interrupted journey is abandoned. Indeed, for the first time in the historiography of their travels, the Two Perfected actually do reach Ma-ku Mountain. But they reach it *before* they arrive at Hua-kai. For Mt. Ma-ku and fully thirty-four other mountains, grottoes, and sites in the larger region of Fu-chou and Chiang-hsi are all now way stations, carefully accounted for, on a winding path even more clearly directed, from the start and at every stage, toward Mt. Hua-kai. The moment of recognition still appears, and still relatively late in the journey.

> They went on to a place called Ch'i-li Mountain, uniquely grand in shape. They looked at each other and said: "This mountain is auspiciously fine in scenery, truly a spot for divine Immortals' cultivation and refinement." Then they continued five *li*, to where the mountains were tall and hard; they saluted left and bowed right. The fine streams faced forward like family branches, spanning a hundred *li*. The thousand hills saluted in rings, like tigers crouching or dragons coiling. The Two Perfected climbed the mountain and perched and rested together. The day now grew late; a pure breeze came softly; a bright moon stood in the void. The Two Perfected took the shade of a pine and chatted and laughed, forgetting to sleep. With first dawn, they looked off to the south at the mountain's summit and made their obeisances and inquiries to the three peaks of Hua-kai. When they were finished, the mists suddenly cleared, and right before their faces stood the three peaks, like a cliff, thrusting out far beyond the skies. The Two Perfected rejoiced: "This is the mountain we saw on Ma-ku! Our master regarded it highly. He must be there."

But this is a very different sort of recognition, for the Two have paid their respects to the mountain even before they realize it is the one their master meant. And the moment has been foreshadowed at four earlier stages, when the Two view and admire Mt. Hua-kai from the distance. The first is at Mt. Yü-ssu, the starting point toward Ma-ku in the earlier versions; another is at Mt. Ma-ku itself. The effect is to turn these, from a national perspective two of the leading Taoist mountains of Chiang-hsi, into viewing platforms for Mt. Hua-kai. The winding journey, ending at Hua-kai and punctuated by views of it, focuses much of the sacred and secular space of Fu-chou and Chiang-hsi upon the mountain, and by treating that space as a series of mere stopping points makes its relation to the mountain one of subordination. The geography of the whole region is arranged along a path that, however it curves, leads in the end to Hua-kai.

Yet this too is only part of the picture. For if these thirty-four sites are subordinated to Hua-kai, they are also glorified one by one in their own right. The text singles them out as places the Two Perfected chose to visit; but more, in many cases it tells us that they visited because they recognized them as special places. We see this above at Ch'i-li Mountain, "auspiciously fine in scenery," but the motif recurs.

> They entered Fu-chou again and bade the prefect farewell. Leaving by the west ford, they gazed off at a mountain, steep and prominent: "This mountain is surely auspicious," said the Two, looking at each other. So they climbed it and looked to the four directions. The streams were fine, the mountains marvelous. They saluted left, bowed right, and rested a while. They took the occasion to

leave a handful of gold, burying it on the mountaintop. "This mountain will someday take its name from this," they said. . . .

. . . Next they came to a place called Left Bridge, where they looked off at a mountain covered in clouds and ethers, its shape like a yellow dragon rising to Heaven. The Two Perfected climbed the mountain, looked back, and laughed. "This mountain too is a worthy place to house people and plant good fortune," they said. . . .

. . . The Two then went out of the city together to inquire of the elders; they observed that this Pa-ling [County] seemed to have many lovely places, that its scenery was rich and fine, its customs pure and solid. "Men will arise here in answer to their times," they said. "Some among them will carry on our Way."

This version of the story, then, applies anew and reinforces the idea already implicit in Yen Chen-ch'ing's inscription: that though the Perfected can make a place extraordinary by their acts there, a place may also be extraordinary in its own right, and it may fall to the Perfected simply to recognize this, and to amplify specialness rather than confer it. Even a whole county may be particularly auspicious—here it is Pa-ling, the administrative ancestor of Ch'ung-jen. Places, as well as the Perfected who travel them, are important.

Even without further word from the text, one would suspect that the sites organized here were all at the time of writing active centers of the Three Immortals cult. This is confirmed by the secondary commentary, evidently of still later Southern Sung date (after 1138), that repeatedly interrupts the primary commentary and much less often the *Veritable Record* itself. While both the *Veritable Record* and the primary commentary, though of Sung date, adopt a narrative voice that could easily be heard as living in the century it reports on, the secondary comments take their stance explicitly in the Sung, updating us on what we shall find at each site "at the present day [*chin*]." What is most important in both commentaries, however, is that in them the traces of the Immortals, and the cult that honors them, unite and define an entire region, which not only spans Ch'ung-jen and Fu-chou but, in reaching out to Mt. Yü-ssu and Mt. Ma-ku, extends to much of eastern and central Chiang-hsi. By the middle of the Southern Sung, when the secondary commentary was written, the cult was evidently not merely local but regional. The earlier texts, including the *Veritable Record*, do not suggest this. But the later texts still magnify Mt. Hua-kai itself. By organizing a whole region's landmarks around it through the Immortals' elaborated journey, they make it even more clearly central. And since the commentaries do not stand apart but flow through the text, any reader of the *Verities* will absorb their version of the story.

The central role *Verities* gives to a single place and its general view of places as important, extraordinary, and numinous in their own right distinguish it sharply from the Celestial Heart texts, which give specific places no attention at all. Where Celestial Heart scriptures portray a free-ranging ritual practice that claims authority everywhere, *Verities* shows us a devotional cult not only local but proud of it. But the texts differ in other ways too, especially in the relations of authority and power they assert. Let us see how.

DIVINE AND HUMAN RELATIONS IN *VERITIES OF THE THREE PERFECTED LORDS*

In the ritual manuals and legal codes of Celestial Heart, as we have seen, the relation of the practitioner to the spirits he confronts or serves is always judicial or bureaucratic. Relations to the people he worked to cure or aid—his customers—are never specifically characterized, but the implication of the texts as a whole is that here too he is an official, serving the welfare of a dependent populace. The bureaucratic model holds with remarkable consistency.

The relations of authority and service we see in *Verities of the Three Perfected Lords*, though less uniform, are very different. The bureaucratic model is not absent, but it is far less prominent and keeps largely to one section of the book. Elsewhere other relationships come to the fore. Like its celebration of place, its treatment of divine and human relations gives the *Verities* a very different tone and meaning from the Celestial Heart texts.

To begin with likeness, let us consider the place of the bureaucratic model in the *Verities*. It shows up most clearly, if rather briefly, in *The Veritable Record of the Two Perfected Lords*, the version of the Immortals' story supposed to have been written by Shen T'ing-jui in the early Northern Sung. Recall that before Lord Fu-ch'iu ascends to Heaven, he tells his two disciples that they are close to their goal. After they have mastered certain crucial remaining techniques, he tells them, "On your behalf I will then *memorialize your names to the Gold Court. When you ascend to the Imperial Site* [*ti-so*], you will be divine Immortals."[16] Soon after, it is time for him to depart. As colorful clouds and strange music fill the sky, a red-shirted messenger arrives "*bearing an edict: The Emperor on High decrees it is time for Master Fu-ch'iu's ascent.*"[17] After Fu-ch'iu is gone, the Two live on without him. "They would often . . . pay respects to the Dipper and *have audience with Heaven.*"[18] And when their own turn came, "*they received a decree from the Jade Emperor commanding them to ascend.*"[19] Finally, after their ascent, "*to the places where the Two Perfected had ruled* [chih], *the Jade Emperor assigned thirty-six Immortal Officials* [hsien yuan] *and eighteen gods of the locality.*"[20] (Emphasis throughout is mine.)

Here the ascent of the Two depends—in good Sung bureaucratic fashion—on Fu-ch'iu's recommendation, presented to the celestial emperor in a written memorial; they are summoned, as Fu-ch'iu is, in a decree (*chao*) from on high; the visits they pay to Heaven are called audiences;[21] and celestial bureaucrats are assigned to their locale after their ascent. The last passage is striking for its reference to "the places where the Perfected had ruled."

This is the only passage in the *Verities* that represents the Immortals' relation to their mountain or region as governmental. The other bureaucratic usages in these passages deal only with the relations of the Three to Heaven—to what is above them, not what is below or around them.

These passages are interesting and surely reflect the strength of the bureaucratic model in Taoism at large. The Three could not be taken seriously as Immortals, perhaps, if their ascent were not an appointment granted by Heaven, if they did not hear from Heaven through written edicts and speak to it in written memorials. Yet the passages are not typical of the book in which they appear. There is not a single similar example in the primary and secondary commentaries of Southern Sung date, and even the main text of the *Veritable Record* more often shows other ways of seeing the Three. Two chief ties place the Three in relation to each other and to the world at large and justify or explain the authority the book attributes to them: academic ties, or the relation of master to pupil, and kinship.

Consider the Three Lords themselves. How are they connected? Are they fellow officials, senior and junior colleagues in a supernatural bureaucracy? Except in the passage above, where Fu-ch'iu memorializes for their appointment, this is not what they are at all. Instead, the Two Lords are Fu-ch'iu's students; this is how they act, and this is how he treats them. In fact their devotion to their teacher, and to learning, is what motivates the journey to Mt. Hua-kai and generates the story the *Veritable Record* sets out to tell. From its first lines, its author places learning and teaching at the center:

> Now, those who study divine Immortalhood have always cultivated their conduct, heaped up merit, and filled up with virtue for generation upon generation. Within, they cultivate their hearts; without, they purify their conduct. Thus for generation upon generation there have been divine Immortals who descend to be teachers to transmit the perfect Way. The Way achieved, one's merit will touch others; one's merit complete, one will ascend and be Immortal. Thus where the Classic says, "In accumulating learning one becomes a Perfected man," this is what it refers to.[22]

Thus, at the outset, the Two appear as young men of special virtue and talent who are attracted to Taoist practice and *set out to learn:* "The Two Perfected held always to humanity and filiality, moral limits and restraint. The excellence of their high purity, their talent and wisdom, no other could approach; and their nature delighted in the divine Immortals' Way. At the beginning they left their homes for the Hsuan-yuan Abbey in their own commandery and made Lord Fu-ch'iu their teacher."[23]

The primary commentary makes even more of their determination, which compels their parents to seek a teacher for them:

> When they grew older, they did not like the things of the dusty world and wished only to leave their homes. Their father and mother could not sway their will,

which was as firm as metal or stone, so they drew up a statement and gave it to the two sons to deposit with a teacher. The Two Perfected carried their father's handwritten statement to the Hsuan-yuan Abbey at Mt. T'ien-chieh in Ta-liang and paid respects to Lord Fu-ch'iu as their teacher.[24]

The theme of teaching and learning recurs throughout the *Veritable Record*. Most interactions between the Two and Fu-ch'iu are acts of instruction or words of praise for study well achieved:

Fu-ch'iu [said]: "You should ponder finely and cultivate diligently; before long your Way will be achieved and I shall grant you ordination."
    ... Day and night [the Two] performed their rites, always in just the same way from beginning to end. Their teacher was delighted with them.
    ... The Master said: "Your will to cultivate Perfection is truly hard to curb." Once again he handed on to them the Way of cultivating Perfection and refining substance.
    ... "You should also study the arts of Three-and-Five-Flying-Paces and the rites of Nine-One-Upper-Clarity so as to aid your time and complete the enactment of your merit." ... The Two Perfected, in accordance with his spoken transmission, studied these.[25]

The Two Perfected, then, are first of all Fu-ch'iu's pupils. But who or what is Fu-ch'iu himself? Is he at least a celestial official ushering two students into the ranks? Again, hardly at all. Shen's *Veritable Record* tells us nothing of Fu-ch'iu's background, only mentioning the names of his two other primary disciples—treating him again as a teacher. But the preceding chapter of the *Verities* fills out the picture a bit. On the one hand, it mentions several other mountains and sites of worship in various parts of China with shrines to Fu-ch'iu, showing him as a figure with some reputation in Taoist and other traditions beyond Mt. Hua-kai.[26] On the other hand, it draws on sources much older than the Sung to offer four brief stories of Fu-ch'iu's life (or lives) in antiquity before he met the Two and came to Mt. Hua-kai. In the last of these, to be sure, we do get a taste of bureaucracy. Here Fu-ch'iu, in A.D. 60 in the Han dynasty, descends with another Immortal to confer texts and arts of the Way on one Wang Pao, a would-be student of Immortality who is pining and failing. Fu-ch'iu's companion Immortal tells Wang: "We manage the Agency of Divine Immortals" (*shen hsien chih ssu*), clearly a celestial bureau.[27] Yet even here Fu-ch'iu is acting as a transmitter of knowledge—a teacher; and it is as a teacher, not a bureaucrat, that we see him in the other three stories. In two he appears in the reign of King Ling of the Chou dynasty (r. 571–545 B.C.) to transmit special arts to the heir apparent Wang-tzu Chin. In the third we find him in the capital city under the Empress Lü in the Han (r. 187–178 B.C.), teaching poetry to an imperial kinsman and high official.[28] Fu-ch'iu consorts with officials and hangs about at court, but the court is an earthly one, and he is not an official. Just as the

Two Perfected are above all students, for this text, the Third, Fu-ch'iu, is above all a teacher.

The first chapter of the *Verities* is of unclear origin and may have been compiled no earlier than the Yuan or Ming dynasties, so we cannot be certain that the assembling of just these four stories of Fu-ch'iu represents a Sung view. Further on in the chapter, however, a transcribed Sung stone inscription draws on some of the same stories to show Fu-ch'iu in just the same light. The author is Li Chung-yuan of the Fiscal Intendancy of Chiang-hsi. He commemorates a grant of imperial honors to Fu-ch'iu in 1099, some years after they had been granted to the Two. Trying to puzzle out the traces of Fu-ch'iu in antiquity, he cites *Biographies of Immortals* (*Lieh hsien ch'uan*) of Liu Hsiang of the Han to the effect that "Wang-tzu Chin encountered Fu-ch'iu, who took him up Mount Sung," and later adds that Liu "recorded only that Wang-tzu Chin *had made Fu-ch'iu his teacher,* but Lord Fu-ch'iu received no biography [of his own]." He points out that "the *History of Former Han* says that Earl Fu-ch'iu (*Fu-ch'iu Po*) was still in Ch'ang-an in the time of Empress Lü, and that Prince Yuan of Ch'u *received poetry instruction from him.*" Finally, he tells us his superior's explanation for seeking honors for Fu-ch'iu:

> [My superior] said: "*Fu-ch'iu was the Two Perfected's teacher,* yet no honors have ever been conferred on him. Surely this is not how to treat the wishes of the high Perfected seriously." So he instructed the head of Lin-ch'uan County to report Lord Fu-ch'iu's case and request appointment from the court; and he assigned his subordinate Li Chung-yuan to review the facts and make a record.[29] [Emphasis here and above is mine.]

Thus Li too treats Fu-ch'iu primarily as a teacher, both in relation to the Two Perfected (like the *Veritable Record*) and in his prior appearances in antiquity (like the first chapter of the *Verities*). The tradition, derived from the *History of Former Han,* that Fu-ch'iu taught poetry recurs in a poem by the twelfth-century high official and Ch'ung-jen County man Lo Tien, who calls him "Fu-ch'iu, poet, and old Immortal earl."

One other passage in the *Verities* gives a sense of Fu-ch'iu's relation to the Two, and indeed to a much larger group of Immortals. The relation is not quite that of student to teacher, but neither is it bureaucratic. The miracle stories that make up the last two chapters of *Verities*, largely gathered by Chang Yuan-shu, include a tale, set in the mid-twelfth century, of worshippers who climb a mountain neighbor to Mt. Hua-kai called Mt. Pa. Their plan is to erect images of four Immortals connected to Mt. Pa, along with images of the Three Lords of Hua-kai and the Twelve Immortals of West Mountain in Hung-chou, the prefecture northwest of Fu-chou. Since Mt. Pa was the Four Immortals' home shrine, they naturally place the images of these Four in the center, with the Hua-kai Three and the West Mountain Twelve ranged on either side. But immediately thunder and lightning burst out all around them.

They know they have made some error but cannot guess what it is. After a series of fruitless inquiries by divination, one of them hits upon the answer:

> "Surely it must be that Mei, Luan, Teng, Yeh [the Four Immortals of Mt. Pa] and the West Mountain Immortals are disturbed that their Sect Leader [*chiao chu*], the Transcendently Responsive Perfected Lord Fu-ch'iu of Hua-kai, is placed in the last seat; and that the many Immortals are yielding in reverence and asking that he take the chief and central place? Is this it? We seek an affirmative divination if this is so." When his words were done they cast [the divining sticks] and received an affirmative reply at once.[30]

I return to this tale in Chapter 5 because it implies much about relations among different Immortals' cults in Chiang-hsi. Here it is important because it offers another way to see Fu-ch'iu's tie to the Two and other Immortals: he is their "sect leader." The Chinese is *chiao-chu*, literally, "chief of a teaching," normally a Buddhist word for the founder of a sect or of a doctrinal descent line, a sort of patriarch.[31] That such a figure is a teacher goes without saying; but he is more, the chief of a whole way of learning, teaching, or practice. There is nothing official or bureaucratic here, however. Like the simple relation between student and teacher, the relation of the sect leader to his followers is hierarchic, but in a way that has nothing to do with rank and office. The notion of the sect leader allows the story's narrator to array a large number of Immortals below Fu-ch'iu, in a position of subordination, without recourse to the image of celestial bureaucracy.

Kinship is not dwelt on in the *Verities* as much as student-teacher or disciple-master relations, but it should not be overlooked. The Two Perfected are not simply fellow students—they are cousins, or even brothers. Shen's *Veritable Record* names them as kinsmen when it first mentions them: "The Two Perfected Lords Wang and Kuo of Hua-kai Mountain were men of Ch'en-liu in Pien-chou by origin. Wang was a distant descendant of [Wang] Fang-p'ing; Kuo was Wang's younger cousin of the same patriline [*tsu-ti*]."[32] Here the *Veritable Record* echoes Yen Chen-ch'ing's eighth-century inscription.[33] The primary commentary places the Two still closer:

> Their grandfather was T'ing-ssu; their father died in the time of Yuan-ti of Chin [about A.D. 320]. He had submitted a book [to court] entitled *Meaning of the Spring and Autumn Annals*. The family was long of high and solid character and had stored up merit through good works. At the age of thirty, their mother, Lady Hsu, happened one evening to dream that the moon's corona filled her room, and a ray of divine light shot into someone. She awoke pregnant and later gave double birth. In spirit and vigor the two sons far exceeded their peers.

Here Wang and Kuo are full brothers, indeed twins. The commentary agrees with the main text, however, on their descent from Wang Fang-p'ing in the Han. Wang Fang-p'ing was an Immortal honored in Taoist traditions far beyond Hua-kai's region.[34] Together, the kinship tie to Wang Fang-p'ing, the student-teacher relation between the Two Perfected and Fu-ch'iu, and Fu-ch'iu's own past activity in Chou and Han connect the Three Lords to a legitimizing wider world of old and nationally honored Taoist traditions, but without any recourse to bureaucratic or official ties, while journeying to Mt. Hua-kai and making their home there roots them firmly in the local and regional setting of Ch'ung-jen County, Fu-chou, and Chiang-hsi.

So far we have been looking at relations among the Three Lords themselves and at their ties to a world or time beyond Sung Fu-chou; most of the evidence for this has come from material in the first two chapters of the *Verities*. Now, for what the book says about the relation between the Three Lords and those they helped—their worshippers and beneficiaries in the region surrounding Mt. Hua-kai—we look to its last chapters, to the twelfth- and thirteenth-century miracle stories collected by the Taoist Chang Yuan-shu. It is hard to put a name to the relationships one finds represented here; for lack of a more particular word, I shall say that they are *personal*. What they are not, almost without exception, is bureaucratic or governmental. There is not a single unqualified indication in the miracle stories that either the Three Lords or their lay worshippers commonly saw the Lords as celestial officials governing mortals as an earthly official governs the common people.

Something like a bureaucratic picture of the Three Lords does appear in one of the twenty-five stories.[35] Here, Chang Yuan-shu tells of his own dream:

In the *chi-hai* year of Ch'un-hsi [1179], on the first of the second month, the [anniversary of the] day that Wang and Kuo rose into the void, I[36] offered fragrant tea and burned a written submission of congratulations. When night came, after the second drum, I dreamed suddenly that I was in the abbey's Hall of the Ascent. All at once I saw the Three Responsive Perfected Lords of Hua-kai. Their visage and form were upright and stern as always. When I looked at their headgear, each had a jewel-fringed crown hanging down [*ke ch'ui liu mien*]. Their garments and the hanging curtain [behind them] too were grand to look upon. When I looked off to the side at the two corners, the myriad figures of the multitude of Immortals each wore an ordinary garment. The beauty of all this was extraordinary. While I was praising and sighing and bowing down in admiration, suddenly I awoke from the dream. I pondered this minutely. Think its meaning through: [the immortals of] Hua-kai would not [ordinarily] have jeweled-crown garb. Now I very much think that the Three Perfected Immortals have been granted an order of appointment by the Emperor on High and, lest the human world be unaware, have informed me by a dream, so that I might inform the faithful and reverent [*hsin ching che*]. Now, Fu-ch'iu's meritorious conduct is renowned as chief among the serried Immortals; but the Perfected Lords Wang and Kuo ought to have further emolument and prestige, lest they again refuse employment by a ruler of Chiang-nan. I now record this here and await any wise gentleman who may have had a confirming dream without previous knowledge [of mine]; then this uncertainty may be resolved.[37]

Much in this story cries out for explanation—"lest they again refuse employment by a ruler of Chiang-nan" is particularly tantalizing, though not relevant to the issue at hand, and I return to it in Chapter 5—but clearly Chang takes the Three Lords' unexpectedly exalted dress in his dream as a sign that they have received promotion from the celestial emperor, and that this should be seconded with new earthly honors: they "ought to have further emolument and prestige." It is crucial, however, that unlike almost all the others in the collection, this story recounts the personal experience of a Taoist professional, a man used to seeing, considering, and communicating with Immortals and divinities in bureaucratic forms and terms; and that Chang Yüan-shu himself expresses considerable uncertainty about his interpretation. This is in any case the only miracle story in the collection that refers to a celestial order transmitted to or by the Three Lords.[38]

Consider now another story from the collection, much more typical in its picture of the Three and their relation to those they help:

> Near the Mountain, at a place called Ch'i-fu, there lived a country commoner whose name I have forgotten. His family had sacrificed to the Three Immortals for generations. Some time in the Shao-hsing period [1131–1162], suddenly a mountain fell down—or as the local people say, "the mountain roared." In front, behind, and to the left and right of where he lived, everything slid down at once. In a single voice the entire family recited the sage-names of the great Immortals, in hope of rescue. All around the house was a deep abyss. This one home remained, as if on a high platform, with no ground to spare. Thus they were saved alive. Afterward they moved their residence, and [what had been] their ground too collapsed.[39]

This is the sparest story, and its picture of the Immortals is hardly detailed. But what is missing is significant. Not only is there no bureaucratic imagery here; there is also no mediation. In the Celestial Heart texts, as in bureaucratic representations in Taoism more generally, the practitioner is above all a mediator between the person in need and the heavenly authorities. He carries the message of need to them and executes their orders; or at his most independent he exercises the authority they have delegated to him. Various other deities play a similar mediating role—the city god and god of the locality above all. Indeed one could say, somewhat too simply, that the bureaucratic model is just a device by which the Chinese represent mediation or intercession in the divine world. In the present story there is none of this. The family prays directly, and on the spur of the moment, to the Three Immortals. The response comes just as directly and immediately. Neither this miracle story nor any other suggests that the power the Three Immortals wield is anything but their own, that they need to consult with any other authority before responding. We are, however, given a hint as to why the Three may have responded to just this appeal: the family "had sacrificed to the Three

Immortals for generations." That is, they had a long-standing relationship to the Three, a relationship that distinguished them from those around them. For the Immortals did not act to save the whole neighborhood—as one might expect Heaven's appointed official to do—but rescued only the family that called on them and that had paid respects to them for a long time.

In a similar story a man is saved from drowning and actually meets two of the Three Immortals when they come to rescue him:

> Below Mt. Hua-kai, at a place called Pi-fu, lived a tenant named Ch'en 4, whose neighbors called him Flowery Fourthling. His family had prayed to the Immortals very diligently. His eldest son went to Kao-yu prefecture [in Huai-nan East circuit] to trade. On the way the boat sank, and everyone else was drowned. His son alone called out the sage-names of the Great Immortals and floated downstream hugging the mast for a day and a night, with no idea where he was. In some rushes near the shore were two old men rowing a small boat. They came to his rescue, pulled him onto the bank, revived him with a fire, and fed him rice gruel. Within two or three days he had regained his senses and was lively and healthy. The two old men had nothing at all in their boat; they gave him their extra provisions and took their leave of him. "There are no people living for some forty or fifty *li* from here," they said. "If you go straight ahead in that direction, you are bound to reach the place you live." He did as they said and headed forward, and just as they had told him came upon a path and went home. His family, thinking him already dead, had provided full filial rites. They had completed the seven fasts [*chai*], and the monks were just finishing when they saw an emaciated figure arrive at the gate, utterly exhausted. The whole family suspected he was some sort of ghost; for a long time they would not believe him. When they did, they asked what had happened to him. "In the moment of peril," he said, "through my merit in reciting the sage-names of the Three Hua-kai Immortals in hope of rescue, I was allowed to live again."[40]

Not all or even most stories imply that one needs a long-term relationship to the Three to receive their aid. But others do show them picking out one person when he calls on them:

> Below Ta-fou Mountain lived a certain Yen-hsien; I forget his surname. In the *chi-hai* year of the Ch'un-hsi period [1179], suddenly there was a noise behind his house. He rushed to look: it was an avalanche, so powerful it was certain to crush the whole household and all its members. The ground shook; there was no sure place to hold on to. So he gathered his whole family, and they looked toward Ta-fou Mountain and begged the Three Immortals of Hua-kai to save them, vowing [to hold] an Offering to pay reverence at the mountain. Their pleas were most pitiable. Suddenly the avalanche stopped. The whole family was saved. To this day the break [in the earth] is still there. The response in this case is particularly clear. Within half a *li* of Yen-hsien's house lived a certain Chang Pang-ch'ang, whose family encountered the "mountain's roar," and half of them were crushed to death. Ah me! When Yen-hsien, who appealed to the Immortals, receives good fortune such as this, while Pang-ch'ang, who did not

appeal, suffers ill fortune such as *that,* how can the people of this age not serve the Immortal Perfected reverently?[41]

Thus, by the very act of appealing, one may establish a special relation to the Three Immortals. In turn, they could give one courage in a fearful moment as easily as life itself. On the way up Hua-kai Mountain, a sharp and narrow ridge often tested pilgrims' confidence; this was the aptly named Sword's Edge Ridge: "Every traveler is so frightened, he says it is like walking on a sword's edge. If with determined heart he calls the names of the Three Perfected and implores them to grant him their aid, then he will walk as on level ground, his heart at peace and his spirit settled, and find no difficulty in it."[42]

In the previous story, it is striking that Yen-hsien's family vows to hold an Offering (*chiao*) in the Immortals' honor in exchange for their aid. Such exchanges are common in these stories:

> A certain Wang, administrative officer in the Department of Ministries, came to the county seat on a visit to Hua-kai and happened to meet me [*Yuan-shu*].[43] . . . Our talk touched on Mt. Hua-kai's scenery. Suddenly Wang said: "Master, have you ever heard of the Old Man from South of the Mountain?" I said I hadn't and asked him why he mentioned this. "He was my former self," he said. When I asked him to explain, he told me:
>
> "My late father had no heir. He prayed everywhere, with no response. When he inquired of those of age and experience, they said: 'If you want a successor, your only course is to disregard all distance and seek at Hua-kai.' He fasted and cleansed himself and set out on his journey. After several days, he reached the very summit and told the Taoists to arrange an Offering. He burned a prayer, promising to visit each year until he had a son, and then to hold a great and splendid affair to repay the Immortals' boon. In the third year, on the night he stayed at the mountain, he suddenly dreamed that three Taoists greeted him, saying: 'Thank you for coming so far. Originally you were to have no son. We now send you the Old Man from South of the Mountain as your heir.' When their words were done, he awoke from the dream and found only himself wrapped in his bedclothes. On pondering their meaning carefully, he was greatly delighted. Not waiting for dawn, he cleansed himself, ascended the hall and made a hundred prostrations of thanks. On the day he came home his wife was pregnant. When her term was full, she bore a son, just as he had been told. From then on he fulfilled his pledge [*chi chih hsin*] by renovating the Immortals' shrine and by holding Offerings at the mountain [*chiu shan hsiu tsao chien chiao*] in thanks for the favor. He never missed a year. When I grew older he would bring me along too, to join him in the visit and obeisances. Later I came alone. I now have five sons. How can I ever repay in balancing measure [*pao ch'eng*] the boon I have borne from the Immortals?"
>
> I heard these words myself and so have reverently written them down.[44]

Most vows are to hold Offerings; but some promise more general obeisance: "In a recent year Wu Ch'eng of Ching-hsiang, seeking blessings for his kin, made a vow to visit the Immortals' peak. After a time, fulfilling his vow, he went to the mountain to give thanks."[45] And one may undertake a vow to avoid punishment as well as to gain rewards:

> At the beginning of Ch'un-hsi [ca. 1174], six brothers from two families in a remote village in Lu-ling went up the mountain to visit and pay obeisance. When they gained the top, it was just reaching noon, so they asked the mountain's manager: "Are there any livestock hereabouts?" The manager said: "These are precincts of splendor, only a few feet from Heaven. How could we make our food of living beings?" "On the way up we never abstained," said the man. "Yesterday, for instance, where we overnighted, we slaughtered a dog. Well, as there's none here, we'll eat plain rice." When their obeisance was finished and evening came, they were also unwilling to sleep below the chapel and insisted on staying below the main altar in the Hall of Immortals. After roughly one watch, those below the chapel suddenly heard a man crying loudly for help. The manager took a torch and ascended to the altar, where by his light he saw five of the men, all knocked senseless by thunderbolts. One, though he had been struck, was partly conscious and asked for help. "All these were struck by lightning," he said. They carried them down into the chapel; he made a vow to hold an Offering in grieving expression of their penitence. Four of the group immediately revived. The two leaders were cold in body and limb; only their hearts and hands were slightly warm, and they could not speak. When dawn came, they hired men to carry them down. After twenty or thirty *li*, the two leaders died. The other four were quite well. From then on, wicked fellows all knew awe and reverence. None who went up the mountain failed to fast and cleanse himself.[46]

The vow is an institution well known to students of saints' and gods' cults outside China. It is most thoroughly studied in Catholic Europe, both medieval and modern, but is present also in Orthodox Europe, in Latin America, in Islamic practice in the Middle East and India, and in deity cults in India and Southeast Asia.[47] Typically, in all these societies, a worshipper seeking a favor promises a gift to the saint or god if the favor is granted. Often the gift is a religious ceremony in the saint's or god's honor (in Europe, a mass; in China, an Offering), though there are other possibilities. Some scholars have argued that the sorts of reciprocity established by vows should be considered according to the structures of secular patronage or (alternatively) the patterns of bargaining and reciprocity among equals that obtain among human beings in each society in question.[48] Seeing Chinese vows to saints and deities in this light is made difficult by the apparent lack of any scholarship on the place and role of vows or promises in secular Chinese life at any period. Still, one may say with certainty that the vows in the Three Lords cult are *not* made by worshippers to their equals. But it would be hard too to argue that they are modeled on human patronage, since I see little evidence that there was any such thing as stable, dyadic patronage or clientage in the relatively developed rural areas of South China in the Sung and after.

In any case, the rather striking parallels and recurrences in vows to saints or gods, and in their surrounding practices, among societies that differ dramatically in their secular social relations, suggest that any single-case explanations may be inappropriate. If structures of secular patronage or the role of secular promises differ in the societies where religious vows are prominent, yet the vows themselves and the practices surrounding them are much alike, are there other similarities among such different societies that can help us understand the vow?

What strikes me as a common feature in all such cases is the presence of a professional religious class with a highly developed theology and cosmology, within which the divinities that laymen usually pray to are secondary, subordinate, marginal, or in some cases even unrecognized, and with a liturgy that places professionals themselves at the node of communication between humans and the divine. In this context, vows serve—even on the occasion of larger clerically managed rituals[49]—as an alternative channel of direct communication and exchange for a lay population, a way of establishing contact that works around or at least supplements the liturgies and mediations of professionals. Thus Pierre Sanchis tells us of modern Portuguese *romarias:* "Involved in the whole practice of vows . . . there is a 'popular' movement of independence, of resistance to the clergy's religious monopoly, and a demand for autonomy so far as relations with the sacred are concerned."[50] According to William Christian, in sixteenth-century Spain "[t]he vow and similar prayers to the saints were forms of direct engagement between the Christian and the divine, with no inquisitive or costly middleman."[51] Jill Dubisch finds Christian's analysis applicable to Orthodox pilgrimage in present-day Greece.[52] Similarly, Marc Gaborieau tells of the suspicion in which personal prayers to Islamic saints, notably including vows, have been held by clerical reformers in India and Nepal, who find the notion of direct prayer to anyone but God idolatrous.[53] Surely we should consider Chinese vows to gods and Immortals in a similar light. A vow was one way—in China not the only way—a lay worshipper could speak directly, and *deal* directly, with a god. The abundance of vows in the Three Immortals stories, then, tells us something important about how worshippers saw the Three and how they hoped to interact with them.

Even without a vow, a favor from the Immortals may require some response by way of thanks:

During the Ch'ien-tao period [1165–1173], in Hu-pei, there was a local strongman whose family property was vast. His household was infected by a seasonal epidemic. Suddenly one day, a man of the Way came to the gate to teach and convert. A servant waved his hand and pointed: "You go away, Taoist! We have nothing! The master's whole house is unwell." "What sickness are they suffering from?" asked the man of the Way. The servant answered: "It's an outbreak of plague." "I can enchant the water," said the man of the Way, "and make the sickness better at once." "If this is so," the servant said, "my master will find out what you want and supply it to you as you command. Now wait until I come back." He reported to his master, who could not contain his joy when he heard. He sent the servant to carry his words, asking the man of the Way to stay and be seated, and immediately drew some water for the man of the Way to enchant. When the man of the Way received the water, he sucked it in and washed and rinsed his mouth several times, then had the servant take it in and give it to the master to consume. If everyone from adults to children drank it, their illness would get better in less than a day. The servant took the water in, and the master knocked his teeth and drank of it and distributed it to all the household. Their pains cleared and cooled and they felt strong and healthy at once. Then he sent the servant in all haste to transmit these words to the man of the Way: that they did not know his lofty surname. "I am surnamed Kuo," said the man of the Way. When asked where he lived, he said "I live in Ch'ung-jen County in Fu-chou." "At what place?" "In a thatched hut below Hua-kai Mountain." When the master learned his surname and residence, he immediately had a room made ready, rice cooked, and noodles made to serve him, hoping that he would stay. The man of the Way said: "I am just stopping by here. I knew there was trouble in the house, so I came to offer help. Now that the sickness is cured, I had already promised a friend of the Way to go on to a famous mountain; I cannot stay long." The master said: "You may live in my poor household; even a year or two would not be too long. Why do you go?" The man of the Way said: "I shall come back in two days. You need not detain me." He did not tarry, but left. The master waited for him for days, months, years, but never saw him return. Finally, he sent men bearing pledges and generous gifts of money to the foot of the mountain, where they searched everywhere for the hut of the man of the Way, Kuo. For days they could not find him. The fuel-gatherers and local elders summoned them. "There has never been any Way-man Kuo's hut below the mountain," they said. "Was this not Perfected Lord Kuo of the mountaintop? He is well known to transform himself in this way. You should go quickly, offer incense and paper money, and hold many Offerings of thanks." The men did as they said, ascended the mountain, and thanked him. They returned to their county and told all their acquaintances. Ah me! So famous is the numinous responsiveness of the Perfected Immortals.[54]

The exchange of vows and Offerings for favors and the promise of thanks for things received should not be viewed cynically. The stories show the devotees as just as sincere in their vows as they are in their thanks afterward. The point, however, is that the stories assume believers can do something for Immortals, just as Immortals can do things for believers. Thus the Immortals who appear to Wang's father thank him for coming so far and seem to give him the unscheduled son in expression of their thanks. Worshippers enter into a direct personal relation with the Three, a relation that makes thanks appropriate on both sides. We have already seen one story in which the Immortals punish someone who offends them. There are several others in the collection. But the Three punish, not with the judicial procedures of the Celestial Heart world, but directly, without formal trappings, with immediate and irresistible force, and sometimes even with humor. Here is an example:

> It was the Ch'ien-tao period [1165–1173]. Ch'en Tsao, also called Wei-ming, a man of Ts'ao-p'ing, visited the mountain every spring and stayed overnight. He would have twenty-odd tenant-serfs prepare his sedan chair, baggage, and such. All who were scheduled to go would fast and cleanse themselves. One of them was a certain Yen Ya-t'ui-erh, whose family had bought a pig's head that day and put it on to boil. His father said: "You're to be taken up the mountain by Inspector-General Ch'en. You should not eat meat." "It's the master himself that's going up the mountain," said the son. "What's that got to do with me?" After eating heartily, he went up the mountain as usual. When the Offering was finished, they headed back, but when they were midway, suddenly he was gone. "I think that servant must be lagging along behind," said Ch'en Tsao. "Surely he's bound to come." By nightfall, he still hadn't arrived. The next morning they sent people up the mountain to search. When they reached Bloody-Tree Hollow, suddenly they found a bamboo hat. There was the barest little path down to Halfway Ridge, where they also found a turban. After a while they found some baggage too. They moved no farther, but drew lots to choose another servant to go back and look everywhere for him. Suddenly, near a place north of the mountain called Chih-wan Gully, there he was, monkey-hanging in the air before the three gates.[55] They untied him and stood him upon the ground; he was without awareness. When evening came, they brought him back and used the heat of a fire to restore his senses. Not till the next day could he speak. When they questioned him, he said: "When I had come about halfway down the mountain, I suddenly saw four strong men clothed in red, who pulled me down. I didn't know how I had come there, but I vowed at once to cleanse my guilt, and begged forgiveness. Only then was I allowed to awaken." Such was the warning.[56]

In a similar story, a certain Cook Liu, who "was always contemptuous of Immortals or Buddhas and did not believe in them at all," finds himself hired for an Offering at Mt. Hua-kai. Spending the night at the Three Immortals Pavilion, he walks about naked before the images of the Three and urinates freely under the eaves. In the middle of the night, he is drawn to a path he has never noticed before and finds himself trapped in a dark and impenetrable thicket of bamboo, where he screams for help for a long time. When at last the assembly rescue him, he realizes that he has committed an offense, but that "in their gracious compassion the Immortal Perfected let me not fall into great harm, simply making known my transgression and making clear their numinous power."[57]

Both these offenses occur during ceremonies for the Three. In Chapter 2, we met Rite-Master Wang from Hung Mai's *I-chien chih*, who "was much employed by the common people because his fees were one-third lower." In his story, a similar offense mars a Celestial Heart ritual. The difference in the result is important:

Wang regularly hired his neighbor Mr. Li to write the memorial and Azure Plaint [for the Offering]. In the second year of the Ch'ing-yuan period [1196], on the fifteenth of the first month, a rich family invited him to hold an Offering for Preservation of Peace at the festival of the first full moon. Mr. Li had gone out with his friends to watch the lamps the night before and had drunk wine and eaten meat. Now he said nothing, but, still drunk, took up his pen; the calligraphy and the seal were neither fine nor elegant.

When the Offering was done, Wang dreamed two red-shirted clerks sought him out and brought him before the court of an officer of Heaven. The officer of Heaven sat upright in fine clothing, his attendants proper and decorous. The clerks led Wang to stand before him. Suddenly, some soldiers led a prisoner in: it was Mr. Li. The officer of Heaven was fearfully angry. "That Azure Plaint you wrote recently," he asked, "how dare you write it after drinking wine and eating meat?" He had [the soldiers] force [Mr. Li] to sit and bare his feet, and sentenced him to over a hundred blows.

Next he questioned Wang, blaming him in the same way. "I was simply superintending an Offering site to realize high merit," Wang replied. "This offense by staff member What's-his-name is something I never knew of." [The officer] shouted an order and withdrew. One of the soldiers raised the stick he was holding and struck [Wang] on the chest, saying, "Go!" Wang awoke in terror with an unbearable pain in his chest.

Before he had a chance to talk with anyone, he heard someone calling urgently outside his gate and sent a boy to check. It was Li's wife. "My husband has suddenly taken sick," she said. "It's very serious. He's asking for the rite master to rescue him." Wang bore with his pain and went to their house, where Li kowtowed to him from a certain distance and said: "I have just received my beating; my suffering is to have no limit. You see it right now. There is nothing more to be said. I hope that for my long service with pen and ink, you will give three thousand cash to buy my coffin." In grief and distress, Wang answered yes. At this, Li died. As for Wang, from then on his chest throbbed and ached more and more, and later he began to vomit blood, till at the end of the fourth month he died.[58]

Perhaps the more severe punishment here is appropriate to the offense. After all, Li is a direct participant in the ceremony, not a cook like Liu or a mere tenant and retinue member like Yen in the previous two stories. More important is how punishment is applied and whom it reaches. The offenders find themselves in a celestial court, headed by a bureaucrat who issues sentences along earthly lines. They undergo the same process that Rite Master Wang must often have applied to wayward spirits himself. But even more striking, though the offense is Li's, Wang must share responsibility and punishment. He is, after all, a bureaucrat, whose Offering is a bureaucratic function, a communication to higher authorities. When a communication is prepared improperly through the malfeasance of his staff, the responsibility is his. Like many a bureaucrat, he claims to know neither of the crime nor even the name of the subordinate; but in his superiors' eyes his subordinates' acts are his responsibility, in fact, his own acts, since the conduct of his office—and an Offering falls precisely in that category—is his own to see to.

The picture is very different in the Hua-kai stories, where only the offenders themselves have offended, and only they are punished. In the story of tenant Yen, we see the Offering, not as a bureaucratic transaction, but, like the other Offerings in these stories, as a personal message from Inspector-General Ch'en to the Three Lords. Yen is Ch'en's subordinate in life, but in matters of personal communication with the divine, this sort of subordination is irrelevant. In this sense Yen is right that it is Ch'en who is "going up the mountain"—making pilgrimage to the Immortals—and not he. What he does not see is that by climbing the Immortals' mountain and entering their shrine, in effect their home, he too is moving at least potentially into a personal relation to them and will be judged by what he—and not his master—does in their presence. There is no need to punish his master for what he does, since neither Yen, his master, nor the Three Perfected appear here as members of a common bureaucratic hierarchy in which each level must be held to account for the level below it. Likewise, when he is punished, and when Cook Liu is punished, it is not in court but simply out of the blue, and in ways—straying into a bamboo thicket that appears from nowhere, hanging upside down waiting for rescue—that however terrifying smack more of whimsy than of the orderly legal processes of the Celestial Heart world. The mysterious "men clothed in red" in Yen's story are undoubtedly a textual echo of the red-shirted clerks in Wang's, figures who appear in many another text and are in fact a sort of *topos* of bureaucratic-style Taoism. But here they are wrenched from their normal bureaucratic context: they are not identified as clerks and act not as escorts to higher authorities but, it seems, as a kind of hired muscle. If there is an earthly parallel to Yen's or Liu's experiences, it is the surly peasant who insults a powerful local gentleman and is beaten by his thugs, not the lawbreaker who runs afoul of the state. The contrast sums up perfectly the different sorts of authority and responsibility, the different sorts of human-divine relations, that operate in the Celestial Heart world and in the world of the Three Perfected.

I have said the Three do not serve as mediators to higher authority. For the most part they need no downward mediation either. There are exceptions: in two miracle stories, the Three speak by "descending into a boy" at their shrine: shorthand for the use of a young medium, who presumably is kept on hand to serve in just this way. We saw the same practice in the Celestial Heart world in Chapter 2. But even where this happens, the story presents it as a direct communication by the Three to those below. And far more often the Three appear much more directly: most commonly in dreams (thirteen times in the twenty-five stories) but several times even in the flesh, as in the story of the Hu-pei family and the plague. Only twice in all the stories do the Three communicate with human beings in writing: once in a poem granted through the planchette, and once by causing a boy they have descended into to write—but they have spoken through him first.

Believers and petitioners too may have their own say directly, by voice, as we have seen in the drowning and avalanche stories. In other stories the means of communication may be less clear: we read that someone went to the mountain and prayed. In practice, prayers may often have been written; but the stories do not tell us so. We learn only twice explicitly of written communications from worshippers to the Three.[59] Most important, in every case, the communication is represented as the appellant's own act: a direct communication with the Three. This is especially striking in a text that so much mentions Offerings.

A word or two of comment is needed here. It is fair to assume that the Offerings held at Mt. Hua-kai as expressions of thanks to the Three Perfected, like all others we know of for this and later periods, were conducted by professional Taoists, and that written communications were central to them. It is virtually certain too that the Taoists who offered them viewed these written communications as memorials to the heavenly government and indeed conceived themselves as communicating not with the Three themselves but with a vast array of celestial bureaucrats and with the Jade Emperor at the top, just as we have seen in the Celestial Heart ritual texts. The point is that the miracle stories, indeed the whole of the *Verities*, never hint at any of this. In the stories we never see an Offering from the inside (as we do, by contrast, in the tale of the punishment of Celestial Heart Master Wang), never read of the actual procedures, communications, and documents that made it up. Rather we see the Offering from the outside, from the perspective of the grateful believer who expresses his thanks or fulfills a vow. It is reduced to a kind of token and as such appears as the believer's own direct communication, or, better, his direct gift, to the Three—and to no one else. This question of the varying meaning of Offerings needs much more attention, and I return to it in Chapter 8. For now I need only stress that in reading about Offerings in the Hua-kai texts, and in the miracle stories in particular, one should attend to the picture the texts themselves draw rather than to what one knows of the Offering elsewhere and from other sources. What is important here is how this text presents them; and it presents them in a way absolutely consistent with the larger picture I have been drawing: as part of a system of direct and unmediated personal relations between worshipper and Immortal.

Two other sorts of relationships portrayed (or not portrayed) in *Verities* need attention here, because they are also important for understanding what the Hua-kai cult—as this book represents it—is about. One, the relation of the Three to the state, I take up in the next section. The other is their relation to other divinities and their cults. There is little of this in *Verities*,[60] but the silence is important. We have seen that the Celestial Heart texts treat the practitioner as controller and often suppressor of local gods and cults, at best subordinating them to the larger Heavenly hierarchy of which he is an active member, at worst burning shrines and destroying false or faithless gods. This is an absolutely typical phenomenon in history: I have already cited R. A. Stein's work showing that promoters and practitioners of religious Taoism had very early assumed this role in relation to local cults.[61] Not a single passage in the *Verities* shows the Three suppressing any other deity or its worshippers. Even in the account of their life on Mt. Hua-kai before the ascent, set in the Chin dynasty, when god-vanquishing Taoists were standard figures, they simply do not do this. The only passage that relates them in any way to another local cult is the story on the arrangement of images on Mt. Pa, where thunder and lightning continue until the worshippers realize they should place Lord Fu-ch'iu in the center and so exalt him over the Four Immortals usually worshipped there. The Four Immortals are not suppressed or denied but are simply subordinated to one (not, apparently, all) of the Three; and this is presented as the wish of *all* the nineteen Immortals enshrined there, including the Mt. Pa four. There is nothing at all here of the cult-suppressing Taoism so prominent elsewhere.

THE THREE IMMORTALS AND THE STATE

Finally, the *Verities* paints a striking picture of the relation of the Three to the state—to the earthly, not the Heavenly, government. The primary commentary to Shen T'ing-jui's *Veritable Record*, in its detailed narrative of the travels of the Two on their way to Mt. Hua-kai, shows them meeting twice with local administrators. They first encounter the Fu-chou prefect—"They entered Fu-chou [city] and visited the prefectural supervisor. He received them with reverent ceremony and sent them with special escort to a retreat east of the prefecture to rest"[62]—and then the county administrator of Pa-ling County, whose jurisdiction at that time included Mt. Hua-kai:

> They entered Pa-ling County and were welcomed to audience by the administrator. He escorted the Two Perfected to a temple west of the county seat and settled them in there. The next day they held a Retreat and discoursed on ritual. When the Retreat was finished, the Two Perfected rested for a bit in their lodging.[63]

This helpful and respectful treatment from the representatives of the state in the area of their travels is interesting but not surprising. Much more surprising is an episode in Shen T'ing-jui's *Veritable Record* itself that for a time brings the Three Perfected into contact—or rather conflict—not with local officials but with the court itself. Lord Fu-ch'iu has already ascended, and the Two are in residence at Mt. Hua-kai, performing their miraculous services for local people and in the meantime working to brew an elixir.

> When the elixir was complete, divine colors and numinous radiance permeated the space among the sun, moon, and planets. Those who saw to heavenly omens

at that time marveled, and memorialized to the ruler of the time: "In Chiang-nan an auspicious ether mounts to the sky. It is the ether of a Son of Heaven." The ruler commanded his ministers and lower officials to offer their views on it. In the court's discussions, no one knew what to say. At this he commanded generals to move an army across the [Yangtse] River to search it out.

At that time the chief general was Li Yen-yuan. When Yen-yuan received the order, he organized his troops for a punitive foray. When they reached the bottom of Mt. Hua-kai, they saw only the mountain, surrounded by purple clouds and auspicious ethers, which wound all about it. He ordered his soldiers to reconnoiter. The Two Perfected heard and laughed. "We are cultivating our will for the void," they said. "How could we wish for anything higher?" They transformed themselves into Immortal troops, who deployed and filled the clouds. They played at fighting with the mortal troops, but though they joined lance points in repeated combat, there was never any injury. When the soldiers shot at them with arrows, they saw the arrowheads simply fall to the ground, where they changed to bits of tile. The troops and commanders were perplexed and fearful. Suddenly black clouds gathered again from all sides into one place, making a thick darkness. The commanders and soldiers trembled in terror; none could advance or retreat. At last [Li] Yen-yuan and the others realized [that these were] divine Immortals. They knocked their heads on the ground and confessed their wrongs, vowing that if they received light they would swear never [again] to commit any offense against the Perfected Sages. In an instant the cloudy ethers rolled up and an auspicious light blazed forth. Then cassia branches and a jeweled bow descended from the void, shedding multicolored light unlike any in the world. Yen-yuan took the bow and assigned a man to bear it to the court, reporting what had happened in full. When the emperor saw it, he was alarmed and ordered his hundred officials to elucidate it. Only the chief minister Li Chung-fu said, in a memorial: "This is a bow that divine Immortals in higher Heaven use for play and amusement. It must be a response called forth by your Majesty's sagely virtue. If a State has a man of perfection, then it receives marvelous treasures." The hundred officers commended his words. An edict ordered Yen-yuan to withdraw his army and sent emissaries from the inner court with a decree of invitation to the Two Perfected. The Two Perfected made their excuses: "We live on the mountain and are to bring fortune and benefit to the common people." In the end they refused [tz'u] the order calling them forth.

... When the decree emissaries returned and completed their report, the emperor sent down another decree deputing the emissary-minister Li Chung-te, along with the Fu-chou prefect [tz'u-shih] Liu P'ing-hui, the Lin-ch'uan county administrator Huang Ssu-hu, and the Pa-ling county administrator Hsia Tzu-ying, to visit Mt. Hua-kai together and offer apologies in personal audience [chao hsieh].[64]

This is extraordinary. The Two Perfected are shown defying the authority of a sitting ruler—to be sure, authority wielded in misunderstanding, and by implication improperly—and even defeating his troops in a battle only they understand is mock, then accepting the apologies of his representatives when the misunderstanding is cleared up. The ruler's misapprehension is that the authority of the Two, made obvious to his court by the emanations their elixir sends up from the mountain, may threaten the authority of his own state. He learns that their power, though unconquerable and utterly legitimate in its own right, is of another category from his own and so no danger to him. He also learns that he cannot summon these men to serve at his court—that they are after prizes not his to grant or to refuse. This lesson tells us much about the Hua-kai cult, and I shall return to it in Chapter 5.

Verities of the Three Perfected Lords is the document of a local deity cult, the cult of the Three Immortals. In the chapter that follows, I use *Verities* and other sources to trace the rise and spread of this cult in Southern Sung Chiang-hsi.

CHAPTER FOUR

The Rise of the Hua-kai Cult

When did the Hua-kai cult first become important in Fu-chou? Let us begin by consulting the tourist guidebooks. Wang Hsiang-chih, who lived in the late twelfth and early thirteenth centuries, finished the book that would make his name in 1227. This was *The Scenery of the Empire Recorded* (*Yü-ti chi-sheng*), a guide to sights and historically interesting spots in Southern Sung China. Wang spent one chapter on each prefecture. His chapter on Fu-chou is typical: a brief administrative geography precedes long lists of scenic spots, "traces of antiquity," worthy officials, famous locals, and so on. Wang came from Wu-chou in Liang-che East Circuit, hundreds of miles across mountains and rivers from Fu-chou. Apparently, he never visited, but worked from written sources alone. Yet he managed a fair amount of detail, much of it right. Out of about fifteen mountains he listed, four are of interest here:

> Mt. Chin-hua. In Lo-an County, thirty *li* northwest of the seat, rising up sharply from level ground, with a stone peak several hundred feet high. Shaped like an overturned calabash. Upon it is a shrine building for the Three Immortals of Hua-kai. When you tread there, it is as if you could hear them. . . .
>
> Mt. Pao-kai. In Ch'ung-jen County. Proclaimed "the utmost summit of Chiang-nan." Shaped like a jeweled canopy, whence [its name]. The *Record of the Territory of the Empire* says: "Upon it is an altar to Master Fu-ch'iu. This is where the Two Perfected Wang and Kuo rose to Immortality." There is a commemorative record by Yen [Chen-ch'ing]. . . .
>
> Mt. Feng-t'ai. In I-huang County, fifty paces outside the north gate. On it is a shrine to the Three Immortals. It is especially responsive to prayers. . . .
>
> Mt. Wang-hsien. In Lin-ch'uan County, ninety *li* north of the seat. Four *li* high and twenty *li* around. On the very summit stands a shrine building. It has been handed down through the generations that [from here] the Two Perfected Wang

and Kuo gazed at Hua-kai, residence of the Immortal Fu-ch'iu. Hence the name ["Gazing Off at the Immortal"].[1]

"Mt. Pao-kai" is an alternate name, used occasionally by locals, for Mt. Hua-kai. Wang Hsiang-chih, again, is an outsider here and hardly well informed. He seems not to know that Hua-kai and Pao-kai are the same, or perhaps even that the Three Immortals of Hua-kai are the same as the Two Perfected and Fu-ch'iu. Yet by hook or by crook, as much his sources' victim as their master, he manages to reproduce evidence that this single cult is very important in Fu-chou, as he writes, spanning at least four counties.

Compare now what a certain Yueh Shih had to say some 250 years earlier. Unlike Wang Hsiang-chih, Yueh was a Fu-chou man himself, indeed a man of Ch'ung-jen County where Mt. Hua-kai stood. He too wrote a guide to the empire, the very first national gazetteer of Sung China, the *Record of the Imperial Domains in the T'ai-p'ing Era*, which he submitted to court soon after the second Sung ruler restored southern China to the empire. Like Wang Hsiang-chih's much later work, Yueh's book goes into some detail on points of cultural, historical, or merely scenic interest. In his chapter on Fu-chou, he too deals with about fifteen mountains, Mt. Hua-kai among them: "Pao-kai Mountain. One-hundred-twenty *li* south of the [Ch'ung-jen] county seat. Shaped like a precious canopy. Also called Mt. Hua-kai. Upon it is an altar to Master Fu-ch'iu. The spot where the Two Perfected Wang and Kuo ascended to heaven."[2] This is the only mention of the Three Immortals and their cult in Yueh Shih's chapter on Fu-chou. Wang Hsiang-chih, an outsider and not an especially well informed one, could name four shrines to the Three in four different counties. Yueh Shih, a native of Ch'ung-jen County, who owned property in I-huang County and had extensive contacts in Lin-ch'uan County as well, mentions only the home shrine on Mt. Hua-kai.

It was not that Yueh Shih did not care about Fu-chou religious life. He cites several other local shrines and sites of occult matters, in some cases going into far more detail than for Mt. Hua-kai.[3] He was clearly interested in Taoism in particular, since he wrote commemorative inscriptions for at least two Taoist temples in his home county: the Ching-yun (Bright Clouds) Abbey near his own home and the Ch'i-chen (Pray to the Perfected) Abbey, to which he donated land. Both appear in *Verities of the Three Perfected Lords* as centers of Three Immortals worship. The Ching-yun Abbey stands nineteenth in a list of thirty-six "auspicious sites" (*fu-ti*) of the cult,[4] and the last of the miracle stories in the closing chapters tells us that a county administrator held an Offering for the Three at this abbey in 1182. Consider then what Yueh Shih, writing ten or so years before the Sung reunification, has to say about it:

> The Bright Clouds Abbey was built under the T'ang, in the Ching-yun (Bright Clouds) era. It is in the northwest corner of Ch'ung-jen. Mt. Pa shades its pillars;[5]

the River Pa washes its gates. The hills and streams screen it all about; the pines and creepers throng in upon it. Scholars and gentlemen praise it as the scenic track of divine Immortals, and their words are not false.

I make my home north of the abbey. When I was a sprout of a boy, I heard my elders pass down the old tale of the abbey's name-board. They had planned to replace it, and on the holiday of the fifteenth of the first month, the Taoist assembly chose one among them who was good at calligraphy. The next day he moistened his brush. That evening a Taoist appeared, his form emaciated, his clothing rough, his manner restless and unsettled. No one was polite to him. He said he was skilled at small seal characters and asked to do the calligraphy. The assembly roared with laughter and would not let him do it. Toward midnight the Taoist hung a lamp in the main hall, set his brush and inkstone to work, and on a leaf of the gate, in large characters, wrote the three words: Bright Clouds Abbey. The next morning [the others] observed the power of his skill with the brush: its splendor dazzled the eye.[6] At this time the county administrator and his deputy came and sighed and exclaimed at it again and again. Though they realized he was an extraordinary person, they never took the time to inquire about him. They asked him to write again on a new board, but he declined, claiming he was unable. When the Retreat was finished, he took his leave and went to the gate. The administrator and vice-administrator and all the Taoists followed and tried to make him stay. "I am Hsiao Tzu-yun," he said. The assembly bowed to him, and when they raised their heads he had vanished....

This Tzu-yun was an attendant worthy of the Yellow Gate who attained Immortality on Mt. Yü-ssu in the Liang dynasty [502–554].... The Abbey also had a censer with the name of the Perfected Lord Hsu inscribed on it, donated, according to tradition, by the Perfected Lord himself, who came in another's shape.[7]

Yueh goes on to tell us of the rebuilding of the abbey in the late 950s. There are immortals here, to be sure, but not the Hua-kai Three. Instead the divine traces on this site all point outward, toward major Taoist centers of national rank: Mt. Yü-ssu to the west of Fu-chou, site of Hsiao Tzu-yun's ascent, and West Mountain to the north, cult center of the Perfected Lord Hsu.

As for the Ch'i-chen Abbey, it too appears in the *Verities*, in Chang Yuan-shu's catalogue of Three Immortals sites. Here is part of its entry, one of the longer ones:

Ch'i-chen Abbey. In the forty-second ward of Ch'ing-yun Canton in this [Ch'ung-jen] county. Originally a shrine of Hua-kai. During the T'ai-ho period [227–231],[8] seven Immortal geese came from the direction of Mt. Hua-kai and landed in the pond outside the gate. During the Ch'ien-te period [963–967] over two hundred of them gathered in the temple's pine grove. During the K'ai-pao period [968–975] they approached again, and the high officeholder Yueh Shih made a record of it.[9]

And what does Yueh Shih's record tell us? Something similar, but hardly the same. His inscription is far too long to reproduce here. Immortal geese are there in profusion, in several visits in the same periods, but Yueh never says they come from Hua-kai. They come, instead, from nowhere in particular—perhaps from the transcendent realms beyond or on high—and they are drawn by the presence and acts of two men, the adept Tu Hsien-hsing in the third century and the officeholder Liu Yuan-tsai in the tenth, each a specialist of a kind in Taoist matters. Though Tu may possibly be a local man—the inscription says only that he is "resident" at the abbey—Liu, like any local administrator, is an outsider, from P'eng-ch'eng County, far away in northern China, and Yueh goes so far as to speculate that because far more geese came during his time, his "connections to the Way" must be stronger than Tu's. As in Yueh's other inscription, that is, spiritual power seems to come above all from outside, from a national sphere of Taoist numen whose worthies, human and otherwise, grace Fu-chou from time to time with their presence. He makes no mention of any Immortals with lasting ties to the region, let alone the Hua-kai Three. The claim of the *Verities* that the abbey was "originally" a center of the Hua-kai cult finds no support here. Either the Three Immortals are not worshipped here, or (and this is most unlikely) Yueh does not know that they are, or he does not find it worth mentioning, even though he takes some pains to fill out this record with points of spiritual interest in the surrounding area.

Oddly enough in all this silence, Yueh Shih may have had a special interest in Mt. Hua-kai. He apparently climbed it at some time in his life and left a record in the form of a poem:

> The palace gates of P'eng-lai adjoin the Bar of Heaven,[10]
> Locking the clouds' pink in a purple-turquoise palisade.
> In the middle of the night the rain awakes the dragon in his cave;
> At sun's setting the clouds part; the cranes return to the mountain.
> At Chessboard Rock the multitude of Immortals of old is inscribed;
> The cinnabar-medicine stove is empty, nine refinings complete.[11]
> On this day I climb to look, and rise into the infinite.
> From here on the pure void divides from the realm of dust.[12]

The poem makes the mountain an important place—the first line seems to identify it with P'eng-lai, holy island of the eastern seas and home of immortal beings—yet talks about it in terms so general that it might be almost anywhere. Cranes, closeness to Heaven, dragons in caverns, stoves for refining elixir—these are the standard vocabulary of poems and stories about Taoist mountains. The only reference that might be specific to this one is to Chessboard Rock[13] (although Immortals who met to play chess on mountains were a commonplace too), and the only reference to Immortals is to a "multitude," not to any in particular, and certainly not to a group of three. We shall see that later poems about Mt. Hua-kai often mention the Three Immortals specifically and tell us a good deal about them. There is nothing like that here. Though we have seen from the *Record of the Imperial Domains* that Yueh Shih knew of the Three Immortals and their tie to Mt. Hua-kai, when he writes a poem about his own experience on the mountain he has nothing to say of them. In sum, in Yueh's writings on Fu-chou and his own Ch'ung-jen County, though he pays close attention to spiritual matters, to Taoism in particular, and even to Mt. Hua-kai itself, he gives no evidence that he found the Hua-kai Immortals cult important, and no evidence that the cult was present anywhere but on or around Mt. Hua-kai.

Much the same picture emerges from the writings of another famous Northern Sung Fu-chou writer, the reforming chief minister Wang An-shih. Unlike Yueh, Wang was not especially drawn to Taoist religion, but he did compose three inscriptions for two Taoist abbeys in his home county, Lin-ch'uan.[14] One of these, the Hsiang-fu Abbey, appears in *Verities of the Three Perfected Lords* as a site of Three Immortals worship.[15] But in two separate records Wang tells us of his love for the abbey ("When I was young I used to go along with my elders to relax there, and delighted in it. . . . Though my body left to serve in office, my heart never left for a moment"), describes its Pavilion of the Nine Illuminators and Hall of the Three Pure, and praises the sponsoring Taoists and local gentleman, without ever mentioning the Three Immortals. "The central images are three, the side images twenty-six: this is called the Hall of the Three Pure."[16] The three images may bring us up short at first, but of course these are the Pure themselves. Who the twenty-six images that join them on the sides may be, we never learn. The third record, for a Chao-hsien Abbey in Ch'ung-jen County, likewise has nothing to say of specific Immortals.

Wang also writes of another site, Mt. Ling-ku (Numinous Gorge), which according to *Verities* and many other later sources was the most important center of Hua-kai Immortal-worship in Lin-ch'uan county. Mt. Ling-ku stands not far east of the county seat, and Wang's maternal uncle, a Mr. Wu, lived nearby. As the author of a collection of poetry, *Poems of Ling-ku*, he asked Wang to write a preface for it. Wang wrote:

> Southeast of our prefectural seat is one Ling-ku, a famous mountain of the south. The spirit of dragon and serpent, the elegance of tiger, leopard, and pheasant, the material quality of cypress, cedar, camphor, and arrow-bamboo, all emerge from this mountain; and spirit woods, ghostly tombs, and holes of goblins, as well as the boasted abbeys of Immortals and Buddhist masters, all join in taking refuge there. As to the ethers, pure and numinous, harmonious and clear, that swirl throughout and build up between Heaven and Earth, whatever [of these] the myriad creatures cannot take is allotted to men. And he, the gentleman in retirement [of whom this essay speaks], was born on this very site. His surname is Wu.[17]

Wang knows the mountain has a reputation for spiritual manifestations, and he knows that Taoists (as well as Buddhists) have lodgings here; but he does not tell us what sort of Taoists, which "Immortals." There is no hint of the Three. If their cult is active on Mt. Ling-ku, Wang does not tell us so.

Another Northern Sung author writes a few decades later about Mt. Chün in Nan-feng County southeast of Fu-chou. The author is Tseng Chao, brother of the famous prose master Tseng Kung, and like him a native of Nan-feng but a sometime resident of Lin-ch'uan County. We shall see shortly that in the Southern Sung, Mt. Chün is a central place of Three Immortals worship. Writing long before Tseng Chao, Yüeh Shih had this to say in the *Record of the Imperial Domains:* "Mt. Chün. Twenty-five *li* northeast of the county seat. Below it is a shrine to a deity who can raise clouds and rain. When the year is one of drought, all prayers and sacrifices are answered."[18] More than a century later, Tseng Chao tells us much more:

> Mt. Chün is the chief mountain of Nan-feng [County].... The virility of its form, the ripeness of its material force, are as the crouching tiger or rhinoceros, the soaring phoenix or *luan*-bird. It is only fitting that it can bring forth clouds and rain, present marvelous phenomena, and provide wealth and resources to the people, so that it is known as the chief mountain of this county.
>
> The old traditions hold that during the Han, when Wu Jui was attacking the southern Yüeh, he camped his army at this mountain. His general Mei Hsuan offered sacrifices there. When the rite was done, a shape like mounted soldiers brandishing weapons enveloped the summit. Thus they named it Mt. Chün [Army Mountain]. It was probably from this time that the county people began to sacrifice there. In T'ang, during the K'ai-yuan era [713–741], it showed numinous evidences again, so they built a great shrine and undertook ceremonies with increased devotion. Later the shrine was several times moved. The present one, north of the Yü River and seven *li* from the county seat, is the remnant of one built under the Southern T'ang, in the third year of the Sheng-yuan era. In the prayers and sacrifices of the whole region, every request is immediately answered.
>
> In over a thousand years no enfeoffment had been granted [to the deity]; the people were dissatisfied at this. A circuit intendant made a request of the court, but for a long time it was unanswered. In the third year of Yüan-fu [1100], on the sixth month's first day, the present assisting councilor Mr. Tseng Pu, then administrator of the Bureau of Military Affairs, offered up a memorial: "Your minister is a man of Nan-feng and has known Mt. Chün for a long time. The words of the circuit intendant were not false. I hope his request may be followed." A decree enfeoffed the deity as Marquis of Excellent Beneficence and named the shrine Army Mountain Shrine of Numinous Sensitivity. When the decree documents came down, the people of the county were excited, praising the god's merit and boasting to one another of the emperor's boon. Then they joined their wealth and strength to enlarge the shrine and renew it. When the shrine was finished, the assisting councilor entrusted his younger brother, [Tseng] Chao, with making a record of it.

> ... Starting in the decline and disorder of the late T'ang, the central plain changed its [ruling] surname five times; but this county, undisturbed, was never touched by the fires of war. When this dynasty inherited the mandate and nourished the people for a hundred and forty years, the population multiplied abundantly, and families prospered and rejoiced. Though the influence of eight sages[19] has bathed and anointed [the county], it is also the hidden aid of the god in bringing good fortune that has made it so. Now that names have been rectified to accord with facts, our praise and affection should be put in writing, to be handed down to eternity. Thus I have written down the whole series of events. I also attach an ode, so that the county people may sing it each spring and autumn when they sacrifice there. The ode goes:
>
> The earth's fertility rises! Flowing streams are rushing on!
> Now the herdsman turns to the fields, along with his wife and son.
> They plow and then they plant the seed, they weed and then they hoe.
> The year's success depends upon this hard beginning toil.
> The fields are free of grubs or larvae, water's in all the ponds.
> If this is not the god's power, then who has made it so?
> Our husks of grain are full now, our kernels now are ripe.
> Wield the sickle, mow, mow, with a sound like wind and rain!
> The storehouse bares its heaps of grain, like river-isles or hills.
> The ears ungathered, left for gleaners, make widows and orphans rich.
> We drink and eat, we pledge with wine, we banish anger and strife.
> But were it not for the god's help, never a crop would thrive.
> Here we have our house and home, all through the god's assistance.
> Here we have our old and young, whose lives the god has lengthened.
> The favor the god confers on us, oh, how far back it goes!
> The god's reward from the ruler, too, we would call it hearty!
> Press the wine, slaughter the ox, lay out the cups so fine!
> Blow the flute; beat the drum, *p'eng, p'eng*, it sounds!
> We, the folk, present our offerings, forever without end.
> A thousand autumns, a myriad years, preserve this our shrine.[20]

This is a fascinating piece. The celebration of locality is striking, and a good deal stronger than in Yüeh Shih's inscriptions. Tseng represents the god both as a local patron and as a sort of silent assistant to the emperor. I shall have more to say about the very important story of the god's first appearance in the next chapter. Here, however, the point is that there is no sign at all of the Three Immortals of Hua-kai. If the cult is present, Tseng Chao cannot or will not tell us so. His only concern is the god of the mountain.

These Northern Sung sources, in saying nothing about the Hua-kai Immortals cult away from its home mountain, diverge little from what we find in Yen Chen-ch'ing's inscription three centuries earlier. Though Yen says "all counties of the region" pray to the Immortals in drought, he seems to mean county governments, and he makes clear that those who prayed came to Mt. Hua-kai. There is no hint that there might be shrines elsewhere. If the cult

THE RISE OF THE HUA-KAI CULT   83

had spread in his time, presumably county administrators (and others) would have gone to shrines near their own seats. There is simply no evidence of this in the T'ang or Northern Sung. And the silence makes the starkest contrast with the abundance of miracle stories and the long catalogue of cult sites in *Verities of the Three Perfected Lords,* for the most part a Southern Sung source. The contrast suggests that the Hua-kai cult, confined largely to its home mountain in earlier periods, first spread throughout the Fu-chou region in the Southern Sung.

I shall argue later that this is true. But to compare the wealth of testimony in the *Verities* with the silence in these Northern Sung records raises problems of method. They are very different sources, after all. The whole aim of the *Verities* is to celebrate the Three; the Northern Sung authors are doing many other things. If one hopes to show change, one should be able to show it within sources of more constant character. In what follows, then, I shall divide the sources into two categories and trace each through time, separate from the other. On one side are the materials in *Verities,* a book produced directly by the Hua-kai cult. On the other is a range of materials like those we have been examining: scattered inscriptions, poems, and other occasional writings of local men, some of religious vocation but mostly of the secular elite. These are preserved most commonly as models of belles lettres in their authors' collected works, but sometimes in collections of odd notes and anecdotes or in the region's local histories. By treating the *Verities* and these other materials separately, one can show that they support a single reconstruction of the history of the Hua-kai cult. The temporal pattern that I am arguing for here is crucial for explaining the cult's rise. I shall begin with the secular records and then turn to *Verities.*

THE CULT IN THE NORTHERN AND THE SOUTHERN SUNG: SECULAR SOURCES

It may be most revealing to begin with the two mountains we have just been considering: Mt. Ling-ku in Lin-ch'uan County and Mt. Chün in Nan-feng County. For both, the belles lettres materials suggest a certain trend. The data on Mt. Ling-ku are few. Tseng Chi-li, a kinsman of Tseng Chao and Tseng Pu whose line had settled in Lin-ch'uan County and who achieved a prefectural degree in 1132, came to the mountain some time between 1117 and the first decades of the Southern Sung and took the occasion to write a poem.[21] His preface tells us precisely what we want to know: "Thirty-five *li* east of the city is a mountain called Fu-chü. ... To its southeast is [Mt.] Ling-ku, its several peaks ringing it about like a screen. It abounds in rocks. Here they sacrifice to the Three Immortals, [at a place] called the Abbey of the Reclusive Perfected. Hsieh Ling-yun's Ink Pond is here." Clearly, by Tseng Chi-li's time, the Three are worshipped here. And here is his poem:

> Hearing it long ago from Po-tzu's *Record*,[22]
> I already knew Numinous Gorge's name.
> In secret stillness gazing over Fu-chou,
> Its strange sights announce the mountain's power.
> The hanging crags' cascading falls fan out
> Like tile gutters built for a high house.
> Beneath the pines that rise a hundred feet
> Are fungi to let one live a thousand years.
> With sidewise step, I walk a path for birds,
> Wishing for handholds in the sky's azure murk.
> Though Immortals' things are vast and hard to fathom,
> In seeking sights I don't forget old ties.
> After the eighth month, in high autumn,
> I chose a fine day and planned my trip.
> A trio or pair of men in yellow hats,
> Freed of feeling, have forgotten earthly form.
> The rosy mists now reach their table and seats,
> The dry ethers have come to their door and hall.
> ... I grieve my handwriting's none to trade for geese:
> I would not dare approach the Yellow Court.[23]
> Perhaps I may join my lines to the Stone Tripod's
> And need not yield my place to Mi-ming.[24]
> With hardly a week left till the tenth month,[25]
> The yellow 'mums are slowly reaching splendor.
> The weather these days, so magnificent!
> A single laugh's not easy to repress.
> I only hope my feet are strong and healthy
> That every year I may here renew my covenant.

Tseng refers to "a trio or pair," a fine thing to call Immortals whose believers sometimes group them as two, sometimes as three. The poem leaves the purpose and nature of Tseng Chi-li's visit not absolutely certain, but the last lines surely imply a pilgrimage: "I only wish my feet to be strong and healthy / That every year I may here renew my covenant." That is, Tseng's visit either fulfills or initiates a vow—the "covenant" he hopes to renew every year. "In seeking sights I don't forget old ties" suggests the vow requites a favor already received. Yearly visits to the mountain are certainly typical of the vows that appear in miracle stories in *Verities of the Three Perfected Lords*, and we shall see more of them shortly. It is likely, then, that Tseng is a participant—or here paints himself as a participant—in the cult of the Three. What is certain—in sharp contrast to the Northern Sung texts—is that the Three are worshipped here, that Tseng knows it, and that he finds them worth celebrating in a poem that records his own visit.

An early Ming source confirms that the rise of Mt. Ling-ku as a center of Three Immortals worship took place after Wang An-shih wrote of it and before Tseng Chi-li visited. Sometime after 1394, Chang Yü-ch'u (1361–1410), the forty-third Taoist Heavenly Master, wrote to commemorate a renovation of the Abbey of the Reclusive Perfected, which Tseng Chi-li mentions in his preface. Chang tells us something of the mountain's history:

> In the *i-ch'ou* year of the Ta-kuan period [1109], tenth month, a man of the mountain, Ch'iu Hu, was gathering wood on the summit and met three men, capped with stars and garbed in mist, playing chess on the ground. They gave him a pear. When the game was done, they shouted at Hu to go home; then they slowly disappeared. When Hu reached his home, three years had passed. Hu went back to the site of the chess game and dug in the earth, where he found three pottery lamps and an incense burner. Everybody marveled at this. Thus they piled up an altar and made statues of three Immortals and sacrificed to them, in the belief that the chess-players were the Three Perfected Lords. In the *ting-yu* year of the Cheng-ho period [1117], the Taoist I An-ning built the first abbey on the mountain, requesting [recognition] from the court, which granted the name Reclusive Perfected. Whenever the people suffered from flood, drought, or sickness, they would pray there and be answered instantly. It was famous at the height of the Yuan dynasty as well.[26]

By Ming times, then, tradition held that Three Lords worship on Mt. Ling-ku had begun only near the end of the Northern Sung—not long before Tseng Chi-li himself made his visit.

For Mt. Chün the evidence is fuller. We have seen Tseng Pu sponsor the god of the mountain to the central government and gain official titles for the god and his shrine in 1100. The god had been worshipped there, however, long before, and the shrine was by this time very old. Other elite men of the county were involved in the cult. Hung Mai retells the story of a Nan-feng County man named Huang Lü-chung, told by his grandson Huang Yüeh:

> Huang Yüeh, whose courtesy name is Yüan-shou, is a man of Chien-ch'ang. He achieved a *chin-shih* degree on the list headed by Wang Yang-ch'en. He says that his grandfather, Lü-chung, having no sons, prayed at the Chün Mountain shrine (*Chün-shan miao*). He dreamed of a man who held three five-colored male phoenixes in a multicolored basket, and one bird in a plain bamboo basket. The man gave both to him. Later his legitimate wife gave birth to three sons, and all attained *chin-shih* degrees. A concubine gave birth to one son, who was no good at anything.[27]

Huang Lü-chung, a minor officeholder, was a rough contemporary and possibly an in-law of Tseng Pu and Tseng Chao.[28] He must have offered his prayer in the middle-to-late Northern Sung, certainly well before its last two decades, when his sons were already grown and earning their degrees. The shrine of the mountain god here bears its usual name, Chün Mountain Shrine; this name had even been included in the official title granted by the government. The man who appears alone to Lü-chung in the dream is clearly the god himself, represented here, as always, as a single figure.

In Tseng Pu and Tseng Chao's time, then, a Huang offered sacrifices to the god of Mt. Chün. Two generations later, members of the family still prayed there, but to different divinities. In 1163, just two years after Hung Mai published the account of Huang Lü-chung and the mountain god, the high official Chou Pi-ta returned from the capital to his home in Chi-chou (also known as Lu-ling) and passed through Nan-feng County. He made a diary of his journey, *Journal of a Return to Lu-ling*. Here is the entry for a day he spent in Nan-feng:

> Early on the *ting-ssu* day, prefectural vice-administrator Huang Yüeh sent someone to inquire after me. He is the father of [Huang] Shih-yung.[29] I went out by the West Gate to pay a visit but did not find him. Later I passed by the Shih-hsien Abbey, ten or so *li* from the county seat. Its official name is Ch'ung-chi. . . . Ill and exhausted, I did not take the time to pay it a visit but came back, passing the Fu-sheng Monastery. . . . Here I went to look at Mt. Chün, which is extremely close by. . . . The *Record of Imperial Domains in the T'ai-p'ing Era* says: "below the mountain is a shrine to a deity capable of making clouds and bringing rain." At the top are sagely traces of the Two Immortals, Wang and Kuo. Huang Yüan-shou says that every year in the ninth month, he goes to the back of the mountain and climbs to the Altar of the Three Immortals. The mountain is steep and not accessible to carriage or horse; at many points he pulls himself up with his hands. "Three Immortals" refers to Wang and Kuo and their master, Lord Fu-ch'iu.[30]

In the middle Northern Sung (or thereabouts), Huang Yüeh's grandfather prayed at the Chün Mountain shrine and dreamed of its god, lauded in Tseng Chao's ode; but by the 1160s, Huang Yüeh himself was making a yearly visit not to the god's shrine but to a Three Immortals altar on the same mountain. For Chou Pi-ta, the mountain god's shrine appears only as ancient matter preserved in the *Record of Imperial Domains*, a book by then almost two centuries old; he gives no hint of active worship there in his own day. Huang's annual visit recalls the "covenant" Tseng Chi-li hoped his feet would be able to keep each year, as well as the performance of vows we have seen in *Verities of the Three Perfected Lords*.

Mt. Chün appears in the writings of still another Nan-feng man: Liu Hsun (1240–1319), who wrote in the late Southern Sung and under the succeeding Yüan dynasty. In a brief piece in *General Views of a Dweller in Reclusion*, he tells of three extraordinary things he has seen with his own eyes. One takes place regularly on Mt. Chün:

> Nan-feng's Army Mountain, high and precipitous, leans against the sky. It is proclaimed the utmost summit of the lands south of the Yangtse. At its top is a stone house enshrining the Three Perfected Lords, Fu-ch'iu, Wang, and Kuo, known as the Three Immortals. When worshippers go there, they sometimes see thick clouds and mist, with a light inside like the sun's corona, as big as a

carriage. People of that neighborhood call it "The Round Light." Inside the light appear the Three Immortals. Their caps and garments and their bodily forms can be made out dimly. Their flying motions are quick and abrupt, now rising, now sinking; in a moment they vanish.

Liu tells us that "worshippers" see this, but also tells us he has seen it himself. The conclusion seems natural that he has been a "worshipper," though we do not know for sure. He leaves no doubt, however, that the Three are regularly worshipped on Mt. Chün; and like Chou Pi-ta he makes no mention of any other current religious activity there. For Chou, getting his information from Huang Yüeh, and for Liu, Mt. Chün was first of all a place of sacrifice to the Three Immortals. For Tseng Chao and for Huang Yüeh's ancestor Lü-chung in the Northern Sung, it had been the home of its own mountain god and his shrine. Like Tseng Chi-li's preface and poem, the Mt. Chün materials suggest that the Three Immortals won new attention from the Fu-chou elite in the Southern Sung.

Other evidence of Southern Sung Three Immortals worship abounds. In the 1180s, a certain Chou Meng-jo came to administer I-huang County. His experiences would make him well aware of the following the Three enjoyed.

> I-huang [County] is 120 *li* from Fu-chou city, wedged into a corner; but its scenery is exceedingly fine, first in all Chiang-hsi. Not five *li* north of the county seat is Mt. Hsien-yen [Immortals' Cliffs], thrusting up among the massed peaks.... Up against the mountain stood the Yuan-pao Abbey....
>
> I came from Liang-ch'i to administer this county. Once, in time spared from the account books and registers, I leaned on my staff and climbed up for a look, marveling that though its dimensions were small its atmosphere was very grand.... I inquired into the abbey's past fortunes, but no one had recorded these things. The Taoist abbot, Hsu Hsun-ch'üan, was calm and generous in nature and took untiring delight in guests. He was especially outstanding among his sort at playing the lute and at chess. He told me what he had learned from what tradition hands on: Under the Chin this had been a byway for the Two Perfected Lords Wang and Kuo. They had searched for their master, had loved the scenic beauty of the landscape, and had made a divination to build here. The ruins and traces they left behind still remain, hidden away....[31]
>
> In the *kuei-mao* year [1183], at the meeting of summer and fall, we suffered drought. The dams and ponds dried, and the grain withered. Everywhere the multitude gazed off into the distance, but no cloud or rainbow appeared. The elders joined in an appeal: "The administrator must travel to Mt. Hsien-yen! The traces of the numinous marvels of the Two Perfected screen and shade this region. It is to them our gentlemen and commoners have long turned. Why not go pray to them?" Thus I chose a [favorable] day, fasted and cleansed myself, and led my subordinates in preparing an Offering of humble gifts. Pulling ourselves along by the creeping vines, we clambered up and presented our sincere confession of faults beneath the starry altar. When the memorial [for the Offering] was first presented, the jade heavens were as if on fire;[32] within a short time,

feather screens of cloud arose all around; then thunder and lightning came all at once. They covered the sun's charioteer in the east and whipped awake sleeping dragons in the vast seas. When the sweet flood came down, by early morning there was enough. The ditches and ponds were overflowing. Heat and drought turned away, and the grains revived throughout ten thousand *ch'ing* of fields in a single day.[33]

Hua-kai worship at about the same period in another county, Lin-ch'uan, is recorded in 1213 in an inscription for still another abbey written by Hsu Cheng, a Lin-ch'uan man and prefectural exam graduate, who begins his long account by setting things in a larger regional context:

> South of the great river, since the time when the lord Fu-ch'iu received the Way on Mt. Hua-kai, such mountains as in their ripe beauty and steep upthrusting are worthy dens for deities and Immortals have always abounded in shrines to the Three Immortals.... Mt. Huang-t'ung is seventy *li* south of the Lin-ch'uan County seat; the mountain has had a shrine to the Three Immortals for a long time.[34]

Hsu goes on to tell of miraculous responses to prayers and of other manifestations by the Three at this mountain, including relief of drought in 1172, circular lights in 1182, and the sudden opening of a curing spring in 1185; he also records the rebuilding of the shrine through local efforts over a period of years ending in 1213. Here the involvement of local "gentlemen" as donors of land, cash, and Taoist rites is especially striking: these include the successful officeholder Hsu Tzu-shih, who had received his *chin-shih* degree in 1199. Another Fu-chou gentleman and officeholder of the late twelfth century, in a commemorative inscription for abbey construction between 1198 and 1202 on Mt. Hua-kai itself, remarked on the currency of Hua-kai worship in terms very much like Hsu's: "Among the famous mountains of Chiang-hsi, Hua-kai yields to no other. Since the time when the Three Immortals left their numen at its summit, those who hear of it believe, and so there is prayer; those who pray are many, and so there are shrines."[35] The writer was Tseng Feng (1142–ca. 1210), a man of Lo-an County. Tseng also wrote an inscription for a friend who had built a tower from which Mt. Hua-kai could be viewed and named it "Tower for Viewing the Immortals."[36]

There is no evidence in Tseng's works that he or his friend worshipped the Three Immortals themselves (though they may have); but they took notice of the cult in a way characteristic of Southern Sung (and not Northern Sung) authors. In the works of Ch'en Yuan-chin of Ch'ung-jen County, a *chin-shih* in 1211, we find more. In Ch'en's epitaph for Ch'en P'eng-fei (not a relative), we read:

> When I lived in my home community and took students, there was a certain Shu, of my own surname, who came to study with me. He took from his sleeve his father's [work called] *T'u-nan shu* and said, "When I was young I was orphaned,

and my uncle raised and educated me. Now that I am grown up, he is much afraid his knowledge is too limited and would have me follow after you, Master, so that I may complete my studies." I sighed and said: "To be rich and still know how to improve one's son with the ways of propriety is to be all the more excellent." Though I did not yet know [Ch'en P'eng-fei], my heart judged him dutiful.

Every other year I ascended Pao-kai. When I did so, the road passed by [Ch'en P'eng-fei]'s gate. He got his sons and nephews to intercept me and invite me back to stay. [Emphasis mine.][37]

Pao-kai, as we have seen, is Hua-kai's other name. Here again we see the journey at regular intervals that Tseng Chi-li hopes for in his poem, that Huang Yüeh reports to Chou Pi-ta, and that *Verities of the Three Perfected Lords* records in abundance. Ch'en Yüan-chin is able to assume that anyone reading the epitaph—a highly educated audience—will understand the passing reference: will know what Pao-kai is and why someone would go there every other year.

These events took place before 1230, and probably before 1211.[38] Around 1222 the noted Taoist and master of thunder rites Pai Yü-ch'an (reputedly 1134–1229) passed through the Fu-chou region. He stopped for a time at Mt. Pi-chia (Brush Rack) in Lin-ch'uan County, and in composing an inscriptional record for a pavilion there noted the mountain's connection to the Three Perfected:

> Of old there was a certain Earl Fu-ch'iu. Was his hiding place on Mt. Hua-kai? He had made a pact with the Two Immortals, Wang and Kuo, that they should look for him, and Hua-kai was a great mountain of Chiang-nan. When first they sought him, they did not find him. Of all the branches of the territory south of the river there was none that they did not pass through then. Mt. Hua-kai in present-day Lin-ch'uan County is where Fu-ch'iu once drove his carriage. Passing east from Hua-kai, north from Lin-ch'uan's seat, there stands a mountain through which Wang and Kuo once passed. Shaped by spirits and sharpened by ghosts, its form is like a brush rack. When you ascend to the mountain's summit, there is an abbey called Yung-hsing. The abbey building is extremely fine. Above is the Tower of Flocking Kingfishers; below is the Pavilion of the Multitude of Immortals. A visitor from Hai-nan heard of it and came to pay a call. When first he visited this mountain, he sighed at how far away Fu-ch'iu had been and marveled that Wang and Kuo had gone there.[39]

The visitor from Hai-nan is Pai himself. The discussion that follows this has nothing to do with the Three and mentions no rites offered to them. Pai simply wants to locate the subject of his commemorative essay in relation to the story and cult of the Three Lords. Clearly, he sees them as the most prominent divinities of this time and region. He writes similarly in another inscription, for a certain Hall of Rejoicing at Rain in Hung-chou, Fu-chou's immediate northwestern neighbor.

> Of old the great Immortal Fu-ch'iu and the two Perfected Lords Wang and Kuo came from the Southern Mount[40] and visited Yü-chang [i.e., Hung-chou]. They

passed Wei pavilion and lodged at Mt. Ma. Mt. Ma is where the Way was handed on to Ma-ku. Later came one who embraced the Way, who some say was named Tao-hsien. He always ate carp and walked like a flying cloud. When someone spied on him in his bath, he was a white dragon. He could bring clear skies or rain. Today on the mountain he is known as the Immortal Lord White Dragon of the Sages' Well. In the *chia-shen* year of the Chia-ting period [1224], on the first day of the first month of autumn, there was no rain for one hundred *li* around, and the people grieved at being sent death. The local spirit mediums had already exhausted their arts. The county gentleman T'ang Chao and his younger brother, a minor official, responded to the times. . . . They used half their family's wealth to carry the Immortal to their household. Right from the beginning there was a fine mist; but the town was still joking and making fun [of them]. When they performed the Offering, the sound of thunder and lightning came in answer. It poured for three days. People had joyous faces, and happy song filled the roads. . . . They escorted the Immortal back to the mountain and on the mountain built the Hall of Rejoicing at Rain.[41]

A nice story. But again the Three are largely irrelevant; the miracle is not theirs. So why does Pai drag them in? Because his reader needs the widely known as context for the new and unknown. By placing the hall and its own Immortal in relation to the Three, Pai reveals the prevalence of their cult in the region in his time.

The same kinds of evidence we have seen so far for the Southern Sung show that local and regional elite interest in the Hua-kai cult continued strong under the Yuan dynasty. In a commemorative inscription for a renovation of the Chao-ch'ing Abbey in the Ch'ung-jen County seat in 1325, the prominent Neo-Confucian scholar and teacher Wu Ch'eng wrote:

> Within a hundred *li* of Ch'ung-jen County are four mountains higher than the normal run: Lo, Pa, Fu-jung, and Hua-kai. All have altars to the numen of Immortals at their summits; but those who believe in and revere the Hua-kai shrine are the most numerous. Wherever a mountain closely resembles [Mt. Hua-kai] in shape, people hurry to establish a branch shrine there.[42]

In the same year, Wu wrote an inscription for another abbey, this one in Lin-chiang prefecture to the west of Fu-chou, and commented similarly but more specifically on the cult's extent:

> South of my home is a mountain called Hua-kai, which enshrines Fu-ch'iu, Wang, and Kuo, the Three Immortals. From far and near, worshippers hasten to it as if to market, all year and every month without cease. At any prominent mountain within the two prefectures of Fu[-chou] and Chi[-chou], people are bound to establish a branch shrine. Often they use "Hua" in its name. Thirty *li* southeast of the Ch'ing-chiang prefectural seat, the lone peak of Yü-hua rears up. In flood or drought, pestilence or sickness, whenever one seeks there, he is answered at once. In the neighborhood it is popularly handed down that this too was a stopping place for the Two Immortals Wang and

Kuo; these are the same Immortals worshipped on Mt. Hua-kai. But Hua-kai has a building for its sacrifices, while there is no building for the sacrifices on Mt. Yü-hua.

Near the mountain, a certain Kuo family respected the divine and loved goodness. Father and son had planned to build a palace for the Immortals but had not managed it. It fell to the grandsons [Kuo] Ju-hsien and Ju-ching to carry out their forebears' intentions. Thus they assembled lumber and stone and began the work.[43]

On another occasion, Wu agreed to commemorate an altar to thunder built on Mt. Hua-kai itself. Though this altar was not for the Three Immortals, Wu noted the importance of their cult: "On the mountain the numen of Immortals is enshrined. The prayers never end, the seekers of good fortune are often unsparing of their wealth. There is a house to enshrine the Immortals; there has been no altar to enshrine the thunder."[44]

Wu refers to the Hua-kai cult in two other places. In a record for the Ch'ing-ch'i Abbey in Lo-an County, written in 1326, he reports the tradition that the abbey began as a branch of the Three Immortals shrine on Mt. Hua-kai; and in a 1321 inscription for the Tzu-hsiao Abbey in Nan-feng County, an institution mainly devoted to quite a different Immortal, he records the presence of an altar to Fu-ch'iu.[45]

Wu tells us that Hua-kai worship reached across two prefectures: not only Fu-chou, but also its larger southwestern neighbor Chi-chou. In the Sung sources, so far, we have seen nothing of this. One bit of evidence, however, does survive from the very end of the Sung. In 1275, the Chi-chou gentleman Liu Ch'en-weng composed an inscription for the Ch'ao-hsien Abbey in Lu-ling County, Chi-chou's seat of government:

> The former Chi-chou administrator, . . . was the first to call Mt. Hsiang-ch'eng Mt. Southern Hua and to make Mt. Southern Hua the site for the Ch'ao-hsien Abbey. "Hua-kai," the Floreate Canopy, is shelter for the Northern Chronogram.[46] High-arched mountains look like it and so become prominent [in their regions]. Today how common is talk of Hua-kai! First there were the Three Peaks among the clouds in Lin-ch'uan Commandery [Fu-chou], proclaimed as Chiang-hsi's highest and most inaccessible point. It is handed down that [there] the recluse Lord Fu-ch'iu ascended riding a crane. But he had promised his disciples Wang and Kuo that he would see them there. These are the Three Immortal Old Men of Mt. Hua-kai; and on any high mountain one comes to, there are traces of the two disciples. So reverent were the ancients to their teachers! Was he here?—there?—there was no way to know. This is why one finds them everywhere. Going upriver from Lin-ch'uan, Yung-feng County has its Mt. Western Hua; farther west, one comes to Chi-shui County's eastern mountain, which is Mt. Middle Hua; and if one ascends fifty *li* from Middle Hua, one finds Lu-ling County's Mt. Hsiang-ch'eng, whose highest point is Mt. Southern Hua. These were all places where the two disciples wandered the white clouds; and the three peaks of Southern Hua roughly resemble those of

Mt. Hua-kai. Beneath it lives the Hu family of Mr. Chung-chien, likewise prominent in Lu-ling.[47] This is why Southern Hua is most flourishing.[48]

Considerably later, in a commemorative inscription by Feng I-weng for the Chia-hui Abbey, also in Lu-ling County, we find:

> In the first year of Huang-ch'ing [1312], the Taoist I To-fu broke ground and built an altar to sacrifice to the Three Assisting Perfected Lords of Hua-kai.[49] The Heavenly Master, manager of the teaching, created the title Perfected of the Celestial Floreate, Teacher to the Imperial House,[50] granted the name Chia-hui Abbey, and had him [I To-fu] manage it. No sincerity went unrequited, no prayer unanswered; the gentlemen and commoners of the whole prefecture rushed eagerly to pay reverence and make obeisances below the altar. Before long the main hall was completed and the images of the Three Perfected Sages erected.[51]

Compare also Chieh Ch'i-ssu (1274–1344), of Feng-ch'eng County in Hung-chou northwest of Fu-chou, writing in 1331:

> In the T'ang dynasty, during the Chen-yuan period [785–804], the Chi-chou prefect Marquis Yen retired to Fu-jung Peak, fifteen *li* east of the prefectural city. It was later handed down that he had gained Immortality there. His descendants became Chi-chou men. . . . Some say that in antiquity the Immortal Fu-ch'iu and his disciples Wang and Kuo also frequented this place; and they say that in the mountain are many light-marvels. . . . In the third year of Yen-yu [1316], the Marquis Yen's descendant [Yen] Hung-i enshrined Fu-ch'iu at this spot, together with his two disciples and the Marquis Yen. . . . The next year, a man of the prefecture, Mr. Tseng, appealed to the Heavenly Master and gained an order creating [the shrine] as the T'ien-hua Abbey.[52]

Clearly Wu Ch'eng was right: by his time, Hua-kai worship, or secular elite awareness of and involvement in it, had spread west to Chi-chou. On Liu Ch'en-weng's evidence, this was already occurring at the end of the Southern Sung.

The Three Immortals found their way into poetry as well. We have seen Tseng Chi-li's effort on Mt. Ling-ku. In the 1160s, a man named Hsieh O came to hold office in Lo-an County. While serving there, he visited the Southern Perfected (*Nan-chen*) Abbey, built just outside the county seat a few years earlier.

> The smoke of men masses together at the ancient creek's head.
> The bamboo trunks bow and rise against the sunset sky.
> Hefting my staff, I pay no mind to the perils of mountain roads.
> Within the Abbey of Southern Immortals I call on Fu-ch'iu.[53]

Some thirty years earlier, Sun Ti, a high official heading into exile, had passed through Fu-chou and visited Mt. Hua-kai, perhaps to seek aid for an illness. He too left a poem:[54]

> The misty vines grow thick enough to let me clamber up;
> Doing without a sedan chair, I've already reached the top.
> Beyond the azure range, the voices of dawn-escorting birds;
> I ask the men of numen to speak among the white clouds.
> Before the hall I still imagine the tracks of paired *luan;*
> At the cave's mouth there still remain patches of purple mist.
> In a latter day, if the cinnabar sand transfigures my bones,
> The wind my car, perhaps I shall yet visit the Metal Gate.

The mention of the paired *luan*-birds shows that Sun Ti knew the story of the Three Lords, probably from the gentlemen of I-huang County he met in Fu-chou and later recalled in epitaphs.[55] His cave with its remnants of purple mist is the Cavern of Purple Tenuity (*tzu-hsuan tung*), a central sacred place at Mt. Hua-kai.[56] Sun also visited Mt. Hsien-yu near the Ch'ung-jen county seat, where his preface for another poem tells us he stopped at a "Taoist shrine" (*Tao tz'u*).[57] This would have been the Chao-ch'ing Abbey, long a center of Hua-kai worship in the Southern Sung; and his poem there refers again to the paired *luan*-birds.[58]

But more important than outsiders' poems are those of local men themselves. The local histories and other sources preserve poems on Mt. Hua-kai or its Immortals by nine Fu-chou men of the Southern Sung and the Yuan.[59] Almost all mention one or more of the Three Immortals by name. Some are very short. Wu I (d. 1198), a Ch'ung-jen man who reached high office but died in disgrace back home, wrote a poem for the Ch'ung-hsien Abbey in the prefectural seat, where Fu-ch'iu was worshipped:[60]

> The sleeves of Immortal Fu-ch'iu are pulled back in the wind;
> Wang-tzu Chin's pipe-playing is heard beneath the moon.
> In rainbow shirts of lotus leaves, they come to visit me;
> Crouched in a car, with spirit horses, I follow after them.[61]

Other poems on the Hua-kai Immortals are much weightier. Perhaps the most notable is by Lo Tien (1150–1197), a man of Ch'ung-jen County who reached high office in the capital before his rather early death. Lo writes, probably in 1182,[62] to celebrate the success of Lord Fu-ch'iu in bringing rain after two other Immortals of his county, Luan Pa of Mt. Pa and Lo Kung-yuan of Mt. Lo, have failed to answer prayers.[63] Here are the poem and its prose introduction:

> The saying goes: "On Mt. Pa's turban and at Mt. Lo's girdle, if there is no rain today, there is bound to be tomorrow." Mt. Pa gets its name from the given name of Luan Shu-yuan; Mt. Lo takes its name from the surname of Lo Kung-yuan. Both are nearby prominences of my neighborhood. Whenever it rains, there are always clouds covering their summits first of all.
>
> The drought was intense. No place offered shade from the blinding whiteness. The county [government] welcomed the images of the Hua-kai Immortals

in procession. The moment they entered the suburbs [of the county seat], the two mountains sent forth clouds, and the city's environs in all four directions were soaked.

> Luan Pa,[64] his cap off, pounds at his double topknot,
> Winding and binding the glossy blue-black, as if he would tether a crow.
> Long-locked, he gazes off at his hair's distant past;
> Day after day, we only hear him feeding on sunset clouds.
> Kung-yuan, of my family,[65] still purer and more refined,
> Is wearing neither belt nor shoes, his garment's all undone.
> He likes the wind; it blows his sleeves, and he lets them flutter about.
> Night after night, we only hear him play with the crescent moon.
> It's not, of course, that cloud-feeding and moon-playing are bad;
> They didn't cause the farmers' fields to crack like diviner's shells.
> The lord magistrate, finely dressed, tells them the people suffer;
> Resting easy, chests bared, they still feel unashamed.
> Respectfully firm in his intent, he welcomes Fu-ch'iu;
> Fu-ch'iu at once takes on the magistrate's concern.
> He calls in haste his horses of wind and drives his car of cloud;
> At last the two Immortals see the error of their nakedness.
> At once they put on caps and turbans, tighten belts too;
> As soon as they see Fu-ch'iu, they bow down in the dust.
> At once they change a cruel harvest into a year of plenty:
> Amid the talk and laughter comes the clatter of pouring rain.
> Though the dense clouds did come from the peaks to north and south,
> Their first beginnings really came from grizzled Fu-ch'iu.
> Fu-ch'iu, writer of poems, ancient Immortal earl,
> Knows enough to grieve for his land and wish a plenteous year.
> Whose the boon, that the county people all eat their fill,
> Fathers shall proclaim to sons, elder to younger brothers:
> "If this rain had come just another four days late,
> They'd now be going to look for you in the dried fish shop."[66]

This is a wonderful document. The celebration of Fu-ch'iu's superiority to the Immortals of two other cults and the extraordinarily personal picture of these two, the one obsessed with his hair and old age, the other given over to feckless nature-loving; Fu-ch'iu's portrayal as confidant and helper of the local administrator; the transformation of the local metaphoric proverb into literal physical imagery in the poem (rain is to be found at Luan's "turban" and Lo's "girdle," meaning the summit and middle slopes of the two mountains; but here a literal turban and belt are *off*—so no rain!)—all combine to make this the richest poem on the Hua-kai Immortals that Fu-chou men have left us. Notice that nothing here suggests any of these Immortals is a bureaucrat. Fu-ch'iu seems rather the concerned and aristocratic old gentleman who turns up in his carriage to remind his juniors that they are not doing what they ought. Their obeisances to him look entirely personal.

THE RISE OF THE HUA-KAI CULT 95

Another long poem comes from Ho I (1129–1209), a degree holder and capital official who, like Lo Tien, lived in the Ch'ung-jen county seat.[67]

> The land's numen pushes Pao-kai
> To tower up astride three counties. . . .
> The South boasts scenes without peer;
> Immortal lords salute Fu-ch'iu.
> The old abbey leans on the mountain's foot;
> The altar of worship caps the highest summit.
> "At long last!" The Two Immortals' thought
> Was to stay on purpose here a little while.
> Arguing whether the spirit-elixir was cooked,
> Who could know the lucky ethers would drift?
> False reports called them heroes' ethers;
> At once was sent an aged official to seize them.
> He tried to meet them in battle beyond the clouds;
> Into the wind he cast his schemes, in vain.
> The sharp points are now shards of tile;
> The brave and valiant, fierce beasts no longer.
> They folded their flags and fled, or yielded in fear;
> The returning troops were willing to take their time.
> The cassia and bow were brought to the inner court;
> The fragrant missive shook the jeweled fringe.[68]
> The arrowheads left behind lie close as teeth,[69]
> The hoofprints dense on the banks they rode across.[70]

Here Ho I celebrates the battle between the Immortals and the imperial troops, and his account almost exactly parallels the story in *Verities* recounted in Chapter 3. The poem goes on to tell of the Two's ascent:

> Once they received the red phoenix decree,
> Together, wrapped in furs of kingfisher-cloud,
> With merit-rushes in three thousand rows,[71]
> And gods stretching right to the Eight Poles,
> Their fore-riders the *luan* bird with the crane,
> They rode astride the yoked tiger and dragon.[72]

Finally, Ho shifts to the present day to give a virtual catalogue of sacred wonders along the route up Mt. Hua-kai, and it becomes clear that he is tracing his own journey. At the end we even learn the purpose of his visit:

> Immortals' music sends new echoes;
> Their fine chessboard, now brittle catalpa.[73]
> The Robe Altar opens a clear expanse;[74]
> Purple Cave encloses deep darkness.[75]
> Fowlery's left its trace at the empty pit;[76]
> Dragon casting keeps to the old pool.[77]
> Demon killing leaves us Bloody Tree,[78]

Which, turned to stone, watches Immortals' Boat.[79]
At Goose's Clay they cleared the flying snow;[80]
At Tea Hollow their heat held off the autumn.[81]
At Losing Heart they've placed a daunting ridge;[82]
At Clean Hands I cup the cold current.[83]
The rocks are clever: they're like ten heads;[84]
The mountain is long, and like a sword's edge.[85]
The path risky, I've walked nine windings;
The terraces tricky, I've taken three rests.
Spirit medicines answer the prayers of men;
The fragrant stoves assure their hopes and schemes.[86]
Three Houses send up auspicious visions;[87]
Five Mounts record the Perfected's travels.[88]
Thunder and lightning come to their beck and call;[89]
Cloudy Heaven lends them shelter and shade.
It's hard to record in full the traces they've left;
I write my lines without wide research.
Four myriad and eight thousand years,
The five cities' walls and dozen mansions.[90]
Nearby, I suppose, they adjoin my Scarlet Palace;[91]
Far off, I imagine, they neighbor the Azure Isle.[92]
I ask the hermit Aged Immortals' views:
Whether here to lay my pin of office down.[93]

Ho has come—whether in reality or in imagination—to ask the Immortals whether he should retire. He may think this an appropriate question for them because they had once refused an emperor's appointment. In any case, it is extremely interesting to find Ho I, Lo Tien, and Wu I as authors of poems on the Hua-kai Immortals. Wu I, in 1186, also rebuilt the Hsing-lo Abbey, a center of Hua-kai worship.[94] If to these three we add Ch'en Yuan-chin, with his journey up Mt. Hua-kai every other year, we assemble a foursome that is far from random. The four came from families closely connected. Elsewhere I have shown the ties that joined the Hos, Los, Wus, and Ch'ens, along with a fifth family of Ch'ung-jen, the Lis, who are not represented in the Hua-kai evidence. Briefly: the Wus had been an established elite family with some history of degrees and offices since the middle Northern Sung, but they reached real prominence in the early Southern Sung. We shall see more of them in the next chapter. The other three families first come into sight in the sources in the same early Southern Sung decades, connected to each other or to the Wus from the start.[95] To find they shared interest in the Hua-kai Immortals is thus partly unsurprising, but it is very important for our understanding of the cult. I shall return to this below.

The poetic evidence, like the inscriptional sources, shows continued elite interest in the Three Immortals in the Yuan dynasty. Two of the most prominent Fu-chou men of the period, Yü Chi and Wei Su, wrote poems celebrating the mountain or its Immortals.[96] Again there is continuity of personal ties: Yü Chi was related to Ch'en Yüan-chin on his mother's side; Wei Su was Yü Chi's own student.

In sum, the inscriptions, journal entries, and poems found in belles lettres collections and in local histories show that the Hua-kai cult was well known to local elite men in the Southern Sung and the Yuan, who both celebrated and worshipped the Three Immortals. Consider the years covered by the prose materials catalogued here (most of the poems are only roughly datable): ca. 1120 (Tseng Chi-li); 1163 (Chou Pi-ta / Huang Yüeh); 1169, 1172, 1182, 1186, and 1213 (Hsu Cheng); 1183 (Chou Meng-jo); 1198–1202 (Tseng Feng); ca. 1211 (Ch'en Yüan-chin); 1222 and 1224 (Pai Yü-ch'an); 1275 (Liu Ch'en-weng); late Southern Sung or early Yuan (Liu Hsun); 1312 (Feng I-weng); 1321, 1325, and 1326 (Wu Ch'eng); 1331 (Chieh Ch'i-ssu).

In the Northern Sung, the same kinds of sources suggest by their silence that the cult had not yet spread beyond Mt. Hua-kai, at least in the religious awareness of the secular elite. The silence of the poets is the most impressive, since poems by Northern Sung Fu-chou men survive in enormous numbers—more in fact than for the Southern Sung. Yet I have found, and more convincingly the compilers of local histories in the Ming and Ch'ing dynasties apparently could find, not one poem about Mt. Hua-kai in the collected works of Northern Sung men from Fu-chou. Wang An-shih, Yen Shu, Tseng Kung, Hsieh I and Hsieh K'o, Jao Chieh, Ou-yang Ch'e: all these, in their thousands of poems, never wrote of Mt. Hua-kai. The only Northern Sung poem I have found, by Yueh Shih, again makes no special mention of the Three Immortals themselves, despite Yueh's considerable interest in Taoism.

THE CULT IN THE NORTHERN AND THE SOUTHERN SUNG: *VERITIES OF THE THREE LORDS*

What about *Verities*? I shall show that it paints the same picture. But it also supplies Northern Sung information crucial for reconstructing the history of the cult. Recall the main layers of this many-layered book. First is *The Veritable Record of the Two Perfected Lords*, written by one Shen T'ing-jui, who lived in the Five Dynasties and perhaps the early Northern Sung. Second is the primary commentary interwoven with the *Veritable Record*, always beginning with the words "Another version says," clearly drawn from an integral extended narrative in its own right, and of unclear date, though evidently written after 1125.[97] Third is the secondary commentary inserted in both the *Veritable Record* and the primary commentary, recognizable by its smaller print and double lines, and unlike them in referring often to "the present day," a time identifiable as falling after 1138 and thus within the Southern Sung.[98] Fourth is the sacred geography entitled *Verities of Mt. Hua-kai* and prefaced by the Taoist Chang Yüan-shu, dating to near the turn of the twelfth and thirteenth centuries. Fifth is the collection of miracle stories in chapters 5 and 6, which bear no title or indication of author but are also largely the work of Chang Yüan-shu. (Both the sacred geography and the miracle stories show some interpolations by later editors in the Yüan and the Ming.) Clearly, the great bulk of this composite work is Southern Sung material. Only the Shen T'ing-jui *Veritable Record* seems clearly of Northern Sung date or earlier; the primary commentary may belong to the very last years of the Northern or to the Southern Sung.

We have seen that moving from the *Veritable Record* to the primary and secondary commentaries brings a considerable widening of geographical scope. The *Veritable Record* mentions only two places in the Chiang-hsi region other than Mt. Hua-kai: Mt. Yü-ssu in Lin-chiang prefecture to the west, where the Two Immortals began their journey, and Mt. Ma-ku in Chien-ch'ang prefecture to the east, where they planned to go. However, the primary commentary traces their path through a large number of sites across several counties and prefectures; and the secondary comments bring us up to (Sung) date on the abbeys and other landmarks found along the way. No leap of intuition is required to suggest that the cult had spread across space between the *Veritable Record* and the commentaries; or at least that a wider network of its sites and sacred places had entered the awareness of literate authors. The problem is to place this expansion in time. The dating of the primary commentary gets in the way, though if its post-1125 date were certain rather than likely, the picture would be much clearer.

Chang Yüan-shu will help us here. For it is the cult's growth in recent times that he cites in his preface to *Verities of Mt. Hua-kai* to justify his project. He mentions the work of Shen T'ing-jui and the stone inscription of Yen Chen-ch'ing as evidence from the past. Then:

> As the years have drawn on, worship of the Three has flourished more and more; there have been foundations and construction that, taking place after Mr. Shen shed his mortal form, were not recorded, so that those who come after will have no basis for discussing them. Rashly disregarding my own commonness and foolishness, I have made further broad searches and inquiries, and whatever has met my eye or whatever I have gotten by hearsay, I have written down and fully recorded.[99]

Chang is writing not long after 1200. He holds that the expansion of the cult over an unspecified period of time since Shen T'ing-jui makes his new work necessary. But what period? Consider the events his succeeding two chapters record and for which they specify a date. These are abbey foundings, donations, and the like—just the sort of thing he says the flowering of the cult requires him to recount. They bear the following dates: 968–75, 1144, ca. 1146, 1168, 1174–1189, 1180, 1181, 1186+, 1188, and 1265.[100]

THE RISE OF THE HUA-KAI CULT   99

The event dated 1265, long after any plausible death date for Chang Yuan-shu, is clearly an isolated later addition by the 1391 editor, Chang Yen, as it deals with the acts of his own ancestors.[101] We are left with one date from the very beginning of the Northern and nine dates from the first six decades of the Southern Sung.

The same picture emerges from the miracle stories in the last two chapters. Only four of them deal with the Northern Sung at all; and one of these concerns events of the 1111–1117 period, very near the end of the Northern Sung, and goes on to treat matters that took place two generations later, or around 1170.[102] Of the other twenty-six stories, all but three include dated events—often several—or are otherwise datable. The dates are as follows (arranged in rough chronological order, but with dates from one story grouped together): 1127–30 and 1134;[103] 1132;[104] 1131–1162 (twice);[105] 1151, 1154, and ca. 1170;[106] 1157–1158;[107] 1158;[108] 1165–1173 (twice);[109] ca. 1173;[110] ca. 1174;[111] 1179 (twice);[112] 1182 (twice);[113] 1184;[114] ca. 1184;[115] 1191, 1200, and 1200+;[116] 1258 and 1260;[117] and 1258, 1260, and 1265.[118] This is almost exactly the same distribution of dates as in the catalogue of sacred sites, but more completely filled in. Here is the same striking gap between a mass of material concentrated in the first several decades (in this case, the first seventy-five years) of the Southern Sung and material dated near the end of the dynasty (in this case, two stories), presumably added by the later editors.[119] If we treat the first mass of material as largely Chang Yuan-shu's and examine it together with the catalogue of sites, the conclusion is inescapable that when Chang set out, through his own witness and by the testimony of others, to research the flowering of the Hua-kai cult since Shen T'ing-jui's time, he could find almost no material from the Northern and a great deal from the Southern Sung.

It may seem especially surprising to find so little early material in the miracle story chapters, since presumably a compiler would want to show his patron Immortals' ancient power by finding (or inventing) stories as old as possible. It is enlightening then to see what the few Northern Sung items in the collection actually have to say. The first, standing at the head of the entire collection, is a biography of Shen T'ing-jui. This tells us a great deal about Shen's life and learning, as one might expect, but makes no mention at all of the Three Immortals. Evidently, it is here only because Shen is the putative author of the *Veritable Record*. Another story is the account of Jao Tung-t'ien's revelation, life, and ascent that we saw at the beginning of Chapter 3, set very early in the Northern Sung. This story certainly glorifies Mt. Hua-kai and the Three Immortals, but it is not a story of their miracles, and it does not document an ongoing cult—no one in it worships the Three.[120]

A third Northern Sung story does treat a miracle (or at least a marvel), but it is not the Three Immortals' miracle. The subject is Chan T'ai-ch'u, a wandering Taoist master of the Hsi-ning period (1068–1077) who settles down for a time at Mt. Hua-kai.

> Chan T'ai-ch'u, whose courtesy name was Yüan-tso, was first a Taoist of the Chung-yu Abbey in the Wu-i Mountains. During the Hsi-ning period in Sung he came to be caretaker[121] at Mt. Hua-kai. One day the county administrator Mr. Kuo Chün asked to pray at the mountain and so left the county seat. T'ai-ch'u welcomed him with a poem:
>
> The cranes report: a starry worthy travels into the caves.
> At once I seize my staff and take my leave of Fu-ch'iu.
> Eagerly I walk out on the white cloud road;
> With skips and leaps I come to greet the lord who governs purely.
> His lucky ethers float far; the mountain phoenix is glad.
> His red garb shines on the heights; the wilderness flowers blush.
> I dare to ask this court pennon to repair to my web of rushes;
> The Purple Shoot and Yellow Essence[122] wish he'd stay a while.
>
> And so they struck up a friendship. Chan also used cinnabar sand to cure [Kuo's] chronic ailment. When the administrator returned, he told his fellow officials. There was a certain County Sheriff Chang who wanted to view the holy precincts and went to inquire of [Chan]. Before he had gone a few *li*, T'ai-ch'u already knew, and met him by the side of the road with a poem:
>
> Immortal Mei[123] buckles his weapons and visits P'eng-lai.
> The wilderness elder, prizing their tie, will meet and entertain him.
> The base of his flag bounds and opens the color of the blue-green ranges.[124]
> His horse's hooves tread and break the piles of white cloud.
> The mountains and streams show their ripeness, forests and woods are twigging;
> Monkey and crane hear the wind and leave their cavern dens.
> There ought to be a Perfected One with whom to laugh and talk;
> The Aged Immortal, truly Lao Tzu's distant scion, comes.
>
> They sat down and had hardly begun chatting when a peasant woman passed by. The sheriff followed her with his eyes and was paying no attention to T'ai-ch'u. "You people of Ch'u are just washed monkeys, with hats on," said T'ai-ch'u. The sheriff grew angry, [but] T'ai-ch'u had already vanished. When he climbed the mountain, he asked where T'ai-ch'u was. His disciples said, "Yesterday he was napping in daylight, when suddenly with beat of drum he took his leave." When he returned to the county seat, the administrator said to him: "Not long after you left, T'ai-ch'u paid a call at the county seat and withdrew from his post." The sheriff was suddenly as if enlightened: with [T'ai-ch'u's] withdrawing from the mountain, resigning his post, and meeting the sheriff on the road, he now believed this was no ordinary sort [of man].[125]

Chan's miraculous comings and goings are his own and owe nothing to the Three Immortals. He tells us he has been with Fu-ch'iu, it is true; but neither Fu-ch'iu nor his disciples are the point of the story, which tells nothing of their cult. No one here is worshipping them, and they are aiding no one. Rather, we see a wandering practitioner much like the Celestial Heart masters, who cares for an abbey on Mt. Hua-kai for a while but cannot be held there, who takes offense easily at the inattentiveness of the locals (his remark about Chiang-nan people, when the sheriff can't restrain his wandering eye, can hardly nourish local pride!) and moves on. Yet it seems this story is the best Chang Yüan-shu or later editors could manage for a Hua-kai miracle tale from the Northern Sung.

Later I shall consider the fourth Northern Sung tale; it is as much of Southern as Northern Sung in any case. We may see more of the Northern Sung situation in a document from another section of the *Verities:* a decree of 1075 granting honors to the Two Immortals and to an abbey on Mt. Hua-kai, preserved in a sort of appendix to the second chapter. On internal evidence the decree looks authentic: the three signatory high officials whose titles and surnames end the document correspond perfectly to the three councilors of state known to have been in power at the time.[126] The grant is also recorded in other Sung sources in a way that confirms this document.[127] But what guarantees authenticity in my view is the unflattering picture the decree accidentally paints of the current state of the Hua-kai Immortals cult, and especially of the knowledge that government officials both central and local possess of it. This is not what a compiler eager to glorify the cult and its history would fabricate. The entire text follows.

> The Secretariat-Chancellery notifies the Ch'ung-hsien Abbey:
> Fu-chou has sent up a memorial:
>
>> We have received the report of the Ch'ung-jen County administrator, Kuo Chün, that he had received, delivered by the man assigned by this prefecture, the two decrees ordering that titles be conferred on the Hua-kai Mountain Perfected Man Wang, as Perfected Lord of Compliant Response, and on the Perfected Man Kuo, as Perfected Lord of Sincere Response, and that [someone] be deputed to go to make sacrifices of announcement and construct a name-tablet to be installed at the Shang-hsien Abbey; that he then personally took charge of [these documents] and went out to make sacrifices of announcement; that *because there was no Shang-hsien Abbey building,* he had on his own authority and temporarily directed the Ch'iao-hsien Abbey to look after the decree documents in his possession; that he had subsequently made inquiries and found that at the foot of the mountain there had once been four Taoist abbeys: the Hsien-lin, Nan-chen, Ch'iao-hsien, and Shang-hsien; that among these, the Hsien-lin, Nan-chen, and Shang-hsien all lack any abbey building; there is only the one abbey, the Ch'iao-hsien, surviving among them; that the decree documents for the two Taoists sent down by the court which he had received were at present on his own authority delegated to the Ch'iao-hsien Abbey to look after; that the aforementioned ancient abbeys had never had officially granted names; and that with attached documents he hereby reported, asking that [the prefecture] submit a memo-

rial asking the grant of a decree of an official name and of funds for a Taoist community, and that the resident head be directed to manage and solely to look after the bestowed documents of decree and see to prayers and sacrifices. [This was] received by the prefectural office.

This official [the prefectural administrator] now reports: We have taken note of the decree sent down by the court, that Perfected Man Wang of Mt. Hua-kai be made Perfected Lord of Compliant Response and Perfected Man Kuo be made Perfected Lord of Sincere Response, and that a name-tablet be erected at the Shang-hsien Abbey. On recent investigation, it has been found that at the foot of this mountain were once the Shang-hsien Abbey and others, each now fallen down and abandoned and its lands confiscated by the authorities. We dare not on our own authority undertake new building. There is only the nearby Ch'iao-hsien Abbey, whose original abbey building and images have been preserved; but as to its name, no official name has ever been granted. Its original 600 or so *pa*[128] of wet fields had also been taken over as colony fields by the authorities because there was no one to receive and carry them on. *For prayers at this mountain of late, there has only been a single Taoist of this county, who resides there and sees to it.* In all humility, as the recently received decree documents for the Perfected Lord of Compliant Response and the Perfected Lord of Sincere Response sent down by the court may only be taken in hand at that site, the prefectural office wishes to request an order that the single abbey that survives be made the Shang-hsien Abbey, that a decree be expressly sent down granting the name, and that it retain as before its original Worthy images and the 600+ *pa* of wet fields; and that one select a Taoist in name and actuality to manage it, to see to occasional prayers and sacrifices, and to look after the decree documents that have been sent down. We await a decree.

We [the Secretariat-Chancellery] have received a decree according entirely with the memorial: that it is proper to make a special grant of the name Ch'ung-hsien Abbey. The documents having arrived, in accordance with the decree we therefore send notification.

Notifying on the eighth year of Hsi-ning [1075], twelfth month, twenty-eighth day.

Executive of the Ministry of Works and Assisting Executive of the Secretariat-Chancellery, Yüan [Chiang].

Executive of the Ministry of Rites and Assisting Executive of the Secretariat-Chancellery, Wang [Kuei].

Left Executive of the Department of Ministries and concurrently Executive of the Chancellery and Executive of State Matters, Wang [An-shih].

What on earth has happened here? Why has the Chinese imperial court, under Emperor Shen-tsung and the reforming chief minister Wang An-shih—a Fu-chou man himself, after all—awarded honors to an abbey that does not exist? There is no error in the source. Not only does *Verities* also preserve the original decree, in which the abbey's name similarly appears as Shang-hsien,[129] but the *Sung hui-yao* quite independently confirms that the target of honors in the first decree was the so-called (and nonexistent) Shang-hsien Abbey.[130] Valerie Hansen has examined on an empire-wide scale the enfeoffing and entitling of deities and temples and has shown for the Southern Sung the thorough bureaucratic checking and rechecking of gods and their miracles that the law required, and that often were applied, before state titles were granted. These were necessary because in many cases the initiative for enfeoffment came not from the government but from the god's local supporters. We have already seen such local initiative in the case of the Army Mountain god whom Tseng Pu supported at court. Like local reports or petitions on any other subject, such claims—particularly once they became frequent—could not be credited automatically, but needed checking; and the contending claims of different cults might need adjudicating.[131]

Now if anything is clear in the case of the 1075 decree for Mt. Hua-kai, it is that no process of checking and rechecking can possibly have taken place and that the first move for the grant cannot have come from devotees or sponsors of the cult in the local community. For had either been the case, the mistake of the nonexistent abbey could not have gone unnoticed. It is not just a matter of a slip of the brush at the capital, where no one could be expected to know one local cult from another. The prefectural and county administrators *themselves do not know* that there is no Shang-hsien Abbey, or that the fields of the Ch'iao-hsien Abbey have been confiscated and it has no means of support, or that there is but one lonely Taoist performing sacrifices—any of this—until Kuo Chün goes to the mountain, decree papers in hand, and discovers he has no properly authorized place to deposit them or to offer his sacrifices of announcement. If they had carried out an investigation before the grant, or if they were being lobbied by supporters of a real and active Hua-kai cult, they would have known these things already.

None of this means that Hansen is wrong. She is quite clear in drawing her picture only for the Southern Sung.[132] Indeed, her count of gods' fiefs through time can help us. As she shows from the records of titles and enfeoffments preserved in the *Sung hui-yao*, in 1075—the very year of the Mt. Hua-kai decree—the court's enfeoffments suddenly leapt to fifty-eight times the average yearly number for the preceding 115 years.[133] This was the direct result of an imperial decree handed down in the eleventh month of the preceding year commanding local administrators to report all efficacious gods and shrines that had never received titles. This decree, and the responses from the prefectures, began the first great flood of enfeoffments in the Sung, which after a pause in the late 1080s and 1090s resumed in redoubled volume under the emperor Hui-tsung (r. 1101–1126). As Hansen points out, these periods of vast increase coincide with the regimes of the great reforming chief minister Wang An-shih and his followers and successors. These are times when the state is reaching out to take more and more of local economic and social life within its grasp: in Hansen's words, "the activism of the reforms on the mundane level was matched by that on a supernatural level."[134]

Imagine now the prefectural administrator who learns that the court is suddenly interested in local cults—much more interested than it has ever seemed before. In effect, he is being ordered, out of nowhere, to find deities and shrines worth honoring. And this is an activist court, whose orders are to be taken seriously perhaps as none other before it in the dynasty. What does he do? Well, he finds something, and quickly. And where will a Chinese official look to find something quickly? Very likely to his books, or the books supplied to his office. In Yüeh Shih's *Record of Imperial Domains*—the work of a Fu-chou man, thus very likely to be available in Fu-chou—he would have found record of the Hua-kai shrine. Yen Chen-ch'ing's inscription, if his works were on hand, would have told him more. In both of these he would have found much on the Two Immortals and little on Fu-ch'iu: is this why only the Two are honored in the 1075 decree? In Shen T'ing-jui's *Veritable Record*, he would have found mention of the abbeys supposedly founded after the Two Lords' ascent. In fact, the *Veritable Record* or something like it seems clearly to lie in the background here, since of all the sources surviving to us today, only it mentions the Shang-hsien Abbey, for which honors were evidently requested and to which they were granted. A memorial, then, is drawn up based on the writings at hand—a later inscription confirms what the surviving 1075 decree does not tell us, that the prefectural government had indeed specifically asked for honors for the Two[135]—and soon after the memorial goes up, in the seventh month of 1075, the first decree comes down. At this point, administrator Kuo Chün in Ch'ung-jen County finds himself having to straighten out the mess the prefecture has made.

We should step back for a moment to consider how this case affects our understanding of the central government's push to enfeoff local gods, and beyond them our view of the great eleventh-century reforms as a whole. The "supernatural level" of the reforms, to borrow Hansen's notion, cries out for further study. We are far from understanding exactly why the enfeoffment of local gods should have become so important, especially since no organized structure of control of the process seems to have been instituted at the same time. We cannot (yet) safely see what is happening here as a realistic attempt by the center to seize control of local religious life. It is tempting to see it instead as an attempt to attract local support. But if this is what it was, the Hua-kai case makes it look extremely ineffectual. A government on the hunt for constituencies will surely seek them out and ask their views, making sure that what it chooses to honor is something they would like to see honored. The fault here may of course lie with prefectural and county administrators, but the point is that the center was not making sure that it acted with knowledge of real local conditions. A rare glimpse here into the local application of a New Laws measure suggests that the top-down character and undiscriminating across-the-board application of the reforms, of which anti-reformers like Su Shih complained bitterly, was in fact a problem. Some of the New Laws were by their nature hard to apply in a way congenial to local elites, for local elites might be their targets. But there was no reason why this should be true of fiefs for local gods: here elite views might be followed without risk to central revenues or the material interests of other locals. The center here is not *interacting* either with its local governments or through them with local constituents; it is simply *acting* upon both, even where it could do otherwise if it chose. A decree to enfeoff gods comes down, and willy-nilly the prefecture must comply, whether it knows legitimate candidates for enfeoffment or not. We need not accept the anti-reformers' own claims to represent local views and interests when they reported "the people's" unhappiness with the effects of this or that New Law. But this enfeoffment case certainly suggests that the reform party's utter failure to make the reform process even superficially consultative opened a rhetorical gap into which the anti-reformers could plausibly step. For if we see at Mt. Hua-kai a fair example of how things were being done, then who on the reform side in the capital could know enough to gainsay them?

But let us return to Mt. Hua-kai itself. The second decree reveals more than just the prefecture's hasty and bookish response and the lack of any full investigation before the honors were granted: it tells us also that the Hua-kai cult was quite undeveloped. For it tells a general tale of abandonment and neglect. Recall its citation of the prefecture's own memorial: "For prayers at this mountain of late there has only been a single Taoist of this county, who lives there and sees to it." Amazingly, this brings these official documents into direct correspondence with the marvel story of Chan T'ai-ch'u in *Verities:* Chan is "caretaker" at Mt. Hua-kai in the Hsi-ning period, when county administrator Kuo Chün comes out to meet him.[136] Presumably, this is a local and supernatural interpretation of the same journey that Kuo Chün's own memorial records. As far as the memorialist can tell, presumably relying on Kuo Chün, there is little activity of any kind at the mountain. Even after visiting and carrying out the investigation that should have happened before the enfeoffment was requested, he does not tell of active patronage by important local families, though this would strengthen his memorial. As we shall see, among the patrons of the cult in the early Southern Sung were the one or two Ch'ung-jen families that were already producing degree holders in the Northern Sung, just the sort of people that a county administrator would have been able to ask once he began asking. Taking this evidence together with the absence of Northern Sung Three Immortals miracle stories in the *Verities* and the virtual absence of Northern Sung material from Chang Yüan-shu's catalogue of sacred sites, the conclusion that the *Verities* documents the insignificance of the Hua-kai cult in the Northern Sung and its considerable expansion in the Southern Sung seems inescapable.

106   THE RISE OF THE HUA-KAI CULT

If we cast our eye back over the list of dates that emerged from an examination of Sung belles lettres, the parallel becomes remarkable. Both the scattered inscriptions in Sung collected works and the rather diverse materials brought together in *Verities of the Three Perfected Lords* suggest that the real rise of the Three Lords cult came only in the Southern Sung.

This is not the only parallel between the two bodies of sources. We have already seen that the belles lettres material suggests that in the late Southern Sung and the Yuan, the cult spread to the elite of Chi-chou to the southwest. *Verities* hints at the same thing, chiefly through its prefaces. Liu Hsiang and Wang K'o-ming, who edited a 1261 edition and whose preface stands third in the present version, identify themselves as men of Lu-ling, Chi-chou's metropolitan county.[137] Chu Huan, author of another 1261 preface, was likewise a Lu-ling man.[138] Chang Yen, who edited the 1391 edition, was a man of Lo-an County—part of Fu-chou, but lying to the southwest, up against the Chi-chou border, and tied by history and geography as closely to Chi-chou as to its own prefecture. Chang's ancestors had rebuilt the abbey on Mt. Hua-kai in 1265, nearly at the end of the Sung. Thus all these late Sung and Yuan preface writers came from a definable region to Fu-chou's southwest.

But the most striking parallel between the *Verities* and the belles lettres material lies in the list of Ch'ung-jen County elite families whose ties to the Hua-kai cult one can reconstruct from both. We have already seen that men of the Wu, Lo, Ch'en, and Ho families, known to form a social circle in Southern Sung Ch'ung-jen, wrote poems about the Hua-kai Immortals (Wu I, Ho I, and Lo Tien), founded an abbey devoted to their worship (Wu I), or made pilgrimages to the mountain (Ch'en Yuan-chin). If we examine only the miracle stories in the *Verities* that obviously deal with men of the secular elite, we find the same Ch'ens, the same Wus, and men surnamed Lo strongly represented, together with a fourth family prominent in the Ch'ung-jen elite, the Hsiungs. One man of the last surname may hold an especially strategic position, because his is the other Northern Sung tale in the miracle stories. The narrator is Chang Yuan-shu himself.

> The Golden Image of Sandalwood Incense represents the case of the Three Immortal Perfected Lords of Hua-kai and the late prefectural administrator Mr. Hsiung. His name was P'u, his courtesy name Po-wen. During the Cheng-ho period [1111–1117], while at the Imperial University, he offered veneration [to them] day and night. After winning his degree, he served as general executive inspector of Jung-chou, where there was a disastrous fire. The wind was wildly, fiercely strong. He dressed in cap and gown and made repeated obeisances. The Image appeared in the air; and at that moment [the wind] suddenly ceased. When he administered Chien-te, there were bandits robbing and stealing; he fasted, prayed, and in the end evaded harm, and became administrator of Hai-k'ang [i.e., Lei-chou].
>
> He would always make scenic tours of the traces of the Immortals of his

home mountain and offer donations to them. He honored the Immortals at Chao-ch'ing Abbey and donated property there. Thus the Image receives its worship at that abbey.

I had always heard of these matters and had thought of carving them on stone to transmit them for ever. One day I met a descendant of Mr. Hsiung, and we spoke of it. Later I got his cousin through a female line, the professor of Li-chou, Wu Tsung, to make a record, and also carved the sagely Image on the stone to transmit it to the four directions.[139]

Just what the "Image" was whose story appears here is not clear: it seems to have been a representation of the visitation of the Three while Hsiung was in Jung-chou.[140] Evidently, it had marvelous powers. Hsiung P'u was a palace degree holder of 1112 and did serve as administrator of Lei-chou in Kuang-tung circuit.[141] His father, Hsiung Chih-ch'ang, had obtained his own degree in 1082;[142] his younger brother, Hsiung Chiang, would receive his in 1115;[143] and six more lineal or collateral descendants would pass the palace examination in their turn between 1166 and 1268.[144] Thus the Hsiungs were one of the most successful families in Ch'ung-jen County in the examinations. Very unusually for a Ch'ung-jen family, they were already successful in the late Northern Sung: three or possibly four members passed the palace exam between 1082 and 1115.[145] One family that nearly matched the Hsiungs' Northern Sung performance was the Wu family: Wu Shan-fu, the great grandfather of the poet and abbey-builder Wu I, passed the palace exam at the capital in 1053, and Wu Yu-lin, who had passed in 1002, was probably also an ancestor.[146] In the Southern Sung, the Wus produced at least another eight palace degree holders as well as many more prefectural graduates.[147]

With their shared and atypical success in the examinations in the Northern Sung, the Hsiung and Wu families would have come to know each other; and the *Verities* shows us that they did. Wu Tsung, the "cousin through a female line" of Hsiung P'u who appears in the miracle story and aids Chang Yuan-shu by making a record of it, was the son of the early Southern Sung poet Wu Hang and a more distant kinsman of the 1053 palace degree holder Wu Shan-fu.[148] The very earliest testimony we have of Hua-kai worship by men of the Fu-chou elite is this miracle story, which shows Hsiung P'u offering his prayers to the Three while studying at the Imperial University in 1111–1112.[149] The next earliest for Ch'ung-jen, from the very end of the Northern or the beginning of the Southern Sung, involves the Wus and appears in a very long story of a visit to hell by a wife of the Wu family, Ms. Chia. The crucial material appears midway:

> Wu Hsun, on the morning of the first day of the fifth month, prepared fragrant paper and delivered to the Eastern Mount [Shrine] a Confession of Faults before the Sagely Emperor and a Confession of Crimes to the Bureau of Good and Evil. When he left the shrine gate, he met his younger brother, [Wu] Ch'eng, . . . who asked him what he was doing. Hsun told him the whole story. His brother

said: "Your grandfather worshipped the Hua-kai {Immortals] very diligently; whenever he prayed to them their answer was like an echo. Long ago, at a place they had passed through, he built a great hall and sculpted the sagely figures of the Three Immortals in clay, with adornment. He named it the Chao-ch'ing Abbey. It is the most imposing Taoist temple of our county. Halls, buildings, gates, corridors, and property for the residents were all your grandfather's donations. Now when [in Ms. Chia's vision] your grandfather says 'Every day I am at the Immortals' Pavilion of the Chao-ch'ing Abbey,' this is clearly the reward for his merit in donating. It seems his hell-quota is already sufficient for him to come back and be born into the world. You should go there again and make a communication about it."

Hsun followed his brother's advice and the next day went straight to the Chao-ch'ing Abbey, recited a scripture, and offered sacrifices. At dawn on the twenty-third day of the fifth month, Ms. Chia gave birth to a son.[150]

These events take place in 1184. The grandfather's donations, assuming thirty years per generation, should fall about sixty years before; and, in another source, we learn that Wu Mien, elsewhere named as a cousin of Wu Hang, composed an inscriptional record for the building of the same abbey in 1127.[151] This would place the donations in the same year or just before. Another story tells us the further adventures of the same Wu Ch'eng.

People are always visiting and paying respects to Hua-kai; there is not an empty day in a year. In the cold of winter and in the height of summer, the clouds and mist abound; this is the rule. On the very summit, with no regard to cold or heat, there are always worshippers. A whirling, sweeping fog then rises to the sun. In a recent year, Wu Ch'eng of Ching-hsiang, seeking blessings for his kinsmen, made a vow to visit the Immortals' peak. After a time, fulfilling his vow, he went to the mountain and gave thanks. For days in succession, there had been thick rain. When he reached an inn, he burned incense and off in the distance saw the Three Perfected. So he prayed for it to clear. The next day, it was just as he had prayed: he went and came back at his ease. Thus he intoned a poem to recount the matter:

A damp week, a freezing rain, a road turned to mud,
At every hour, filling the sky, the snow and sleet flew.
Thank the Perfected: the wind is held, the shadows screened away;
The tops of the myriad peaks gush a clearing brilliance upward.[152]

Thus Hsiung P'u and his in-laws the Wus were the first men of the Ch'ung-jen County elite to leave a record of their devotion to the Hua-kai cult, and their earliest records fall at the end of the Northern and the beginning of the Southern Sung. Men surnamed Lo turn up in the miracle stories not long after:

In the county town lived a certain Lo Pin, administrative officer of a military intendancy, who had no heir. Every day he prayed secretly to Hua-kai. On the first and fifteenth of each month, he would go to the Offering at the Chao-ch'ing [Abbey] and send up prayers of various kinds, begging for a dream in reply. In the *hsin-wei* year of Shao-hsing [1151], he suddenly dreamed that a single purple-garbed Taoist presented him with three plums, one slightly spoiled. The next day he visited Hua-kai to give thanks for the dream. This, he thought, represented three sons. In the next year [1152], he did indeed have a son. In the *chia-hsu* year (1154), he had another. Later he had one more son, named [Lo] Yeh, who although he grew up and entered school did not escape an early death; this proved to match the dream of the one spoiled plum. This is how efficacious the Immortals' dream answers are.[153]

The story does not tell us that this man is of the same family as Lo Tien. But we know that Lo Tien maintained a residence in the county town, where this man lived; that his lineage was extensive; that men of his surname began appearing in office and among donors to temples and the like in the first decades of the Southern Sung; and that he and his brothers all had names written with characters bearing the fire radical, which appears also in the only name given for one of Lo Pin's sons: Yeh.[154]

A later miracle story introduces others of the same surname:

Dragon Spring Mountain lies directly south of the Ch'ung-jen County seat. . . . As a rule its divine protection is stern: at the slightest offense, wind and thunder will strike accordingly. During Shao-hsing [1131–1162], the retired gentleman Mr. Lo Chang, together with the Taoist Tsou Ts'ung-chou, set up figures of the Immortals there. On the night of the day the work was finished, there was a circular apparition with three arch-like lights; the lamps illumined the sky like a boat, like a bridge, and a wondrous fragrance emanated four times from night to daybreak. Lo was moved to say, in a prayer of thanks, "Auspicious signs and circular luminaries only manifest the numinous and constant Way; no well-omened light or dazzling illumination can exhaust the transforming spirits. Reverence and respect are requited; where is an end of the joy and gladness? The mild breeze of a thousand years [ago] moves again; the old foundations of the Three Immortals are glorified anew. If ever after there are any who defile it, there will be disaster from Heaven once more. This indeed is the intent of the sages above: to clear away the old and spread the new."

In the *hsin-hai* year of Shao-hsi [1191], the Taoist Huang Tsung-i gathered a multitude to make renovations. On the seventh night, when the neighborhood gentleman Mr. Lo Wu-i was resting a moment with Huang Ch'ung, Huang Chen, and Lo Tou-nan of the county seat, they suddenly saw three heavenly lights rise blazing from the mountain. At midnight when they climbed the writing tower to look at them, there were several hundred. Thereafter they emerged from time to time, but only in threes or fives or tens or so.[155]

Lo Tou-nan appears on the Ch'ung-jen examination lists as a prefectural graduate in 1192.[156] Again we are told nothing of these men's kin ties. With the

Ch'ens, the last of this cluster of families to appear in the miracle stories, we are in a better position.

> On the precious mountain of Hua-kai, in the spring of the *wu-hsu* year of Pao-yu [1258], through the spread of a brushfire, the shrine building and abbey were all burned down, leaving not even a scrap of tile. Though people raised a rough and hasty shelter against the wind and rain, the old Abbey was entirely lost. In *keng-shen* of Ching-ting [1260], in mid-spring, the sojourning-resident officeholder and son of Military Intendant Ch'en, Judicial Inspector [Ch'en] T'ung-tsu, hearing that matters on the border were in crisis, brought his family to live at their estate at Ku-ling. His mother, the Lady Yü, had an old illness of the ethers, and through worrying over the alarms of the time, this grew more severe; she was disturbed and at a loss for what to do. At this time the judicial inspector made a visit to the Altar of the Immortals to appeal for sagely water to relieve her illness. After taking this, in her sickness she saw blurrily three Taoists, wearing many-colored clothing and riding many-colored clouds. They gradually descended into the estate compound. There was a Taoist with a beautiful beard and luxuriant cheeks. He came to her seat and handed Ms. Yü a pair of bronze chopsticks, saying: "The Lady is troubled by an illness. Now we give you these chopsticks; you shall be at ease and happy at once and cease to worry." When his words were done, they bowed and were gone. Ms. Yü then awoke; her body was light, her ailment quickly eased. She only smelled a strange fragrance.... At this Ms. Yü called together the whole household and told them her story. Nobody understood it. After thirteen days, Ms. Yü and her sons ascended the mountain to give thanks for the water. When they reached the Hall of Ascent, they offered incense and looked up to the Three Perfected. She said: "These Immortals are the ones I saw before, when I was sick." At this they held a great Offering and feast to give thanks for the boon, and departed. Later they also hired artisans to erect a precious hall—the name-boards, sage-table, cups, and drums were all made anew—to answer the sages' bestowals.[157]

There is no doubt who these people are. Ch'en T'ung-tsu is Ch'en Yuan-chin's son. The Lady Yü, Ch'en Yuan-chin's wife, comes from the family that will produce the Yuan dynasty scholar and imperial adviser Yü Chi, who as we have already seen wrote his own poem about the Hua-kai Immortals.[158] Ch'en Yuan-chin's own testimony, again, places his biennial journeys up Mt. Hua-kai in the years before 1230. The miracle story shows the family continuing its devotions some thirty years later.[159]

Here, then, is one more parallel between the materials drawn from belles lettres and the testimony of the *Verities:* in both, local elite men named Wu, Lo, and Ch'en are shown as actively involved in the celebration and worship of the Hua-kai Immortals. For the men named Lo, identity can only be presumed; but for the Wus and Ch'ens, there is no doubt: these important elite families of the Ch'ung-jen County seat were important worshippers and donors of the Hua-kai cult. Alongside them, according to the *Verities,* was a family named Hsiung, whose connection to the Wus is clear from other evidence as well. I shall pursue the reasons behind these families' involvement more closely in the next chapter.

CONCLUSION

The two categories of sources yield consistently parallel findings. First, the cult of the Hua-kai Immortals, though known and recorded in a Sung text as early as the *Record of the Imperial Domains in the T'ai-p'ing Era*, does not appear prominent in local elite life in the Northern Sung. Authors and poets of note from Fu-chou had nothing to say of it, even when they turned their attention to religious life and to Taoism in particular. Officials at the prefectural and county level, when required to report on deserving local cults to the central government in 1075, could come up with the names of the Hua-kai Immortals but knew nothing of their cult and proceeded to request honors for an abbey that did not exist. Second, the cult begins to appear important among the Fu-chou elite in the transition from the end of the Northern to the Southern Sung: in this period, roughly, the abbey on Mt. Ling-ku was built and Tseng Chi-li paid his visit; worship of the mountain god on Mt. Chün was displaced (at least insofar as elite attention is concerned) by a shrine to the Three Immortals; and perhaps earliest of all, Hsiung P'u and the Wu family worshipped the Three at the Chao-ch'ing Abbey in the Ch'ung-jen county seat. Third, after these beginnings, under the Southern Sung and through the Yuan, there is abundant evidence of elite involvement with the cult. Observers like Chou Meng-jo in the Southern Sung and Wu Ch'eng in the Yuan called it the most important cult of the region, and books devoted wholly to the mountain and the Immortals—the *Verities* itself is one—were several times edited and reedited, sometimes by members of the secular elite. Fourth, the same three Ch'ung-jen County families emerge as important Southern Sung supporters of the cult in the *Verities* and in secular sources. And, finally, both source categories document a new wave of Three Immortals worship in the Chi-chou region and Fu-chou's southwestern corner in the late Southern Sung and the Yuan.

The ability to construct narratives so closely parallel from the very different source bases of the *Verities* and the highly miscellaneous and scattered secular materials is very significant. It strengthens one's confidence in the narrative both categories yield, by suggesting that its broad outlines at least have not been too drastically shaped by the historiographic peculiarities or special concerns of one source base or the other. What is most striking here is that the parallel narratives emerge from contemporaneous bodies of material *without including a single contemporary miracle, event, anecdote, story, or poem in common*:[160] they tell the same broad story without ever overlapping in specifics. That is, if one imagines a pool of miracle tales, poems, proverbs, and other current material attesting to the power of the Three Immortals and all circulating orally or in writing among the secular and religious elites of the Fu-chou region in the Southern Sung and the Yuan, then one must look at the *Verities* and the body of secular sources as representing two samplings from that pool. For two samplings of reasonable size to yield not even one piece of material twice must require a very large pool, and gives some measure of the depth and breadth of the Three Immortals cult in the region.

Perhaps moderating the very confidence that the matching narratives otherwise strengthen, the parallels between the two source bases suggest something else very important: that they grow out of the same religious world. Let me explain what I mean. Chang Yuan-shu, in the preface to his own *Verities of Mt. Hua-kai* included within the larger *Verities of the Three Lords*, presents himself as bringing the evidence of the Three Immortals' power and wonders up to date for the sake of a readership of "gentlemen" (*shih*), and specifically gentlemen who may be interested in focusing their prayers close to home. Let us take up his words from just before we left them off:

> Rashly disregarding my own commonness and foolishness, I have made further broad searches and inquiries, and whatever has met my eye or whatever I have gotten by hearsay I have written down and fully recorded, so as to expose and raise up the reputation of the Perfected and to follow and honor [their] sagely transformations, [and] *so that the gentlemen of the four quarters, in their sacrifices and prayers, may pay respects to them each according to his quarter.*[161] [Emphasis mine.]

That is, Chang is writing for the secular local elite. And many of the miracle stories that follow *Verities of Mt. Hua-kai*, and that largely come from Chang's hand as well, recount dreams, visions, and other experiences of men and women of this same elite (including the four families we have already seen). Some tell us that Chang himself heard the story from the man it happened to, or that he was present himself, or that he is a friend of a friend of the man in question, and so on. That is, he presents himself both as writing for the secular elite and as living among them and telling the tales he heard them tell. The strong parallels between the materials in the *Verities* and the materials in secular sources suggest that Chang is telling the truth: that he is serving here as a faithful recorder for secular elite views of a secular elite cult. To return to the metaphor of sampling: Chang himself is a professional Taoist, but in writing for local gentlemen and from local gentlemen's testimony, he is giving us a sample that, though distinct from the sample offered in belles lettres sources, is not wholly independent.

This matters. We have seen already that there were social and religious worlds in Sung China that were not the secular elite's, and that Taoist sources do not always so neatly jibe with secular elite views. The differences between the *Verities* account and the Celestial Heart texts' account of the site of the Celestial Heart revelations, or of the nature of the Three Immortals themselves—

stable and continuous beings with a permanent and chosen connection to the mountain for the former, mere temporary incarnations of the abstract Three Pure for the other—make this clear. It is an interesting question, then, why a professional Taoist like Chang Yüan-shu should have chosen to convey so faithfully a picture of local divinities that has in it so little specifically Taoist flavor, so little of bureaucracy, heavenly courts, divine appointments and promotions, and so on. It sharpens this question if we recall that in the miracle stories he transcribes, the *only* clear instance of a bureaucratic representation of the Three Immortals is *his own* dream.[162] The dream, that is, is precisely what one would expect of a Taoist, and confirms that Chang thinks naturally in Taoist ways; but the other stories he transcribes, and the whole enterprise of his *Verities of Mt. Hua-kai*, are in the service of lay views.

I suspect that "in the service" has more than metaphoric force here, and that Chang Yüan-shu may be in important ways a man of a particular time. Perhaps we can imagine him a sort of "tame" Taoist, attached to a particular local cult and its shrine, and more crucially to a circle of lay elite devotees: hence his everyday contact with the subjects of his stories. The Southern Sung was a time when such an attachment was particularly likely. Through much of the Northern Sung, the legal status of a professional Taoist (*tao-shih*) and the ordination certificate that endowed it proceeded from demonstrating one's knowledge of Taoist texts in an examination at the capital. The examination's content was under the control of high-ranking government Taoists, also at the capital. From late in the Northern Sung, however, the government began selling Buddhist and Taoist ordination certificates to gather revenue. The practice increased with time, and by the Southern Sung, vast numbers of certificates were flowing into the private sector in exchange for cash. This had important effects. Ordination was now to be had for money, and—to a commoner in the Sung—a great deal of it. Clergy or groups of laymen could, of course, band together and pool funds to buy a certificate for an aspiring candidate. But the cost of ordination—which increased steadily through the dynasty—also created new channels of religious patronage, as wealthy laymen bought certificates and gave ordination to Taoists, sometimes to perform particular religious tasks for them. Examples abound in Sung sources. As we shall see in Chapter 5, a Li family of Ch'ung-jen County more than once ordained a Taoist to care for a shrine to the Immortal Mei Fu, whom they worshipped near their home.[163] The certificate thus became a means of attaching certain individual Taoists, as men indebted to patrons for their status and livelihood, to lay elite projects and institutions.[164] Chang Yüan-shu may be just such a Taoist.

But a larger question remains. Why had the Hua-kai cult grown to such prominence among lay elites in the Southern Sung? I take up this question in the next chapter.

CHAPTER FIVE

Explaining the Rise of the Hua-kai Cult

Huang Chen was a man of Ming-chou, on China's eastern coast.[1] In 1271 he came to Chiang-hsi to govern Fu-chou in severe drought. In such years, by custom, an administrator would offer prayers for rain at the major shrines under his jurisdiction. Huang made inquiries to learn where the locals expected him to pray.

> When the clerks told me what people had prayed to in the past, it was all improper worship [*yin ssu*]. "So this is how it is!" I said, and I prayed instead to the land and grain and the gods of the famous mountains and great rivers. Fortunately, the rains responded at once; yet we were still not drenched. But in the prefecture's southwestern mountains, as I gazed out at them, clouds rose day after day. The rainy ethers constantly obscured that entire region.

Clouds and rain in Fu-chou's southwest, as we have seen, often brought credit to the Three Immortals of Mt. Hua-kai. But Huang Chen does not mention Hua-kai here.

> Everyone said: "That is the numinous power of the Four Immortals of Mt. Hsiang. When drought is severe, we bring them here to worship them." I followed their words, and the rains came all around for a thousand *li*. The next year was drought, and the next year drought again. I prayed, and the rain came as before. Again and again I thought of setting foot on the peak to thank the gods on our people's behalf, but for a long time I could not. One day the mountain's resident Taoist, Lo Tuan-ying, asked me for an inscription for the altars of the Four Immortals. "The Four Immortals' spiritual force is crystal clear," I thought. "In all three years in Fu-chou I have personally received their numinous responses. How lucky I am to be able to send them thanks on another's behalf!"[2]

We have seen how far the Hua-kai Immortals' cult had spread across Fu-chou and its region by this time, and how thoroughly it had penetrated the lives and writings of the local elite. When he asked to whom he should pray, Huang Chen would surely hear of the Mt. Hua-kai Immortals. When clouds gathered in the southwest—Mt. Hua-kai was in the same direction as Mt. Hsiang but a bit higher and farther away—he would surely hear of them again. Did he consider their cult "improper worship"? Other evidence shows that his disregard was a deliberate choice. In 1272, he traveled the countryside urging the farmers to plant wheat along with their beloved rice, and he had occasion to climb Mt. Ling-ku, not far from the city, where he found the same Yin-chen Abbey that Tseng Chi-li had visited a century and a half before him.

> The Taoist Ch'iu Shou-ching came out to welcome me in startled pleasure. "Since the former prefect Chang Yü-hu," he said, "for a hundred years the cranes and monkeys of this mountain have not heard a carriage. This abbey, projecting loftily halfway into the void, was unable to bear the battering of the winds; it was almost completely ruined. And now the Prefect chances to come just when I have finished restoring it. Is this fate? I hope that you will make a record of it for the Perfected Immortals." I said: "Of Perfected Immortals I can know nothing. But this mountain is the leading peak of the prefecture.[3] This abbey houses the sacrifices for the mountain. This is just as in the *Sacrificial Statutes* for a prefecture. It is appropriate to write [for this]."[4]

Huang goes on to argue the same case that we shall see he argues for Mt. Hsiang: that "Immortals" is really only modernity's ill-chosen name for the real, nameless, quasi-physical mountain spirits the ancients worshipped, to whom prayer should properly go today as well. I shall say more of how this claim serves his own approach to local religion, and how it fits his current role in Fu-chou. But what is important here is a difference. Huang *names* the Four Immortals; he acknowledges them, at least as their worshippers misunderstand them. By contrast he does not, evidently will not, name the "Perfected Immortals" for whom Ch'iu Shou-ching requests an inscription on Mt. Ling-ku. Indeed, he does Ch'iu a sort of discourtesy by explicitly refusing to write his inscription in their honor, commemorating the abbey but not its dedicatees. We know from Tseng Chi-li's poem in the twelfth century, from the *Verities of the Three Perfected Lords* in the thirteenth, and from the Heavenly Master's inscription in the early Ming that the Perfected Immortals worshipped on Mt. Ling-ku were the Three of Hua-kai. Here is direct evidence that Huang Chen did hear of the Three but would not honor them.

This is strange. In Chapter 3 we saw a story of Mt. Hsiang—there called Mt. Pa—in which the Four Immortals of that mountain willingly yielded the center to Lord Fu-ch'iu, first of the Hua-kai Three. The story may reflect a rivalry between the two cults, resolved by compromise but in the Hua-kai Immortals' favor. In any case, one can take it as testimony that at that time on Mt. Hsiang, the Three and Four were displayed together, with Fu-ch'iu in the center.[5] Huang's decision to honor the Four but not the Three looks even odder against this background. Furthermore, it does not agree with the acts of the central government: the Four received no enfeoffment until 1231, with a promotion in 1234,[6] whereas the Hua-kai Three, after their first enfeoffment in 1075, received further honors in 1099, 1117, and 1237.[7]

Why did Huang Chen snub the Three Immortals? I shall argue that his reasons for not choosing them were the same as the Fu-chou elite's reasons for choosing them: that the spread of the Hua-kai cult in this region throughout the Southern Sung and the choices made by Huang Chen in 1271 share one explanation. The Three Immortals had come to embody authority that was locally rooted; in the Southern Sung, such a symbol corresponded well to the needs of the Fu-chou elite; and the Three were peculiarly well suited to play the part. But this was the last sort of symbol Huang Chen needed.

THE FU-CHOU ELITE AND THE STATE

In earlier work I have shown that from the Northern to the Southern Sung, the elite of Fu-chou changed considerably in their involvements, self-conceptions, and relation to their own locality and to the state. Broadly speaking, elite strategies that in the Northern Sung had been directed with some consistency toward officeholding, and toward high central office in particular, gave way in the Southern Sung to strategies devoted more decisively to attaining and maintaining local position: prestige, power, and wealth within Fu-chou, or, more precisely, within a single county. The change expresses itself most strikingly in marriage, but also in residence and migration, in building and religious donation, in descent group organization, and even in the identity of the officials, heroes, and teachers enshrined in county and prefectural Confucian schools.[8] There is good reason to believe that the change was not peculiar to Fu-chou. Indeed the notion of a shift from the Northern to the Southern Sung along such lines may make intelligible a whole field of changes in the cultural and intellectual life of the Sung elite and in the nature of the Chinese state in the Sung and even after.[9] For my purposes here, however, it is crucial only that the change took place in Fu-chou and its surrounding region.

One can easily imagine that an elite grown more local in its concerns might turn toward local and popular religious cults and practices. On this argument, as Fu-chou gentlemen grew generally more interested in the various gods and saints of their own region, they grew interested in the Perfected Lords of Mt. Hua-kai simply as three among many. But there is more to it than this. I have said the Three were "peculiarly suited" to attract elite attention in this period. To begin to explore why, we must consider certain events of the late Northern Sung that made the relation of locality to center, of the local gentleman to his government, and of religious life to both especially acute issues in the early Southern Sung and for Fu-chou men in particular.

In the eighth month of the first year of what would later be called the Southern Sung, with the emperor Kao-tsung only recently installed after the Jurchen seizure of the north, state executioners in the temporary capital beheaded a man named Ou-yang Ch'e. He was a strange criminal. Though a man of no official standing, over the previous two years, he had sent up three long letters to the throne, offering detailed proposals to save the dynasty from its peril. His suggestions, which touched on the personal unfitness of several ministers, earned him execution. Within a few years, Kao-tsung would regret Ou-yang's punishment, which (we are told) one of his ministers had ordered without his knowledge, and would issue two extraordinary decrees blaming himself and granting honors and lands to Ou-yang posthumously and to his widow and orphaned son.[10] But in this year of 1127, the news of his execution must have shocked and frightened the elite of Ch'ung-jen County. For Ou-yang Ch'e was a Ch'ung-jen man, and a man with important friends at home.

Before his martyrdom Ou-yang Ch'e was known in Ch'ung-jen chiefly as a poet. His works include countless "social" poems written in travels or poetic exchanges with friends and companions. Certain names pop up again and again. One is Wu Ch'ao-tsung, who appears in the titles or prefaces of twelve poems.[11] Ou-yang travels with him, trades poems with him, and borrows his rhymes for his own poems. Now in a collection of "poetry talk" by Wu Hang of the prominent Wu family, whose involvement with the Hua-kai Immortals cult we have seen, we learn that this Wu Ch'ao-tsung is none other than Wu Mien, Wu Hang's elder cousin, the very man who recorded the building of the Chao-ch'ing Abbey and its shrine to the Hua-kai Immortals in 1127.[12] In a preface to Ou-yang's works, Wu Hang himself tells us: "When I was a boy, I heard that Mr. Ou-yang Te-ming [Ch'e's courtesy name] could memorize several thousand characters a day, and that whenever he put brush to paper he made something worth seeing.... Recently I obtained from his younger brother Kuo-p'ing the writings he left behind."[13] This was written in 1156. Some thirty years after Ou-yang Ch'e's death, Wu Hang was still in contact with the Ou-yang family, as his cousin Wu Mien had been while Ch'e was alive. A connection between the two seems to have been recognized a good deal later as well: in 1223, Wu Hang and Ou-yang Ch'e were enshrined together in the newly rebuilt county school. Other evidence tends in the same direction.

Another name much mentioned in Ou-yang Ch'e's poems is "Te-hsiu." No surname is given, but in two places the name occurs alongside Wu Ch'ao-tsung—that is, Wu Mien. It never occurs together with any other name. Perhaps "Te-hsiu" is somehow specially connected to Wu Mien? Here we meet a striking piece of evidence. Wu Hang and three brothers, also known for their poetry, all had courtesy names built on a single pattern. Wu Hang's courtesy name was Te-yuan; his eldest brother Wu T'ao's was Te-shao; his next eldest brother, Wu Kuang, was called Te-ch'iang; and his youngest brother, Wu Hsieh, was Te-shen. In both places where Ou-yang Ch'e mentions the name "Te-hsiu" together with Wu Mien, "Te-hsiu" stands second, as he would if he were Mien's younger kinsman. Finally, we can consult Hung Mai: "Lo Ch'un-po [Lo Tien] was a man of Ch'ung-jen in Fu-chou. In the *chia-wu* year of Ch'un-hsi [1174], he took up the post of family teacher to a man of the county seat, Wu Te-hsiu. Several generations of the family studied with him. Wu dreamed . . . "[14]

The story goes on to tell of the various apparitions and omens that foretold Lo Tien's examination success. We have already seen Lo Tien's own long poem to the Hua-kai Immortals. Here, acting as his host, is a Wu Te-hsiu, living in the same western quarter of the county seat as Wu Hang and his brothers, bearing a courtesy name built on the same pattern (Te-X) and identical to that of the man who appears in Ou-yang Ch'e's poems alongside Wu Mien. Surely, all these sources refer to one man: another Wu, brother or cousin of Wu Hang, who traveled and exchanged poems with Ou-yang Ch'e.

We saw in Chapter 4 that the Wu family belonged to a cluster of elite families tied to each other and focused on the county seat in the Southern Sung— the Wus, Ch'ens, Hos, Los, Lis, and Hsiungs—and that their multiple involvements connected the members of these families, all except the Lis, to the Immortals of Mt. Hua-kai.[15] The Wus were not the only one of the group with ties to Ou-yang Ch'e. In the epitaph of a man of the Li family, Li Yen-hua (1112–1192), we find:

> Ou-yang Ch'e, the family of Wu Hsieh and Wu Hang, and Yen Ssu-i were all [Li Yen-hua's] neighbors. He studied with Yen, and Ou-yang and the Wus were his close friends. . . . When Ou-yang sent up his letters asking for the punishment of the six knaves and died along with Ch'en Po-yang, while the old fellows and friends of the powerful evildoers were removing the traces and covering their tracks, [Li] and his fellow students had him encoffined and buried.[16]

Thus both Wus and Lis had ties to Ou-yang. There is no evidence as certain for the other families of the cluster, but Ou-yang's mother was surnamed Lo and his wife Ch'en; and, as we have seen, Lo Tien served as household tutor to Wu Te-hsiu, who traveled and traded poems with Ou-yang. All the families were tied so closely—Ho I was teacher to Li Yen-hua's son and formed a poetry society with kinsmen of Wu Hang; Ch'en Yüan-chin's grandfather was a member of the same poetry society; Hsiung P'u, first known worshipper of the Hua-kai Immortals in Ch'ung-jen, intermarried with the Wus and donated to the same abbey—that any member who had not known Ou-yang personally would have known of him through his fellows. Ou-yang also took the prefectural examination in Fu-chou city at least once.[17] At the examination hall, he would have met sons of many of the leading families of his county and prefecture. After his death, the memory of his virtue and heroism was preserved and proclaimed by his enshrinement in schools first in the prefectural city and then at the county seat.

Ou-yang's death was one the Ch'ung-jen and Fu-chou elite would have found hard to forget, even if its leading families had not been his friends. Political executions were very unusual in Sung China. The case of the general Yueh Fei, for example, attained such fame partly because it departed so seriously from the norms of political life; and Yueh Fei was still alive when Ou-yang Ch'e died. Here was a gentleman of Ch'ung-jen who had spoken out on issues of the day; now he was dead. Though it was not usual for a "commoner" to submit letters to the throne, it was certainly not unheard of. Ou-yang had no reason, and his friends at home had no reason, to expect that he would die. The local elite of Ch'ung-jen and Fu-chou could hardly fail to feel assaulted and threatened by his execution. One of their own had talked to the court, and the court had sent him back in two pieces. This brought court politics and the state's lethal power rather too close to home.

Ou-yang Ch'e had not died alone. At around the same time that he sent up his letters, a student at the Imperial University, Ch'en Tung, did likewise. The two met their deaths together. Ch'en Tung was not from Fu-chou or its region, so his execution could not have the personal resonance for Fu-chou men that Ou-yang's had.[18] But it had meaning of its own. During the last decades of the Northern Sung—more precisely, from 1102 to 1121—the civil service examinations as they had existed up to that time gave way to a new system: a pyramidal structure of schools in the counties, in the prefectures above them, and at the capital. Movement through the local schools, into the Imperial University at the center, and from there into office still required students to pass tests at each level. But men who graduated at the prefecture now not only traveled together to the capital as before, but lived and studied together as fellow students at the Imperial University. Every prefectural graduate from Fu-chou over a period of twenty years—about three hundred men—was at least for a time a university student in the capital.[19] Again these included the sons of most of the leading families of Fu-chou and Ch'ung-jen County. Li Yen-hua was an Imperial University student in this period; so were Wu Mien and Hsiung P'u. Though by 1127 the school system was six years gone, replaced by a revived examination system, killing an Imperial University student was to kill a sort of man that most in the Fu-chou elite were father or brother or uncle to—a sort of man that many of them, in fact, had been. This second perspective on the 1127 executions, of course, was common to office-seeking local elites throughout the empire. But Ou-yang Ch'e's roots and connections made the catastrophe special for Fu-chou men, and for Ch'ung-jen men most of all.

Ou-yang Ch'e's execution was perhaps the most catastrophic single direct visitation of state power on the Fu-chou elite in the period from the late Northern to the early Southern Sung. That his story meant something to

Fu-chou men for decades and more is clear from his enshrinement fifty and almost a hundred years after the events.[20] Wei Liao-weng, who wrote Li Yen-hua's epitaph sometime after 1214, could assume that its readers would still care 87 years later that Li had been on Ou-yang's side. But Ou-yang's was hardly the only ill encounter with state power in his time and region. In the years immediately after the fall of the North, Fu-chou several times fell in the way of marauding imperial troops, who were more adept at devastating the countryside than at fighting the still threatening Jurchen. These, at least, were not deliberate acts of the center; the troops had shed discipline and were acting on their own, while Ou-yang Ch'e's death came by direct order of officials at court. Another intervention was deliberate. This came earlier and was both less lethal and less special to Fu-chou, but directly touched matters of religious life, enshrinement, and sacrifice. In Chapter 2, I noted the rise of Divine Empyrean Taoism under the emperor Hui-tsung (r. 1101–1126). With the guidance of the Taoist Lin Ling-su (d. 1119) and Lin's associate and successor Wang Wen-ch'ing,[21] the emperor sponsored and promulgated throughout the empire a new form of Taoism: the religion of the "Divine Empyrean" (*shen-hsiao*). New court liturgies were instituted. A new canon of Taoist scriptures was compiled. For a few years, Buddhism was abolished as a separate entity, and its clergy nominally taken into the Taoist clerical hierarchy as an inferior suborder. But most important here, new temples were built. In 1117, the court ordered all prefectures to build Divine Empyrean temples to house images of the Great Emperor of Life Everlasting. This "Great Emperor," son of the Jade Emperor, was the deity through whom the Divine Empyrean scriptures had been revealed; his younger brother was even now governing heaven; and his most recent earthly incarnation, according to Lin Ling-su, was the emperor Hui-tsung himself.[22]

Thus Lin and the emperor had managed, for the only time in Sung history, to establish a living emperor as a god, and a very high god indeed—the brother of the ruler of Heaven. His worship was not to be confined to the court: the Divine Empyrean temples and images were its local vehicles. We have no record of the Fu-chou elite's response; but again, the new dispensation must have caused some shock. No emperor had asked them to see him as a god before. For many of them, the emperor was quite visibly a man, however exalted: they had seen him in the flesh and spoken with him, or with his predecessor, when they took the palace examination that confirmed their *chin-shih* degree. Now his godly image stood in their own prefecture, in a temple that was supposed to rank above all other temples, abbeys, and shrines of their cities and countryside. Some Fu-chou gentlemen already took their own local divinities rather seriously. Hsiung P'u had worshipped the Three Immortals while studying at the Imperial University in 1112. Tseng Pu had supported the enfeoffment of the god of Mt. Chün, describing him as an aide to the emperor and indispensable for local prosperity, in 1100.

These deities had pasts that reached back in local reckoning to the Chin and Han dynasties. Now they were upstaged by the image of a living man. Other local elite men were attached enough to older forms of Taoism or to the abolished Buddhism to have built abbeys and monasteries themselves. We may have a hint of local response to the Divine Empyrean "reform" in the sort of temple actually built in Fu-chou. While in some prefectures the finest Taoist temple in the seat of government was converted to serve the purpose, in Fu-chou the building that became the Divine Empyrean temple was an insignificant Buddhist monastery in the subordinate county of I-huang.[23] Thus the nominally highest-ranking Taoist temple of Fu-chou, housing the emperor's own image, stood in a rustic corner, out of everyday sight of most of the local elite. After the Chin invasions in 1126, the succeeding emperor, Ch'in-tsung, abandoned the Divine Empyrean enterprise, and Fu-chou's temple reverted to its original condition along with all the others in the empire.

In the first years of the Southern Sung, then, the Fu-chou elite had recent and specific reasons to feel ambivalent about the court and emperor and their relation to its own goals and projects. A broader ambivalence or pessimism about state, office, and national involvements, founded partly in transformed real conditions of officeholding and office-seeking, led, as I have suggested above and argued at length elsewhere, to a general elite reorientation toward the locality throughout the Southern Sung. What could the Three Immortals of Mt. Hua-kai offer an elite skeptical and perhaps fearful of the center, less drawn to the pursuit of high office than before, and more concerned with its position in its home communities? A number of peculiarities of the lives and character of the Three, already evident in the earliest accounts we have of them, would have appealed precisely to such an elite, and just those peculiarities are magnified and elaborated in *Verities of the Three Perfected Lords* and other Southern Sung and Yuan writings by Fu-chou men. To make this argument, I shall have to travel again over material presented in the preceding two chapters.

WHY THE THREE IMMORTALS?

The Three Immortals were not officials. This characterization has two sides: earthly and divine. First, they had not been officials on earth. The earliest account of them, Yen Chen-ch'ing's eighth-century inscription, presents the Two Immortals Wang and Kuo as traveling Taoists, cousins, pursuing the cultivation they had begun under their teacher Fu-ch'iu. In *The Veritable Record of the Two Lords*, from the early Northern Sung or earlier, Fu-ch'iu enters the story directly, but again as a teacher, and the Two are above all his students. This is how they appear again in Li Chung-yuan's inscription of 1090, which echoes the earliest sources on Fu-ch'iu by showing him as teacher to princes and officials at the Chou and Han courts. Finally, Yen Chen-ch'ing and the later sources all present Wang and Kuo as distant collateral descendants of Wang Fang-p'ing, eremitic devotee of the Way in Han times. The claim links Wang and Kuo, by descent, both to national Taoist traditions and to a tradition of abstention from office. Wang Fang-p'ing was an official before he withdrew to the mountains and sought the Way, but his withdrawal was deliberate, and he steadfastly refused to come to court thereafter; when forced to come, he refused to speak.

In this teacher and his two students, this tutor of officials and the two cousins descended from a man of high spiritual and official rank in a former dynasty, we find personal embodiments of two status-defining principles crucial to the lives of the Southern Sung local elite in Fu-chou: the transmission of learning—the tie of student to teacher and of student to fellow student—and kinship or descent. A third potential principle, official standing, is simply missing. I have suggested elsewhere that as the national marriage network of the Northern Sung dissolved, academic ties gained by compensation a special role in forming elite social networks beyond the locality, and that this expresses itself in the strongly intellectual and academic orientation of the major factional crisis of the Southern Sung, the prohibition of the False Learning faction—known to its own members as the fellowship of the Learning of the Way, *Tao-hsueh*—in 1195.[24] Student-teacher ties were at least as important a glue of elite social life at the local level as well. Men who would not or could not define themselves as officeholders or office-seekers could see themselves as proper *shih-ta-fu* by defining themselves through their common education; and for this, who had taught them mattered.

As to descent and kinship, there is considerable evidence that local elite men in Southern Sung Fu-chou were turning their attention more and more toward ties of common descent and the chartering and promoting of lineage organization.[25] This turned the ties that joined adult brothers and cousins, and men descended from more distant common ancestors, into fundaments of identity and (sometimes) action. Even apart from this, it was commonplace in epitaphs and elsewhere for Southern Sung Fu-chou men to claim descent from some famous man or family of a long-ago dynasty, without troubling—just as the sources on the Three Immortals do not trouble—to fill in the intervening generations. In sum, the ties that joined the Three to one another, to the state (through Fu-ch'iu's tutoring of princes and officials), and to the distant past and common national traditions, and in these ways largely defined their status, were precisely the ties by which Southern Sung Fu-chou men were more and more likely to define or celebrate themselves. And these aspects of the Three are present in the earliest documents we have—present before elite gentlemen took up their cult, and so available for them to consider in taking up this one rather than another.

The commentary on the *Veritable Record* tells also of Wang and Kuo's more immediate ancestry: "Their grandfather was T'ing-ssu, and their father died in the time of Yuan-ti of Chin [r. 317–322].²⁶ They had submitted a book to court called *Meaning of the Spring and Autumn Annals*. The family had long been of high and solid character and had stored up merit from good works."²⁷ This account of a family of good social standing, with scholarly achievements in the generation or two preceding the protagonist, might come from any epitaph of a Southern Sung man who was the first in his family to achieve real fame. Indeed, several members of the Ch'ung-jen County Wu family submitted writings to the throne before they held office. Note as well that the book the grandfather and father submitted is not a work of Taoism or occult study but falls into a solidly conventional genre, commentary on a Confucian classic, and a classic—the *Spring and Autumn Annals*—strongly associated in the Sung with political conservatism and moral seriousness. The passage only strengthens the parallel I am drawing.

All this touches only the Three Immortals' earthly status, their position while alive and active on Mt. Hua-kai. But we have seen that in their divine role, too, they are not for the most part treated as officials: that the standard Taoist model of celestial bureaucracy has very little place in the hagiographies, miracle stories, inscriptions, and poems on the Three. This again is true from the earliest source, Yen Chen-ch'ing's inscription, which uses no bureaucratic imagery at all. The *Veritable Record* brings bureaucracy in here and there, as we have seen, but it is far from the dominant image in the text. The model disappears from the later expansion of the Three Immortals' life story in the commentaries to the *Veritable Record* and is almost entirely missing as well from the sacred geography and miracle stories—many of them about our cluster of Ch'ung-jen County elite families—assembled by Chang Yüan-shu in the Southern Sung. Indeed, in the miracle stories the only taste of the Three as divine bureaucrats is in the dream of a Taoist professional, Chang Yüan-shu himself. His special status immediately sets the imagery off as atypical, since all the other dreams, visions, communications, and encounters retold in the stories are the experiences of laymen. Elsewhere the stories represent the interactions of worshipper and Immortal as personal, not bureaucratic—most typically as vows, gifts, or spoken appeals by worshippers, requited directly in miraculous boons from the Three Immortals; and the power of the Three is personal, inherent power, not derived from a higher authority. They are not mediators or intercessors.

Where then does this power come from? What grounds or justifies the Three Immortals' authority? To judge from these texts, it is again their learning and cultivation; their ties, by descent and (in Fu-ch'iu's case) by direct activity, to antiquity; and their ability to do good for the people of the locality and the region by granting prayers and performing miracles. In this last respect their power authorizes itself—they are entitled to wield power for good (and to deal out punishment) in the surrounding communities because they *can*.

Yet their power has another basis: their special connection to place. Several peculiarities of their story made them a particularly appropriate focus of *local* celebration. First was the journey that brought them to the mountain. We have seen that in Yen Chen-ch'ing's inscription, the Two Immortals interrupt what was to be a journey from Mt. Yü-ssu to Mt. Ma-ku when in the distance they see Mt. Hua-kai. They recognize it as an extraordinary place, end their journey, and stay. They never travel farther. Thus the earliest surviving text of the cult grounds it in an act of settling down, renouncing a life of movement for a stopping place that becomes, for the rest of earthly life, a home. And what motivates this is their recognition that there is something originally and inherently notable about Mt. Hua-kai. Here every place is not just like every other: this place is special. Their eventual ascent to Heaven from the mountain only emphasizes and amplifies the quality that they have already discovered there.

Later versions, as we have seen, change the story of the journey, but in ways that still stress the specialness and centrality of the mountain and its region. The early Northern Sung *Veritable Record* turns the journey into a search for the teacher Fu-ch'iu, who chooses the mountain as a meeting place—again signaling that it is a special place to begin with—but leaves it to his students to discover it. This version brings all Three Immortals together on the mountain; places Fu-ch'iu's ascent to Heaven there, as well as his disciples'; and makes the mountain the place where the disciples acquire their full powers. Here we begin to see the organizing of a more extensive space around the Three, as the narrative lists and celebrates a series of places for their roles in the Immortals' lives. And the longest expansion of the story, in the primary commentary to the *Veritable Record*, carries this still farther by organizing the whole region between Mt. Yü-ssu and Mt. Ma-ku—much of central and eastern Chiang-hsi—as a series of carefully named and celebrated stopping places on a circuitous route leading inexorably to Mt. Hua-kai. Thus each successive version of the Immortals' journey brings new resources to the task the device of the interrupted journey had performed in Yen Chen-ch'ing's inscription: to give centrality and finality to a single place. Each presents the story of a long journey ended and a final dwelling place chosen for its special character.

Now just such a story—often told in the briefest terms, even as a mere sketch—organized the past of almost every Fu-chou elite family. Hardly any claimed to have been natives of Fu-chou in the very distant past. Almost all claimed to have come—as most of them very probably had—from outside and settled there. Often we read that, like the Three Immortals, they had chosen Fu-chou, or one of its counties, not by chance but for its special character: an ancestor had "marveled at the beauty of the scenery," say, and settled down on that account. The narratives of the Three Immortals' journey thus elaborated a motif commonplace in the elite's story of itself. In the Southern Sung and the Yuan, as promotion of lineage ties became more and more central to elite strategies and self-views, the story of the coming of the first ancestor to what was now the lineage home became a key element in genealogies and their prefaces, and sometimes in epitaphs.[28] The journey might again be a winding one—the founder (or his own ancestors) might have passed through a number of different regions for longer or shorter periods along the way; but the point was that the present home was where he had stayed, where his journey had ended—it was assumed—once and for all.

This was a peculiarly Southern Sung and post-Southern Sung view of things. The Northern Sung elite certainly did not assume that Fu-chou, let alone the particular village some ancestor had settled down in, put a final stop to a family's travels. Quite the contrary: the Northern Sung families most successful in office set up second long-term residences in faraway parts of China, usually in the capital region or near the junction of the Yangtse River and the Grand Canal, and most left Fu-chou behind well before the fall of the North. This sort of family departure for points more central simply did not happen in the Southern Sung and Yuan Fu-chou: the most successful families stayed. Indeed, without the assumption that even important people—or perhaps important people especially—would stay put, lineage strategies could not have become important in elite life in this period.

It is important, then, for the parallel I am drawing that the Three Immortals did stay on Mt. Hua-kai, that they never truly left. In their earthly lives, this is clear: the hagiography of the Three, from Yen Chen-ch'ing's inscription on, agrees that the mountain was where they stopped for good. As we shall see, this set them off from other Immortals and divinities of the region. But the notion that the Three were Taoist Immortals who had ascended to Heaven made the question of their presence on the mountain more problematic. How could they be on the mountain if they were in Heaven? The question arose even for sympathetic observers. Chou Meng-jo, whom we have seen as administrator of I-huang County in the 1180s praying successfully to the Three Immortals for rain, closed his inscription celebrating their boon with these thoughts:

> Ah me! When the Two Perfected Immortals mounted azure *luan*-birds and harnessed white cranes to travel far off to the vast regions of the Peach Springs and the isles of P'eng-lai, it would seem that they had moved apart and would have no contact with the dusty and the ordinary. Why is it then that now, when we call, they answer; when we want, they grant, turning drought into abundance, changing sorrow and sighing into joy and music, as [immediately as] shadow copies shape or echo answers sound? How can it be that spirits dwelling together in the obscure and mysterious distance would with their every thought's concern never once forget men? In my inquiries I learned that when the Two Perfected Immortals found their teacher Fu-ch'iu on Mt. Hua-kai, were instructed in the secrets of cultivating Perfection and refining their substance, and followed after

him in flying upward, among their words were the following: "We live on the mountain and are to bring fortune to the people," and "After we have gone, to any who encounter locusts, fire, drought, or flood or are in dire straits from sickness and pray about it at this mountain, we shall respond with the blessings of good fortune." From their words we know their hearts. How lucky our people are in this![29]

Chou offers two solutions and seems not to choose between them: on the one hand, the Immortals have said they are *on the mountain* and will serve people; on the other, they have promised to respond to all prayers at the mountain after they have gone. The promise serves to keep them present in influence; in fact, it establishes a personal tie to the region. We may even see the promise as a model and a legitimizer for the vows people offered the Immortals: if the cult is founded on a promise, promises are a natural expression for the cult to take. Something of the same problem seems to concern Chu Huan, who prefaces the 1261 edition of the *Verities,* though he puts it in different terms:

Who dies and has spiritual force is called a god [*shen*]. Who lives long without dying is called an Immortal [*hsien*]. Their paths are not the same. A god can often guard against natural disaster and calamity to protect the living. The Immortal's intent lies only in cultivation and refinement and in his flight of ascent: rare is one who so extends his virtue as to touch others. But the Three Immortals of Mt. Hua-kai are different. When we pray for rain, the rain responds. When we pray in illness, the illness is cured. We seek an heir and receive an heir; we seek medicine and receive medicine. Those of all quarters who have received good fortune are a multitude. This is why, in a host, they pour out their hearts to offer up reverence.[30]

The problem here is not only that the pursuit of Immortality, as Chu portrays it, is selfish, but that, while gods are often conceived as inhabiting more or less forever the sites they make powerful, Immortals' "flight of ascent" takes them *away*. Yet Hua-kai worshippers commonly treated the Three Immortals as still present on the mountain or at the many other sites they had visited on their journey. People see them there; poems talk of going to the mountain to meet them; they visit people in dreams or visions; they tell people who meet them in the (apparent) flesh that they live on the mountain. Neither the hagiographies nor the miracle stories ever show them in Heaven. Though having ascended implies that they are—at least some of the time—elsewhere, their miracles and all the traces of their activity show that they are—at least a great deal of the time—here. They frequent the mountain and wander the counties they had traveled so many years before. They are, above all, Immortals *of* Ch'ung-jen County and Fu-chou.

There is a tension here, which Chou's and Chu's ruminations reflect. But again a like tension informed the lives of local elite men themselves. For these men, even in the Southern Sung, had hardly given up office as one aspect of a gentleman's life; and many of those we have seen involved with the Hua-kai Immortals held office, even high office, for at least a time. The point was, in the new conditions of the Southern Sung, that even when one went off to office, one was still, and above all, a man of Fu-chou or Ch'ung-jen County; even while away in the flesh, one was still (one hoped) present in influence and authority. Though ascent to the (earthly) court might still be a shaping ambition for some men, even those who ascended expected—as they had not necessarily expected in the Northern Sung—to come back. The peculiar, perhaps-up-there-and-yet-clearly-also-down-here character of the Three Immortals could resonate for the Southern Sung official stretched between state duties and home commitments as it would not have for the Northern Sung minister, who did not assume he would return home.

But the story of the Three Immortals' journey not only attached them to one place: in its later development, it also celebrated and organized around a central focus a whole series of other important places that the Immortals had passed through. This development fully exploited a potential inherently strong in the first version of the story. The very idea of a journey by wandering, mountain-searching Taoists from Mt. Yü-ssu in Lin-chiang prefecture to Mt. Ma-ku in Chien-ch'ang prefecture—a journey spanning a considerable distance on a prefectural scale—implied ground covered in between: the Immortals must have stopped at many places, especially mountains, along the way. This gave the story a peculiar capacity to combine a unifying regionalism, through the celebration of a single central site, with a quite diverse and individuated localism of specific sacred places. That is, no matter how closely elite localism might hug the ground in the Southern Sung and Yuan Fu-chou, the image of the Three as travelers allowed virtually any locality, however small and otherwise insignificant, to assume the position of a sacred place in the Three Immortals' cult. At the same time, the focused character of their journey gave a common center to these sacred places and so allowed those who lived there to feel, and through common participation in the cult to *be*, joined to a larger regional community of elite devotees. To say this is not mere speculation; Chang Yüan-shu, editor of the catalogue of sacred places in *Verities of Hua-kai Mountain*, around 1200, states the case in his preface in terms not foreign to mine:

> Rashly disregarding my own commonness and foolishness, I have made further broad searches and inquiries, and whatever has met my eye or whatever I have gotten by hearsay, I have written down and fully recorded so as to expose and raise up the reputation of the Perfected and to follow and honor [their] sagely transformations, [and] *so that the gentlemen of the four quarters, in their sacrifices and prayers, may pay respects to them each according to his quarter.* . . . This is what is meant by "The Way is near, and need not be sought far off." . . . Now, where there are numinous traces of Hua-kai, and where there have been, *each according to its*

quarter, manifest responses of the Three Perfected, whether these be cavern-heavens, auspicious sites, abbey buildings, peaks and ridges, or even foundings of altars, I list them all completely below.[31] [Emphasis mine.]

Because the Three had traveled far to reach Mt. Hua-kai and had wandered along the way, the "Way" of their cult was indeed near—through sites they had touched directly—no matter what "quarter" one lived and prayed in. For an elite more and more openly attached to its respective "quarters," this meant something. Here was a Way that resided in every byway.

The idea that certain places were special, and that a divinity might attach itself to a special place for the place's sake, does seem to have grown more important in elite religious life in the Southern Sung, not only in Fu-chou but elsewhere as well. A fascinating example, strikingly reminiscent of the "automobile" saints of European popular Catholicism, comes from the cult of the god of Ta-ch'ien in nearby Shao-wu prefecture, Fu-chien, whose growing popularity Hung Mai attests in several stories in the *I-chien chih*.[32] The late Southern Sung and Yuan dynasty Fu-chou man Liu Hsun (1240–1319) made notes on *The Veritable Record of Ta-ch'ien*, a Sung hagiography of this god, which are now the best near-contemporary record. The book told how the god found his resting place, later the site of his shrine:

> An old stela records that when the prince had completed his term at Ch'üan-chou and was returning home, he took a route through Shao-wu, tied up his boat on the bank of the Ta-ch'en Creek, and with his wife, Ms. Ts'ui, wandered and viewed the ripeness and fineness of the landscape. He vowed: "This auspicious land deserves a temple and sacrifices." He returned to his boat and continued for several *li*. Wind and waves arose in force and capsized the boat. The whole family sank and was drowned. His and his wife's remains were left on the shore, [but] then floated along the stream, back to where he had made his vow about a temple and sacrifices. The people of the locality were astounded. They shipped his remains downstream, twenty *li* to the east. The next morning they had moved, against the current, back to the place where he had stopped. The people of the locality again shipped him downstream, a greater distance, and the next day he was back again at the place where he had stopped. "This is a worthy and wise man," someone said, and led the multitude in burying him with full ceremony on the bank. Ten years later, when there was famine and plague, the people worshipped him for the first time and built a shrine and sculpted an image.[33]

Thus in life this god, like the Hua-kai Immortals, recognized the place at which people would eventually enshrine him as a worthy and special place in its own right, and when he died he chose it, against strong and repeated resistance by river currents and local folk alike, as his final resting place.[34]

But to return to Chang Yuan-shu's preface, what was the "Way" that local elite devotees of the Three Immortals could seek close at hand? No doubt much of the elite's attention to the Three centered on favors sought and received, whether for a single family or for a wider community. Yet the Hua-kai texts do have ethical content. Recall the advice Wang and Kuo leave behind for the "local people" (*hsiang jen*) when they ascend to Heaven in the *Veritable Record:*

> If you can simply be loyal and filial to lord and parent, restrain your heart, be impartial and honest, aid the poor, and rescue those in need, each of you acting according to your own capacity, this will be a great merit. As to whoever is disloyal, unfilial, undutiful, inhumane, a hateful and envious or flattering and false fellow, though he exhaust his wealth and use up his property to offer sacrifices, and though he come [to us] having cut his hair and burned his body, if he cannot confess and change, we shall never respond to him.[35]

Chang Yüan-shu gives these words central importance when he echoes them in his preface: "If one can follow the words left to us by the Two Perfected, one will 'be impartial and honest, be loyal and filial, aid the poor, rescue those in need, each according to his own capacity.' Act in this way and the response will be immediate." And the miracle stories collection presses the Celestial Heart exorcist-founder Jao Tung-t'ien—here reduced to a mere auxiliary to the Three Immortals cult—into service to offer similar advice at his own transformation: "To rescue people from disease, disaster, famine, flood, and drought is the highest merit. Loyalty, filiality, harmony, submission, humanity, and trustworthiness are fundamental conduct. For any who realizes these, accordance with the Way will be secretly determined, and though he has never made obeisance to T'ai-shang, he too will live among the Immortals."[36]

Now these virtues and charities are of the most conventional kind. One might call them "Confucian" if they were not, in Sung times and long before, so general to Chinese culture as not to need the label of a particular tradition. But they are also virtues and charities that a man may embody and perform without leaving his home—specifically, without holding office. They are just the sorts of virtues, including just the sort of charitable service to the community—"to rescue people from disease, disaster, famine, flood, and drought"—that Neo-Confucians stressed more and more in the Southern Sung. Peter Bol has argued for the Neo-Confucian side, too, that such emphasis on homely virtues appealed to Southern Sung literati partly because it suggested that good performance and high standing as a gentleman were possible without bureaucratic rank or political achievement.[37] Jao Tung-t'ien makes an exactly analogous promise in Taoist terms: Immortality is available through virtue and beneficence, even if one has never "made obeisance at T'ai-shang"—that is, even if he has never, as an ordained celestial *official*—a professional Taoist—appeared in audience at the imperial court of Heaven. Read literally as advice about the Heavens, the promise laicizes Immortality; read as a metaphor for earthly striving, it privatizes success—in both cases through the exercise of everyday virtues. And the Hua-kai Immortals not only recommend these virtues but also embody them: in their youth "the Two Perfected held always to humanity and filiality, moral limits and restraint."[38] Fu-ch'iu teaches them that virtue must express itself in performance: "Your Way now is near achievement. But if you have no means to benefit the people, your merit cannot be complete."[39] They take his words to heart and go on to "benefit the people" immensely, not as celestial bureaucrats but as virtuous and powerful community patrons.

To sum up the argument so far: the Three Immortals, even as the earliest sources present them, are "pre-adapted" to embody authority that is locally based: authority that resides in the locality, maintains close touch with the communities it serves, draws force from one place, is committed to remain there, and acts in direct and personal rather than bureaucratic or judicial terms, from a foundation of personally transmitted knowledge, textual learning, self-cultivation, virtue, and descent, rather than official standing. This was power that came from within, not from without. The later elaborations in Southern Sung versions affirm precisely these sides of the Three Immortals' authority. In particular, the miracle stories in the *Verities* and the poems of local elite authors show elite worshippers in direct personal contact with the Three Immortals. In several ways the terms and narratives used to portray the Three parallel rather neatly the terms in which the Southern Sung elite of Fu-chou saw and presented itself. I am arguing that the Southern Sung elite of Fu-chou were drawn to the Three Immortals' cult and that the cult became by far the most important local cult in the period because the Three embodied a sort of authority the local elite was coming more and more to see as its own.

WHY NOT OTHER GODS?

Can this notion help us understand the relation of Three Immortals worship to other local cults? I think it can, and that the history of one cult in relation to the Three suggests the peculiar relevance of the experiences of the early Southern Sung and in particular the death of Ou-yang Ch'e. Recall the case of Mt. Chün—Army Mountain—in Nan-feng County. In 1100, Tseng Pu appealed to the court to enfeoff the god of the mountain, and his brother Tseng Chao's inscription dwelt at some length on its protection of the county through the centuries, with a hymn celebrating it as a necessary assistant to the emperor. This is the earliest evidence of serious elite sponsorship of a local cult in Fu-chou. Around the same time, Huang Lü-chung, probably Tseng Pu's in-law, was praying successfully to the Mt. Chün god for sons. Yet within fifty years, Huang's own grandson went yearly to the same mountain to pray not to its god but to the Three Immortals of Mt. Hua-kai, and Tseng Pu's kinsman Tseng Chi-li sought out the Three at Mt. Ling-ku in another county. And in the late Sung or the early Yuan, Liu Hsun too describes Mt. Chün only as a site of Three Immortals worship. We need not assume that worship of the mountain god had died out on Mt. Chün; but in the writings of local gentlemen, it had given way to the cult of the Three Immortals.

Why should this have happened? The god of Mt. Chün might seem a strong candidate for elite attention in the Southern Sung. It was unassailably local—as far as anyone could say, it had always simply been "the god of the mountain." It had the prestige of antiquity, having first shown itself under the Han dynasty. Tseng Chao had praised it in terms that made it virtually an equal of emperors in protecting the county: "Though the influences of eight sages [i.e., the eight emperors of Sung up to that time] have permeated [the county], it is also the hidden aid of the god in bringing good fortune that has made it so."[40] The god even had official neglect to its credit. Tseng tells of the ill feeling the court had created by not responding to requests for enfeoffment before 1100—possible grist for a promoter's mill, surely, in the atmosphere of the early Southern Sung. But this was not the whole story. Recall the god's first miracle. Under the Former Han, the regional official Wu Jui had moved south to attack the southern Yueh and had camped near Mt. Chün. His general Mei Hsuan offered sacrifices at (to?) the mountain. When the sacrifices were done, "a shape like mounted soldiers brandishing weapons enveloped the mountain." The mountain took its name—*chün* means "army"—from this highly auspicious response, which clearly signaled divine approval of the armed force here levied against southern barbarians.

Wu Jui, an early supporter of the first Han emperor, was a former official of the Ch'in dynasty who rebelled, joined the Han forces, and helped to subdue the major Han rival, the great general of the state of Ch'u, Hsiang Yü.[41] For his services, he was created king of Ch'ang-sha. Now the early Han kingdoms represented a temporary revival of an older feudalism in backlash against the centralism of Ch'in and did involve real devolution of authority to regional leaders, at least to begin with. Yet Wu Jui, as an early supporter, was a Han man through and through; the wars against the Yueh were Han wars; and Wu Jui in this story stands unambiguously for dynastic power.[42] It would go too far to speculate that the elite of Fu-chou in the Southern Sung secretly rooted in hindsight for the state of the southern Yueh, or (more plausibly) for the state of Ch'u and its heroic son Hsiang Yü—though Chianghsi men in the Southern Sung were fond of calling themselves "men of Ch'u." But it does seem fair to think that a founding miracle that showed a god as cheerleader for lethal imperial force directed southward might have seemed distasteful to an elite that in 1127 had lost a poet and neighbor to imperial executioners and in the years immediately afterward had watched government troops, almost accidentally, bring disorder and occasional destruction to their region.

This may seem the merest speculation; but I think it is not. It draws considerable force from another piece of the Three Immortals hagiography, presented in Chapter 3. Like the Mt. Chün god, the Three Immortals were present when an imperial army entered the Fu-chou region to subdue a southern threat. But *they* were the threat, and they turned the army back. Recall the story from the Northern Sung *Veritable Record*, which Ho I, member of the Ch'ung-jen cluster of families connected through the Wus to Ou-yang Ch'e, made into poetry in the twelfth century. The Immortals Wang and Kuo, after Fu-ch'iu's ascent, continue refining their elixir; the ethers drift into the sky and are noted at the court of the "ruler of the time." On being advised that these are imperial ethers, he sends a large army south on what his general turns into a punitive expedition. The Two Immortals confound the attackers with ghostlike Immortal troops—here are soldiers in the sky again—who fend them off but do not hurt them, and all the attackers' arrows change to tile and fall harmlessly to the ground. Realizing what they are up against, the imperial troops beg for forgiveness; the Immortals send them back to court with marvelous gifts for the ruler, who now receives better advice and invites the Immortals to join him at court. They refuse his offer with the words: "We live on the mountain and are to bring fortune and benefit to the people." These, of course, are precisely the words that Chou Meng-jo quoted in considering whether the Immortals could really still be on the mountain. But in their original context, as a refusal tendered, however amiably, to a ruler who has sent an army to destroy or capture them and whose attack they have utterly foiled, the words assert independence of imperial power rather directly. If we view the cult of the Three Immortals in the light of this story, which we know Southern Sung men paid attention to (since Ho I told it in poetry and Chou Meng-jo quoted from it), then the displacement of the god of Mt. Chün by the Three in elite worship seems significant indeed. On "Army Mountain," named for its god's approving sign to an army sent south, men of the Southern Sung elite now worshipped divinities who had defeated another such imperial army and who had then, by way of afterthought, refused to attend the emperor's court. This elite, again, had experienced the central government's lethal capacities at the beginning of the period, through the execution of a man who himself, with his letters to the throne, had implicitly asserted the authority of someone without office—someone not normally in attendance at court—to speak and be heard on the issues and official personalities of the day. This elite had ceased to celebrate the god who had seconded imperial force and now celebrated the Immortals who had turned it away.

One would, of course, like to have direct evidence that Southern Sung men connected to the Three Immortals cult themselves drew a parallel between the "ruler of the time" in this story of the army and their own imperial court. Fortunately, the evidence exists. Though most accounts of the

Three Immortals place their stay on Mt. Hua-kai in the 290s, or under the Western Chin dynasty, another tradition puts them there decades earlier; the primary commentary on the *Veritable Record* tells us that "another version" dates Fu-ch'iu's ascent to 260, under the Wu kingdom in the period of division we now call Three Kingdoms. In Chang Yüan-shu's story of his 1179 dream of the Three Immortals—the only miracle story in the *Verities* that uses bureaucratic imagery—he concludes from the Immortals' appearance before him in jewel-fringed headgear that they must have received a promotion from the celestial emperor. He goes on to suggest that they ought now to receive new earthly honors as well, "lest they again refuse employment by a ruler of Chiang-nan." That is, Chang is accepting the alternate tradition and placing the two Immortals' refusal in a time when China was divided and the "ruler" governed only "Chiang-nan," the land south of the Yangtse River. (This reading actually makes the usage "ruler of the time" [*shih chün*], rather than "emperor," a good deal more intelligible.) In suggesting that they might "again refuse employment by a ruler of Chiang-nan," he both acknowledges that his own emperor governs only the south (this might have been seditious in an official context but was commonplace in private writings) and directly compares him, on that account, to the emperor whose army had attacked the Two Immortals. He is also saying that, just as the Two Immortals refused to serve an ancient ruler, they can now—if they are not properly honored—refuse to serve a modern one. In sum, the potential parallel between the court of that time and the court of their own was available to Southern Sung men, and at least one drew it in writing.

It is important to see what sort of authority the Immortals Wang and Kuo are claiming in refusing the ruler. Their actions against the troops that attack them clearly show they have a kind of power that an emperor and his army can do nothing about. Yet they use this power, not to harm the army or the emperor, but only to avoid harm to themselves and to preserve the space within which they can pursue their own cultivation and aid their community. Their gifts to the court show they mean no challenge to its authority in its own sphere; and their words when they are about to be attacked show that their ambitions belong to a different sphere entirely: "The Two Perfected heard and laughed, saying: 'We are cultivating our will for the void. How could we wish for anything higher?'" The message is thus one of resistance of a limited kind, but also of reconciliation: a wise court will see that there need be no conflict between the kinds of power the Immortals wield and the kinds of power a court wields. Each side has authority in its own sphere. The parallel to the way in which the Southern Sung elite saw—or hoped to see—its own position within its home locality would have made the story seem a very happy one.

The Mt. Chün god was, of course, not the only one that a Southern Sung elite drawn to local involvements and community patronage could have chosen to favor. There were also the Four Immortals of Mt. Hsiang, whom Huang Chen chose to honor for drought relief in 1271. Evidence suggests from the mid twelfth century on that this was an active cult known to elite recorders of local life. Its Immortals received state enfeoffment in 1231 and 1234; it was sponsored by other local administrators before Huang Chen; and it continued to attract literate attention under the Yuan dynasty from commentators as notable as Yü Chi. Yet there is nothing like the wealth of material on the Four that one finds for the Hua-kai Three. Though Mt. Hsiang, like Mt. Hua-kai, stood in the southern reaches of Ch'ung-jen County, closer to the county seat in fact than Mt. Hua-kai, and though its two leading Immortals could claim ties to the county and prefecture dating back to the Han dynasty, it did not attract even from Ch'ung-jen families the patronage that the Hua-kai cult commanded. Indeed, of the Ch'ung-jen elite families with close ties to one another who have proved so important in the history of the Three Immortals cult, only one left evidence of active involvement with the Four Immortals of Mt. Hsiang. Perhaps significantly, the same family is the only one of the cluster with no record of ties to the cult of Mt. Hua-kai: the Li family of White Sands in southern Ch'ung-jen.

These Lis are the family of Li Yen-hua, who was a friend of Wu Hang and his brother Wu Hsieh as well as of Ou-yang Ch'e, and whose son Li Hu (d. 1214) studied under Ho I, author of the poem celebrating the Three Immortals' defeat of the imperial army. The most successful member of the family in official terms was Li Liu, Li Hu's son, who received his palace degree in 1208. The family home lay just north of Mei Peak, one of the peaks of Mt. Hsiang. At some unspecified date, Li Liu and his younger brother Li Po-ku gave funds to build a shrine on Mei Peak, bought land for its support, supplied sacrificial vessels, and paid to ordain a certain Hu Shou-chen as a Taoist practitioner to serve as guardian and offer sacrifices to Mei Fu, one of the Four Immortals and the man the peak was named for.[43] Mei was already enshrined with the rest of the Four on the main peak; the Lis' act singled him out for separate sacrifices at the new shrine. Li Liu's son Li Hsiu and nephew Li T'ao later took up their fathers' role of patron and ordained a new Taoist to succeed Hu. In the disorder of the Sung-Yuan transition, the guardianship of the shrine fell empty. When order was restored, Li Liu's great-grandson Li Yun-ssu found a new guardian and ordained him. Thus four generations of Lis maintained a strong connection to the shrine, treating it virtually as their own. Insofar as their acts formed a tie to the cult of the Four Immortals, it was a very special one. The Lis did not, as far as we know, join in the regular worship of all Four on the main peak; they singled one out for particular and more or less private worship. The peak named for Mei Fu, again, was right next to their home. Thus the one Ch'ung-jen elite family known to have any connection to one of the Four Immortals was the one most likely to see the Four as local (and personal) divinities in the narrowest possible sense.⁴⁴ That this family alone among the local elite is known to have paid homage to Mei Fu thus hardly undermines a localist reading of the rise and spread of the Three Immortals cult.

How early the Four Immortals were worshipped at Mt. Hsiang is unclear. Yü Chi, writing in the Yuan, tells us that the prefectural administrator Chang Hsiao-hsiang had recorded the marvels of the Four on stone; this was around 1165. (By Yuan times the stone was lost.) Near this time, according to the *Verities,* the miracle of the seating order occurred: the Four Immortals would not allow their own images to hold the central place in the Mt. Hsiang shrine and insisted that Fu-ch'iu of the Three Immortals take it instead. The story at least shows that the Four Immortals cult was active at this time. Around 1182, Lo Tien wrote the poem in which Fu-ch'iu reminds the feckless leader of the Four Immortals, Luan Pa, of his duty to relieve drought. Again the poem shows that the Four Immortals cult was present, but, like the seating story, it clearly subordinates the Four to the leader of the Three. The Four were enfeoffed by the state in 1231 and again in 1234. In 1265, a "sojourning gentleman in the county," one Shih Te-yü, currently serving as administrator of Shao-wu prefecture next door and not a Fu-chou man, asked the court for further recognition, apparently with no result.

Who were these Four Immortals, whose cult clearly had some following in Fu-chou but who consistently played second fiddle in local elite writings— and a distant second at that—to the Three Immortals of Mt. Hua-kai? Can their stories tell us why they commanded less attention than the Three, though they were enshrined together with them in at least one spot? The materials that survive (though the best of these date only from Yuan times) make clear that two of the Four were always chief, the other two far less important to the cult. The two subordinate Immortals were Yeh Fa-shan and Teng Tzu-yang, T'ang dynasty Taoists said to be men of this region who had cultivated themselves near the mountain. They earn hardly any attention from Fu-chou men in the records that survive, though in one miracle story the Three Immortals do tell a dreamer that they are planning to get together with Teng and Yeh. But the two leading figures among the Four are Luan Pa and Mei Fu, both men of the Han dynasty. Luan had administered Yü-chang Commandery, which in Han times governed the territory that would later be Fu-chou; Mei had served as sheriff (*wei*) of Nan-ch'ang County in the same commandery. Thus they were just what the Three Immortals were not: representatives of the outside power of the state, governing the people of what would someday be Fu-chou.

But there is more to Luan and Mei than this; these were not just any officials. As sheriff, of course, Mei was especially closely associated with punishment and physical force. His biography in the *History of Former Han* unfortunately has little to say of his time in Nan-ch'ang. Yü Chi, however, tells us that Mei visited the Ch'ung-jen region because he "had someone to catch and punish." He goes on to give an account of Mei and Luan as a pair:

> The two gentlemen possessed specialists' arts in the Way of the Immortals, which aided them in administering and transforming [this territory]. They did away with heterodox outrages and prohibited immorality and defilement, so that the people would not encounter what [Mei and Luan] did not approve and would distance themselves from evil and injury. Therefore [the people] recognized their virtue and did not forget them.

We do not learn a great deal more about Mei from Yü or in other Fu-chou sources, but the general drift is clear. Of Luan Pa more can be said. His life is filled with fascinating stories: probably the best is that while drinking and chatting with the emperor one day, he suddenly turned and spat his wine out across the mats. (See the woodcut on the jacket of this book.) The emperor was enraged and wanted to punish him; but Luan told him he had done it to rescue his home commandery from drought. The emperor sent fast riders out to learn the truth, and they returned bearing the news that indeed there had been drought; that on the day Luan Pa spat wine, it had finally rained; and that the rain tasted like wine. Luan, then, was a man of extraordinary powers. Not all the stories make him appear so harmless: here is Yü Chi again (recall that Mt. Hsiang was also known as Mt. Pa):

> Luan Pa . . . was fond of the Way, and under the emperor Shun-ti [126–144] served in the imperial side-palace and advanced to prefect of the Yellow Gates. . . . [Later] he was made grand administrator of Yü-chang. This commandery abounded in mountain and river demons; the little people wasted their wealth in sacrifices and prayers. Pa had long been in possession of the arts of the Way and could make demons and gods his servants. He destroyed all their side-shrines and reduced and controlled licentious spirit mediums. Weird and uncanny phenomena then ceased of themselves. The common people were at first much afraid at this, but in the end all were at peace with it. It was at this time that they divided off the eastern area of Yü-chang and created Lin-ju County: this was the territory of the present Fu-chou. But it is handed down that Luan Pa had come here when suppressing magicians. Thus the people thought of him and did not forget, and used his name to name this mountain.

Yü Chi follows Luan Pa's biography in the *History of Later Han* rather closely. This is the view of Luan that would be available to any literate Sung man. Clearly, the governing theme of his story, in relation to Fu-chou, is of repressive power brought from outside and directed especially at local religious practices he judged heterodox.[45] In this respect, Luan occupies just the position the practitioners of Celestial Heart Taoism took up (see Chapter 1): disciplinarian to gods and demons on behalf of higher authority—in the Celestial Heart case, the Heavenly court; in Luan Pa's case, the earthly one. Recall that Huang Chen began his inscription for the Four Immortals in 1271 with the announcement that the other cults recommended to him by locals for prayers in drought had all fallen in the category of "improper worship"—just what the first among the Four had spent his term in this area suppressing. Huang Chen, a Neo-Confucian scholar in love with books,[46] would hardly have sponsored Luan Pa and the others of the Four without consulting the histories about them. His talk of improper cults was not only talk: his works preserve records of his active suppression of the popular practice of sending off plague gods in paper boats. We have seen that the texts of the Three Immortals cult, by contrast, never show the Three suppressing improper cults or gods.

Earlier evidence also suggests a local official might choose to see the Four Immortals, and Luan Pa in particular, as representing outside, official, and relatively impersonal authority. We have seen that the name of Mt. Hsiang was originally Mt. Pa. The old name continued in local use well into the Yuan. But in 1156, the current Ch'ung-jen County administrator, Cheng Mao, had decided the name was improper. Again Yü Chi tells the story:

> He proclaimed to the people: "The men of the Chou dynasty used personal names when they dealt with gods, but these names were not given to mountains or rivers. That the mountain is named Pa has long been, I fear, a source of unease to the common people. At Tung-t'ing there is a mountain; because it was the dwelling place of the Lord [*chün*] of Tung-t'ing, they call it Mt. Chün, Lord Mountain. Lord Luan went on from Yü-chang to be prime minister [*hsiang*] in the kingdom of P'ei; might we not call [this mountain] Mt. Hsiang, Minister Mountain?" Then he poured out wine to inform the god, and the god was pleased. He revealed it to the people, and the people went along [*ts'ung*]. Thus the name was changed to Mt. Hsiang.

What has happened here? People have been calling the mountain by Luan Pa's first name: his familiar name, the one a close friend or confidant might use, or what he might call himself. This practice seems too personal, disrespectful, in fact, to administrator Cheng. In its place, he offers the official title "minister," which Luan Pa held in another part of China after he left this region—the highest office, in fact, that he ever achieved. The effect is to change the mountain's name-giver from a familiar friend to a high official, a servant of the emperor; and also to reemphasize that Luan Pa not only came from outside but left to hold high office outside again: he was, after all, never a "minister" when he was in Fu-chou. We are told the local people "went along," but this is exaggeration at best: the older name is commonplace in later texts. It seems doubtful that the older name had "long been a source of uneasiness among the common people."

WHY HUANG CHEN IGNORES THE THREE

My case is nearly made. It may help to say a bit about the situation Huang Chen found himself in. He had come to Fu-chou to relieve drought and famine. But he soon concluded that the chief obstacle to famine relief was the local elite itself, or specifically the wealthy "upper-grade households" who would not sell their stored grain to hungry neighbors, as Huang would have them do, but preferred to hold it till prices went still higher or to ship it secretly out of the prefecture.[47] Huang's approach, as these things went in the Sung, was confrontational: he insisted the rich sell their grain at a price he judged reasonable, prohibited shipping grain out of the prefecture (thus violating Sung law himself), and in specific cases sent officials to seize the grain and administer its sale. The families he confronted reacted with everything from passive hostility to vigorous resistance. Thus from his first week in office Huang found himself in direct conflict with the wealthiest families of Fu-chou, and there is remarkably little evidence in the documents he left behind that he managed to establish cooperative relations with more than a few. On his best day, Huang Chen would not have found most local religious practices in Sung China congenial. But in a conflict with the local elite, one could hardly expect him to look kindly on Immortals whose cult texts commemorated their resistance to imperial authority; whose own authority was that of insiders, not outsiders, and personal, not official; who had never held any office themselves; and whose sponsors and patrons for generations had been leading families of just that local elite he now treated as a selfish antagonist. Huang Chen, it seems, could see Luan Pa and Mei Fu as representing authority very much like his own: external, official, and largely confronting and punitive. And it was just this side of the Four Immortals, I suggest, that had kept them subordinate to the Three Immortals of Mt. Hua-kai in the writings of the local elite. By his choice of the Four Immortals and refusal of the Three, Huang Chen supports the interpretation of the Three I am proposing here.

On this point, again, there is more evidence. Huang Chen did not worship only the Four Immortals while he was in Fu-chou. His collected works preserve ten prayers for rain or prayers of thanks for rain he offered to a variety of divinities. Two address gods of the state cult: one the gods of soil and grain, which had been associated with central authority and dynastic fortunes from time immemorial and whose worship by local administrators replicated the emperor's own rituals at the capital; the other the god of the soil again and with it the city god, who had special associations with bureaucratic authority. In the former prayer, Huang specifically treats the worship of the gods of soil and grain as a direct alternative to the worship of "improper cults": "Why is it that recent generations address the gods of improper cults, while to the gods of soil and grain, by contrast, they are lax in prayer? Since I was made administrator, my reverence is only for the gods of soil and grain." He goes on to draw a precise parallel between the position of prefectural administrator—his own—and the role of the gods he is praying to: "I vow [*yuan*] to join with [you] gods in fulfilling each our office [*chih*]. To give the people peace with one another, that is my work; to bring the people a [successful] harvest, that is the gods' boon: so that before High Heaven we may both have no shame."⁴⁸ The last words invoke an authority—Heaven's—higher than Huang's or the gods' and to which both are responsible, referring their power upward to a source outside their own sphere. The second prayer also draws a picture of multilevel authority, but in a somewhat different way: "Bowing down, I ask that [you] brilliant gods may oversee the serried sages [*lieh sheng*] in conferring mercy."⁴⁹ Here "the serried sages" refers to gods at large—in this context, certainly local gods—subject to the oversight of the state's own god of the soil and city god.

Four of Huang's prayers bear no god's name in their titles, but their texts convey to whom or to what they are addressed. In the first, it is the creative force in the universe: "Unless the creator-of-things [*tsao-wu*] grant its concern and call forth [*ch'i*] with all urgency the spirit dragons of the pools and springs, I fear the early-ripening grain may all be ruined . . . and the late-ripening grain too may not reach fruition."⁵⁰ Again Huang looks to a universal higher power to move local deities (here, the dragon guardians of the water sources) to act. In a second prayer, from the following year, he addresses Heaven: "Bowing, I ask that August Heaven oversee the serried sages in conferring humane kindness."⁵¹ And in two prayers offering thanks for rain already received and appealing for more, Huang addresses the classical Lord (or Emperor) on High (*shang ti*), in popular and Taoist thinking often identified with the Jade Emperor: "Now who am I that I might compel Heaven's heights [*t'ien kao*] to listen and comply? That I have received sweet watering extending over successive weeks is only because [your] great virtue loves the living and so allows a minor servant to escape blame. . . . Bowing, I ask that the Lord on High confer his mercy and in his high perfection oversee";⁵² and "Bowing, I ask that the Lord Above hand down his mercy and oversee the five grains' ripening."⁵³ Once more Huang appeals to highest authority, and here the middlemen, local gods, are simply left out.

Only two of Huang's prayers, and perhaps a third, address divinities who are not part of the state cult throughout the empire, gods special to the Fu-chou region. The uncertain prayer is entitled simply "At the Several Shrines" (*chu miao*); these may be shrines of state gods or of local gods, and the text does not settle the issue. But whoever they are, Huang treats them as his allies in changing the ways of the locals he is at odds with: "The wealthy houses are closing off grain purchases. May [you] gods induce them to come to their senses. By current custom, people do not plant wheat but simply wait for the autumn harvest. . . . May [you] gods think on both these things."⁵⁴ Of the two prayers clearly addressed to local deities, one is Huang's prayer to the Four Immortals,⁵⁵ while the other addresses a deity that, while "local," is no longer local to Fu-chou. This last case deserves special attention.

Immediately before the prayer to the Four Immortals in Huang's works, we find a prayer entitled "Praying for Rain to the Perfected Lord of Hemp Spring."

> In antiquity, when the feudal lords sacrificed to the mountains and rivers of their territories, it was because the mountains and rivers could raise clouds, bring rain, and anoint our people. Over the generations since, the ancient rites have not survived, false doctrines have misled the people, and even the governing officials have gone along with these doctrines unawares. When praying for rain, they often do not turn to the mountains and rivers, but refer instead to dolls of wood and clay, taking these for gods. Pondering in my grief that Fu-chou has had drought for three years in a row, and that now once again it is the highest heat of summer, I made urgent inquiry of the names of the famous mountains and great rivers that should be prayed to, but the officials and people had no idea where to turn. The prefecture had a vice-administrator, namely the monastery registrar, Mr. Lü, who told me: "Of old when Yen Chen-ch'ing[56] administered Fu-chou, he once said: 'At the valley's mouth, there is a god; when one prays for rain, he answers at once; his numen is still as new today, after a thousand years.' 'The valley's mouth' is Hemp Spring. Though today it has been divided off and falls in the jurisdiction of Chien-ch'ang prefecture, in reality it is one of our old mountains and rivers; it should not be looked on as from outside, as a [mere] neighbor. In a recent year, assigned to administer Chien-ch'ang, I once went to the valley to pray for rain; the response was indeed immediate." I was now desperate at having no strategy for praying for rain, and so from afar took [Yen] Chen-ch'ing's words by intermediary and from near at hand accepted Mr. Lü's instruction, and have thus caused Mr. Lü, in disregard of distance, to go and make announcement. I hope that the god will show a concern for our Fu-chou people just as intimate as in former days.[57]

As Huang makes clear here, Hemp Spring lies not in Fu-chou (in its Sung form) but in Chien-ch'ang prefecture to the east, created of Fu-chou territory under the T'ang. In fact, Hemp Spring is at Mt. Ma-ku, the famous Taoist mountain to which the Three Immortals were heading when they interrupted their journey and stopped forever at Mt. Hua-kai. To a Sung Fu-chou man, the Perfected Lord of Hemp Spring is divine power that lies *outside* his own prefecture. Whether in choosing a god from Mt. Ma-ku Huang intends a subtle comment upon the Three Immortals—that they should have continued their journey to a place of proper and larger authority or that their cult ought not to claim a prestige superior to a national Taoist center—is unclear. But in bringing Yen Chen-ch'ing into the picture, he leaves no doubt that again the choice to worship one divinity is at the same time a choice *not* to worship the Three. He seems almost to circle warily and deliberately about them, always looking elsewhere while aware that they are there. For Yen Chen-ch'ing, as we saw at the outset and as Huang certainly knew, had commemorated the shrine to the Three Immortals in the same year as the shrine at Hemp Spring. If Huang were searching for mountains to pray at as innocently as he suggests here, then relying on Yen Chen-ch'ing's testimony would mean praying at Mt. Hua-kai too.

But we may look at the choice of the Hemp Spring deity from yet another angle. If we consider again Huang's strategy in his practical efforts at famine relief among the people of Fu-chou, we find that in several places he proclaims his intention of relying upon "sojourning gentlemen" in Fu-chou as mainstays of aid and support. Huang seems to have feared that gentlemen native to Fu-chou would be too bound by ties of kin or neighborhood to the wealthy resisting families to be reliable agents for him.[58] "Sojourning gentlemen" were men of official standing from other prefectures, or indeed other regions entirely, who for one reason or another found themselves living in Fu-chou for a time. Their political status made them social equals of Fu-chou men of rank, and so able to act with some realistic claim to authority where men of rank were resisting. It seems that Huang not only sent Vice-Prefect Lü to pray at Hemp Spring but later brought the god's image to the Fu-chou prefectural seat for a time.[59] In doing so, he made the Hemp Spring god himself into a "sojourning gentleman." In seeking help from an outsider, but an outsider with some connection to Fu-chou, Huang chose his god just as he chose his men.

This angle of view will clarify another sacrifice Huang performed while in Fu-chou: not a prayer for rain or even a prayer at all, but a rite of offering and veneration to Chu Hsi, the Neo-Confucian thinker and Learning of the Way leader who had died more than seventy years earlier.[60] A shrine to Chu—a typical artifact of the Southern Sung "worthies' shrines" movement whose nature and history Ellen Neskar's work has brilliantly revealed[61]—stood in the prefectural city at the Lin-ju Academy, a private academy devoted to Chu Hsi's curriculum of study, and here Huang offered his sacrifices. Chu Hsi, of course, was not a Fu-chou man himself. In fact, a Fu-chou man had been one of his leading rivals: this was Lu Chiu-yuan (Lu Hsiang-shan) of Chin-ch'i County. A shrine to Lu stood in the prefectural city at the time Huang served, yet it appears he did not offer sacrifices there. This was not because he did not think of Lu; in fact, he devotes a large part of his prayer of offering to Chu Hsi to the rivalry between Lu and Chu and suggests that the differences between them were less profound than at times they, and certainly their followers, may have been willing to believe. Huang celebrates the readiness of Fu-chou men in his time to follow Chu's teaching even though Lu was of their own prefecture. His message here, clearly, is conciliatory. Yet if conciliation were his only aim, he could sacrifice to Lu as well. But in the sphere of intellectual-spiritual authority, Chu Hsi, or his spirit enshrined in the Lin-ju Academy, is a precise analogue of the "sojourning gentlemen" on whom Huang relies in the world of the living. He is not a Fu-chou man, but in his image, in spirit, and through the local following for his teachings, he resides there. He is an outsider with authority inside.

Huang's prayers and sacrifices in Fu-chou, then, embody a number of recurring themes: that authority comes from outside the local sphere or from a plane higher than that of local gods; that higher authority may direct lower authority; that local people do not know whom to worship; that the local administrator in choosing his gods must therefore beware of "improper cults," whose local following does not justify them; that gods and spirits are, or should be, the allies of the local administrator; or that they are his divine analogue. Almost any one of these by itself might be enough to motivate the choice of the Four Immortals of Mt. Hsiang over the Three Immortals of Mt. Hua-kai. Taken as a whole, they make the choice look fated.

It is in the light of these themes and concerns that we should approach Huang's commemorative inscription for the Four Immortals. It is a complex document. Huang does have a problem with the Four Immortals, even if he is willing to celebrate them and not the Three: they are Immortals, and so Taoists. As a good Neo-Confucian in Chu Hsi's line, he cannot fully affirm their power, or even their reality. But if we read what he says with care, it is clear that issues of inside and outside are on his mind. His solution to his difficulty is striking and offers no solace to elite worshippers of local cults. Let us take up his text from where we left it:

> I have heard that when the world speaks of "Immortals," it means those who mount yonder white clouds to go to the land of the [Heavenly] Emperor. These are thus transcendent [*ch'ao-jan*], living in the dwellings of celestial music of the Purple Court in the Pure Capital. How could they be on this mountain always and forever? Is it actually that the traces they may have left behind are protected by the mountain's spiritual force? Or is it rather their divine spiritual force [itself] that will never be gone? Or is it that what we today call the Four Immortals are precisely the spirits of the maker-and-transformer of the mountains and rivers? That is to say: since Heaven and Earth began, and the mountains and streams were arrayed, the raising of clouds, the emission of vapor, the multiplication of the populace have all been accomplished by the spirits of the mountains and rivers. This is what the *Tso Chuan* means when it says, "Ghosts and spirits are the traces of the maker-and-transformer." It is what the *Rites* means when it says, "What benefits the people, sacrifice to that." Mt. Hsiang is in Fu-chou; it is twenty-six *li* high; it thrusts up elegantly halfway to Heaven; it towers over all the four directions; it is the greatest peak in the territory. This truly is a place where divine intelligences reside and where the maker-and-transformer is housed. Of the Four Immortals, both Immortal Mei Fu and Immortal Luan Pa were men of Han; Teng Ssu-huan and Yeh Fa-shan were men of T'ang. Their first enfeoffment was in the fourth year of Shao-ting [1231]; their further enfeoffment was in the first year of Tuan-p'ing [1234]; all this is found in full in previous accounts. But the "Four Immortals," in my humble opinion, represent nothing other than the spiritually efficacious marvels of the gods of the mountains and rivers; they represent nothing other

than the traces of the maker-and-transformer. This being so, what I wish to say is to cause the men and gentlemen of Fu-chou, from now and henceforth, always to make one what their hearts incline to.

Huang here offers the believer in the Four Immortals, in effect, two choices, one of which, of course, he greatly prefers. One may see the Four as Immortals. But in this case one must admit that they are not on or of the mountain; they must be far away, in the celestial court and capital. (Here is Chou Meng-jo's puzzle again, not resolved but reaffirmed and exploited.) That is, Huang here introduces the bureaucratic model and proposes it *as the only model available for the worship of Immortals*. If they are Immortals, they are away, up, out there, with the Emperor of Heaven. In my terms, they cannot in any sense be local; their authority is not of the inside; they are with, and of, an authority higher and farther away than any human can know. On the other hand—and this is Huang Chen's choice—one may see them as the classical gods of the mountains and rivers. This will grant that they are in some way in the mountain: the Neo-Confucian model of the classical gods is of an essentially feudal hierarchy, and its gods cannot be denied locality in an important sense. But in the particular interpretation Huang offers, to recognize the Four as such gods has two implications, which largely take back what he has yielded. One he spells out: the gods of the mountains and rivers are only so many expressions or manifestations or instruments of the single "maker-and-transformer"—the creative force or principle of the entire universe. The implication is that their locality is only partial or temporary, or not ultimate; what is really behind them is everywhere, total, by no means an aspect or effect of this particular locality; and above all, it is one. The rhetorical tactic is not different from the Celestial Heart move of making the Three Immortals temporary incarnations of the Three Pure. This or that spirit of this or that mountain or river, Huang tells us, is no different, or even really separate, from the spirit of some other mountain or river. This is why "the gentlemen of Fu-chou" should "make one what their hearts incline to," what they honor or revere or worship: their hearts should "incline to" the one unifying creative and transforming principle, and not to its mere particular manifestations. There is no true space here for a local god as an expression of locality itself. Thus the effect of Huang Chen's argument, I believe quite deliberate, is to deny local worship as such.

The same conclusion can proceed by another route: this is the implication Huang Chen does not draw out, but it would be there for Sung readers. Accept for the moment that the gods of the rivers and mountains are just that; do not pursue them to their root in the single creative principle, but regard them as elements in the classical feudal structure of worship, as Sung Neo-Confucians believed it was practiced in antiquity. The crucial feature of this ideal classical structure was that it defined precisely who was entitled to worship which gods, at which level. At every level the authorized worshipper belonged to the structure of *government*. That is, the emperor could worship the gods at his level; the highest feudal lords those at their level; and so on down the line to the governors of the smallest units in the system, who were solely entitled to worship the gods of the local rivers and mountains. Lu Chiu-yuan, a Fu-chou man himself, had complained that in his day just anybody worshipped gods, and that this ought properly to be the task of officials alone.[62] This was the true classicist position held by many Neo-Confucians, at least in theory.

Thus in saying that the Four Immortals were really just the gods of the rivers and streams, Huang Chen made available the implication that, if things were to be done properly, the local elite really ought not to be worshipping them—or any other gods or Immortals—at all. Not only in choosing which Immortals to worship, but in trying to redefine those Immortals as such out of existence, Huang Chen argued and acted so as to rob the Fu-chou elite of any special connection to their divinities and to deny their authority to choose whom to worship.

CONCLUSION

I have argued here that the rise of the Three Immortals cult expresses a local elite's new construction of itself as locally rooted and locally concerned, that it reacts specifically against expressions of central power such as the imposition of Divine Empyrean Taoism and the execution of Ou-yang Ch'e, and that this view of the Three Immortals' meaning for the elite makes intelligible both their own relative lack of interest in certain other divinities and the religious choices made by Huang Chen when he confronts the elite in time of famine. To see Three Immortals worship as only *reacting against* central power, however, may miss an important aspect of its relation to the state. Consider again the early history of the cult. In 1075 and 1100, the central government enfeoffs the Three Immortals, and within twenty years of the second enfeoffment, we see the very earliest evidence of local elite patronage in both Lin-ch'uan County (Tseng Chi-li) and Ch'ung-jen County (Hsiung P'u). Was it the state's attention, however ill informed, that first stimulated elite interest in the Three Immortals? I suggest that it was, and that in taking up the worship of the Three the Fu-chou elite both adopted an object of state concern as their own and turned it to their own purposes, in many ways opposed to the state's.

This is certainly no paradox, but it is complicated enough to be interesting, and belongs, I think, to a larger historical pattern at the interface of the Northern and the Southern Sung. Clearly, state patronage was not enough to make the elite take up a god for the long term; we have seen the Mt. Chün god, enfeoffed in the late Northern Sung at local urging, fade into the background in the Southern Sung even on its own mountain, and there is no evidence that the late Sung enfeoffment of the Four Immortals of Mt. Pa gave them a wider local audience in the Yüan dynasty. But there is so little sign of Fu-chou elite interest in specific local divinities *before* the great enfeoffment project of the 1070s that one wonders whether perhaps state patronage created the very idea of elite patronage. If this was so, it was only one aspect of a much larger tendency. The New Laws, and the smaller measures of reformist precursors in earlier decades, especially in education, opened up whole new fields or modes of action for the state at the local level. And again and again, Southern Sung elites or their intellectual leaders moved to replace or build parallels to these by taking action or creating institutions in the same fields and modes, which had not earlier been part of local elite life or at least its public expressions. Along with others, I have elsewhere argued the case for certain prominent examples: for the government schools so greatly expanded by Wang An-shih and his reformist predecessors and successors, we have in the Southern Sung the private academy; for Wang's Green Sprouts farm loans, the community granary; for state-organized mutual surveillance organizations like *pao-chia*, the "community compact," if only on paper; and so on. All are conscious institutional alternatives to state action, sponsored by Chu Hsi and his fellows in the Learning of the Way movement. But in other cases, state action under the New Laws regime may simply have revealed opportunities or needs that local elites later more or less spontaneously took up. In the 1070s, the state organized a local militia in Fu-chou, of which nothing at all is later heard; but fifty years later, at the fall of the Northern Sung, important families in Chin-ch'i County organize a private militia of their own that is crucial for Fu-chou's defense for more than two centuries. Local sources suggest that this was an entirely new organization; but did it, in fact, build on the experience, the structure, or even the membership of the units the state had founded? Perhaps the New Laws taken as a whole had proposed, implicitly and explicitly, a conception of what needed doing and a notion of what it meant to take leadership in the localities, and perhaps this conception was powerful long after the New Laws themselves were no more. Perhaps certain functions came to seem important partly because the reformist state had first shown their possibility and then either performed them in ways hostile to elite interests or withdrawn. Perhaps the sponsorship of local gods was one of these.

Whatever its motive, the state's own first route of entry into this arena, enfeoffing gods already held to be locally powerful, offered little threat to local interests; provided local elites with a potential channel through which they could act, by sponsoring gods for the state to enfeoff; and implicitly presented a question—which local gods are the worthy and important ones?—that local elites could claim the authority to answer. I argue in Chapter 7 that the "feudal" model of relations between center and god articulated by the enfeoffment process differed sharply from a bureaucratic model precisely by minimizing the assertion of imperial authority *over* the gods and in recognizing gods' authority as something that existed before enfeoffment. The attention that enfeoffment gave to local gods was thus a kind of attention that local elites need not feel any reason to abstain from, let alone resist, though they might disagree with and seek to influence the choices made among gods. The later and much more assertive claim to central authority over local religion that Divine Empyrean Taoism embodied was far more likely to seem a threat, and it makes sense that a local elite might react against it by cleaving further to just such local gods as the earlier central drive to enfeoffment had held up as important.

I am not arguing that enfeoffment was the prime goal at which elite patronage aimed or the prize it needed to survive; it is interesting that after the Hua-kai Immortals become central figures in local elite religious life, there are no further enfeoffments of the Three till very near the end of the Southern Sung. I am arguing rather that the rise of state enfeoffment under the New Laws called attention to local gods as something for the elite to take seriously, not simply in the capacity of private devotees but in a more public arena of proclamation, sponsorship, donation, and community-minded beneficence. Once they did so, their choice of gods and the godly virtues and character they proclaimed and celebrated could, of course, diverge very widely from, or indeed express resistance to, the state's own conceptions and interests. This is precisely what happened with the Three Immortals of Mt. Hua-kai.

CHAPTER SIX

Taoists, Local Gods, and the Transformation of Wang Wen-ch'ing

At the close of the Northern Sung, a leader of the court Taoist establishment, Wang Wen-ch'ing, who had rendered divine aid to the emperor Hui-tsung for several years, left court and capital and returned to his home in Nan-feng County, settling near the same Mt. Chün where the cult of the Three Immortals would flourish in the Southern Sung. For the next three decades, he practiced the Five Thunders arts in his home county, in other parts of Chiang-hsi circuit, and in the neighboring circuit of Fu-chien, attracting disciples and performing exorcisms, cures, and weather miracles for clients public and private. In 1153, he "was transformed away,"[1] and his disciples buried his mortal remains near the mountain, at Spirit Turtle Ridge. But his service to his community continued: he repeatedly answered local prayers for rain, and the people of his prefecture built shrines to him, perhaps by the 1220s and certainly no later than 1292.[2]

This is the sketch of Wang's life and afterlife that emerges from reports dating from the Southern Sung, Yuan, and Ming. The details are far from secure. Only one mention of Wang survives in a source that may be contemporary with his own life,[3] and the fullest accounts, especially of his career at court, come from documents written almost two centuries after the events they claim to record. Yet certain records lie close enough in years to make the broad outlines plausible; and the sources in their range across time are worth examining for themselves, because they trace the transformation of a professional Taoist practitioner, close cousin to the Celestial Heart masters, into a local divinity akin to the Three Lords of Mt. Hua-kai. In this transformation we can see with much more precision than we have so far how Taoist writings represent the Taoist practitioner, and gauge more precisely the balance of the bureaucratic and the personal in clerical Taoism.

WANG WEN-CH'ING AS TAOIST PRACTITIONER

We may be lucky enough to have Wang Wen-ch'ing's own words preserved in a book called *Household Talk of the Void-Soaring, Mystery-Penetrating Imperial Attendant, Master Wang* (*Ch'ung-hsu t'ung-miao shih-ch'en Wang hsien-sheng chia-hua*).[4] This very brief work, bearing no date or preface, presents a dialogue between Wang and his disciple Yuan T'ing-chih on Five Thunders practice. Boltz seems to accept it as authentic,[5] and I cannot find any special reason to doubt that it is more or less what it claims to be. It shows familiarity with the geography of the county that Wang lived in. It glorifies Wang, as one would expect, but represents Yuan T'ing-chih and disciples of his generation in a not very dignifying light, far from what one would expect if it were the product of later Sung or Yuan followers of Wang's teachings, all of whom claimed direct spiritual descent from this first generation of students. It is thus plausible that it was written by a disciple of the first generation who properly represented himself and his fellows in an unflattering light before their teacher. Even if the text is later, it is invaluable as a representation by Five Thunders followers of the sort of man a teacher like Wang ought to be. In effect it is a self-portrait of Five Thunders masters in their daily interaction with one another and with the divine. This alone would make it worth examining.

Much of *Household Talk* treats the details of Five Thunders practice. A longish extract will convey the flavor:

> [Yuan] asked: The quickness of spirit envoys is indeed divine; as for instance when a single one emerges from one's ancestral palace and can be employed anywhere. But in the dark and obscure stillness of the void, how is one to verify [*yen*] whether the spirit envoy has come or not?
>
> [The imperial attendant] answered: According to the rite, one is to knock one's teeth silently, grasp the Thunder Office, and summon the envoy in accordance with the rite; recite silently to oneself the sounds of the incantation; and hold the brightness in one's mouth, perfectly silently. When the space between one's eyebrows tingles, the envoy has come.
>
> [Yuan] asked: Your disciple previously received the master's instruction and transmission in rites and mantras, and while healing illness at the house of Ch'en Tzu-shih of I-huang County, similarly in mystery and darkness I summoned a spirit envoy to punish the spirit-ill. As I sat fixed, suddenly a cool wind struck my two feet. Afterward I gave the sick person a talisman and saw the envoy display his shape. Why is this verification [*yen*] somewhat different from what the master has said about the space between the eyebrows?
>
> [The imperial attendant] answered: Thoughts arise from a single point. Responses are verified upon the whole body. The head is round and images Heaven; the feet are square and image Earth. In the case of verification in the space between the eyebrows, the envoy comes from the gate of Heaven; in the case of verification on the soles of the feet, the envoy arrives from the door of Earth. Probably the spirit-ill's shadow and echo were present in the world of the

living [but it?] resided in the earth. That is why the envoy came by breaking through the door of Earth to catch the spirit-ill. But the verification for mobilizing thunder cuts into the space between the eyebrows in order to reach the five organs.[6]

There is much more of this, nearly impenetrable to the uninitiated and hard to read with security even when one has read a great deal of it. But other passages bear directly on my central issue: the bureaucratic model of the divine. As one would expect, Wang consistently presents his own position and procedures in bureaucratic terms. He stresses the care with which one must treat the various official communications through which one acts:

[Yuan] asked: What are the essentials of mobilizing thunder and stirring thunderclaps?

[The imperial attendant] answered: Thunderclaps are the orders of Heaven. They must not be employed except on the most urgent and important business. It is just as when the [earthly] Bureau of Military Affairs issues an order to the Receivers in the Edicts Office of such-and-such a place: they must act according to the order.[7]

[Yuan] asked: ... How is it that rite-officers and ordained Taoists of today offer one memorial after another, of which not one is responded to, and without any verification or effect? Why is this?

[The imperial attendant] answered: In the end, the memorials one sends up all go to the same place; one ought not to multiply them unnecessarily. It would be as if people today, whenever they had a problem, went straight to the Drum-Court for Reporting Grievances [*teng-wen-ku yuan*]. When The One Above proclaims drought by the quotas of Heaven, if you thoughtlessly memorialize for your own private reasons, this will automatically be sent down to the circuit spirit authorities and in turn to the spirit prefecture and county, for them to investigate how things stand, before any measures are taken. If you are awaiting an order from The One Above and it turns out that it was just on the day of your memorial that rain was to be sent down, won't you be ashamed? This is why the Fire Master taught me the Way to fly my spirit and appear in audience before the [Jade] Emperor. All matters of rain-prayer fall under the jurisdiction of the Celestial Lord of the Limpid Waves. In each case one simply memorializes to the Celestial Lord asking that he grant the favor of reporting this in turn to the Jade Emperor and obtaining an edict to the Palace of Perfection of the God of the Earth to open the depths [*k'ai t'an*], release the water, and relieve what is scorched and parched.[8]

Just as in Celestial Heart practice, bureaucratic forms govern the practitioner's interactions both upward and downward:

[Yuan] asked: Thunder shakes a hundred *li*. How is it that it cannot reach everywhere—so much so that while township A has rain, township B has none; or that township C has none, while township D is soaked and its drought reversed?

> [The imperial attendant] answered: When you perform a rite, you first issue a summons to the earth god of that place or township to receive you formally. If the people of that place or township are fully sincere, and further the township's earth god receives you and memorializes in response, their rain will surely be torrential. If the people of that place have so ripened in evildoing as to produce a drought with not even the tiniest drop of water, their earth god too will not receive you. The principle is the same as when, in the world of the living, one sends an official someplace to grant special relief: if the prefecture or county office complies with his wishes, then the special relief is forthcoming without fail; while if the local officers do not perform their duties, then the relief process is mere paperwork.[9]

In this last example a disruption of proper bureaucratic relations explains a failure to reverse drought: the gods staffing the lowest-level local offices (influenced by their populace's evil character) do not respond to the practitioner's official summons. This is a use of the model we have not seen before. Other passages suggest the limits that bureaucratic norms may place on the practitioner's authority to act and so on his power to help. In one case, a superior in the know fills Wang in on the channels (as it were!) he may use to get around a prohibition on rain.

> [The imperial attendant] answered: ... Long ago when I entered Yin [County], I met the Fire Master again, who said: "You are going to the [earthly] court and for a weighty assignment, so I have come to report to you. This year, however, the quotas of Heaven require manifestations of drought. This is not something you can affect with prayers." I appealed to the Fire Master as to how he could instruct me. "All the world's dragon pools and springs have been sealed off by the Jade Emperor," the master said. "Even with talismanic rites this will be hard to affect with prayers, until the quota is filled." Again I asked the master how he could instruct me. "When you undertake this," he said, "only the Yellow River will not have been locked shut. Your only appropriate course is to detail a spirit messenger to the Yellow River to borrow water to relieve the drought." I followed his instructions: when I reached the capital, the court did in fact command me to pray for rain. I assigned a thunder spirit to borrow three feet of water from the Yellow River and relieve the drought. Later, the capital circuit authorities memorialized to the emperor that all the rain that fell was muddy. From this I saw that the Fire Master's words were correct.[10]

Here Wang is successful. In another case, his similar circumventing of proper lines of authority accomplishes little:

> [Yuan] asked: The quotas of Heaven are high and powerful. Even though one hold to inward cultivation, how can one shift or turn them?
>
> [The imperial attendant] answered: The quotas are, to be sure, determined in Heaven. Any thought of shifting them will depend on acting at the crux and responding to change. For instance, in former days before I went to the capital, the prefectural administration wanted me to pray for rain. Before I acted, the

prefecture had carried out prayers and sacrifices everywhere without response. One day, while I was quiet and settled, a spirit envoy suddenly appeared in the air and secretly reported: "The quota of Heaven requires drought; this cannot be dealt with by rites. Now, within fifty *li* of the prefectural seat, there is a thunder pool, at the place called Ripe Spring in Chien-ch'ang prefecture. Though the thunder god within has already received the order to seal the pool, in your rites of the Way you still have the capacity to compel. You should use a talisman to order him raised." I understood and proceeded to use a talisman to order a spirit envoy to seek the god out. I went in again, and then I saw, in a dazzling flash, an old fellow suddenly come onto the altar and suck up from the basin a mouthful of black water that was covering the sun.[11] Before long Heaven and Earth were in shadow, and down came a brief fall of rain, then stopped. I realized that I had not managed to reverse the drought. Later, I asked the spirit envoy, and he said the old fellow was simply the dragon-god I had raised; he had come out of his cavern in violation of celestial orders; the brief fall of rain that came down was just the mouthful of pure water from the altar. It was simply a one-time response within the limits of my rite. At this I sent off a memorial and flew to report to the Perfected King and request a decree. Later, I received a decree from the [Jade] Emperor sending down three days of rain; only then was the drought reversed.[12]

That bureaucratic status could limit as well as empower was of course also clear in the codes of Celestial Heart, which listed punishments for masters who exceeded their own authority. An anecdote in Hung Mai's *I-chien chih* shows the same for a student of Wang Wen-ch'ing's, though here the punishment is ad hoc:

When Wang Wen-ch'ing of Chien-ch'ang had made a name for his arts of the Way, his disciple, Taoist Cheng [Cheng *tao-shih*], received the Five Thunders rites and traveled in the vicinity of Yun- and Fu-chou. He requested rain and suppressed spirit-ills for people, and when he called upon the thunderclaps, the response was like an echo. At the beginning of Shao-hsing (ca. 1130) he came to Lin-ch'uan, and several guests called on him, hoping to see his reputed Thunder Gods. He resisted but could not hold out against them and so proceeded to chant and write charms as always, grasping his sword and shouting. After a time a hidden wind blew softly, and, partly obscured by a smoky mist, a deity with a high hat stood before him, grasping an axe. "I, your disciple, am a Thunder God; I have received the master's call and would hear what he directs." Cheng said: "I sent an assistant to call you because several people wanted a chance to see you; nothing else." The god was enraged. "Whenever I receive an order," he said, "I must appear before Heaven above before I dare come; when the matter is done and I return, I must report to Heaven again. Now you have used me as aid for a jest; with what excuse shall I answer Heaven? This axe may not be borne in vain. It is the master who must make good for it." Then he raised the axe and struck Cheng on the head. All those sitting there, speechless, fell to the ground in fright. After a while they came to; Cheng was dead.[13]

This story, one of five Hung Mai gathered about Wang Wen-ch'ing, first appeared in print in 1171. Clearly practitioners of Wang's line, like Celestial Heart masters, were subject to stern official discipline not only in their own ritual and legal texts but sometimes in the stories that laymen told about them.

The same picture emerges from a much later text, the very long biography of Wang in *Comprehensive Mirror of the Successive Generations of Perfected Transcendents and Those Who Embody the Way* by the Yuan dynasty Taoist master Chao Tao-i (fl. 1294–1307).[14] Here the first special knowledge Wang acquires after he has wandered the world is "the method of flying up with a memorial [*fei-chang*] and having audience with the [Jade] Emperor," handed on to him by an "extraordinary man [*i-jen*]."[15] Once he has learned this, "every half-hour he would fly up with a memorial and secretly pay court to the Emperor on High."[16] When people suffer harm from spirits, he sends spirit officers to drive them away. At the capital, when he acts to end a plague of fox demons, in the middle of the night his fellow Taoists see "military officers and government clerks" driving the demons before them. When he brings the muddy rain for the drought—just as in the dialogue text—he explains to Hui-tsung that "the Yangtse and the Huai have both been interdicted by the Emperor on High; only the Yellow River's water is not."[17] When he prays on Hui-tsung's behalf for peace from Sung's threatening northern neighbors, communicating with Heaven and learning its will require an exchange of memorial and edict:

> The emperor sent the inner commissioner Huang Yao to present to Wang the emperor's incense-letters, all the vermilion memorials sealed in a single box-envelope, and Wang went to the Jade Emperor Hall in the Nine-Yang Palace for Overseeing the Perfected to burn them [and so send them up to heaven]. . . . The emperor asked how the vermilion memorials he had sent up had been answered. In tears, the master reported: "In Your Majesty's memorial you vowed: 'If a gentleman who possesses the Way is sent out to manage the world, I shall give up my own life in thanks.' In response to this I received the edict: 'If you are removed there will be no regrets.'" . . . On the twenty-third day of the twelfth month, the emperor abdicated his throne at the Eastern Palace.[18]

After Wang withdraws from the (secular) capital and returns home, he travels to Shao-wu prefecture in drought and witnesses a local god's own audience in Heaven. We hear the story in his own words:

> Recently, Shao-wu had a drought. I secretly paid court to the Emperor on High about this, and at the site of my audience, somebody called the God of Beneficent Response was appealing most powerfully to the Jade Throne on the people's behalf. The Emperor told him that the quotas required it; but Beneficent Response stood and said: "The prefecture is poor and exhausted; the people cannot go without grain for even a day." His words were most

intense, and in the end his request was granted, and that year's harvest was a good one.[19]

Here a local god acts just as a compassionate county administrator might, pleading directly to the throne for relief for his people. Finally, when Wang dies, he "orders the god of the earth" to protect the ritual texts and seals he has hidden away in a cave. Imperial and bureaucratic language by no means saturates Chao's long biography, but it punctuates it crucially, leaving no ambiguity about Wang's role and place in the world.

I may seem to belabor the obvious here: from all we have seen, how could a professional Taoist not be represented as a divine official? But I devote so much space to this way of representing Wang precisely because there is another, preserved most purely in writings roughly contemporary with Chao's biography. Before we consider these, it is important to see that Chao presents Wang as practitioner and as transmitter of his arts, *and as nothing else.* Consider his account of Wang's death:

> One day in the twenty-second year of Shao-hsing [1152], the master said to his disciple Chu Chih-ch'ing: "I shall go into seclusion." He took his ritual texts and seals, went into the Stone Cavern of Mt. Chün, and hid them. He further ordered the god of the earth to guard them and to wait for one with the conduct of the Way to find them. In the next year [1153], on the twenty-first day of the eighth month, the master took his leave of the county administrator. On the twenty-third day he arose early, composed an ode, and inscribed it on the wood of his coffin: "My body is pretense / The pine planks are not true / They snare the worldly eye / While I escape red dust." When the ode was done, he was transformed in seclusion at the Hall of Hsu Ching-yang's Refining in the county's Ch'ing-tu Abbey. At that instant, there was a single clap of thunder, and the master was transformed away.
>
> His disciples Hsiung Shan-jen, P'ing Ching-tsung, Yuan T'ing-chih, and others buried him at Black Turtle Ridge. In the third month of the next year, Taoist Kuo of Mt. Lung-hu came to the county. "On the evening of the fifteenth of the first month," he said, "I was performing rites at a temple, and the imperial attendant was living at the hall. After three days he left." Later, a traveler on the way back from Ch'eng-tu-fu met the master coming into Szechwan. From time to time, some also have met the master and had the rites of the Way transmitted to them.

Everything about Wang's departing moment suggests a man leaving permanently, "escaping red dust" and leaving only illusory signs of continuing earthly presence—the body, the pine planks. In fact, his leaving, even in this story, is not quite so final. In keeping with a common motif in Taoist hagiography, he still makes brief mysterious appearances to survivors who can recognize him. Most of these fleeting manifestations, however, have no earthly consequence but to prove Wang's immortality to those left behind; and when he does act in the world, it is only to pass on his rites to new generations. What Chao's biography does not even hint is that Wang might still be active as a benefactor in the world of men, still helping the human community as he did when he was alive. This is a striking omission, because by Chao's time (he was probably writing in about the 1290s), people in Wang's home county and prefecture were worshipping Wang as a beneficent and active local patron. It is in the documents of his local cult that we find, in its purest form, the second way of representing him.

WANG WEN-CH'ING AS LOCAL GOD

Suggestive but not conclusive evidence of Wang's cult comes from no later than the 1220s, when the traveling Taoist master Pai Yü-ch'an, probably on his way through Chiang-hsi, wrote a poem about an "image" (*hsiang*) of Wang. Painted or sculpted images were the common apparatus of local shrines, and it is hard to imagine where else Pai might have seen Wang's portrait. The poem itself finds Wang still beneficently active in the world of the living:

> Drunk, he grasps his iron staff and calls the wind and thunder;
> The silken word of the Jade Lord: to summon back the rain.
> As soon as there are no more demons hiding in the world,
> Once again he's crooning at the eight western towers.[20]

Pai Yü-ch'an is a professional Taoist. Even at a shrine in Wang Wen-ch'ing's honor, he shows Wang executing the decrees of his bureaucratic chief, the Jade Emperor. But in a record from the 1290s, a gentleman living in Wang's county paints a different picture. The author is Ch'eng Chü-fu, earlier a sojourner in Chien-ch'ang prefecture for some years.

> In the spring of the *jen-ch'en* year of the Chih-yuan period [1292], I was about to undertake my mother's burial. I went home, consulted the omens, mowed the grass, excavated the vault, hodded away the earth, wheeled away the stones. With matters at a critical stage, accumulated rain and mudslides made me much afraid I could not complete the burial. I hurried all around to streams and hills [to pray], when my father said: "In this county once lived the imperial attendant Wang, who people say controls the handles of cloud and clearing. The registrar Teng Shih, called Ping-chien, has inherited his rites. Any prayer to Wang gains instant response. Why not appeal to him?" In the second month, on the day *chia-tzu*, at the new moon, I went and made my plea. In the morning, it was still cloudy and dark, the rain hanging, hanging, ready to fall; before long, the clouds broke, the sun filled the sky, and it cleared. From then on, it did not rain again for two weeks. On the *chia-shen* day we covered the vault, and when it was done, it rained for a full month. "A wonder!" I sighed. One day the registrar came and said to me: "The imperial attendant's Way-rites could make wind and rain by inhaling and exhaling. In the Sung, he was received at the courts of both Hui-tsung and Kao-tsung. He died, yet the people of his county serve him as if he were alive. In the drought of the year

chi-ch'ou [1169, 1229, or 1289] they prayed, and it rained; in the drought of *hsin-mao* [1171, 1231, or 1291] they prayed again, and it rained. His shrine at the T'ien-ch'ing Abbey, below the veranda, is poor, ill-kept, and unworthy of him. Now people are going to enshrine him instead on the ground where once he lived, to the left of the abbey. This is so as to repay him." And he sought writing from me for a record.[21]

Here, just as we have seen with the cult of the Three Immortals of Huakai, the celestial bureaucracy is simply missing. Supplicants offer prayers to Wang, and he responds "like an echo." He "controls the handles of cloud and clearing"; this language, and the image, could easily fit a bureaucratic context, but the context is absent, leaving Wang as a lone actor who grants Ch'eng Chü-fu a personal favor because Ch'eng asks him to. Ch'eng responds by helping with the project to rebuild Wang's shrine and so "repays" Wang for the favors he and others have received. The language of personal exchange is something we have seen before. Ch'eng clearly represents Wang as a professional Taoist who performs "Way-rites" that a follower can "inherit" from him; but the crucial apparatus that surrounds Taoists' practice as they themselves see it is gone. Wang is simply a local god or saint, though especially cherished. He acts on his own for those who pray to him.

We see the same Wang about forty years later in a commemorative essay by Yü Chi. In the 1330s Yü granted the request of a recent Nan-feng County administrator, P'u Ju-lin, that he write in honor of Wang Wen-ch'ing, who had answered P'u's prayers in drought and brought rain to Nan-feng. Yü first reproduces P'u's own story of the drought and Wang's intervention:

> In the *keng-shen* year of the Yen-yu period [1320], I was administering Nan-feng when in the third month there was great drought there. I prayed to the mountains and rivers without response. A local man told me: "There is an altar to the imperial attendant, Mr. Wang, at Spirit Turtle Ridge, at what they call the Abbey of Marvelous Numen, several *li* from the Nan-feng seat. The imperial attendant returned in the time of Hui-tsung of the Sung and passed away in his home region. His spirit has rendered numinous wonders to this day. Why not pray to him?" I took the rain as my responsibility and went in person to pray there. When I received an answer to my divination, I asked for numinous water in a jug and climbed into a boat to come home. There was a winding, turning serpent that came floating along the water, with a red glow all brilliant, and with cloudy ethers following behind. The district clerk coaxed it into a vessel; once it was there, it coiled up and did not move. When we reached the county gate, the rain was beginning to fall; by the time we reached the government offices, it was coming down in quantity. That year was a ripe one. The next year there was drought again. Because my previous prayer had been answered, the clerks and people laid it upon me to go again; the response was as the year before. That year too was a ripe one. The elders of the county came to me and said: "The imperial attendant's grace must not go unrewarded. Alive, he possessed arts of the Way renowned in his own time; departed, he still sheds

benefit upon his people. This should be reported to the court, which has the means to mark him out."²²

Like Ch'eng Chü-fu, Yü stresses Wang's benefactions for his home region after his death, benefactions resting on "arts of the Way" that he treats simply as Wang's own. Yü goes on to offer a broader account of Wang's life:

> According to the local histories for Lin-ch'uan and Nan-feng Counties, during the Hsuan-ho period [1119–1125] there was a man of Nan-feng, Wang Wen-ch'ing.... From birth he was of unusual character: he once composed a poem to tell his father he had ambitions for the extraordinary. When his father died, Wang took leave of his mother and wandered far away, crossing the Yangtse River. The crossing passed through a wild marsh, and in the rain and mist he lost his way. He saw what seemed to be lamplight and went toward it. He came upon an old dame who kept a roadside inn, where he found a text of several chapters. This he read by firelight. The rain cleared up, the fire died down, and when the dawn grew bright he was under a tree; there was no roadside inn. The book was about how to bring thunder and lightning and employ ghosts and spirits. By these means, he helped multitudes, and his name was known throughout the Yangtse and Lakes region.
> At this time the emperor Hui-tsung was celebrating the Taoist teachings and dreamed that he had found a divine man. He searched for him by his countenance, found the imperial attendant, granted him an audience, and praised him greatly. A decree honored him as *t'ai-su ta-fu* and redactor of archives at the Palace of Condensed Spirit.²³ ... Foxes were causing weird mischief in the capital, and people erected a shrine to the fox king. At Precious Ford Pond, too, there were weird incidents, the fault of a black carp. Wang received an order to investigate; foxes and carp all died from thunderstrokes. [Another time] there was to be a ceremony at the Hall of Light, but it would not stop raining. When the Lord prayed, it cleared at once. A decree commended him and honored him with titles and offices. [At another time] the circuits north and south of the Huai River reported a lack of snow. The emperor, concerned for the wheat crop, informed the imperial attendant. Afterward there was a great snowfall, and the wheat ripened. He was granted gold and silk but would not accept it. When bandits rose in Shan-tung, their bands attracted huge followings, and the prefectures and counties could not suppress them. Their power grew to great proportions. Wang was called to audience at the Palace of Ease, and the emperor spoke of it to him. He replied: "I shall aid the attack with spiritual might." Some days later, a courier reported that there had been great thunderclaps in the sky and that the bandits had then dispersed. The emperor gave the credit to the imperial attendant. But the imperial attendant foreknew Heaven's quotas and made repeated appeals to reform the government and train the army; yet the emperor did not take the time to listen to his views. He asked to return to his fields and village but was refused. One day, with a shake of his sleeves, he set off home for Nan-feng. Before long the Sung [lost the north and] moved south.
> In the twenty-third year of Shao-hsing [1153], on the twenty-third day of the

eighth month, he prepared wine and food and invited his neighbors to drink at his departure. He composed an ode and quickly passed away. After he died, when they bore his coffin to bury him, it was very light. For it was said he had shed his husk. Spirit Turtle Ridge is his tomb. Examples of his numinous wonder-working have been passed down ever since.

The imperial attendant died, yet was able to bring good fortune to the people of his home [*hsiang*]. Mr. P'u left for another office, yet did not forget that his former people had received the imperial attendant's grace. Their humanity and beneficence deserve commemoration. Thus I write this down, so that the people of the region may be able to consult it.[24]

Here the reason for recording Wang's acts is that he "was able to bring good fortune to the people of his home" after his death, something Chao Tao-i never tells us. The content of his parting poem, which in the other version so emphasized his departure's finality and the unreality of the world he left behind, is here unspecified. Once again, earthly government is very much present, but celestial government is not. Wang simply acts, sometimes at the earthly emperor's decree, sometimes when the emperor tells him of a problem with which he can help. In one case, we read that he "prays," but what or whom he prays to we never learn. The point becomes even clearer if one compares passages from Yü Chi's account to directly corresponding parts of Chao Tao-i's biography or *Household Talk*. In the episode of the fox demons, where Chao tells us that "in the middle of the night the Taoist officers saw military officers and state clerks driving red-clad demons before them in fetters" and shows Wang reporting to the emperor that he has "prohibited" the foxes' manifestation, Yü notes only that "foxes and carp all died from thunderstrokes." Where Chao paints the background for Wang's departure with the elaborate story of the memorials to Heaven and Heaven's decree that prompts the emperor's abdication, Yü tells us merely that Wang "foreknew Heaven's quotas." And consider Yü's sole mention of a specific authority higher than Wang, which appears not in the inscription itself but in a lengthy postscript offering information that has come Yü's way since he wrote it:

> When the Yang-chou administrator reported drought and had prayed for rain with no response, the Lord of the Way [the emperor again] questioned the imperial attendant, who replied: "The people below have sinned much; the Lord on High is thunderously angry; water is not to be had." The Lord of the Way pressed him, but he said, "There is none. Yet just a couple of feet might be borrowed from the Yellow River." In a few days, envoys from Yang-chou arrived and reported that they had had rain, all muddy and silty; and when they calculated the time, it was the very day when he had memorialized in reply.[25]

This account, which, unlike the information in the inscription itself, Yü tells us he got from a professional Taoist practitioner, preserves just a trace of the multilevel relations of delegation and communication that form the

Taoist bureaucratic model, but comparison with the other two versions shows how much is missing. Yü says nothing of the means Wang uses to "borrow" the Yellow River water, and so allows us to imagine that the power to do so is simply his own. The knowledge that the Yellow River water is available emerges as Wang's informed answer to the emperor's query, not as something Wang learns from other authority. In contrast, as we have seen, *Household Talk* shows Wang, on the Fire Master's advice, dispatching a spirit envoy—one of the complement of official underlings who take orders from a member of the celestial bureaucracy—to get the water for him. Chao Tao-i gives yet a third account:

> Later, Yang-chou had a long drought. The emperor ordered prayers for rain. The master petitioned for a sword and water basin and received a decree granting them. He squirted out a mouthful of the water and intoned: "The august emperor of great Sung has ordered this minister to pray for rain. The rain must soak and soak; the wind must uproot trees; for a thousand *li* around, Yang-chou all must be thoroughly drenched. I now borrow three feet of the Yellow River. Urgently, urgently, according to the code and the ordinances." After a few days, the Yang-chou administrators reported: they had received rain, and it was all yellow and muddy. The emperor asked the master why the rescuing rain that had been sent down was yellow and muddy. The master said: "It was because the Yangtse and the Huai had both been interdicted by the Emperor on High; only the Yellow River's water had not been interdicted."[26]

Here we see the words of Wang's dispatch, with its characteristic endpiece of fossilized Han-dynasty bureaucratese: "urgently, urgently, according to the code and the ordinances." Both these versions, unlike Yü Chi's, make clear that Wang can get around the prohibition on the empire's waters only because he is a celestial bureaucrat with a staff of underlings and the authority to issue government dispatches according to codified law. For Yü Chi, by contrast, Wang simply acts. In sum, in Yü's record and in Ch'eng Chü-fu's we find the same abstention from the language of bureaucracy and see instead simply an extraordinary man, powerful enough to help the emperor while he lives and the people of his home region when he dies.

In Yü's account, Wang's special character is inborn ("from birth he was of extraordinary character"), but it grows through contact with others as special as he. I have argued that the records of the Three Immortals of Hua-kai speak in a language of personal relations, among which the relation of teacher and disciple is especially important. The same is true of Yü Chi's account of Wang Wen-ch'ing. The only example in the inscription itself is Wang's encounter with the mysterious old dame at whose vanishing inn he finds the texts that teach him his practice. But Yü's postscript, recording further details passed on to him by other Taoist practitioners, has more to say about Wang's teacher:

When the imperial attendant took leave of his parents and left Nan-feng for the Yangtse, it was the Fire Master he met and received a book from. The Fire Master is a divine being of high antiquity, and the person whom the world has by tradition referred to as Mr. Wang Tzu-hua was in fact only his incarnation. Among his injunctions to the imperial attendant were: 'One's own body is all of Heaven and Earth; Heaven and Earth are all *yin* and *yang*. All that that rests with oneself is grasping the crux. You are to use this to respond to the subtlety of the obscure and aid a brilliant ruler; I shall await you in the Divine Empyrean.' The imperial attendant withdrew and cultivated this to the south of Army Peak in his home country.[27]

The Fire Master, or his incarnation Wang Tzu-hua, appears in Chao Tao-i's biography (though there not by name) and in *Household Talk* as well, but in both what he hands over are the first rudiments of the celestial bureaucrat's techniques of communication. "He met an extraordinary man who handed on to him the methods of flying up with a memorial and paying respects to the Emperor on High" (Chao Tao-i); "before I received the thunder text, I had already visited Mr. Wang at the Yangtse River, who handed over to me the Way to fly my spirit and have audience with the [Jade] Emperor" (*Household Talk*). We have already seen how the Fire Master, again in *Household Talk*, guides Wang in the bureaucratic possibilities in the matter of the muddy rains of Yangchou. Again there is none of this in Yü Chi's postscript, where the Fire Master teaches only to cultivate and manipulate the internal resources of the self.

If a personal encounter with a teacher brings Wang the knowledge he needs, personal encounters and in some cases previous personal ties also carry that knowledge down to later generations after his death:

> Long after the imperial attendant died, his grandnephew, driven by poverty, accompanied a merchant into Szechwan, where he personally met the imperial attendant on the road. Unrecognized, the imperial attendant grasped his hand and by the banks of the river transmitted much to him. "Tomorrow, when you cross the river," he said, "you may look for me at Such-and-Such Abbey." The next day they reached the abbey, which was abandoned, with no one about, and in the high hall was a painted image; this, it turned out, was a shrine to the imperial attendant. Only then did he know the transmitter he had met was his granduncle. The next day he met him again, and the imperial attendant gave him a length of paper. "When you reach home, deliver magical aid [*miao chi*] to my maternal grandson Shang-kuan Miao-chi through this piece of my calligraphy." He returned home and told Shang-kuan about it. Shang-kuan would not believe him; but when he took out the calligraphy and showed it to him, Shang-kuan knew the handwriting. Much moved, he cried out, and they made a space for him to instruct him in everything. In Ning-tsung's reign, Shang-kuan's rites too were widely known, and he was granted the appellation Miao-chi Master. His given name was Ssu-wen ("Practices Writing"). For in his early years, Miao-chi had not known characters very well, and "practice writing" too was something the imperial attendant had commanded on the banks of the River.

There was also a certain Sa Shou-chien, similarly devoted to the Way, who met the imperial attendant at Mt. Ch'ing-ch'eng and received his divine secrets in full. He traveled the southeast praying and putting down spiritual anomalies. Others were visited by the imperial attendant and later traveled to Chiang-hsi and stopped at Spirit Turtle Ridge, only then realizing that the imperial attendant was the man they had met decades earlier. Before, when the imperial attendant was in K'ai-feng, he lived in temples and abbeys and saw that the Yellow-Hats often peddled falsehood and trucked with the noble to show themselves off. He pondered this, and most of them did not receive his doctrines. When he returned home, the one who received what he handed down after he had grown old was Kao Tzu-yü, who handed it on to Hsu Tz'u-hsueh of Lin-chiang, whence next it came to Nieh T'ien-hsi of Chin-ch'i. Later, the recipient of transmission who became the most well known was T'an Wu-lei of Lin-ch'uan.[28]

What is important here is not simply that to make a man like Wang takes personal transmission, but also that personal qualities are crucial for receiving it. On the one hand, the first to receive Wang's posthumous transmission are his grandnephew and maternal grandson: we have already seen that descent is one of the relations the Hua-kai cult texts bring to the fore in providing status for their Three Immortals. On the other hand, we learn that faults of personal character can disqualify obvious candidates: the "Yellow-Hats," an informal term for ordained Taoists, whom Wang meets in the abbeys of the capital, do not receive his knowledge because they "peddled falsehood and trucked with the noble to show themselves off." Finally, that this passage leads directly into a list of the men Wang did make transmissions to *after he returned home*, all from the region immediately surrounding Nan-feng, suggests that a third important quality may be local or near-local origin itself. (Kao Tzu-hsu is from Nan-feng, the others from the neighboring counties of Chin-ch'i and Lin-ch'uan and the nearby prefecture of Lin-chiang.) Thus a possible reading might run: Corruption and impurity infest court and capital, but men of quality and character wait in one's own countryside.

Much of this is only implied; but at the end of Yü's postscript, the importance of personal character, descent, and even obscurity becomes explicit. The new information the postscript records comes to Yü from a Taoist named Hsueh Hsuan-ch'ing, whose letter to Yü takes up most of the text. Hsueh writes to tell Yü what he has learned of Wang and his disciples from yet another of Wang's followers, Hu Tao-hsuan. Hu is a direct inheritor of Wang's arts (from one Hsiao Yü-hsuan, from a certain Lo Hsu-chou, from T'an Wu-chen, and so on back to Wang). He has traveled the important sites of Chiang-hsi, paying a visit to the chief Hua-kai Immortal, Fu-ch'iu, at Mt. Hua-kai along the way, and delivering rain and other boons to those who ask his aid. The last bit of Yü's postscript quotes the concluding paragraphs of Hsueh's letter, a portrait of this living spiritual descendant of Wang Wen-ch'ing:

When he visited me, his hair was parted in three braids, and a single sword swung behind him. In a short-skirted garment of sackcloth, he sat solemn through all the wind and snow of the day and an extremely cold night. The lamp flame failed, yet a fine warmth filled the room. His eyes were divinely clear, yet his divine gaze penetrated in all directions. Self-inhabiting and set apart from things, he was without restraint, yet his firm resolution was inviolable. This too must be a perfected cultivator of immortality! He had a piece of poetry from the imperial attendant's hand, evidently a talisman passed down in their turn by T'an and Lo. And he said: "I shall go into hiding; but I must find someone to hand things on to. One whose restraint in conduct is like ice and frost; whose will once set is like iron and stone; the lodging place in whose breast is like the moon in water; the signs of whose material substance [*ch'i*] are like the sun and the spring; and who also, though he come of noble descent, still has accumulated virtue in obscurity for generations; who studies at a quiet, pure gate yet in his own person has auspicious force—to him, then, I shall hand it over. It's only—as one would expect—that he is hard to find!²⁹

Here again is a very special man, whose remarkable qualities are inherent, personal, and so powerful as to transform the man's surroundings. At the same time, he carries with him in Wang Wen-ch'ing's poetry the evidence that some of what he is comes to him through a line of extraordinary teachers. And his description of the man he looks for shows the same fine weave of the inherent with the inherited: restraint in conduct, will, the lodging-place in the breast, material substance, auspicious force in his person, on the one hand; noble descent refined by generations of virtue in obscurity, and study with a proper teacher (the "quiet, pure gate"), on the other. In its larger context, which after all is a discussion of Wang Wen-ch'ing himself, we may take the portrait of Hu, and Hu's description of the man he seeks, as a recipe for a man of Wang Wen-ch'ing's sort. We may also read Yü's entire piece—P'u Ju-lin's story of Wang's miracle in Nan-feng, Yü's background biography, and the quoted letter from Hsueh with further details on Wang's life and disciples—as proclaiming that Wang Wen-ch'ing is doubly active in the world: through the continued practice of the disciples who have personally inherited his Way; and through his own miracles, still granted to those who pray.

To sum up my argument so far: the records of Wang Wen-ch'ing that come to us directly from Taoist practitioners—*Household Talk* and Chao Tao-i's biography—repeatedly show Wang as a celestial official in regular communication with both superiors and underlings and treat his acts as exercises of delegated power commanded or authorized by a celestial court and emperor. They neither present him as a local divinity nor mention his posthumous aid to any community. But other records have come to us from members of the secular elite who lived in Wang's home region and who took part in (Ch'eng Chü-fu) or endorsed (Yü Chi) his posthumous cult. In these, anything like a model of celestial bureaucracy simply vanishes, and Wang appears not as an official responsible to higher authorities but simply as a spiritually extraordinary man, who in life and afterlife aids first his emperor and later his local community with powers founded partly in his own special character and partly in the instruction of a powerful teacher. The contrast neatly parallels what we have already seen in the two religious manifestations connected with Mt. Hua-kai: the cult of the Three Immortals on the one hand, patronized in the Southern Sung by lay gentlemen of Ch'ung-jen County and the surrounding region; and the Celestial Heart sect of professional exorcist practitioners on the other. Wang's case confirms that when Southern Sung and Yuan gentlemen of the Fu-chou region adopted Taoist practitioners as local divinities—whether these were real practitioners of their own age, like Wang Wen-ch'ing, or legendary masters of deeper antiquity, like the Three Immortals—they largely erased the bureaucratic model from their representations and celebrations of their cult.

Yet the contrast I have just drawn is only a first approximation. To do the world of Taoist practitioners justice, one must complicate the picture. There are not simply bureaucrats wielding delegated authority on one side and inherently powerful "extraordinary men" on the other. If the bureaucratic model is largely missing from lay elite representations of Wang, a model of inherent personal force and direct personal relations is certainly *not* missing from the representations we receive from professional Taoists. To expose a real and strong contrast, I have skipped over this point, but we must now return to the same texts to see how for Taoists the personal supplements the bureaucratic.

BUREAUCRAT AND EXTRAORDINARY MAN IN TAOIST SELF-REPRESENTATIONS

In Chao Tao-i's biography, the motif of the inherently extraordinary man is clearest in the story of Wang's childhood and youth:

> When he was growing up, he was intelligent and sharp-witted. He once wrote a poem that included these lines: "For the wealth and praise of red dust, I have no heart to pine / To the Purple City's perfect Immortals, I have a will to climb." One day, he suddenly announced to his father: "Last night I dreamed I came to a many-storied abbey, towering grandly. A huge snake lay coiled on the ground. I tried to tread on its head, and the snake surged up and climbed almost to the Milky Way." "This means you are to carry on the line of our Immortals," said his father. The master continued to love purity and emptiness. His will was only to nourish his simplicity; he did not covet fame or profit. He distanced himself from the [worldly] dust's toil and always delighted in idle wandering to numinous regions and scenes of beauty. With kerchief and bamboo staff, he traveled the world far and wide.[30]

The reader can hardly wonder that a man so described should meet, in the very next line, an "extraordinary man" (*i-jen*) who reveals important secrets to him. The extraordinary meeting is prepared by Wang's extraordinary character and conduct. We learn a good deal about Wang's extraordinary meetings in *Household Talk*, which also uses the disciple's voice to explore fundamental questions of the interrelation of personal endowment, teaching, and technique:

> The imperial attendant said: Long ago I traveled the famous mountains, stopping at more than two hundred. Once I came to the Cavern of Pure Perfection in Chin-ling. This in the T'ang was where the Heavenly Master Yeh cultivated Perfection. At twilight there was no sign of any human habitation I might resort to. I looked far off into the mountains, where suddenly appeared the light of a lamp. So I hurried in the direction of the lamplight and came to a thatched hut. Within, it was lonely and abandoned; there was no one. My heart was greatly alarmed. Under the lamp, on a table, was a piece of writing. I opened and looked at it: its title was Writings on Exhaling Wind and Rain. I thought this must be the dwelling of the thunder; now my heart was easy. I took brush and ink and copied the text onto wooden slips. When the copying was nearly done, suddenly I heard the sound of a cock's crow, and in an instant an old lady appeared. I asked her surname. "I have no surname," said the old lady. "This is where thunderclaps dwell. One must not tarry here long." I asked how there could be a cockcrow here. "That was the crow of the golden cock within the earth," the old lady said. I understood and left. After a few steps, I turned back to look, and I could not see the thatched hut. Less than a *li* farther on, I reached the cavern-heaven. It was at the Cavern of Pure Perfection that I first received a thunder text.[31]

Notice how little suggestion there is here of anything bureaucratic. Wang enters a humble thatched hut, not a palace or government bureau. He suspects it is the "dwelling" of the thunder—not the thunder's office or seat of rule. The old woman confirms this: "This is where thunderclaps dwell." She herself lacks not only title but surname too. Wang receives his text not by some decree but simply by copying writings he finds lying open—and nothing suggests this is an official document. The image is of a man stealing into another's home and copying from his valuable books. Of course, we are not to think—and this becomes clearer through the disciple's interpretation of Wang's story further on—that Wang could do this without the permission of those to whom the text belongs: the old woman herself partly plays this authorizing role in the story. But the passage does not represent the implicit permission as something in any way official or formal.

Wang's disciple, Yüan T'ing-chih, now asks: "If the master received the thunder text at the cavern-heaven, it would seem that the master's Immortal breath (*hsien feng*) and Way-bone (*tao-ku*) were sheer Heaven-granted destiny. But in antiquity one could not be saved except by a teacher. Is it possible even without a teacher?"[32]

An interesting mix of notions presents itself here. "Immortal's breath" and "Way-bone" both suggest properties very much Wang's own. "Bone" plays a major role in Chinese conceptions of biological descent from parents and ancestors, and more specifically, even today, in notions of the hereditary transmission of Taoist priestly status.[33] Similarly, the word I translate very roughly as "destiny" (*yuan*) refers to karmic connections passed down from previous generations by rebirth. Yet Yuan's question represents "breath," "bone," and "destiny" as things "Heaven-granted"—seemingly lent to Wang ad hoc. The apparent tension is probably a misreading: in Chinese conceptions, there need be no contradiction between something's being granted by Heaven and its being "naturally" inherited through biological descent or rebirth, since Heaven's acts can be seen as not ad hoc interventions but rather moments in a larger cosmic and natural process. Yuan is simply taking the discovery of the text as evidence that something larger than any mere teacher has been at work here. The tension he means to query is between a different pair of possible views of a Taoist's power: that it emerges from Wang's independent resources (whether these were acquired through descent, rebirth, Heaven's grant, or more likely all three), or that it depends on external transmission from a teacher. Wang's answer enlists his own teacher to resolve the tension:

> The imperial attendant said: Before I received the thunder text, I had already visited [the Fire Master][34] at the Yang-tzu River, and he had handed over to me the Way to fly my spirit and present myself before the [Jade] Emperor. Later, I traveled to the Cavern of Pure Perfection and received the text. After an interval of three years, I visited the Fire Master again in an inn at Army Mountain. Afterward, we visited a Ch'an monastery, and he spoke with me about how my Way . . . was progressing. I answered him: "Three years ago I came to the Cavern-Heaven of Pure Perfection. It was near evening, and I did not know where I was. In a rustic grass hut, on an abandoned table under a lonely lamp, I found the Writings on Exhaling Wind and Rain. So I noted them down on wood slips on my person and now present them to you." The Fire Master said: "You are truly a reborn Immortal. The old woman back then was the Mother of Thunder. Since you have received the text, I should speak to you." I then received his instruction and transmission. When the transmission was done, he called spirit envoys for me to distribute orders to in midair. This was my education by the Fire Master.[35]

Wang here affirms the importance of a teacher: he has learned from Mr. Wang *before* he stumbles upon the hut and finds the text. But in turn his teacher, when they meet again, reads his receipt of the text as a sign precisely of an extraordinary personal endowment: Wang has been an Immortal in a past life. And it is this that persuades the teacher to take Wang on again and confer presumably more significant transmissions upon him. The implication is that to make a Wang Wen-ch'ing takes *both* original personal quality *and* teaching. Wang himself confirms this when he derides would-be practitioners of his own day who perform rites without the necessary foundation:

> People of today, with no reborn bone and never encountering an enlightened teacher, in their own deception hand on deception, and, [as foolishly] as one who would buy a horse from its picture, without regard to whether something is important or not but to win praise and fame or to chase profit and wealth, take vain action and covet the credit due Heaven as their own. In a crisis they can achieve nothing.[36]

Here "reborn bone" (*su ku*) echoes both the "Way-bone" (*tao-ku*) of Yuan's first question and the "reborn Immortal" (*su hsien*) of Mr. Wang's judgment, confirming that "Way-bone" can descend through rebirth. Again, the false practitioners fail because they lack *both* this special inheritance from earlier ages *and* a proper teacher in their own lifetime.

Further on, Yuan T'ing-chih worries that he must fail too: "The master has Immortal's breath and Way-bone; as for me, I am just an ordinary fellow. The master had the extraordinary encounters with the Fire Master; but if I, in later days, should have doubts or difficulties, what shall I have to rely on?"[37] By "later days," Yuan presumably means a time when Wang Wen-ch'ing will no longer be available to him. Wang's reply is to the point: "What you say about Immortal's breath and Way-bone is right, to be sure; but in the encounter with a man of Heaven, we are the same. If, indeed [in later days], you should lack the virtue to call forth a worthy as teacher, you should go into your house and sit in meditation to verify [*yen*] whether your own power of creative transformation [*tsao hua*] is adequate."[38] Wang seems to admit that not every successful practitioner need be, like him, a reborn Immortal (and he reminds Yuan that he too has encountered a "man of Heaven"—Wang himself!), but he immediately returns the focus to Yuan's own qualities: his "power of creative transformation," which may be tested or "verified," as well as developed, through meditation.

Elsewhere, he suggests a process of refinement and development, in which practitioners may move through various stages:

> [Yuan] asked: Your disciple has seen that his two altar-fellows Yu and P'ing share this [your] method. Why is it that when they perform, they are successful only six or seven times out of ten? This mechanism is incomprehensible.
>
> [Wang] answered: The tie of your two friends Yu and P'ing to the Way[39] is shallow and thin, their practice of the techniques not yet pure and ripe. Doubting thoughts interpose themselves in their hearts. That is why their responses are only six or seven out of ten.[40]

Through all of this, we see again and again not only the personal qualities the practitioner needs but also the personal relations through which his knowledge must pass. The Fire Master tells Wang that the mysterious old woman at the hut who sanctions his copying is the Mother of Thunder: not bureaucratic hierarchy but parental authority turns up here at the fount of Five Thunders practice. Wang visits the Fire Master at an inn and travels with him to a monastery: these are not the official movements of bureaucrats but the informal joint travels typical of Sung gentlemen (who might of course also be fellow officials). Yu and P'ing, other disciples of Wang, are Yuan T'ing-chih's "altar fellows" or "friends."

Robert Weller has pointed out for modern Taiwan that the same Taoists who describe the divine world in bureaucratic terms characterize their own ties to their earthly teachers and disciples as personal relations, indeed, often as (fictive) relations of blood.[41] But it is important to see that these same personal relations penetrate the Taoist divine world as well, since acts of revelation or transmission from divinities to practitioners are often represented in the same personal terms.[42] Indeed, my distinction between divine and earthly here is partly faulty, since Taoists present themselves and their living teachers and disciples as Immortals or Immortals-in-the-making. In principle, the difference between Wang Wen-ch'ing's relation to the Mother of Thunder or the Fire Master (who had last lived on earth in the T'ang dynasty) and his relation to Yuan T'ing-chih or his other disciples is a difference not of kind but of degree: the relative spiritual advancement that the disciples and teachers have attained. Wang Wen-ch'ing himself continues to form new teacher-disciple relations after he is dead (or, rather, Immortal). There are not, in Taoist texts, a divine world of bureaucratic relationships on the one hand, and a secular or mortal world of personal relations on the other; rather, there is a divine and secular world, in which important relations are represented either in bureaucratic or in personal terms, or in both.

Even the teacher-student relation itself need not always appear as a personal one. In Chapter 2, we saw in the Celestial Heart spirit code the form a master must use in recommending his disciple to Heaven's authorities for ordination, with its disciple B and officiant A and its blanks for filling in names and ranks: there was no hint of a personal content in the relation between the two. I have found no suggestion anywhere in the body of Celestial Heart rites and laws of a personal side to the practitioner's relations with anyone at all. Yet even these texts, perhaps the most doggedly thorough expression of the bureaucratic model, touch on the personal view of transmission/revelation in their prefaces. Recall that Jao Tung-t'ien, after he discovered the buried texts of Celestial Heart, could not understand them. Then, according to Teng Yu-kung's preface to the *Correct Rites of Celestial Heart,* "he met a divine man who directed him to take as his teacher Master T'an, whose name was Tzu-hsiao, and receive transmission of his way."[43] Teng goes on to tell of the further transmission by which the rites eventually reached him: "When [Jao] ascended to Heaven, he transmitted the rites to his disciple, Abbey Superintendent Chu, named Chung-su; Chung-su in turn transmitted them to Yu Tao-shou; Tao-shou in turn transmitted them to the *t'ung-chih-lang* Tsou

Fen; Tsou Fen transmitted them to my first teacher, Rite-Master Fu, named T'ien-hsin. With me the transmission has reached the present day."[44] There is not much here about the personal content of these relationships, to be sure. But the transmission is not represented, as for instance it might have been, as a passage of documents between celestial officials. Rather it is a passage of secrets between men, who appear, not under their celestial titles, if any, but (with the exception of Rite-Master Fu), under whatever name or appellation will best identify them, including titles of the earthly government (*t'ung-chih-lang* Tsou and very likely Abbey Superintendent Chu). Continuing, Teng treats the transmission as incurring a personal debt that he can now attempt to repay:

> I grieved at the decline of the Way, and cried out: having undertaken my master's instruction and personally received the secret essentials and amulet-texts of the four-graded canon-registers of the Supremely High, dare I fail to attend with care to passing on these divine treasures? Lest I turn my back ungratefully on the former sages, I have thus taken the marvelous Way I received and have recompiled one full set of the *Correct Rites of Celestial Heart*.[45]

All of this, I must stress, is far from peculiar to the Celestial Heart and Five Thunders teachings. A glance over the biographical materials in the Taoist canon, or at the preface to almost any text that represents itself as a revelation or transmission from earlier masters, will show that the twin notions of inherent extraordinary personal character and personal encounters or acts of transmission are common Taoist property, especially in accounts of the hero's early life and his first spiritual advancement, and even in contexts where the bureaucratic vocabulary is just as clearly present. The "extraordinary person" is as much a part of the Taoist worldview as the "celestial official."

THE THREE IMMORTALS: WHY TAOISTS?

All this, I think, makes it important to step away for a moment and take a look back at the cult of the Hua-kai Immortals. For what we have seen here puts the special character of the Hua-kai texts, of which we saw so much in Chapter 3, in a partly different light. The Three Immortals, after all, are Taoist practitioners in their lifetimes; and it emerges from the discussion here that almost all elements of the representation of the Three Immortals in the Hua-kai texts are at least *available* in Taoist practitioners' own habits of self-representation: special personal character or inherent power; direct personal handing-on of learning from a teacher; refinement and cultivation, through what one has learned, of the resources already present in the self; and even physical inheritance of those resources from previous generations, either through rebirth or through descent. In all these ways, the Three Immortals are not a different sort of creature but recognizably Taoist figures. The Hua-kai texts give most of these elements particularly strong emphasis, to be sure. But to notice the large common ground with standard Taoist representations is to see even more clearly that two points set the Hua-kai materials off: one an omission and the other an addition. The first, of course, is the near absence, which in the light of all that is shared looks more than ever like a *removal,* of the Taoist's bureaucratic side. The second and equally important—the two are in fact, I think, closely connected—is the Hua-kai texts' strong stress on locality.

The celebration of the special place in itself is of course far from unusual in standard Taoist texts, even if it is not much a part of Celestial Heart or Five Thunders teaching. Lists of auspicious sites of the empire (typically thirty-six) and the wonders that have marked them out, celebrations of mountains like Mt. Mao or Mt. Lung-hu or Mt. T'ai, are common. What is special in the Three Immortals cult is the notion that a practitioner or Immortal has a peculiar *and constant* relation to just one place, bears an inherent responsibility for a particular community or region. For Taoists, an Immortal, crucially, transcends earthly location; and it is central to Taoist notions of the relation of god (let alone Immortal) to locality that a god, even if now responsible for someplace in particular, is an *appointee* whose superiors can therefore move him to another someplace. Consider again the case of the god of Ta-ch'ien, the same god Wang Wen-ch'ing saw pleading for Shao-wu prefecture before the Jade Emperor's throne in Chao Tao-i's biography, but whom we have also seen as an "automobile" god choosing his own resting place in Chapter 5. Here is Liu Hsun again, telling us what he has read in a devotional history called *The Veritable Record of Ta-ch'ien:*

> According to the *Veritable Record,* Shao-wu saw no peace for many years after the disturbances of the *keng-shen* year of the Shao-ting period [1230] in the Sung dynasty. In the *chia-wu* year of the Tuan-p'ing period [1235], the Chin-hua man Wang Yeh, courtesy name Tzu-wen,[46] became prefectural administrator and joined with other gentlemen sojourning there to lead the local people, both gentle and common, in escorting the Prince of Auspicious Goodness [i.e., the Ta-ch'ien god] to the prefectural seat, where they held an Offering of the Yellow Register. They invited Heavenly Master Chang of Mt. Lung-hu. At that time the sojourning gentleman Tu Kao, courtesy name Tzu-hsin,[47] was making his home near the shrine, and he joined with Wang in directing the Offering. They ordered the Taoist Lin Hsiao-yao to present the memorial. When he first attempted to present it, it did not get through. Hsiao-yao performed his rites and went again. Then he fell down on the ground and did not rise from morning to late afternoon. Suddenly, before the prefectural offices, it rained heavenly flowers. The whole city rushed to see them. The sky was a confused mass of them, but when they fell to the ground they disappeared. When people caught them in their skirts, again they were gone. After an hour they stopped. Finally, Lin rose and, with a happy expression filling his face, told the assembly:

"I have just been to the gate of Heaven, where I met the Prince of Auspicious Goodness, who said, 'I have already been granted my request by the Emperor; you may go home.' He had presented a report to the Emperor on High on the purity and sincerity of Shao-wu's Offering and had been specially granted forty years of peace for Shao-wu. The two Fast Officers will both receive generous rewards." From this time on the prefecture did indeed have peace and rest, and its population increased daily. . . .

In X year of the Hsien-ch'un period [1265–1274],[48] the two aboriginal bandits Huang and Liao rose. The gentlemen sojourning here took counsel with each other, saying: "The forty-year period is past. Should we not hold a Yellow Register [Offering] again, to beseech the god?" The assembly put forward the [missing title] of the Directorate of Education, Wu X, and the [title partly missing] -ta-fu, Tu Wu, courtesy name Po-t'ang, to direct it. Po-t'ang, you see, was Minister Tu Tzu-hsin's [kinsman]. [At the Such-and-Such] Abbey, they ordered the Taoist Hsieh X to present the memorial. When he arose, he went straight into the prefectural office and, with a fixed expression, spoke secretly to Tu and Wu: "I have just received the response: Shao-wu will suffer great hardship. The Emperor on High has ordered the Prince of Auspicious Goodness to go to Fu-jung City, not to return for twenty years. This is most frightening." That night when they burned the prayer, a host of crows clamored, and the assembly all paled. The next year indeed brought great military disaster, and after the *ping-tzu* year [1276], bandits repeatedly violated the city; there was not a year of peace.[49]

Shao-wu suffers disaster because the god who protected it in the past has been transferred from his post. (Note that the story attributes this news to a professional Taoist practitioner.) A like story is hard to imagine in the Three Immortals texts or in Yü Chi's or Ch'eng Chü-fu's picture of Wang Wen-ch'ing. Wang and the Three are not, for their worshippers, simply *in* the region: they are *of* it. We have already seen that both promoters of the Hua-kai Immortals like Chou Meng-jo or Chu Huan and opponents like Huang Chen found the idea that an Immortal should be permanently responsible for a single place strange or surprising; it is certainly missing from the Celestial Heart and Five Thunders texts, and I do not think it is common in Taoist practitioners' texts in general. But it is prominent in secular elite discussions of Wang Wen-ch'ing as local saint; and it is central to the cult of the Three Immortals.

Finally, what we have seen in this chapter may help to answer what otherwise might seem puzzling about the popularity of the Hua-kai Immortals cult among the secular elite of Fu-chou and Chiang-hsi: why Immortals? Which is to say, why Taoists? There were certainly other local gods available. But the Taoist representation of Immortals already had within it the very notions of personal power, learning and refinement, textual and teacherly transmission, and dignified descent that I have argued were central to the self-representation of a secular elite thinking through its independence from the state and feeling its local oats. Torn as they were from any larger context of bureaucratic divinity, these were as much Neo-Confucian as Taoist values. Above all they were *elite* values, and Taoism itself was a learned and literate tradition. To treat Immortals like the Hua-kai Three as embodiments of locality and of a power that modeled in ideal form the local gentleman's own real and wished-for power, only two changes were necessary: to emphasize the chosen and permanent quality of their local connection, and to erase or ignore almost entirely the notion that Immortals were also bureaucrats subject to higher power. In other respects than these, their Taoist character was not an impediment to their rise, but an advantage.

CHAPTER SEVEN

The Bureaucratic Model: A Speculation

I would like to ask an impossible question. Why do Celestial Heart and Five Thunders masters use the bureaucratic model? More broadly, why is the model central to clerical Taoism? The question may seem pointless by seeming to invite tautology: Taoists use the bureaucratic model because they are Taoists. As observers, we recognize Taoists in large part by the model they use. More important, as participants, Chinese recognized Taoists in the same way: one might plausibly argue that after organized Taoism first arose in the religious upsurge of the later Han, no one would have called Taoist any practitioner who did not draw on bureaucratic vocabulary in acting upon the divine world. Even if one begins the story with the Sung, one must see that the practitioners we call Taoist and who called themselves Taoist were simply continuing a stable tradition that long preceded them when they identified themselves as celestial officials and saw the world as governed by a bureaucratic Heaven.

Yet the question has a point. Religions change; traditions end. Clerical Taoists might have ceased to exist—the Mohists did, and took their syllogisms with them. Or people might have called themselves Taoists but abandoned those parts of earlier traditions that constructed a celestial bureaucracy. One cannot take continuity for granted.

I should make clear what I am not asking here. I am not trying to explain the origins of the bureaucratic model, which long predates the Sung and parts of which may predate organized Taoism.[1] Rather, I am trying to explain its continuing and perhaps even increasing power in the conditions of the Sung, conditions in important ways new. I am trying to identify sources of its continuing or growing strength in a changed setting. For what gives the question further point is that in the Sung, the older Taoist traditions did not simply continue: many new "traditions" were revealed. New forms of practice emerged, with new texts and new rituals, in an upsurge of religious creation unparalleled since the Six Dynasties. Celestial Heart and Five Thunders are only two examples. These new Sung traditions were particularly enthusiastic in deploying and elaborating bureaucratic and especially judicial vocabulary. And it is frequently the new Sung traditions and texts that inform the rituals of modern Taoists, as they have been studied in Taiwan in particular. Such continuities over a thousand years, without anything really approaching a centralized church or clerical body, themselves invite explanation.

The explanatory urge of this book, as I made clear in the Introduction, is to see models of the divine world—indeed all cultural artifacts—not as tightly bound strands in a unitary and enveloping mental web for a whole society, but as plural and differing *pieces* of culture taken up from a repertoire of possibilities and applied by religious actors, speakers, and writers in ways made sensible by their own locations in time, place, and social or cultural action. For such a view, a thousand-year continuity, even within a distinct social group, poses fascinating problems. A way to rework my question that makes this motive clear might be: how did it happen that in China for a thousand years (to restrict one's view to the Sung and after) a class of religious practitioners has reproduced itself, whose members have persistently found it fitting, or useful, or simply correct, to define themselves and their gods as celestial bureaucrats? It is rash to answer such a question from the vantage point of the Sung and Yuan alone. What I shall propose here I offer as something between speculation and hypothesis: a speculation that I can partly ground in evidence, but a hypothesis that I do not have full means to test.

Two possibilities are worth clearing away at the outset. One is that Taoists' image of a celestial government supported a project of alliance with or legitimation of the secular state. Against this I shall argue that Taoists could as easily use their heavenly bureaucracy as an instrument to delegitimize earthly government or to assert superiority to it; that relations between professional Taoists and the court changed significantly over time in the Sung without change in the Taoists' model of the divine; and that relations with local officialdom too were variable and ambivalent. The other possibility is that Taoists simply took up, while perhaps elaborating, an imagery and vocabulary that were common property: that the bureaucratic model is not specifically Taoist but simply Chinese, and that Taoists used it because their audience/clientele took it for granted in its own religious representations and expected its religious professionals to do so too. What we have seen should already have undermined this notion at least for secular elites. I argue that instead we need to see professional Taoists as positive promoters, in effect and sometimes in intent virtual salesmen, of the bureaucratic model to a populace that in the Sung (and in this century too, I argue in the next chapter) might take it but was just as likely to leave it.

TAOISM AND THE STATE: THE COURT

There is no doubt that the acts of Taoists at court and the installation of a Taoist sect as national religious orthodoxy under the emperor Hui-tsung amounted to an alliance between Taoist clergy and emperor. Taoists sanctioned and magnified the emperor's authority by proclaiming him the direct incarnation of a high member of their own celestial hierarchy, while the emperor supported the Taoists' claim to special status for their own rituals and texts. But the Taoist position was ambiguous. Hui-tsung, under the Divine Empyrean dispensation, was revealed as Great Lord of Long Life, Sovereign of the Divine Empyrean, in a new incarnation on earth, and his image stood in the new public shrines established throughout the empire. But this Great Lord of Long Life was, according to Lin Ling-su's revelation, the Jade Emperor's son. Masters of Lin's own Five Thunders rites, like those of Celestial Heart and other Taoist teachings, through their own bureaucratic position had the authority to appear in direct audience before the Jade Emperor—to go right over the head of the secular emperor's divine self. The revelation thus both raised Hui-tsung to heights unimagined for Sung emperors before him and at the same time *subordinated* him—not through bureaucratic hierarchy but through the father-son tie—to a higher divine figure, to whom Taoists had direct access. Thus, for Taoists, the system of which they were a part held power over the emperor.

This reading is not mine alone: we have seen it already in the way Taoist sources represent Wang Wen-ch'ing's role at court. Recall how Wang acts as the channel for Hui-tsung's display of his own subordination before the Jade Emperor when the dynasty is in crisis:

> The emperor asked how the vermilion memorials he had sent up had been answered. The master, shedding tears, reported: "In Your Majesty's memorial, you vowed: 'If a gentleman who possesses the Way is sent out to manage the world, I shall give up my own life in thanks.' In response to this memorial, I received the edict: If you are replaced, there will be no regrets.'" ... On the twenty-third day of the twelfth month, the emperor abdicated his throne at the Eastern Palace.[2]

Wang can report that the emperor's services are no longer required because he is officer of an authority that governs the emperor too. Elsewhere, we have seen that Wang's position gives him knowledge superior to the emperor's own, as when he borrows water from the Yellow River. Oddly, a story recognizably the same was told also about Hui-tsung and Lin Ling-su, and here the emperor's inferior understanding is played up considerably:

> Lin Ling-su transmitted the art of employing spirits of Five Thunders. The capital was once suffering fierce heat and had had no rain for two months, and it was decreed that the commissioner [i.e. Lin] apply his rites to it. He replied: "Heaven's intent does not yet wish rain; the four seas and hundred streams and

springs are all sealed off, and one is not permitted to take of them except by order of the Emperor on High. Only the Yellow River has not been prohibited, but it is unusable." "People are on fire," the emperor said; "if they could just get some sweet moisture to bathe them, what harm if it were muddy?" Lin followed the order and went directly to the Palace of Upper Purity, where he ordered the Han-lin Academician Yü-wen Ts'ui-chung to oversee it.[3] Lin took a basin of water, grasped his sword, performed the steps of Yü, recited an incantation several times, and said to Yü-wen: "You may go." . . . Yü-wen went out the gate and mounted his horse, and a fan-like cloud was rising in the sky; in a moment it was like a blanket, and a sound of shaking came from the earth. The horse was frightened and hurried on, and just when they reached home, the rain came in great quantity, with sudden thunderclaps. After two hours it stopped. The tiles and drains of people's houses were all filled with mud, and water had accumulated on the ground to a foot or more, yellow, muddy, and undrinkable; it did the crops no good at all.[4]

Because on earth Lin is the emperor's subordinate, he must obey his order to get rain from the Yellow River. Because he has access to the will of Heaven—a more powerful force than the emperor's desire to relieve his people—he knows beforehand that it will do no good. These stories, of course, were told long after the fact, if fact there was, and we need not assume that the emperor often allowed Lin and Wang to represent themselves in his presence as agents of a power superior to him—though we should also not assume he didn't. The point is rather that when Taoist practitioners from the Southern Sung on joined all other literate commentators in recalling Hui-tsung as a misguided and overreaching ruler, their accustomed bureaucratic model could serve as neatly to show themselves his superiors as it had once served to magnify him. Using that model was not a function of their real relation or attitude to imperial authority.

In any case, Sung Taoists' relation to imperial authority, or what Taoist writings tell us of it, seems to have changed over time. Wang Wen-ch'ing's story is suggestive. The first half of his career, in the late Northern Sung, seems to point inevitably to his arrival at court and his service to the emperor. He gives up court life and returns home just as the north is about to fall. After the dynasty moves south, the first Southern Sung emperor invites him to court several times, but he refuses and lives out his life serving his neighbors and traveling to other regions of China, but never to the capital. The first part of Wang's life seems to parallel that of his patron Lin Ling-su and of other famous Taoist practitioners of the Northern Sung: origin in a backwater, a period of travel to well-known Taoist sites—the grand tour we have already seen with the Three Immortals—then a final journey to the capital, service and fame at court, practice among the admiring capital elite. The second part—a life as a provincial practitioner and teacher, who travels, but not to the capital—seems to anticipate the life-course of the much better known Southern Sung thunder master, indeed probably the most famous Taoist of the period, Pai Yü-ch'an.[5] Pai's biographical annals record his long and recurring residence at Mt. Lo-fu in his home region of Kuang-tung and his frequent travel to important sites in Fu-chien, Hu-nan, Szechwan, and Chiang-hsi. The parallel to Wang's later life breaks down, if only briefly, in 1218, when Pai, already eighty-five years old, is summoned to the capital for an audience with the emperor; but he stays only a short time, then "disappears" and resumes his travels in Fu-chien and Chiang-hsi.[6] Activity at court or in the capital is no more a central part of his career than it is of Wang's life after the Northern Sung falls. Rather, like Wang after 1127 but more so, he gathers fame in the provinces as teacher, traveler, and largely private miracle worker. The contrast with Lin Ling-su, or with earlier court Taoists of the Northern Sung, is strong.

Early in my research for this book, these seeming patterns in the lives of a few prominent Taoists of the Sung reminded me of the shift from a capital-centered to a locally or regionally centered life and self-definition between the Northern and the Southern Sung that I had observed in my work on the secular elite of Fu-chou. To see whether the contrast was general—whether Taoist practitioners of the Northern Sung as a group were more likely than their counterparts in the Southern Sung to spend the peaks of their careers in the capital—I gathered the biographies of Sung Taoists preserved in the Taoist canon. What I found proved more complicated than what I was looking for, but still has real import for the relation of Taoist to state in the Sung. The biographies of Taoists do draw a picture of real changes across the dynasty. Briefly, while the proportions of Taoists who spent part of their careers in the capital hardly differed between the two halves of the dynasty—46.4 percent in the Northern and 43.1 percent in the Southern Sung[7]—the circumstances of their capital visits, and the character of those who visited, changed considerably. Slightly more than half (27 of 51, or 52.9 percent) of those who spent time in the capital in the Northern Sung had come (we are told) at an emperor's invitation. Since an imperial invitation is rather likely to draw mention in a biography, we may probably assume that the other 47 percent came to the capital on their own. But in the Southern Sung, Taoists invited by the emperor (Pai Yü-ch'an among them) make up fully 78.5 percent (22 of 28) of those who come to the capital, while only six may have come by their own choice. The difference becomes even more striking when one asks where those who come to the capital have come from. As Maps 3 and 4 show, in the Northern Sung both those who come to the capital and those who do not are drawn from a wide geographic range. In the Southern Sung, on the other hand, Map 5 shows that the great majority of those coming to the capital hail from a small number of prefectures concentrated around the capital itself. Of this group a definite subconcentration appears around the prefecture of Chien-k'ang (modern Nanjing): these are all masters of Shang-ch'ing Taoism attached to Mao-shan (Mt. Mao) near Chien-k'ang city. Outside the broad capital region, a much smaller cluster is visible in Hsin-chou in Chiang-hsi: these are all members of the Celestial Master line at Mt. Lung-hu. In fact, fully sixteen of the Taoists who came to the capital in the Southern Sung—57 percent of those in the capital and 73 percent of those invited—were masters of the Mao-shan or Celestial Master sects, invited to court to perform specific rituals on the government's behalf. All of these returned to the provinces immediately after the ritual was done. These findings do not simply reflect a bias in the sources for Taoists in the Southern Sung; as Map 6 shows, Southern Sung Taoists who *did not* come to the capital are scattered much more widely in their geographical origins than those who did.

The capital, that is, seems to have been a gathering point in the Southern Sung mainly for Taoists from a much narrower regional span than in the Northern Sung, and from two centers of organized Taoism in particular. These centers drew from pools of practitioners themselves strikingly regional, to a degree not always appreciated in the literature on Taoism. Map 7 shows the places of origin of all the Southern Sung Mao-shan masters with biographies in the canon, and Map 8 shows those of practitioners associated with the Heavenly Master sect who appear in the *Gazetteer of Mt. Lung-hu*. Both sects drew most of their practitioners from areas right around their home mountains. Thus if—as it appears—the Southern Sung state was interested chiefly in Mao-shan or Heavenly Master practitioners for ritual aid, by this preference alone it introduced a strong regional bias into its invitations to Taoists. As to the larger picture, there is no way to know from my evidence whether Taoists in the Southern Sung were less interested in capital careers or the capital was less interested in them. Did the Mao-shan and Celestial Master Taoists who left right after completing their rituals go home because they wanted to or because the state now preferred them home when they were not doing its business? One can imagine reasons for either. The fall of the north, the excesses of Hui-tsung's reign that were said to have caused it, and the frequent domination of the Southern Sung court by the anti-war party may have tainted court service in provincial Taoist eyes (as in some others). Also possible, though, was that the ill precedent of Hui-tsung's virtual capture by Taoists made later emperors and ministers more wary of encouraging Taoist practitioners to work the capital market. It would take deep research into sources I have only skimmed here to disentangle these possibilities. But it does appear that the relation between Taoist practitioners' careers and the state—at least as we see it in the canon—changed considerably from the Northern to the Southern Sung. If there was a state-Taoist "alliance" in either period or both, it could only involve a much more limited segment of the Taoists of the empire after 1127 than before. This too

Map 3. Places of origin of Northern Sung Taoists active in the capital

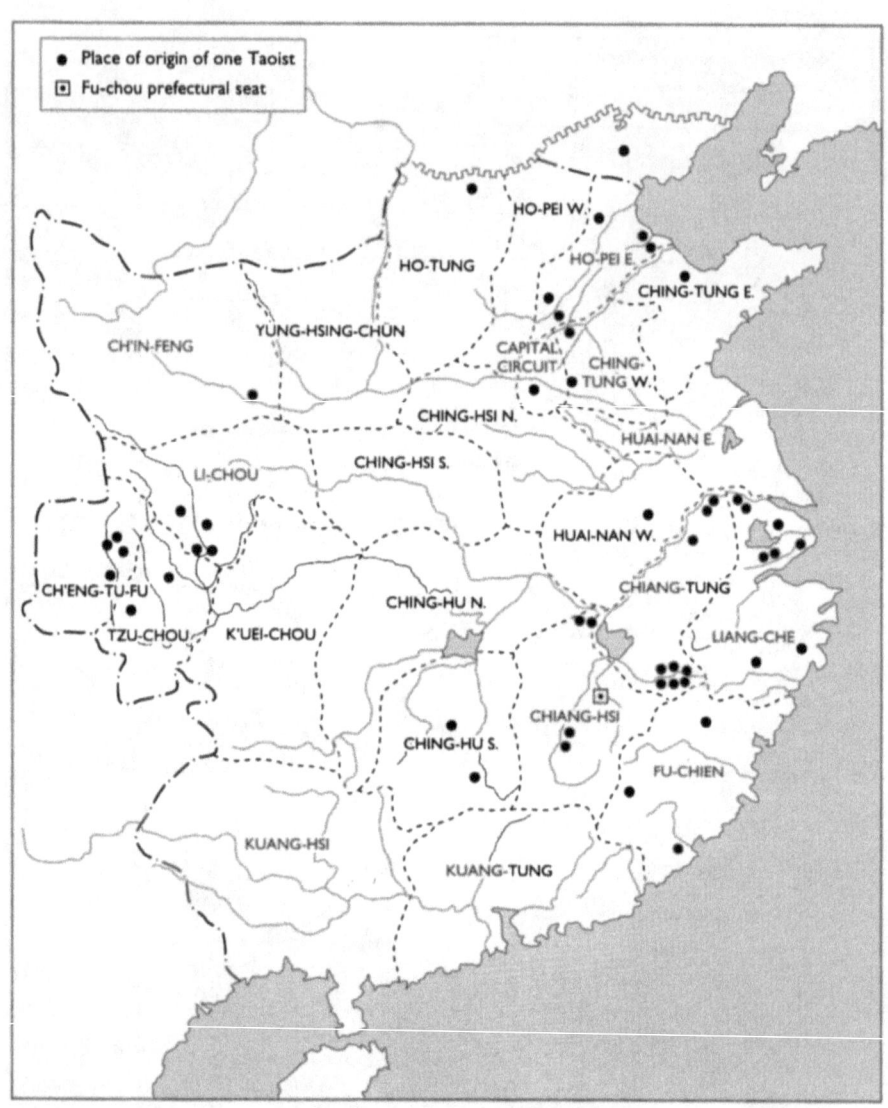

Map 4. Places of origin of Northern Sung Taoists not active in the capital

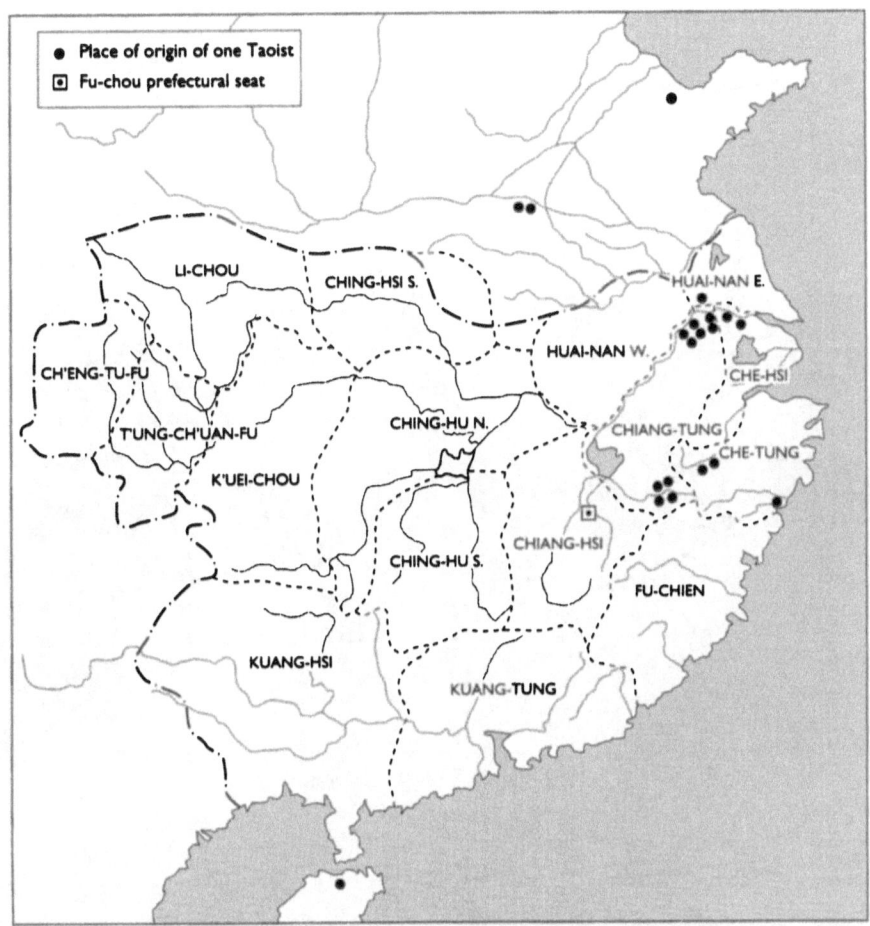

Map 5. Places of origin of Southern Sung Taoists active in the capital

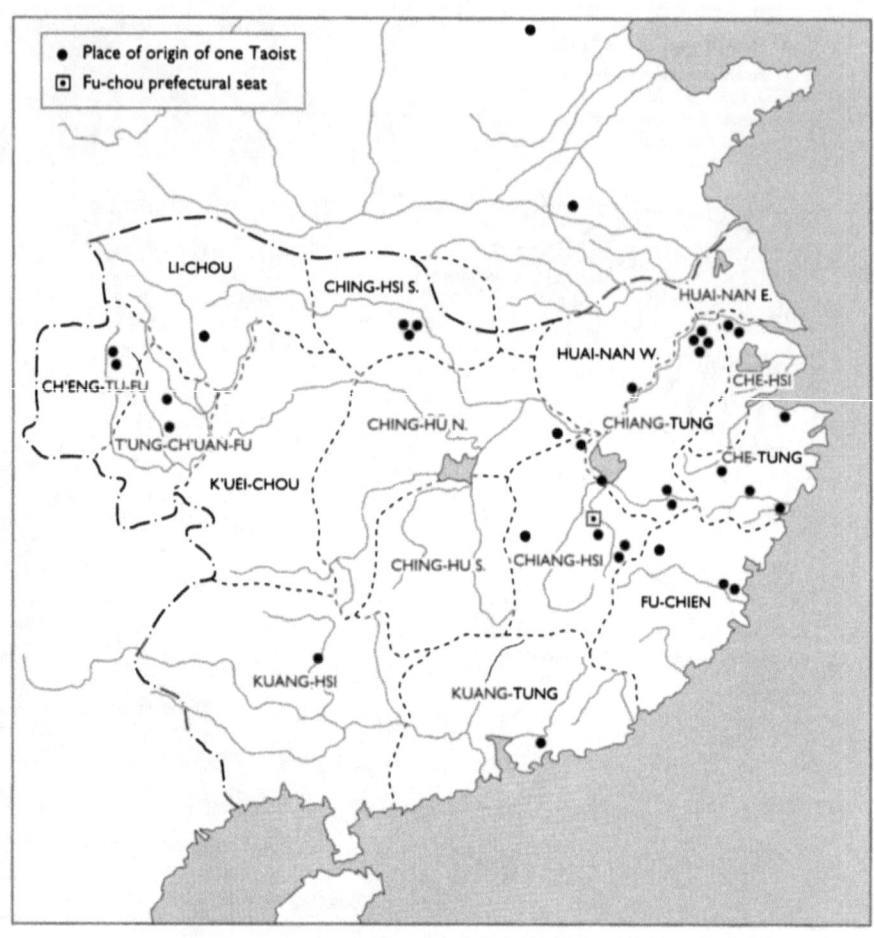

Map 6. Places of origin of Southern Sung Taoists not active in the capital

suggests that it was not real relationships with the earthly state that motivated or the Taoist image of a celestial bureaucracy.

TAOISM AND THE STATE: ENFEOFFMENT OF GODS

We may reverse my question about the relation between the Taoist bureaucratic model and the secular state to ask whether the state itself promoted bureaucratic images of gods and Immortals. Of course, it did so in effect when it specifically promoted Taoism or held Taoist rites; but it is interesting to consider its other, much more frequent interventions in the divine. The state, after all, "enfeoffed" local gods and Immortals. Did this articulate a bureaucratic relation to divinities? In Chapter 4, I noted that we hardly yet understand the aggressive projects of enfeoffment that seized the Northern Sung state under reform regimes and were routinized into regular procedures in the Southern Sung. Here I shall only introduce evidence that the "feudal" stance the state took up in rewarding local gods was serious, consistent, and very different from the bureaucratic stance of an appointer to office.

To begin with simple things, the titles Sung enfeoffments granted—marquis (*hou*), duke (*kung*), and prince or king (*wang*)—are precisely those of the feudal lords of antiquity. At least at this superficial level, the metaphor of enfeoffment was held to quite literally. The government did not, in Taoist fashion, attach the names of celestial bureaus to the gods' titles, did not use the titles to indicate posts in a functional hierarchy. (There were separate titles for divinities seen as specifically Taoist, but these too—Perfected Man and Perfected Lord—carried no specific functional implication.) Hierarchy there certainly was, expressed both in the three-level lordly titles and in the descriptive phrases prefixed to them, which could comprise two, four, or eight characters—the more characters the greater the honor.[8] But nothing in the titles or the prefixes suggested duties that the state assigned by its enfeoffments, and nothing in any of the writings surrounding enfeoffment suggests that hierarchy among gods was a hierarchy of tasks and posts, of ascending nested jurisdictions, or of reporting lines. Rather, this was a hierarchy of *honor* and *recognition*. The prefixes described, extremely vaguely, the character of past accomplishments and capacities for future accomplishment that the god had shown. Thus our old friend the Ta-ch'ien god advanced through successive enfeoffments (between the 1040s and 1258) from Marquis of Penetrating Response, to Duke Who Assists the People, to Prince of Broad Assistance, and thence ultimately to Prince of Brilliant Response, Awesome Sageliness, and Heroic Beneficence, Who Brings Fortune to the Good.[9] If this was a bureaucrat, it seems odd that his "appointers" saw no need to convey his specific duties and relations to colleagues. The titles and the enfeoffment process suggest an effort to reward merit already shown and to grant

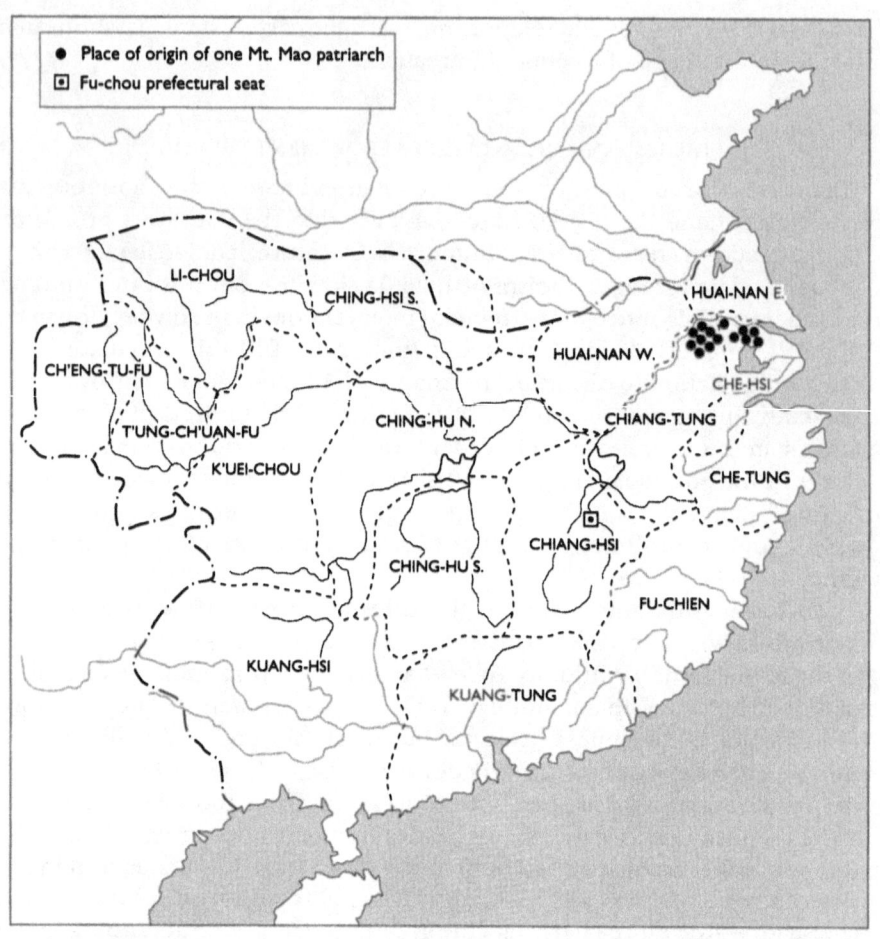

Map 7. Places of origin of Southern Sung Mt. Mao patriarchs

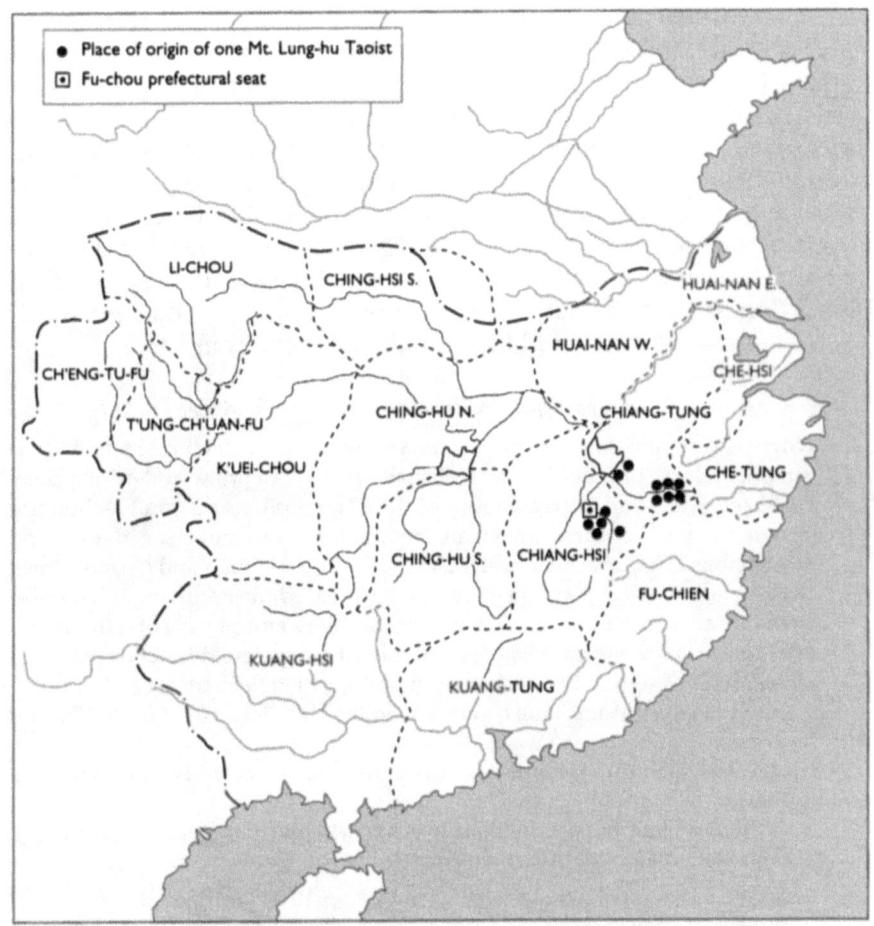

Map 8. Places of origin of Southern Sung Mt. Lung-hu Taoists

sanction to local powers already in place—one important way in which "feudal" (*feng-chien*) models of rule were interpreted in the Sung and before.

There is no doubt that some state agents saw enfeoffment partly as an assertion of authority. Wang Ku, in the 1080 memorial that first proposed the strict system of graded fiefs, argued that "the bestowal of titles will manage the gods." But this was "managing" by rewarding independent beneficence as it emerged from below, not by assigning and enforcing duties. This is clear if we compare the decrees that enfeoffed gods to the decrees that appointed officials. They are very different documents. Consider the decrees of the Three Immortals' enfeoffments, from 1075, 1100, 1117, and 1237 respectively. (For ease of reference I have numbered them from 1 to 4.)[10]

1. *Decree-letter of the edict enfeoffing the Two Perfected, Wang and Kuo [1075]*

    Where divine spirits reside, the people rely on their protecting shade. When their beneficent unction is reported, shall I neglect to praise and display them? Perfected Wang and Perfected Kuo of the Shang-hsien Abbey in Fu-chou are lofty and exalted in their Immortals' breath, luminous and clear in their virtuous boons. They lived afar on Hua-kai's famous mountain and partook deeply of Fu-ch'iu's magical Way. They traveled and viewed the entire region, no place so distant that they did not reach it. The sacrifices and prayers of a thousand *li*, if sincere, they answer. Shall [I] not raise them to fine titles of heavenly ascent, so as to signal the hidden merit of their beneficence?

    On Perfected Wang shall be conferred the title Perfected Lord of Soaring Response;

    on Perfected Kuo shall be conferred the title Perfected Lord of Sincere Response;

    so that we may expect the people of faraway places to enjoy forever the good fortune of health-bringing prayer.

2. *The August Emperor Che-tsung enfeoffs Master Fu-ch'iu as Perfected Lord of Transcendent Response [1100]*

    The Way itself has no mind; in mystery it responds. Where refined spirit is moved, it issues from obscurity. Fair indeed have been the anointments from the Three Immortals upon the entire nation! They have given life to what was withered, set flowing what was dried up, and rewarded us more than once with years of abundance. Having already exalted the enfeoffments of Hua-kai, one ought to display the learning of Fu-ch'iu. The title of a Perfected of transcendent ascent will soothe popular feeling. Let him be specially enfeoffed as Perfected Man of Transcendent Response.

3. *Precious patent of the title of enfeoffment of Perfected Lord Fu-ch'iu decreed by the August Emperor Hui-tsung [1117]*

    In magnifying the invisible and inaudible intent of the Grand Beginning to commend and favor the myriad quarters, on the one hand [We] invite from great distances the neglected and overlooked gentlemen of woods and hills to guide [Us] their pupil, while on the other [We] also hold up for mention those of the Way in remote antiquity and display and reward them. This is so as to make clear [Our] genuine respect and reverence and to increase the good fortune of all under Heaven. The Perfected Man of Transcendent Response at the Ch'ung-hsien Abbey of Ch'ung-jen County in Fu-chou has refined his essence, has viewed mystery, has known transformation, has plumbed spirit, has soared and wheeled in the Grand Void, and he is looked up to by later generations. It is Our will to add to his praise, increase his honor, and strengthen his name; thus [We] grant a letter of praise to express [Our] sincere regard. Let him be specially enfeoffed as Perfected Lord of Fu-ch'iu.

4. *Patent-order of supplemental enfeoffment as confiding and assisting, correcting and assisting, and manifestly assisting perfected lords by the August Emperor Li-tsung [1237]*

Pao-kai[11] is the utmost summit of Chiang-nan. It has an inscription by Yen Chen-ch'ing of the T'ang preserved upon it. In recent years the numinous benefactions of the Perfected Lords of the Ch'ung-hsien Abbey of Mt. Hua-kai in Ch'ung-jen County in Fu-chou, Fu-ch'iu and others, have been much noted. In protecting the people and fending off bandits, they have shone afar. Rising into the clouds, they have sucked up water to cleanse painful illness and drive it away east of the mountains.[12] Thus [I] embellish their titles to repay their vast blessings. [I] have heard further that the plowing and delving people most fear the tyranny of drought. Consider the village proverb: "Commit no insult of the gods." Let them be specially enfeoffed, in accord with the aforementioned, as the Confiding and Assisting Perfected Lord of Fu-ch'iu, the Correcting and Assisting Perfected Lord of Soaring Response, and the Manifestly Assisting Perfected Lord of Sincere Response.

Consider how these edicts name the interaction between the decreeing emperor and the Three. What does the emperor actually do to or for Immortals? Apart from the clauses that enact the enfeoffment itself, the key passages are these: From number 1: "Shall I neglect to praise and display [*pao hsien*] them?" and "Shall [I] not raise them to fine titles of heavenly ascent, so as to signal [*ching*] the hidden merit of their beneficence?" From number 2: "Having already exalted [*ch'ung*] the fiefs of Hua-kai, one ought to display [*hsien*] the learning of Fu-ch'iu" and "The title of a Perfected of transcendent ascent will soothe popular feeling [*wei yü ch'ing*]." From number 3: "and also hold up for mention [*shang lun*] those of the Way in remote antiquity and praise and display [*pao hsien*] them;" "This is so as to make clear [*chao*] [Our] genuine respect and reverence [*ch'in ch'ung chih shih i*]"; "It is Our will to add to his esteem [*chia shang*], increase his luster [*tseng p'i*], and strengthen his name [*ch'iang ming*];" and "thus [We] grant a letter of praise [*tsan shu*] to show [*shih*] [Our] utmost regard [*chih i*]." And from number 4: "[I] embellish their titles [*tseng mei hao shih*] to repay [*pao*] their vast blessings."

Almost all of this is language of *communication*. More precisely, notice how much of what the emperor is doing here communicates with a third party: with a watching populace. When he "praise[s] and display[s] the Immortals"—

one might capture the original Chinese more closely with "display them by praising" or "display them with praise"—he is displaying (*hsien*) them, not to themselves, of course, but to others who may not yet know of them; and he can do this by "holding them up for mention." When he "signal[s] the hidden merit of their beneficence," the "signal" (*ching*—literally a flag or banner) is not to the Immortals themselves, from whom their own beneficence could hardly be "hidden," but again to an audience at large. Likewise, when he "adds to [Fu-ch'iu's] esteem, increases his luster, and strengthens his name," he is communicating more with that audience than with the Immortals: it is the audience that will see Fu-ch'iu's luster (because the emperor has increased it), hear of his name (because the emperor has strengthened it), and so accord him added esteem. But the emperor's communication aims as well at the part of the audience that already knows the Immortals and wishes them honored: thus their new titles "will soothe popular feeling." Once one sees how much of the communicating here is framed in terms that direct it at persons other than the Immortals themselves, one realizes that even phrases that seem to involve direct address of the Immortals can be read otherwise. "This is so as to make clear (Our) genuine thoughts of respect and reverence" could mean that it is the Immortals one hopes to make things clear to; but one might want just as much to make one's respect and reverence for the Immortals clear to the people. And likewise, "[We] grant a letter of praise to show [Our] utmost regard"—though "grant" indicates an act aimed directly (and here downward) at the Immortals—can be read as "showing" one's regard for the Immortals either to the Immortals themselves or to an interested audience.

This ambiguity is possible because *the edicts nowhere unmistakably address the Immortals directly*. Appointment edicts are very different. Vast numbers of these survive in the collected works of the drafting officials who composed them for the emperor's use. To make clear how different they are from the Three Immortals' enfeoffment decrees, I have translated three below, two from the Northern and one from the Southern Sung. The first, drafted by Ou-yang Hsiu, appoints a certain Li Yuan-fang as assistant justice of the High Court of Justice:[13]

> The hall of the vice-ministers is the trunk of the empire's governance. As what I entrust to a minister is weighty, so selecting the officer for it is difficult as well. There are statutes of preferment both for rewarding his labor and for encouraging his capacities. Because you [*erh*] have now been the reviewing policy adviser for a long time, with a diligence ever more notable, cautious never to leak secrets, careful never to err, therefore when your [*erh*] term is complete, [I] cause [you] to assist at the Court of Officers. Exert [yourself] and calculate so as to be effective hereafter, and do not dishonor the splendor of this grace.

The second edict, composed by Wang An-shih, moves one Li Tui to the position of administrator of Teng-chou:[14]

> Teng[-chou] is a key city in Ching-hsi. To administer it and lead its troops, [I] regularly select a major officer, who also bears additional titles to honor and glorify his acts. The [holder of X office] So-and-So, mild and serene, honest and sincere, from censor moved next to be policy critic. He tarried in the ranks of the ministerial attendants, then held the trust of a commander and prefectural administrator. He has had brilliant success, expressed in real accomplishment. Let him be moved in sequence to the glory of the Eastern Department [i.e., the Chancellery] and entrusted with the weight of Nan-yang [i.e., Teng-chou], to soothe and pacify officials and gentlemen, rule the army, and shepherd the people. Proclaiming [my] decrees and articles abroad and setting manners and customs in order will depend on your [*ju*] capacities. Go and exert [yourself] thereto!

Finally, as a Southern Sung example, consider an edict drafted by Chang Hsiao-hsiang, naming Huang Jen-hung as fiscal vice-intendant of Liang-che Circuit:[15]

> The fiscal intendancy of the capital region is much weightier than appointments in other circuits. You [*erh*], through your penetrating talent, have been moved more than once to hard employment [there]. [I] pluck [you] from the treasury bureau and cause you to undertake [your] former office. Go and be reverent in it! Afterward, there may be further appointments by way of praise.

Each of these edicts—and a search of the hundreds that surround them in the works of these authors will show that they are typical—addresses itself in at least one passage directly to the appointee, using the word *erh* or *ju* (you). Each ends with a direct admonition or instructions for the appointee to follow. The emperor tells the man receiving his grace to "go and be reverent in it," "go and exert (yourself)," or "[do not] dishonor the splendor of this grace." With direct address goes particularity of assignments. Each edict traces the appointee's previous career through at least one specific office, usually more, and then turns to specify the new post that is being granted him. Each at least touches on his precise tasks in past or present offices. This locates the appointee and his office not only in his own career trajectory but in a framework of posts, bureaucratic relationships, and responsibilities. And consider some of the vocabulary that expresses the emperor's action upon the recipient: "entrust," "select," even "pluck." These edicts show the emperor taking up a man, moving him simply and directly into a new position, and assigning him definite tasks.

All this is foreign to the Three Immortals' enfeoffment edicts. Nothing suggests the emperor is assigning them responsibilities. Rather, he is recognizing and, perhaps more important, causing others to recognize achievements that were, in effect, unasked for. He does not do this without expectations. There is a sense of exchange here—a sense that, just as the emperor can "repay" the Immortals for their grace to his subjects (no. 4), so they may requite his honors with continuing grace in the future. But the edicts do not use "repay" for what the Immortals may later do,[16] let alone treat the expectation of future benefit as an assignment of tasks or a "selection" of appointment candidates. They imply exchange in language as vague and nonimperative as can be: "*that we may expect the people of far-off places to receive forever the fortune* of health-bringing prayer"; "this is so as to make clear [Our] genuine thoughts of respect and reverence *and to increase the good fortune* of all under Heaven." On the one hand, "that we may expect," "so as . . . to increase"; and, on the other hand, "go and exert yourself," "be resolute in your duty." The emperor never approaches the Immortals he enfeoffs as he approaches the bureaucrats he appoints. He neither selects them for offices nor assigns them duties. Rather he honors and proclaims them, makes known their already active power, and expects that they will respond by continuing to act.

This is not to deny the possibility that when the state gave local gods titles, it might promote, however inadvertently, the notion of a celestial officialdom among people at large, especially those unlikely to read edicts of appointment and enfeoffment. Public celebrations probably greeted either sort of edict when it came down, and ordinary people certainly might draw analogies between the offices granted to men of their local elite and the titles granted to their local gods. And yet even ordinary people could surely also see important differences. They knew, after all, that the local gentleman went away and served somewhere else when he received his office, and only for a limited time; their god, however, even after the state honored him, stayed ever at home. They knew that the state did not pick up and remove their gods to other places when it honored them, as it picked up and moved their local gentlemen about and as Taoists claimed their bureaucracy could move local gods. The difference surely touched what was most crucial in local worship. It may be that in adopting a feudal metaphor and carrying it through consistently, the court responded appropriately to the nonbureaucratic way in which local worshippers, whether gentle or common, imagined their gods. Were feudal conceptions central even to popular belief? To think in this direction might call into question other indicators that scholars have thought pointed to bureaucratic conceptions—the "official dress" of god images, for example. But this is work for another place. Here it is enough that the state itself neither represented itself as an appointer of gods nor treated gods as bureaucrats, but used quite different vocabulary and took quite a different stance. State officers and Taoist practitioners were precisely the literate observers who would have understood the difference. This, I think, further weakens any notion that the Taoist bureaucratic model might be related to an alliance of mutual legitimation with the state; the state itself proclaimed a different model.

TAOISM AND THE STATE: LOCAL OFFICIALS

In talking of "the state," so far, I have meant the court, and we must also consider the relations of professional Taoists and state agents in the countryside. Here again, variety and ambivalence strike the eye. The local official and the Taoist might certainly join in a common purpose: indeed, they might be the same man. Judith Boltz has explored the use of exorcism and other techniques of Celestial Heart and related schools by officeholders who sometimes seem more or less fully trained practitioners, and has suggested that secular and divine office were parallel and therefore easily combined roles. The cases she has identified in Hung Mai's *I-chien chih* are important, but I cannot agree that they often show local administrators "rearming" themselves by acquiring supernatural powers to aid them in their governmental duties, as Boltz suggests. Only a very few stories, I think, may be read in anything like this way. An excellent example is the story of Ch'ien Tang and the Bee King.

> In Nan-ling County in Hsuan-chou there used to be a shrine to a Bee King, whose origin no one knows. A medium-priest [*wu chu*] used it to draw a huge following, proclaiming it extremely efficacious; and local custom was to serve it most assiduously. When they built the shrine, they had also exalted and adorned a niche-hall to house the god. At all periodic festivals and amusements, they would hold processions and escort the god afar. At the beginning of Shao-hsing [ca. 1131], Ch'ien Tang of Lin-an administered the county. Soon after he arrived at his post, he had occasion to pray for rain, and the clerks and local people told him: "This god is dependable." So he prepared a ceremony and led it into the county seat.
>
> When it had ascended the hall, Ch'ien burned incense and offered his respects. When he looked inside, there was no image, but only a single bee, as big as a fist but flying about just as a bee would. Ch'ien had long practiced [*su hsi*] the Correct Rites of Celestial Heart and knew this was some occult deception [*kuai wang*]. So he spoke to it in a great voice: "You are a wiggly little vermin. You should content yourself with holes and burrows. How can you turn to demonic malefactions [*yao-sui*] to enjoy blood sacrifices from men?! I now make this compact with you: in today's affair there can in reason be no outcome to both our good. If you are truly efficacious, you shall [*tang*] come out at once and sting me, and I shall not shrink from death itself. Otherwise I shall burn you to ashes and thus cleanse deluded custom."
>
> When he had finished speaking, it was as if the bee had not heard. Ch'ien had, in fact, already stored up dry sticks; he ordered these piled outside the shrine, the door of the niche-altar tied shut, and the niche-altar carried out and set on fire. The bee inside clamored and knocked against the walls, with a noise of grief and rage [*sheng yin ai yuan*], but in a while everything was burnt up. Then he burned the shrine too, and from then on the county people never again dared talk of it.[17]

This passage depicts an almost perfect coming together of Celestial Heart practice and state responsibilities. Suppressing local gods was routine stuff for Celestial Heart masters and could often be the state's concern as well. Why then should a county administrator not arm himself with the latest spiritual and ritual techniques to serve a cause that he and the professional Taoist shared? That the Taoist represented himself as a heavenly bureaucrat, it would seem, could only strengthen the resonance of Taoist and state interests here. And so, the argument might run, men like Ch'ien Tang took on the technical apparatus and the divine worldview of the religious professional. At least ten other anecdotes in Hung Mai's collection deal with officeholders who regularly practiced or borrowed the rites of Celestial Heart or similar schools.

Yet to argue even here for an alliance between official and Taoist roles, supporting and supported by the image of a divine bureaucracy, one must ignore important things in the story. In the first place, Ch'ien Tang does not defeat the bee god with Celestial Heart rites. The crucial passage— "Ch'ien had long practiced the Correct Rites of Celestial Heart, and knew [the bee god] was some occult deception"—suggests that his Celestial Heart training equips him to distinguish divine gems from demonic paste. One might then expect him to proceed to a rite of summoning and interrogation, which enacts the punishment of an ill spirit in wholly bureaucratic-judicial terms. What he does instead acts out quite a different relation: he addresses the Bee King directly and personally, without any suggestion of official standing, and makes "a compact." Now a compact or contract (*yueh*) is an arrangement that in the "real" world joins private parties whom it defines at least for that transaction as rough equals—not as superior to subordinate—and binds not in any official capacity but as persons. Ch'ien treats the bee god not as a formal subordinate but simply as an adversary, whom he invites to a personal contest of strength. His insults too are highly personal—"wiggly vermin," "content yourself with holes and burrows"—and have nothing of the flavor of the courtroom or the government office about them.

Of course in other stories of local officials' spiritual combats, we do find an office or courtroom flavor. Recall the story we saw in a different context in Chapter 2. A certain "minor official named Yao, who had bought his office by contributions of relief grain" and "was a capable practitioner of the rites of Five Thunders and Celestial Heart," comes to heal Hung Mai's young cousin, orders a spirit officer to summon the god of the locality, and eventually ferrets out the offending ghost mother, whereupon he "notified the city god and placed her in its custody."[18] The bureaucratic-judicial model is clearly central to this officeholder's Taoist practice. It is worth noting, though, that Yao is not a local administrator, but a native of the prefecture where the story takes place, who thus cannot hold office there. His official rank, a very low one at that, gives him no formal authority at all in this county. There is no direct parallel in this instance, then, between his status as an official and his role as a celestial bureaucrat. He is not pursuing official duties and reinforcing himself with divine armament. He is simply a private Taoist practitioner, hired like any other to serve the needs of some household, but who happens separately to hold a minor office. He may certainly have seen the parallels between divine officialdom and the secular state of which he was a particularly lowly part; but there is neither combining of roles nor active alliance of Taoist and state here.

Elsewhere in Hung Mai's stories, it is sometimes hard to tell whether an officeholder who performs Celestial Heart rites is practicing, like Ch'ien Tang, in the place where he is posted or, like Yao, in his native place, where he cannot hold office. A story of practitioner Chao Tzu-chü identifies him as a local military official (*ping-ma chien-ya*):

> At the end of Ching-k'ang [1126], there was a high official (note: I do not wish to write his name) who administered prefectures in the region of Ch'ing and Ch'i, and by some misfortune died. More than ten years later, his son dreamed he was going along a thoroughfare where elms and willows lined the way and there was no other traveler. He heard a great noise rising up ahead of him, like hundreds of drums. Little by little, it grew nearer. Thinking it was a great force of soldiers coming toward him, he hid hurriedly in an earthen hut by the side of the road and peered stealthily out through the window. When it came, it was several hundred ghosts, carrying a great grindstone that never stopped turning. A man's head stuck out of the wheel's top, blood pouring from him. When the son looked closely at him, it was his dead father. He was horrified. The sound then began again as before; when [this second force] drew near and he looked, there was the lady, his mother. He let out a great cry unknowing, and with that he awoke. Afraid this was a fearful sign from the underworld, he went in haste to Yen-chou and with several hundred strings of cash held a great Yellow-Register Offering inviting the imperial lineage member and minor military official [Chao] Tzu-chü to manage it.
>
> That evening all the assembled saw somebody outside the bathhouse, standing at the foot of the flag dressed in a purple robe and with a golden girdle about a foot long, his eyebrows and eyes just as in life and easily recognizable. After a bit, he entered the bath. When the Offering was finished, Tzu-chü sent up a memorial to ask for life and said to the man's sons: "I am not willing to tell your father's business abroad; I shall let you and your brothers examine it yourselves." He took a large box, spread ashes inside it, sealed it all around with mud, and had them wait a day before opening it and looking. When they opened it, they found written characters, just like those in the normal world: "Mr. X preyed upon his country and harmed his people; his crime is one of those not amnestiable." The sons wept pitiably and left. When this high official was in office, no one had heard of any great misdeeds. Given that he died a sudden death, and yet the condemnation on the other side was still so severe, can the cause have been anything but three-generations' karma?[19]

Like the story of Yao, this one does show a secular official practicing Celestial Heart rites, and bureaucratic-judicial vocabulary is obvious: "his crime is one of those not amnestable." But the story does not tell us whether Chao held his post in Yen-chou or in some other place, so we cannot tell whether his secular and divine personae are congruent here. (It is worth noting that a *ping-ma chien-ya* could not send memorials to the secular emperor, so at that level any parallel breaks down.) But Chao, like Yao, is *not* acting simultaneously as secular official and divine bureaucrat: he too has been hired privately and is serving private, not official, aims.

Most of the other stories of officeholding Celestial Heart practitioners Hung Mai retells, like these two, deal with men whose offices are simply incidental to what they do in the divine sphere: they are practitioners who happen also to hold an office, their ritual practice takes place in the private sphere, and there is no combination of secular function with divine role. In such cases, again, there is neither a "rearmament" of local officials through Taoism nor an alliance or mutual support between Taoist and secular bureaucrat.[20] The parallels between the two bureaucracies may sometimes have made them mutually legitimating de facto, but this neither grew out of nor produced any regular relationship of support and cooperation. Indeed, Hung Mai's stories sometimes show official and practitioner in conflict.

> Chang X, a spirit medium of Huai-chin canton in Wu-yuan, was skilled in occult arts and could deliver disaster or good fortune.[21] He was always demanding money and grain from rich families, and if they would not do just as he wished, he would leap and turn in the air, which he called: "striking a muscle Dipper."[22] The family would then fall ill with boils and sores, sometimes even perishing. For this reason everybody feared him. The gentleman Wang T'ing-jui, admiring his success at ill-gotten gain, followed and assisted him. He wrote a signboard in large characters: "The Gate of Heavenly Audience," and hung it in front of his dwelling. The spirit medium wore a high hat, dressed in broad sleeves and purple robes, tied on a great yellow belt, and every day ascended his high seat and chattered freely of good fortune and ill. His followers and disciples numbered more than thirty. A county employee, Wang Tsao, once stopped at his gate. Chang grew angry that he burned no incense and sent a man to seize him and bring him back for questioning. "Allow me to cleanse my hands and offer reverence," Wang Tsao said. After he was done burning incense, Chang still ordered his assistants to beat him and tie him up. "This won't do," said Wang. "If you have talismanic powers, you should have shadow-troops lift me into the air to beat me. If not, I'll go inform the county administrator." Thus he won his release. He went straight off to draw up a complaint and went to the county seat to hand it in. The county administrator, Hung Ying-hsien, had them arrested and brought to his court, where he examined their occult deceptions. Chang replied: "What I practice are the Correct Rites of Celestial Heart, which are of the utmost good for healing the sick. They are by no means ill magic" His words and manner were haughty and arrogant.

THE BUREAUCRATIC MODEL   193

"You know how to 'strike a muscle Dipper,'" said the administrator. "If you can leap over the drum tower, I shall let you go." Then Chang shivered in fear, bowed hurriedly, and begged him for mercy. The administrator ordered him jailed. The next day he went in person to interrogate him, holding in his hand a Demon-Subduing Seal of the Cheng-i Register, and said to him: "You have often said that by your divine powers you can know things yet to come: tell me then what this is in my hand." Confused and amazed, Chang had no answer. At once he was beaten twenty strokes and banned from the territory.[23]

One could object that it is only a *false* practitioner this local administrator sets out to suppress, but the story is told from the official's point of view, and an official inclined to suppress illegitimate shows of divine power may not have cared to distinguish false from real. Note again in this story that the official does not use divine or occult methods against the practitioner. That he palms a Cheng-i Taoist talisman may mean he has some acquaintance with that teaching, but in this story its only use is as something hidden, which a practitioner who claims clairvoyance should—perhaps especially because it is a divine object itself—be able to detect. Other stories suggest that the two roles—Taoist master and secular bureaucrat—may be fundamentally incompatible:

Ch'en Yuan-ch'eng was a Fukien man endowed by Heaven with a love of the Way. During the Shao-hsing period [1131–1162] he served in the entourage of the military intendancy of Han, the prince of Ch'i. Later, hated by Assisting Councilor Ch'in [Kuei], he was expelled from office for many years. Giving up all thought of the officeholding road, he cleared brush beside Ta-mao Peak in Chü-jung, built a hut there, and forswore his wife and concubines entirely. He built a Platform of the Eight Trigrams and paid court and cult to the Dipper day and night. At rest, he conserved his spirit and looked inward, kept tranquil, and abridged his desires. He bought several dozen *mou* of fields below the mountain to support wandering gentlemen in esoteric pursuits. Every spring in the second month, on the Great Lord Mao's birthday, gentlemen, commoners, and those of the Taoist sort would converge, and fully seventeen temples would hold Offerings, with not a seat empty. But the sacrifices of the Yuan-fu Wan-ning Temple north of the mountain were the most abundant, and Ch'en would go every day to offer reverence. He met a traveler, very tall, with blue-green eyes and square pupils, his bearing and manner free and easy, wearing a garment of oak leaves and holding an eight-cornered fan, who blocked the way and begged for alms. In Ch'en's bag he had a single cash of the Large Coinage of the Ch'ung-ning period, which he tossed to him. The traveler took it, and after a moment said: "Your Honor has given me money; I cannot fail to repay your Honor." And he handed the money back to Ch'en. Ch'en looked at the coin in surprise, and it turned into two. When he looked back to the traveler, he was gone. When he returned to his hut and took the money out, there was golden coin in quantity, and he wondered all the more. That night, he dreamed the man came and told him: "I am Lü Tung-pin. Because you have an Immortal's bearing, I made sport of you. Though your will to learn the Way is intense, your success in applying it to things of the world is not yet striking. Why not work harder at that?" So he taught him the rites of swallowing ethers, refining Perfection, making talismans fly, and healing the sick, and agreed to meet him again in thirty years. When Ch'en awoke, he gave up all meat and wine and drilled himself in performing the Correct Rites of Celestial Heart. Strange spirit-ills and weird calamities were cured at once when people received his talismanic waters. He also conducted Retreats and Offerings for people, with most abundant success. He dwelt in the mountains for years and years, his tread as light and powerful as if he flew, and Taoists and laity alike treated him with great reverence. After Ch'in [Kuei] died, those in power were Ch'en's friends, who urged him to come out again. At first he held to his will and refused them, but in the end he was impelled by the entreaties of his sons and nephews to offer ancestral sacrifices at home. When Liu Hsin-shu served in Chiang-Huai, he made Ch'en his advisory officer. Later, Ch'en administered two prefectures, then returned to his first post. His attention to the Way grew increasingly lax, and his special arts were no longer effective. In his later years, he took concubines again, his back grew bent, his sight and hearing dark and dim; he was nothing like what he had been before. He happened to be getting into a bath, with burning coals beside it, when suddenly he saw a divine spirit cursing and scolding him. He fell onto the bed of coals, burned himself over half his body, and so died.[24]

Ch'en's return to officeholding is a clear step toward the loss of his powers as a master, indeed, a step in his willing abandonment of his proper Way, for which the spirit scolds him before his death. It is only one step in an interesting sequence: taking up the domestic ancestral cult again; taking office again; taking concubines again; which leads finally to the aging that adhering to the Way might have spared him. Each of these steps recommits him to some new form of secular involvement and entanglement: first to family, then to social-political responsibilities, then to sensuality; but the second step, entry into office, is crucial. A similar idea is at work in another story:

Sung An-kuo was military supervisor of Che-hsi and took lodging in Hu-chou. His practice in Celestial Heart rites was still not abandoned. A commoner family of Te-ch'ing was disturbed by a spirit-ill and invited Sung to their home, but his treatment was ineffective; in fact he was humiliated by the ghost. Sung was infuriated, and went to a Taoist abbey in a nearby village, where he fasted and cleansed for seven days, wrote talismans, and recited incantations, extending his skill and concentration to the utmost. Then he seized his sword, covered his hair, and went into the great trees behind the commoners' house, where he stepped like Yü, turning and winding. Suddenly a quaking thunder arose in Heaven, and a tree several fathoms tall and ten spans around split in two from top to bottom. It thundered again several times, and the tree trunks, both large and small, were broken and split like tallies, covering the ground in heaps. Thereafter the strange happenings vanished without a trace.[25]

The implied moral here is not as transparent, but the story tells us that "his practice in the Celestial Heart rites was still not abandoned," implying that one would expect it to be when a man entered office; and Sung's laughable ineffectiveness and need for a period of solitary recommitment and renewed self-discipline suggests again that secular and divine office were hard to combine. It adds an interesting twist that in the story of Ch'en Yüan-ch'eng, his training under Lü Tung-pin appears not as a further withdrawal from the secular world but as a move back toward it, though along a special unworldly path: "Though your will to learn the Way is intense, your success in applying it to things of the world is not yet striking; why not work harder at that?" One can imagine a Neo-Confucian scholar immersed in his studies hearing similar advice, urging him toward secular office. Here the eremitic Taoist is urged to become less eremitic, to help the world with the divine skills Lü will train him in. The Taoist Way appears here not simply as an escape from the secular world (though from other angles it may be one) but also as a nonsecular route to beneficent action within it. It is this parallel to more worldly endeavors, including office—the fact that like these, the practitioner's role can offer ways to aid the world—that here makes Taoist practice appear precisely and strongly an *alternative* to normal worldly power. In this light, it makes sense that it is difficult to combine with worldly responsibility and authority.

But in a broader sense, this is the very same picture we have already seen of court Taoists: that the parallel between earthly and celestial hierarchy was two-edged. On the one hand, it could serve to make Taoist and bureaucrat look alike and so seem capable of mutual accommodation, but on the other it could serve to distinguish the Taoist, to elevate him above the earthly bureaucrat, even the emperor. In being *parallel,* the Taoist's claims to authority were also *separate* from the state's claims and derived from a separate source, which Taoists could represent not only as separate but also as higher. If the two bureaucracies in many respects resembled each other, for that very reason they could be in tension, sometimes even in competition for the services and commitment of the same man.

GOD WORSHIP AND THE BUREAUCRATIC MODEL

If the Taoist bureaucratic model does not serve primarily to legitimate state authority or to support an alliance between clergy and state, then does it simply reflect the understanding of the Chinese populace? Did Taoists treat gods as officials because that is how the people they served saw gods? Did the elite devotees of the Hua-kai Immortals, in leaving bureaucracy almost entirely out of the picture, distinguish their cult not only from Taoist but also from popular conceptions? Was the bureaucratic model common property in the Sung? Put in this temporally specific form, the question is not easy to answer with certainty, since our sources for the religious views of Sung commoners are both limited and skewed. But on the available evidence, the answer seems to be no. Valerie Hansen, in her pathbreaking study of Sung deity worship, certainly found no general tendency to view gods, the relations among them, or their relations with human beings as bureaucratic. Ordinary people's gods and their roles, on her evidence, are as various as can be—as various, perhaps, as human roles and identities—and furthermore lack the clear hierarchy that Taoists ascribe to them: "In the Daoist hierarchy, gods are not thought to seek promotions, and lower gods remain subordinate to higher gods. Lay people did not accept these hierarchies; they prayed to gods who were efficacious, regardless of their purported rank."[26] More recently she has pointed to the gods of walls and moats, or city gods, as special examples of gods of bureaucratic or officeholding character and, while tracing their source ultimately to models provided by deities of Buddhist origin (the god Vaisravana in particular), has suggested that itinerant Taoist clergy played some role in promoting their rise and the view of them as bureaucrats. Here she notes: "Office-holding gods were by no means the only gods worshipped in medieval China. The first extant lists of divinities from Southern Sung . . . gazetteers show that most of the gods worshipped did not hold office of any type."[27]

My own survey of Hung Mai's anecdotes set in the Chiang-hsi region confirms Hansen's flexible view of Sung gods and their roles.[28] Bureaucratic motifs—supernatural beings as officials, multiple levels of hierarchy, formal mediation between one level and another, written orders and records—are universally present in only one context: stories of the underworld.[29] That purgatory is a bureaucracy is a commonplace of Chinese religion from long before the Sung. The question at issue here is not the underworld but the heavens: are *gods*, not just the gods who specialize in handling the dead but the gods of heaven and of earth more generally, bureaucrats? To this, Hung Mai's stories as a collection seem to answer: only sometimes. The large majority of nonpurgatorial gods in the stories do not appear as bureaucrats.[30] Of those who do, about two-thirds fall into two characteristic contexts: (1) they appear in stories that feature Taoist practitioners as major actors, or they themselves are gods customarily associated with Taoist views and rituals—in particular the city god and the god of Mt. T'ai; (2) they act as dealers of death or assigners of souls. In the first category, it is usually explicitly the Taoist himself who represents the god's acts or words in bureaucratic terms, and even where this is not explicit, the Taoist's presence as participant and usually as the resolver of the crisis makes the anecdote likely to be colored in specifically Taoist ways. The second category is a good deal more interesting. Here gods not themselves purgatorial are dealing with just the questions of the wronged dead and the sorting out of their grievances that the bureaucrats of purgatory so often treat. It may be that when believers imagined a god dealing with these issues, it was easy to imagine him as a bureaucrat, and vice versa. Was the state so associated with punishment and death in the minds of Sung laymen that when a god dealt with these issues, he must take on the lineaments of a government official or judge?[31] There may be interesting insight here into the peculiar sort of legitimacy that the Chinese state had for ordinary people. Adding these cases in with the stories of hell, we find that most of the stories that show gods as bureaucrats show them as punishers and as associated with death;[32] and we have already seen in previous chapters that Taoists too, and their gods, are accustomed to approaching both gods and ghosts in punitive ways, often consigning them to unpleasant fates in the underworld. Only a small proportion—about a fifth—of the bureaucrat-god stories do not deal either with purgatory, with Taoists or Taoists' gods, or with death and the souls of the dead,[33] and these amount to less than a tenth of all the god stories.[34]

Bureaucratic gods, then, in Hung Mai's stories are for the most part creatures of rather special contexts. The very same gods may, of course, appear in other stories with no hint of bureaucratic character.[35] Alongside them are many gods who never appear as bureaucrats and whose relations with each other and with human beings are as often as not personal relations, relations of exchange and favor and promise and gratitude—just the sort of relations we have already seen in the elite cult to the Hua-kai Immortals. Why then, we may ask again, do Taoist practitioners consistently express and promote a model of divine roles that in the populace at large is at best one among a variety of competing and coexisting models? Why do the Taoists tell their clients and themselves that gods are officials?

TAOISM AND THE MARKET

To offer my own answer to this question, I must consider the position of Sung Taoist professionals within a growing national market for religious services. I choose the word "market" carefully. It is crucial for the character of Sung religion, and indeed Chinese religion of most periods, that it was far beyond the capacity of the state to regulate. The effort under Hui-tsung to make Taoism a national religion with the emperor its center, and to suppress Buddhism by drawing its practitioners into the Taoist clergy under new names and as a second-class stratum, collapsed utterly within a few years. The government's attempts from the beginning of the dynasty to regulate both clergies by monopolizing the right to ordain them may have achieved a sort of rough quality control (or more precisely, literacy control) through examinations, but when, in the late Northern and Southern Sung, exams gave way to purchased ordinations, even this check on the clergy's membership broke down. The mass enfeoffment of local deities over the same period may have begun as an attempt to "manage the gods," but by the Southern Sung, the sheer, and surely unmanageable, numbers suggest that the multiple tail of devotee constituencies was wagging the dog of state sanction. Religion, then, did not inhere in a network of more or less stable institutions and associations supported or imposed by the state or a statelike church on the pre-Reformation European model, but rather circulated as a *commercial good* in a relatively free market, where, as Hansen has also shown, "consumers" could pick and choose whose service to buy—perhaps a condition closer to our own. I argue that Taoist practitioners' peculiar place in this market in important ways supported, and was supported by, the image of divinity they drew.

Promising to explain something religious in these terms raises the specter of economic and social reductionism. I believe the picture I propose here is not reductionist. A Taoist practitioner in the Sung traveled in two worlds, both real for him. Both powerfully conditioned the ways he acted. On the one hand, there was the world of gods and ghosts, in which he acted as the appointed officer of the highest powers. On the other, there was the world of mortals, in which he lived as a religious entrepreneur, selling aid and services to lay customers for a fee. I am arguing not that his situation in the latter *caused* his view of the former but that there was a *resonance* between the two, between the bureaucratic model of divinity that Taoists lived within and their position in the religious market. The resonance could allow causation to run in either direction: a man drawn for personal and internal reasons to a view of gods as bureaucrats and of the supernatural world as a government would find himself drawn to the market position that most Taoists in fact occupied; and a religious practitioner occupying that market position would find the bureaucratic model, and so Taoism, congenial and supportive of his enterprise. The image of a market is not mine; indeed if we take Sung sources at their word, it is no image. Recall the story of Rite-Master Wang, which made a point of his lower fees and the advantage they offered in competition with ordained Taoists. Stories of practitioners make the economic character of their calling very clear, may even dwell on it, sometimes while denying it as a motive for one special man. We may see this in two other stories:

> The son of officeholder Hsu . . . was of sincere and solid character from the time he was a boy. When he grew up, he pondered how his relatives had sometimes been plagued by demons and spiritual perversities, and so fixed his mind on serving the Way and practiced the Celestial Heart rites of summoning and interrogation [*k'ao-chao*], curing and rescuing others. His numinous efficacy was extraordinary, and he sought nothing at all, even providing the incense and paper money himself. He did not distinguish rich or poor, high or low. . . . [36]
>
> Liu Tzu-hsu, a Taoist of the Tzu-chi Abbey in Fu-chou [Fu-chien], used the Correct Rites to control spirit-ills for others. Though he was very effective, his nature was given to extravagant boasting, he devoted his thoughts to wealth and fees, and he liked to talk big and sell himself. Whenever he met a customer he would proclaim: "Last month at so-and-so's house at the West Gate, I was

interrogating and suppressing [*k'ao chih*] and with my own hand beheaded three ghosts. Their blood covered my sword and axe. A few days ago, I was at so-and-so's house in the eastern part of the city and beheaded two more; their blood too flowed as red as red. In an average month, I execute no fewer than several dozen ghosts."[37]

Here is one practitioner coveting his fees and advertising his skills, another forgoing the payments that the story assumes to be normal. That the market was highly competitive is implicit in the second story and explicit in Rite-Master Wang's case, and this runs through a great deal of the miracle-story literature. Taoists, operating in this market as performers of Offerings, exorcisms, cures, rites of salvation, and communications with gods, faced a sturdy array of competitors, both from their own ranks and from spirit mediums and others. It is a cliché of miracle stories that a family consults a whole series of practitioners, who seem to come out of the woodwork until just one succeeds:

> The family of County Magistrate Chang Te-lung of Hou-kuan County had five maidservants. One of them was possessed by some spirit-ill, and . . . the whole family suffered from it. They called the local medium, Rite-Master Wen, to examine her. Wen ran a wineshop, and when he arrived the maidservant covered her face and laughed. "Your whole body is surrounded by the ethers of dregs and yeast," she said; "how are you going to get to me?" Wen withdrew in shame. They next called Lin T'e-ch'i. Lin was the elder brother of Chang's wife, who had actually driven off a weird manifestation for them once before. . . . Lin's back was a bit bent, and this time the maid said: "Just a banana leaf! I'm not afraid of him!" After this, the ill influence became all the more foul. Chang invited Rite-Masters Shang Jih-hsuan and Liang Kun to cure it.[38]
>
> . . . The county administrator Pi Tsao had just finished his term, but his boat had not left yet, and when he heard Mr. Lu had come, he came to pay his respects. "At home is my middle daughter," he said, "the unlucky victim of a ghost. I have brought Way-men and rite masters one after the other to treat her, but they are turned back with indignities and insults or even driven away with beatings. Now the illness has worsened; none but the Perfected Officer can save her. I hope you will deign to step in my boat and have a look at her."[39]

But to picture Taoists competing only with other practitioners underestimates the complexity of the Sung landscape. Among their main "competitors" were their prospective clients themselves, who, when they needed divine force on their side, might go straight to the force's mouth. For another cliché is that in time of need people go on their own to pray to the gods they think may help them. They may try god after god and shrine after shrine before they resort to a professional:

> The wife of the younger brother of Judicial Intendant Wang X fell ill; possessed by something, she cursed Mr. Wang's name, shouting and scolding, never silent.

This went on for more than year, and there was no place so distant that they did not go there to pray and offer sacrifices, but she was not helped at all. They heard [of Sun Shih-tao] and sent for him. Sun asked the whole house to fast and cleanse for seven days; only then did he cap and belt himself, burn the incense, personally draft a petition, and deposit it at the Hall of the Celestial Pivot.[40]

In Ch'en-chou, because it had not rained for six months, they had prayed everywhere with no response. The elders went to the prefectural administrator, saying that it was already too severe a drought and that no one but Vice-Prefect Lu would be able to bring rain.[41]

We saw exactly the same pattern in Chapter 6 in Ch'eng Chü-fu's efforts to get good weather for his mother's burial. But there, of course, the solution to a series of unanswered prayers was not a professional cleric, but one more prayer, to a more efficacious god. This is crucial for understanding the cultural landscape in which Taoists moved and the demands it placed upon them. People could reach the gods themselves, could seek solutions to their problems directly, and they did.[42] What is more, stories sometimes suggest direct appeal might be more efficacious than appeal through professionals. In one, a practitioner, Lu, has taken testimony from the ghost possessing a young woman, has found that it is her own sister, and has learned the just grievance the ghost seeks to avenge: "Mr. Lu thought deeply for a long time. 'Her case is a strong one,' he said. He looked back at Administrator Pi, 'Your honor ought to use the strength of his own goodness to pray for forgiveness for her himself. This is not something [my] rites can control.' "[43]

In another story a man learns by trial and error that his own words may influence gods more than the efforts of Buddhist monks and Taoist priests alike:

> The registrar of Chin-ch'i County in Fu-chou, Wu Shih-liang, when his term was done, housed his family in the Dragon's Head Monastery in a nearby village. In the night, someone threw a stone against his window. Thinking the monks of the temple had done it, in the morning he scolded them. The monks were reluctant to respond but with cautious speech finally said: "The gods of this county called the Three Worthies are very well known; they must have been offended." Wu did not believe them. The next day, all through the monastery, tiles and shards fell from the sky helter-skelter, never stopping. At the time, it happened to be snowing, yet the objects cast down were all dry, almost like things one would find in an ancient tomb. Now Wu grew alarmed and summoned the monks to recite sutras and offer prayers of apology, but the marvel continued, till the flying stones filled the air. His father picked up a brick and scratched a message on it, then threw it, with the prayer: "If we have really offended you Three Sages, let this come back." In a moment, it was there again, with the inscribed part unchanged. Unable to stop it, Wu moved from the eastern suburbs to the west to escape [the gods'] anger. Before their luggage was even put away, the problem was back. So he moved his entire household

into the county town and lodged at the Magical Sounds Taoist Monastery. There the marvel resumed just as seriously, so he called the Taoists to hold an Offering to give reverence, but this did not stop it for a moment. Wu grew angry, called out the gods' names, and cursed them: "You are gods! You should be intelligent and upright. Why would you commit such outrages against me? From now on, I shall fear you no more!" When his words were done, all sounds ceased.[44]

With stories like this one current, Taoists needed to be able to explain to ordinary people (and perhaps even more to themselves) why they needed a professional's services to gain aid from the gods: why they should hire instead of pray. And more, they needed to tell people who had gone from god to god at shrine after shrine why the next step should be in their direction. In a world where direct access to gods was common, Taoists needed to explain and justify mediation.

With all this as background, we may move to the question: what in fact was the "market position" that Taoists took up? A would-be mediator between people and gods might naturally take up a position *between* them: to speak spatially, a position above ordinary people and below the gods ordinary people would appeal to. Interestingly, this is not the position Taoists normally (or ever?) take up: instead, as we have seen, they claim a position either above or to the side of popular gods. The position between gods and humans, if it is filled, may be filled instead by spirit mediums, *wu*, through whom gods may speak by descending into their bodies. Interestingly, again, there is a sense in which what happens here looks like "mediation" only from outside the system, since participants see the god as borrowing the medium's body to speak directly, and since in many cases the god's words require no interpretation by third parties. One might argue, then, that the position between gods and people is occupied precisely, and paradoxically, by a *non-mediator*, leaving a would-be mediator to find his place elsewhere.

I pause here in my argument to offer a historical just-so story explaining *why* mediums and Taoists hold the positions they do. It is a just-so story because the work to show it remains to be done (if the sources are there to do it). But the story, which I think is roughly true, would go like this. An extensive large-scale commercialization of religious services for most ordinary people ("extensive," "most," and "ordinary" are crucial words) is, in fact, a new phenomenon of the Sung, or more likely of the T'ang-Sung transition, and is just one part of the larger commercialization of rural and town life. That is, as money becomes more and more part of ordinary people's daily life, and as the general wealth of society increases enough to allow even those not extraordinarily rich (or some of them) to add new goods to their household consumption, this opens opportunities for people to offer, and for others to buy, new routes of access to supernatural and divine aid that before they would have had to seek at home, or closer to home. "At home" might mean from ancestors (we know too little about ancestor worship and its role in the postclassical but pre-T'ang period) or from household gods; "closer to home" means (in this imagined picture) from the gods of local shrines or from local spirit mediums, diviners, or other village specialists who find a place in such small-scale monetary or barter economy as a pre-T'ang community may support. Spirit mediums and other village practitioners, in this story, are an old and largely permanent part of the religious landscape, at least in South China. What are new, *for most ordinary people,* are the multitudes of higher-level, literate, Taoist, quasi-Taoist, and Buddho-Taoist practitioners who move into the greatly expanded opportunities that the monetizing economy offers for religious entrepreneurship. At the same time, the expansion of literacy and quasi-literacy that printing allows increases the number of would-be practitioners who might be drawn specifically to a literate tradition and its textual depth and prestige, who flow in turn toward the new opportunities in country and town. If something like this story is right, then religious Taoists, in the long period between the collapse of the true religious communities represented by the Five Pecks of Rice movement and the changes of the T'ang-Sung transition, are largely elite clerics serving mainly the court and the wealthy or powerful; and their religion, to speak in even more crudely economic terms than I have done so far, is a luxury good. Taoists, then, move into a religious landscape where spirit mediums and other village practitioners *already* occupy the position of direct mediator (or vehicle) between specific gods and people. The fact that the slot is filled makes the literate and text-bearing Taoist's choice of another—in his own view, higher—position inevitable. The stories in which people pray to one shrine after another or appeal to one practitioner after another usually put things in a definite and recurrent order: direct prayer precedes the appeal to a professional; among professionals, a spirit medium will come before, never after, a Taoist or other literate figure.[45] It may not go too far to imagine that ontogeny is in effect recapitulating phylogeny: that the roles most recently added to the village religious world stand last in order of consultation, though highest in status and expense.

My account of the post-T'ang Taoist's position is still incomplete. We can see an essential part of it in the peripatetic lives of the Celestial Heart practitioners in Chapter 2: the stories about them, or their autobiographical sketches in the prefaces to their texts, show them traveling across prefectures, circuits, or even all of China, both to gain cultivation and to offer service to others. The people such sources record are, of course, especially prominent, and we cannot assume that all Celestial Heart masters or all Taoists had horizons so broad. But their movement writes large a pattern crucial to the Taoist role at all social levels: the capacity to cross community boundaries freely. At the same time, we have seen in their liturgical texts that Celestial Heart men and other Taoists have no special attachment to any single god. On the contrary, they represent themselves as able to deal equally with any of the multitude of gods they may meet in the exercise of their responsibilities. This too distinguishes them from spirit mediums, many of whom provided contact with only a single god, a god who had chosen them by possessing them earlier in their lives. Spirit mediums, that is, are often specialists, and their relation to a god is often personal and permanent. In sum, the Taoist practitioners of the new Sung sects, and Taoists at large, hold a position in the religious market that as to place is *translocal* rather than local, and that as to gods is *generalist* rather than specialist. A Taoist, unlike many spirit mediums and unlike most of his clients, is someone whose access to the divine has nothing to do with place and little to do with divine individuality. The service he offers is *general, multiple,* and *impersonal* mediation. Finally, Taoists are, probably unlike spirit mediums, an occupational *network* (in market terms, perhaps a cartel, since they keep their methods secret),[46] ultimately even national in scope: they are tied to each other as student to teacher, as fellow to fellow student, and they often come together apart from other people, at abbeys, at privileged spots along the grand tour of peripatetic cultivation, and so on.

Now one might argue that translocality by itself could force governmental models into a group's self-conception: what else in China is organized and cuts across local lines but the state? Occupational networks that cross geographic boundaries in China do often make government part of their charter myth. Physicians, for instance, claim professional descent from ancient sage-kings and in their books constantly equate keeping a body healthy with governing. But they do not imagine doctors as an alternative bureaucracy. The Learning of the Way of the Southern Sung, not quite an occupational network but an academic and political one of some cohesion, was intimately concerned with images of rulership even while occupying the political periphery for most of the period, and traced its spiritual descent, in some versions, to the duke of Chou, certainly a governmental figure. But one could argue that Neo-Confucianism handled the statelike implications of organized translocality not by imagining itself a shadow government but by translating rulership down into each individual—something one might call "imitation of emperorship" often seems to lie at the heart of Learning of the Way views of the relation between person and society. To account for the Taoist solution, or rather for its extraordinary vitality and elaboration in the Sung, one needs to add to translocal organization a particular form of *mediation.*

We have seen that Taoists offer mediated access to divine aid in place of the direct access that was widely available; but we have seen that they do not, for whatever reason, take up the expectable position of direct mediator between god-worshippers and their gods. Rather, they claim an outsider's access to—and perhaps, if their customers are to be interested, must claim privileged *influence* over—all gods. In a world where anyone can go to a shrine and beg a favor from a god, a customer does not need somebody else to beg for him: he should be getting something better than begging necessarily provides. He does not need a clearer channel of communication to hear the answer to his begging: he can get that from a spirit medium. That is, practitioners in the Taoists' position are structurally motivated to claim specially *privileged* access to divine power; their position outside the two-party person-god relation must somehow be a higher or stronger position. (And this perhaps all the more when, as is clearly beginning to happen in the Sung, a Taoist *employs* a spirit medium to serve as vehicle for communications from a god or other spirit. The relationship to the medium and his god must be justified by the Taoist's superior position, or what is the Taoist there for?) But where will the power or authority come from to support a position higher than a god's? By the market position they took up and the services they sought to provide, Taoists presented themselves as able to influence any god and claimed power in any local venue. But to claim this, when people know that even gods' power is often limited to one region, is to place oneself above those gods and to claim access to an authority higher (because broader) than theirs. And to posit such higher authority, with power over all local gods, is logically to propose that ordinary gods themselves are mediators too, and that their power is not inherent but derived. But to claim this is in turn logically to paint a picture of a *multilevel* structure of mediating authority, with at least two distinct levels of mediators (local god and Taoist) and at least four levels in all: Source of Higher Authority, Taoist, local god, layperson.

But such a multilevel structure of mediation had to be *pictured* somehow. What I am finally arguing, then, is that if, with the inherited resources of pre-Sung Chinese culture, one tried to imagine a translocal network of mediators fitted into a structure of multiple ascending levels of authority, the one ready-made model that would come to hand is the bureaucratic state. An entrepreneur with nonlocal interests and ties, entering upon a local scene from the outside, treating it as one in a succession of local scenes upon which he had entered or would enter, and claiming to wield translocal authority that was neither personal nor individual but transcended or superseded the personal and individual forms of authority present locally, was simply *acting like* a local official. If his sphere of operation was religious and supernatural, how apt that he should claim to be, and feel himself to be, the agent of a supernatural state.

The bureaucratic model of Taoism, then, as it long preexisted the T'ang-Sung transition, was an ideal conceptual language for a burgeoning stratum of commercial purveyors of religious aid to a new greater-than-local market: it was, as it were, *preadapted* to this new situation and ready to thrive in it. We may see it as obvious and natural that financial or commercial models within religion—the notion of the loan of divine money that every soul carries with it into life and must repay, for example, which first gains prominence in the Sung—should emerge from a rapidly commercializing economy.[47] What I am suggesting is that a commercializing situation can as easily support and find support in cultural models that in their literal content are anything but commercial.[48]

This argument may also help explain how Taoists' varying conceptions of divinity are distributed within their own lives. We saw in Chapter 6 that in their relations among themselves, in legitimizing the special character and authority of their teachers, and in aspiring to similar character and authority themselves, Taoists make extensive use of models of divine power and its transmission that are not bureaucratic at all but personal, descent-based, founded in teaching, and even locally rooted. Poul Andersen has suggested that Taoist use of the bureaucratic model is, in fact, limited to liturgical contexts, to the rituals that Taoists performed for and upon non-Taoists and their gods, and that it finds little place in their notions of self-cultivation or even always of the life of the achieved Immortal.[49] I think that Andersen overstates a bit here, since even the Taoist's own body, as the object of his cultivation, was often conceived as a country or state governed by god-officials in the various organs.[50] But as to the proportions in which bureaucratic models appear in different contexts, Andersen is surely right: they are more universally present where Taoists concern themselves with the contexts in which they would deal directly with laymen, the contexts of public and private ritual. But this makes perfect sense, in fact, is precisely what one would predict, if the bureaucratic model serves particularly to conceive and shape relations with a clientele. Taoists do not need, perhaps, to spend a great deal of time affirming bureaucratic models to one another if in the first place they are bureaucrats mainly vis-à-vis their lay customers.

In the next chapter I leap into the twentieth century and examine in ethnographic and other recent materials whether the implications of the argument worked out here can help us understand the relations of Taoist and lay views and action in modern contexts.

CHAPTER EIGHT

God Worship and the *Chiao*

It is time to pick up loose ends. In Chapter 3, a question remained dangling about the meaning of the Offering ritual as a favor to Immortals. Consider again the simple story of Yen-hsien of Mt. Ta-fu. An avalanche is about to bury Yen-hsien's house. He gathers his family, and they call out to the Three Immortals to save them, vowing that they will hold an Offering to repay their rescue. The avalanche stops, and Yen-hsien and his family are saved. Not far away, Chang Pang-ch'ang's family is crushed by the same avalanche. Chang Pang-ch'ang, we see, had not prayed to the Three Immortals.[1]

I have already pointed out, in stories involving Offerings in *Verities of the Three Lords,* the potential tension between worshippers' views and Taoists' views. It is potential, but in these stories never actual, since only the worshippers' view appears. Let me sharpen the tension by redescribing the story, which encompasses a paradox. People in danger call out to divinities to save them, and they are saved. Others do not call out, and they are not saved. The attention to those unsaved is unusual, but in other ways the story resembles many in the *Verities*. The directness of the appeal—its immediacy in both senses—is important.

And this is precisely the paradox. Yen-hsien and his family appeal *directly*, with no mediation but their own language, to Immortals. They ask for help and receive it. But in asking they have made a promise: to hold an Offering for the Three Immortals, as a way to "pay them reverence." But the Offering as liturgy embodies typically Taoist notions of authority: authority in which, as we have seen again and again, complex and almost obsessively *mediated* hierarchy is crucial, and that expresses itself in explicitly bureaucratic terms. Ultimately, an Offering is not about anything personal, individual, or really anything particular at all—not about one person's act of worship; not about a boon from a particular god. In Offerings as we know them from studies of modern Taiwan, the gods of everyday life, the gods people usually worship, are deliberately subordinated, through the physical displacement of their images, to a vast celestial officialdom, of which they are redefined as lowly members at best, and ultimately to the supreme and abstract god-principles Taoists know as the Three Pure; but they are subordinated also to the Taoist practitioners, who hold their own positions in Heaven's bureaucracy. The purpose of the ritual, in Taoists' view, is to reestablish the harmony of the cosmos on behalf of the whole world of men. To sum up the paradox: the miracle stories of the Hua-kai Three tell us that people may communicate directly with their local gods, who respond directly to aid their worshippers, out of a power and authority that are their own. The Offering tells us that local gods at best convey people's appeals to their celestial superiors, who are to them as the highest earthly officials are to the lowest; and that this needs the further mediation of the Taoist, a member of the same heavenly officialdom. Our two models are in direct contact, and it seems conflict, here.

Is it not odd, then, that a family in danger, seeking immediate aid from familiar local divinities, should promise as thanks an Offering? Are they promising to foot the bill for a ritual display of the subordination, the utterly marginal cosmic relevance, of the gods they are asking to help them? Is it for this that the Three save them? Do Immortals like looking small? How does a ritual that proclaims bureaucratic hierarchy fit into a cult whose texts give little place to bureaucracy, or to any hierarchy not personal and dyadic? How does worshipping the Three Pure thank the Three Immortals? How does an Offering "pay them reverence"?

There is, of course, an implicit historical question here, of which my own question is only a special case. That is: how did it happen that a Taoist Offering came to be a standard vehicle for addressing, propitiating, rewarding, and thanking the gods worshipped among lay Chinese at large? I speculate on this question further on, but for now I want to put it aside to deal with the apparent paradox of meaning.

There are at least two ways to solve my paradox quickly. One is to tell it to go away, to say that it presents no problem. Someone who said this might mean that the historical question is really the only question to be asked— that once Offerings became conventional vehicles for addressing gods, that is what they became for their lay users, whatever the Taoist officiants may have thought they were expressing in the ritual performance itself; that there is no reason to expect consistency of meaning, in the observer's terms, between the different aspects or uses of a ritual, and no reason to examine inconsistency closely when one finds it; that meaning is not the point, *doing* is the point; and so on.

The other quick answer—which might be elaborated at considerable length but is still "quick" in its effect on our approach to this sort of problem—

would be that what the lay worshipper does in his or her direct approach to a particular divinity and what the Taoist practitioner does in his ritual performance are part of a *single system* of meanings, within which apparent conflict or difference hides truer unity. One strategy of argument here might be that apparent difference dissolves at a higher level of generality—that the things the worshipper and the Taoist do and mean, details aside, are similar in ways that show their membership in one community of meanings, one culture. For instance, both the Taoist and the god-worshipper believe in gods, and lots of them; both believe there is hierarchy among gods; both conceive hierarchy among gods (and between gods and people) in ways that parallel hierarchy among people; both believe in relations of response or resonance between the world of gods and the world of men; both use physical images to represent gods; the images both use look much alike—a list could grow long. Both the Taoist and the worshipper, such an account might conclude, are Chinese. I indicate my unease with this style of argument in the Introduction.

A different strategy, but one that still finds a single system of meanings, would resolve the difference entirely at ground level: the worshipper's god and the Taoists' gods *already* make one system, namely the Taoist celestial hierarchy of deity-officials, topped off by the three godly abstractions; the more earthly Three Immortals find their appropriate place near the bottom of this structure and, as participants in it, acknowledge and embody its rightness and power; what the common worshipper treats as Three Immortals' own acts, he treats so either from ignorance or as a customary shorthand, because these are really the acts of the heads of the celestial bureaucracy, to whom the Three Immortals appeal on worshippers' behalf in heavenly audience; and so on. Professional Taoists, in this reading, are the cultural experts who understand the system and on whom worshippers rely for an understanding they do not have themselves.[2] Thus one simply fills in the blanks in *Verities of the Three Lords*. Taoism, on this view, *is* the larger common system within which local god-worshipping fits and must be understood.

In this book so far, and in what follows, I avoid all these ways of arguing, not because I think all of them are wholly wrong, or wrong equally often, but because I believe that in this case they avoid or short-circuit analysis. The first proposes that a ritual communication that seems to have meaning should be treated as having none in practice. This avoids knotty problems, no doubt, but it offers no way to recognize *when* the apparently meaningful is really not, unless the answer is, whenever seeing it so will avoid knotty problems. Arguments of the second class, the single-system-of-meanings arguments, may fail in other ways. Moving to a higher level of generality will, tautologically, find similarity not evident at a lower level; but it remains unclear why and within what sort of unit similarity-seeking should be privileged; how one knows what level of generality suits a particular question; and where, or why, the process of level-raising should stop. Even the hypothetical list of similarities I have offered, after all, quickly ceases to seem so very "Chinese"—ceases to identify a single shared culture—when one considers the Indian parallels to virtually every item. One could even raise one's level of generality so high as to construct "fundamental similarities" between Chinese and Christian religion (indeed, we do this simply by using the word "religion"); and would this show that both were part of a single system of meanings?

The one-level solution—that Taoism *is* the system that frames or supplies meaning for deity worship—instead evades difference by subsuming one member of a contrasting pair under the other. This again is easy to do; but I am troubled by the fact that to my knowledge hardly anyone in the Sung or modern China ever does this, ever explicitly offers this sort of "synthesis," *except professional Taoists*. (There is, after all, not a word about higher celestial authorities, about the Three Immortals' offering memorials or appearing in audience, about intercession by anyone with anyone for anyone about anything, in the miracle stories in *Verities of the Three Lords*.) Thus in leaping to offer it oneself, one is simply taking sides. To argue that lay worshippers understood only in part what professional Taoists understood as a whole invites the answer, "Who says so?" Well, professional Taoists say so, that's who. And what do others say? "Filling in the blanks" can mean that the people one studies can never knowingly and with good reason leave something blank—in other words, that no silence is meaningful.

There can indeed be experts to whom people defer for their knowledge of particular cultural fields, and when they do so it may be fair to say that the experts' knowledge embodies the position of the culture as a whole. Roy D'Andrade makes this point for medical knowledge in modern American culture:

> The *germ* schema held by most Americans is a simplified version of the findings of scientific medicine. When pressed for more detail about germs, respondents typically say that they are not doctors, and if you want to know all about germs go to a doctor or read a book on medicine. Most of the schemas by which Americans understand illness seem to be derived from scientific medicine, rather than coming from an independent folk tradition.[3]

But expertise and deferral to it are not the only possibility when knowledge differs. Starting from the similar example of research science in medicine, Fredrik Barth argues:

> Note that the conventions governing the credibility of Dr. Salk's scientists are valid only within a small circle of specialists. A few minutes' walk from the laboratory one finds other people, in other circles, who maintain a robust world view anchored in a locally based identity and who feel free to mock and reject the truths of the scientists.... Martin (1987) reports class differences in the degree of abdication to medical authority in urban populations.... All I

urge at this stage is that we . . . seek to discover, in each case, how particular persons or populations actually cope in the face of ontological incompatibility between coexisting traditions. . . . (1) There may be deep variations in the criteria for judging the validity of the kinds of knowledge accepted in a local population, particularly as between different circles and as between specialists and nonspecialists. (2) Knowledge produced within a tradition of knowledge is judged by the criteria of validation of that tradition and not necessarily embraced in other contexts or by the population at large. (3) There may be relations of inequality between different traditions of knowledge, whereby some people will grant hegemony to knowledge from one of the traditions—at times quite independently of the actual extent to which they themselves have a command of the knowledge in question.[4]

Only the third of Barth's three conditions would give us license to take one group's knowledge as authoritative for another. To defend the claim that Taoism is the common overarching system that makes sense of the Offering, one must assume that Taoists, at least in the context of this ritual, hold authority in Chinese religion as great as the authority doctors hold in American medical culture—that they are the experts to whom others defer for explanation of an action's meaning. In this case, if one asked ordinary people what the Offering is for, they ought, when pressed, to say "go ask the Taoists." We shall see that people say something like this when asked what *the Taoists themselves* are doing, but that as to the whole Offering celebration, in which ordinary people participate, they say both in words and in ritual action a great many other things. "Go ask the Taoists," I shall try to show, is simply not an adequate solution to the question "What is happening at an Offering, and what does it mean?"

It is worth pursuing this last "solution" further, since it underlies much excellent work on Taoism's place in Chinese history and society done over the past twenty years. Understandable frustration with earlier neglect of religious Taoism in Chinese history has led some scholars to grant even more to Taoism than it deserves. Michel Strickmann's claim that Taoism is China's "indigenous higher religion" is reasonable if "higher" simply means literate, clerical, and congenial to social elites (sometimes, and among others); it is wrong if it means instead that Taoism absorbed or spoke for the hundreds and thousands of deity cults that dotted China. The explicit claim occurs less in print than in scholarly conversation, but versions of it crop up in prominent places. In the introduction to their volume on T'ang and Sung religion, Patricia Ebrey and Peter Gregory tell us: "In the Sung the Taoist pantheon became merged with the popular pantheon into one vast bureaucracy whose reaches encompassed both terrestrial and celestial postings. . . . And it was the Sung transformation of the pantheon that defined the basic contours of Chinese religion for the remainder of the imperial period."[5] Now this can be true only if it refers to how Taoists themselves drew the pantheon. Taoists *asserted* the unity of the pantheon, and we saw in Chapter 2 that the way they wrote the gods of most of the populace into their god lists, lumping them together at the bottom of their hierarchy, included them mainly to subordinate them. These amalgamated and unnamed god-positions are nothing like the richly individual figures local worshippers understood their gods to be. Is their inclusion in Taoist liturgical lists an *absorption* or rather an *explaining away*? As we shall presently see, John Lagerwey's evidence suggests even more: that local gods today are constructed as entirely outside the Taoist pantheon, mere demons, permitted to watch and learn as the real structure of authority in the universe displays itself. In Chapter 7, we saw that the god-worshippers who told stories to Hung Mai only sometimes described their gods as bureaucrats, and then chiefly in rather specific contexts. Indeed, it is hard to find convincing evidence that Sung laypeople habitually thought in terms of "pantheons" at all. They certainly were only vaguely aware of the vast panoplies of gods whom the Taoists claimed as their own. Where then is the "merging" of Taoist and lay pantheons? Ebrey and Gregory cite Terry Kleeman, but Kleeman's own formulations are much more measured: "Taoism had long rejected the traditional bureaucracy of otherworldly officials . . . in favor of . . . a celestial bureaucracy culminating in the Three Pure. Now in the Sung the two bureaucracies were reinterpreted as being different levels of one continuous administration. . . . In a parallel development, during the Sung Taoism claimed a role of caretaker in relation to the popular pantheon, a role it maintains to this day."[6] A role it *claims* to this day would be more precise; but clearly Kleeman is talking of Taoist interpretations and Taoist claims, and there is no reason to read him as confusing these with simple truths about Sung religion.

In a book on deity cults in contemporary Fujian province, Kenneth Dean has built a richly detailed case for one version of the view I am challenging here. For Dean, Taoism is the organizing and unifying force in the devotional and ritual activity of local cults: "Taoism *provides the liturgical framework* which enables local cults to expand and develop";[7] "communal celebrations *structured by* Taoist rituals marked social hierarchy while maintaining communal integration";[8] "[in] each case study . . . I point out the role of Taoist ritual specialists in *providing a framework* for the universalization of the local cult" (emphasis mine).[9] Dean is a superb ethnographer, and his descriptions scant none of the complexity, difference, and contradiction that local cults and their interactions with Taoist professionals can display, but his analysis contains all this complexity, rather precariously, within the notion of the Taoist "liturgical framework."

> These different points of view result in a theological identity that becomes highly contradictory. These contradictions are clear to many of the participants, but the contradictions are not allowed to erupt: a taboo against con-

fronting contradictions seems to take effect.... That all this holds together is primarily due to the fact that Taoism never imposes doctrinal dogma. This is a fundamental principle of Taoism, which spontaneously recognizes in all these different aspects so many facets of its pantheistic worldview. These different aspects of the deity have their place in the liturgical framework.[10]

It may be true, on a very strict construction of the words "doctrinal dogma," that this is something Taoism rarely attempts to impose; but to conclude that Taoism is inherently inclusive and tolerant of difference looks wildly wrong against the background of the Sung, when court Taoists briefly succeeded in abolishing Buddhism and officially Taoicizing its clergy, and when Taoists were as likely as state agents or Neo-Confucians to try to suppress local cults. The de facto tolerance with which Taoists then and now have often approached local cults is a fact not about Taoism but about the political and social situation Taoists have found themselves in (and all religious professionals with them), lacking the power to impose their views, constrained instead to wheel and deal as one would-be monopoly among many in China's expanding religious commerce. I shall have more to say in what follows on how Dean argues for the "liturgical framework" in the Offering. Here I shall observe only that the "framework" seems to mean different things in different cases, and sometimes may boil down to no more than the undeniable fact, which Dean states early on: "At every central point in [cult groups'] liturgical practice ... the participation of one or more Taoists is indispensable." (Even here he may approach tautology by defining the points at which Taoists participate as central points.) To turn sheer presence and the variety of roles that Taoists play in relation to local cults, even in Dean's own evidence, into a constant "framework" that "structures" cult rituals may, I think, be nothing but an especially deft way of taking the Taoists' side.

My point, again, is that all these arguments prematurely resolve the tension that the use of the Offering as an instrument of local god-worship displays; they resolve it by redefining it, either as without real meaning or as dissolved in a higher unity. Here I prefer to explore tension and difference and see where that gets me. But I am a bit ahead of myself. I should begin by showing that what I have called a paradox—the occurrence of the Offering in a context where direct personal interaction of person with god is the point—recurs frequently in *Verities of the Three Lords* and in other Sung testimony. Of the twenty-five miracle stories in the *Verities*' final chapters, nine mention Offerings. Some of these we have already seen. Brief summaries of all nine follow.

In the first story that mentions an Offering, Lo Pin, an official in the regional military administration, prays daily to Mt. Hua-kai for a son: "On the first and fifteenth of each month, he went to the Offering at the Chao-ch'ing Abbey and offered prayers of various kinds, begging for a dream in answer." Finally, he dreams that a Taoist gives him three plums, one slightly spoiled.

In time, he has three sons: two are highly successful, but one dies young.[11] In a second story, a strange wandering Taoist cures the family of a Hu-nan man of plague and tells them he is Kuo of Mt. Hua-kai in Ch'ung-jen County, Chiang-hsi. When he vanishes, the man travels to the mountain to find and repay him; the locals realize that he was none other than Immortal Kuo, one of the Three Immortals, and tell the man to hold an Offering of thanks, which he does.[12] A man named Wang, in a third tale, seeks an heir at Mt. Hua-kai. "After several days, he reached the peak and commanded the Yellow-Hats [i.e., professional Taoists] to hold an Offering. He burned a prayer, promising to pay one visit each year until he had a son, and then to hold a great and splendid affair to repay the Immortals' boon." That night, three Taoists appear in his dreams, thank him for coming so far to see them, and tell him they are sending him a son in return. After the son (who tells the story) is born, Wang holds an Offering every year to express his thanks, and his son continues the annual ritual after him, remarking, "How can I ever repay in balancing measure the boon I have borne from the Immortals?"[13] In the story of the Four Immortals and the dispute over the images' seating, the worshippers who climb the mountain hold an Offering to dedicate the images.[14] A wealthy man in another story climbs the mountain and holds an Offering each year to pay his respects to the Three.[15] The six rustics who are punished for eating dog meat on the way up the mountain promise to hold an Offering "to offer grieving acknowledgment of their repentance."[16] The seventh story is the tale of Yen-hsien and the avalanche. The eighth is the story of Mr. Yü's mother: when she recognizes the images of the Three Immortals as the Taoists who gave her chopsticks and helped her in her dream, her family holds "a great Offering and feast in thanks for the boon."[17] In the last story, a drought hits Ch'ung-jen County. The county administrator, his subordinates, and gentlemen and commoners of the county join in escorting the images of the Three Immortals to the county seat and holding a series of rites in their honor, culminating in an Offering; the rains come at once.[18]

Two things are interesting about these Offerings. First, we have learned from anthropologists to think of the Offering as a collective community ritual. According to Steven Sangren: "The *chiao* is an elaborate ritual celebration of communal renewal that occurs periodically . . . when a temple is built or restored."[19] Kristofer Schipper: "Since the end of the war, the three hamlets have collaborated in a Great Communal Sacrifice, *ta-chiao*, every twelve years."[20] Kenneth Dean: "the regular performance of Taoist [Offerings] at least once every sixty years is required in most villages."[21] David Faure: "To most villagers, the [Offering] is an event that must be realized every so often, usually every ten years, because it has to be done, because it has been promised (to the deities) by the ancestors, and because it is feared that ill-fortune will follow if the practice is abandoned without the deities' express approval."[22] But at most two of the Sung Offerings here are community rites:

the one performed for drought relief at the Ch'ung-jen county seat, and possibly the one performed on the first and fifteenth of each month at the Chao-ch'ing Abbey. Only the latter has the cyclical character noted by Sangren, Schipper, and Dean.[23] Aside from these, all the Offerings in the stories are offered by individuals or particular groups for quite personal or specific reasons, with no suggestion of benefit for a larger community or the cosmos. Second, the stories treat the Offering as serving three functions in relations between men and the Three Immortals: as an *object of exchange,* or proposed exchange—as when someone promises an Offering to the Three if some favor is granted; as a *token* of thanks or apology; or as a *setting* for personal prayers to the Three. In the first two functions, the Offering becomes simply a kind of gift from men to Immortals.

There is nothing exceptional about this in Sung sources. In my corpus of Chiang-hsi stories from Hung Mai's *I-chien chih* (see Chapter 7, n. 28), fifteen Offerings appear. Of these, two may be regular communal rites: one held to celebrate the birthday of the city god of Jao-chou,[24] and one at the T'ien-ch'ing Abbey in the same city, evidently for the salvation of the dead.[25] The other thirteen are all personal rites held by or for individuals, usually in response to personal or family crisis. A Lo-p'ing County man troubled by ghosts hires Taoists to hold an Offering and pray on his behalf.[26] A Taoist performs an Offering for his disciple, the victim of strange light-apparitions.[27] The administrator of Nan-k'ang prefecture is deathly ill, and when his doctors give up, he calls on the Taoists of the T'ien-ch'ing Abbey to hold an Offering for him at the prefectural seat.[28] Another Lo-p'ing man, summoned to hell and granted an extra six years of life, holds an Offering to express his thanks.[29] The judicial secretary of Fu-chou holds one to gain forgiveness for his dead wife, who had killed his concubine.[30]

Part of the difference from ethnographic testimony here may be a matter of sources. Anthropologists of Chinese religion tend naturally to stress "structures" (the recurrent, the culturally required) over individual agency (contingency, the historical or personal moment). The stories in Hung Mai's book are about crisis, the fate of the individual in occult emergency. It is not surprising that rites that are regular and cyclical, that respond to no sudden need of the moment, should be rare here. And yet the complete ethnographic silence on personal Offerings does make one wonder whether such rites simply no longer occur.[31] Their absence would represent a tremendous change in the economy of religious ritual between the Sung and the present day. The question certainly deserves investigation.

To return to the stories of the Three Immortals: one cannot speak of unmediated contact here, since the Offering itself is mediating congenial relations between men and the Three, communicating or guaranteeing to the Immortals specific feelings or intentions of human beings. But the quite different sort of mediation that the Offering as we see it in Taiwan or in Taoist ritual manuals embodies is missing—the mediation of local gods or Immortals, as celestial officials, between human subjects and the truly authoritative highest gods; the required mediation of Taoist professionals between worshippers and any gods at all; the bureaucratic and documentary character of both. It is missing because the ritual here is a sort of black box; we see it only from the outside, from the vantage of the relationships it serves. We see that people offer it and that Immortals must be glad to receive it, or how could it play the gift-like role it plays? But we do not see inside it; we do not see what happens. Even the professional Taoists who presumably are the performers of every Offering in the stories appear explicitly only once, when Mr. Wang, who wants a son, "commands" (*ming*) the "Yellow-Hats"—Taoist practitioners—to prepare the Offering at which he makes his vow. This is the Offering as mere setting; and the word "commands" clearly subordinates the Taoists to the worshipper, turning them from mediators with gods into the instruments Wang uses to create conditions for communicating personally with the Three.[32]

It would be wonderful to know "what was really happening" in these Offerings. Other Sung texts, notably the ritual manuals preserved in the Taoist canon, record something very like what Taoists and their anthropologist observers describe today. In the Sung as now, a written memorial, modeled on earthly memorials from officials to the emperor, was crucial to the rite;[33] and then as now the deities the Offering (or its sister rite, the Retreat) honored made up a vast pantheon-government, dwarfing and obscuring the particular gods worshipped in any specific place. We saw this in *Ceremonial Forms for the Performance and Completion of the Unsurpassed Grand Retreat of the Yellow Register* in Chapter 2. In brief, this picture of the divine world is much the same as that drawn in the liturgy of the modern Offering. What we do not see in Sung ritual manuals is how the liturgy and its performers fit into the larger celebration that all modern examples suggest an Offering involved, and that Mr. Wang's promise to hold "a great and splendid affair" suggests as well. While the Taoists were chanting their texts and delivering their memorials, where were they standing? When an Offering was held for specific local or regional figures like the Three Immortals, what was the physical relation of the Taoist ritual performance to the images of the gods who were receiving the gift? What role did lay worshippers play in the formal ritual? What else did they do while the ritual was going on? None of these questions find answers in any Sung source I have seen. Yet they are crucial. There is difference and tension between the representations of divinity offered in the texts of the Hua-kai cult and the representations constructed by the formal liturgy; and the tension is evident even in the way the Hua-kai texts represent the rite itself. It is likely that there should be such tension wherever the Offering ritual became a prominent part of lay celebration of specific local gods, since as liturgy it dealt with local gods largely by subordinating them.

But if there was tension, and if the formal liturgy's relatively unchanging character (which seems to be historical fact at least from the Sung on) and its monopolizing by professional Taoists made it unable to express, mediate, or resolve it, then one would expect to find it expressed or worked out in just those other aspects of the Offering that the Sung texts tell us nothing about: in the physical and participatory relation of lay worshippers to the ritual, and in the relation of the Taoists and their rite to the deities and their temple. And where different parties bring conflicting views to a ritual, these will be worked out or expressed differently in different times and places, depending on the relations of power or other resources between the two parties, and depending on the past and present processes of haggling, co-optation, monopoly, or coercion that have produced the ritual.[34] I cannot trace such processes here, because ethnographers have told us little about them, but I think one can make some progress by examining their product in different settings. Academic understanding of the Offering has largely depended on research done in Taiwan. Most of this work suggests a ritual all of a piece, without evidence of tension or contradiction. But I shall try to show that even in this century, the Taiwan Offering is not "the" Offering, and that comparing it to Offerings in other places can at least hint at the sorts of power relations and processes of negotiation that need to be explored.

ETHNOGRAPHIC EVIDENCE: TAIWAN

Let us begin with Taiwan and go from there. John Lagerwey's book on Taoist rituals is an extraordinarily detailed and informative guide to their performance and meaning. Lagerwey's study under Kristofer Schipper and his work with the Tainan Taoist master Chen Rongsheng give his account the authority of an insider's voice. When he tells us, for example, that the lay community representatives who pay for an Offering "watch it . . . without really understanding what it is they are watching,"[35] one is surely hearing the professional Taoist's point of view. Here I focus on two elements of Lagerwey's description: first, the bureaucratic character of the picture of the divine world the liturgy projects; and, second, the subordination of local gods that it asserts.

One document Lagerwey reproduces nicely conveys the bureaucratic flavor of the Taoist priests' written communications to heaven during the Offering. It is an especially good example because it lists a series of other documents the Taoists submit (by burning) to various divinities:

> Announcement (dispatch!): Office of the Great Method of the Numinous Treasure. This office today worships the Way and prepares an Offering to give thanks and pray for peace. Being charged with maintaining the order of the Three Heavens, the office-holder [refers to the Taoist officiant himself] is enrolled in the ranks of the five recordkeeping bureaus. The antiquity of canon law ensures that sincerity penetrates the high [heaven] and the thick [earth]; the

luminosity of the ritual texts makes certain that the somber heavens [water] reach both the dark [earth] and the light [heaven]. All our earnest petitions must be transmitted by an honorable office-holder if they are to be executed with dispatch. Those who must receive this announcement are as follows:

—five box envelopes [*fang-han*] with invocations, invitations, and presentations are respectfully sent to:

> the [Metal] Gate in the Jade Capital: respectfully invoked;
>
> the gate of the Four Bureaus of the Three Realms: respectfully invited;
>
> the Bureau of the Great Sovereign of the Office of Heaven: respectfully presented;
>
> the Court of the Celestial Pivot in the Highest Purity: respectfully presented;
>
> the Office of the Eastern Peak Tai: respectfully presented.

—two box envelopes with letters of presentation are respectfully forwarded to:

> the offices of the Six Masters of the Numinous Treasure: respectfully forwarded;
>
> the offices of the Four Saints of the North Pole: respectfully forwarded.

—four box envelopes with missives of offering are respectfully presented to:

> the officers of merit who transmit symbols,
>
> the various gods who assist the Way,
>
> the gods of the soil and of the walls and moats,
>
> the gods to whom is rendered a cult recognized by law: to each, presented.

—seven letters, cards, and notes are respectfully passed on to:

> the officers, generals, clerks, and soldiers of the various offices of the thunder and lightning of the Numinous Treasure in the Court of the Law of Highest Purity;
>
> the various officers, generals, clerks, and soldiers of the altar where gather the gods of the Three Realms in the Chamber of Spontaneity for Communication with the Perfected;
>
> the host of immortals who bring catastrophes during the various parts of this year;
>
> the venerable god of supreme virtue in charge of the Great Star [T'ai-sui];
>
> the venerable gods of the walls and moats of the district and the prefecture of Tainan;
>
> the gods and keen-eared ones from above, below, far, and near who receive sacrifices in this neighborhood;
>
> the six gods of the soil and directors of destiny of the incense burners of each family.

The above documents have all been duly stamped, sealed, and completed. We look to the divine powers on high to transmit them for us. Let the mounted gods gallop each in his own direction and give [his documents] to the right office, penetrating on high into the Golden Gate of the Jade Capital and below into the bright waters and dark earth. May our sincerity be communicated directly on high and a response be forthcoming. Let there be no delays: it must reach those concerned.

The above is announced to the jade lasses of the Three Heavens charged with transmission, the messengers of the roads through the clouds of the Nine Heavens, the officers of merit of Orthodox Unity, the great generals of the molten and fiery bells, the potent officers in charge of memorializing on this day, the clerks mounted on the fiery dragons—all the gods of transmission.

In the *keng-shen* year of heaven's revolution, the 11th month, the 20th day, dispatched.

In charge of the execution of the rituals: Ch'en Ts'un-hsin.[36]

There is much here, of course, that does not sound bureaucratic to secular or Western ears—the dragons, the jade lasses, and so on—but much else that does: the document's name; the identification of the Taoist priest as an officeholder; the capital; the graded series of bureaus, courts, and offices, and the careful grading of the documents to go to each; the box-envelopes, modeled on the boxes Ch'ing dynasty officials used for secret memorials to the emperor; and the date and seal. What is crucial here is that, just as in the Sung listing of gods for the Yellow Register Retreat, the local gods likely to be worshipped at or near the temple where the rite is performed appear very near the bottom: "the venerable gods of the walls and moats of the district and the prefecture of Tainan" and "the gods and keen-eared ones from above, below, far, and near who receive sacrifices in this neighborhood." Indeed, the fact that for these gods no offices are mentioned suggests that they stand outside the heavenly bureaucracy itself; that they represent a "commoner" stratum and so fall even more distinctly to the bottom of the divine heap. (After all, they receive no official box-envelope, but simply "cards, letters, and notes"; and Lagerwey tells us that "the primary hierarchical distinction is between gods who receive their invitation in a 'box-envelope' and those who do not.")[37] If this is the right reading, then the subordination of local gods, their remoteness from real celestial authority, is even greater here than in the Sung register, which did not set off local deities qualitatively but simply relegated them to positions at the bottom.

This relatively extreme subordination of local gods expresses itself directly in the physical layout of Lagerwey's Offering. Central importance goes to the five highest Taoist gods: the Three Pure, flanked by the Supreme Sovereign, Jade Emperor, and by the Great Emperor of the Purple Empyrean. Portraits of these five hang at the north, or imperial, end of the temple, facing south like all Chinese rulers. They are thus the primary recipients of the "offering" that the rite literally accomplishes. Lining the walls to east and west, farther south but still in the northern end of the temple relative to the audience, are portraits of other recipients: the officers (*guan*) of Heaven and earth. Still farther south on the same walls, in the "outer altar" now and thus inferior to the Taoist officiants themselves, but serving as their aides, are portraits of a variety of other specifically Taoist gods. Finally, in the southernmost and thus most inferior position stand a large number of images arrayed on bleachers, behind a table that holds sacrificial goods offered to them by locals (not by the Taoists), the Table of the Three Realms: "Here are deposited the divinities brought by the people from their homes, *as well as the divinities of the temple in which the ritual is being performed*" (emphasis mine).[38] These temple gods (and the others on the table), unlike any other deity present, thus take up the role of supplicant with respect to the five gods at the north end and the role of audience with respect to the performance of the Taoists: they are specifically and expressly *not* recipients of the Offering. This wrenches them out of their normal position and reverses their usual role, since they would usually occupy the place of honor the five Taoist gods now hold. Also behind the Taoists are the human "representatives of the community," the wealthy donors who have paid for the Offering: they too take the role of audience.[39]

That all this deliberately subordinates the temple gods and other locally worshipped divinities, not only to the Taoists' gods but to the Taoists themselves, Lagerwey makes clear:

> A re-presentation, as we shall see, of the origin and structure of the universe, the ritual reminds the assembled gods of their proper role as local parts of a great Whole. In a certain sense, this goal is already achieved simply by setting the gods on the bleachers, for the Table of the Three Realms is also called the Table of the Three Officers, and the gods are thus at once placed under the jurisdiction of and assimilated to the Three Officers [heaven, earth, and water, and their respective gods—], that is to the deep structure—the order—of the natural universe.... The Offering provides the local gods—who are none other than the "obstructed souls" of Feng-tu, the demons of the Six Heavens—with a glimpse, through this doorway, of how the Way works. Just to see it is already to be transformed, humanized, integrated. But they will get no more than a glimpse for ... they are not yet ready to be enrolled on the Taoist's register.[40]

Thus the local gods become mere demons, eagerly seeking instruction from the ritual performed by the Taoists and gaining a chance to stand before the Taoists' universal gods. Lagerwey's account is especially eloquent, but others have remarked on the gods' displacement and interpreted it in roughly the same way. Thus according to Schipper, for an Offering "the statues of the deities normally worshipped in the temple are removed from their niches, situated at the noble side (opposite the entrance), and placed on the exact opposite side, with their backs turned toward the closed doors."[41] According to Steven Sangren, "One of the most revealing and central of the many rituals included in [Offerings] involves the physical manipulation of deity images in the temple. All the gods in the temple ... normally face south, absorbing *yang*. During the Offering, however, they are moved back toward the temple doors, facing north, in the position normally occupied by their worshipers. The gods' normal positions are then occupied by the Taoist gods of 'prior heaven' (*hsien-t'ien*). These gods, mysterious to nonspecialist Chinese, are thus *yang* in relation to the regular pantheon's temporary *yin* status."[42] According to Stephan Feuchtwang, "The performance of the [Offering] turns the territorial cult itself inside out, bringing into its centre the [D]aoist's own altar and furthering the [D]aoist master's initiation into his esoteric knowledge. The objects of the cult normally at its centre are displaced into positions of supplicant community representatives and underlings in a cosmological hierarchy of purity."[43] There is no doubt that we are dealing with a general pattern.

I would like, for ease of reference in the rest of this chapter, to call this pattern of Offering performance the "Taoist-on-top" pattern. I trust the reason is clear. The arrangement of human and divine participants puts the Taoists and their gods foremost, subordinating not only the local gods but the community representatives as well: both are mere watchers of the ritual the Taoist performs and the Taoist gods receive. While the ritual subordinates the Taoist to these supreme gods too, it simultaneously exalts him above local gods and leaders of the temple community. Here physical layout simply confirms what the words and documents of the liturgy express: there is a celestial government; the Taoist is part of it; the community representatives and, in Lagerwey's rite, even their gods stand below it. That the ritual presents itself as a renewal of the whole cosmos through the restoration of unity and harmony cannot obscure the stark, unidirectional hierarchy it imposes.

As we shall see, the Taoist-on-top pattern is not the only way to run an Offering. And this makes it even more interesting to ask why the wealthiest and presumably most powerful members of a Chinese community, those who initiate and pay for the Offering and in fact hire the Taoist officiants, should accept a ritual of this form—why they should act out their own subordination and the subordination of the gods they and their neighbors worship daily. Part of the answer may be that there is more than one way of looking at what is going on even here, and that the community representatives do not have to look at it in the same way that the Taoists do. It is important in itself that the Table of the Three Realms bears offerings to the local bleacher-gods, to whom the Taoists themselves make no offering. That is, it is built into the very structure of this celebration that the community representatives are making offerings to different gods, gods the Taoists treat only as audience. There is a hint of differences of view, too, in Lagerwey's remark that the community representatives "watch it ... without really understanding what it is they are watching." Perhaps what to the Taoist seems lack of understanding is simply understanding that differs. Schipper tells us that the deities removed to the back of the temple "are said to be 'inspecting the sacrifice,' *chien-chiao*."[44] The phrase could as easily be translated "supervising the sacrifice," a very different picture of the local deities' role than Lagerwey offers. One wonders by whom these words "are said," and whether Schipper heard them from community representatives rather than from the Taoists. Or perhaps there is more than one view even among Taoists themselves.

Still, there is a question here. That north-south orientation symbolizes political authority is a commonplace of Chinese culture. It would be amazing if the "community representatives" did not recognize that a rite performed in Taoist-on-top fashion appears to subordinate their gods and themselves radically to religious specialists and the pantheon "mysterious to nonspecialist Chinese" (Sangren) that the specialists represent. I would argue that what makes this acceptable to men who would see themselves as community leaders is that it accomplishes a second subordination at the same time. The entire ritual in its Taiwan version, in fact, is founded on exclusion. All the members of the community who would normally have access to the temple as a place of worship, *except* the wealthy "community representatives" in attendance, are forbidden to enter the temple or to witness the ritual. (This does not mean they are not part of "the Offering" in other ways; on this, more below.) Although the ritual may reduce local gods to mere audience, at the same time, "audience" is an exalted role in relation to the community as a whole. The community representatives are licensed to occupy the same role; in effect, they take up a position that (again in relation to the community) is parallel to that of their own gods. We seem to see a sort of bargain between religious practitioner and local powerholder (or perhaps sometimes only would-be powerholder) by which the former accepts a position that subordinates him and his gods in return for having his superiority to his neighbors symbolized in the same ritual. This may be especially important where community leadership, or indeed the unitary character of the community itself, is no certain thing. Taiwan "communities," often lacking lineage identity or other clear political organization, may throw up "leaders"—in the case we have seen we are talking perhaps only about men of relative wealth and status—who need to call on all possible sources of standing in freewheeling competition with other contenders. Stephan Feuchtwang, in an extremely useful account of an Offering he studied near Taipei in 1967, found the ceremony itself an object of controversy among the politically ambitious:

> The orthodox master was employed by the town's wealthy and in particular by those seeking political status, converting their wealth into votes via prominent funding of the temple's repair and sponsorship of its [*ch*]*iao*. Yet the winner of the elections for township mayor, soon after the [*ch*]*iao*, took no ritual role in it, nor killed a pig for the feast. He deplored the extravagance of the occasion,

convincingly adopting the official nationalist (KMT) view of it as wasteful, while his election agents made quite sure voters would know that he had contributed substantially to the rebuilding of this and every other temple in town. He was a member of the temple committee, but not a manager of the [*ch*]*iao*. His rival, on the other hand, was a manager of the [*ch*]*iao* and acquired one of the leading ritual roles in it.[45]

Here, incidentally, is more evidence against the notion that the Taoists' bureaucratic model is a religious prop for the secular power of the state, for here the state and its party's representative oppose the very rite that proclaims the model. But the point is that when a ritual role becomes a resource in the competition for status, as it must often have been in Chinese history, it is plausible to consider the subordination of the community representative a bargain with the Taoist for a hoped-for elevation above others. To read the rite as I am reading it is not necessarily to claim that a literal "bargain" is historical or present fact, although since the "community representatives" or other wealthy locals do *hire* the Taoists, bargaining of some sort is not simply metaphoric. Nor can we take the status of the "community representatives" for granted. In Lagerwey's example, they are wealthier members of the community and funders of the ceremony, but this need not always be the case. The role of organizer, the role of funder or financial contributor, and the role of "community representative" participant are in principle separable and in practice sometimes separate. Only the first two clearly require wealth and position in the community, though it does still seem common for the last to be relatively wealthy. In an Offering that Kenneth Dean observed, not in Taiwan but in Zhangzhou, Fujian, in 1985, the *hui-shou*, community members present in the in-temple ceremony, were chosen by lot, and moneys for the occasion came equally from all village households; but one wonders if this egalitarianism of both funding and representation reflects the influence of Communist conceptions of community since 1949.[46] At the Offering Myron Cohen witnessed in 1963 in Mei-nung, a rural community in southern Taiwan, the community members who lived for a week in the temple and took part in the ceremonies were all rich farmers or businessmen who had paid for the role.[47] For Feuchtwang's Offering, the representatives were chosen divinely—that is, by lot—but from a short list preselected for wealth and status.[48] In a general account, Kristofer Schipper notes: "The representative dignitaries or 'Chiefs' are the only members of the community to participate in the [in-temple] ceremonies. . . . The Chiefs are mostly the elderly heads of large and wealthy local families. They are not necessarily the organizers of the [Offering] . . . [who] normally do not have their names entered in a special way on the memorial. But the custom of including them and their functions is gaining acceptance."[49] Indeed, as Feuchtwang's evidence shows, we cannot assume that the "community" is a single unit in relation to the rite, or that as a unit it preexists its representation there.

But it is precisely such things that we need to know, for any local tradition or even for any single instance of the Offering, to get at what is happening in it. We surely cannot understand Lagerwey's and other Offerings without knowing more than we do about the working out of relations of status, power, and conflicting or common interest between Taoists and local elites and between each and a larger populace. To put things back in the terms of my original paradox, I am arguing that the Offering and its representations have to be understood as an interaction between two different models of divine-human relations, carried at least in part by different participants in religious life. The form it takes in Taiwan is one way of combining in a single ritual a model of direct contact between individual humans and specific local gods and a model of a universal, impersonal, mediated, bureaucratic hierarchy of divinities. Even in the Taiwanese case, and even within the temple, both models express themselves (recall the unmediated offerings to local gods on the Table of the Three Realms); yet one is clearly and profoundly subordinated to the other. I am arguing that we must understand this subordination simply as one possible outcome of the interaction and urging that we begin to ask about its specific historical roots in political and social exchange, sometimes competitive, sometimes collusive, between Taoist professionals and lay worshippers.

ETHNOGRAPHIC EVIDENCE: THE NEW TERRITORIES

To make this plausible, of course, there must be other outcomes. The evidence that there are emerges from work on the Offering in another part of China—broadly, the Hong Kong New Territories region. It is not clear why this other work has not influenced our picture of the Offering and the place of Taoists in local religion as deeply as work done on Taiwan. Consider David Faure's description of a rite he attended in 1980 in Fan Ling, a village cluster in the New Territories whose residents share one surname. In part of what I quote below, Faure is concerned with different issues from mine (in particular, with the relationship between lineage identity and territorial identity), and my quotations here are torn from this context. In one place Faure provides a list of the gods invited to the Offering (in Cantonese, *ta-tsiu*):

> It is the practice in a *ta-tsiu* to invite to the altar all the deities held in esteem by the villagers in common. On this occasion, the villagers invited *the three deities of the village temple who, represented by their statuettes, were given central positions*. In addition, they invited seventy-five other deities and spirits, represented by slips of red paper bearing their names. These obviously held secondary positions. Some of these secondary deities, such as the Jade Emperor or the Goddess of Mercy, were not related to any locality in particular. Some, such as the Ch'e Kung and the Hung Shing, were recognized as deities of south China. Others included the protector deities of Fan Ling and the vicinity, such as the rain god of Shui

Moon Shaan, the earth gods of Tin Ping Shan, Wutong Shan, Ngau Lo Hau, Ngau T'aam Shaan, the Shui Long Kung, Mau Chau, the walled village of Fan Ling itself, the two other villages just by the village walls known as Naam Pin and Pak Pin, nearby Kwun Po, inhabited by another segment of the lineage, and an unspecified "brother village," in addition to "the earth gods of the mountains" and "all the earth gods within our territory." Also invited were Governor-General Chau and Governor Wong, the two officials who petitioned the emperor to ask that the coastal evacuation policy in the late seventeenth century be rescinded. The founding ancestor of the lineage was also invited, but was represented as a single slip of red paper among the seventy-five slips. . . . What is significant here is that this list of spirits and deities represents, in religious terms, the villagers' mental map of their community and its vicinity.[50] (Emphasis mine.)

The centrality of the villages' own temple deities, not only spatially but in their representation by images rather than only as slips, makes this ritual very different from the Taiwan cases recorded by Lagerwey, Schipper, Sangren, and Feuchtwang. The other gods form no clear hierarchy, but rather a loose network stretching outward to the larger region and ultimately to China as a whole. But where are the Taoists and their higher gods? Elsewhere Faure tells us:

As a religious occasion, the foci of the *ta-tsiu* are the deities, and they are invited to an altar placed in a matshed especially constructed for the purpose. Near this matshed is one for the operas, built so that the stage faces the deities' altar. *Nearby is also an altar for the saam-ts'ing* . . . [i.e., the Three Pure], *the deities of the village priests*. This "hall" set up for the *saam-ts'ing* is *appropriately adorned with the village priests' paraphernalia, notably pictures of the ten layers of the underworld and, nearby but not in the "hall," a picture of the Heavenly Master (T'in-sz)*. Because the "isolated spirits" (*ku-wan*), that is spirits unattached to ancestral shrines, are also invited to partake of the burnt offerings, an effigy of the *taai-sz-wong* [*ta-shih-wang*, "great scholar-gentleman king"] is erected to maintain order, a smaller effigy of the magistrate (also referred to as the city god) stands in a smaller matshed nearby accompanied by two *yamen* orderlies, and banners (*faan-kon*) are posted at the major crossroads leading into the site of the *ta-tsiu* . . . .

Within the confines so prepared, the rites are executed. In an earlier chapter, it has already been noted that the deities of the entire territory holding the *ta-tsiu* are invited to the deities' altar, the invitation being a representation of the territory. The presence of the city god, and his surrogate, the *taai-sz*, blends the territorial deities back into the official hierarchy that reflects the political order. *The deities from the territory have been invited to the altar by the villagers themselves, but the effigies of the taai-sz and the city god, along with the representations of the saam-ts'ing set up in a special matshed, are brought along to the ta-tsiu by the village priests*. Throughout the ceremonies, unnoticed by the villagers, it is the rites of the priests—such as bringing into the festival the presence of the *taai-sz*—that place the villagers' deities in a wider setting than the confines of the village. However, to the villagers, and to the priests themselves, the centering of their activities on the matshed of the *saam-ts'ing* only serves to demarcate them from the villagers. The villagers come into the site of the celebration, insert incense sticks into the burners in front of their territorial deities, and lose themselves in the crowds that stand around and chat, or proceed to the opera matshed to watch the opera, leaving the priests to their own rites.[51] (Emphasis mine.)

This is extraordinarily interesting. One needs more: the opera matshed faces the temple deities' matshed, but how is the matshed of the "village priests"—that is, the professional Taoists—oriented? How does it relate to the local gods and to the celebration as a whole? But already there is no doubt that this is a very different sort of Offering. The unified, centered structure that in Taiwan puts the Taoists and their liturgy at the core, right in the middle of the local gods' temple itself, and assembles not only the Taoists' gods and the displaced and subordinated local gods there but the "community representatives" too, is utterly missing here. The local gods are moved from their accustomed position again, but only to be placed in a special matshed, which, as far as the villagers' side of the ritual is concerned, becomes the central focus. But "as far as the villagers' side of the ritual is concerned" needs emphasis, since what Faure is really showing us are two separate rituals, simultaneous and adjacent. One is the villagers' ritual, centered on individual prayers offered directly to their local gods and on the operatic performance for which the villagers and their gods join as audience. (Note the difference from the way the role of audience is used to build complex hierarchy in Lagerwey's rite.) The other is the Taoists' own rite, which for all we can tell may be exactly like the Taiwan version or a Sung Offering in its formal liturgy, and which, like those, focuses on the Three Pure above all. Most significant for my argument, here it is the Taoists and only the Taoists who bring the symbolic vocabulary of celestial bureaucracy and a hierarchy of gods into the picture, and they do so virtually ignored by the villagers. Here, then, the pattern is not "Taoist on top" but perhaps "Taoist alongside."

Whatever historical "bargain" Taoist and villager may have worked out here must be far different from the one that produces the Taiwan rite. And yet there is a sense of a bargain here too: the Taoists have not simply horned in and performed their own rite at the same time that the villagers are performing theirs, for the villagers do see Taoists and their rites as essential for a proper Offering:

> To most villagers, the *ta-tsiu* is an event that must be realized every so often, usually every ten years, because it has to be done, because it has been promised (to the deities) by the ancestors, and because it is feared that ill-fortune will follow if the practice is abandoned without the deities' express approval. It is almost characteristic of the *ta-tsiu* that villagers are not bothered by their lack of understanding of what the priests perform. It matters, and the villagers are confident

of the fact, that the priests do perform a set of ceremonies that amount to a *ta-tsiu*, and that the villagers themselves may integrate into them their own practices.[52]

"Integrate" seems an exaggeration here: nobody is integrating his rites into anyone else's, as far as I can see in Faure's data.[53] But it is interesting and important that villagers see the Taoists' presence as a requirement for their own celebration. "Lack of understanding" may be a less problematic notion here, where locals are simply taking no part in the rites the Taoists perform, than where some play a direct role, as in Taiwan; but it is still an issue worth pursuing further on. In the meantime, the crucial point is that direct, personal contact between men and local gods and the acting out of celestial bureaucracy and official mediation coexist here, through entirely separate practices, within what advertises itself as one celebration, the *ta-tsiu*. There is no expression, at the level of the whole,[54] of the subordinating of one model to the other, or indeed of any specific relation between them at all. There is no indication that wealthy members of the Fan Ling community are using their relationship with Taoist professionals to clinch their own authority or dominance symbolically through the very shape of the ritual, as I have suggested for Taiwan. Yet the rite in this case was organized and paid for, not by some spontaneous act of the villagers, but by the ancestral trust of the lineage that dominates Fan Ling, an agency generally managed by the wealthy and informally powerful.

One wonders again what kinds of negotiation, cooperation, and competition have generated the present situation, in which Taoists are recognized as essential but do not get to shape the ritual as a whole to their model. An organized lineage leadership in a village cluster like Fan Ling may simply be safer in its authority, less needy of Taoists' aid for religious legitimization, than the individual wealthy and powerful members of a temple community in Tainan. We should notice also that, according to Faure, for the Fanling villagers the entire ritual fulfills a promise their ancestors made to the local gods generations ago, a promise strongly reminiscent of the vows Mr. Wang and others in *Verities of the Three Perfected Lords* make to hold Offerings if the Three Immortals help them. The ritual thus commemorates an original direct interaction between ancestors and gods; and since the lineage trust stands for the relation of the villagers to these ancestors, it is not surprising that direct contact with gods is the focal point of the celebration the lineage trust sponsors. But what, then, is the function of the Taoists and their gods, and what has brought them to accept the collateral position they hold here?

That New Territories Offerings do not follow the Taoist-on-top pattern is clear from other work as well. Tanaka Issei, in his massive studies of ritual and theater and their connections with lineage organizations and associations, offers descriptions and maps of a number of Offerings, which vary a good deal both in physical layout and in the relation between the Taoists' rites to their divinities and the prayers and operas offered to local gods.[55] For the Offering of the Lin Village Alliance, the local temple god, T'ien Hou (Ma Tsu), was moved temporarily, as in Faure's example, out of her temple and into a temporary "god shed" (*shen-p'eng*); but unlike in Faure's case, the officiating Taoists' gods were placed in the T'ien Hou temple.[56] So far we might imagine we were in Taiwan. But consider first that the Taoist gods did *not* stand in the place normally occupied by T'ien Hou in the central hall of her temple, but instead one hall off to the side, in the place of two of the temple's *subsidiary* gods, thus off-center both in space and in status; while at the center—the ritually dominant position—the hall that usually housed T'ien Hou remained empty, as if signaling that she *could not* be replaced. Second, T'ien Hou did not become audience and supplicant at the Taoists' rites as in Taiwan, because the "god shed" in which she now stood faced, not toward the temple where the Taoist rites were taking place, but perpendicular to it, toward the massive shed where operas would be performed for her own entertainment and honor. Third, the special sheds set up for the city god (often a Taoist-associated god) and the great gentleman-king (*ta-shih-wang*, the *taai-sz* in Faure's materials, there likewise brought by the Taoists) also faced the opera house from the opposite side, and were thus oriented toward T'ien Hou herself, rather than toward the temple with the rites and higher gods of the Taoists as one might expect. Fourth, the other regional and local gods brought from shrines and temples nearby, who in Lagerwey's example were also treated as supplicant audience for the Taoists' gods, here took up their own subsidiary positions in the "god shed" alongside T'ien Hou and so like her received the community's own gift: the opera. And if we turn back to Lagerwey's case, we find that his opera house faces the temple from the outside, but from the same direction as the in-temple audience, so that the operas here are offered implicitly as much to the Taoist gods as to the gods of the community.[57] The contrast is thus stark. In Lagerwey's case, everything, from the local gods as audience to the opera presented ostensibly in their own honor, is organized around the Taoists. In Tanaka's example, the ceremony has two axes, one lying through the temple and the Taoists' performance—but with centrality even there denied them by placing their gods in the side hall—and the other lying through the god shed and the opera house. Although here (as in Lagerwey's example, but apparently not in Faure's at Fan Ling) the community sends representatives to the Taoists' rite, who become supplicants of the Taoist gods as in Taiwan, the rite involves no physical subordination of the community's gods, who receive their separate homage some distance away and from a different angle. As in Faure's example, the impression that two separate rituals happen side by side, or in this case, rather at right angles to each other, is very strong.

Tanaka supplies other examples that strengthen this impression. At the

Offering of the Teng lineage of Lung-yueh-t'ou, the Taoists took over the ancestral hall instead of T'ien-hou's temple, setting up their own god images in a position of honor but not, as in Taiwan, at the most northern point of the shrine: for the images normally there, the Teng lineage ancestors, remained in place and thus implicitly became recipients of the offering along with the Three Pure and other Taoist figures.[58] In the meantime, T'ien Hou, as elsewhere, was moved out of her nearby shrine to a special matshed, where she stood along with a stone stele bearing a list of other gods of the region, also moved from the ancestral hall. These gods thus became available for individual offerings along with T'ien Hou. The opera house in this case, however, was built not facing T'ien Hou's god shed but facing her now empty temple, so that the operas offered in her honor were performed not to her image but to the space she normally occupied. Tanaka explains this oddity convincingly: in the past, the operas at this rite had been puppet shows, which required only a very small stage, easy to fit in front of the god shed; but this time the community had invited a real opera troupe, and the large theater it needed would not fit there and so was built facing the vacated temple instead.[59] Thus the norm was, as in Tanaka's previous example, to aim the operas at T'ien Hou. On this occasion, the aim was a bit indirect, via the shrine where she normally stood; but again the structure was biaxial, with no conversion of community gods to audience in the Taoist rites, with the inclusion of ancestors as recipients in their normal position, and with no spatial subordination of any of the community's usual divinities to the rites and gods of professional clerics.

In another of Tanaka's examples, a rite offered by the T'ai-k'ang Teng lineage, no divinity occupies any permanent structure. Both the local gods and the Taoists' gods are on temporary altars; the two face each other, so that the local gods do become audience to the Taoists' ritual; but the Taoists then leave, and their altar turns into the stage from which operas are offered to the local gods: the biaxial form is thus produced in time rather than in space.[60] The separation of Taoist from village ritual—meaning by the latter both the operas and the sacrifices and prayers individuals offer to local gods—occurs again and again. Since Tanaka is interested in the influence of lineage-based ritual and drama on other sorts of associations, he does not investigate the relations or negotiations between the sponsoring committee and Taoists, but both the variety of his material and its sharp divergences from the Taiwan pattern suggest there is matter here worth investigating.

Faure and Tanaka are not the only authorities to whom one can turn for materials from this region of China. Francis Hsu, in a book again devoted to other issues (the relation of "magical" to "scientific" thinking), has provided a very useful account of the Offering (he spells it *chiu*) in two communities in the far south of China, well separated in space and time.[61] Both aimed at protecting the communities from plague. The later one took place in Shatin, again in the New Territories region, in 1975. Again the main local god leaves his permanent temple to reside in a temporary structure for the whole celebration, but as in Faure's case he remains central, and Taoist divinities do not replace him:

> The biggest temporary poles-and-matting structure (*p'eng*) constructed for the meeting was the Cantonese opera-house.... Directly opposite the opera-house was a large pavilion honoring Che Kung and his spouse. Part of the role of Che Kung was that of [plague god] ... he was credited with clearing Shatin of its infectious disease at the request of the populace. His was the main shrine, most elaborate in its construction and decoration.... [S]ituated closer to this main temple but still outside its front steps was a large offering table on which were a lantern and three modest sized incense burners for worshippers to insert sticks of incense into at all times. A cushioned platform about one foot high was in front, for worshippers to kneel in prayer or to kowtow after they made the offering of incense. Draping this table was a red skirt with the embroidered words, "Gratitude to Gods for Favors." ... In the inner sanctum [of the main temple] sat images of Che Kung and his spouse, under a red and yellow canopied enclosure. In front of them were two more tables. The smaller one, closest to them, was laden with the usual incense burner, candlesticks, and food offerings. Next to it was a much larger table (about twelve feet by twelve feet) which filled the rest of the hall all the way to the front entrance.[62]

Further on, Hsu tells us the function of the large table:

> Instead of scripture recitation and chanting, the offerings here [i.e., in the Che Kung temple], aside from the inevitable and constant lighted incense sticks, were mainly food. On [the table] were displayed a variety of polychromatic animals: roosters, fishes, horses, pigs, goats, tigers, ducks, and so forth.... All of these animals were made of flour. On the last day of the *chiu* meeting, each contributor who gave $50 or more and who wished to do so could take one home. In addition to these lively animal figures, also displayed on this table were heaps of oranges and stacks of pastry and many-layered cakes, red and white roses, and a variety of figurines of gods, angels, and other immortals, also made of flour.
>
> All of these items were blessing-givers in anyone's home. The edibles were blessed because they were first offered to (and presumably eaten by) the gods; the other articles because they were associated with them.[63]

Thus here, as in Faure's material, the central deity, who has a long-standing connection to this community, is the focus both of personal offerings and of an opera, which entertains him and his worshippers together. This entertainment, Hsu tells us, was "an essential ingredient of any expression of gratitude to gods and spirits for favors."[64]

Again, of course, there are Taoists, though here they may have more competition than in Fan Ling:

> Other structures in the *chiu* ground were a number of side shrines: (1) one for five Taoist deities; (2) one for three Buddhist deities; (3) one for fifty Village

Guardian Gods (Chun Shen) [ts'un shen], lorded over by the Earth God; (4) one for souls of deceased ancestors by descendants who paid to have them uplifted; and (5) one for Cheng Huang or District God [the city god], flanked by Earth God (Tu Ti) on his right; on his left was an assistant god named Ta Wu Chang, a figure with white hair and a pointed hat. Of these five the shrine housing the Taoist deities was the largest and the one for Buddhist deities the next largest, while the others were much smaller.[65]

It would be useful to know whether the more bureaucratic deities—the city god, the earth god, and so on—arrived with the Taoists, as in Faure's community, or were installed by others. It is interesting in any case that their shrines, like that of the five Taoist deities, are clearly secondary in size and centrality (Hsu calls them "side shrines") to the temple of Che Kung and his spouse. But the Taoists center their efforts on their own shrine: "Although Che Kung and his spouse occupied the main temple and the *chiu* meeting was staged in the name of gratitude for their favors, the priests' ritual activities were concentrated at the side shrine for Taoist deities. Here polychromatic pictures of various Taoist gods were hung on the main wall."[66]

In sum, here is the same separation as in Faure's and Tanaka's evidence between the rites of the professional Taoists, aimed exclusively at their own deities, and devotions to the local god, from which worshippers expected personal benefits—the blessed foodstuffs that those who had been especially generous in their donations could take home, food in effect shared with the god; but also the boons that worshippers sought in their personal prayers and with their personal offerings of incense. During most of the Offering, the Taoist rites are only one show among many for lay participants, who circulate on the grounds, visiting whatever building they choose and making offerings "to any image of any spirit in any shrine."[67] Again, the celebration as a whole has none of the unified and focused ritual structure of the Taiwan examples Lagerwey et al. describe. Hsu tells us little about the content of the Taoists' rites, but it is clear that for most people at the Offering the figures of Che Kung and his wife, not the gods or the Taoists, are central. These Taoists do in the end move to the fore a bit more: on the last night, they lead a ritual and procession to offer charity to wandering ghosts without descendants, which draws an enormous attendance, even though the opera is still going on. But there is nothing in Hsu's description that suggests that the Taoists' own view of this rite, whatever it may be, attains special status in the form of the procession. This is simply not the same sort of centered, hierarchy-embodying ritual practiced in Taiwan.

In these New Territories Offerings, then, we see a way of structuring the relation between professional Taoist and lay worshipper, between their respective gods, and between alternative models of divine-human interaction that leaves the members of each pair on an equal footing, or at least leaves the question of hierarchy open. It certainly leaves them looking quite separate, capable of articulating distinct domains of religious action without, in some cases, much interaction at all. Yet, on the Taiwan evidence, the two models can also be structured into an intimate relation that is strongly unequal. The differences between the New Territories and Taiwan versions suggest that my strategy of treating the two ways of conceiving and interacting with the divine as distinct and potentially in tension is a useful one. The New Territories cases in particular confirm that celestial bureaucracy and mediated god-human contact are the baggage of professional Taoists;[68] thus we see in Taiwan an Offering that is powerfully shaped in specifically Taoist directions. To historians of Taoism itself, this may seem a strange notion. Since the Offering is, historically, originally a Taoist product, an Offering "shaped in specifically Taoist directions" may seem simply an Offering in its most natural, original, and thus proper sense. But the New Territories evidence shows that with time things have become more complicated.

THE OFFERING OUTSIDE THE TEMPLE

The physical organization of the ritual—its structuring, or not, around the performances and gods of Taoists—is not the only medium in which differing models can express themselves. Here we may turn to Hsu's other Offering, which he observed in West Town (not its real name), a small community in western Yunnan province, in 1942. In this instance, the community was much smaller, and very different from the communities in the Taiwan cases. It had, for example, no local shrine of its own in which to hold the ritual, and as far as one can tell no strong cults to local deities whose images could be repositioned. Yet the fundamental rituals in which members of the populace and professional Taoists both took part were as firmly centered on the Taoists and conveyed subordination of the community representatives just as clearly as in Taiwan. Here, after the Taoists issued public notices that presented the relation between the gods and the community as entirely a disciplinary one, a series of rites took place, including most notably one in which, while the chief Taoist read scripture and prayers to an image of the plague god (apparently supplied by the Taoists themselves and not a god with local connections), a leading community member "knelt just behind him and kowtowed at regular intervals following each chant . . . during the entire performance without intermission, which lasted one and a half hours." The performance left his trousers torn and knees bloody.

This is a more grueling demonstration of subordination to the god and to the Taoist himself than the equivalent community representatives in Lagerwey's Offering ever undertake; and in this and every other public ritual moment, the community participants simply followed the Taoists' lead. Yet Hsu finds abundant evidence that the rite had very different meaning for these townspeople than for the Taoists they followed. Perhaps his best evidence, since it involves deliberate action, is a separate altar the local "managers" erected—again, those responsible for initiating the Offering and for hiring the Taoists. This alternative center of worship was sited in what may have been a strategic way: it stood directly opposite one of the Offering altars, which, unlike it, had been erected according to the Taoists' instructions.[69] The special altar (see figure) assembled a number of Buddhist and other god-images, with an incense burner in front for individual offerings and a fountain of "angel water" (Hsu's translation of *hsien-shui;* "Immortals' water," I believe) that when consumed would save one from illness. It "was created in a moment's enthusiasm by individual worshippers," and no Taoist had any part in it or in any offerings made before it. Thus we have here a spontaneous expression of lay notions, or at least an expression that laymen represented to Hsu as spontaneous. The images stand in a way that certainly suggests hierarchy of a sort: a rough, wide-rimmed circle of smaller figures surrounds a more robust image of the Buddha. But hierarchy here is far vaguer than in the Taoist god-lists, as there is no clear ranking of the images away from the center. In fact, this looks not at all like the pyramidal hierarchy of the Taoists but like a sort of radial web of dependencies—a circle of one-on-one relations of subordination to the Buddha, the sort of dyadic relation a worshipper might hope to form for himself. The altar is a difficult document to read; but the presence of at least two images of Kuan-yin, goddess of mercy, and the frequent association of the Buddha himself with free grace and goodwill, suggest an emphasis rather different from the disciplinary tone of the Taoists' public proclamations. Faure has shown elsewhere that professional Taoists may become quite defensive about the emphasis that laymen give to Kuan-yin, for one.[70] But what is certain is that townspeople—indeed, the very initiators of the Offering itself—here made a religious artifact whose meaning is utterly independent of the Taoist rites in which they involved themselves at the same time, and which, like the villagers' half of the rites at Shatin and Fan Ling, was the setting for direct appeal to divinity and direct receipt of benefits by worshippers. In effect, they created on the spot, in a place where there were strictly speaking no local gods, a miniature parallel to the local gods' axis in the New Territories Offering. Is an axis of direct lay worship something that simply *must* be present whenever laymen and Taoists come together in ritual?

Hsu's work on West Town, particularly when read with the New Territories evidence fresh in one's mind, suggests that one should examine Taiwan practice anew. For there too a great deal happens at an Offering that is not directly connected to the in-temple Taoist ritual. That in Taiwan this ritual occupies the physical and symbolic center of the celebration and admits leading laymen should not, if West Town is any guide, discourage us from looking at all the other lay activities, entertainments, and ritual acts that take place at the same time, on the periphery as it were, and from asking what model

Special altar at West Town. From *Exorcising the Trouble Makers: Magic, Science, and Culture*, by Francis L. K. Hsu. Copyright 1983 by Francis L. K. Hsu. Reproduced with permission of Greenwood Publishing Group, Inc., Westport, Connecticut.

is being acted out, what hierarchies built or unbuilt in these. Yet to discourage this is the effect that the systematic, unified, and focused character of the central rite has had on inquiry in Taiwan. We may draw on Lagerwey here again: "a Taoist ritual is not only what goes on inside the temple, it is also what goes on outside.... Outside the temple there is theater, often two or three competing companies.... There are processions, of youth squadrons..., of neighboring communities who have brought their gods..., of the community itself carrying its gods on an inspection tour." Lagerwey chooses not to concentrate on any of this: "But all this excitement we will have to ignore in order to concentrate on what is going on behind closed doors, in the magic mountain of the Tao."[71] For a scholar of Taoism itself this is a reasonable choice, but the scholarly community as a whole has lost something by its omission. We have already seen how one of the outside elements Lagerwey notes, the opera, and the siting and orientation of its stage, may speak of the relative place of local gods and Taoist gods in the celebration. Serious analysis of the out-of-temple activities might make it possible to show that the Taiwan Offering is not as different from the New Territories Offering as a concentration on the within-temple ritual can make it seem. Perhaps even in Taiwan, the hierarchy and subordination that the Taoist officiants achieve there, and the redirection of lay worshippers' focus at least partly toward their own celestial bureaucracy, do not reach much beyond the temple itself, or beyond the circle of community leaders who fund the temple ritual.

A few investigators have attempted such analysis. Especially interesting is Donald Sutton's study of the god processions that take place both at Offerings and at other celebrations for gods in Taiwan. On their face these processions, which escort specific gods of local shrines from the troupes' own communities, must surely express a different view of gods and their relation to localities and individuals than professional Taoists take when they perform the Offering. Sutton shows that in contrast to the Taoist liturgy, which aims at the harmony of the entire cosmos and downgrades local gods, processions act out notions of locality, often exclusive and competitive. He argues that at the same time the processions, too, seek unity with a larger cosmic order; but his material makes clear that this cosmic order is not conceived of bureaucratically. If the drama of *Water Margin* heroes that procession troupes act out is, as Sutton suggests, concerned with a larger order, then to any audience that knows the story it is an order constituted by personal relations, founded on heroic individual choice, and preserved by the eminently dyadic and personal virtue of loyalty. (That the story is concerned with a larger order is very plausible, since the participants, often numbering only 36, nonetheless represent at once the 108 human heroes of the story and the 36 earthly and 72 heavenly star spirits in the universe.) But I believe that some of the dramas Sutton observes also offer subtle commentary on the notion of mediation, central to Taoist practice. Sutton argues persuasively that the paired god-general figures Fan and Xie and the infernal generals, main characters of the "tragic" procession dramas, are *mediating* figures, because as purgatorial bailiffs they are go-betweens from gods to men. These are, by the way, the only figures in all the dramas who embody a bureaucratic model of the divine, and they are, as in my survey of Hung Mai stories in Chapter 7, gods of purgatory. For the moment, however, let us consider them merely as mediating figures and note that they are mediators associated with danger, violence, and death. It is striking that mediators appear in some of Sutton's comedies as well. One deals with a pretty young woman accosted by the boatman she is relying on to get across a river. Not only is a boatman a literal go-between, someone who brings one from one place to another, but the word for "ford" or "cross" in the title of this performance (*tu*) is interchangeable with the word for the "salvation" (*tu*) the Taoists obtain for wandering souls and others. For a boatman to symbolize a Taoist would not be far-fetched. The "Interfering Maid" drama shows a family victimized by a reckless matchmaker—another go-between. "Simple Orchid Gets Married" shows a bride wandering aimlessly behind her matchmaker, who obviously has not really found her a match—again advice to families that they ought either to do without or exert proper control over go-betweens, who may claim to make a connection they cannot make. Thus, while at the center of the Taiwan Offering hired clergy act as mediators in a rite founded on bureaucratic models, at its edges local amateurs show only dangerous and hellish figures as divine bureaucrats and hold mediators up as figures of danger or of fun. Is this significant? Do the dramas comment not only on the morality of daily life, as Sutton suggests, but also on the rite going on inside and the hired mediators performing it?[72] Even if the message were simply "Rely on your own efforts in making important connections," this would undermine the message of the Taoists.

Sutton has also studied the spirit mediums who perform in god processions. He shows that the medium is a representative of local community from the very beginning of his career. His difficult initiation is a process closely guarded by the community as a whole, and his successful achievement of full status an occasion for celebration and personal congratulation by community members. The god who possesses the medium has chosen him individually from among the villagers, and in his performances of possession and self-mortification during Offering processions, the medium *becomes* the god, in direct contact with his community: "In its full form this mortification ritual uses a symbolism which patently identifies community, territory, and god through the medium's person. Advancing at the head of the sumptuously decorated god's sedan or, more rarely, sitting on top of it, he manifests the community's pride in its native place and the awesomeness of its protecting god."[73] Again the difference of concern between this lay rite and the rites of the

Taoists, which pay next to no attention to specific communities and place the local god at the bottom of the pantheon or outside it, is clear and profound.

"FRAMEWORKS" AND THE MEANING OF THE OFFERING

Kenneth Dean, again, has made one of the most sophisticated attempts to reconcile the differences in meaning between what lay worshippers do and what Taoists do at an Offering or in other rites. (Dean's work deals not with Taiwan but with contemporary Fujian province, the ancestral home of much of Taiwan's population, its rituals clearly in important ways allied with their Taiwan equivalents.) Dean recognizes, even celebrates the differences—"These different points of view result in a theological identity that becomes highly contradictory"—but treats contrasting elements in the ritual as "structured" by the Taoist liturgy and sees differences as encompassed by a uniquely ecumenical Taoist mind-set, which "spontaneously recognizes in all these different aspects so many facets of its pantheistic worldview."[74]

> Should one interpret Taoist ritual as a symbolic affirmation of local authority, appealing to the cosmic spiritual hierarchy that encompassed the imperial order? In that case, Taoism could be seen to serve the imperial metaphor. . . . Or one can see to a deeper level, at which Taoism refuses to be drawn into either the bureaucratic metaphor erected by the despotic signifier, or the local codes of territoriality and blood ties. Perhaps Taoism served to scramble the codes, creating floating signifiers that distinct groups in Chinese society could fix upon to fashion their own interpretations of the significance of their own participation in the ritual festival.[75]

There are a number of problems here. First, I have suggested that ecumenism is a practical effect, not an animating cause; that it reflects the open, largely uncoerced, and competitive religious field Taoists and other professionals found themselves in historically, where no state enforced its orthodoxy or authority upon communities. Second, Taoist liturgy—the in-temple rite that is entirely the Taoists' own—precisely and explicitly *denies* local authority, whether of men or of local gods, in favor of upward-pointing and highly centralized cosmic unity. That local elites and others use the celebration and even take part in the Taoist rite itself to affirm or assert local authority, or their own, should not confuse us about the Taoists, who know that their own rite is effective in both affirming and establishing *real* authority, and who therefore, when circumstances force coexistence on them, can treat local assertions as ignorant, deluded, and thus irrelevant. Third, it seems to me simply wrong to suggest that at any level Taoism "refuses to be drawn into . . . the bureaucratic metaphor," when both now and in the past Taoists have employed the metaphor with greater consistency and in finer detail than any other Chinese religious actors.[76] That they can treat this in turn as mere metaphoric dress, or shift to speak of more abstract forms of authority at a higher level (as we shall see further on in Kristofer Schipper's Twelve Kings rite), does not change the fact that it is very thoroughly *their* metaphoric dress. Finally, "signifiers" in rites for gods, whether floating or not, were clearly "created" by many participants besides Taoists. The signifiers the Taoists created in their own liturgy, far from being "fixed upon" as the object of multiple lay interpretations, were according to all testimony either ignored or "not understood" by laymen; and free or multiple interpretation of ritual signifiers was something that did not need the permission of Taoist liturgy or worldviews to proceed. Unless we simply redefine everything that went on at an Offering as Taoist, "codes" were "scrambled," not by *Taoist* liturgy, which on the contrary offered an exceptionally consistent coding of authority in the universe, but by the coexistence and confrontation of multiple codes and indeed multiple liturgies at the same celebration.

As to Dean's notion of the "Taoist liturgical framework," I have suggested but not explained my unease; it is worth exploring here. Dean suggests that Taoist liturgy "structures" in three different ways: "At the most obvious level, the timing of [the] different aspects of the festival is determined by the timing of the Taoist ritual. At a deeper level, the ritual organizes distinct groups along parallel lines. Finally, at the level of the cultural construction of reality, the liturgical framework generates a complex process model of spiritual power in a multifaceted interaction with local systems of power."[77] The phrase "process model of spiritual power" does not recur when Dean elaborates this three-part formulation, but the promissory note it writes appears to be cashed by the discussion of contradiction and signifiers I have just quoted. As to his first two points, timing and the organizing of groups along parallel lines, questions arise again.

> Prior to the afternoon and evening performances of the regional repertoire, short ritual plays are performed. These performances are timed to coincide with certain Taoist rites. Ch'u Kunliang . . . has charted the synchronous correspondences between ritual presentations by a *Beiguan* troupe and a Taoist ritual sequence during a three-day [Offering] in northern Taiwan. Three out of six ritual presentations were obligatory performances at the beginning and end of ordinary theatrical shows. The other three were linked to rituals going on inside the temple. The first took place simultaneously with the opening rituals on the first night. The second took place just prior to the Presentation of the Memorial. The third was the exorcistic dance of Zhong Kui, itself modeled on the Taoist Sealing of the Altar, which was performed on the evening of the last day during the reopening of the doors of the temple.[78]

First, the synchrony of drama and Taoist rite here is not overwhelming. Of six ritual plays, only three are "timed to coincide" with what Taoists are doing; and note that the "ordinary theatrical shows" for which the other three are obligatory, and which apparently also lack synchrony with the Taoists' rite, are performed just as surely as the others for the gods' entertainment and honor and so are very much a part of the lay population's own ritual. But second, it is not clear why any mutual dependence means it is the Taoist rites that "provide the framework." Why not say the lay rites—the dramas—are "providing the framework" for the Taoist? Or much better, why not say that *two* frameworks have been built so as to correspond at a few strategic moments, and ask who built them? Why not explore how the correspondence was negotiated—as it must have been—and who negotiated it? There is nothing automatic about this relation of drama to rites, since at one of Tanaka's Offerings the platform for the Taoists became the stage for the dramas only after the Taoists were done, making synchrony impossible. On the notion of two frameworks I say more below. As to how the ritual "organizes distinct groups in parallel ways," Dean points out that "priests, the community representatives, and the entire community follow parallel prohibitions during the course of the ritual." But of course such prohibitions are common to almost all Chinese dealings with gods, whether Taoists are present or not, so they can hardly be part of a Taoist "framework." Faure has shown that there may even be disagreement between local worshippers and Taoists over what prohibitions are appropriate, and that the villagers' view may win out.[79] Dean next points out that "[m]ost groups are marked by special clothing; the community representatives make a brave showing in traditional Qing scholar robes while the Taoist priests are decked in embroidered vestments . . . performing arts and militia troupes dress up for the procession of the gods." But all these groups wear *different* clothing. It is "parallel" only in that it is all "special," which tells us only what we already knew, that a celebration is happening and various sorts of people are all celebrating. Calling *different* kinds of special clothing *parallel* is a brilliant way of making difference into likeness. There is no evidence that the Taoist liturgy in the temple somehow structures the choice of clothing by the drama troupes in the god processions, or even that villagers dress up because the Taoists dress up. Dean moves on to point out that the community representatives in the temple follow the Taoists' lead in their movements. But that the *in-temple* rite is structured by Taoist liturgy we already know—in fact it *is* Taoist liturgy—while Dean's point, and what he needs to show, is that other parts of the celebration are similarly structured. Finally, Dean turns to the performances of the ritual master (*fa-shih*) (recall Chapter 2) outside the temple:

> At various points in the ritual, outside the temple, in traditional times and when possible nowadays, the Ritual Master leads spirit mediums in recitations of chants detailing the hagiographies of the local gods. Manuscripts of these chants are often written in vernacular Chinese. Occasionally the medium will go into a trance and enter into the temple. This usually occurs at some point in the ritual that calls for dramatic emphasis. The rites performed by these groups are complementary to the rituals performed by Taoist priests.[80]

On the "complementarity" of *fa-shih* rites to Taoist priests' rites, Dean cites Schipper's 1985 article, in which Schipper discusses at length the differences between the two—including the distinctly personal relation the *fa-shih* has with the local god or gods of the temple[81]—but then notes a number of important similarities and suggests the two traditions have common origins.[82] But for his purposes here, Dean needs again to show more than similarity-within-difference, let alone mere common historical roots: he needs to show that the in-temple liturgy somehow structures or determines what the ritual master is doing outside. Here he falls back on timing again, but what he is able to say, that the incursion into the temple "usually occurs at some point in the ritual that calls for dramatic emphasis," implies that sometimes it does not; it is also rather vague (are there not a great many points in the Offering liturgy that might call for dramatic emphasis?) and in no way touches on what the *fa-shih* and mediums are doing when they are *not* rushing into the temple. And once again synchrony cannot by itself tell us which side is doing the "structuring" or whether instead a cooperative interaction or even antagonistic negotiation between the two sides has picked out these moments.

In sum, Dean's evidence cannot do the job he wants it to do. That in Taiwan there are points of contact or coordination (or conceivably of competition, confrontation, and mutual response, which could also generate synchrony) between in-temple and out-of-temple rites is not in doubt. That these mean the Taoist liturgy is "structuring" or "providing the framework" for the rest does not follow. Dean's approach implicitly assumes that variety can never feed back upon the meaning of the encompassing framework and thus encourages him to report variety but not to analyze it. Early on he lists six separate ritual traditions of Fujian, differing in some cases in whether Taoists or Buddhists or "lay liturgical groups" perform particular rituals,[83] whether elaborate Offerings are present at all, or whether a national figure or a local deity is credited with the tradition's founding.[84] The list is tantalizing because these are just the sorts of things one might expect to affect (or respond to) the relation between clerical and lay roles and views in the rite, but Dean does not attempt to analyze the differences and instead moves four pages later to describe a sort of average of the fifteen Offerings he has observed.[85] Yet his own accounts of specific rituals later in the book show differences that tantalize again. In his chapter on the Patriarch of the Clear Stream, a local deity of Penglai township, Dean includes a photograph that shows the image of the Patriarch and other local deities in place in the Patriarch's shrine at the time of a Taoist rite. The paintings of Taoist deities hang at the back of the hall, exactly where one would expect them from Lagerwey's account. But the Patriarch and the other local gods also still stand on an altar at the back of the temple, thus in the position of co-recipient, not in the position of audience and supplicant they hold in Lagerwey's version. In other words, although the Taoist gods have been installed in the position of highest honor, the local gods have not undergone the reversal of role and stripping of status that we see in Taiwan. Dean does not tell us why, and his notion of a single Taoist framework that structures local rites, though it allows for such variation, cannot explain it.[86]

Stephan Feuchtwang, in his study of the 1967 northern Taiwan ritual, provides material that allows a different approach to the notion of "framework." He documents another framework, that of the Offering's organizing committee, comprising wealthy and influential lay householders, who in this capacity hire the Taoists. It is the instructions in this document that, according to Feuchtwang, "order the community for the duration of the [Offering]." There is not room here to reproduce the very interesting list of matters in the document or Feuchtwang's discussion, but his closing summary covers what is important.

> These documents indicate the parts of [an Offering] which are important for those outside the inner circle [by which Feuchtwang means the performers of the in-temple rite]: the processions bringing in the figures from surrounding temples, the outside altars, the lantern masts, the procession to the waterside and the lanterns' release, the *dou* lamps and the commemorative memorial of the community and its representatives—patrons of the [Offering], the offerings and rites performed at the outside altar to Heaven, the furnishings of this and the altars in the temple, the theatre and the performances, the weights of the sacred offering pigs, and most involving of all, the rite of general salvation and the propitiation of hungry ghosts on the third day when hundreds of meters of tables were laden with offerings brought out from every household and not supplied by the [Offering] fund. . . . They are furthest out in terms of a lack of interest in the ordering liturgy and in being entirely left to community representatives.[87]

If all of these matters—virtually the whole content of the out-of-temple rites, or at least their structured and scheduled components—are under the control and direction of the lay committee that sponsors, funds, and organizes the Offering, and if that committee also hires the Taoists who will govern the in-temple rite, then surely we should speak of *two* "frameworks" that *in coming together* structure the Offering: the framework of the Taoist liturgy and the framework of the lay organizers' plan.[88] Faure has also closely examined the process by which a rite is organized, and shows that the lay organizers' framework is the more encompassing, at least temporally. In the example he observed in Lam Tsuen in 1981, offered to the local instantiation of Tin Hau or the Empress of Heaven (*T'ien-hou* again), the organizing committee constituted itself eleven months before the ceremony was to be held and very soon chose the "leaders of worship" (the community representatives who would serve in the Taoists' rite), or rather allowed them to be chosen by the goddess herself through divination blocks.[89] Thus the first ritual act of the Offering process was a direct interaction with the local god by members of the community, under the lay organizers' supervision, with not a Taoist to be seen. The committee then hired both the Taoists and an opera troupe, and on the appointed days, the Taoists performed their rites to their gods and the opera troupe offered their performances to the local goddess. The committee then concluded the process, a month after all rites were completed and the Taoists dismissed, by meeting again "to celebrate" and to settle accounts.[90] Here is a "framework," with clear bounds and a beginning, middle, and end; but it begins long before the Taoists are on the scene and ends well after they are gone. And this framework provides abundant opportunities for lay worshippers to honor their goddess directly, in both scheduled and unscheduled ways:

> Over the next few days, villagers from all over the valley came to burn incense to the gods. In Lam Tsuen, a rota was worked out whereby the villages of each village group would be responsible for keeping watch one day, and during that day, the unicorns [village god processions] from those villages would come down to the [Offering] site to pay their respects. These unicorn dances were part of the ordinary martial arts training of the young men of the villages and were performed at most important village festivals. The practice for the [Offering] was for the unicorn to leave the village in the morning, to worship first at the ancestral hall, to be driven by car to the ta-tsiu site, to dance its way to the Empress of Heaven Temple to pay its respects, and then to pay respects to the other gods.[91]

If we think of an Offering as always involving at least these two structuring frameworks, which contrast in important ways, yet in each instance must be negotiated and find a way of relating to one another, then we may be able to see Taiwan Offerings and New Territories Offerings through a single lens. The biaxial rite that Faure, Tanaka, and Hsu have found displays the two frameworks as particularly independent—I have suggested the metaphor of acting "at right angles" to each other. In the Taiwan and apparently the Fujian version, however, the axes the two frameworks form are rotated until, at their intersection within the temple, they lie very close together and—again *within* the temple—the Taoist axis assumes dominance. Outside the temple the distinctness and power of the lay organizers' framework is still clear. And the crucial point is this: whatever the relation of the two, the lay framework is in each case the one that finds a place for local gods as independent recipients of sacrifice and for direct individual contact between humans and gods.

Frameworks may sometimes be more than two. Among specialists in Taoism Kristofer Schipper has given the greatest attention to the differences between lay and Taoist viewpoints in rites for local gods. "Taoist ritual in no way expresses concern with local cults. The pantheon is abstract, the prayers impersonal. . . . Most of the participants [in the out-of-temple ceremonies] are completely taken up with these celebrations [processions, dances, etc.]

and are quite unconcerned by the Taoist rituals going on simultaneously."[92] But Schipper has analyzed one rite in which the differences of view are especially striking because the organizing committee seems to have adopted a typically Taoist position, the Taoists yet another, and laymen outside the committee perhaps a third. This is the Offering of the Kings (*wang-chiao*) held for the twelve Royal Lords (*wang-yeh*) every three years at Hsi-kang on Taiwan's southern coast.

Schipper shows that for the committee of wealthy local elders (whom he calls "chiefs") who organize the Offering of the Kings, the twelve are "emissaries from heaven, commissioned by the first among gods, the Emperor of Heaven and ruler of the universe, the Jade August, in person. 'Divine Inspectors Commissioned by Heaven' (*Yü-ch'ih tai-t'ien hsun-hsiu*):[93] thus the reverential title the chiefs give the Kings." Their story is an extraordinary one: they were twelve holders of the highest imperial degree (*chin-shih*), whom one day an emperor commanded to play music in the palace cellars. Then he called the Heavenly Master, chief of all Taoist priests, and (apparently in an antic mood) demanded to know why there was such an unholy racket when the Heavenly Master was responsible for keeping demons away. The Heavenly Master wrote and burnt a talisman; the noise ceased at once; and when the Heavenly Master left, the emperor found the twelve degree holders were all dead. Their wronged souls appealed to a higher authority, the Jade August (or Jade Emperor), who named them Divine Inspectors in recompense and placed the entire region around Hsi-kang under their permanent jurisdiction.

> This jurisdiction is exercised in their name by the chiefs, who divide up a certain number of directing functions. The most prestigious of these is that of officer of the Tablets of Commandment, that is to say agent for the power of the Kings, [which] corresponds to that of a magistrate charged with security and justice. It is given to that chief who makes the largest contribution to the celebration.... [H]e holds a court of justice at which all the cases of the region may be arbitrated.... The court of justice, the tours of inspection, the audiences before the Kings, all are the object of an imposing ceremony, which the chiefs know perfectly through having studied expressly and learned by heart. One should note that the text of this ceremony is not in their local language (Hokkien), nor in the classical language of the Taoists, but in Mandarin, the official language of central government functionaries.[94]

For the Taoists whom the chiefs hire, on the other hand,

> the sacrifice of the Kings is a service of propitiation: in brief, a ritual of exorcism. For the Kings are gods who sow epidemics and particularly the plague. In the Taoist pantheon ... the Royal Lords are negative cosmic energies, breaths of death, tied to the cycle of time.... Three times a day the masters briefly leave their sacred space to appear in the main hall of the temple, where the Kings

have their residence. They are now supposed to render homage to the Lords in the chiefs' presence. But this homage is in form only. In reality, the ritual formulas—always in classical Chinese—do not concern the Kings, or hardly, but the pantheon in its entirety.[95]

Among themselves the Taoists express their utter alienation from their service to the kings with a pun: instead of *ken tiao*, "audience," they call it by the similar words *ken ciao*, "submitting to humiliation." Finally, for ordinary participants in the celebration, Royal Lords are low-level gods whom they worship and around whom they form local cults in a regular way, personal benefactors but dangerous ones, often originating as bandits killed at their trade. If, for the chiefs, the twelve Royal Lords leave in boats at the end of the celebration in keeping with their role as patrolling inspectors for Heaven, for other locals, Royal Lords, whether twelve or thirty-six or three hundred sixty, are regularly and routinely present to the community. We may perhaps call this a third ordinary lay "framework." There is some uncertainty here, because Schipper leaves unclear which, if any, aspects of this ritual are shaped by the broader lay view, and in keeping with Dean's original usage it seems to me most useful to reserve the notion of "framework" for views or plans that actually condition or shape a ritual. But if god processions or other typical community manifestations act out this view at this rite as at others, there is a third framework at work.

The framework of the chiefs, in the meantime, is unusual in a number of ways. They have elaborated a bureaucratic view of the Royal Lords that one might ordinarily expect from a Taoist, and they have taken for themselves the role of bureaucratic agent and divine adjudicator on earth that the Taoist also usually assumes. Yet they preserve a typically lay view in focusing the rite on specific gods with a connection to their region, and in conceiving the connection as permanent. They are making an incursion upon what is usually Taoist territory, but on behalf of lay authority. In the extraordinary story of the twelve Royal Lords' origin, degree holders—the ideal type of the local gentleman sent up by his community to serve the ruler and nation—fall victim to the combined capriciousness of the Taoist par excellence and central political authority, but win vindication from a divine ruler more reliable than his earthly counterpart. The use of the degree holder as a symbol of locally rooted high status reflects the late imperial origins of the story,[96] but of course modern locals of wealth and ambition may easily assimilate themselves to this type. Here the bureaucratic model, of all things, is used in modified form to exalt local lay authority as against both real state *and* Taoist. The Taoist, in turn, with the ground of divine bureaucracy wrested away from him in the service of gods of questionable moral standing, retreats skyward into a more purely abstract view of gods always available in his tradition. The move shows how essential the very separateness of their own framework may be to the self-understanding of the Taoists. But Schipper's material also shows something of a reversal of the Taiwan pattern we have seen so far. There we saw community representatives and their gods subordinated in a temple ritual dominated and shaped by Taoist views; here we see Taoists "submitting to humiliation" in a ritual known, run, and dominated by laymen. The case is further evidence that there are outcomes other than the standard Taiwan version, but it shows too that the differences of role that participants bring to the Offering express real differences of view, to which they may hold with some determination. Schipper insists upon the importance of these differences, noting that "the ritual is for [the Taoists] something that they are obliged to live, but not necessarily to think" and that "the position of the chiefs and that of the Taoist masters . . . were irreconcilable." They signal their extreme discomfort with the ritual but also assert their own view of the situation with their pun on "holding audience" and "submitting to humiliation." With such talk and through their own rites, separate from the chiefs' and kept secret in content and meaning, they distance themselves from the chiefs' ritual and deny the chiefs' authority to define it.

But of course two can play at distancing and denial. To see this, we may return to Hsu's work to consider the answers he received to direct questions about the Offering's meaning. Most notably, *all professional Taoists and only professional Taoists* gave a bureaucratic-mediative interpretation: the plague god was punishing the people on the orders of his superiors, sending out his own subordinate spirits in turn to do the infecting; to end the plague one must appeal to the superiors, who would then order the plague god to end the plague; "the petition papers burned during the [Offering] meetings were like petitions to our officials in this world"; and so on.[97] From the lay managers and participants, however, Hsu received an extraordinarily wide variety of answers. Some had nothing to do with gods—it should be remembered, again, that the town had few deity-worshipping traditions of its own. Some answers simply invoked custom; some focused on the charitable character of participating in the ritual for the community's benefit; but none suggested any notion of celestial officialdom or of mediation by one god with others. Most interesting among Hsu's list of common answers, however, is this: "What the priests did in these [Offering] meetings were their professional secrets. They were only paid to do a job."[98]

We have already seen claims that laypeople are ignorant or uncomprehending before the rituals of the Taoists. Hsu's "professional secrets" answers, however, suggest ignorance of a special kind. It would be good to have the original texts of the answers his informants gave and to know the phrases Hsu is translating as "professional secrets" and "do a job." But I would argue that when a Chinese man of some standing in a community, certainly in imperial times but even in this century, says that other people possess "professional secrets" and are "paid to do a job," he is not simply pleading ignorance. Rather, he is classifying the people he refers to as specialists, artisans, or hired men: as people whose knowledge is of a kind not worth other people's bothering about, especially not worth the time of a leading man of the community. Because one does not wish to know about such things, one hires others to take care of them; and because one hires others to take care of such things, one does not wish to know about them. The Taoists' knowledge, that is, looks two different ways, depending on who is looking. Taoists wear their knowledge and its secrecy as a badge of rank, and their texts sometimes liken it to the knowledge that a high official needs to govern men. But their customers can always make an equally culturally characteristic move: to treat some knowledge as the knowledge of hirelings, which it is proper and dignifying not to possess. To speak of a form of knowledge in this way is to treat its possessor as one's subordinate—thus, in this case, to reverse the subordination symbolized by the kneeling and kowtowing in the rite itself. Knowing, that is, is in China not always a good thing, and not knowing is not always shameful: everything turns on the kind of knowledge and on the sort of person who would normally have it.[99] What is going on here, perhaps, is a sort of mutually co-opting agreement by the Taoist and his customer: agreement that the Taoist knows and will continue to know what the customer does not know and will continue not to know. But it is essential for the agreement that they do *not* agree on the meaning of not knowing; for by his interpretation of this each asserts his superiority to the other. To confuse the customer's side of this bargain with mere "lack of understanding" is, I think, a mistake, and seriously underestimates the opportunities that all lay Chinese had, especially the literate, to learn in a general way what the significance of Taoist rites was to the Taoists themselves. (Consider the public disciplinary notices the Taoists issued on this occasion.) The Taoists' customers, perhaps, were not ignorant: they ignored. Thus they did for themselves what the humiliated Taoists do in Schipper's Twelve Kings case.

A colleague has suggested that what I am describing is a sort of "zero degree of resistance," in which power otherwise irresistible is resisted by being redescribed or ignored, and finds this of interest for students of the ways, say, peasants or intellectuals may have oriented themselves to the power of both imperial and more recent Chinese states.[100] I am far from hostile to drawing such connections. But in talking of "resistance" one must exercise a certain care. It is easy when talking of power and resistance to imagine that one knows where the power is, that it is all in one place, and that resistance must be on the other side. But I have been considering cases in which different participants bring different sorts of power to the field, and where "resistance" is mutual. It is worth elaborating this point.

A gentleman patron of the Hua-kai Immortals in the Southern Sung who described and dreamed his own relations with the Immortals in direct and personal rather than mediated and bureaucratic terms may indeed have been engaging in symbolic resistance of the bureaucratic state and its attempts to make governmental relations supreme among political and social relations. Such redescriptions of ideal power may have held great appeal for men living in a world where significant bureaucratic careers had grown difficult to achieve. This forms a large part of my argument in Chapter 5 on the rise of the Hua-kai cult in the Southern Sung. But at the same time this gentleman often exercised power that was quite real in his own locality—all the more since assertions of state power in the localities were less vigorous than they had been earlier in the Sung—and need not be at a disadvantage in all confrontations with state representatives in that arena. Indeed, his accounts of how the Hua-kai Immortals acted provided a positive model of a sort of power—inherent, not delegated; personal, not official; direct, not mediated; informal, not law-governed—that he could see as much like his own. When gentlemen and the state acting at the local level upheld different images of the divine, who was resisting whose power? The question is even more acute when we consider relations between gentleman and professional Taoist. Without a centralized clerical hierarchy or a religiously committed state backing him up, the Taoist practitioner often really stood in the relation of mere hireling to employer with the powerful local gentleman who paid him to perform an Offering. In this setting, a gentleman's claim that the Taoist was "merely hired to do a job" and his disregard of the Taoist's own "knowledge" of what the job meant looks less like resistance of Taoist power than like the power to state facts. And one can read the Taoist's ritual assertion of celestial bureaucracy as a claim to a higher, formal, merit-based power that could overmatch or rise above the merely personal power of the man who was, in the cold hard worldly world, his boss. Yet we have also seen in the modern evidence that Taoists are *necessary* to the Offering, and this certainly looks true in the Sung as well. Their necessity supplies them with power of their own, power that perhaps expresses itself most clearly in the Taiwan pattern, and that might need to be denied in turn by being redescribed or ignored. I am arguing, from the evidence of both the Taiwan and New Territories Offering, that the lay bearers of a model of direct human-divine relations and the clerical bearers of a model of bureaucratic divinity are each "resisting" the other's power. The ways in which the two models end up coexisting in a single ritual grow precisely out of the different working out of this mutual resistance in different settings.

If indeed the Offering is a recurrent interaction of two different and often mutually resistant frameworks, it is interesting to ask how this interaction first came into being. From evidence brought forward by Kristofer Schipper and Florian Reiter, the crucial historical moment seems again to lie in the T'ang-Sung transition, though whether already in the late T'ang or not until the Sung remains unclear. As early examples of Taoist rituals performed for local cults, Schipper points to the Retreat of the Yellow Register held in

T'ang to celebrate the birthday of Hsu Sun, immortal and patriarch of the Taoist sect called the Way of Filial Piety, and to the Ritual of Declaring Penitence to Heaven and Earth of the Pure Retreat of Ling-pao associated with the Taoist saint Wang Fa-chin and practiced, apparently in her honor, by ordinary people of Szechwan and neighboring regions in the late T'ang.[101] Reiter explores the worship, through Offerings and other Taoist rites, of the god called the Investigation Commissioner of the Nine Heavens (*chiu-t'ien shih-che*) in the middle T'ang and after.[102]

The evidence for a "local cult" is extremely weak in Reiter's case. In the material he presents, at the start the cult of the Investigation Commissioner was clearly an imperial effort in cooperation with court Taoists to counter Buddhist presence at the mountain while also providing a centrally sanctioned alternative to existing local god cults.[103] That is, the court and its Taoists are not instituting Taoist rites for local gods, but instituting new gods to replace them and performing Taoist rites for the new. On this point, the scripture reads: "The blood-eating spirits of the famous mountains, the holy mountains, and the marches are being treated as patrons deserving religious sacrifices. T'ai-shang [Lao-chün] holds them to be false. Having the might to do good, they use it to harm the common people. He dispatched the superior perfected ones to supervise and to be actually present at the rivers and mountains, and so there are perfected lords on the five mountains." This testimony comes from the earliest source Reiter adduces, a late T'ang work.[104] The vague evidence of local initiative in the founding comes from much later texts, in particular one written in 1154, precisely the period when one would expect authors to begin to be interested in demonstrating or implying local roots for any important religious activity in their region.[105] Even so, this text too has abundant evidence of top-down action, including imperial promotion of a T'ang-period Offering. Even assuming some local involvement, the god was still a new one promoted by court and clergy and imagined very much on professional Taoist models. The case is far from the evidence of Taoist rites for indigenous gods that one would like to find: instead, it is evidence of imperial and Taoist worship precisely of a *Taoist* god. It may be no less important for all that, as we shall see.

Schipper's evidence is closer to what we are looking for. His two deities are indeed in some sense local gods, who considerably predate the rituals that celebrate them. But what is striking, and what makes his cases at least partly parallel to Reiter's, is that these too are clearly from the beginning (Wang Fa-chin) or from early in the history of their cult (Hsu Sun) specifically *Taoist* deities, held as objects of cult by specific schools of Taoist practitioners and devotees. That is, we have here local figures adopted or identified by Taoist sects as founding figures of their own liturgical tradition, and then celebrated in specifically Taoist rites such as Retreats and Offerings. What we do not quite see, again, is a *non-Taoist* divinity, of local roots and constituency, honored by Taoists with their own rites. The fact is that in a modern (post-Sung) setting, this happens only if lay devotees of a god hire Taoists to honor him, since left to themselves Taoists do not honor non-Taoist gods, and indeed even when they are hired for the purpose, the literal meaning of their rites still *does not honor* them. In contrast, there need not have been two competing frameworks when Hsu Sun's own direct spiritual descendants in the T'ang honored him with an Offering.

But Reiter's and Schipper's materials, and to some extent Schipper's own argument, do suggest how a demand for Taoist rites for non-Taoist gods might have arisen. If in the T'ang we first see Taoist rites honoring individual gods in provincial settings, even if these are still specifically Taoist gods by origin or adoption, this sets the stage for worshippers of other gods—of "really" local gods—to notice the Taoist rites, to be impressed by them as ritual display, to see that such rites may be held in honor of a single god, and so to want similar rites for their own gods. In the Sung, the evidence for such rites becomes abundant. I have already argued that the T'ang-Sung commercialization of village life gave added life to the bureaucratic model for Taoists in the Sung. It is easy to imagine that it also, by creating new wealth and by accustoming villagers to look outside the village for the goods and services of daily life, created new demand among local gods' followers for professional ritemongers, a demand that Taoist professionals were able to fill. But the demand that produced the modern Offering was not for new religious ideas, not for a faith to which one could convert, not even for new gods—though all these demands existed too in various realms of Sung and post-Sung religious life—but for interesting, impressive, and prestigious rites with which to honor one's own gods, gods one was already worshipping in other ways. Taoist rites had a good deal that could make them interesting, impressive, and prestigious. Taoists were literate, wore strange and expensive clothes, performed mysterious movements and dances, spoke mysterious words; and their rites were, after all, acts of submission to gods, even if not the gods of local worshippers. The ceremonies for Hsu Sun or Wang Fa-chin or the Investigation Commissioner would have taught people this much.[106]

One can imagine, at the beginning, lay god-worshippers allowing Taoists to direct their movements and shape the celebration strictly around a ritual that was unfamiliar but that they wanted and had paid for. But with time, as Offerings became required for specific gods through individual or community vows, and then through imitation became standard rites for any god, the different purposes of the two sides would have found expression, producing the two frameworks that we find in a variety of relations at Offerings today. If inviting a Taoist in to perform his rites for one's own god was inviting in a religious worldview and a whole pantheon not one's own, accepting the invitation was in principle an even larger step for the Taoist himself, who was being asked to honor gods who in his eyes might be demons or worse.

But Taoists knew the efficacy of their own rites, and knew that these could work, could bring order and harmony to the universe of gods and men, even if their meaning was lost on those who gathered around. The work of the Offering did not depend on who believed. It is not a cynical view of ordinary people's use of Taoist rites to propose that it began from a demand for impressive rituals and not from religious conviction, because what we are trying to explain is precisely how a ritual comes to include two groups, one of whom *does not* attend to or believe in or even know just what the other group believes in. It is not a process of conversion we are trying to explain—villagers are in every important sense *not* Taoists—but the entry into cooperation of what are, as Faure has put it, virtually two different religions.

It is interesting to imagine a China in which this deal had never been struck. But we do not need to imagine it, for the Taoist-lay accommodation, it seems, did not occur everywhere, or always with the same consistency. Even within southeast China, Paul Katz has shown that Taoist priests played little or no role in the frequent festivals for the plague god Marshal Wen in Wen-chou and Hang-chou, being brought in to hold Offerings to him only in times of epidemic.[107] But David Johnson has explored for southeastern Shansi a kind of god-worshipping ritual possibly typical of a much larger area of northern China: the *sai*, or Sacrifice, in which Taoists played no part at all.[108] Ritual specialists operated there—the *yin-yang* masters who served as masters of ceremonies and the music households (*yueh hu*) who performed operas for the gods—but on Johnson's account, both seem to have been largely village-based, living among the lay populace and serving lay religious needs without a distinct ritual tradition or self-cultivating practice of their own. Most important—and perhaps this most clearly distinguishes them from Taoists and Buddhists—they did not have their own *gods*. When religious specialists were not using the bureaucratic model to elevate clerical gods above local gods, did it become more available and attractive to laypeople for their own religious purposes (as the lay chiefs of the Twelve Kings rite made it their own by dominating the Taoists they hired)? Or did it fade from the picture in favor of a personal model? One can imagine either outcome, but on Johnson's evidence, the answer seems to be: some of each, but perhaps more of the second. Scattered elements of the *sai* ritual process do provide at least some gods with certain characteristics of officials—an entourage of yamen runners, for example. Yet as a coherent *model,* bureaucracy seems hardly present. Gods do not appear in a clear hierarchy with respect to one another. The farewell prayer at the end of the ceremony suggests a simple scattering instead of a graded return to a neatly stepped hierarchy of governing seats: "Heavenly gods, return to Heaven / Earthly gods, return to Earth / All you holy gods, / Go back to your proper places."[109] The prayers offered to gods seem to address them directly, without the written or spoken apparatus of officialese: "We are here to invite Lord Earth God to come to the great *sai*."[110]

And the ritual does not assume the form of an audience at court but of a *party:* "the model for a great *sai* was the birthday banquet of a powerful person."[111] The other gods invited to a god's *sai* were his guests and he their host; in this respect, the *sai* is reminiscent not only of Sung Neo-Confucian guides to ancestor worship, as Johnson points out, but also of much more ancient ancestral rites, as represented in the *Book of Odes* and even in Shang oracle bones. As Johnson makes clear, there is much still to know about the *sai* and particularly about the precise scripts of liturgies and invocations that guided it, but at a first glance, in its intense and direct focus on the local god and in the central place it gives to operatic performance, it has something of the look of a New Territories Offering from which the Taoist axis has been removed, or into which it has never entered. Here, unlike in Taiwan or the New Territories, there may be only one religion at work: the religion of local god-worship.

We have come a good distance and can now return to the question I began with. We have seen enough to know that an Offering taken as a whole celebration need not enact the subordination of the local god to whom it is offered. Direct contact between worshipper and god finds expression in the parts of the Offering that lie outside the formal Taoist liturgy; it manifests itself secondarily even in the in-temple section of the Offering of Taiwan. It seems safe to assume that this was true in the Sung as well—that a two-framework analysis of the Offering can shed light on the sources' silence on the content of Offerings to the Three Immortals. But Hsu's evidence on what informants could tell him about their rite suggests even more; it suggests that even where an Offering takes a strongly hierarchical and subordinating form, the lay god-worshipping participant is not without recourse. For Hsu shows that Taoists and lay worshippers may reconstruct the meaning of their mutual relations and of the rituals they take part in just as surely by what they say or do not say about each other and about the rites as through physical layout or liturgical script. This may hold all the more for what they write, given the more public and formal character of writing—again regardless of how the ritual they write about was actually structured and performed. One way to give meaning to a rite was by shaping its performance, by renegotiating its form with or imposing it on the other participants. But another way was simply to read, or better still to write, the meaning of the ritual in a particular way. This may have been especially important where different participants brought interests to the ritual that were difficult to negotiate. I began with the miracle stories in *Verities of the Three Lords*, texts that present Offerings as gifts or barter currency between men and gods or as mere tokens of thanks or apology from one to the other, and that never explore what internally an Offering says or does. I have already complained that there is no other entry into what actually was happening in the rites the texts mention. We cannot discover, for example, whether these were Offerings on a

New Territories model, in which direct address of the local god happens at right angles to the rites of Taoists, or perhaps an even more "laicized" form in which, one might imagine, the Taoist rites are actually subordinated symbolically to the worship of the local god. But perhaps knowing this is irrelevant to understanding what the *Verities* stories have to say. When the authors of the tales in the *Verities* treated the Offering as a mere gift or token, as something defined by the external relations it entered into but without perceptible internal content, perhaps they did so because writing in this way (and talking and thinking and dreaming in this way) allowed them to assert that its meaning lay exactly and simply in what they used it for, and not in what somebody else might say or do in performing it: that the Offering belonged to them and to the Three Immortals, and not to the hireling Taoists, who merely knew how to do it.

THE BUREAUCRATIC AND THE PERSONAL IN MODERN CHINA: BEYOND THE OFFERING

In this book I have tried to show that we may understand Chinese ways of viewing the divine and its connection to the human by positing two "models" that compete, interact, sometimes combine or intertwine, in different contexts and to serve the purposes of different religious actors. In the notion of lay and clerical "frameworks," building on but diverging from the interpretation of Kenneth Dean, I have proposed a way to think of the interaction of the two models, the bureaucratic and the personal, in a single context, the ritual called an Offering. It should be clear, however, that the two models and the two frameworks are not the same things, not necessarily coextensive. Even leaving aside the possibility that more than two frameworks may shape a ritual—in the Twelve Royal Lords case, a Taoist framework, a lay organizers' or "chiefs'" framework, and perhaps an ordinary lay framework—the lay framework need not use only the personal model, and the Taoist framework need not embody only (or at all—again see the Hsi-kang case) the bureaucratic model. The notion is intended to encompass the possibility of such pure or extreme cases, to show, for example, how one can conceive of an Offering that serves deities imagined so unbureaucratically as the Three Immortals of Hua-kai. But frameworks may instead take the form of different *combinations*, different *proportions*, of the two models: a framework here is an overall plan or view of how a particular ritual should proceed, why, and for whom or what. Such a plan when conceived or when applied will allot opportunity for expression in the ritual to one or the other, or to both, of the two models of divinity. Clearly, lay frameworks are more likely to find room for the personal model, Taoist frameworks more likely to embody only the bureaucratic model. But Feuchtwang's detailed documentation of the lay organizers' framework for his 1967 Offering includes gods represented as bureaucratic, and the Twelve Royal Lords case involves lay organizers who adopt great portions of the bureaucratic model for themselves. Yet in each case, the framework the lay organizers provide remains sharply distinct from the framework offered by the Taoist liturgy.

One can, of course, explore the relative place of the two models in recent times through evidence other than the Offering; and the complexity of the relation between framework and models in these modern examples makes this worth doing. Setting my examination of Hung Mai's stories against the evidence of modern ethnography, it is tempting to think that in lay conceptions and practices the bureaucratic model occupied smaller ground, appeared in more tightly limited contexts, in the Sung than it does today. I strongly suspect that this is true, and that Taoist promotion of the bureaucratic model, precisely in such settings as Offerings for local gods, has succeeded over the centuries in "selling" it to the lay population (who have put it to uses of their own, to be sure) and making it a more important part of common Chinese conceptions than it was in the Sung. But the evidence for the two periods is so different that this reconstruction would be hard to demonstrate. And in any case, what modern ethnographic evidence has shown about the place of the bureaucratic model in recent or modern Chinese religion is not unambiguous. Let us review some of what the ethnographers tell us.

Anthropologists had, of course, noticed the correspondence of gods to bureaucrats before Arthur Wolf's seminal article. Bernard Gallin in 1966 reported that the villagers of Hsin Hsing

> consider the hierarchy of gods to be fashioned on the order of the imperial court of traditional China. They are thus, as described by one of the better educated older villagers, "what would be the equivalent of an emperor, ministers, marshals, and generals. In this hierarchy T'ien Kung is the emperor. Right under T'ien Kung are the three brother gods, San Chieh Kung: (1) T'ien Kuan, the god of heaven; (2) Ti Kuan, the god of earth; and (3) Shui Kuan, the god of water." In addition, the gods which reign in the underworld are regarded as high and powerful gods. After these is a whole series which inhabit local areas such as villages. . . . [These] function as intermediaries or "ambassadors" between ordinary people and higher gods, since mere mortals cannot take their prayers or wishes directly to the highest gods.[112]

One wonders what sort of education this educated man had had, who gave Gallin such a Taoist-sounding picture of gods; but there is no reason to doubt that other villagers too told him that gods were like officials. Still, one may notice that some of the relationships village people enter into with gods seem hard to account for in this bureaucratic-mediative vocabulary. There are certainly personal relations between gods and men:

GOD WORSHIP AND THE *CHIAO*   253

> For years [one man in the village] had been plagued by bad luck. He had no children and could not make an adequate living. One stormy night, walking through a wooded area, he was frightened by a flash of lightning, which showed him the form of a man in ancient costume high up in a tree. Fearing for his life, he claims that he immediately vowed to build a statue in the image of the vision and worship it as a god. In the twenty years since that day his fortunes have changed, and today he is a wealthy man with many children.[113]

Spirit mediums too, in Hsin Hsing as elsewhere, have specific personal ties to gods who have "chosen" them as their mediums.[114] But it is striking also that since gods have no temples (the village is too small and poor), they reside in private homes instead, some of them in rotation from household to household over the years, some of them permanently in the houses of families who have bought god images.[115] One wonders how the families that house these gods conceive of them and of their own relations with them: are these really simply celestial officers quartered with the people? Or are they honored guests? In the case of households caring for a god temporarily, the god is said to choose the household at his birthday celebration each year, and sometimes to laugh at candidate families during the divination. Is this a bureaucratic process? Does the choice establish a tighter connection of the god to this family than to others? Gallin does not tell us what language the villagers use for these special relationships, or whether they always speak the same way as when they are talking of gods in the abstract and collectively.

David Jordan, in his study of the village of Bao-an, tells us more about household-god relationships. On the general picture, he echoes Gallin: "The gods are conceived as occupying positions in a celestial government very similar, at least in broad outlines, to human governments. The traditional view, and the one most often expressed by Chinese, is that the hierarchy is a sort of mirror of the Chinese governmental structure of imperial days. . . . Today, some Taiwanese explain it, and perhaps conceptualize it, as resembling the Republican government, ruled over by a president, vice-president, various underlings and directors, and divided into divers ministries and commissions."[116] Jordan goes on to note, however, that the specific hierarchy is notably hard to pin down, and his phrase "perhaps conceptualize it" is a clue that his villagers have other ways of treating gods:

> One official of the Nankeunshen shrine at Peimen, one of the major shrine centers in Tainan county, suggested to me that one should not worship too broadly, but rather concentrate one's adoration on one or a few divinities. The rationale was simple: if you worship a great host of gods, he explained, then when you bring one of them a problem he will just say: "you often worship old So-and-So; why not bring this problem to him instead of bothering me with it?" But if you worship only one or a few gods, it is harder for them to shift the responsibility for helping you to their co-divinities, and it is easier for you to get action.[117]

The way one god is here imagined speaking of another god—as "old So-and-So," much as one village elder might talk of another—does not seem very bureaucratic. Bureaucrats do pass the buck, perhaps obsessively. It is not bureaucratic buck-passing we see here, though, but a man's refusal to help somebody without a strong and specific tie, of the kind that would be formed by regular devotion and worship. The shrine officer is recommending forming an individual and personal relation with a god. Of course, one can form a regular personal relation with a bureaucrat too, as through bribery: but the relation bribery forms is not itself a *bureaucratic* relation; it lies outside bureaucratic norms and procedures, founded in another model. The shrine officer in any case is not seeing regular worship of a single god as anything like bribery; he is talking about finding a patron. And as Jordan shows, patron-client relations are the normal way families who hold and worship god-images in their homes construct their tie to the god.

> It is not unnatural in such a system that certain people, and certain families, should find that they have good success in appealing to a certain god, and that they should develop with him a standing relation of patronage. . . . The possession of a joss marks a special relationship of reciprocity with the god it represents, entailing both a responsibility on the part of the god for the general welfare of the family that has acquired and maintains the statue, and a responsibility on the part of that family to worship the statue at regular intervals. . . . God-worshipping groups seem to be recruited on a number of different principles and to be used for a wide variety of kinds of solidarity, but always in the basic religious context of establishing relationships of reciprocity with a god. Some groups seem to recruit their member families entirely on the basis of kinship. . . . Others recruit more widely. The cult of the Great Saint . . . unites most of the transriverine families in the ritualization of a group clearly based on locality.[118]

Thus not only are gods also conceived of through the dyadic and personal relation of client to patron, but the identity of the group they protect can be based on kinship or common locality, just the principles we have seen defining the relation of god to human and god to god in the Hua-kai Immortals cult.

Other ethnographic authorities sometimes transmit quite conflicting testimony on the character of even one god. Stephan Feuchtwang tells us, "Everyone whom I asked about the nature of Tudi Gong [*t'u-ti kung*, the god of the locality] either referred to the republican and colonial or to the imperial administrations, saying he was like the local official."[119] But Kristofer Schipper, in his study of Taiwan neighborhood cult associations, notes, "His statues always show him as an old gentleman with a flowing beard. He is always seated, wearing a 'dragon robe.' More important is his cap. *Most often he wears the* yuan-wai-miao *of the wealthy country gentleman, one who carries no official rank but great local influence.* In one hand he invariably holds an ingot,

GOD WORSHIP AND THE *CHIAO*   255

in the other sometimes the long walking stick of a country patriarch" (emphasis mine). Schipper goes on to recount several myths of the *t'u-ti*'s origin, of which one does make him a former county official later deified, but others make him a local gentleman who responded voluntarily to an emperor's call for aid, a servant who sacrificed himself for his master's daughter, a slave who carefully guarded his master's money, or an old man transformed into a tomb guardian. Finally, Schipper sums up: "In Taiwan even today, the heads of traditional communities are preferably elderly gentlemen whose virtue and experience have earned them the respect of all. One calls them *lao-ta* or *ch'i-lao*, and the community that includes a man worthy of the name is considered fortunate indeed. T'u-ti-kung is the perfect *ch'i-lao*."[120]

Emily Martin Ahern's important work on the political implications of Chinese ritual bases her central insight, that ritual and religion are a "teaching and learning game" in which peasants learn the rules of government and the ways of officials, on the similarity between gods and bureaucrats. Ahern devotes considerable space and attention, for instance, to the ways in which communication with gods is like communication with officials, sometimes to the neglect of the many ways it is not. Yet Ahern also supplies one of the most striking—and most systematically gathered and reported—pieces of evidence for another model:

> I asked a sample of Chinese villagers which human relationship most resembles that between man and god: student-teacher; child-parent; citizen-official; patient-doctor; upper-lower generations; or sister's son—mother's brother. Half expecting them to choose "citizen-official," I was startled to find that the choice was almost invariably "child-parent." The following explanation is representative: "Parents teach their children to do good and the gods do the same. If you were sick your parents would want to help you. The gods are the same. As long as you do good deeds and respect them, they will exert their strength to the utmost to help. Parents will do likewise, if you are obedient and good . . . "
> Further questioning about relations between men and officials and men and gods led to shocked denials. I asked whether giving a local official a "red envelope" in return for a favor was like making an offering to the gods. These are the kinds of answers I got: (1) The two things are entirely different. Giving red envelopes involves people mutually taking advantage of each other. Each party has a hold over the other: I can report the policeman [for bribery] and he can report me. Gods aren't the same at all. They will not help more as we give more. These are entirely different sorts of things. (2) Red envelopes are not given for no reason. The point is to make the other party be good to us and not make trouble for us. So police act one way to people who give them red envelopes and another way to those who do not. But gods are not like that. It is not that the more things you do for them the more they will help you. It is only necessary to do good deeds and burn three sticks of incense and they will be enormously happy. A god is a being with a very upright heart. He is fair and just, rewarding without favoritism. (3) Offering things to the gods is just like taking

a gift to one's host. A stranger won't necessarily help you no matter how nice a gift you bring, and a good friend will help even if you bring nothing at all.[121]

The answers in categories (1) and (2) directly contradict the view offered by the shrine officer in Jordan's example, as well as the patron-client practices of Jordan's families and god-worshipping groups. They also seem inconsistent with vows offered in expectation of help. Answer (3), though, parallels Jordan's material in suggesting that there may be gods who are strangers and gods who are friends: that a personal tie, however established, is crucial. It is interesting that Ahern did not include friend-friend or elder brother–younger brother among her choices, or attempt to find an example that could typify the relation of patron to client. But the important question is not whether people are consistent in the details of their explanations; the striking datum here is that Ahern's informants "almost invariably" chose a *personal* relationship as the earthly parallel to their own relations with gods, and that one of the three explanations she gathered proposed two other personal relations—friend to friend and guest to host—to amplify the point.

Ahern explains these findings by differences in the organization of the earthly and heavenly bureaucracies. Her informants, she argues, believe that:

> High officials are in actual practice virtuous, upright, impartial, benevolent, and attentive. But they are blocked from access to ordinary people by a lower layer of rapacious underlings who accept bribes, carry on extortion, and bring every manner of legal entanglement or financial ruin on those who cannot avoid dealing with them. . . . In the world of spirits, upright gods may have corrupt underlings, but men have direct, unimpeded access to the highest gods. . . .
> The puzzle over the responses to my question would then be resolved this way: high officials *and* high gods are impartial, benevolent and attentive. So offerings to high gods are not payments but tokens of respect given to perpetuate a valued relationship like that between parents and children. In contrast, low gods and ghosts, like low officials and their underlings, are open to the influence of special gifts, and care is taken to see they get them.[122]

Ahern's solution is ingenious and may be partly correct (though it is unclear why informants asked a question about gods should have answered only about high gods). But it seems to me to address the motives of people's conceptions of gods and not the content. People want, and believe they have, direct access to high gods; and this is, as Ahern points out, a difference from their view of earthly bureaucrats. But her data show that the *way* people conceive direct access to high gods, the way they authorize it, is by switching from a bureaucratic to a personal model. That is, people are equipped with (at least) two different ways to conceive gods, and they bring one or the other forward in response to different situations. Ahern's material is so striking because it contradicts what many other anthropologists have told us about what people actually *say* about gods. We have seen Gallin's, Feuchtwang's, and Jordan's testimony; Robert Weller confirms that "[m]any informants also make an explicit analogy between the gods and the government. The Jade Emperor, they say, is like President Jiang, Co Su Kong is like a governor, the Earth God is like a policeman, and so on."[123]

Ahern's evidence makes one want to know what questions elicit such statements, and whether closer attention to context, treating the anthropologist's own questioning too as just one of a variety of contexts, might weaken the general force that they seem to carry. Is it that when asked to characterize gods in the abstract, apart from their own concrete and specific interactions with them, the bureaucratic model comes to mind, or that Martin has asked them instead to characterize *human relations* with gods, something in which they have their own experience to call on? Perhaps they do not usually ask themselves the question "What are gods?" Does the bureaucratic model belong mainly to informants' *passive* religious vocabulary?[124] By "passive" here, I mean that informants have absorbed the model from its numerous expressions around them, from religious professionals and others; that they have it available in their heads, and that it can be stimulated into expression by the right question or by certain religious situations; but that in their own active dealings with gods, and their experience of gods' dealings with them—when they have to *act for themselves* toward gods, that is—they draw much more frequently on a different model. This is obscured by the symbol-making power of religious professionals; for in many of ordinary people's interactions with gods, they are using tools or acting in settings—written petitions drawn up by Taoists or others, temple architecture—that have been provided or recommended to them and sold as goods and services by specialists and so express specialist views. Ahern sees this and concludes that their actions contradict their testimony: that they really do *treat* gods as officials, though they say they see them as parents. But perhaps this way of treating gods is not fully their own.[125]

When the contemporary Religion of the Yellow Emperor movement set out to attach the god shrines of Taiwan's communities to itself by inviting them to register voluntarily as affiliates, it argued: "The various deities of Taiwan include the Yellow Emperor himself under other names, the Yellow Emperor's Royal Mother under other names, *and deities who are his descendants,*" thus attempting to define relations between its own god and community gods (when not simple identity) as ties of kinship.[126] A bureaucratic pyramid might seem a natural image for a would-be national religious organization centered on an imperial figure, but apparently when approaching the lay constituencies of local gods a union through personal ties came more easily to mind, or seemed more likely to succeed. Recall some of the (relatively) spontaneous interactions between laypeople and gods we have seen. Community representatives in a Taiwan Offering place their own gods, including those of the temple itself, on the secondary table in the audience's section of the temple, and there bring offerings of their own to these gods outside the formal Taoist ritual. Community members in Faure's New Territories Offering wander among the temporary shrines set up to a variety of gods and offer direct personal prayers to whichever they choose, without written forms or clerical mediation; at the same time, the community's organized representatives offer operas as gifts to the main god of the local temple. A man is possessed by a god—chosen directly, individually, and permanently—and becomes from then on the direct channel for the god's patron-client relation to his community. A procession outside the temple at an Offering celebrates a village's god in a way that at the same time dramatizes the village's competitive relationship with a neighboring village and its own god. A family buys a god-image and keeps it in its house, and the god becomes the family's patron or the patron of a larger group joined by kinship or locality. A man frightened by—a ghost?—in a tree makes a vow to worship it as a god, takes it into his home, and prospers ever after. And a family threatened by sudden death makes its own vow to Immortals to hold a great ceremony in their honor, and lives.

The last example, of course, is the Sung dynasty story I began with, but the others are all twentieth-century cases from the ethnography of Taiwan and southern China. They tell us that specific persons or groups can have ties of their own to specific gods, who become their patrons; that gods are deeply connected and paternally devoted to specific places, not merely temporarily appointed; that prayers can be offered directly and orally, not only through mediation or in writing; that gods will help one in exchange for personal promises; that gods' relations to people and to one another are dyadic and direct. Surely we can take all this as making up a second model, a personal model of divinity, a model that *more deeply informs* laymen's independent acts and choices than the bureaucratic model. That they have the bureaucratic model available too, can draw on it for their own purposes as well as for abstract discussion, and live easily among religious institutions and practices that reflect its acting out and promotion by Taoists and other professionals should not obscure the personal model's crucial importance for their own religious acts and views. It seems no less vital today than in the Sung.

This conclusion may also help shed new light on a piece of modern religious talk that has already been the subject of interpretation by two major figures in the field. Arthur Wolf has told us how his informants explained why, when arranging images, they placed the stove god in a higher-ranking position than the god of the locality, despite his lower bureaucratic rank:

> The view of the gods as bureaucrats is so pervasive that evidence to the contrary is itself explained away in bureaucratic terms. . . . I asked: "But how is it that a little god like the Stove God can report directly to T'ien Kung [the Lord of

Heaven]?" Another old man answered: "The Stove God is not a small person like T'u Ti Kung [the god of the locality]. He is T'ien Kung's younger brother." The apparent departure from bureaucratic principles is thus explained away as nepotism.[127]

Steven Sangren has expressed dissatisfaction with this explanation, as with Wolf's notion that "the gods are modeled on bureaucrats and nothing more." Sangren's own explanation, however, makes the stove god a special exception because of his association with fire.[128] An explanation in terms of two models can, I think, find here not an exception but an example of a much broader range of phenomena, including those we have already seen. The stove god above all is a family representative who is not a family member. This is the starting point for my own interpretation of Wolf's conundrum. Sangren notes that "it is not bureaucratic hierarchy per se that is invoked to gloss inconsistency but an image of nepotistic behavior attributed to celestial bureaucrats," but does not build on this promising beginning. Wolf, indeed, argues as if to explain something as nepotism were to explain it on bureaucratic principles. But it is not. Nepotism, in the Chinese view as in ours, is not a simple expression of bureaucratic principles but an interaction or tension between two *different* principles: a principle of impersonal, merit-based, rule-governed bureaucratic hierarchy and a principle of *personal relationship,* more specifically kinship. That is, when Wolf's informants tell him that the stove god is placed where he is because, although he governs a lower unit than the place god, he is the son of the man at the top and so has more direct access, they are saying that in this context, for this god, personal ties are *more important* than bureaucratic rank.

But why might they want to think so? Let us return to who the stove god is. We know the pessimistic view of the stove god: he is a spy in the bosom of the household who reports the household's sins as well as its virtues to the top of the celestial government. A spy is the agent of a bureaucracy, if anyone is, and enters into personal relationships only for that bureaucracy's purposes. But there is an optimistic view of the stove god available as well: the stove god is a guest in one's home, who if treated well as a guest will treat one well in return. Though not a family member, he stands in a personal relation with the family he lives with. Now let us assume that ritual acts such as the placement of images on an altar are often to be read (as I forget who once said) not in the indicative but in the subjunctive mood: not as "it is so" but as "let it be so." Then I think it becomes easy to argue that when Chinese assert, by the placement of the stove god and by their explanation of it, that personal ties mean more in the stove god's case than bureaucratic principles, they are saying: *Let* personal ties overcome bureaucratic principles; *let* the stove god act according to a personal, not a bureaucratic model. To say this is to say implicitly, with regard to the stove god's relations in the other direction, his relations with the family itself: Let the stove god be more guest than spy; let him honor his personal obligations to his hosts more than his official duties to his superiors. In sum, let him report well of us, as a loyal guest would, and protect us before Heaven. That is, here again, Chinese laymen infiltrate the personal into the ostensibly bureaucratic.

CHAPTER NINE

Conclusion
The Two Models

The notion of two separate, independent models, neither one utterly monolithic yet both fairly coherent and tending to travel as wholes, on which religious actors draw as resources in varying, flexible, sometimes even momentary or individual, yet broadly patterned ways, is to my eye the best way of making sense of the range of religious representations and expressions we find in China, whether in the Sung or in this century. Other ways have been proposed. Steven Sangren and Robert Weller in particular have anticipated some of what I say here and, although working on modern Taiwan have produced the work on Chinese religion probably closest to my own in concern. Both are attentive to the evidence for nonbureaucratic ways of conceiving and interacting with gods. Both handle this evidence differently than I have done here, although very differently from each other as well. Without discussing the differences at length, it is fair to say that Sangren takes a more unified and unifying view of Chinese religious culture than I do. Sangren treats differences in participants' interpretation of gods and religious action as the expression of real ambiguities built into a cultural process of dialectical generation of religious "structures of value" that are no less coherent, unitary, and pervasive for containing or allowing ambiguity. The structures are both real and shared, though people can interpret them in varying ways. Thus, for example, for Sangren a nested hierarchy of god territories is a cultural reality, continuously regenerated, which holds within it the double possibility of being read as a strictly bureaucratic structure in which power flows down to communities and gods act on behalf of higher authority, or as a sort of ladder of ascending communities in which power "bubbles up" from below and gods are the representatives and gentry-like protectors of their own localities.[1] My own view would be that insofar as people recognize and act within a nested hierarchy, it may offer these opportunities for interpretation. But the nested hierarchy of god territories itself is only real insofar as people think it, talk it, write it, or act it out, and it is in question whether in any specific case of religious action or expression this is what they are doing. *Nested hierarchy itself* is an idea that people are most likely to entertain and express when using a bureaucratic model, of which it is an essential part. They may also reinterpret others' representations of nested hierarchy in the terms of a personal model, with which as Sangren shows it is not absolutely incompatible. But some or much of the time, people are not thinking of or acting upon nested or multilevel hierarchies at all, but dyads and dyadic networks.[2] The example may serve as an emblem of a difference of approach to the problem.

With Weller, my differences may lie almost in the opposite direction, though his approach, skeptical of system and supportive of a nonunitary view of culture, lies closer to my own. Weller treats systematic or "ideologized" models as characteristic of literate, elite, and culturally powerful actors, and pragmatic interpretation and action as characteristic of most other participants in social and religious life.[3] Since the bureaucratic model is promoted and elaborated with detail and consistency by professional Taoists and in Weller's view (here we differ) by the state, there remains a sense in Weller's work in which the bureaucratic model is (leaving aside Buddhist views) the only coherent "model" in play, while other views and implicit views are the pragmatic, momentary, situation-dependent interpretations of the sorts of actors less likely to systematize and ideologize. Thus there is not a "personal model" in Weller's work of equivalent weight and coherence to the bureaucratic model, though there are more or less ad hoc personal interpretations. I think this underestimates the consistency and coherence of nonelite models as well as the strength of pragmatic and situation-dependent interpretation among elites and professionals. The bureaucratic model too is subject to varying, reshaping, and idiosyncratic backing-and-filling.[4]

Two possible objections to my analysis have occurred to readers of this book as it came into being, and to me as I wrote it. One is that in distinguishing a bureaucratic from a personal model, I impose ideal types upon a flexible Chinese culture that can see both personal patron and bureaucrat in one god as easily as in one earthly official—that the Chinese simply have no need to separate the bureaucratic from the personal at all. The other is that my two models are out of balance, representing disparate levels of generalization, the "bureaucratic" well specified but the "personal" a conglomerate of distinct relations—parent-child, friend-friend, teacher-student, patron-client. Why think all these belong together from a Chinese point of view? I can respond to these objections in part with the arguments already presented in this book, but it will be helpful to draw on recent work from outside the sphere of religion.

To deal with the first objection first, real Chinese bureaucracies, like real bureaucracies elsewhere, were riddled with personalism of every kind: nepotism, bribery, and the sorts of backdoor relations summed up in the common (though incomplete) understanding of the modern term *kuan-hsi*, literally "relationships," but often translated as "connections." When Sung gentlemen in Fu-chou or modern peasants seek personal ties to gods, or describe gods in personal terms, why should we suppose this means they see gods as other than bureaucrats? Why not suppose they are seeking from gods exactly what they seek from real officials? Should we accept Wolf's view of the divine world as a simple "projection" of the earthly government, with the proviso that the divine government admits all the personal ties that its earthly model allows? Does separating the personal from the bureaucratic impose an alien ideal-type analysis?

The bureaucratic and personal models do have something of the ideal type about them. But my claim is that these are *Chinese* ideal types, not my own. I do not doubt that peasants, for instance, saw real officials as both bureaucrats and persons, or as bureaucrats to whom they needed to form personal ties, at least in the few moments in peasants' lives when they had to (or could) deal with real officials at all. I do doubt that they simply reproduced in their view of gods whatever mix of qualities real officials presented to them, and this book is partly an argument against that claim. If peasants can recognize earthly officials at once as bureaucrats and as potential personal patrons or allies, it does not follow that they cannot distinguish the two aspects, that they cannot disentwine in their heads what is entwined in real life, that they must hold a model that melds all the aspects of real officials into one mush: bureaucrat-patron-fathers. To assume that the Chinese simply projected into the divine sphere an officialdom just like the real one paints their mental processes as merely mechanical and their gods as pure epiphenomena. To see instead that peasants and others could distill from complex reality and their messily varied cultural furniture two distinct models, two spheres of relationship and interaction, grants them an intellectual life that a notion of mere projection denies them.

In the successive chapters of my book, I have shown that the Chinese performed just this distillation. Again and again, we have seen that those who used the models could and did separate them. First, either could be used to the exclusion of the other: the bureaucratic model in the liturgical manuals and divine law codes of the Celestial Heart sect, or the personal model in the miracle stories of the Hua-kai immortals cult. Second, a single group, the Taoist clergy, assigns the two models to separate contexts: the bureaucratic to the performance of rituals for their clients or to constructing rituals and ritual codes in their liturgical texts; the personal to their own relations to one another and their experience of revelation. Third, the two models appear in sharply different proportions in the words and acts of the two sorts of participants in a single ritual: professional Taoists and laymen.

264   CONCLUSION

Fourth, I have tried to reanalyze ethnographic testimony to show that the two models can be shown at work both separately and in combination in contemporary lay testimony and practice. But the strongest evidence that the Chinese could distinguish bureaucratic from personal lies in their pictures of hell. We have seen that hell is bureaucratic with almost absolute consistency. Here is a realm where, though mistakes are sometimes made and the occasional underling may be corruptible or susceptible to personal ties, again and again, in the end, the rules are followed, the registers consulted, and decisions made by the formally responsible officers in a quite impersonal and in fact infallible, though often unpleasant, way. Indeed, storytellers sometimes directly contrast the impersonality and impartiality of the bureaucracy of hell with the corruptibility and nepotism of the real earthly government. Unless Chinese commoners had a conception of bureaucratic order intellectually separable from the real workings of a nepotistic and highly personal earthly officialdom, how did they imagine hell as they did? We have also seen repeatedly that commoners and others often, perhaps usually, imagined the gods to whom they prayed and from who they sought protection as *very different* from the genuinely bureaucratic hell gods, represented them as acting out of personal concern elicited through individual ties, and represented this *not* as a grant of favoritism by bribed officials but as the proper protective behavior of patrons, parent-figures, or powerful friends. Again and again, the Chinese imagined and constructed religious arenas in which the bureaucratic and the personal were more clearly separate than they were on earth.

Yet they could separate them on earth too. In his book on Lukang, Donald DeGlopper searches for the categories the Chinese use to conceive human relationships beyond or apart from family and descent. He joins other investigators, especially Morton Fried, in pointing out the fundamental role of the notion of *ch'ing*, or "sentiment" (more or less interchangeable with its compound *kan-ch'ing*, and appearing also in the term *jen-ch'ing*, "human sentiments"), in Chinese descriptions of reliable social relationships. *Ch'ing* is "the affective, variable component of any two-person relation"; it "can be strengthened or lost, one has more or less of it, it is good, very good, not bad, or absent."[5] Compare the line I have translated as "I do not forget old ties" in Tseng Chi-li's twelfth-century poem, which says, more literally, "I do not forget *ch'ing*." DeGlopper's analysis of *ch'ing* is important in a number of ways, but his most original contribution is to propose a category with which the Chinese contrast *ch'ing* in a polar pair: this is *li* or "principle."

> I believe that they contrast ties based on ch'ing with a category of relations based on what we might call "principle" or "rationality." ... Ch'ing and li are polar terms. Li connotes reason, regularity, equity, and strict impartiality. Ideally the bureaucrat and the shopkeeper follow li, as does anyone who goes by the book and follows general, codified principles. ... While li implies following the rules,

which are the same for everybody, ch'ing implies evaluating another as an individual and a total person. It is associated with notions of trust and long-term reciprocity, and with mutual support in a wide and undefined range of contexts. . . . As I see it the concepts of ch'ing and li provide a way to understand the form of Chinese associations.[6]

It is tempting to suggest that DeGlopper's *ch'ing* and *li* and my personal and bureaucratic models are simply different versions of the same pairing: that the bureaucratic model, for instance, is the rendering of his *li* into a specific imagined physical and social form in the religious sphere. It may be premature to go so far. DeGlopper's *li* includes contractual relations, for example, while I have treated the vow-based exchanges we find in miracle stories as hallmarks of a personal model. The difference may be that the contracts he means are formal *written* documents, whereas my vows are represented as oral; and even where they may have been offered in written prayers, the absence of the god as signatory, or indeed of any written response from the god, would make the written vow seem closer to a promise made in a letter than to a contract. In any case, it does not go too far to say that his distinction bears striking parallels to the contrast of models I have drawn. It certainly suggests that the Chinese had all the conceptual apparatus they needed to distinguish a bureaucrat in his capacity as bureaucrat from a bureaucrat in his capacity as patron, ally, or backdoor partner, and indeed to imagine bureaucracies that were purely bureaucratic or personal relations that were purely personal. For when functioning as polar terms, *ch'ing* and *li* are precisely ideal types; and their use in Chinese analysis of the secular world makes it plausible that the same people could parse a divine world into ideal types as well.

DeGlopper uses *ch'ing* and *li* to talk about relationships outside of kinship, so his analysis itself cannot support my lumping parent-child, friend-friend, and teacher-student relations together in the single category of the "personal." For evidence of a category just so embracing, however, one may turn to the extremely important new analysis of Chinese village social networks by Yunxiang Yan. Many scholars have used the term *kuan-hsi*, literally "relationships" or "connections," mainly for single-purpose ties formed instrumentally—for the "back door." Yan shows that this seriously distorts its meaning—that in his village in North China, people use the term to refer to their whole in-village network of relatively reliable social relationships, ranging from family ties through friendship to colleagueship.[7] For these villagers the word *jen-ch'ing*, "human sentiments," seems equally broad in scope: "in certain contexts, [*jen-ch'ing*] is used as a synonym for [*kuan-hsi*]. People may talk about how much [*jen-ch'ing*] they possess when in fact they are referring to the size of their [*kuan-hsi*] networks."[8] The division between this field of relatively sentiment-rich relationships and the thinner, more distant, and more instrumental ties villagers also take part in is marked by a difference in forms of gift-giving: "expressive" giving on the one hand, which marks and celebrates existing relationships, and "instrumental" giving, the direct exchange of gifts for personal favors. The villagers have different words for the two, and the second is more likely to mark relationships outside the village.

> [A] clear line can be drawn between the village community and the outside world, paralleling the distinction between expressive and instrumental gift-giving activities. . . . [A]ll except the last three categories of gift exchange ["indirect payment," "flattery gifts," and "lubricating gifts"] belong to the expressive type of gifts, and all instrumental gift-giving relations go beyond the village boundary. Thus far, scholarly attention has focused primarily on the latter three categories, especially gifts of lubrication. . . . Earlier studies based solely or even mostly on analysis of lubricating gifts therefore hardly grasp the totality of [*kuan-hsi*] networks in social life.[9]

Yan's analysis sheds new light on Emily Martin Ahern's informants, who indignantly denied that their relations to gods were like their relations to officials, or that gifts to gods were like gifts (or bribes) to officials. In insisting that gods were more like parents, friends, or hosts to human beings, and that they did not help people more as they received larger gifts, Ahern's informants were placing gifts to gods within the sphere of "expressive" giving, and placing gods themselves within the field of reliable and multipurpose social relationships that in their earthly life lay mainly within the village. Real officials lay quite outside that sphere, and the gifts given them were indeed instrumental. Note that the relevant contrast here is not between the personal and the bureaucratic—the real-world relations with officials they were considering and rejecting as a model were not the formal relations of administrator to subject—but between two sorts of extra-bureaucratic relations: the full and truly personal ties of the expressive gift-giving field, and the temporary and single-purpose ties built by bribes and other instrumental gifts. The point is that the field of expressive gift-giving encompasses family, broader kin, friends, colleagues, or indeed anybody to whom one may be joined by a recurrent or stable connection. Kin or non-kin, all are part of one's effective *kuan-hsi* network, a network mediated by human sentiments. Again the point is not to claim that the scope and content of my "personal" model and of Yan's expressive gift-giving *kuan-hsi* are identical. But Yan's materials show that the Chinese can and do frame a social category that brings together kin and non-kin relations in the secular world, in much the same way that I have argued the personal model does for the interactions of humans with gods.[10]

If the argument of this book is correct and the personal and bureaucratic make up two distinct models,[11] how are we to think of their relative cultural and historical places, their respective roles, and their distribution among religious actors? From what we have seen, it is surely critical to distinguish three elements that condition their use: (1) the god, (2) the representer or actor, and (3) the context. This may seem like a hopeless truism, but in fact the discussion has not always proceeded on this basis, and if one fills out these elements with some concrete content, one may go far toward making new sense of Chinese religious representations. The first element is, of course, the identity and special character of the god. We have seen that certain gods are especially likely to appear as bureaucrats. The purest examples are, of course, the gods of hell or purgatory; but among the gods of earth and heaven, we also find examples of "particularly bureaucratic" gods: the city god is one, the god of Mt. T'ai another, the Jade Emperor himself perhaps another. Likewise, there are particularly unbureaucratic gods: the goddess of mercy, Kuan-yin, for example, who apparently can make hell itself a domain of personal relations.[12] Yet even the most bureaucratic or the most unbureaucratic god may be represented as the opposite given the right actor and context.

The second element is the *representer* or *actor:* who is doing the talking, praying, or sacrificing? Certain groups of people, or certain social roles, are clearly associated with greater or lesser likelihoods of using bureaucratic or personal models. I have devoted most of my attention to one very broad such division: professional Taoists and lay god-worshippers. But an important task is to find and examine such divisions at finer levels of focus. We have seen, for example, that even for Taoists and even for lay worshippers, Celestial Heart practitioners and Three Immortals worshippers embrace particularly strong forms of the bureaucratic and personal models respectively.

But the most interesting variations are variations in *context*. The category itself is vague and must be broken down into finer elements such as occasion, setting, and purpose. Expanding on a point that Weller had exposed, I have argued that Taoist professionals themselves often adopt personal models, founded in descent, incarnation, teaching, and gift rather than in appointment or delegation, when they talk or write about relations between Taoists both living and dead, and especially when they talk about acts of revelation or of initiation into the divine. We have seen that in Schipper's Royal Lords Offering, the officiating Taoists withdraw upward from bureaucracy into abstract numerology when the god is not one they approve of and when the lay organizers have made bureaucracy their own model. Just what in the circumstances of the Royal Lords rite prompts a lay appropriation of divine bureaucracy remains uncertain—it may be simply that gods of plague are easily assimilable to gods of death—but it is surely important that the charter myth of the organizers uses divine bureaucracy to elevate their own kind above Taoists and to affirm their local authority. For laypeople we have also seen, in Hung Mai's several hundred stories set in Chiang-hsi, that a leading context for the bureaucratic model in lay worship is the imposition of death and the handling of souls of the dead. Such examples only begin the exploration of contexts that one would need to undertake in order to understand fully who uses what model, when, and for what.

When one considers these three elements—god, representer, and context—the thought occurs that the first, "god," is a problematic category and perhaps reduces to the latter two. We are dealing, after all, with *representations* of gods here, and trying to establish the elements that determine representations. It may then seem odd to say that the god partly determines his own representation, since unless we actually believe in Chinese gods, a god simply *is* his or her representations. Perhaps what one means by "the god" here, as distinct from any current representation at the moment, is the history of previous representations of the god, or rather their varying histories, which are multiple for any god; the repertoire of representations of any god that have been thrown up by past worshippers and are circulating and available for use in the present time. Then one might further say that the previous representations are the result of who did the representing and when—representer and context again—and so reduce the three elements, at least in the historical dimension, to two. There is something to this argument, but I prefer to step back from it at this stage, in particular because it neglects the *power* that people attribute to gods as they have learned of them from the circulating representations available. Worshippers may often believe that a god would not allow himself to be represented in just any way, and this gives real power to the crystallized representations that have come down to them.[13] Thus there continues to be sense in treating "the god" as an independently determining element, and insisting that one needs to consider the *interaction* or *conjunction* of god, representer, and context to understand how, in different historical situations, models of divinity and of divine-human relations are used and expressed.

I have built this book around the difference between lay and local conceptions of gods and the conceptions of a professional clergy. That there are such differences and that they are important, even in a society whose religious professionals have real power and authority of their own, should not seem strange. In the history of European religion, the differences between lay and clerical ideas about the Christian god; about Christianity's local divinities, called saints; about the liturgy; and about the clergy itself are the subject of a large body of work.[14] I have already touched on parallels between Chinese vows to gods and European vows to saints. Peculiar parallels arise, too, when in Europe a mass, a rite whose liturgy has nothing to say of any divinity lower than the Trinity, is offered to a local saint, just as in China an Offering is held for a local god. It may not be wrong to say that a mass, like an Offering, is a clerical rite for the highest ruling divinities, which through historical compromise the laity has adopted for its saints.

A parallel that is also a contrast emerges from Stephen Wilson's work on saints' cults and images in Paris churches. Here there is a division between the space of the priests in the eastern part of the church, and "the people's space" in the middle and to the west. Like the Taoists' gods and the local gods at an Offering, different saints stand in the two spaces. "The authentically popular cult may enter by the door quite literally . . . ; it may then progress into the body of the church, where it tends to remain in the middle area, the people's space, rather than move into the clergy's eastward space. . . . Cults which do progress, or are taken at once, into the east end tend to be those which are taken up officially by the clergy"[15] This process may take decades, as a saint with lay support inches her way through the church and, in some few cases, is finally "taken up" by the clergy and installed in the position of higher status at their end. There she may even replace a saint who had clerical patronage before her. The process is often long and slow because the clergy are an organized spiritual bureaucracy, backed by the coercive bureaucracy of the state; because these bureaucracies run the churches; and because changes in the approval of saints depend on shifts in the relative power of semi-organized laity and organized clergy and in the power balances within church and state. Yet saints in the long run can and do move, even change places. In China, as we have seen in the Taiwan examples, gods may move and change places for an Offering, then change back in a matter of days, as power in the temple shifts from laity to clergy and back again. Here too there are clerical gods and lay gods, and here too, during the Offering, their images stand in places of higher and lower status. But here the temples belong to the laity; the state does not impose a single clergy; and the clergy themselves are not a centralized bureaucracy, but hired specialists. Thus relations between laity and clergy depend not on the glacial shifts and collisions of bureaucracies in response or resistance to popular sympathies, but on private commerce. That a market can effect some kinds of change more quickly than a bureaucracy can should not, at this date, surprise us. The Offering itself, and the reversal of gods that it undertakes, is each time the result of a commercial transaction between lay organizers and Taoist clerics, and to get the ritual done the transaction can go through even though neither group wholly acknowledges the other's gods. China may offer a revealing test case of how an organized and literate professional clergy functions when it does not have the effective backing of either a state or—what the Chinese state *was* strong enough to prevent—a powerful, centralized, statelike church.[16]

We cannot know whether at an Offering for the Three Immortals of Huakai Mountain their images moved into a subordinate position during the rite while the Three Pure of the Taoists moved to the fore; whether the Three Immortals remained supreme in their own shrine while the Three Pure had to receive their honors elsewhere; or whether Taoists avoided the issue by redefining the Three Immortals as incarnations of the Three Pure. But we may guess that which of these or other things happened depended on current dealings or continuing relationships between Three Immortals worshippers and Taoists, not on the dictates of a higher clerical or political authority. Gods may rule stably or change only slowly when one side lays down religious law. They may trade places in a day when two sides haggle.

Appendix
Source Issues

TENG YU-KUNG AND THE *CORRECT RITES* AND *SPIRIT CODE*

In Chapter 2, I suggest that Teng Yu-kung's *Correct Rites of Celestial Heart from Shang-ch'ing* and *Spirit Code: A Numinous Text from the Marrow of Shang-ch'ing* are works of the late Northern Sung. As I note there, however, Judith Boltz, whose dissertation on Celestial Heart opened the field, disagrees and argues that the author of those texts, Teng Yu-kung, is the same man as a Teng Yu-kung of Nan-feng County attested elsewhere, who lived from 1210 to 1279. For Boltz, these two works are thus products of the late Southern Sung.

No argument I make in this book depends on this question. Virtually all the material in Teng Yu-kung's two texts appears nearly verbatim in Yüan Miao-tsung's *Secret Essentials of the Most High on Assembling the Perfected for Relief of the State and Deliverance of the People*, whose preface addressed to the emperor Hui-tsung dates it firmly to 1116. Thus whenever Teng Yu-kung lived, it is clear that the materials in his books had taken the form in which he conveys them by the late Northern Sung. For the Southern Sung we have the abundant testimony of Hung Mai's stories in the *Record of the Listener* (*I-chien chih*) that Celestial Heart practice was thriving in his time, again whether Teng's work may serve (as Boltz believes) as Southern Sung evidence or not. But since the dating of these texts has achieved the status of an ongoing controversy in the field since Poul Andersen's 1991 dissertation challenged Boltz's views, it is worth giving here the reasons why I agree with Andersen and not with Boltz. The case is far from sure, and new discoveries may yet change the picture, but as it stands the evidence seems to me clearly to favor the Northern Sung.

Boltz summarizes her reasons for thinking the two Tengs are one in a note to *Survey of Taoist Literature, Tenth to Seventeenth Centuries*, in which she refers to my own early communication with her on this issue:

> Teng Yu-kung's prefaces are undated, but I identify him with the Teng Yu-kung (1210–1279) of Nan-feng (Kiangsi) cited in Ch'ang Pi-te et al., 1974–76: 3730.

In the preface to HY 566, Teng traces his heritage back five generations to Jao Tung-t'ien, Chu Chung-su, Yu Tao-shou, Tsou Pen, and Fu T'ien-hsin, Teng's own master. This is the number of disciples one would expect from the time of Jao's putative discovery to the time of Teng Yu-kung. On 18 November 1983, Dr. Robert P. Hymes of Columbia University wrote, questioning the authenticity of this identification of Teng. Hymes takes the position that the compiler Teng is not the Teng Yu-kung documented in the index to Sung biographies of Ch'ang Pi-te et al. 1974–76 but rather another person of the same name who lived during the 12th century. But external and internal evidence seems to suggest he was more likely to have been writing during the reign of Sung Li-tsung (r. 1225–1264) than of Hui-tsung. If Teng were in fact Yuan Miao-tsung's near contemporary, I find it strange that Chin Yün-chung (fl. 1224–1225) would not mention him in his discussion of other compilers of T'ien–hsin ritual. Chin seems to be familiar only with Yuan and Lu Chen-kuan (i.e. Lu Shih-chung). The latter he identifies as responsible for the reedition of T'ien-hsin rites (HY 1213 *Shang-ch'ing ling-pao ta-fa* 43.16b ff.; on this text see Chapter 1, section 5). Moreover, a close investigation of the texts ascribed to Teng Yu–kung in the Canon suggests that they are works of the 13th, not the 12th, century. For example, Teng identifies Hei-sha (Black Killer) with the spirit Hsuan-wu (HY 566, 3.6b), whereas the two cosmic forces were regarded as distinct in texts as late as the ritual corpus compiled by Lu Yuan-su (fl. 1188–1201) and a disciple in 1201 (HY 1216 *tao-men t'ung-chiao pi-yung chi* 7.6a; on this text see Chapter 1, section 7).[1]

It is beyond my competence to comment specifically on Boltz's last point, the chronological implications of the identification of Hei-sha with Hsuan-wu, since I have not surveyed the surviving material with anything like Boltz's thoroughness or depth. It does strike me, however, that since we have extant only a fraction of the Taoist texts that must have circulated in Southern Sung China, to hang dates on points of doctrine is dangerous. There may at any one time have been separate textual traditions that took different positions on the status of figures like Hei-sha and Hsuan-wu, and of which we now can know nothing. The dates of Teng's texts are in fact one of the many things we would have to know to have an adequate picture of the range and distribution of doctrinal views and assumptions among Taoists at different periods in the Sung: we surely do not know enough yet to reason in the opposite direction. Similarly it does not seem very odd that Chin Yun-chung, in commenting on and criticizing Celestial Heart practice in his time, should have nothing to say of Teng Yu-kung. After all, if we accept Boltz's identification of Teng Yu-kung, then he comes on the scene long after Yuan Miao-tsung and some time after Chin Yun-chung, yet he mentions neither of them, or indeed any other previous compiler. If this sort of argument serves equally well for either side, then it serves for neither. Perhaps Teng's own texts were no longer circulating in Chin's time, or perhaps he had not come across them. As to the five steps of textual transmission separating Jao Tung-t'ien and Teng Yu-kung, Boltz finds it plausible that these should cover a period of about 250 years: from 994 (the date of the revelation to Jao) to perhaps 1240, when her Teng Yu-kung was thirty years old. Poul Andersen finds this unlikely, and it is worth considering the point. Here is what Andersen says on the *Correct Rites:*

The [*Correct Rites'*] author, Teng Yu-kung, appears to have been active around
the end of the eleventh century. . . . [He] refers to [Mt. Hua-kai] as his own,
pen-shan, and gives a line of transmission of the methods from Jao through four
(otherwise unknown) masters to himself . . . and refers to the Ch'iao-hsien Kuan,
i.e. the monastery representing the ancient residence of the two disciples. . . .
The name of the monastery was changed to Ch'ung-hsien Kuan by an imperial
decree of 1075 . . . and it may be significant that Teng Yu-kung uses the old
name. A date of the preface before 1075 would be consistent with the line
of transmission described by the author, yet the text of the book itself shows
evidence of a later date. Thus the book incorporates material adopted from
the Shen-hsiao tradition, which did not emerge until around 1117. Furthermore the description of a set of talismans (3.9b–20a) is said to be copied
verbatim from the text edited by the 30th Celestial Master, Chang Chi-hsien
(1092–1127). It seems likely that the preface originally belonged to an earlier
version of the book. Note also that in the preface the author introduces the
book by saying that he has divided it into two ch. (pre. 3A), and that a book
with the same title is listed in the *T'ung-chih lueh*, where it is said to consist
of three ch. It would appear that the present seven-ch. Book is an expanded
version, no earlier than the middle of the twelfth century, of a work compiled
by Teng Yu-kung toward the end of the eleventh century.[2]

Andersen moves on to discuss the *Spirit Code* and there develops his arguments further:

> Teng Yu-kung seems to have lived on Hua-kai shan in central Kiang-hsi (cf. 566
> *Shang-ch'ing t'ien-hsin cheng-fa* pre. 2B, where he refers to this mountain as his own,
> *pen-shan*). He seems not to be identical with the man by the same name who lived
> 1210–1279 and in the same area. . . . In [ibid.] pre. 1B–2a he describes the trans-
> mission of the texts revealed to Jao Tung-t'ien in 994 through four masters, the
> last of them, Fu T'ien-hsin, being his own master, *pen-shih*. It seems impossible
> to make this line of transmission stretch over a hundred years. Furthermore
> the information contained in his preface to the present book seems rather to
> indicate that he was active before 1116. . . . Teng relates that he searched for
> copies in monasteries in Hung-chou (Nan-ch'ang), Nan-k'ang (Hsing-tzu), on
> Lu-shan, and in Shu-chou. . . . He says that in this way he obtained "five versions
> of the Shang-ch'ing code," . . . and that he edited the present version on the
> basis of a collation of the se five versions, arranging the entries in accordance
> with the original form (pre. 3A). . . . Another version of the code is included in
> [HY] 1227 *Tsung-chen pi-yao* [ch.] 6, which was edited by Yuan Miao-tsung in
> 1116, and where it is said to be copied faithfully from the original, *chiu-pen*. . . .
> In fact, though lacking certain paragraphs . . . the text of this version corresponds
> quite exactly to the text of the present book. The account given by Teng concern-
> ing his own procedure implies a certain amount of active editing and thus ex-
> cludes the possibility that he could have simply extracted the work from [HY]
> 1227 *Tsung-chen pi-yao*. If we believe his account, it follows that [the latter] was
> derived from the form of the code established through his editing, and it may
> be concluded that this editing took place before 1116. Note also that in connec-
> tion with the group of talismans attached to the *Pei-ti fu* (. . . *Tsung-chen pi-yao*
> 2.21a–b), Yuan Miao-tsung states that in the original, *chiu-pen*, these talismans

were transmitted along with (and not as part of) the *T'ien-hsin cheng-fa,* and compare [HY] 566 *Shang-ch'ing t'ien-hsin cheng-fa* pre. 3A, where Teng states that in fact he edited the *Pei-ti fu-wen* separately.[3]

Andersen's arguments have considerable persuasive force, but in fairness I cannot say they utterly exclude Boltz's alternative view. It is conceivable that Teng Yu-kung exaggerates his role as editor and that the five texts he examined differed little; that all five of them were later recensions of Yuan Miao-tsung's own work; or that only one was Yuan's work and Teng relied on that to the near exclusion of the others. He might separate the *Pei-ti fu* from the rest of the work because Yuan's comment tells him that is how an "old edition" had done it and he hopes to restore the tradition to its purer earlier form. In other words, it remains possible to construct a historiographic story in which Yuan came first and Teng is writing long after, even in the middle or late thirteenth century, as Boltz argues. Andersen's own view of the evidence—that the *Correct Rites* has a preface written before 1075 preserved in a work that was updated in the middle twelfth century—makes the story at least a bit complicated. But other evidence, some of which Andersen touches but does not dwell on, does persuade me that in broad outline he is right: that Teng Yu-kung was a man who wrote in the late eleventh to early twelfth century.

One apparently hopeful piece of evidence should be gotten out of the way at the start because it leads nowhere. As Boltz points out, *Verities of the Three Lords* preserves mention of Teng Yu-kung in a context that might suggest a temporal framework: the secondary commentary I discuss in Chapter 3, appearing as double lines interspersed through both the main text and the primary commentary of Shen T'ing-jui's *Veritable Record*.[4] Here, after a mention of rites that Fu-ch'iu is urging the Two Lords to practice, the secondary commentator inserts: "The ritual texts encased in stone gotten by Jao Tung-ch'i [evidently a mistake for Jao Tung-t'ien] at Mt. Hua-kai, which in the present day [*chin*] Teng Yu-kung submitted to the throne, are precisely these [rites]."[5] The hopeful element here is the word *chin,* "in the present day," which might seem to indicate that the author(s) of the commentary is (are) contemporary with Teng Yu-kung. Boltz believes the commentary may be the work of Liu Hsiang and Wang K'o-ming, authors of the 1261 preface to a printed edition of *Verities of the Three Lords* (or more properly a text partly or in some degree ancestral to our present *Verities*), or of Huang Mi-chien, an otherwise unidentified and undated Taoist whose older work Liu and Wang had edited and engraved for printing, and uses the Teng Yu-kung comment as tentative and partial support for the point: "If we accept Teng's dates as 1210–1279 . . . that would date the commentator to the generation of Liu Hsiang and Wang K'o-ming."[6] In principle, one might also attempt to work in the other direction: if one could arrive at a plausible date for the secondary commentary, this would yield a plausible date for Teng Yu-kung. I give my reasons below for thinking it unlikely that the secondary commentary comes from a hand as late as Boltz suggests, but in any case the commentary's expression "in the present day" is of only very limited use for dating purposes. When the Two Immortals rest at a retreat in the eastern part of the commandery seat, the secondary comment tells us: "*In the present day* there has been established an abbey called T'ien-ch'ing."[7] But this must have happened in the Ta-chung-hsiang-fu reign period (1008–1016), when T'ien-ch'ing Abbeys were established all over the empire by imperial decree after the discovery of letters from heaven to the emperor.[8] Where the Two spit clouds to form a bridge, the secondary comment adds: "Therefore the abbey was called Ch'iao-hsien [bridging the Immortals]. *In the present day* by decree this has been changed to Ch'ung-hsien."[9] But this change of name, as we know, took place in 1075. And where Lord Wang waits at a bridge for Lord Kuo to arrive, the secondary comment is: "In the present day in Nan-feng County there is a bridge called Hui-kuo [meeting Kuo];" but it is known from other sources that this bridge was not built until 1127.[10] Thus from internal considerations we know that the commentary cannot have been written before 1138,[11] yet its author uses "in the present day" for events that took place over a range of years from 1008 through 1075 to 1127. One should note that the comment is thus *consistent with* the date of 1075 that Andersen suggests for Teng's preface; but it is consistent with at least a 130-year range of other possible dates as well, and possibly much more. In fact we would have to know exactly how late the commentator lived to deduce the range that "in the present day" actually encompasses for him. My own view is that "in the present day" in this commentary is properly understood simply as establishing a modern—which is to say Sung—temporal viewpoint in contrast to the basic text and primary commentary it is attached to, both of which take their narrative stance almost perfectly consistently in the third century of the Three Lords' own lives: the commentator uses "in the present day" to let the reader know he is now reading a Sung man talking of Sung things. This of course makes the term nearly useless as an indicator of time.

As to the issue of the number of transmissions: Andersen thinks five transmissions from Jao Tung-t'ien (who received his revelation in 994) to Teng Yu-kung are consistent with a date of 1075 for Teng; Boltz finds them consistent with dates of 1210–1279. The disagreement is extreme and partly reflects the real difficulty of arriving at useful time estimates from numbers of generations, whether of biological descent or of discipleship. In principle, five transmissions could indeed span eighty-one years or, assuming that the ostensible Teng Yu-kung received it in 1240, when he was thirty years old, 246 years. But in this case again, although eighty-one years seem a bit short, Boltz's alternative seems the more extreme. In the year 994, Jao Tung-t'ien, a prefectural judicial clerk with some reputation, surely cannot have been less than thirty years old. For five transmissions after him to span fifty years each, every master in the succession must receive the transmission as a young man (or he will not live long enough afterward to hold it for fifty years) and live to a considerable age: receive at twenty and live to seventy, receive at thirty and live to eighty, or the like. A reduction of this span for any single master would require its increase for another to achieve the total span of 250 years. It seems unlikely that masters would always live so long and always hand on their knowledge to a young man instead of to a disciple who had matured in their service, for example. (Technically, of course, the transmission itself can occur at any time; the point is that each master must outlive his predecessor by an average of fifty years.) Eighty-one years requires a transmission span of about sixteen years, considerably closer to the generation-length of twenty to twenty-five years that one might typically expect.

But all this has to do only with plausibility. The strongest definite evidence in my view comes from Teng's own prefaces, though we have already seen that it is not without possible contradictions. As Andersen points out, Teng's preface to the *Correct Rites* mentions the Ch'iao-hsien Abbey, whose name was changed by imperial decree to

Ch'ung-hsien Abbey in 1075; yet certain contents of the *Correct Rites* seem to require a later date; and Andersen solves the problem by suggesting in effect an origin stretching over a period of time but still confined within late Northern and early Southern Sung, long before the (presumably) other Teng Yu-kung lived. Another point in the preface suggests Andersen is right to find complexity here; for if the name Ch'iao-hsien points back before the 1075 enfeoffment, this points forward: "[The Three Lords'] titles of enfeoffment and talismanic wonders are handed down quite clearly in inscriptions on stone; here I shall not recount them superfluously."[12] No source suggests any enfeoffment of the Three Lords before 1075, when the abbey's name also changed; so there is a conflict here that may require Andersen's solution.

Place-name references in the prefaces, however, strongly support an early date for Teng. In the preface to the *Spirit Code*, Teng lists the abbeys where he has searched for texts and mentions abbeys in Hung-chou and Shu-chou among others. Hung-chou's name was officially changed to Lung-hsing Fu in 1165, and Shu-chou's to An-ch'ing Fu in 1195.[13] Both of these changes were not in name alone but promoted the prefectures to higher status (to *fu*, "superior prefecture," from *chou*, simple "prefecture") within the imperial network of administrative divisions. In fact both prefectures gained their promotion because they had once been the residences of men who later became emperors: for Hung-chou, Hsiao-tsung (r. 1163–1189), and for Shu-chou, Ning-tsung (r. 1195–1224). Past imperial presence demanded marking, and the promotions accomplished this. Teng explicitly addresses his *Spirit Code* preface to an emperor, whom he asks to promulgate the text among Taoist practitioners at large.[14] In this highly formal context, which demanded care and humility of expression, it seems extremely unlikely that he would use unofficial names and so at one stroke demote two of the emperor's prefectures and slight two of his ancestors. This makes it extremely improbable that this Teng Yu-kung is the man who lived from 1210 to 1279, and instead indicates a time before the promotion of Hung-chou in 1165. This in turn would seem to point to Hui-tsung (r. 1101–1126) as the emperor most probably addressed, since Hui-tsung's larger project of promoting Taoism and inviting and collecting Taoist texts would make him, more than most emperors, seem likely to undertake the distribution of a scripture to all the rite masters of the empire. All this strongly supports Andersen's general position.

But even stronger evidence in my view is the way in which Teng describes Mt. Hua-kai itself. In the preface to *Correct Rites*, Teng remarks: "Hua-kai, a precinct of the Void where the Three Pure were incarnated, has only a Transcendent Altar to the August of the Void; it does not even have any of the Taoist sort in residence; thus people of our time do not know the name Hua-kai." Now, a claim that people at large "do not know the name Hua-kai" would have been utterly fantastic in the late Southern Sung when Boltz's Teng Yu-kung lived, when Hsu Cheng could write "South of the great river, since the time when the lord Fu-ch'iu received the Way on Mt. Hua-kai, mountains such as in their ripe beauty and steep upthrusting are worthy dens for deities and immortals have generally abounded in shrines to the Three Immortals," and when some of Fu-chou's most prominent officials and their families were devotees of the cult and wrote poems on the Three. On the other hand, Teng's description is almost eerily reminiscent of the way the administrators of Ch'ung-jen County and Fu-chou described the site when the county administrator visited it to present the imperial grants of titles in 1075:

On recent investigation, it has been found that at the foot of this mountain were once the Shang-hsien Abbey and others, each now fallen down and abandoned and its lands confiscated by the authorities. We dare not on our own authority undertake new construction. There is only the nearby Ch'iao-hsien Abbey, whose original abbey building and images have been preserved; but as to its name, no official name has ever been granted. Its original 600 or so *pa* of wet fields have also been taken over as colony-fields by the authorities because there was no one to receive and carry them on. *For prayers at this mountain of late, there has only been a single Taoist* of this county, who resides there and sees to it. [See Chapter 4 for complete text.]

The authorities tell the same tale of obscurity and inactivity that Teng tells; they find "a single Taoist" in residence where he finds none, but we have already seen that the Taoist the authorities mention is probably Chan T'ai-ch'u, who departed the mountain shortly after the county administrator visited him. Since Teng is aware of the enfeoffments, the preface must date at least in part from after 1075—thus presumably after Chan's departure; but it surely belongs to the same early period, when Mt. Hua-kai had not yet begun attracting the attention of local gentlemen (or was only just beginning to) and when the cult had not yet spread throughout the Fu-chou region. Since these beginnings fall precisely in the decades of Hui-tsung's reign and the first years of the Southern Sung, Andersen's estimate of a late Northern Sung date for Teng's life and an early Southern Sung date for the completion of his texts in their present form gains perhaps its strongest support here.

DATES AND AUTHORSHIP OF *VERITIES OF THE THREE LORDS*

In this book I have treated all of the last four chapters of *Verities of the Three Lords* as largely or almost wholly the work of the Taoist Chang Yuan-shu, whose book *Verities of Mt. Hua-kai* is incorporated into the larger work beginning with chapter 3, the first page of which bears that title and his name. Since in this I diverge in part from the attributions of other recent commentators on *Verities of the Three Lords*, I should explain my reasons. Judith Boltz recognizes the third and fourth chapters, which together form what appears to be a continuous list of the famous sights and landmarks of Hua-kai and its region, as Chang's work.[15] This accords well with Chang's own description of his work, and I am at one with Boltz on this point. Florian Reiter sees the fourth chapter as separate—"Chapter 4, which opens without any note of authorship, is of independent origin"[16]—but does not give his reasons for thinking this of a chapter so very strongly connected to the one that precedes it, or for speculating that it may be the work of the 1261 editors Liu Hsiang and Wang K'o-ming. Boltz and Reiter come together, however, on the two chapters that follow, which begin with the biography of Shen T'ing-jui and pass rapidly into the collected miracle stories of which we have seen so much in Chapters 3 and 4 above. Here is Boltz: "The last two chapters comprise a selection of biographical and narrative accounts. The provenance of this segment of the text is not indicated, but most of the narratives appear to date to the first five reign periods of the Southern Sung (1127–1189), which suggests they may have come directly from the edition printed by Liu Hsiang and Wang K'o-ming."[17] This is puzzling, since Liu and Wang did their work in 1261, seventy years after the period in which Boltz correctly places the miracle stories. Similarly, Reiter, after attributing chapter 4 to Liu and Wang, suggests "[t]he same authorship might in any case hold as well for the two chapters that follow,"[18] though he does note that several of the pieces in chapter 5 come from the hand of Chang Yüan-shu.

I discuss in Chapter 4 above the strong parallel between the dates of events recorded in chapters 3 and 4, which Boltz and I agree are Chang Yüan-shu's work, and the dates of the items in chapters 5 and 6. In both cases, apart from a relatively small amount of Northern Sung material and isolated material from around 1260 (which in the case of chapters 3 and 4 clearly originates with the 1391 compiler; see above in Chapter 4 n. 110), we find a mass of material bearing dates from the first few reigns of the Southern Sung, or between about 1140 and about 1200. The striking temporal correspondence of the two sections would by itself make one wonder if they came from the same compiler. But more: in the miracle stories chapters, it is only within this temporally more focused mass of material, and never in the Northern Sung or ca. 1260 material, that one finds a recurrent voice that comments on the story just told;[19] or that uses time expressions in a way that relates to a definite narrative present ("down to the present day,"[20] or "lately,"[21] or "in a recent year"[22]); or that refers to itself in the first person ("I foolishly forget his name," and other first-person formulas[23]); or that both narrates in the first person *and* refers to itself quite explicitly as "Yüan-shu."[24] Together these devices, which sometimes occur together in the same story, establish a specific individual narrative voice, and the stories they occur in make up well over half the collection. The stories set themselves off in certain important ways. First, no story that uses either first-person reference or a definite temporal stance for the narrator supplies any name for the teller other than Chang Yüan-shu's. Second, the first story in the chapters to use clear first-person reference immediately precedes the first to bear a date falling within this period and forms a clear boundary between the biographies unconnected to the Three Immortals that precede it and the real miracle stories that follow; in fact it is the first item in these two chapters that actually refers to current worship of the Three.[25] Third, the latest-dated story to use any of these devices also bears the latest date in this whole mid–Southern Sung group (1200, with context that identifies the teller's own time as not long afterward); and the story that immediately follows it is the last to use any of the narrative devices, a reference to "a recent year."[26] Fourth, a sharp temporal break separates this group from the earliest story that follows (1258),[27] with no stories at all set in the six decades between. Thus there is a group of a certain integrity here. In other words, a single recurrent set of self-referential narrative devices runs through the body of stories that belongs to the same period that the material in Chang Yüan-shu's earlier chapters comes from, and some of the stories from this body—in both chapters—explicitly identify themselves as told by Chang Yüan-shu. Because the Three Immortals stories in these chapters also directly serve the purpose Chang Yüan-shu outlines in his preface to *Verities of Mt. Hua-kai,* namely to supply testimony to the responses and miracles and other doings of the Three Immortals in more recent times, there seems to me good reason to conclude that at least this whole body of Southern Sung miracle stories in these chapters, aside from the two dating from the very end of the Sung, come as a group from Chang's hand.[28] Whether the Northern Sung materials—the biographies of Shen T'ing-jui, Jao Tung-t'ien, Chan T'ai-ch'u, and Way-man Mao—also come from Chang, there is no way to know; but the fact that they do not glorify the Three Immortals but only the mountain and so do not serve the purposes he outlines in his preface, and that they use none of the narrative devices of the Southern Sung group, suggests that they may be a later interpolation. But the evidence is strong that Liu Hsiang and Wang K'o-ming, or perhaps the unknown Huang Mi-chien to whom they give credit, had acquired and incorporated (either as an independent book or as part of an earlier edition of the larger work) a text of Chang Yüan-shu's *Verities* that included both the sacred geography that now makes up chapters 3 and 4 and the miracle stories that are the bulk of chapters 5 and 6.

A remaining mystery is the identity of the author of the secondary commentary in *Verities of the Three Perfected Lords*. Boltz and Reiter both suppose it must have been supplied by Liu and Wang in 1261. But as Chapter 3 above makes clear, the comments mention nothing datable after 1138. It seems strange that men writing 123 years later should find no more recent event worth mentioning in updating a body of text (the *Veritable Record* and its primary commentary) that mentions a considerable number of the important sites of Hua-kai worship. Chang Yüan-shu himself, writing shortly after 1200, would move us sixty years closer; but this too leaves a considerable gap, especially when one considers the extent of his research into events that occurred in the several decades after the 1130s. But Chang's own testimony may possibly help us here. In his preface he tells us:

> There are the stela [*pei*]) of Yen Lu-kung [Chen-ch'ing] and the Veritable Record of Venerable Immortal Shen [T'ing-jui], whose records are very detailed. In the Sung, during Hsi-ning, the administration of this prefecture made a memorial about the inscription to the court, which expressly conferred precious appellations.
>
> Now as to the places where the Three Perfected manifested transformations, I do not know how many there are of them. The mountains and gorges of our own county at least may be thoroughly investigated; the traces left in other localities are hard to search out exhaustively. I, Yüan-shu, since the time I first wore a cap and serge, have in this regard inquired into the knowledge acquired by my honored elders in the tiniest detail. It has been over twelve years now. [I] have thought and thought on the traces of the Three Perfected and have not been able to ascertain the facts. Now Heaven has given me the good fortune to be able to find a complete text. I have further obtained the annotations [*chien-chu*] made by Mr. Li Kung-yen before me [*tsai ch'ien*]. All are well grounded in evidence.[29]

Chang does not say *of what* he has obtained a complete text, but the context suggests it must be Shen T'ing-jui's work, perhaps with Yen Chen-ch'ing's inscription and the 1075 memorials and decrees attached as well. But the reference to "annotations" is striking. Li Kung-yen's name does not appear elsewhere in *Verities of the Three Perfected Lords*, and I have not been able to find him in any other source. But one wonders if we have here the compiler/author of *both* the primary and secondary commentary, whose internal datable material does not differ too sharply (1125+ and 1138+ respectively)[30] to allow a single author for both. If Li's text had been around for some years before Chang Yüan-shu, 1138 as a latest date in the secondary commentary would not be implausible.

The effect of all this would be to make the 1261 preface-writers Liu Hsiang and Wang K'o-ming appear mere recompilers of materials already either acquired or written long before them by Chang Yüan-shu. This is in fact broadly consistent both with Liu's and Wang's self-description in their preface and with the very small amount of material in the *Verities* that can definitely be assigned a date near their own.[31] But it does make it strange that their preface has nothing to say of any book by Chang and mentions only Huang Mi-chien as a predecessor. And yet, perhaps Chang is really there too? As far as I know, no one who has studied these texts has pointed out the significant lacuna in our surviving version of Wang's and Liu's preface. They tell how the resident Taoist on Mt. Hua-kai, Ch'en Yüan-ying, when they visited in 1260, asked them to see to a new *Veritable Record* because the old one had been destroyed in a great fire in 1258.[32]

> When we finished we returned home and sought copies [editions: *pen*] of it everywhere. Only then did we find one compiled by the Taoist Huang Mi-chien. *Its narrative records [chi-tsai] were rather brief and summary. It fully recounts the enfeoffments and titles received by the Three Perfected through the successive dynasties, the prefaces and records of famous gentlemen through the ages, the narratives of the refinement and ascent, and the actual traces of numinous and manifest responses in more detail than the Huang edition, but each has its advantages over the other.* We, not ashamed of our foolishness and commonness, have brought together the strong points of both versions and arranged them into fourteen chapters. [Emphasis mine.][33]

Clearly something is simply missing here. We are first told that the Huang edition is too brief and summary, then suddenly we are reading that "it" is more detailed than the Huang edition—than itself?—then that the compilers have combined the best points of "both" editions, when we have never heard of another version! Obviously, at some stage in later copying, a passage between the second sentence and the third has fallen out, in which Liu and Wang introduce a second edition they have found, which they are here comparing favorably to the Huang Mi-chien edition. It is overwhelmingly likely that this edition, which by accident of text transmission remains unidentified, is in fact the work of Chang Yüan-shu so abundantly represented in our surviving *Verities*.

Notes

CHAPTER ONE. INTRODUCTION

1. The name Hua-kai, translated as "Floreate Canopy" by Edward Schafer among others, refers to a flowered ceremonial parasol or umbrella under which an emperor traveled. Its origin, according to one source, was a story in which the legendary Yellow Emperor, fighting a battle, was protected by a parasol-like shaped five-color cloud. The name was also applied to a constellation of nine stars, in our terms part of Cassiopeia, forming a rough umbrella shape and said to be a canopy for Heaven's August Great Emperor, represented by the star we call Polaris, as he traveled through the heavens on the carriage formed by the Big Dipper. It is presumably this astral meaning of the name the two traveling Taoists were reacting to, for its associations with heavenly imperium and so on. The possible worldly political associations of the mountain's name—implying aid or protection to emperors on the one hand but conceivably also *power superior to* an emperor's and so capable of protecting him on the other—are never exploited in any way in any source I have seen. Indeed the occasional but apparently random substitution of the name Pao-kai, "Precious Canopy" or "Jewel Canopy," a similar ceremonial canopy associated in legend with Buddhas and bodhisattvas rather than emperors, suggests that the name did not have special significance, at least for Sung writers. All who dealt with the question maintained that the mountain received the name because of its shape—presumably the shape of the highest of its three peaks, which does have a striking form. Interestingly, when the cult of the Three Immortals became prominent in the Sung and the Yuan, and other mountains of the region came to be named for Hua-kai (either for their shape or for their place in the constantly ramifying legend of the travels of the Three Immortals), it was the element *Hua-*, "flowery," rather than *-kai,* "cover, canopy," that traveled, an element that would have shed all specific associations with umbrellas for emperors and instead tended to imply an analogy between Hua-kai and Mt. Hua, one of the five great mountains of ancient Chinese history and culture. When I trav-

eled to Ch'ung-jen County in 1985 to visit the mountain, local officials knew it as Ta-hua "Great Hua," a version of the name already attested in the Sung, rather than as Hua-kai. For the Floreate Canopy in its earthly and astral senses, see Morohashi, *Dai kanwa jiten,* 9: 710 (p. 10,064 in the dictionary's continuous pagination), item 31214–46; Schafer, *Pacing the Void,* pp. 45–46, 119; and Bokenkamp, "Sources of the Ling-pao Scriptures," p. 468.

2. The description is a typical instance of the highest form of ascension for an Immortal, escorted broad-daylight ascent. The combination of the paired *luan*-bird escort with the crane-steeds, however, though a variant of the common motif of *luan* escorts or steeds and of *luan*-crane combinations, is as far as I have been able to determine special to the Three (or rather at this moment Two) Immortals among the immortals' cults of this region. On the three levels of ascent for an Immortal—by celestial chariot and with celestial escort as in the Two Immortals' case; by simple vanishing; and by leaving one's corpse, or some material substitute, behind—see Kohn, *Taoist Experience,* pp. 303–4 and, for examples, pp. 325–32. On the third form of ascent see also Robinet, "Metamorphosis and Deliverance," esp. pp. 57–66; and for an example see the story of Wang Wen-ch'ing in Chapter 6 of this book. On the *luan*-bird and its uses in Taoist and other literature, see Hargett, "Playing Second Fiddle," esp. pp. 252 ff.

3. Yen, *Wen-chung chi, shih-i* 2/29–30.

4. Hartwell, "Demographic, Political, and Social Transformations"; Hymes, *Statesmen and Gentlemen,* chs. 3 and 4; Ihara, "Sōdai kanryō no kon'in no imi ni tsuite."

5. Feuchtwang, "Domestic and Communal Worship," p. 127.

6. A. Wolf, "Gods, Ghosts, and Ancestors," p. 175.

7. For other work see in particular Shahar and Weller, *Unruly Gods,* which shows nicely the range of work on the problem. My own chapter in that volume, "Personal Relations and Bureaucratic Hierarchy in Chinese Religion: The Case of the Three Lords Cult of Mt. Hua-kai," adumbrates a number of the arguments I work out at greater length in this book.

8. Simona Cerutti has written aptly of "a certain culturalist history, of American imprint, which has dissolved social behavior into the general and generalizing idiom of the cultural universe in which it is inscribed." She continues: "This historiographic current has often proceeded by taking acts away from the social actors who have produced them, to make them the elements of a language that is superindividual and, in its totality, coherent." Cerutti, "Normes et pratiques," pp. 127–28. To what extent the products of Clifford Geertz's influence actually reproduce Geertz's own views is of course, as always with matters of influence, uncertain, though certainly Roy D'Andrade (in the passage quoted later) attributes a view to Geertz recognizably akin to the view that has inspired so much work in cultural history in recent decades.

9. On Geertz's influence, see, e.g., Levi, "I pericoli del geertzismo."

10. Barth, *Balinese Worlds,* pp. 4–5.

11. Geertz, by the way, is wrong about the octopus, which is a very well integrated creature as creatures go, the most intelligent and highly organized invertebrate and capable of social learning. He may be thinking of the starfish, a much closer relative to culture-bearing humans than the octopus is, but not nearly as integrated as either.

12. D'Andrade, *Development of Cognitive Anthropology,* p. 249.

13. Freedman, "On the Sociological Study of Chinese Religion," p. 38.

14. Smith, "Afterword"; the direct quotations from Smith are from p. 341; his quotation of Turner/Rosenberg on p. 347. Smith attributes the Turner/Rosenberg passage to Rosenberg and draws it from a citation in Turner, *Dramas, Fields, and Metaphors,* p. 14; in that original context it appears as Turner's own approving paraphrase of what Rosenberg "has often argued," but without more specific citation of Rosenberg.

15. A. Wolf, *Religion and Ritual in Chinese Society,* "Introduction," p. 9.

16. Lepetit, "Histoire des pratiques," pp. 10–11.

17. Ibid., pp. 19–20.

18. But note that Barth is cited approvingly in Cerutti's contribution to the collection: see Cerutti, "Normes et pratiques," n. 10.

19. Shweder, "Preview," pp. 8–9.

20. Leach, "Ritual," in *International Encyclopedia of the Social Sciences,* 13: 525. I came across the citation in Skorupski, *Symbol and Theory,* p. 21.

21. This was also Melford Spiro's argument in answer to Geertz at the same conference: "We don't want to fall into the other trap. In the first place we don't know, except for our own scientific *Weltanschauung,* that the Hopi rain dance doesn't have an effect causally. Even if we do accept our scientific *Weltanschauung* as valid, we don't have to go to the Hopi for examples of its rejection. Two years ago there was a drought in southern California, and the mayor of San Diego declared a day of prayer, not so we could express our feelings that we were suffering but rather to influence God to bring rain. . . . [I]f San Diegans can believe, whatever the wishful thinking involved, that prayer can affect rainfall, it is not counterintuitive for me to believe that the Hopi might have the same belief." Shweder, "Preview," p. 10.

22. Skorupski, *Symbol and Theory,* p. 165.

23. For an exhaustive and sometimes exhausting treatment of the difficulties that the idea of belief may raise in encounters with other cultures, see R. Needham, *Belief, Language, and Experience.* For support for the view that belief and doubt are very much at issue in Chinese religion, and an argument that the character of miracles is partly accounted for by the need to assuage doubt and assure belief, see Jordan, "Chinese Signs and Wonders."

24. Hymes, "Truth, Falsity, and Pretense."

25. For examples, see Wu Ch'eng's views on sacrifices to mountains in Chapter 4, n. 43, and Huang Chen's implicit attack on Three Immortals worship in Chapter 5.

26. Kohn, *Taoist Experience,* pp. 100–101. My translation slightly modifies Kohn's.

27. Bacon said "the magnet" but counted it important specifically for its use in navigation. Bacon, *Novum Organum,* bk. 1, aphorism 129, cited in J. Needham, "Science and China's Influence," p. 242.

28. Written civil service examinations were not a Sung invention but were expanded by the Sung government to be the primary means to a career. On their possible transmission westward, see J. Needham, "China and the Origin of Qualifying Examinations."

29. Mintz, *Sweetness and Power.* On sugar cane and cane sugar in the Sung, see Freeman, "Sung," p. 147; on tea, pp. 145–46, 147, 151, 156.

30. See, e.g., Elvin, *Pattern of the Chinese Past,* p. 70.

31. For all this see my *Statesmen and Gentlemen,* esp. chs. 4–7.

32. I do not provide citations for the quotations appearing here because all of

them come from passages quoted at greater length and cited fully in the chapters that follow, especially Chapter 4.

33. Raoul Birnbaum has informed me that this sort of apparition is characteristic of Mt. Wu-t'ai in the T'ang and after; this may ultimately be the source of the tradition of such sightings at Hua-kai.

CHAPTER TWO. CELESTIAL HEART TAOISM

1. This story is reconstructed from the partial accounts given in Teng Yu-kung's prefaces to *Shang-ch'ing t'ien-hsin cheng-fa* (TT 318–19, HY 566; hereafter cited as THCF) and *Shang-ch'ing ku-sui ling-wen kui-lü* (TT 203, HY 461; hereafter cited as LWKL). I have not here drawn on Jao's biography in *Hua-kai shan Fu-ch'iu Wang Kuo san chen-chün shih-shih* (TT 556–57, HY 777), since I argue in a later chapter that this paints a picture slightly but significantly different from the one drawn in Teng's texts. If Judith Boltz is right in placing these two in the Southern Sung—in the Appendix, I give my reasons for thinking that she is wrong—then one cannot be sure that all the details in my account above were already part of the story of Jao Tung-t'ien under the Northern Sung. That some such story was nevertheless already in circulation then is shown by the mention of Jao in connection with the Celestial Heart founding texts in Yuan Miao-tsung's preface to *T'ai-shang tsung-chen pi-yao* (TT 986–87, HY 1217; hereafter cited as TCPY), which is firmly dated to 1116.

2. Judith Boltz disagrees and places Teng Yu-kung in the late Southern Sung, but I find Poul Andersen's evidence and certain other indications of a Northern Sung date persuasive. For all this evidence, see the Appendix.

3. Yuan combines in one work and in different order the materials—often in precisely the same words—that Teng allots to two books. The two authors choose different points to elaborate on in some places; and more generally, Yuan provides considerably more detail than Teng; but the material as a whole forms a single body joining all three texts. Judith Boltz, *Taoist Rites of Exorcism*, pp. 72–74.

4. Most of this evidence is found in Hung Mai's *Record of the Listener (I-chien chih)*, hereafter cited as ICC. I am indebted to Judith Boltz for her work in tracking down Celestial Heart materials in Hung Mai's collection. See ICC *i* 6: 232, 235–36, 236 (two stories), 7: 237, 244, 16: 320–21, 19: 347; *ping* 5: 403–4, 8: 429–30, 13: 479, 16: 504–5; *ting* 2: 549–50, 4: 568, 14: 653–54, 18: 684–85, 691; *chih-chia* 5: 745; *chih-i* 5: 830, 831–32, 832–33, 7: 846, 9: 866–67; *chih-ching* 2: 890; *chih-ting* 1: 971, 4: 995; *chih-wu* 5: 1089–91, 6: 1101; *chih-keng* 6: 1181, 7: 1191; *chih-kuei* 4: 1252–53, 5: 1260, 10: 1298–99; *san-chi* 8: 1362, 1362–63; *pu* 5: 1594, 15: 1693–94, 17: 1710–11, 20: 1736, 22: 1755, 23: 1759–61.

5. Strickmann, "Taoist Renaissance" and "Longest Taoist Scripture."

6. See Strickmann, "Taoist Renaissance," pp. 26, 28; Boltz, "Taoist Literature. Part II," p. 154.

7. ICC *i* 7: 236.

8. ICC *chih-i* 5: 832–33.

9. THCF 1: 4a–b.

10. THCF 2: 1a ff. and 2b ff. respectively.

11. THCF 2: 7a.

12. THCF 3: 12a, 16a, 18a, 29b–31a; 4: 1a–12b, 14b–19a; 5: 13a–14a.

13. THCF 6: 1a–3a, 3b–5a, 5a–6b and ff., 15a–17a.
14. Boltz, "Taoist Rites of Exorcism," p. 74.
15. THCF, preface.
16. On memorializing to the Emperor on High see, e.g., THCF 3: 1a, which names "secret memorializing" (*mo tsou*) as one step in the process of using any talisman; 6: 5a, which instructs the practitioner: "Whenever flying up a memorial and submitting a communication [*fei-chang pai-piao*], first imbibe a Talisman for Opening the Heart, next imbibe a Talisman of the Three Pure and the Perfected of the Three Regions; and let the divine ethers mix together [in you] so that you may appear in secret in audience to the Emperor on High"; 6: 3b, where memorializing is part of the process of setting up a Platform for Rebirth in Heaven; and 4: 1b, where "appearing in secret audience before the Emperor on High" is one step in a detailed procedure set forth for treating madness. Cf. also TCPY 1: 2a–8a, which gives basic instructions for nine essential tasks that may be undertaken by the Celestial Heart practitioner and lists "flying up and memorializing to the Emperor on High" as one step in each of the nine.
17. For the use of writing in Taoist ceremonies in general, see Schipper, "The Written Memorial" and "Vernacular and Classical Ritual."
18. Kleeman, "Land Contracts."
19. See, among other places, THCF 4: 1a–b, which mentions the sending of dispatches to the city god and god of the locality. On these, see also the section on "Celestial Heart and Local Cults" further on in this chapter.
20. TCPY 10: 5b–7a.
21. Referring to the Bureau for the Expulsion of Perverse Forces, of which the Celestial Heart master is a commissioner.
22. TCPY 10: 1a–2a and 3a–4a.
23. TCPY 10: 4a–5a.
24. TCPY 10: 8a–b and 8b–9b.
25. TCPY 10: 10a ff. See also the forms in TCPY 6: 23a ff. and in LWKL *hsia* 11b ff.
26. The first penal compilation of the Sung, the *Sung hsing-t'ung*, although it did not bear the name *lü*, was modeled directly on the code of the T'ang. See McKnight, "Chinese Law and Legal Systems."
27. LWKL *shang* 6a; TCPY 6: 6a, where the same material is divided between two separate articles.
28. LWKL *shang* 7b–8a; TCPY 6: 8a.
29. LWKL *shang* 5a; TCPY 6: 5a.
30. LWKL *shang* 1b; TCPY 6: 1b.
31. LWKL *shang* 8a; TCPY 6: 8a.
32. LWKL *shang* 7b–8a; TCPY 6: 8a.
33. LWKL *chung* 1b; TCPY 6: 11b.
34. LWKL *shang* 2b; TCPY 6: 2b–3a.
35. ICC *chih-kuei* 4: 1253.
36. ICC *chih-i* 5: 831–32.
37. ICC *pu* 15: 1693–34.
38. For an example of a Celestial Heart master who suppresses a local cult, see ICC *chih-i* 5: 830.
39. LWKL *shang* 9a–b; TCPY 6: 9a–b.

40. LWKL *shang* 9b; TCPY 6: 9b–10a.

41. This in one sense paralleled the state's own view of things, or at least its own practice. Gods that had not found their way into the *Statutes* were often tolerated or even patronized by administrators. The point is where the authority to make such decisions in conflict with the *Statutes* was seen to lie. When officials discuss these matters, they generally assume that it lies with them, or with popular consensus, or perhaps with the emperor. The *Spirit Code* clearly hands it over to Celestial Heart Taoists. On these issues, see also Hymes, *Statesmen and Gentlemen*, p. 188.

42. TCPY 10: 15a–16a.

43. See, e.g., LWKL *shang* 2b–3a; TCPY 6: 3a.

44. ICC *chih-i* 7: 846. We are to understand that the woman blamed here for the possession of the Hung boy is not of good family, since the story refers to her as Hsun's "natural mother," indicating a concubine or maid.

45. ICC *chih-kuei* 5: 1260. Though the passage is unclear, it is possible that the god of the locality in this case is also regarded as the god of the local *she* shrine, or else is called to testify alongside him. The *she* was the classical god of the soil, which had largely slipped into the background, except in government sacrifices, in the Sung. On the tendency for the *she* to give way to the god of the locality and to the city god, see Johnson, "City-God Cults," pp. 397–99. It is also conceivable that in the story quoted the word *she* simply means the temple of the god of the locality itself.

46. See, e.g., THCF 4: 1a and 8a.

47. TCPY 10: 13b–16a.

48. Johnson, "City-God Cults."

49. On enfeoffment of gods, see "Taoism and the State: Enfeoffment of Gods" in Chapter 7, pp. 181–88.

50. This issue has its own complications. Some Immortals gained their immortality by "shedding the husk" of their mortal body—that is, in our terms, by dying and leaving behind a visible and palpable corpse—in order to ascend in their immortal form. (This notion coped with the inescapable and observable fact of the earthly death of many men viewed during their lives as Taoist masters and so as Immortals-to-be.) Others ascended directly, leaving behind no "husk." See Chapter 1, n. 2.

51. In fact there is no reference in any of the Celestial Heart scriptures to local cults of Immortals or Perfected at all. Yet these were commonplace in the Sung. See, e.g., the numerous enfeoffments in *Sung hui-yao chi-pen*, *li* 20: 50a–56b.

52. THCF, preface: 1a.

53. By contrast there is a good deal of evidence of the practice of Celestial Heart's sibling sect, Five Thunders, in Fu-chou (see Chapter 6).

54. TCPY, preface: 1b.

55. LWKL, preface. Men who submitted writings to emperors, as Teng did, very often came to the capital to do so in person; but Teng's preface leaves unclear whether he himself did so.

56. ICC *i* 6: 235–36 and *ping* 16: 504–5.

57. Seidel, "Imperial Treasures"; see also her "Image of the Perfect Ruler."

58. Stein, "Religious Taoism"; see also Miyakawa, "Local Cults around Mount Lu," esp. pp. 91–94.

59. Strickmann notes this in "Taoist Renaissance," p. 10. My reading of Steven Bokenkamp's work on the Ling-pao scriptures suggests that Strickmann is referring

to LP #8, *Major Precepts of the Upper Chapter of Wisdom* (*Chih-hui shang-p'in ta chieh*), which contains three sets of regulations on the dead, their crimes, their punishments in hell, and the means for their release from hell; to LP #18, *Precepts of the Three Primordials* (*San-yuan p'in-chieh*), which deals with the agencies judging the dead and lists the crimes falling under their jurisdiction; and perhaps to LP #11, *Ordinances of the Luminous Perfected* (*Ming-chen k'o*), which lists the various sorts of meritorious and harmful records that can have been accumulated by the dead while they were alive. Strictly speaking, none of these works seems closely parallel to the Celestial Heart *Spirit Code*, because all deal only with the spirits of the dead currently in hell, while the *Spirit Code* treats spirits, demons, and deities of all kinds insofar as they are active in the earthly sphere, including the armed spirit entourage of the practitioner and extending even to the practitioner himself and his human disciples. In the general notion of penal statutes directed at spiritual beings, however, these Ling-pao texts do provide forerunners of what seems more fully developed in the *Spirit Code*. See Bokenkamp, "Sources of the Ling-pao Scriptures," pp. 481 and 483.

60. Chiang, *Wu-shang huang-lu ta chai li-ch'eng i*, 52: 26a and 16a respectively.

61. These appear in *Sung hui-yao chi-pen*, *li* 20 and 21. Note as above that those in 20: 50a–56b are specifically Taoist Immortals and Perfected; but even of these, few are represented in Chiang Shu-yü's list.

62. Chiang, *Wu-shang huang-lu ta chai li-ch'eng i*, 53: 30a.

63. Ibid., 56: 28b.

64. In the discussion that follows, I almost always give *tao-shih*, often simply translated as "Taoist" or "Taoist priest," its full literal translation as "gentleman of the Way" in order to be clear about what exactly it is I am comparing to the "rite master," *fa-shih*. Since "gentleman of the Way" is an unwieldy phrase, however, elsewhere in the book I translate *tao-shih*, or refer to the social type that would bear this Chinese title, simply as "Taoist," "professional Taoist," or "ordained Taoist," depending on the context.

65. Schipper, "Vernacular and Classical Ritual," pp. 37–38.

66. See, e.g., THCF 4: 8b, line 4. I owe the reference to Boltz, *Taoist Rites of Exorcism*, p. 169.

67. ICC *chih-keng* 6: 1181. Schipper misreads the second sentence here as follows: "But he was not a *tao-shih*; hence this appellation (of *fa-shih*)." It would be a violation of all the normal rules of classical Chinese of Sung or other times for the elements *sui* and *erh* in this passage to have the functions Schipper gives them when he translates them as "But" and "hence" respectively. This translation of course yields quite opposite implications from my own, and Schipper follows these out. See Schipper, "Vernacular and Classical Ritual," p. 37.

68. ICC *chih-wu* 6: 1101. On this story too, I differ with Schipper, who says, "Because of this transgression, Master of Rites Wang was severely punished by the gods and suffered an untimely death." The implication again is that the *tao-shih*'s functions were not normally available to the *fa-shih*, so that their usurpation by a *fa-shih* could be cause for divine punishment. But Schipper misunderstands the story, which makes it clear that Wang is punished because on one occasion his assistant drinks wine and eats meat before a *chiao* and so bungles the job. There is no indication at all that the celestial authorities who judge Wang are offended by his performing a *chiao* in itself.

69. ICC *chih-wu* 5: 1089–91.
70. ICC *chih-kuei* 5: 1260.
71. Schipper, "Vernacular and Classical Ritual," pp. 27–28.

CHAPTER THREE. HUA-KAI MOUNTAIN AND ITS IMMORTALS

1. Shen T'ing-jui, *Hua-kai shan Fu-ch'iu Wang Kuo san chen-chün shih shih* (hereafter cited as HKS) 5: 4b–5b.

2. This is HKS; see n. 1 above.

3. The Celestial Heart materials are in Teng Yu-kung's prefaces to THCF and LWKL.

4. Compare the discussion in Chapter 2, where I argue that placing the light at the Altar of the Three Pure serves to reinforce an association of Celestial Heart with the Three Pure that is elsewhere established by the claim that the Hua-kai Immortals are the Three Pure's incarnations—and thus to tie Jao's texts to abstract divinity rather than to specific Immortals.

5. For my views on controversial or uncertain points in the history and contents of the *Verities*, see the Appendix.

6. The original is a bit more precise, though hard to incorporate into a translation without awkwardness: *ts'an luan chia hao* indicates that the *luan*-birds are acting as the outer two of a team of birds four abreast; the inner two are the cranes the Two Perfected are riding.

7. HKS 1: 5a–6b; but in one place I have corrected this to follow the version in Yen Chen-ch'ing's own collected works. Where I have "were about to suffer drought" (*chiang han*), the HKS version has *chiang chün*, "general [of an army], command an army," which makes no sense in context and is undoubtedly a corruption influenced by the repeated occurrence elsewhere in the text of *chün chiang*, here translated as "army commander."

8. HKS 2: 2a–b. The ellipsis at the beginning of the next paragraph indicates the omission of the commentary (*chu*) that separates these two sections of Shen's work and that purports to supply material from "another version" (*i pen*) of the story. I am treating what is here presented as Shen's own work as a continuous narrative apart from the commentary.

9. HKS 2: 3b. Again the immediately following ellipsis represents the omission of the commentary only.

10. HKS 2: 7a.

11. HKS 2: 7a–8a.

12. The ellipsis represents the omission of one line of secondary commentary: see n. 14 below.

13. HKS 2: 10a–b.

14. The commentary, though in both style and temporal point of view generally indistinguishable from the main text (except that its upper margin is indented one character from the top of the page) appears on a single piece of internal evidence to date from after about 1125. See HKS 2: 6a, line 3, where the primary commentary has "later, the people who lived here named it the Yung-ch'ung Way-hall." According to the local histories of Ch'ung-jen County, the Yung-ch'ung Abbey did not receive this name until the Hsuan-ho period; before that its name was the I-hsing

Abbey. See TCCJ 2d: 6b. This primary commentary is to be distinguished sharply from the further, double-lined comments that periodically interrupt either it or (far less often) the main text—what I shall call the "secondary commentary." These comments move the point of view sharply forward in time, referring repeatedly to events of "the present day" (*chin*) as matters clearly distinguished from the events and period described in the main text and primary commentary, and dealing with matters that in fact imply a date of composition no earlier than 1138. HKS 2: 3a, in the secondary commentary, locates Mt. Chung-hua in Kuang-ch'ang County. The county was not created until 1138.

15. The Chinese is "*i pen yun.*"
16. HKS 2: 7b.
17. HKS 2: 8a.
18. HKS 2: 8a.
19. HKS 2: 9b.
20. HKS 2: 10b.
21. The Chinese is *ch'ao t'ien*, "have audience with Heaven."
22. HKS 2: 1a.
23. HKS 2: 2a.
24. HKS 2: 1b–2a.
25. HKS 2: 2a, 7a–b.
26. This discussion appears in two articles standing at the beginning and end of the Fu-ch'iu material in the first chapter: HKS 1: 1a–b and 4a–b.
27. HKS 1: 3a–b. No source is indicated for this story.
28. HKS 1: 1b–2a, 2a–b, and 2b.
29. HKS 1: 7a–9b. For the *History of Former Han* reference to Fu-ch'iu, see Wang Hsien-ch'ien, *Han Shu pu-chu*, p. 951 (*Han Shu* 36/1a).
30. HKS 5: 12a.
31. For *chiao-chu*, see Morohashi, *Dai kanwa jiten*, 5: 504 (p. 5142 in continuous pagination), item 13212-83.
32. HKS 2: 1a.
33. Actually, Yen's account is very slightly different: he makes Wang the "collateral descendant" (*tsai-ts'ung*) of Wang Fang-p'ing, rather than his direct descendant. See HKS 1: 5b.
34. Indeed, Wang was in Taoist lore the elder brother—thus the ritual superior—of Ma-ku herself, the Hemp Lady, patron Immortal of Mt. Ma-ku, to which the Two Immortals had intended to travel before their journey was interrupted by their discovery of Mt. Hua-kai. Tracing Immortal Wang's descent to Wang Fang-p'ing thus not only tied the Two to national traditions but more specifically placed them in a line superior to the patroness of a more famous nearby Taoist mountain. There may be a regional as well as a national status claim being made here.
35. There are several more than twenty-five separate items in HKS chs. 5–6. What I am calling "miracle stories" here are only the last twenty-five items, beginning on 5: 6b and continuing right through ch. 6, which deal specifically with the Three Lords. Earlier items treat various other figures associated with Mt. Hua-kai, chiefly in the Northern Sung. The last twenty-five items form a clear group not only as to subject but as to time, since all but the last one or two date (when they are datable) from between about 1150 and the early 1200s. I trace in the Appendix the evidence that

these stories were gathered by Chang Yuan-shu, the Taoist who edited *Verities of Mt. Hua-kai*, which makes up chs. 3 and 4 (and I believe also chs. 5 and 6).

36. Here as often elsewhere Chang refers to himself by name: "Yuan-shu." I translate this as "I."

37. HKS 5: 10a–b. What I have translated here as "a written submission of congratulations," *he shu*, could conceivably be read as a "memorial of congratulations." This would strengthen the bureaucratic tinge of this story. However, *shu* is a rather general term for a statement rendered in writing to a superior; it can also mean simply a prayer. (Whether the meaning "prayer" derives etymologically specifically from the meaning "memorial," via Taoist notions of communication with the supernatural, is a separate issue.) Furthermore, in the Sung the normal bureaucratic terminology for a congratulatory communication sent in an official context to a superior would be either *he piao* or *he ch'i*, depending on whether the addressee was (respectively) an emperor (or emperor's family member) or a fellow bureaucrat of higher rank. Vast numbers of these are to be found in the collected works of Sung men who held office. The term *he shu* simply does not appear in regular bureaucratic contexts.

38. One other story contains matter that might suggest a bureaucratic identity for the Three Immortals, but I think this would be a misreading. Here a woman of Ch'ung-jen County loses consciousness for a time, then tells her family of her visit to hell, in some detail; later in a series of dreams she receives visitations that follow up on her experiences there. In hell, she meets three men:

> I saw three men come in [and stand] in front of my bed. One man wore purple, one wore green, and one wore white. The one in purple told me to ask [Wu] Hsun: "Why do you not demand the twenty strings of cash from Lady Three-eight?" And again to ask: "The Liu family has much money and much land. Why do you not demand it?" Hsun knocked his head and said: "I fear Heaven and fear its punishment and reward. Other people's things I dare not demand." Purple-Garb said: "These two things were only to test you," and he pointed out another house full of money and rice and showed it to me, saying, "This is your husband's. For some time it has been locked." Then he gave me three keys: I put them aside on my family's table. The two [*sic*] men in purple further said to me: "We are the two judges of good and evil of the Eastern Marchmount. Your ten stars are reduced by eight; you get only two; and you get one, and further receive the rescue of your husband's stars and the return of your Granddad; this is why the time has not yet come for you to go away; if it were otherwise, you would go away for a long time."

After her return to life, she has a series of dreams. In one, she sees "three Taoists come in. Two of them alit on a flower vase; a purple-garbed Taoist came straight to her bed and said: 'We are the Two [*sic*] Immortals of Hua-kai, come to see your little boy. For two nights, he has cried at night. From this night on, he will not cry.' When she awoke it was so." If one were to identify the "three men" encountered in hell with the "three Taoists" seen in the dream, on the basis of the purple garb in both cases, then one would have here a case in which the Three Immortals appear as bureaucrats in hell. But I doubt that the teller of the story intends this: the different term used ("men" vs. "Taoists"), the reference to a long beard for one of the dream figures but not for those in hell, and the fact that the three in hell never mention any Hua-kai connection themselves all tend to work against it. Nowhere else in any miracle story or other text do any of the Three Lords appear as judges of good and evil of the Eastern Marchmount, or indeed explicitly as judges in the formal sense at all. More significantly, no one in any other story or text ever encounters the Three in hell. In fact one can read Wu Ch'eng's advice to his brother as telling him that he ought to be appealing to the Hua-kai Immortals *instead of* (as he has already done) to the Eastern Marchmount, or at least in addition to it. If the Eastern Marchmount judges of good and evil in hell were the same as the Three Lords, why appeal to the Three Lords when he has already appealed to the Bureau of Good and Evil at the Eastern Marchmount shrine? In Ms. Chia's dreams (where the Three Lords do explicitly appear), as opposed to her visits to hell, there is nothing specifically bureaucratic going on.

39. HKS 5: 15a.
40. HKS 5: 14a–b.
41. HKS 6: 1b–2a.
42. HKS 3: 4b.
43. The narrator is Chang Yuan-shu, who refers to himself here by his own first name. This is common practice in premodern Chinese texts; the best English equivalent for the name in such passages is the first-person pronoun.
44. HKS 5: 10b–11b.
45. HKS 6: 12a–b.
46. HKS 6: 1a–b.
47. For vows to saints in Europe, see Wilson, *Saints and Their Cults*, esp. his introduction, pp. 13, 21, and Hertz, "St. Besse," pp. 59–60, 90; DeLooz, "Towards a Sociological Study of Canonized Sainthood in the Catholic Church," p. 208; and Sanchis, "Portuguese 'romarias,'" pp. 267–72. See also Badone, *Religious Orthodoxy*, esp. her introduction, pp. 16–17, and Brettell, "Priest and His People," pp. 58, 66; and Dubisch, "Pilgrimage and Popular Religion," pp. 120, 126. See, too, Christian, *Local Religion*, pp. 23–69, and his *Person and God*, pp. 118–35. For vows to Islamic saints in India and Nepal, see Gaborieau, "Cult of Saints," esp. pp. 296 and 299. For vows to Hindu deities, see Bhardwaj, *Hindu Places of Pilgrimage*, pp. 154–62. For individual promises to spirits and fulfillment of promises in spirit cults in Thailand, see the treatment of *pa ba* rites in Tambiah, *Buddhism and the Spirit Cults*, pp. 269–70.
48. Wilson, "Introduction," p. 21.
49. This is the case, e.g., with the father who receives the "Old Man from South of the Mountain" as his son: he offers his vow at the time of an Offering that he has ordered (*ming*) Taoists to perform; but he offers it in his own individual prayer.
50. Sanchis, "Portuguese 'romarias,'" p. 270.
51. Christian, *Local Religion*, p. 32.
52. Dubisch, "Pilgrimage and Popular Religion," p. 126.
53. Gaborieau, "Cult of Saints," p. 299.
54. HKS 5: 8a–9a.
55. Though the passage is unclear, the picture seems to be of a man tied and hanging upside down at the end of a rope by his feet or legs.
56. HKS 5: 15a–16a.
57. HKS 5: 9a–10a.
58. ICC *chih-wu* 6: 1101.

59. One is Chang Yuan-shu's memorial or prayer of congratulations (see n. 37 above); another is a prayer burned by the father-to-be of the Old Man from South of the Mountain.

60. The only clear mention in the miracle stories of any relationship at all between the Three and other divinities, apart from the story of the order of seating of the Immortals at Mt. Pa, appears in a description of the wonders of Dragon Spring Mountain, also in Ch'ung-jen County. One of the wonders is a "Coin Storehouse," and thereby hangs a brief tale:

> The mountain has a "Money Storehouse": this is where the Perfected Lords have employed the gods of the earth [*ti shen*] to yield up money to aid those in poverty and distress. Once there was a fuel-gatherer who came to this place and espied a stone that had opened. Inside was money of incomparable abundance. There were also three hundred or so cash scattered on the ground. Having nothing to carry it in, and also fearing that others might come to know of it, the man planned that he would return home with the extra and come and take it that night. Accordingly, he piled up earth and stones as a marker. When he came again, the stone had closed. He went home and dreamed of a Taoist who said to him: "These are the things we use for relieving the poor; they are not to be taken wildly. The extra money will repay you for sealing up the storehouse, and that's all."

Note that the Three are said to have "employed" (*i*) the earth gods, not to have ordered or directed them. The term is used in Celestial Heart and other Taoist sects for the act of putting to work subordinate divinities of various kinds. Here, however, the bureaucratic context that would have clarified the usage is missing. In the Sung, the verb was used very broadly for private employment arrangements: a nonspecialist reader would have been more likely to read it as "hired" or "employed" than as "commanded to work." The Immortals treat the fuel-gatherer too as someone who has performed (however unwittingly) useful employment for them and who ought therefore to be paid. See HKS 6: 9b–11b.

61. Stein, "Religious Taoism."
62. HKS 2: 2b.
63. HKS 2: 5b.
64. HKS 2: 8a–9b.

CHAPTER FOUR. THE RISE OF THE HUA-KAI CULT

1. Wang Hsiang-chih, *Yü-ti chi-sheng* 29: 5a–6a.
2. Yueh, *T'ai-p'ing huan-yü chi* 110: 6b.
3. See the notes on Mt. Ying-chü (ibid., 110: 3b), on Mt. Lei-kung (4a), on the Stone Granary (4a), on the altar to Lady Wei (4b), on Mt. Ching (5a–b), on the tomb of T'ao K'an's mother (6a), on Mt. Feng-ts'ai (6b), and on Mt. Chün (7b).
4. HKS 3: 15a.
5. This is puzzling, and my reading may not be correct. Mt. Pa lies far to the *south* of the county seat, some sixty *li* according to Yueh Shih himself in the *T'ai-p'ing huan-yü chi* (110: 6b; here the mountain is called Mt. Lin-ch'uan, but Yueh notes that Mt. Pa is its older name), so it is hard to see how it can "shade" an abbey that stands in

the county's northwest quarter. It is possible that more than one mountain bore this name at various times. Or perhaps Mt. Pa seemed to Yueh a landmark so important and so epitomizing of Ch'ung-jen County's identity that any spot in the county could be said to be in its "shade." Alternatively, and perhaps more probably, Yueh may be referring here not to the mountain but to the county town itself, as older names of the county were Pa-shan ("Mt. Pa") and Pa-ling ("Pa Ridge"). Finally *ts'ui*, which I am reading "shades" (an odd reading anyhow), may be a miswriting of a different character (with the same phonetic but a different radical), also pronounced *ts'ui*, meaning "to collect or bring together." Then the passage would read "Mt. Pa assembled its pillars," which would presumably mean that the pillars were cut and brought together *on* Mt. Pa before being shipped to the abbey site.

6. This is *she jen mu:* literally, "shot into men's eyes."

7. *(T'ung-chih) Ch'ung-jen hsien chih* (hereafter cited as TCCJ) 2b: 1b–2b.

8. My date assumes that this is the T'ai-ho period of the Wei kingdom. The Eastern Chin dynasty also had a year-period called T'ai-ho, beginning in 366 and ending in 371. The text says: "During the T'ai-ho period in the Sung," but "in the Sung" is an error, perhaps inserted by Ming editors: there was no such period in the Sung, and the commemorative record by Yueh Shih that the entry cites says only, "In T'ai-ho." Further on in Yueh's record, however, he says: "From T'ai-ho to Ch'ien-te, for roughly [a] hundred and forty years." Since neither T'ai-ho period is anything like as few as 140 years before Ch'ien-te, clearly a preceding digit is missing: this should read "for X-hundred and forty years." As Ch'ien-te falls in the 960s, it is roughly 600 years after the T'ai-ho of the Chin but about 740 years after the T'ai-ho of the Wei. If we are looking for a span of years ending in forty, the earlier T'ai-ho period in the Wei kingdom's calendar seems the right one. All this is complicated by the fact that Fu-chou and Ch'ung-jen County never fell within the Wei kingdom's territory, belonging instead to its southern contemporary, the kingdom of Wu. However, it was commonplace afterward to refer to events occurring in any of the three kingdoms of this time using the calendar of the Wei.

9. HKS 4: 1b.

10. For Heaven's Bar, a Taoist name for the divinity whose visible form was the seventh star of the Dipper (our Big Dipper, recognized as a constellation by the Chinese as well), see Schafer, *Pacing the Void*, p. 51.

11. In the original: *"Chiu chuan huan."* The reference is to the so-called *chiu chuan tan* or *chiu chuan huan tan*, literally, "nine revolutions' elixir" or "nine-revolution-turning elixir," an elixir said to yield immortality on its ninth cycle of refining. Thus the last part of the line literally means "the ninth revolution is turned."

12. This poem is preserved in a recent edition of the genealogy of a Yueh family of modern Ch'ung-jen County, along with a variety of other materials on Yueh Shih. Officials at the county's Cultural Bureau kindly allowed me to examine their photocopy of sections of the genealogy when I visited in May 1985.

13. This might refer to Chess-Playing Terrace, listed in Chang Yuan-shu's sacred geography in *Verities* with the comment: "The place where the Two Perfected played chess." See HKS 3: 4a.

14. These are the record for the Chao-hsien Abbey, written in 1047 (*Lin-ch'uan hsien-sheng wen-chi* 83: 872); the record for the Pavilion of the Nine Illuminators (*Chiu-yao ko*) at the Ta-chung Hsiang-fu Abbey, undated (83: 875–76); and the

record for the Hall of the Three Pure (*San-ch'ing tien*) at the same abbey, dated 1050 (83: 877).

15. HKS 3: 14b.

16. Wang An-shih, *Lin-ch'uan hsien-sheng wen-chi* 83: 877. For this record, see also Jonathan Pease's very useful study of Chiang-hsi writing, "Lin-ch'uan and Fen-ning"; his partial translation appears on p. 61.

17. Wang An-shih, *Lin-ch'uan hsien-sheng wen-chi* 84: 881. I had the privilege of reading Jonathan Pease's unpublished translation of this preface (since published in Pease, "Lin-ch'uan and Fen-ning," p. 69), and my own translation benefits from his, though it differs in several places.

18. Yueh, *T'ai-ping huan-yü chi* 110: 7b.

19. Refers to the eight emperors who had so far reigned in the Sung.

20. Tseng Chao, *Ch'ü-fu chi* 4: 4a–6a.

21. Chi-li's great-grandfather Tseng Tsai (1022–1068) was the elder brother of Pu and Chao by fourteen and twenty-five years respectively. For Tseng Tsai, see his epitaph in Tseng Kung, *Yuan-feng lei-kao* (SPTK, first compilation) 46: 11b–12b. For Tseng Chi-li, see the biographies in TCLC 43: 5a–b and KHNF 7: 19b; the farewell composition for him in Chang Shih, *Chang Nan-hsuan hsien-sheng wen-chi* (TSCC ed.) 3: 53–54; and the colophon to his collected letters in Chu Hsi, *Chu Wen-kung wen-chi* (SPTK, first compilation) 83: 17a. The date of Tseng Chi-li's visit is difficult to pin down. Tseng studied under Lü Pen-chung (1048–1145) and "traveled with" both Chang Shih (1133–1180) and Chu Hsi (1130–1200). His own dates are thus hard to estimate precisely. He was dead by 1194, when Chu Hsi wrote a postface for his collected letters. His great-grandfather Tsai died in 1068 at the age of only forty-six, so it is hard to imagine that Chi-li's father (Tsai's grandson) can have been born much before that date. Assuming 1068 as the earliest birthdate for the father, Chi-li could have been born as early perhaps as 1090. His visit to the mountain, if he was still fairly young, might thus have fallen in the last decades of the Northern Sung as easily as in the Southern Sung. All of this is based on very optimistic assumptions, however; and one doubts that he would be described as "traveling with" Chu Hsi if he had been fully forty years older than Chu. An early Southern Sung date for the mountain visit thus seems much more likely. As we shall see, Ming testimony places the building of the Abbey of the Reclusive Perfected in 1117—ten years before the fall of the Northern Sung—whence my *terminus a quo*.

22. The reference is to the *Record of Lin-ch'uan* by Hsun Po-tzu, a man of the Liu Sung state (420–478) of the medieval southern dynasties. Tseng cites this work in his preface to the poem.

23. The reference is to the calligrapher Wang Hsi-chih (321–379), said to have traded a copy of *Classic of the Yellow Court* (or, in many versions, a copy of *Tao Te Ching*) in his own calligraphy to a Taoist for a flock of geese. Tseng is offering a piece of writing to Taoists and regrets that, because as a calligrapher he is no Wang Hsi-chih, he cannot offer something as fine in trade to them as Wang's *Yellow Court* transcription. There is an implication here, as elsewhere, that Tseng has received or hopes to receive favors from the Three.

24. This alludes to "Preface to the Couplets of the Stone Tripod" by the T'ang poet Han Yü (768–824), recounting the tale of a Taoist named Mi-ming who chal-

lenges two gentlemen to compose poetry about a tripod cooking vessel of stone standing in the fireplace, and amazes them with his ability to rattle off strange couplets in response to their own attempts. See Han, *Han Ch'ang-li ch'üan chi* 21: 15b–18a, and for the poem 18a–19a.

25. The Chinese is "there are not ten days"; I've made it "hardly a week" for meter's sake.

26. Chang Yü-ch'u, *Hsien-ch'üan chi* 2: 68b–70b. The record mentions events that took place in the twenty-seventh year of the Hung-wu period, or 1394.

27. ICC *chia* 9: 74. The collection in which this story appears was first published in 1161. Huang Yueh's *chin-shih* degree fell in 1135, when the highest qualifier in the palace exam was indeed one Wang Yang-ch'en (Cheng Yueh et al., *[K'ang-hsi] Nan-feng hsien chih* [hereafter cited as KHNF] 5: 4a; Ma Tuan-lin, *Wen-hsien t'ung-k'ao* 32: 306). Hung Mai renders the name of the mountain as *chün* "commandery" or "prefecture," rather than as *chün* "army," but the reference is clearly to the same Mt. Chün because there is no "Commandery Mountain" in the region. The mistake is understandable not only for sound but also for meaning: *chün* "army" was the official title of one of the four official ranked categories of prefecture in the Sung (the others were *fu*, *chou*, and *chien*), and in fact the prefecture Chien-ch'ang, to which Nan-feng County belonged, fell in this category at the time and so was called Chien-chang Chün, literally "Chien-ch'ang Army," but understood by contemporaries as Chien-ch'ang (Military) Prefecture. *Chün* "commandery," on the other hand, was in the Sung used both as an alternate official and mainly ceremonial or decorative name for many prefectures (thus Fu-chou's alternate official name was Lin-ch'uan Commandery) and in unofficial usage as a general term for any prefecture, useful in everyday speech or writing because it cut across the four official categories and identified a single administrative level. Both words *chün*, then, had "prefecture" as one possible meaning.

28. The funerary inscription of Huang Yueh's son Huang Wen-sheng (1137–1187) and an examination record for his other son, Huang Wen-ch'ang (1128–1165), confirm that Yueh's grandfather was Huang Lü-chung, who had by some means reached office and served as police inspector of K'ang-chou (Lu, *Hsiang-shan ch'üan chi* 28: 2b–3b). Two of Lü-chung's three degree-holding sons can be identified: they are Huang Fu, *chin-shih* in 1112 (Yueh's father), and his brother Huang Yang, *chin-shih* in 1118 (KHNF 5: 3a, 3b; Li Kuang-jun et al., *[Min-kuo] Nan-feng hsien chih* [hereafter cited as MKNF] 19: 7b). Other Huangs of Nan-feng obtained degrees in 1088 and 1128; one of these may be the third son of whom Hung Mai tells us (KHNF 5: 2b, 4a). Huang Lü-chung may well have been Tseng Pu's in-law: his son, grandson, and great-grandson all married women surnamed Tseng, and the tie would explain his access to office when he held no degree. Assuming thirty years per generation and counting back from Huang Wen-sheng and Wen-ch'ang, Lü-chung would have been born in the late 1030s (Tseng Pu was born in 1036) and would have been in his early sixties when the shrine was renovated (Lu, *Hsiang-shan ch'üan chi* 28: 2b–3b). His prayer, of course, was offered before any of his sons was born; with *chin-shih* degrees in 1112 and 1118 they cannot have been born later than the 1090s.

29. "Shih-yung" here is Huang Yueh's son Huang Wen-ch'ang, a *chin-shih* in 1148.

30. Chou, *Wen-chung chi* 165: 15b–21a.

31. Neither this episode in the Two Immortals' travels nor the abbey itself is

recorded in Shen T'ing-jui's *Veritable Record* and its commentaries or in the miracle stories in the last chapters of *Verities*.

32. That is, it was very hot and dry.

33. Chang Hsing-yen, *(T'ung-chih) I-huang hsien chih* (hereafter cited as TCIH) 45b: 18a–20a. Note that the Yuan-pao Abbey in this inscriptional record is the very same as the site of Cook Liu's misfortunes in the miracle story from *Verities* (set in 1173, or ten years before this record) cited in Chapter 3, n. 57.

34. T'ung Fan-yen et al., *(T'ung-chih) Lin-ch'uan hsien chih* (hereafter cited as TCLC) 19: 34a ff.

35. Tseng Feng, *Yuan-tu chi* 19: 21b–23a.

36. Tseng Feng, *Yuan-tu chi* (Sung edition) 22: 1a–2a.

37. Ch'en Yuan-chin, *Yü-shu lei-kao* 6: 6b–7a.

38. The epitaph goes on to tell of later events that took place during the extensive banditry in Fu-chou in 1230 (ibid., 6: 7a–b). Ch'en got his degree in 1211 and seems to have been in office continuously for a considerable period thereafter, so regular activities in his home county narrated in this inscription probably took place before his degree. On the 1230 banditry, see Hymes, *Statesmen and Gentlemen*, pp. 144, 147, 149, and 321 n. 46(b).

39. Pai, *Sung Pai chen-jen Yü-ch'an ch'üan chi*, pp. 68–70 (1:52–54 in Chinese pagination). The *nien-p'u* in the appendix (*fu-lu*) of this collection (p. 769) places Pai's visit to Mt. Pi-chia in 1222.

40. Mt. Heng in Hu-nan. This detail is not mentioned in the versions of their travels in *Verities of the Three Lords*.

41. Pai, *Sung Pai chen-jen Yü-ch'an ch'üan chi*, p. 84 (1: 68 in Chinese pagination).

42. WWC 47: 8b–10b. "Branch shrine" is my translation of *hsing tz'u*—literally, a "shrine that has traveled" from its original location.

43. WWC 46: 4b–6a. Wu himself is clearly not a believer in Immortals. In this inscription he goes on to take up the problem of the difference between ancient sacrifices at mountains, which were directed to the mountain, and modern sacrifices at mountains, which are directed to men (i.e., Immortals). He discusses the true source of numinous power and comes down, in good classicist fashion, on the side of the mountains themselves. Compare Huang Chen's discussion of similar issues in Chapter 5.

44. WWC 50: 13a–14a. This record is undated. The donor of the altar was Cheng Sung of Lo-an County, Wu Ch'eng's neighbor but more importantly his protector for a number of years in the early Yuan, when Wu moved into the mountains and lived in retreat on Cheng's estate. The text of this inscription may well have been composed during those years. On Cheng Sung see WWC 74: 3a–5a and end matter; Yü Chi, *Tao-yuan hsueh-ku lu* 44: 2b–17a; Ho Hsi-chih, *Chi-lei chi* 5b: 7b. See also Hymes, *Statesmen and Gentlemen*, pp. 74, 83, 127, 128, 148, 149–50, 169, 286 n. 7, 304 n. 9, 321 n. 46.

45. WWC 47: 6a–7b, 48: 1a–31.

46. These are astronomical phenomena. The Northern Chronogram is our Polaris, also known as Heaven's August Great Emperor, for whom the Floreate Canopy—Hua-kai—made of stars of our Cassiopeia, was a sheltering parasol. See Chapter 1, n. 1.

47. "Mr. Chung-chien" (*Chung-chien kung*) is Hu Ch'üan (1102–1180), scholar

and officeholder of Lu-ling, who passed the *chin-shih* examination in 1128. For materials on his life, see Ch'ang et al., *Sung jen chuan-chi tzu-liao so-yin*, pp. 1573–75.

48. Liu, *Hsu-ch'i chi* 3: 29b–30a. The inscription is also preserved in Ting Hsiang et al., *(Kuang-hsu) Chi-an fu chih* (hereafter cited as KHCA) 8: 70b–71b. See also Liu's inscription for the Chu-ling Kuan in *Hsu-ch'i chi* 1: 38b–41a, written around 1290, which similarly touches on the tendency in Chi-chou to name mountains after Hua-kai.

49. The word "Assisting" here reflects titles granted the Three in the Yuan.

50. This title probably applied only to Fu-ch'iu, who supposedly taught Wang-tzu Chin, son of the king, in Chou times and a number of imperial family members and officials during the Han. See Chapter 3, "Divine and Human Relations in *Verities of the Three Perfected Lords*." But note that in granting "Teacher to the Imperial House" as a title, the Celestial Master, the Taoist practitioner par excellence, bureaucratized Fu-ch'iu's role as teacher, which in other sources appears quite informal and personal.

51. KHCA 8: 67b.

52. KHCA 8: 72b–73a.

53. Chu K'uei-chang et al., *(T'ung-chih) Lo-an hsien chih* (hereafter cited as TCLA) 2: 43a.

54. The Fu-chou gazetteers preserve the poem that follows and report that it was written on (about, to) Mt. Hua-kai but provide no information on the context (Lo Fu-chin, *[Yung-cheng] Fu-chou fu chih* [hereafter cited as YCFC] 45: 44b–45a). *Verities*, in contrast, places the same poem in a story of Sun's visit, not to Mt. Hua-kai but to Mt. Hsien-yu in the same county, and specifically to cure his illness (HKS 6: 12b–13a). The last couplet of the poem is consistent with the story of illness (if the "cinnabar sand" refers to Immortals' medicine received on the mountain); but other things in the poem, especially the reference to the tracks of paired *luan*-birds, suggest the setting is Mt. Hua-kai. Sun Ti's collected works confirm his visits to both Mt. Hua-kai and Mt. Hsien-yu but preserve poems different from the one found in the gazetteers and the *Verities*. See Sun, *Hung-ch'ing chü-shih chi* 1: 9a–b and 10a–b for two pairs of poems on Mt. Hsien-yu and 1: 10a for a poem on Mt. Hua-kai.

55. See the epitaphs of T'u Ta-hsiang, Tsou Tsung-mo, Tsou T'ao, and Tsou Kai in ibid., 35: 30a–32b, 36: 17b–19b, 37: 29a–31b, and 37: 31b–33b respectively. Each of these epitaphs dates Sun's stay in Fu-chou to 1132, when banditry in neighboring prefectures delayed his progress south; and the terms in which they describe his stay agree closely with his preface to the first pair of poems on Mt. Hsien-yu, indicating that the poems belong to the same period. Sun also had connections to the Wu family of Ch'ung-jen County, who as we shall see in Chapter 5 were major sponsors of the Hua-kai cult. See the extended account of Wu Hang's poetic development, the *Huan-ch'i shih hua*, which tells us: "One day a friend returned from seeing Minister Sun (*Sun shang-shu*) at Mt. Ts'ao" and goes on to report Sun's views on poets and poetry (see Wu Hang, *Huan-ch'i shih hua* 1b–2a). "Minister Sun" is the correct title for Sun Ti at this period; Mt. Ts'ao is a mountain in I-huang County; Sun Ti's visit there is abundantly attested in his collected works.

56. See, e.g., HKS 3: 2b–3a.

57. Sun Ti, *Hung-ch'ing chü-shih chi* 1: 9a–b and 10a–b.

58. Ibid., 1: 9a–b (the first of two poems).

59. Apart from the three Sung men whose poems follow immediately, these are Teng Ch'ih-ju and T'ang Yuan-ling of the Sung (YCFC 45: 44b–45a), and Yü Chi (YCFC 45: 11a–b and 45: 53b), Wei Su (works in Nanjing 1: 5b–6a and 1: 9b–10a), Ho Chung (YCFC 45: 12a), and Ching Ch'i-p'eng (YCFC 45: 44b) of the Yuan.

60. For Wu I's death date, see ICC *san-jen* 1: 1468–69. The bare facts of the end of Wu's official career that Hung notes are confirmed in *Sung hui-yao chi-pen*, p. 4588 (*hsuan-chü* 21: 5b), p. 4015 (*chih-kuan* 72: 54b), and p. 4050 (*chih-kuan* 73: 68a). Wu received his *chin-shih* degree in 1163; see Hsu Ying-jung, *(Kuang-hsu) Fu-chou fu chih* (hereafter cited as KHFC) 42: 11a, Ch'en Ch'ien et al., *(K'ang-hsi) Ch'ung-jen hsien chih* (hereafter abbreviated as KHCJ) 1: 49b.

61. TCLC 18: 26a (where we are told that the abbey was a site of sacrifices to Fu-ch'iu); YCFC 45: 74a–b.

62. A drought, the escorting of the Three Immortals to the Jade Purity Hall in the Chao-ch'ing Abbey in the Ch'ung-jen County suburbs under the leadership of the county administrator, and successful prayers for rain to the Three are recorded in a miracle story in *Verities*, dated 1182. See HKS 6: 14b–15a.

63. For Lo Kung-yuan and his cult in Szechwan, see Verellen, "Luo Gongyuan."

64. The original has "Shu-yuan," Luan Pa's courtesy name; I translate this as Luan Pa for clarity's sake.

65. Lo Kung-yuan shares the surname of the poem's author, Lo Tien; hence "of my family."

66. An allusion to *Chuang Tzu* XXVI (*Wai wu*): 2, where Chuang Tzu tells the marquis of Chien-ho, who has promised him funds in some vague future, how he once met a perch stranded high and dry on the road, who asked him for a dipperful of water. When he promised the perch to change the course of the West River in his favor on an upcoming trip to the north, the perch (so Chuang Tzu tells the king) replied angrily: "If you can get me a dipper of water, I'll be able to stay alive. But if you give me an answer like that, then you'd best look for me in the dried fish store!" I follow the translation of Watson in *Complete Works of Chuang Tzu*, p. 295.

67. YCFC 45: 83a–b. On Ho I see KHFC 47: 23a–24a; KHCJ 4: 23b–24b; Huang Tsung-hsi, *Sung-Yuan hsueh-an* 97: 9b; Wang Tzu-ts'ai, *Sung-Yuan hsueh-an pu-i* 97: 4a.

68. "The jeweled fringe" refers to the ruler, whose headdress might bear such a fringe. Their missive "shook" the fringe—that is, it caused the ruler's head to shake in amazement, surprise, or fright.

69. See HKS 3: 9a, under "Wonders and Marvels," which lists the following: "Tile arrows: the Two Immortals transformed all the arrows that Li Yen-yuan's troops shot. When they fell to the ground they were transformed into tile. To the present day they are there on that spot. There are still people who find them."

70. See HKS 3: 10a, again under "Wonders and Marvels," which lists the following: "Horse tracks: right at Battle Plain. This is the ground where at that time Li Yen-yuan battled. Down to the present day the horse tracks and camel tracks still remain on the stone."

71. This translates *kung p'u san ch'ien hang*. I have been unable to find the term I translate as "merit-rushes" (*kung p'u*) in any dictionary or reference work. Some sort of ceremonial insignia seems to be meant; compare the account of the ascent in Shen T'ing-jui's *Veritable Record* (HKS 2: 10a): "with Immortals' music and ceremonial in-

signia escorting them in front and rainbow flags and numinous officers pressing them on behind." A *kung-pu*, literally "merit cloth," is a sort of flag borne before a funeral procession (see Morohashi, *Dai kanwa jiten*, 2: 1449, entry no. 2295-103); probably something analogous is referred to here. *P'u*, "rushes," may simply indicate what the insignia or flags in question are made of. Alternatively, there may have been a substitution of *p'u* for *pu* here.

72. I have found no other reference to these mounts. Elsewhere the Two are said to have ascended on the *luan*-bird and crane (HKS 2: 10a) or on *luan*-birds escorted by cranes (HKS 1: 6a). Chang Yuan-shu's sacred geography does list a Tiger-Track Rock, with the comment: "Near the Shang-hsien Abbey. It was at this spot that the Two Perfected Wang and Kuo rode tigers day after day. Where they rested a while, they left tracks, which still remain." See HKS 3: 10a–b.

73. Evidently a reference to Chess-Playing Terrace, listed in Chang Yuan-shu's sacred geography with the comment: "The place where the Two Perfected played chess." See HKS 3: 4a.

74. A reference to the Altar of the Putting on of Robes, marking the spot where the Two Immortals were said to have donned robes and met their teacher. See HKS 3: 5b.

75. A reference to the Cavern of Purple Tenuity, where the Three were said to have dwelt. See HKS 3: 2b.

76. Evidently a reference to Golden Fowl Grotto, where the Two Immortals were said to have raised chickens, and at the mouth of which a charcoal-gatherer had recently (as of Chang Yuan-shu's writing) found a golden tail feather. See HKS 3: 6a–b.

77. *Lung t'ou an chiu ch'iu:* apparently a reference to Dragon Casting Pond, to which it was said the T'ang court had sent emissaries to make sacrifices by casting jade tablets and golden dragons into the pond, and where (presumably similar) sacrifices for rain were still common at the time Chang Yuan-shu wrote. See HKS 3: 11b.

78. A reference to Bloody Tree Hollow, to which the Two Immortals were said to have sent soldiers to capture and execute demons, whose blood struck the tree. See HKS 3: 4a.

79. Perhaps a reference to the Golden Boat (though the character is *ch'uan*, not *chou*, as in the poem—but of course in the poem *chou* is required by the rhyme scheme), listed under "Auspicious Omens" in Chang Yuan-shu's sacred geography, HKS 3: 10b.

80. A reference to Lord Goose's Clay, listed in Chang Yuan-shu's sacred geography with the comment: "The place where immortal geese spread their wings. At the present day, Immortal Geese Pond." For the Immortal geese and their pond, see Yueh Shih's inscription, quoted earlier in this chapter. The reference to the clearing of snow remains obscure. See HKS 3: 8b.

81. A reference to Tea-Brewing Hollow, listed in Chang Yuan-shu's sacred geography with the annotation: "It was at this spot that the Three Perfected, Fu-ch'iu, Wang, and Kuo, brewed tea. The name has survived to the present day." See HKS 3: 4a.

82. The reference is to Losing Heart Ridge (*t'ui-hsin ling*), listed in Chang Yuan-shu's sacred geography with the annotation: "When one first climbs Mt. Hua-kai, halfway up at the mountain's waist a ridge spreads out across it; the higher one goes

the steeper it gets. When gentlemen who come to pay their respects reach this point, if they are not of earnest intent they cannot help losing heart at the difficulty and the height. Hence the name." See HKS 3: 4b.

83. I am reading *ching shou*, which I translate as Clean Hands here, as the name of a place, according to the pattern of the preceding lines, although I have been unable to trace any place on Mt. Hua-kai that bears this name. In fact, "Clean Hands" is surely a mistake for "Clean Water" (*ching shui*), which is the name of a gully listed in Chang Yüan-shu's sacred geography with the comment: "At this spot Gentlemen who visit the Perfected wash their hands and rinse their mouths [*kuan shu*] to cleanse their pollutions [*ching hui*]." See HKS 3: 5a. Ho I depicts himself washing his hands at the appropriate spot.

84. I can find no reference in other sources to clarify this line.

85. The reference is to Sword's Edge Ridge, which we saw in Chapter 3. The line is a recognizable though somewhat exaggerated description of the path leading between the Three Peaks of Mt. Hua-kai as it appears today. The version of the poem that I am using, preserved in the Yung-cheng era Ch'ing dynasty gazetteer of Fu-chou (YCFC 45: 83a–b) has *chien ch'un*, literally "sword spring," at the place I am reading *chien-chi*, "sword's edge." Since the character for "spring," *ch'un*, would be an easy scribal error for "edge," *chi*, and since "Sword's Edge" is an attested place-name on Mt. Hua-kai and "sword spring" would be of no clear meaning at all, I have confidence in this emendation.

86. Under "Wonders and Marvels" (*ch'i i*) Chang Yüan-shu's sacred geography lists both "Immortal Medicines" (HKS 3: 11a) and "Omen Stoves" (HKS 3: 9b). Under "Immortal Medicines" we find: "Grasses and trees on top of the Three Peaks. Through the ages, when there have been sick people who prayed and then picked and took [these as medicine], they have been healed without exception." Under "Omen Stoves" we find: "Natural formations [*tzu ch'an chih wu*] on top of the Three Peaks.... Their form is very ancient. They can ward off plagues. Thus they are called Omen Stoves. If one knows how to pray with the greatest sincerity and then digs in the ground wherever he likes, he will find one. If not, then he will search the whole day without finding one. From Chin down to today, for who-knows-how-many years, the more people have dug the more the Omen Stoves have responded. They have never been exhausted. They are as round, regular, hard, and glossy as if they had been fired by a potter. It is the transformation of the sages that makes them so."

87. For the "Three Houses" (*san lu*) that topped the Three Peaks of Mt. Hua-kai, see, e.g., Tseng Feng's early thirteenth-century inscription commemorating their renovation by the abbot P'ei Sheng-chung between 1198 and 1202, in Tseng Feng, *Yüan-tu chi* 19: 21b–23a. For auspicious visions (*jui hsiang*) in their vicinity, see the list "Auspicious Omens" in Chang Yüan-shu's sacred geography, HKS 3: 10b–13a, which includes such apparitions as the "Golden Lamp," the "Golden Boat," and the "Round Lights" seen by worshippers of the Three Immortals over the generations.

88. The reference is to the Altar of the Five Mounts, one of six altars on Mt. Hua-kai listed in Chang Yüan-shu's sacred geography (HKS 3: 5b). Evidently one or more of the stelae commemorating the acts and movements of the Three Immortals stood at this spot.

89. At both of the shrines to the Three Immortals that I was able to visit in 1985— the parent shrine on Mt. Hua-kai and a shrine in the Yün-lin Mountains in Chin-ch'i

County—images of deities of thunder and lightning hung high above the Three Immortals' altar, flanking it to the right and left. The association of the Three with thunder and lightning is well attested in other Sung and Yuan sources.

90. A traditional description of the abode of the Immortals on Mt. K'un-lun.

91. A term for an imperial palace, in Taoist usage often applied to a palace of the Immortals in Heaven; but even more often to that palace's equivalent in the divine layout of the human body, where it is identified with the heart. It appears that Ho I must be referring to his own heart here; otherwise it is hard to understand why he would place the Scarlet Palace "nearby."

92. *Ts'ang-chou,* a term for the distant Land of the Immortals.

93. What I translate "pin of office" here is *tsan,* the hairpin customarily worn by officeholders. "Removing the hairpin" (*t'o tsan*) and "casting down the hairpin" (*t'ou tsan,* which Ho uses here) were conventional metaphors for retiring from office.

94. TCCJ 2d: 42b; see also HKS 4: 4a.

95. In the same period, a Li family was connected to this group as well. For all five families, see Hymes, *Statesmen and Gentlemen,* pp. 77–79, 301–2.

96. See n. 59 above.

97. On this date see Chapter 3, n. 14.

98. For dating issues see Chapter 3, n. 14; see also the Appendix.

99. HKS 3: 1a–b.

100. As follows: 968–75 for the founding of the Hua-kai shrine on Mt. T'ien-pao, HKS 4: 10b–11a; 1144 for the naming of the Sung-shan Abbey, HKS 4: 8b; ca. 1146, or "the middle of the Shao-hsing period" (1131–1162), for the visit of Tseng Yen-t'ung to Mt. Hua-kai, HKS 3: 11b; 1168 for the building of the Immortals' Pavilion at Mt. Hsin-hua, HKS 4: 10a; 1174–1189—the Ch'un-hsi reign period—for Chang Yuan-shu's inscription for the Ling-hsing Abbey, HKS 4: 2a; 1180 for the rebuilding of the Hua-kai Immortals' Altar at Mt. Chai-mao, and 1181 for the building of the Round Light Pavilion at the same mountain, HKS 4: 11a; 1188 for the beginning of Hua-kai worship at Mt. Chü-hsien, HKS 4: 16a; and 1265 for the rebuilding of the Yü-t'ing Abbey by the Chang family of Nan-ts'un in Lo-an County, HKS 3: 7a. The 1186+ date follows from the mention of the Hsing-lo Abbey as an active institution in HKS 4: 4a; the abbey was rebuilt in 1186 by Wu I, after having been abandoned since the T'ang (see TCCJ 2d: 42b).

101. Chang Yen's preface (HKS, prefaces, 6b) tells us that his fourth-generation ancestor Yuan-feng restored the Yü-t'ing Abbey. He also identifies himself as a man of South Village (*Nan-ts'un*). The South Village Changs of Lo-an County are well documented in the examination lists and biographies in the local histories for Lo-an: they produced twenty-seven prefectural graduates and five palace degreeholders between 1150 and 1270 (TCLA ch. 7; Fang Chan et al., *[K'ang-hsi] Lo-an hsien chih* [hereafter cited as KHLA], ch. 5). The note on the rebuilding of the Yü-t'ing Abbey in Chang Yuan-shu's catalogue of sites again mentions Chang Yuan-feng (whose given name it records as Hsi-i), as well as Chang Yen-fa, who appears as a South Village man in the local histories' exam list (in the entry for the prefectural exam of 1264, TCLA 7: 24b and KHLA 5: 14a) and is also mentioned in Wu Ch'eng's funerary inscription for his nephew Chang Yuan-ting; see WWC 79: 2a–3b. The record in Chang Yuan-shu's catalogue sticks out like a sore thumb for its uniquely late date.

102. HKS 5: 12b–13a. This is the story of Hsiung P'u and the miraculous image; see below.
103. HKS 5: 3b–4b.
104. HKS 6: 12b.
105. HKS 5: 11b–12b and 5: 15a.
106. HKS 5: 6b. The 1151 and 1154 dates are recorded explicitly; the story goes on to deal with events that take place about fifteen years later, whence ca. 1170.
107. HKS 5: 13a–14a.
108. HKS 6: 5a–b.
109. HKS 5: 8a–9a, 5: 15a–16a.
110. HKS 5: 9a–10a.
111. HKS 6: 1a–b.
112. HKS 5: 10a–b, 6: 1b–2a.
113. HKS 6: 2a–5a, 6: 14b–15a.
114. HKS 6: 5a–8b.
115. HKS 6: 12a–b. The story is not dated explicitly, but the protagonist is Wu Ch'eng, mentioned in the story in HKS 6: 5a–8b above with a date of 1184. Hence "ca. 1184" for this story as well.
116. HKS 6: 9b–11b.
117. HKS 6: 13a–14a.
118. HKS 6: 14b.
119. Possibly Chang Yen again, judging by the similarity of the dates to the date of his ancestors' building project in the catalogue of sacred sites.
120. HKS 5: 4b–5b.
121. Literally, to "sprinkle and sweep" (sa–fu).
122. Respectively, a high-quality tea and a drug—presumably what Chan is serving Kuo.
123. Mei Fu, one of the Four Immortals of Mt. Pa, on whom I say more in Chapter 5. Mei Fu served in his earthly lifetime as sheriff of the county that was Ch'ung-jen County's administrative ancestor. Hence in greeting a modern sheriff of Ch'ung-jen with a poem, Chan T'ai-chu refers to him as "Immortal Mei."
124. I am happy to admit that I do not understand this line even in my own translation.
125. HKS 5: 2b–3b.
126. First in the list of three comes "the executive of the Board of Works and assisting executive of the Secretariat-Chancellery, Yuan"; this corresponds to Yuan Chiang, who then held just these positions at court. Next is "executive of the Board of Rites and assisting executive of the Secretariat-Chancellery, Wang"; this would be Wang Kuei. Last is "left executive of the Department of Ministries and concurrently executive of the Chancellery and executive of state matters, Wang"; this would be none other than Wang An-shih. For the titles of the three and their service in this year, see T'o T'o et al., *Sung shih* 211: 5486–90.
127. The *Sung hui-yao* preserves the record of a decree that corresponds perfectly to one referred to in the present document: "Under Shen-tsung, in the eighth year of Hsi-ning [1075], in the seventh month, it was decreed that the Shang-hsien Abbey in Ch'ung-jen County, and the Two Immortals Wang and Kuo, be expressly awarded titles of enfeoffment" (see *Sung hui-yao chi pen* vol. 2: *li* 21: 64a). As we shall see, the

present document is dated in the twelfth month of the same year and specifically refers to an earlier decree that had granted just these honors; the problem now is to correct the first decree, since the Shang-hsien Abbey does not exist!

128. A land measure apparently customary in the Fu-chou region and referred to in a variety of surviving documents, especially in legal judgments in local administrators' collected works and in the judicial collection *Ming-kung shu-p'an ch'ing-ming chi*. I have never been able to determine its equivalent in more common units. The underlying meaning of the term *pa*, to grasp, a handle or a handful, suggests a quantity of land sufficient to produce a handful or perhaps a sheaf of grain.

129. HKS 2: 11a–b.

130. *Sung hui-yao chi pen* vol. 2: *li* 21: 64a.

131. Hansen, *Changing Gods in Medieval China, 1127–1276*, pp. 79–104.

132. Ibid., pp. 91–95.

133. Ibid., pp. 176–77. See also the table on p. 80, which graphs the same figures. The actual numbers are 37 in 1075 as compared with .63 per year from 960 through 1074. These are gross underestimates, however, as Hansen points out (p. 79) on the basis of her closer examination of the enfeoffment history of Hu-chou. If these figures were multiplied by Hansen's ratio of the enfeoffments known from other Hu-chou records to those listed in the *Hui-yao* (91 to 7, or a multiplier of 13)—a rough-and-ready method to be sure, but sufficient for an educated guess—the figure for 1075 would grow to 481 and the average for preceding years to about 8. The figure of 481 for 1075 is not at all implausible: it would mean about 1.5 enfeoffments per prefecture in the empire at that time. A prefectural administrator under pressure to come up with gods for enfeoffment would presumably think recommending one or two an adequate response. Applying the same multiplier to later years would suggest that between 1075 and the end of the Northern Sung, the state officially recognized 11,986 deities: about 39 per prefecture, 230 per year, and about .77 gods per prefecture per year. The total number seems staggering, but with annual and prefectural numbers much short of these, it would be hard to understand the concern, emerging (as Hansen shows) by the 1090s or early 1100s, that the process of enfeoffment required rationalization and regulation.

134. Ibid., p. 81.

135. This is Li Chung-yuan's *Record of the Three Perfected* of 1099, in HKS 1: 7a–9b. The relevant lines are as follows: "During Hsi-ning the prefecture reported the matter of Wang and Kuo's wonders to the court, and August Emperor Shen-tsung decreed that Wang be enfeoffed as Perfected Lord of Compliant Response and Kuo as Perfected Lord of Sincere Response. But by chance they neglected the case of Lord Fu-ch'iu; thus honors did not extend [to him]." After this chapter was completed, I was able to examine at the Library of Congress a Ming-period text on Mt. Hua-kai, the (*Ch'ung-hsiu*) *Chiang-nan Hua-kai shan chih* compiled by Hsu Yün-sheng in 1555. By remarkable good fortune, this work, though a mere fragment in its present form, preserves the original memorial from the prefectural authorities asking enfeoffment for the Two Immortals.

> Fu-chou is in receipt of the articles of the act of grace of the twenty-fifth day of the eleventh month of the seventh year of Hsi-ning [1074], to the effect that all altars or shrines in the empire where prayers and sacrifices have received

numinous verification and that have not yet received honors or titles are to be reported by name, and that one should consult and advise on the granting of special ceremonious orders. For any that have received honors and titles but whose praise and veneration have not been [sufficiently] made known, memorials are also expected. Below we make a careful statement in accordance with the above.

This prefecture has investigated and learned of the case of the Two Perfected Wang and Kuo of the Shang-hsien Abbey at Mt. Hua-kai in Ch'ung-jen County. The people of this county have directed their sacrifices to them for a very long time, and down to today prayers and requests are answered. The good fortune extends to the entire prefecture. They have long been proclaimed as Perfected, but they have never borne the court's grace in titles of honor showing ceremony of praise and veneration. Having received the instructions in this act of grace, we reproduce as accompaniment to our statement one copy each of the text of the stela by the T'ang dynasty prefect of this prefecture, Yen Chen-ch'ing, and the *Veritable Record* of the Taoist of Mt. Yü-ssu, Shen T'ing-jui, and hereby report by memorial, humbly begging that the court expressly send down an edict granting titles of honor to be recorded in the *Sacrificial Statutes*. We humbly await the edict.

Memorializing on the 28th day of the 3rd month of the eighth year of Hsi-ning [1075]:

> Prefectural Staff Supervisor Li Chao-i;
> Prefectural Judge Chia Tsai;
> Prefectural Vice-Administrator Ting Chin;
> Prefectural Administrator Liu Kung-ch'en

This conveniently confirms that the administrators were basing themselves on Yen Chen-ch'ing's inscription and Shen T'ing-jui's *Veritable Record*, since they submit copies of just these two documents as support for their request. It is very satisfying evidence for the speculative reconstruction of the local administrators' conduct I have offered here.

136. Kuo Chün's service is well attested elsewhere; he appears in the full list of Sung administrators of Ch'ung-jen County in the Fu-chou gazetteer (KHFC 35: 19b).

137. HKS, prefaces, 3b–5b.

138. HKS, prefaces, 3a–3b. For Chu Huan, recognizable beyond doubt here because he uses both his given name and his studio name, Yueh-shan, see Ch'ang et al., *Sung jen chuan-chi tzu-liao so-yin*, p. 579.

139. HKS 5: 12b–13a.

140. A painting seems more likely, if the "sagely image" that Chang Yuan-shu has carved on stone represents the same subject, as it seems to. Chang would be less likely to think a sculpted image—a work in a more durable medium—needed special "transmission" to posterity through reproduction in a stone engraving.

141. KHCJ 1: 46a. See also ICC *chih-ching* 9: 6a–b.

142. TCCJ 7b: 1b; KHCJ 1: 44b.

143. TCCJ 7c: 3b; KHCJ 1: 46b.

144. For the Hsiungs, see Hymes, *Statesmen and Gentlemen*, p. 226.

145. The possible fourth is Hsiung T'ien-ch'ang, a palace degree holder in 1097. The gazetteers do not specifically identify him as Hsiung P'u's relative, but the similarity to the name of P'u's father, Hsiung Chih-ch'ang, makes a connection plausible.

146. TCCJ 7c: 1b; KHCJ 1: 43b. The local histories do not tell us that Wu Yu-lin was a member of the same Wu family as Wu Shan-fu and the rest; but like them he lived in the county seat, and he was disinterred and reburied by the county administration during the Shao-hsing (1131–1162), just when the Wu family was becoming most renowned locally for its academic prowess and examination successes. Honors such as those given to Wu Yu-lin were usually reserved for men whom powerful local constituencies promoted; it is easy to believe that the Wu family, more prominent than ever in the early Southern Sung, managed to obtain laudatory reburial for its ancestor, and hard to explain otherwise why Wu Yu-lin won the local administration's attention at just this time, more than a century after his death.

147. On the Wus, see Hymes, *Statesmen and Gentlemen*, p. 242.

148. The connection may have passed through one Wu Ch'ih, whose funerary inscription Ch'en Yüan-chin composed and who married Hsiung P'u's granddaughter; or more than one marriage may have joined the two families. On Wu Tsung, see TCCJ 7b: 3a and 7c: 7a; KHCJ 1: 50b; and Lou, *Kung-k'uei chi* 52: 11b–13b; on Wu Hang, see KHFC 59: 4a; TCCJ 8e: 1b; his own preface to Ou-yang Ch'e, *Ou-yang hsiu-chuan chi*, prefaces, 1a–2a, and Wei Ho's record for a shrine erected to him in ibid. 7: 16a–19a; also Wei Liao-weng, *Hao-shan ta ch'üan chi* 62: 16a. For Wu Ch'ih's funerary inscription, see Ch'en Yüan-chin, *Yü-shu lei-kao* 6: 18b–20b.

149. The story indicates only the reign period, which extended from 1111 to 1117; but since Hsiung received his degree in 1112, we know he cannot have been at the academy after that year. As we have seen, Tseng Chi-li's visit to Mt. Ling-ku cannot have taken place earlier than 1117, when the abbey he mentions was built, and may have been a good deal later, in the first decades of the Southern Sung.

150. HKS 6: 5b–8b. That this is the same Wu family that Wu I and Wu Tsung belong to is shown by a later inscriptional record for the Chao-ch'ing Abbey by Wu Ch'eng (not the same Wu Ch'eng as in the story, nor any relation). Wu tells us: "It has been handed down that the site, mountain, and fields were all donated by the Wu family of the county seat.... In the autumn of the *ting-wei* year of the Chien-yen period, the prefectural graduate Wu Mien made a record, but the stone is broken and incomplete and cannot be read." (See WWC 47: 8b–10b.) In the Southern Sung and Yüan context, "the Wu family of the county seat" identified unambiguously the family of Wu I, Wu Tsung, et al; there were other prominent Wu families, including Wu Ch'eng's own, but not with their main place of residence in the county seat. (For material on other Wu families in Ch'ung-jen, see Hymes, *Statesmen and Gentlemen*, pp. 242–43.) If this were not certain enough, Wu Mien, author of the inscription that commemorated the donations and very possibly the donor himself, was the elder cousin (*ts'ung-hsiung*) of Wu Hang: see Wu Hang, *Huan-ch'i shih-hua* 9a. Wu Mien passed the prefectural examination in 1119 (TCCJ 7c: 4a; KHCJ 1: 47a). Note also that the brothers Wu Hsun and Wu Ch'eng in the miracle story share the earth radical as generational marker in their names. Now Wu Ch'ih, husband of Hsiung P'u's granddaughter (see n. 126 above), has the same radical in his own name and also has a courtesy name built on the same pattern as that of Wu Ch'eng in the story:

Tz'u-chou vs. Tz'u-yang. His funerary inscription also tells us that he had two elder brothers. Thus he may very well be the younger brother of Wu Hsun and Wu Ch'eng, or at worst a more distant kinsman of the same generation. That the Wus had some degree of lineage identity and organization, which would have made the use of such generational characters likely even for kin more distant than brothers, is suggested by two pieces of evidence. Ch'en Yuan-chin's funerary inscription for another kinsman, Wu Hao, tells us that "the lineage of the Ch'ung-jen Wu family was large" (see Ch'en Yuan-chin, *Yü-shu lei-kao* 6: 17a–18b). And an anecdote about Wu I in Hung Mai's *Record of the Listener* shows him drawing up his final instructions to his sons: "His first words were that his lineage's charitable school was not to be abandoned" (see ICC *san-jen* 1: 1b–2a).

151. See n. 150 above.

152. HKS 6: 12a–b. For other stories of local elite men surnamed Wu, who may be of the same family but cannot be surely identified as such, see HKS 5: 13a–14a, in which Wu Ching, an officeholder, encounters the Three on Mt. Hua-kai; and HKS 6: 2a–5a, in which Wu I-o receives texts from the Three in a dream. The events in these stories are dated 1157 and 1182 respectively.

153. HKS 5: 6b.

154. On the Lo family, see Hymes, *Statesmen and Gentlemen*, pp. 231, 301 n. 89, 302 n. 100.

155. Excerpted from HKS 6: 9b–11b.

156. TCCJ 7c: 7b; KHCJ 1: 51a.

157. HKS 6: 13a–14a.

158. All of these relationships are confirmed in Yü Chi's own funerary inscription for a Ms. Huang, wife of one of Ch'en T'ung-tsu's sons. There Yü tells us that Ch'en Yuan-chin's wife was the sister of his own great-uncle. See Yü, *Tao-yuan hsueh-ku lu* 20: 1b–3a. For Ch'en T'ung-tsu, see also the funerary inscription of Ch'en Yuan-chin's father and mother in Ch'en Yuan-chin, *Yü-shu lei-kao* 6: 4a–6b. For the Lady Yü, see also KHCJ 4: 46a–b.

159. For another story about a Ch'ung-jen elite man surnamed Ch'en, see HKS 5: 15a–16a; this is the story of the meat-eating servant and his punishment, already reproduced in Chapter 3. The servant's master is an officeholder named Ch'en. There is no way of knowing whether he is of the same family as Ch'en Yuan-chin.

160. I say "contemporary" deliberately: *Verities* and the secular material—Ho I's poem is an example—do in some instances reproduce the same stories of the Immortals' lives and acts in the Chin dynasty, but these form the central myth of the cult and are in a different category from tales of specific miracles the Immortals have performed in one's own time or for one's own family.

161. HKS 3: 2a.

162. Chapter 3, n. 37.

163. Wu Ch'eng, *Wu Wen-cheng chi* 46: 1a–3a.

164. The best work on the sale of ordination certificates is that of Chikusa Masaaki, in particular "Sōdai baichō kō." Like many commentators on this phenomenon, however, Chikusa tends to see it from the perspective of doctrinal orthodoxy and purity and thus to associate the sale of ordination with Buddhist (and implicitly Taoist) intellectual and religious decline. That a decentralization of religious authority was accomplished here, and that this may bear some of the credit for the strikingly diverse

new religious movements and tendencies of the Southern Sung, is a point that seems usually to be missed. See also Kenneth Ch'en, "The Sale of Monk Certificates during the Sung Dynasty."

CHAPTER FIVE. EXPLAINING THE RISE OF THE HUA-KAI CULT

1. Ming-chou is modern Ningbo. Huang came from Tz'u-hsi County in the north of the prefecture, on the shore of Hang-chou Bay. He was born in 1213, received his palace degree in 1256, and died in 1280 under the Yuan. For sources on his life, see Ch'ang et al., *Sung-jen chuan-chi tzu-liao so-yin* 4: 2870–71. Huang's collected works, *Huang shih jih ch'ao*, contain an unparalleled wealth of documents from the time of his service in Fu-chou.

2. Huang Chen, *Huang shih jih ch'ao* 88: 33b–34a.

3. "Leading peak" is a weak rendition of the untranslatable *chen*, used for mountains of particular height and reputation that came to represent or be identified with the prefecture or county they stood in. Literally *chen* means "to press or hold down," and the application to mountains seems to derive from the idea that certain peaks were of such weight, both physically and spiritually, as to "hold down" or stabilize a whole region.

4. Huang Chen, *Huang shih jih ch'ao* 88: 5a–6b.

5. To avoid confusion, I use the name "Mt. Hsiang" uniformly in what follows, though some sources use "Mt. Pa."

6. Huang Chen, *Huang shih jih ch'ao* 88: 35a.

7. HKS 2: 11a–15b.

8. On descent groups, see Hymes, "Marriage, Descent Groups, and the Localist Strategy"; for the rest, see Hymes, *Statesmen and Gentlemen*, esp. chs. 3, 4, and 8. On changes in the figures venerated in Confucian shrines, only touched on in my work, see the important dissertation by Ellen Neskar, "Cult of Worthies." My own work elaborated and, for Fu-chou, to a great extent confirmed a thesis first put forward by Robert Hartwell in "Demographic, Political, and Social Transformations of China, 750–1550." The chief difference is that what Hartwell described as an absorption of one social group, the "professional elite," into another, the "local gentry," I prefer to call a change of strategies within a single group: from the vantage point of the local level in Fu-chou, Hartwell's two groups never appear clearly separate. In marriage patterns, a Northern Sung–Southern Sung shift was first identified in published work by Ihara Hiroshi; see his articles listed in the bibliography.

9. On changes in the state, Hartwell is again the pioneer; but on all these issues, see also Hymes and Schirokauer, *Ordering the World*, esp. the Introduction and the articles by Peter Bol, Paul Smith, and Richard von Glahn; Bol, "This Culture of Ours," esp. pp. 58–75; and Liu, *China Turning Inward*. For a partial challenge to the notion of a Northern Sung–Southern Sung difference, but one that does not, I think, affect the argument of this book, see Bossler, *Powerful Relations*.

10. For these directives (*chih-hui*), see Ou-yang Ch'e, *Ou-yang hsiu-chuan chi* 7: 2a–4a.

11. He is referred to as "Wu Ch'ao-tsung" in one poem, and simply as "Ch'ao-tsung" in the other eleven. See Ou-yang Ch'e, *Ou-yang hsiu-chuan chi* 4: 9a, 11a, 11b, 13b, 14b, 15a (twice); 5: 14a, 15b, 18b, 19a; 6: 5a. Wu's full name appears in 4: 14b.

12. Wu Hang, *Huan-ch'i shih-hua* 9a.
13. Ou-yang Ch'e, *Ou-yang hsiu-chuan chi*, prefaces, p. 1a.
14. ICC *chih-i* 2: 2b–3a.
15. Later in the text I discuss the connection of the Lis to a different group of Immortals, perhaps because of the proximity of their shrine to the Lis' home.
16. Wei Liao-weng, *Hao-shan ta ch'üan chi* 79: 4a–6a.
17. See the preface to his poem in Ou-yang Ch'e, *Ou-yang hsiu-chuan chi* 4: 2a: "Last year, in the seventh month, while I was awaiting the examination at Lin-ch'uan, two or three friends accompanied me to the Sun-ch'i Pavilion." "Lin-chuan" here refers to the metropolitan county, where the prefectural seat of Fu-chou was located; the prefectural examination was administered there. It seems that Ou-yang did not pass this examination, since he does not appear on the prefectural exam lists in the Ch'ung-jen County local histories.
18. The materials on Ou-yang Ch'e's life and death assembled from various sources in the last chapter of Ou-yang Ch'e's collected works detail the story of Ch'en Tung as well. See Ou-yang Ch'e, *Ou-yang hsiu-chuan chi*, ch. 7, esp. 1a–b, 4b–6a.
19. We do not know the total number who graduated at the prefectural level in each examination during these years. In the early Southern Sung, however, the per-examination quota of prefectural graduates from Fu-chou was set at 49. Assuming that the number of men sent up in each of the seven examination years between 1102 and 1121 was slightly smaller, the total should be around 300 men ($49 \times 7 = 343$).
20. See Ou-yang Ch'e, *Ou-yang hsiu-chuan chi* 7: 16a–19a, for the enshrinement at the county school in 1223, and TCLC 16: 10a ff. for the earlier enshrinement along with nine other local worthies at the prefectural seat.
21. On Wang Wen-ch'ing, himself a man of the greater Fu-chou region, see Chapter 6.
22. On all of this, see Strickmann, "Longest Taoist Scripture."
23. Chang Hsing-yen, (*T'ung-chih*) *I-huang hsien chih* (hereafter cited as TCIH) 13: 2b. The monastery may even have been abandoned long before it was chosen for conversion: there is no earlier mention of it in Sung Fu-chou sources.
24. See Hymes, *Statesmen and Gentlemen*, p. 122. On the False Learning prohibition and the factional conflict surrounding it, see Schirokauer, "Neo-Confucians under Attack." In calling the *Tao-hsueh* group a "fellowship" I follow Hoyt Tillman in his important *Confucian Discourse*.
25. See Hymes, "Marriage, Descent Groups, and the Localist Strategy."
26. This is a surprising date, because the same source places Wang and Kuo's ascent in 292. Perhaps the author implies that their father survived them (in earthly terms) by twenty-five years, or perhaps he had in mind Yuan-ti of the preceding Wei kingdom, who reigned from 260 to 265.
27. HKS 2: 1a–b.
28. See Hymes, "Marriage, Descent Groups, and the Localist Strategy."
29. TCIH 45b: 18a–20a.
30. HKS, prefaces, p. 3b.
31. HKS 3: 2a.
32. For the Ta-ch'ien god, see ICC *ting* 15: 664; *chih-chia* 5: 749–50; *chih-i* 10: 871; *chih-wu* 7: 1103; *chih-kuei* 6: 1266; *chih-kuei* 6: 1269; *san-chi* 5: 1336; *san-hsin* 8: 1442;

san-jen 1: 1470; *san-jen* 2: 1480; Suppl. pp. 1687–88. For several of these references I am indebted to Judith Boltz.

33. Liu Hsun, *Yin-chü t'ung-i* 30: 311–14.

34. For comparable tales of European "automobile" saints, see, for instance, Christian, *Apparitions in Late Medieval and Renaissance Spain,* pp. 16, 18, 20; Wilson, "Introduction," p. 11; and in the latter work compare the following stories in Hertz, "St. Besse," and Spiegel, "Cult of St. Denis and Capetian Kingship." From Hertz, p. 69:

> According to my informants in the Soana valley, who are doubtless echoing the tradition as maintained at Ozegna, as it left the village, the wagon carrying the relics would not move forward; to get it to continue on its way, one of the saint's little fingers had to be cut off, and this has stayed at Ozegna. According to Baldesano, who himself gleaned the story from oral tradition in Ivrea, before it reached its destination, and just as it was crossing the bridge over the Dora, the sacred body halted its vehicle again; the citizens of Ivrea had to solemnly vow to place it in a crypt below the main altar of the cathedral. As soon as they had done so, the extraordinary weight which the relics had acquired was lightened, and St. Besse took possession of his new domain.

And from Spiegel, p. 143 (and see p. 161 for the Latin text):

> There then occurred the famous miracle with which St. Denis is so particularly associated. For no sooner had the severed head fallen to the ground than St. Denis reached down, picked it up and, accompanied by a host of angels singing God's praises, walked five miles to his chosen burial place, the site of the present church dedicated to him.

For other European cases, see Rothkrug, "German Holiness and Western Sanctity," p. 166. Rothkrug argues that automobile saints are a phenomenon specific to Germany and characteristic of its earthbound or locality-bound view of sanctity, in contrast to western Europe, a position that the evidence from Christian, Hertz, and Spiegel would seem to undermine. For comparable Islamic cases, see also Wilson, "Introduction," p. 41: "The phenomenon of automobile relics or corpses is also found in Islam. Lane relates that the corpse of a dead saint not uncommonly indicated in the course of its funeral procession where it wished to be buried." The work cited is Lane, *An Account of the Manners and Customs of the Modern Egyptians,* pp. 523–24.

35. HKS 2: 9b–10a.
36. HKS 5: 4b–5b.
37. Bol, *"This Culture of Ours,"* esp. pp. 341–42.
38. HKS 2: 2a.
39. HKS 2: 7b.
40. Tseng Chao, *Ch'ü-fu chi* 4: 4a–6a. See Chapter 4, first section.
41. For Wu Jui's biography, which mentions his general Mei Hsuan, see *Han Shu,* ch. 24. The biography has nothing to say about campaigns against the southern Yueh. See also n. 42 below.
42. Note however that the story seems to have no basis in fact. Wu's biography tells us he died a year after taking up the position of king of Ch'ang-sha, apparently very shortly after the Han unification. The kingdom of Nan-yueh was recognized in 196 B.C., without any previous conflict as far as the *Han Shu* can tell us, and war did

not break out until 185. It is true that the southern Yüeh ruler Chao T'o's attack in that year was directed against the Ch'ang-sha kingdom, which directly bordered his own; but Wu Jui was surely long dead by this time if his biography is accurate. The *Han Shu* names a different man, Chou Tsao, as the officer sent to attack southern Yüeh at this time.

43. WWC 46: 1a–3a. The word I am translating as "ordain" here is *tu*. Since neither Li was himself a Taoist practitioner, this can only mean that they saw to Hu's ordination indirectly, presumably by buying the ordination certificate he needed to have official standing as a Taoist, with its accompanying tax exemptions and other privileges (not to mention the higher fees that the state-ordained could draw, as we saw in Chapter 2). On this practice, see Chapter 4, "Conclusion."

44. It is tempting to imagine a still more personal and familial connection: that the family was drawn to Mei because of the similarity in their surnames. Though botanists place the "flowering plum" (*mei*) closer to what we call apricots (which the Chinese call *hsing*) than to the "Japanese plum" (*li*), all three fall in one subgenus of the genus *Prunus,* separate from the subgenera comprising their more distant relatives peaches and cherries.

45. On Luan Pa as an example of official and Taoist-inspired efforts against local god-worship, see also R. A. Stein's "Religious Taoism and Popular Religion," in particular pp. 79–81.

46. A large portion of Huang's collected works, the portion from which they take their name of *Huang shih jih ch'ao,* Mr. Huang's Daily Notes, comprises his reading notes on a vast range of books ancient and modern.

47. I have explored Huang's handling of this crisis elsewhere; see Hymes, *Statesmen and Gentlemen,* ch. 6.

48. Huang Chen, *Huang shih jih ch'ao* 94: 12a.

49. Ibid., 94: 17a–b.

50. Ibid., 94: 14b–15a.

51. Ibid., 94: 17a.

52. Ibid., 94: 17b–18a.

53. Ibid., 94: 18a–b.

54. Ibid., 94: 14b.

55. Ibid., 94: 16a–b.

56. Huang refers to Yen Chen-ch'ing here and below by his appellation Yen Lu-kung, "Lord Yen of Lu." I have translated this as Yen Chen-ch'ing for clarity's sake.

57. Huang Chen, *Huang shih jih ch'ao* 94: 15a–16a.

58. Hymes, *Statesmen and Gentlemen,* pp. 157–60, 171.

59. Immediately after the prayers to the Hemp Spring deity and the Four Immortals of Mt. Hsiang in Huang Chen's collected works is a prayer entitled "Praying for Rain and Escorting to the Two Shrines." The text makes clear that the prayer is offered to gods whose images have been moved temporarily to the prefectural seat and sacrificed to there without success and who are now being sent back to their home shrines with further prayers. Since the preceding prayer to the Four Immortals notes that they are being brought to the seat in just this way, theirs is clearly one of the "two shrines"; in view of the order of the prayers in the collection, and since there is no other prayer to a deity whose shrine would have stood outside the prefectural seat, it is very likely that the other of the "two shrines" was the shrine at Hemp Spring and

that its god too had been brought to the prefecture for offerings. Huang Chen, *Huang shih jih ch'ao* 94: 16b.

60. Ibid., 94: 12a–13b.

61. Neskar, "Cult of Worthies."

62. Lu, *Hsiang-shan ch'üan chi*; Hymes, *Statesmen and Gentlemen*, pp. 196–99.

CHAPTER SIX. TAOISTS, LOCAL GODS, AND THE TRANSFORMATION OF WANG WEN-CH'ING

1. This is the date given in a thirteenth-century hagiography. See Chao Tao-i, *Li-shih chen-hsien t'i-tao t'ung-chien* 53: 16a ff.

2. See the poem by Pai Yü-ch'an, dating from the 1220s at latest (see n. 20 and the 1292 commemorative record by Ch'eng Chü-fu in the section of this chapter titled "Wang Wen-ch'ing as Local God").

3. One brief mention in non-Taoist sources comes probably from the early years of the Southern Sung at latest, and from the hand of a man who seems likely to have been in the capital when Wang was serving Hui-tsung. This appears in the "Biography of (Lin) Ling-su" in the *Pin-t'ui lu* of Chao Yü-shih (1175–1231). Chao says he has here copied "without daring to add or change a single character" the work of Keng Yen-hsi, who served in capital posts in the late Northern Sung and retired to a temple sinecure around 1127 (see Ch'ang et al., *Sung jen chuan-chi tzu-liao so-yin*, p. 1878). Chao was an accomplished bibliographer; if his judgment that the biography in his possession was Keng's work was accurate, we are in possession of a reference to Wang Wen-ch'ing in a text probably written no later than the 1120s. If Chao was mistaken, the text he reproduces can still be no more recent than the Chia-ting period (1208–1225), since Chao's own postface tells us he wrote down the notes that became the *Pin-t'ui lu* over a period of months in that reign period. These earliest and latest possible dates for the biography neatly bracket the dates at which current stories about Wang Wen-ch'ing appeared in various installments of Hung's *Record of the Listener*: 1161, 1171, between 1171 and 1189, 1195, and 1196. The crucial passage in the biography reads: "The next year [apparently 1120, since a closely preceding passage deals with the anti-Buddhist decrees of 1119], the capital had great drought, and they commanded [Lin] Ling-su to pray for rain, but there was no response. Ts'ai Ching memorialized that he was a fraud. The emperor secretly summoned Ling-su and said: 'I have listened to you in all things; now pray for three days of rain for me, to block the slanders of the great ministers.' *Ling-su asked that he urgently summon the Taoist of Nan-feng in Chien-ch'ang prefecture, Wang Wen-ch'ing, who was a leading divinity of the Divine Empyrean and concurrently managed the Bureau of Rain; and together they would report to the Emperor on High. When Wen-ch'ing arrived, he bore a document decreeing rain, and indeed they received three days of rain. The emperor was pleased and granted Wen-ch'ing too [the rank of] imperial attendant of the Palace of Concentrated Spirit.*" (Emphasis mine.) See Chao Yü-shih, *Pin-t'ui lu* 1: 4–6, for the biography, and 10: 138, for Chao's postface; ICC.

4. HY 1240, TT 996. "Household talk" is my tentative rendering of *chia-hua*. I know of no other text that entitles itself this way; nor does the phrase seem to have been a set construction in this period or at other times. It may be modeled on *chia-yü* in *K'ung Tzu chia-yü*, "Household Talk of Master K'ung," a lost text of Han date that re-

putedly contained daily conversations of Confucius with his students. "Void-soaring, mystery-penetrating imperial attendant" (*ch'ung-hsu t'ung-miao shih-ch'en*) was the position Wang was said to have achieved in the imperial Taoist bureaucracy created by the emperor Hui-tsung during the ascendancy of Lin Ling-su and Shen-hsiao Taoism. See Chapter 2, p. 27.

    5. Boltz, *A Survey of Taoist Literature*, p. 306 n. 338.

    6. *Ch'ung-hsu t'ung-miao shih-ch'en Wang hsien-sheng chia-hua* (HY 1240; TT 996; hereafter cited as *Chia-hua*), pp. 3b–4a.

    7. Ibid., p. 2a.

    8. Ibid., pp. 13b–14a.

    9. Ibid., pp. 14a–b.

    10. Ibid., pp. 10b–11a.

    11. Presumably a pictured sun in the basin on the altar?

    12. *Chia-hua*, pp. 12b–13b.

    13. ICC *ping* 14: 487.

    14. Chao Tao-i, *Li-shih chen-hsien t'i-tao t'ung-chien* (TT 148, HY 296) 53: 16a–21b. For Chao and his work, I rely on Boltz, *Survey of Taoist Literature*, pp. 56–59.

    15. Chao Tao-i, *Li-shih chen-hsien t'i-tao t'ung-chien* 53: 16b.

    16. Ibid., 53: 16b.

    17. Ibid., 53: 18b–19a.

    18. Ibid., 53: 20b.

    19. Ibid., 53: 21a. The God of Beneficent Response, also known as Ta-ch'ien for the place in Shao-wu prefecture, Fu-chien, where his main shrine was located (the Shrine of Beneficent Response), was an important regional god in northwestern Fu-chien and adjacent areas in the Sung and Yuan. The most informative contemporary source is a set of notes that the Yuan scholar and Nan-feng County man Liu Hsun made when he came across a devotional history of the god and his cult. The notes appear under the heading "*The Dream Record of Ta-ch'ien*" in Liu's collected jottings, the *Yin-chü t'ung-i* (30: 311–14). Anecdotes treating the Ta-ch'ien deity also appear in Hung Mai's *Record of the Listener* see ICC *ting* 15: 664; *chih-i* 10: 871; *chih-wu* 7: 1103; and the supplement (*pu-i*), p. 1739. B. J. ter Haar has examined the history of this cult in "Genesis and Spread of Temple Cults in Fukien," pp. 363–65.

    20. Pai, *Sung Pai chen-jen Yü-ch'an ch'üan chi*, p. 372. Pai died in 1229 in Chien-ch'ang prefecture, Wang Wen-ch'ing's home, at the end of a journey that had carried him through neighboring Fu-chou in 1222. We have already seen in Chapter 4 the commemorative inscriptions he wrote at that time mentioning the Three Lords of Hua-kai. It is very likely the poem was written on this Chiang-hsi trip; thus I date it to the 1220s. It cannot, obviously, date from later than 1229. If it should predate the 1220s, this, of course, would simply give a still earlier first date for evidence of local worship of Wang Wen-ch'ing.

    21. Ch'eng, *Hsueh-lou chi* 11/3a–b.

    22. Yü, *Tao-yuan hsueh-ku lu* 25: 15a.

    23. For the special Taoist title "redactor of archives" (*hsiao chi*), the rank just below imperial attendant for each of the palaces (*tien*) to which Hui-tsung's Taoist officers were attached, see the article in Ch'en Pang-chan, *Sung shih chi shih pen mo*, 51: 512.

    24. Yü, *Tao-yuan hsueh-ku lu* 25: 15b–16a.

NOTES   313

25. Ibid., 25: 17a.
26. Chao Tao-i, *Li-shih chen-hsien t'i-tao t'ung-chien* 53: 18b–19a.
27. Yü, *Tao-yuan hsueh-ku lu* 25: 16b–17a.
28. Ibid., 25: 17b–18a.
29. Ibid., 25: 18a–b.
30. Chao Tao-i, *Li-shih chen-hsien t'i-tao t'ung-chien* 53: 16a.
31. *Chia-hua*, pp. 1a–b.
32. Ibid., p. 1b.

33. See, e.g., Schipper, "Written Memorial in Taoist Ceremonies," p. 311: "The Tou-su [*tao-shih*: Taoist priest] is colloquially called *sai-kong*, master. His position is normally hereditary. Adoption is possible, but it is rare and difficult. In order to become a priest, one has to have the bones, *sai-kong-kut*." And in Schipper, "Vernacular and Classical Ritual in Taoism," p. 25: "The quality of Mastership does not concern only the social body, but also the physical body. One must have 'the bones' (the skeleton of an Immortal), that is, a certain genetic quality, in order to qualify for the dignity of being the representative of heaven and the administrator of the Gods."

34. This, as we have already seen, is the title of Wang Tzu-hua, Wang Wen-ch'ing's teacher. The text here and elsewhere has "Mr. Wang" and not "the Fire Master." I have taken the liberty of substituting Wang Tzu-hua's more exalted title for "Mr. Wang" throughout these passages so as to avoid any confusion with Wang Wen-ch'ing himself, whose surname is not even written with the same character as his teacher's.

35. *Chia-hua*, pp. 1b–2a.
36. Ibid., pp. 2a–2b.
37. Ibid., p. 11a.
38. Ibid.
39. Or their "Way-destiny" (*tao-yuan*).
40. *Chia-hua*, pp. 6b–7a.
41. Weller, *Unities and Diversities in Chinese Religion*, p. 100.

42. Kenneth Dean cites a Taoist scripture of interest in this connection, the *Tu-jen ching*, which presents the normal life of a scripture as comprising three important stages. The numbers inserted in the text are mine: "(1) In the beginning the primordial breath, [*ch'i*], filled the Void. The Breath gradually congealed into immense cloud-seal characters. These emitted light and sound. (2) Eons later they were transcribed by heavenly scribes on gold tablets, and preserved in libraries in the stellar court. (3) After more eons they were revealed to the Taoist elect, usually in the context of a visitation from a divine messenger, a 'hierogamy.'" Here the stages marked (1), (2), and (3) constitute what one might call "cosmic," "bureaucratic," and "personal" stages in the passage of a text respectively. Dean, *Taoist Ritual and Popular Cults of Southeast China*, p. 48.

43. THCF *hsu* 1b.
44. THCF *hsu* 2a.
45. THCF *hsu* 3a.
46. On Wang Yeh (palace degree 1220), see the entry in Ch'ang et al., *Sung jen chuan-chi tzu-liao so-yin* 1: 167.

47. For Tu Kao (1173–1248), see ibid., 2: 794. Tu is called a "sojourning gentleman" because his grandfather, Tu To, had been a K'ai-feng man who moved to Shao-wu at the time of the fall of the North in 1127. Many other migrant northern-

ers in the Southern Sung identified themselves fully with the places they moved to, and we find the Tus too identified as Shao-wu men in other contexts; but the continuing pull of K'ai-feng identification was especially strong, since K'ai-feng had been the capital in the Northern Sung and remained officially the Sung capital in cherished theory and in government propaganda. To admit that one was no longer a K'ai-feng man—that one would not be going back—was in a sense to admit that the Sung was no longer the legitimate government of all of China, an admission that was nearly seditious in the Southern Sung. To call oneself a "sojourner" was thus in this context an expression of loyalty to one's emperor and his state. For Tu To, see Ch'ang et al., *Sung jen chuan-chi tzu-liao so-yin* 2: 808.

48. Presumably the year was 1274, since 1235 through 1274 makes a period of forty years, and since, at the end of the passage, we find "next year" and 1276 mentioned in a way that could imply direct succession.

49. Liu Hsun, *Yin-chü t'ung-i* 30: 313–14.

CHAPTER SEVEN. THE BUREACRATIC MODEL: A SPECULATION

1. For the pre-Taoist roots of bureaucratic constructions of divinity (in the underworld particularly) and of other important strands of the organized Taoist religion, see the very important dissertation by Peter Nickerson, "Taoism, Death, and Bureaucracy in Early Medieval China." Pre-Taoist bureaucratic images of (in some cases) even heavenly gods are discussed especially in his second chapter. Nickerson notes, of course, that the grave-securing writs in which bureaucratic models and language are found must already have been the work of literate ritual specialists (p. 266), which makes his own term "proto-Taoist" seem particularly apt.

2. Chao Tao-i, *Li-shih chen-hsien t'i-tao t'ung-chien* 53: 20b.

3. For Yü-wen Ts'ui-chung, see Ch'ang et al., *Sung jen chuan-chi tzu-liao so-yin*, 1: 559–60.

4. ICC *ping* 18: 518.

5. On Pai, see Berling, "Channels of Connection in Sung Religion."

6. Pai Yü-ch'an, *Sung Pai chen-jen Yü-ch'an ch'üan chi, fu-lu*, p. 768.

7. The raw numbers are 51 of 110 in the Northern Sung and 28 of 65 in the Southern Sung.

8. *Locus classicus* for this graded system of enfeoffments is a 1080 memorial by Wang Gu preserved in *Sung hui-yao, li* 20: 6b. For this memorial and on enfeoffments in general, again see Hansen, *Changing Gods*, pp. 79–104; the text of the memorial is translated on pp. 81–82.

9. Liu Hsun, *Yin-chü t'ung-i* 30: 311–14.

10. These appear in HKS 2: 11a–15b along with the 1075 decree officially recognizing the Ch'ung-hsien Abbey. The source contains full texts of the edicts, with surrounding notations about dates, names of signatory officials, the movement of documents among the throne, bureaus, and local authorities, and so on. For the sake of my comparison of these with the edicts of bureaucratic appointment that follow, which all appear in draft form in the collected works of their drafters and without the similar surrounding apparatus that would have accompanied them when they were finally issued and transmitted beyond the court, I omit all but the heading and basic text of each edict from my quotation of the Hua-kai Immortal enfeoffment orders.

11. Recall that "Pao-kai" is another name for Hua-kai.

12. The allusion is unclear. A specific instance of epidemic disease is presumably meant, but I have found no record of epidemics in Fu-chou that would correspond to this. "East of the mountains" probably refers here to Fu-chien circuit, which lay east of Chiang-hsi across mountains. It could possibly refer instead to the Shan-tung region, since Shan-tung literally means "east of the mountains," but Shan-tung is so far from Chiang-hsi that this seems unlikely.

13. Ou-yang Hsiu, *Ou-yang Hsiu ch'üan chi, wai-chih chi* 3: 173.

14. Wang An-shih, *Lin-ch'uan hsien-sheng wen-chi* 49: 516.

15. Chang Hsiao-hsiang, *Yü-hu chü-shih wen-chi* 19: 189.

16. This, of course, did not prevent other observers from representing future aid from deities in such terms. Hung Mai's collection preserves an anecdote of exam candidates who appeal to the Ta-ch'ien god to suppress bad weather along a river course so that they may travel to the examinations. Their prayer refers to the god's previous enfeoffment by the state (*kuo*), and ends by saying if he grants a boon to them this "will also be a way to repay [*pao*] the state." ICC *chih-kuei* 6: 1266.

17. ICC *chih-i* 5: 830; cited in Boltz, "Not by the Seal of Office Alone," p. 262.

18. ICC *chih-i* 7: 846.

19. ICC *ping* 16: 504–5.

20. ICC *ting* 2: 549–50, 14: 653–54; *chih-chia* 5: 745; *chih-ching* 2: 890, 9: 949–50; *chih-ting* 4: 995; *san-chi* 8: 1362–63.

21. Here I follow the alternate reading given in the commentary in the text.

22. In modern Chinese, this term means simply turning head over heels, turning a cartwheel. It is unclear what it means as the practitioner's technical term in the present context. Hence, I illustrate it literally.

23. ICC *chih-ting* 4: 995.

24. ICC *chih-ching* 9: 949–50.

25. ICC *ting* 4: 568.

26. Hansen, *Changing Gods*, p. 26.

27. Hansen, "Gods on Walls," p. 102 n. 5.

28. I examined 499 stories set in Chiang-hsi in the first three volumes of the Chung-hua shu-chü edition of Hung's *Record of the Listener;* 179 of these deal with gods. I counted as a "god" any entity that satisfied one of the following conditions: (1) the story, or characters in the story, referred to it or addressed it as a *shen;* (2) characters in the story prayed to it for aid of some sort; (3) it appeared as a powerful actor in purgatory or in Heaven; (4) it was the dedicatee of a shrine. These conditions might seem restrictive (or, to some eyes, too lenient), but in fact there were very few cases in which it was not instantly clear whether a god, in our common understanding of the notion in Chinese culture, was involved, and I am reasonably certain that any other reader would have classified the stories almost precisely as I have. The god stories appear in ICC *chia* 1: 2, 4: 28–29 and 32, 8: 70, 9: 73 and 74, 12: 102, 13: 120 and 121, 15: 132, 16: 140; *i* 4: 211, 6: 228, 8: 252, 10: 271, 14: 299, 303, 303–4, and 304–5, 17: 326, 18: 338, 19: 351, 20: 358; *ping* 5: 406–7, 6: 418, 9: 444–45 and 445, 11: 457–58, 458, 459, and 460–61, 12: 471–72, 13: 475, 478, 15: 490, 18: 515, 517, 19: 527, 528–29; *ting* 2: 546, 547, 551, 3: 555, 559, 10: 622, 624, 12: 635, 14: 657, 15: 660, 667, 16: 670, 17: 677, 18: 687, 19: 695–97, 20: 701, 703–4, 705, 706, and 708; *chih-chia* 3: 732, 733, 733–34, 735–36, and 737, 4: 744 (two stories), 5: 746, 748 (two

stories), 749, and 750, 6: 755, 758, 759, 760 (two stories), and 761 (two stories), 7: 762–63, 764, 765, 766, and 768, 8: 773 and 776, 10: 788, 792, and 793–94; *chih-i* 2: 808, 810–11, and 811, 3: 813, 815, 818, and 819, 4: 827, 5: 832–33 and 834, 7: 849, 850–51, and 851–52, 9: 864, 10: 871, 872, and 876–77; *chih-ching* 1: 886, 2: 888 and 893, 5: 920–21 and 921, 7: 937–38, 8: 946, 952–53, and 953, 9: 955, 955–56, and 959, 10: 963, 963–64, and 964; *chih-ting* 1: 968–69, 2: 983, 3: 984, 7: 1020, 1021–22, 1022–23, and 1025, 8: 1034 (two stories), 10: 1044–45, 1045–46; *chih-hsu* 2: 1063, 3: 1076, 4: 1082, 1082–83, and 1084–85, 7: 1104 and 1108, 8: 1114–15 and 1116, 10: 1133–34; *chih-keng* 1: 1139, 4: 1162, 6: 1181, 7: 1186, 1188–89; *chih-kuei* 1: 1224–25, 2: 1235–36, 3: 1244 and 1247, 5: 1255, 1258–59 and 1260, 6: 1266–67, 1268, 1268–69, and 1269, 7: 1276, 8: 1283, 10: 1295–56, 1300; *san-chi* 2: 1318–19, 5: 1343, 6: 1349 (two stories), 8: 1366–67 and 1367, 9: 1371–72, 1373–74, and 1374, 10: 1378, 1379, 1382–83; *san-hsin* 1: 1388–89, 1390, and 1393, 2: 1395 and 1396–97, 5: 1422.

29. Eighty-one of the 179 god stories (45 percent) contain bureaucratic motifs, but of those 31 are purgatory stories (38 percent of the bureaucratic group, 17 percent of the total). Amazingly, there is also *one* purgatory story out of 31 with no trace of bureaucracy: perhaps not surprisingly, there the active god is the merciful Kuan-yin, who helps a woman escape from hell. See ICC *chih-ching* 5: 921.

30. If we exclude purgatory stories from the group of god stories, which then numbers 147, then 97 of these 147, or 61 percent, contain no bureaucratic motif. The nonbureaucratic stories are in ICC *chia* 1: 2, 9: 73 and 74, 13: 121, 15: 132, 16: 140; *i* 8: 252, 14: 299 and 303, 18: 388; *ping* 5: 406–7, 6: 418, 9: 444–45, 11: 457–58, 459, and 461, 12: 471–72, 13: 475, 15: 490, 18: 513 and 517, *ting* 2: 547 and 551, 3: 555 and 559, 10: 624, 15: 660, 18: 687, 19: 695–97, 20: 701 and 705; *chih-chia* 3: 732, 5: 746, 748, and 750, 6: 759, 760, and 761, 7: 764 and 766; *chih-i* 2: 808, 810, and 811, 3: 813, 818, and 819, 4: 827 (two stories), 5: 834, 7: 849, 850–51, 9: 864, 10: 871, 872, and 876–77; *chih-ching* 1: 886, 2: 893, 8: 952–53, 9: 955, 10: 959 and 963–64; *chih-ting* 1: 968–69, 2: 983, 7: 1021–22, 1022–23, 1025, and 1034, 10: 1045–46; *chih-hsu* 4: 1084–85, 7: 1108, 8: 1114–15, and 1116, 10: 1133–34; *chih-keng* 1: 1139, 4: 1162, 6: 1181, 7: 1186; *chih-kuei* 2: 1235–36, 4: 1247, 5: 1255, 1258–59, 6: 1266–67, 1268, 1269, 10: 1295–96, 1300; *san-chi* 8: 1366–67, 1367, 9: 1371–72, 1373–74, and 1374, 10: 1378; *san-hsin* 1: 1390, 2: 1396–97. Of these, only 15 (15.5 percent) involve female gods.

31. Compare Stephan Feuchtwang's comment on popular gods: "The rites of petition performed in procession festivals were quite separate and distinct from those of the officially favoured instructive veneration and recompense. If they replicated imperial power, it was the martial and terrible aspect which they portrayed." Feuchtwang, *Imperial Metaphor*, p. 78.

32. The hell stories and death-related stories together are 44, or 54 percent, of the 81 stories with bureaucratic gods.

33. Other god stories with bureaucratic motifs number 17, or 21 percent, of the 81 bureaucrat-god stories.

34. The 17 non-Taoist, non-death-related, nonpurgatory stories with bureaucratic motifs amount to 9.5 percent of all the god stories Hung Mai records for Chiang-hsi, or about 11.5 percent of the stories of nonpurgatorial gods. These stories appear in Hung Mai, *ting* 2: 546, 10: 622, 12: 635, 17: 677, 20: 708; *chih-chia* 5: 749, 7: 765

and 768; *chih-i* 7: 851–52; *chih-ching* 2: 888, 5: 920–21; *chih-ting* 10: 1044–45; *chih-hsu* 2: 1063, 4: 1082–83; *chih-kuei* 7: 1276; *san-chi* 5: 1343, 6: 1349, 10: 1379.

35. Or bureaucratic relations and personal relations may be thoroughly mixed together in a single story involving a single god. In ICC *ting* 20: 708, a bride from a family of hereditary spirit mediums is harassed by the god she and her family have previously served. The god ceases and desists when his mother tells him to let the bride go. In support of her command, the mother tells him, "High Heaven has ordered it" (*shang t'ien yu ming*), and it is on this basis—a god's referring upward to the authority or command of a higher god—that I class the story in my bureaucrat-gods group. But we see the god living in his splendid house with his mother; the god seems to see the bride as his own promised wife: the whole framework of the story, apart from the one reference to High Heaven, is a framework of kinship and marriage relations between god and human and between gods: *personal* relations.

36. ICC *chih-i* 9: 866–67.

37. ICC *chih-kuei* 10: 1298–99.

38. ICC *chih-kuei* 4: 1252–53.

39. ICC *i* 7: 237. For comparable cases, see also *ting* 18: 684–85, *chih-i* 9: 866–67, and *san-hsin* 2: 1396.

40. ICC *ting* 2: 549–50.

41. ICC *san-chih* 8: 1362–63.

42. Ebrey and Gregory suggest that the possibility of direct access to gods by ordinary people was new in the Sung. But miracle stories in pre-Sung texts like the *Sou-shen chi* or those preserved in the *T'ai-p'ing kuang chi*, I believe, also very often show people praying to gods on their own.

43. ICC *i* 7: 237.

44. ICC *ting* 3: 555. I have not been able to find these Three Worthies or Three Sages in other sources. It is tempting to imagine they may be the Three Immortals of Mt. Hua-kai, here viewed in a rather new light.

45. I have not found a single case in Hung Mai's Chiang-hsi stories in which laymen call on a Taoist *before* they call on a spirit medium (*wu*), and there are a number of cases of the opposite order.

46. For Taoists as monopolists, see Dean, *Taoist Ritual*, p. 40, which reproduces a proclamation of 1909 quoting the complaint of local gentry: "Buddhist and Taoist priests set up their own vulgar rites in order to obtain wealth by deceit. They even dare to falsely claim that each ward belongs to a particular *shizhu* [main temple, lit. 'master of dispensation'], and that they have hereditary relationships with [these temples] due to the fact that their forebears have conducted sacrifices and established merit within the ward, so that whenever anyone within the ward wants to hire a Buddhist or Taoist priest, that matter must be handled by the main temple, and people may not hire anyone else [but them], nor may anyone else take the job for personal profit."

47. On the relation of the notion of divine money to a commercial economy, see Gates, "Money for the Gods." See Kohn, *Taoist Experience*, pp. 343–50, for a translation of the *locus classicus* of this notion, the *Scripture on the Loan of Life from the Celestial Treasury Following the Words of the Heavenly Venerable of Numinous Treasure*, TT 333. Kohn (p. 343) notes that the text's ideas "can be related to the emergence of a full-fledged monetary economy in the twelfth century." The scripture of course combines

financial models—loan of life and its repayment—with the standard bureaucratic model, since the loan issues not from a divine merchant, landlord, or other typical moneylender, but from a Celestial Treasury bureau with an administrator and staff of subofficials.

48. It is not even essential to the argument I am proposing that the commercialization of Taoists' and other religious specialists' services, and the movement of Taoists into the market niche of generalist divine mediator for ordinary people, happened first or all at once in the T'ang-Sung transition. Peter Nickerson, in his dissertation and in "Shamans, Demons, Diviners," has traced convincingly the evolution of Taoists from a "church" or "community" organized on bureaucratic lines here on earth as well as in relation to Heaven—essentially the condition at the time of the Heavenly Masters movement in Han—to a "guild" of professional ritual specialists serving a lay clientele. This transformation, he argues, also convincingly, was more or less complete by the fifth century, and the prohibition in Lu Hsiu-ching's *Abridged Code* at that time against Taoists' "traveling the villages" to offer their services does suggest that some may have been doing so. Nickerson's emphasis on Taoist competition with spirit mediums and diviners at this period is similar to the argument I have been making here. What remains hard for me to believe, however, is first that Taoist penetration of rural life can really have proceeded very far in the conditions close to natural economy that historians have so far presumed held in much of the Six Dynasties countryside, and second that Taoists before T'ang-Sung were already offering laypeople aid in dealing with *laypeople's own gods*. On the latter point Nickerson notes: "At least by the T'ang and Sung, Taoist priests began to oversee festivals for local deities," citing work of Kristofer Schipper that I touch on in the next chapter. That his own extensive work on Han and Six Dynasties Taoism has apparently turned up no evidence of direct Taoist involvement with local gods suggests that the T'ang-Sung transition is indeed a time of considerable intensification of the interaction between Taoists and ordinary laypeople away from court and capital. On Taoist incorporation of spirit mediums into their own rites, Nickerson cites work as yet unpublished by Ned Davis, which again focuses on the Sung, and the text in which he finds possible pre-T'ang evidence of such incorporation survives, as he notes, only in a late T'ang redaction and so despite its apparent inclusion of Six Dynasties material *may*—there is no certain conclusion available here—also mainly reflect T'ang-Sung conditions. But my essential point is only that *whenever* large numbers of religious specialists took up the role Taoists routinely occupied in Sung texts, especially those of the Southern Sung, the bureaucratic model would have provided a divine expression (or equivalent) of and justification for that role. See Nickerson, "Shamans, Demons, Diviners," esp. pp. 42, 63–65.

49. Andersen, letter of June 18, 1991.

50. Schipper, "Taoist Body," p. 355: "The body as a 'country' has an administration with a ruler and officials (*kuan*)."

CHAPTER EIGHT. GOD WORSHIP AND THE *CHIAO*

1. HKS 6: 1b–2a.

2. Compare the view of Steven Sangren, not talking specifically about Taoists in this case: "Although it may be true that relatively few individuals construct rational-

ized cosmologies or worldviews, it is generally the few 'rationalizers' in any local tradition or cult who are most responsible for the form it takes" (Sangren, *History and Magical Power*, p. 201).

3. D'Andrade, *Development of Cognitive Anthropology*, p. 129. Even so, D'Andrade goes on to point out that some of Americans' ideas about medicine not only do not come from medical science but contradict its findings. There is no contradiction between the point he makes and the point cited from Fredrik Barth in what follows: that such acceptance of expertise is only one possible way cultural actors may handle systematic differences in knowledge.

4. Barth, *Balinese Worlds*, p. 309.
5. Gregory and Ebrey, "Religious and Historical Landscape," p. 9.
6. Kleeman, "Expansion of the Wen-ch'ang Cult," p. 62.
7. Dean, *Taoist Ritual*, p. 17.
8. Ibid., p. 14.
9. Ibid., p. 18.
10. Ibid., pp. 13–14.
11. HKS 5: 6b. For a full translation, see pp. 108–9.
12. HKS 5: 8a–9a. For a full translation, see pp. 67–68.
13. HKS 5: 10b–11b. For a full translation, see p. 65.
14. HKS 5: 11b–12b. For a fuller account of this story, see pp. 60–61.
15. HKS 5: 15a–16a.
16. HKS 6: 1a. For a full translation, see p. 66.
17. HKS 6: 13a. For a full translation, see p. 110.
18. HKS 6: 14b–15a.
19. Sangren, *History and Magical Power*, p. 56.
20. Schipper, "Written Memorial," p. 113.
21. Dean, *Taoist Ritual*, p. 15.
22. Faure, *Structure of Chinese Rural Society*, p. 80.
23. Even in the second case, it is hard to be sure that a collective community ritual is meant: it is possible that the priests at the Chao-ch'ing Abbey simply performed a *chiao* twice a month regardless of community participation. In any case, the cycle is much shorter than those cited by the anthropologists.
24. ICC *chih-ting* 9: 1034.
25. ICC *san-chi* 2: 1319.
26. ICC *i* 14: 304–5.
27. ICC *ping* 5: 406–7.
28. ICC *chih-chia* 6: 761.
29. ICC *chih-ching* 10: 963.
30. ICC *san-chi* 5: 1341. The other eight stories are in ICC *i* 17: 326; *ting* 2: 551; *ting* 3: 555; *chih-i* 1: 801; *chih-ting* 2: 983; *chih-keng* 1: 1139; *chih-kuei* 5: 1260; and *san-hsin* 5: 1422.
31. Sangren touches on the sorts of personal motives that generate *chiao* in Sung sources, though not as stimulus to the *chiao* itself: "participants in public rituals will often say that they are fulfilling a promise to a deity or thanking it for help rendered. . . . Another opportunity for individuals to testify publicly is afforded by annual inspections of community boundaries (*yu-ching*) undertaken by most territorial-cult gods. Individuals often fulfill promises to the god by taking on the role

of soldier or retainer in such ritual processions." Sangren, "Dialectics of Alienation," p. 79.

32. HKS 5: 10b–11b.
33. Schipper, "Written Memorial."
34. On negotiation as a process by which religious representations and practices are constructed when actors with different assumptions about their meaning must come together, see Sangren, "Dialectics of Alienation," p. 72.
35. Lagerwey, *Taoist Ritual*, p. xiii.
36. Ibid., pp. 65–66.
37. Ibid., p. 67.
38. Ibid., p. 45.
39. Ibid., pp. 37–48.
40. Ibid., p. 46.
41. Schipper, "Written Memorial," p. 317.
42. Sangren, *History and Magical Power*, p. 171.
43. Feuchtwang, *Imperial Metaphor*, p. 151.
44. Schipper, "Written Memorial," p. 317.
45. Feuchtwang, *Imperial Metaphor*, p. 179.
46. This makes it hard to understand Dean's statement that when the *hui-shou* bring home the lamps from the ceremony and hang them in their houses, the presence of the lamps in just these homes "revealed the inner structure and hierarchy of the community," a claim that would seem more plausible where the role of community representative reflects wealth or other special status in the community rather than chance selection. Dean, "Field Notes," p. 209.
47. Cohen, "Mei-nung," pp. 16–17.
48. Feuchtwang, *Imperial Metaphor*, pp. 166–79. The same system holds in the "Sacrifice of the Kings" Kristofer Schipper observed at Hsi-kang. See Schipper, "Seigneurs royaux," p. 32.
49. Schipper, "Written Memorial," pp. 318–19.
50. Faure, *Structure of Chinese Rural Society*, p. 9.
51. Ibid., pp. 80–82.
52. Ibid., p. 80.
53. In more recent, as yet unpublished work, which he has been kind enough to share with me, David Faure agrees: "Insofar as the priests and the villagers can accommodate one another, and yet draw their strength from different deities, their religions meet but are not integrated" (Faure, "Priestly Tradition," p. 8). In electronic mail of June 14, 1995, in response to questions about his work, Faure confirmed this interpretation: "What I have always found with the NT jiao is that you don't find one unified set of rituals, but two quite separate sets of rituals—one might say two religions—going on at the same time."
54. There is, of course, every reason to imagine that, within the Taoists' own part of the celebration, they may continue to represent the villagers' gods as subordinates of their own gods and of themselves. The point is that the lack of a unified, focused ritual structure like that in Taiwan gives them no opportunity to make this representation stick at the level of the whole population of participants.
55. Tanaka, *Chūgoku no sōzoku to engeki*. I am deeply grateful to David Faure for

calling my attention to Tanaka's work and for spelling out the significance for my project of several of the *chiao* Tanaka records.

56. Ibid., pp. 380–402, but see especially the maps of overall layout and of the individual buildings on pp. 385, 386, and 390.

57. This becomes clear in Lagerwey's account of the Presentation of the Memorial, during which the Taoists make the opera stage their own, treating it as a symbol of Heaven to which they climb. Lagerwey, *Taoist Ritual*, pp. 149–67.

58. Tanaka, *Chūgoku no sōzoku to engeki*, pp. 609–32, but see especially the maps on pp. 613, 617, and 627.

59. Ibid., p. 631.

60. Ibid., p. 163. A *chiao* of broadly similar pattern is mapped on p. 211.

61. Hsu, *Exorcising the Trouble Makers*.

62. Ibid., pp. 91–92.

63. Ibid., pp. 99–102.

64. Ibid., p. 96.

65. Ibid., pp. 94–95.

66. Ibid., pp. 96–97.

67. Ibid., p. 97.

68. Others have argued this as well, without treating the *jiao* itself in the way I am treating it here. See Sangren, *History and Magical Power*, but also Robert Weller, *Unities and Diversities*, esp. pp. 97–100.

69. Hsu, *Exorcising the Trouble Makers*, pp. 48–49.

70. Faure discusses local interpretations of the ghost-eater, a god whose image the Taoist priests brought to the *chiao* he observed at Lam Tsuen. "The villagers had two stories of his origin. He was said by some to be the reincarnation of the Buddhist Goddess of Mercy (the Bodhisattva Koon Yam) [i.e., Kuan-yin], and by others a mountain ghost who had come under her spell and was made to help her suppress evil ghosts by eating them. In either story, therefore, the Buddhist goddess was given a crucial role. This caused the senior Taoist priest Mr. Lam some concern, and he explained without our asking him that in the dispute between the Buddhists and the Taoists in history, it was brought out that the Goddess was no more than the reincarnation of a stable-boy for the Tai Shang Lo Kwan, i.e. the philosopher Lao Tzu, the first Taoist master." Faure, "Ta-tsiu," p. 35.

71. Lagerwey, *Taoist Ritual*, pp. 52–53.

72. Sutton, "Ritual Drama," esp. pp. 538–46.

73. Sutton, "Rituals of Self-Mortification," p. 110.

74. Dean, *Taoist Ritual*, pp. 13, 14.

75. Ibid., pp. 52–53. The term "despotic signifier" leaves it unclear who in particular Dean believes "erected" the bureaucratic metaphor if not Taoists—is the despotic signifier the despot himself?—but suggests he may believe it was the state. A paragraph in his concluding chapter, though again ambiguous, suggests the same view (p. 184): "The Imperial system gathered up particularistic communities by organizing them along standardized patterns, as bricks in the edifice of empire. The Imperial system entered into every aspect of life and diverted it toward itself. The power of the Imperial system is all in the hands of the despotic signifier—the Emperor's word is Law. Imperial power comes to inform every aspect of society. This is

most evident in the bureaucratic metaphor, with its Heavenly palaces and hierarchies, its ranks of immortals, its dangerous ghosts and demons, and its tribunals in the Underworld. As a model for conceiving the world, teaching political truths, or inculcating obedience, the bureaucratic metaphor is omnipotent.... Taoism reacted to this architectonic of the state by scrambling the codes." I think most historians, particularly of late imperial China, would now think this a fantastic overestimate of the power, political or cultural, of the Chinese state or, within that state, of the emperor. Agency is unclear again in this paragraph, but there is at least a suggestion that the bureaucratic metaphor was fundamentally the state's own. I show in Chapter 7 that, at least in the Sung, the state did *not* use a bureaucratic metaphor when it enfeoffed local gods. And this whole book is devoted to showing that the bureaucratic metaphor, though important, was not "omnipotent" in any capacity or sphere.

76. David Faure notes that the Taoists at his *chiao* in Lam Tsuen understood even the Three Pure, according to sophisticated textual Taoism primordial cosmic abstractions, bureaucratically: "[T]he priests looked upon the supremacy of the Three Pure Ones in more worldly terms. They were simply emperors, who were highest in the hierarchy of gods, above even the Jade Emperor. The Empress of Heaven and other gods were far below them, and by deriving their own authority from Heavenly Master Cheung, who had access to them, the priests came as representatives of a source of authority even above the Empress of Heaven." Faure, "Ta-tsiu," p. 38.

77. Dean, *Taoist Ritual*, p. 50.

78. Ibid., p. 51.

79. "In Lam Tsuen, the villagers issued a notice to 'close the hills' for the several days of the [*chiao*], forbidding grass or tree cutting, or taking lives of any kind. It was said that during those few days, the birds became exceptionally quiet. But only vegetarian food could be had. *The priests claimed that the rule did not apply to their meals, but the villagers demanded it of all meals served in the villages, including the non-indigenous villagers.*" Faure, "Ta-tsiu," p. 31; emphasis mine. Further on (p. 39) it becomes clear that the Taoists did honor this prohibition.

80. Dean, *Taoist Ritual*, p. 52.

81. Schipper, "Vernacular and Classical Ritual," p. 27.

82. Ibid., pp. 46–48.

83. See also Dean, *Taoist Ritual*, p. 100, which notes that the 1980 consecration of a temple "was performed by Buddhists, though Taoists can do it as well. There is a considerable overlapping of ritual functions by the two groups in the countryside"; and p. 128 for similar material on the distribution of ritual roles among various professionals. Surely who performs what ritual, or the fact that distinct groups compete to offer the same services, might affect ritual content, or for that matter the relative strength of supplier and consumer in the religious market, with consequences again for the ritual.

84. Ibid., p. 42.

85. Ibid., p. 46.

86. Ibid., p. 102. This seems to be the ritual described on p. 111. It is not a *chiao*, but it is a liturgy with Taoists officiating and with Taoist services of some sort.

87. Feuchtwang, *Imperial Metaphor*, p. 173.

88. Paul Katz argues the same view: "[I]nstead of viewing festivals ... as possessing a structure revolving around the rituals of one particular group, it might be best

to view them as arenas where a variety of competing rituals and representations of deities come into play." Katz, "Welcoming the Lords," p. 57. Katz's work on plague deities is extremely important and I consistently find myself, as here, in strong agreement with his approach to the variety and richness he finds in his materials.

89. Faure, "Ta-tsiu," pp. 39–40.
90. Ibid., p. 49.
91. Ibid., p. 45.
92. Schipper, "Taoist Ritual," pp. 831–32.
93. A closer translation of *Yü-ch'ih tai-t'ien hsun-hsiu* might be "Imperial Inspectors, Surrogates of Heaven by Jade Decree."
94. Schipper, "Seigneurs royaux," p. 34.
95. Ibid., pp. 36–38.
96. Schipper (ibid., p. 43) has found the twelve in a Ming liturgical manual under the same surnames by which the chiefs of Hsi-kang know them today.
97. Hsu, *Exorcising the Trouble Makers*, p. 56.
98. Ibid., p. 60.
99. By saying "in China," I certainly do not mean to imply that the same attitude toward knowledge is not found elsewhere. Consider the attitude of European nobility at some periods toward specialized knowledge or skill of almost any kind; of some upper-middle-class Americans in the late twentieth century to the knowledge of plumbers or auto mechanics; of male employers in many offices to knowledge of typing or (now) computing; of feminists of a certain cast of mind to knowledge of professional football. To claim specific ignorance is often, in many cultures and many situations, to claim superior status. In fact, this is simply one more in the range of possibilities proposed by Fredrik Barth of how an unequal distribution of knowledge may be handled and interpreted socially.
100. Personal communication from Theodore Huters.
101. Schipper, "Taoist Ritual."
102. Reiter, "'Investigation Commissioner.'"
103. For the cult's origin in imperial decrees, see ibid., p. 276, the portion of the translated scripture beginning, "Now, this tradition has its roots in the *Chen-hsing t'u*, and so in the period. . . ."
104. The *Lu-i chi* of Tu Kuang-t'ing (850–933), HY 591, TT 327. (Note that Reiter consistently gives as TT numbers what are actually HY numbers.)
105. The *Lu-shan T'ai-p'ing-kung ts'ai-fang chen-chün shih-shih*, HY 1276 (Reiter makes this TT 1286), TT 1006–7. Reiter places this work "after 1124"; for the precise date of 1154, see Boltz, *Survey of Taoist Literature*, pp. 81–82.
106. This account shares a good deal with Schipper's own, but I believe I depart from him in the emphasis I place on the purely Taoist character of the T'ang examples he has uncovered.
107. Katz, *Demon Gods*, esp. p. 171.
108. Johnson, "Temple Festivals."
109. Ibid., p. 697.
110. Ibid., p. 656.
111. Ibid., p. 672.
112. Gallin, *Hsin Hsing, Taiwan*, pp. 235–36.
113. Ibid., p. 237.

114. Ibid., p. 242.
115. Ibid., pp. 240–41.
116. Jordan, *Gods, Ghosts, and Ancestors*, p. 40.
117. Ibid., p. 103.
118. Ibid., pp. 104–13.
119. Feuchtwang, *Imperial Metaphor*, p. 96.
120. Schipper, "Neighborhood Cult Associations," pp. 660–61, 664.
121. Ahern, *Chinese Ritual and Politics*, pp. 98–99.
122. Ibid., pp. 100–101.
123. Weller, *Unities and Diversities*, p. 49.

124. It should be clear that my notion of "passive vocabulary" here is neither the same as nor in conflict with Robert Weller's very interesting idea of active and passive models in his work *Unities and Diversities in Chinese Religion*, on which more below.

125. Compare Christian Jochim, in his work on the Religion of the Yellow Emperor movement in Taiwan today: "[A]cknowledging that people are attracted by 'elite' teachings and ceremonies is not the same thing as saying that they are willing or able to share in the elite style of interpretation of those teachings and ceremonies. In other words, it is one thing to find attractive the outward symbols of someone else's cultural style of interpretation but quite another to adopt and, moreover, understand that style as one's own." Jochim, "Flowers, Fruit, and Incense Only," p. 31.

126. Ibid., pp. 18–19; emphasis mine.
127. Wolf, "Gods, Ghosts, and Ancestors," pp. 138–39.

128. Sangren argues that the stove god is associated with fire, and that fire is known to mediate between Heaven and earth, as when incense and prayers are burned; thus the stove god stands (in rank) between the place god and the Lord of Heaven on the altar. Sangren remarks on other mediative or transformative functions of fire, such as the conversion of the raw to the cooked or (in the ancient myth of archer Yi) of wilderness into civilized ground. My difficulty with this explanation—aside from the fact that a two-models account will bring this case together with a wider range of other cases—is that as far as I know the stove god's association with fire is not with the fire that sends prayers and incense to Heaven but with the fire that cooks the food that feeds the family; and the significance of that cooking, for Chinese who speak of stoves and stove gods, is, as far as I understand it, not so much that the raw is transformed into the cooked or the natural into the cultural as that the food is provided that the whole family eats together. Thus the stove is preeminently the symbol of the family as a unit, of family togetherness. It is by this connection that the god of the stove can be conceived of as the governor of the family and its fortunes.

CHAPTER NINE. CONCLUSION: THE TWO MODELS

1. Sangren, *History and Magical Power*, esp. ch. 8.
2. It seems to me that Sangren has also shown this, especially in his discussion of pilgrimage, for example, and horizontal integration; ibid., pp. 91 and 99.
3. Weller, *Unities and Diversities*, esp. chaps. 3, 4, and 5.
4. Weller is aware of these issues, of course, and by no means claims that the different styles of interpretation absolutely or exclusively characterize the respective groups he treats: see esp. ibid., pp. 10–11. Our divergence is thus a matter of degree.

5. DeGlopper, *Lukang*, p. 31.
6. Ibid., pp. 34–35.
7. Yan, *Flow of Gifts*, pp. 98–121.
8. Ibid., pp. 123–24.
9. Ibid., p.102.
10. For a generally similar picture of gift-giving, *kuan-hsi*, and *kan-ch'ing* in another northern Chinese village, see Kipnis, "Language of Gifts."
11. Nothing I have said should be taken to imply that these are the only two models; they are two prominent ones, but may be two of several or many. I have suggested that the state, in its "enfeoffment" of local gods, should be taken literally as employing a "feudal" model of state-god relations. Such a model may be present in the shadows of other models in other contexts as well: some popular images of gods suggest local lords more than either administrators or local gentlemen. Stephan Feuchtwang, in his very important *Imperial Metaphor*, suggests that popular deity worship is founded on the image of a "command hierarchy"—that is, a hierarchy of relations of military-style command, coercion, and violence, distinct from the bureaucrat's hierarchy of Taoism and the state. While military and martial images are extremely common in lay religion, they play an important part in Taoist notions as well: consider the ubiquitous "spirit soldiers" and "spirit officers" with which the bureaucrat-gods of Taoism, like their earthly counterparts, are endowed. I would suggest that military imagery is not so much a third model as a style of representation compatible with either the bureaucratic or the personal model and cutting across both; and that what Feuchtwang calls a "command hierarchy" is really a militarized version of the bureaucratic model. However, I also think that Feuchtwang sees "command hierarchy," implying multilevel ordering and a highest central authority, wherever he finds martial images of command between gods or between gods and men, and that in fact in many cases the materials themselves do not show that people are operating according to a multilevel hierarchy at all.
12. See Chapter 7, n. 29.
13. This point may share something with Prasenjit Duara's notion of "superscription," in which successive reinterpretations of the same deity by different cultural actors (the state being one) in effect add a new layer on top of the sedimented older layers of previous interpretations in a cumulative process; see Duara, "Superscribing Symbols." I agree with Paul Katz that Duara assumes the cumulativity of this process too completely and neglects the possibility of real independent creation and coexistence of utterly alternative versions (what Katz calls "cogeneration") or of erasure rather than superscription; but that the range or cultural power of previous interpretations sometimes or often (but when? under what conditions?) puts bounds to the interpretations that come after there seems little doubt, and I think Katz would agree as well. See Katz, *Demon Gods and Burning Boats*, pp. 113–14.
14. For a useful set of studies on this topic see Badone, *Religious Orthodoxy*. It is also the focus of virtually the entire oeuvre of William Christian, Jr.: see his *Apparitions in Late Medieval and Renaissance Spain, Local Religion in Sixteenth-Century Spain*, and *Person and God in a Spanish Valley*. Divergences between lay and clerical religion are also important in many of the studies, some already cited in Chapter 3, in Wilson, *Saints and Their Cults*. See also Wolf, *Religious Regimes*.
15. Wilson, "Cults of Saints," pp. 252–53.

16. As the studies already cited show, of course, a distinct lay religion does not disappear when there is a powerful centralized church; but it may be driven into the interstices and margins of the official religion, or into the interior space of the individual, in a way it is not in China. Susan Tax Freeman, writing about Spain, argues: "Spain has, over the centuries, been christianised . . . to the extent that officially sanctioned collective ritual in sacred space has virtually no unofficial rivals—no major pagan rites, no reformed churches. The real rival is the insistence that faith may be expressed through communication with the divine outside the collective context as well as within it. This includes much of what goes on at [saints'] shrines, apart from the periodic collective festivals at them, and also what goes on within the person, as a believer, privately—without reference to a collectivity or a defined time and place in which to worship. . . . It may be that forms of private exercise of faith—private worship, reflective religion—grow up precisely where collective and public ones become subject to official dicta and associated with a church's temporal power." Freeman, "Faith and Fashion," p. 120.

APPENDIX: SOURCE ISSUES

1. Boltz, *Survey of Taoist Literature*, p. 265 n. 65.
2. Andersen, "Taoist Ritual Texts," pp. 81–83.
3. Ibid., pp. 89–90.
4. See Boltz, *Survey of Taoist Literature*, p. 287 n. 217.
5. HKS 2: 7b.
6. Boltz, *Survey of Taoist Literature*, p. 287 n. 217.
7. HKS 2: 2b.
8. On the Heavenly Letters episode and the establishment of these temples, see Cahill, "Taoism at the Sung Court."
9. HKS 2: 8a.
10. Li Kuang-jun et al., (*Min-kuo*) *Nan-feng hsien chih*.
11. As Boltz points out, the commentary refers to Kuang-ch'ang County, which was created from territory of Nan-feng County in 1138. Boltz, *Survey of Taoist Literature*, p. 287 n. 217; see also HKS 2: 3a.
12. THCF, preface, 1a.
13. In personal correspondence (November 29, 1983) Boltz suggested that Shu-chou's name change came even earlier, to Te-ch'ing Chün in 1115. But in fact this name-change applied to the prefectural military establishment only, representing an upgrading of the military responsibilities of the prefectural administrator from a simple "military affairs" (*chün-shih*) grade to the "provincial military governorship" (*chün-chieh-tu*) grade. (See Wright, *Alphabetical List*, p. 146.) After this change the prefecture itself was still called Shu-chou, but the administrator's title in official usage now included the phrase "Te-ch'ing Chün-chieh-tu." In the same communication Boltz noted that Hung Mai's *Record of the Listener* continues to use the name "Shu-chou" in stories containing internal dates of 1146, 1154, 1155, 1175, and 1189, which on the assumption of a name change in 1115 suggested that new prefectural names were not always honored even in published work; but the correct date of 1195 for the first change in the name of Shu-chou *prefecture* brings these usages into perfect correspondence with official nomenclature, as Boltz found was the case for Hung's ref-

erences to Hung-chou ("Hung-chou" in stories with internal dates of 1141–1153 but "Lung-hsing Fu" in stories with dates of 1180 and 1182). But even if it should be shown on more complete investigation that place-names in private sources such as the *Record of the Listener* do not always reflect intervening changes in official names, the crucial point will remain that in his preface to the *Spirit Code* Teng Yu-kung is addressing *an emperor* in a communication in effect public and official.

14. LWKL, preface, 3b.
15. Boltz, *Survey of Taoist Literature*, pp. 80–81.
16. Reiter, *Grundelemente*, p. 110.
17. Boltz, *Survey of Taoist Literature*, p. 81.
18. Reiter, *Grundelemente*, p. 110.
19. HKS 5: 6b, 6b–7a, 8a–9a, 15a–16a, 6: 1b–2a, 2a–5a, 8b–9a.
20. HKS 5: 7a–b, 13a–14a, 6: 1b–2a. Note that the last also uses first-person reference.
21. HKS 6: 9b–11b.
22. HKS 6: 12a–b. Note also that this story concerns the same man mentioned in 6: 5b–8b, which uses first-person reference in the narrative.
23. HKS 5: 5b–6a, 15a, 6: 1b–2a, 5b–8b, 8b–9a
24. HKS 5: 10a–b, 10b–11b, 12b–13a, 6: 2a–5a, 5a–5b.
25. This is the account of the miraculous herbs and medicinal plants that grow on Mt. Hua-kai; HKS 5: 5b–6a. The account ends, "At the present day surrounding the mountain there are also spots with naturally occurring marvelous medicines, of which [I] regret that I do not know all the names. Now I will write down a certain number I have heard of and reverently record them below."
26. HKS 6: 11a–b, 12a–b.
27. HKS 6: 13a–14a.
28. HKS 6: 13a–14a, 14a–b.
29. HKS 3: 1b–2a
30. See Chapter 3, n. 14.
31. See, e.g., the mentions in the sacred geography chapters of an administrative unit called Fu^2-chou; three cases in HKS 4: 8a, one in HKS 4: 18a, three in HKS 4: 20a–b, one in HKS 4: 23a; and the three mentions of Chi-shui-chou in HKS 4: 21b–22a. Fu^2-chou is a name and administrative status given to Feng-ch'eng County in Hung-chou only during the Yuan dynasty, and Chi-shui-chou is the similarly upgraded Chi-shui County in Chi-chou.
32. For this fire see also the miracle story of Ch'en T'ung-tsu and his mother already treated in Chapter 4, HKS 6: 13a–14a.
33. HKS, prefaces, 3b–5b.

Bibliography

Ahern, Emily Martin. *Chinese Ritual and Politics*. Cambridge: Cambridge University Press, 1981.
Andersen, Poul. "Taoist Ritual Texts and Traditions, with Special Reference to *Bugang*, the Cosmic Dance." Ph.D. diss., University of Copenhagen, 1991.
Badone, Ellen, ed. *Religious Orthodoxy and Popular Faith in European Society*. Princeton, N.J.: Princeton University Press, 1990.
Barth, Fredrik. *Balinese Worlds*. Chicago: University of Chicago Press, 1993.
Berling, Judith. "Channels of Connection in Sung Religion: The Case of Pai Yü-ch'an." In *Religion and Society in T'ang and Sung China*, ed. Patricia Buckley Ebrey and Peter Gregory, pp. 307–34. Honolulu: University of Hawai'i Press, 1993.
Bhardwaj, Surinder Mohan. *Hindu Places of Pilgrimage in India: A Study in Cultural Geography*. Berkeley and Los Angeles: University of California Press, 1973.
Bokenkamp, Stephen R. "Sources of the Ling-pao Scriptures." In *Tantric and Taoist Studies in Honour of R. A. Stein*, vol. 2, ed. Michel Strickmann, pp. 434–86. Brussels: Institut belge des hautes études chinoises, 1983.
Bol, Peter. *"This Culture of Ours": Intellectual Transitions in T'ang and Sung China*. Stanford, Calif.: Stanford University Press, 1992.
Boltz, Judith. "Not by the Seal of Office Alone: New Weapons in Battles with the Supernatural." In *Religion and Society in T'ang China*, ed. Patricia Ebrey and Peter Gregory, pp. 241–305. Honolulu: University of Hawai'i Press, 1993.
———. *A Survey of Taoist Literature, Tenth to Seventeenth Centuries*. Berkeley: Institute for East Asian Studies, 1987.
———. "Taoist Literature. Part II. Five Dynasties through Ming." In *The Indiana Companion to Traditional Chinese Literature*, ed. William Nienhauser, pp. 152–74. Bloomington: Indiana University Press, 1986.
———. "Taoist Rites of Exorcism." Ph.D. diss., University of California, 1985.
Bossler, Beverly Jo. *Powerful Relations: Kinship, Status, and the State in Sung China*

(960–1279). Harvard-Yenching Institute monograph series, 43. Cambridge, Mass.: Council on East Asian Studies, 1998.

Brettell, Caroline. "The Priest and His People: The Contractual Basis for Religious Practice in Rural Portugal." In *Religious Orthodoxy and Popular Faith in European Society*, ed. Ellen Badone, pp. 55–75. Princeton, N.J.: Princeton University Press, 1990.

Cahill, Suzanne. "Taoism at the Sung Court: The Heavenly Text Affair of 1008." *Bulletin of Sung and Yuan Studies* 16 (1980): 23–44.

Cerutti, Simona. "Normes et pratiques, ou de la légitimité de leur opposition." In *Les formes de l'expérience: Une autre histoire sociale*, ed. Bernard Lepetit, pp. 127–49. Paris: Albin Michel, 1995.

Chang Hsiao-hsiang 張孝祥. *Yü-hu chü-shih wen-chi* 于湖居士文集. SPTK ed.

Chang Hsing-yen 張興言. *(T'ung-chih) I-huang hsien chih* 同治宜黃縣志. 1871. Cited as TCIH.

Chang Shih 張栻. *Chang Nan-hsuan hsien-sheng wen-chi* 張南軒先生文集. TSCC ed.

Chang Yü-ch'u 張宇初. *Hsien-ch'üan chi* 峴泉集. SKCSCP, fifth collection.

Ch'ang Pi-te 昌彼得 et al.. *Sung jen chuan-chi tzu-liao so-yin* 宋人傳記資料索引. 6 vols. Taipei: Ting-wen shu-chü, 1973.

Chao Tao-i 趙道一. *Li-shih chen-hsien t'i-tao t'ung-chien* 歷世真仙體道通鑑. HY 296, TT 148.

Chao Yü-shih 趙與時. *Pin-t'ui lu* 賓退錄. Shanghai: Shanghai guji chubanshe, 1983.

Ch'en Ch'ien 陳潛 et al. *(K'ang-hsi) Ch'ung-jen hsien chih* 康熙崇仁縣志. 1673. Cited as KHCJ.

Ch'en Pang-chan 陳邦瞻. *Sung shih chi shih pen mo* 宋史紀事本末. Peking: Zhonghua shuju, 1977.

Ch'en Yuan-chin 陳元晉. *Yü-shu lei-kao* 漁墅類稿. SCKSCP, first collection.

Ch'en, Kenneth. "The Sale of Monk Certificates during the Sung Dynasty." *Harvard Theological Review* 49 (1956): 307–27.

Cheng Yueh 鄭鉞 et al. *(K'ang-hsi) Nan-feng hsien chih* 康熙南豐縣志. 1683. Cited as KHNF.

Ch'eng Chü-fu 程鉅夫. *Hsueh-lou chi* 雪樓集. Microfilm ed. at Starr East Asian Library, Columbia University.

Chiang Shu-yü 蔣叔輿. *Wu-shang huang-lu ta chai li-ch'eng i* 無上黃籙大齋立成儀. TT 278–90, HY 508.

Chikusa Masaaki 竺沙雅章. "Sōdai baichō kō 宋代賣牒考." In *Chūgoku bukkyō shakaishi kenkyū* 中國佛教社會史研究. Kyoto: Dōhōsha, 1982.

Chou Pi-ta 周必大. *Wen-chung chi* 文忠集. SKCSCP, second collection.

Christian, William. *Apparitions in Late Medieval and Renaissance Spain*. Princeton, N.J.: Princeton University Press, 1981.

———. *Local Religion in Sixteenth-Century Spain*. Princeton, N.J.: Princeton University Press, 1981.

———. *Person and God in a Spanish Valley*. Princeton, N.J.: Princeton University Press, 1972.

Chu Hsi 朱熹. *Chu Wen-kung wen-chi* 朱文公文集. SPTK, first compilation.

Chu K'uei-chang 朱奎章 et al. *(T'ung-chih) Lo-an hsien chih* 同治樂安縣志. 1871. Cited as TCLA.

Ch'ung-hsu t'ung-miao shih-ch'en Wang hsien-sheng chia-hua 沖虛通妙侍宸王先生家話. HY 1240, TT 996. Also cited as *Chia-hua*.

Cohen, Myron. "Mei-nung: State and Community in Rural Taiwan." *Third World Review* 2, no. 1 (Spring 1976): 1–22.
D'Andrade, Roy G. *The Development of Cognitive Anthropology.* Cambridge: Cambridge University Press, 1995.
Dean, Kenneth. "Field Notes on Two Taoist jiao Observed in Zhangzhou in December 1985." *Cahiers d'Extrême-Asie* 2 (1986): 191–209.
———. *Taoist Ritual and Popular Cults of Southeast China.* Princeton, N.J.: Princeton University Press, 1993.
DeGlopper, Donald. *Lukang: Commerce and Community in a Chinese City.* Albany: State University of New York Press, 1995.
Delooz, Pierre. "Towards a Sociological Study of Canonized Sainthood in the Catholic Church." In *Saints and Their Cults: Studies in Religious Sociology, Folklore, and History,* ed. Stephen Wilson, pp. 189–216. New York: Cambridge University Press, 1983.
Duara, Prasenjit. "Superscribing Symbols: The Myth of Guandi, Chinese God of War." *Journal of Asian Studies* 47, no. 4 (November 1988): 778–95.
Dubisch, Jill. "Pilgrimage and Popular Religion at a Greek Holy Shrine." In *Religious Orthodoxy and Popular Faith in European Society,* ed. Ellen Badone, pp. 113–39. Princeton, N.J.: Princeton University Press, 1990.
Elvin, Mark. *The Pattern of the Chinese Past.* Stanford, Calif.: Stanford University Press, 1973.
Fang Chan 方湛 et al. *(K'ang-hsi) Lo-an hsien chih* 康熙樂安縣志. 1683. Cited as KHLA.
Faure, David. "The Priestly Tradition and Its Place in the Village Culture of Hong Kong's New Territories." MS. N.d.
———. *The Structure of Chinese Rural Society: Lineage and Village in the Eastern New Territories, Hong Kong.* Oxford: Oxford University Press, 1986.
———. "Ta-tsiu: A Festival to Thank the Gods and Feed the Ghosts." MS. N.d.
Feuchtwang, Stephan. "Domestic and Communal Worship in Taiwan." In *Religion and Ritual in Chinese Society,* ed. Arthur P. Wolf, pp. 105–29. Stanford, Calif.: Stanford University Press, 1974.
———. *The Imperial Metaphor: Popular Religion in China.* London: Routledge, 1992.
Freedman, Maurice. "On the Sociological Study of Chinese Religion." In *Religion and Ritual in Chinese Society,* ed. Arthur P. Wolf, pp. 19–41. Stanford, Calif.: Stanford University Press, 1974.
Freeman, Michael. "Sung." In *Food in Chinese Culture,* ed. K. C. Chang, pp. 141–92. New Haven, Conn.: Yale University Press, 1977.
Freeman, Susan Tax. "Faith and Fashion in Spanish Religion: Notes on the Observation of Observance." *Peasant Studies* 7, no. 2 (1978): 101–23.
Gaborieau, Marc. "The Cult of Saints in Nepal and Northern India." In *Saints and Their Cults: Studies in Religious Sociology, Folklore, and History,* ed. Stephen Wilson, pp. 291–308. Cambridge: Cambridge University Press, 1983.
Gallin, Bernard. *Hsin Hsing, Taiwan: A Chinese Village in Change.* Berkeley and Los Angeles: University of California Press, 1966.
Gates, Hill. "Money for the Gods: The Commoditization of the Spirit." *Modern China* 13, no. 3 (1987): 259–77.
Gregory, Peter, and Patricia Ebrey. "The Religious and Historical Landscape." In *Religion and Society in T'ang China,* ed. Patricia Ebrey and Peter Gregory, pp. 1–44. Honolulu: University of Hawaii Press, 1993.

Haar, B. J. ter. "The Genesis and Spread of Temple Cults in Fukien." In *Development and Decline of Fukien Province in the Seventeeth and Eighteenth Centuries*, ed. E. B. Vermeer, pp. 349–96. Sinica Leidensia, 22. Leiden: E. J. Brill, 1990.

Han Yü 韓愈. *Han Ch'ang-li ch'üan chi* 韓昌黎全集. SPPY ed.

Hansen, Valerie. *Changing Gods in Medieval China, 1127–1276*. Princeton, N.J.: Princeton University Press, 1990.

———. "Gods on Walls: A Case of Indian Influence on Chinese Lay Religion?" In *Religion and Society in T'ang China*, ed. Patricia Ebrey and Peter Gregory, pp. 75–113. Honolulu: University of Hawai'i Press, 1993.

Hargett, James. "Playing Second Fiddle: The *Luan*-bird in Early and Medieval Chinese Literature." *T'oung Pao* 75 (1989): 235–62.

Hartwell, Robert. "Demographic, Political, and Social Transformations of China, 750–1550." *Harvard Journal of Asiatic Studies* 42 (1982): 365–442.

Hertz, Robert. "St. Besse: A Study of an Alpine Cult." In *Saints and Their Cults: Studies in Religious Sociology, Folklore, and History*, ed. Stephen Wilson, pp. 55–100. Cambridge: Cambridge University Press, 1983.

Ho Hsi-chih 何希之. *Chi-lei chi* 雞肋集. Ch'ing printed edition at Seikadō, Tokyo.

Hsu, Francis K. *Exorcising the Trouble Makers: Magic, Science, and Culture*. Westport, Conn.: Greenwood Press, 1983.

Hsu Ying-jung 許應鑅. *(Kuang-hsu) Fu-chou fu chih* 光緒撫州府志. 1876. Cited as KHFC.

Hsu Yun-sheng 許雲昇. *(Ch'ung-hsiu) Chiang-nan Hua-kai shan chih* 重修江南華蓋山志. 1555 edition at Library of Congress

Huang Chen 黃震. *Huang shih jih ch'ao* 黃氏日鈔. SKCSCP, second collection.

Huang Tsung-hsi 黃宗羲. *Sung-Yuan hsueh-an* 宋元學案. SPPY ed.

Hung Mai 洪邁. *I-chien chih* 夷堅志 [*Record of the Listener*]. Peking: Zhonghua shuju, 1981. Also cited as ICC.

Hymes, Robert. "Marriage, Descent Groups, and the Localist Strategy in Sung and Yuan Fu-chou." In *Kinship Organization in Late Imperial China, 1000–1940*, pp. 95–136. Berkeley and Los Angeles: University of California Press, 1986.

———. "Personal Relations and Bureaucratic Hierarchy in Chinese Religion: The Case of the Three Lords Cult of Mt. Hua-kai." In *Unruly Gods: Divinity and Society in China*, ed. Meir Shahar and Robert P. Weller, pp. 37–69. Honolulu: University of Hawai'i Press, 1996.

———. *Statesmen and Gentlemen: The Elite of Fu-chou, Chiang-hsi, in Northern and Southern Sung*. Cambridge: Cambridge University Press, 1986.

———. "Truth, Falsity, and Pretense in Sung Religion: An Approach through the Stories of Hung Mai." Presented at the conference "The Fascination with Performance," UCLA, November 18, 1995.

Hymes, Robert, and Conrad Schirokauer, eds. *Ordering the World: Approaches to State and Society in Sung Dynasty China*. Berkeley and Los Angeles: University of California Press, 1993.

Ihara Hiroshi 伊原弘. "Nan-Sō Shisen ni okeru teikyo shijin—Seidofuro-Shishūro o chūshin to shite 南宋四川における定鋸士人—成都府路·梓州路を中心として." *Tōhōgaku* 東方學 54 (1977).

———. "Sōdai kanryō no kon'in no imi ni tsuite 宋代官僚の意味について." *Rekishi to chiri* 歷史と地理 254 (1976): 12–19.

———. "Sōdai Meishū ni okeru kanko no kon'in kankei 宋代明州における官戸の婚姻關係." *Chūō daigaku daigakuin ronkyū* 中央大學大學院論究 1 (1972).

———. "Sōdai Ushū ni okeru kanko no kon'in kankei 宋代婺州における官戸の婚姻關係." *Chūōdaigaku daigakuin kenkyū nenpō* 中央大學大學院研究年報 6, no. 1 (1974): 33–42.

Jochim, Christian. "Flowers, Fruit, and Incense Only: Elite Versus Popular in Taiwan's Religion of the Yellow Emperor." *Modern China* 16, no. 1 (1990): 3–38.

Johnson, David. "The City-God Cults of T'ang and Sung China." *Harvard Journal of Asiatic Studies* 45, no. 2 (1985): 363–457.

———. "Temple Festivals in Southeastern Shansi: The *Sai* of Nan-she Village and Big West Gate." *Min-su ch'ü-i* 91 (1993): 641–734.

Jordan, David. "Chinese Signs and Wonders: Reflections on the Anthropology of Believing." Paper presented at Cornell University, dated May 17, 1988.

———. *Gods, Ghosts, and Ancestors: Folk Religion in a Taiwanese Village*. Berkeley and Los Angeles: University of California Press, 1972.

Katz, Paul. *Demon Gods and Burning Boats: The Cult of Marshal Wen in Late Imperial Chekiang*. Albany: State University of New York Press, 1995.

———. "Welcoming the Lords and the Pacification of Plagues: The Relationship between Taoism and Local Cults." Presented at the Association for Asian Studies Annual Meeting, Boston, March 24–27, 1994. N.d.

Kipnis, Andrew. "The Language of Gifts: Managing *Guanxi* in a North China Village." *Modern China* 22, no. 3 (1996): 285–314.

Kleeman, Terry. "The Expansion of the Wen-ch'ang Cult." In *Religion and Society in T'ang China*, ed. Patricia Ebrey and Peter Gregory, pp. 45–73. Honolulu: University of Hawai'i Press, 1993.

———. "Land Contracts and Related Documents." In *Chūgoku no shūkyō: shisō to kagaku* 中國の宗教：思想と科學, pp. 1–34. Tokyo: Kokusho kankōkai, 1984.

Kohn, Livia, ed. *The Taoist Experience: An Anthology*. Albany: State University of New York Press, 1993.

Lagerwey, John. *Taoist Ritual in Chinese Society and History*. New York: Macmillan, 1987.

Lane, Edward William. *An Account of the Manners and Customs of the Modern Egyptians, Written in Egypt during the Years 1833–1835*. London: East-West Publications, 1978.

Leach, E. R. "Ritual." *International Encyclopedia of the Social Sciences*, 13: 520–26. New York: Macmillan, 1968.

Lepetit, Bernard. "Histoire des pratiques, pratique de l'histoire." In *Les formes de l'expérience: Une autre histoire sociale*, ed. Bernard Lepetit, pp. 9–22. Paris: Albin Michel, 1995.

Levi, Giovanni. "I pericoli del geertzismo." *Quaderni storici* 58 (1985): 269–77.

Li Kuang-jun 黎廣潤 et al. *(Min-kuo) Nan-feng hsien chih* 民國南豐縣志. 1923. Cited as MKNF.

Liu Ch'en-weng 劉辰翁. *Hsu-ch'i chi* 須溪集. SKCSCP, fourth collection.

Liu Hsun 劉壎. *Yin-chü t'ung-i* 隱居通議. TSCC ed.

Liu, James T. C. *China Turning Inward: Intellectual-Political Changes in the Early Twelfth Century*. Harvard East Asian monographs, 132. Cambridge, Mass.: Council on East Asian Studies, Harvard University, 1988.

Lo Fu-chin 羅復晉. *(Yung-cheng) Fu-chou fu chih* 雍正撫州府志. 1729. Cited as YCFC.

Lou Yueh 樓鑰. *Kung-k'uei chi* 攻媿集. SPTK, first compilation.
Lu Chiu-yuan 陸九淵. *Hsiang-shan ch'üan chi* 象山全集. SPPY ed.
Lu-shan T'ai-p'ing-kung ts'ai-fang chen-chün shih-shih 廬山太平公採訪真君事實. HY 1276, TT 1006–1007.
Ma Tuan-lin 馬端臨. *Wen-hsien t'ung-k'ao* 文獻通考. Taipei: Hsin-sheng shu-chü, 1962.
McKnight, Brian. "Chinese Law and Legal Systems: Five Dynasties and Sung." Forthcoming in *The Cambridge History of China*, vol. 5, ed. Denis Twitchett. Cambridge: Cambridge University Press.
Mintz, Sidney. *Sweetness and Power: The Place of Sugar in Modern World History*. New York: Penguin Books, 1985.
Miyakawa, Hisayuki. "Local Cults around Mount Lu at the Time of Sun En's Rebellion." In *Facets of Taoism*, ed. Holmes Welch and Anna Seidel, pp. 83–101. New Haven, Conn.: Yale University Press, 1979.
Morohashi Tetsuji 諸橋轍次. *Dai kanwa jiten* 大漢和辭典. Tokyo, 1955–1960.
Needham, Joseph. "China and the Origin of Qualifying Examinations in Medicine." In id., *Clerks and Craftsmen in China and the West*, pp. 379–96. Cambridge: Cambridge University Press, 1970.
———. "Science and China's Influence on the World." In *The Legacy of China*, ed. Raymond Dawson, pp. 234–308. Oxford: Oxford University Press, 1964.
Needham, Rodney. *Belief, Language, and Experience*. Oxford: Basil Blackwell, 1972.
Neskar, Ellen. "The Cult of Worthies: A Study of Shrines Honoring Local Confucian Worthies in the Sung Dynasty (960–1279)." Ph.D. diss., Columbia University, 1993.
Nickerson, Peter. "Shamans, Demons, Diviners, and Taoists: Conflict and Assimilation in Medieval Chinese Ritual Practice (c. A.D. 100–1000)." *Taoist Resources* 5, no. 1 (1994): 41–66.
———. "Taoism, Death, and Bureaucracy in Early Medieval China." Ph.D. diss., University of California, 1996.
Ou-yang Ch'e 歐陽澈. *Ou-yang hsiu-chuan chi* 歐陽修撰集. SKCSCP, fourth collection.
Ou-yang Hsiu 歐陽修. *Ou-yang Hsiu ch'üan chi* 歐陽修全集. Hong Kong: Kwong Chi Book Co., n.d.
Pai Yü-ch'an 白玉蟾. *Sung Pai chen-jen Yü-ch'an ch'üan chi* 宋白真人玉蟾全集. Taipei: Sung Pai chen-jen Yü-ch'an ch'üan chi chi-yin wei-yuan-hui, 1975.
Pease, Jonathan. "Lin-ch'uan and Fen-ning: Kiangsi Locales and Kiangsi Writers during the Sung." *Asia Major*, 3d ser., 4, no. 1 (1991): 39–85.
Reiter, Florian. *Grundelemente und Tendenzen des religiösen Taoismus: Das Spannungsverhältnis von Integration und Individualität in seiner Geschichte zur Chin-, Yuan-, und frühen Ming-Zeit*. Stuttgart: Franz Steiner Verlag, 1988.
———. "The 'Investigation Commissioner of the Nine Heavens' and the Beginning of His Cult in Northern Chiang-hsi in 731 A.D." *Oriens* 31 (1988): 266–89.
Robinet, Isabelle. "Metamorphosis and Deliverance from the Corpse in Taoism." *History of Religions* 19 (1979): 37–70.
Rothkrug, Lionel. "German Holiness and Western Sanctity in Medieval and Modern History." *Historical Reflections/Réflexions Historiques* 15, no. 1 (1988): 161–249.
Sanchis, Pierre. "The Portuguese 'romarias.'" In *Saints and Their Cults: Studies in Religious Sociology, Folklore, and History*, ed. Stephen Wilson, pp. 261–89. Cambridge: Cambridge University Press, 1983.

Sangren, Steven. "Dialectics of Alienation: Individuals and Collectivities in Chinese Religion." *Man* 26, no. 1 (March 1991): 67–86.
———. *History and Magical Power in a Chinese Community*. Stanford, Calif.: Stanford University Press, 1987.
Schafer, Edward. *Pacing the Void: T'ang Approaches to the Stars*. Berkeley and Los Angeles: University of California Press, 1977.
Schipper, Kristofer. "Neighborhood Cult Associations in Traditional Tainan." In *The City in Late Imperial China*, ed. G. William Skinner, pp. 651–76. Stanford, Calif.: Stanford University Press, 1977.
———. "Seigneurs royaux, dieux des épidémies." *Archives de sciences sociales des religions* 59 (1985): 39–40.
———. "The Taoist Body." *History of Religions* 17, nos. 3–4 (1978): 355–81.
———. "Taoist Ritual and Local Cults of the T'ang Dynasty." In *Tantric and Taoist Studies in Honor of R. A. Stein*, vol. 3, ed. Michel Strickmann, pp. 812–34. Brussels: Institut belge des hautes études chinoises, 1985.
———. "Vernacular and Classical Ritual in Taoism." *Journal of Asian Studies* 45, no. 1 (1985): 21–57.
———. "The Written Memorial in Taoist Ceremonies." In *Religion and Ritual in Chinese Society*, ed. Arthur Wolf, pp. 309–24. Stanford, Calif.: Stanford University Press, 1974.
Schirokauer, Conrad. "Neo-Confucians under Attack: The Condemnation of *Wei-hsueh*." In *Crisis and Prosperity in Sung China*, ed. John Haeger, pp. 163–98. Tucson: University of Arizona Press, 1975.
Seidel, Anna. "The Image of the Perfect Ruler in Early Taoist Messianism: Lao Tzu and Li Hung." *History of Religions* 9, nos. 2–3 (1970): 216–47.
———. "Imperial Treasures and Taoist Sacraments—Taoist Roots in the Apocrypha." In *Tantric and Taoist Studies in Honor of R. A. Stein*, ed. Michel Strickmann, pp. 291–371. Brussels: Institut belge des hautes études chinoises, 1983.
Shahar, Meir, and Robert P. Weller, eds. *Unruly Gods: Divinity and Society in China*. Honolulu: University of Hawai'i Press, 1996.
Shen T'ing-jui 沈庭瑞. *Hua-kai shan Fu-ch'iu Wang Kuo san chen-chün shih-shih* 華蓋山浮丘王郭三真君事實. TT 556–57, HY 777. Cited as HKS.
Sheng Ch'üan 盛銓 et al. *(T'ung-chih) Ch'ung-jen hsien chih* 同治崇仁縣志. 1873. Cited as TCCJ.
Shweder, Richard. "Preview: A Colloquy of Culture Theorists." In *Culture Theory: Essays on Mind, Self, and Emotion*, ed. Richard Shweder and Robert LeVine, pp. 8–9. Cambridge: Cambridge University Press, 1984.
Skorupski, John. *Symbol and Theory: A Philosophical Study of Theories of Religion in Social Anthropology*. Cambridge: Cambridge University Press, 1976.
Smith, Robert J. "Afterword." In *Religion and Ritual in Chinese Society*, ed. Arthur P. Wolf, pp. 337–48. Stanford, Calif.: Stanford University Press, 1974.
Spiegel, Gabrielle. "The Cult of St. Denis and Capetian Kingship." In *Saints and Their Cults: Studies in Religious Sociology, Folklore, and History*, ed. Stephen Wilson, pp. 141–68. Cambridge: Cambridge University Press, 1983.
Stein, R. A. "Religious Taoism and Popular Religion from the Second to the Seventh Centuries." In *Facets of Taoism*, ed. Holmes Welch and Anna Seidel, pp. 53–81. New Haven, Conn.: Yale University Press, 1979.

Strickmann, Michel. "The Longest Taoist Scripture." *History of Religions* 17 (1978): 331–54.
———. "The Taoist Renaissance of the Twelfth Century." Paper presented at the Third International Conference on Taoist Studies, Unterägeri, Switzerland, 1979.
Sun Ti 孫覿. *Hung-ch'ing chü-shih chi* 鴻慶居士集. SKCSCP, twelfth collection.
Sung hui-yao chi-pen 宋會要輯本. Taipei: Shih-chieh shu-chü, 1963.
Sutton, Donald. "Ritual Drama and Moral Order: Interpreting the Gods' Festival Troupes of Southern Taiwan." *Journal of Asian Studies* 49, no. 3 (August 1990): 535–54.
———. "Rituals of Self-Mortification: Taiwanese Spirit-Mediums in Comparative Perspective." *Journal of Ritual Studies* 4, no. 1 (1990): 99–125.
Tambiah, Stanley. *Buddhism and the Spirit Cults in Northeast Thailand*. Cambridge: Cambridge University Press, 1970.
Tanaka Issei 田中一正. *Chūgoku no sōzoku to engeki* 中國の宗族と演戲. Tokyo: Tōyō bunka kenkyūkai, 1985.
Teng Yu-kung 鄧有功. *Shang-ch'ing t'ien-hsin cheng-fa* 上清天心正法. TT 318–19, HY 566. Cited as THCF.
———. *Shang-ch'ing ku-sui ling-wen kui-lü* 上清骨髓靈文鬼律. TT 203, HY 461. Cited as LWKL.
Tillman, Hoyt. *Confucian Discourse and Chu Hsi's Ascendancy*. Honolulu: University of Hawaii Press, 1992.
Ting Hsiang 光緒 et al. *(Kuang-hsu) Chi-an fu chih* 吉安府志. 1876. Cited as KHCA.
T'o T'o 脫脫 et al. *Sung shih* 宋史. Peking: Zhonghua shuju, 1977.
Tseng Chao 曾肇. *Ch'ü-fu chi* 曲阜集. *Ch'ien-yen tsung-chi chün-shu* edition.
Tseng Feng 曾丰. *Yuan-tu chi* 緣督集. SKCSCP, second collection.
———. *Yuan-tu chi*. Sung edition at Seikadō Library, Tokyo.
Tseng Kung 曾鞏. *Yuan-feng lei-kao* 元豐類稿. SPPY ed.
Tu Kuang-t'ing 杜光庭. *Lu-i chi* 錄異記. HY 591, TT 327.
T'ung Fan-yen 童範儼 et al. *(T'ung-chih) Lin-ch'uan hsien chih* 同治臨川縣志. 1870. Cited as TCLC.
Turner, Victor. *Dramas, Fields, and Metaphors: Symbolic Action in Human Society*. Ithaca, N.Y.: Cornell University Press, 1974.
Verellen, Franciscus. "Luo Gongyuan: Légende et culte d'un saint Taoïste." *Journal Asiatique* 275, nos. 3–4 (1987): 283–332.
Wang An-shih 王安石. *Lin-ch'uan hsien-sheng wen-chi* 臨川先生文集. Hong Kong: Chung-hua shu-chü, 1971.
Wang Hsiang-chih. 王象之. *Yü-ti chi-sheng* 輿地紀勝. Taipei: Wen-hai ch'u-pan-she, 1962.
Wang Hsien-ch'ien 王先謙. *Han Shu pu-chu* 漢書補注. Peking: Zhonghua Shuju, 1983.
Wang Tzu-ts'ai 王梓材. *Sung-Yuan hsueh-an pu-i* 宋元學案補遺. Ssu-ming ts'ung-shu edition.
Watson, Burton, trans. *The Complete Works of Chuang Tzu*. New York: Columbia University Press, 1968.
Wei Liao-weng 魏了翁. *Hao-shan ta ch'üan chi* 鶴山大全集. SPTK, first compilation.
Weller, Robert. *Unities and Diversities in Chinese Religion*. Seattle: University of Washington Press, 1987.
Wilson, Stephen. "Cults of Saints in the Churches of Central Paris." In *Saints and Their*

Cults: Studies in Religious Sociology, Folklore, and History, ed. Stephen Wilson, pp. 233–60. Cambridge: Cambridge University Press, 1983.

———. "Introduction." In *Saints and Their Cults: Studies in Religious Sociology, Folklore, and History*, ed. Stephen Wilson, pp. 1–53. Cambridge: Cambridge University Press, 1983.

———, ed., *Saints and Their Cults: Studies in Religious Sociology, Folklore, and History*. Cambridge: Cambridge University Press, 1983.

Wolf, Arthur P. "Gods, Ghosts, and Ancestors." In *Religion and Ritual in Chinese Society*, ed. Arthur P. Wolf, pp. 131–82. Stanford, Calif.: Stanford University Press, 1974.

———, ed., *Religion and Ritual in Chinese Society*. Stanford: Stanford University Press, 1974.

Wolf, Eric, ed. *Religious Regimes and State Formation: Perspectives from European Ethnology*. Albany: State University of New York Press, 1991.

Wright, Hope. *Alphabetical List of Geographical Names in Sung China*. Paris: École pratique des hautes etudes, Centre de recherches historiques, 1956.

Wu Ch'eng 吳澄. *Wu Wen-cheng chi* 吳文正集. SKCSCP, second collection. Cited as WWC.

Wu Hang 吳沆. *Huan-ch'i shih hua* 環溪詩話. SKCSCP, separate collection.

Yan, Yunxiang. *The Flow of Gifts: Reciprocity and Social Networks in a Chinese Village*. Stanford, Calif.: Stanford University Press, 1996.

Yen Chen-ch'ing 顏真卿. *Wen-chung chi* 文忠集. TSCC ed.

Yü Chi 虞集. *Tao-yuan hsueh-ku lu* 道園學古錄. SPTK ed.

Yuan Miao-tsung 元妙宗. *T'ai-shang tsung-chen pi-yao* 太上總真必要. TT 986–87, HY 1217. Cited as TCPY.

Yueh Shih 樂史. *T'ai-ping huan-yü chi* 太平寰宇記. Taipei: Wen-hai ch'u-pan-she, 1962.

Glossary of Chinese Characters

A-ch'üan	阿全	Chao Po-wu	趙伯兀
An-ch'ing Fu	安慶府	Chao Tao-i	趙道一
An-jen	安仁	Chao Tsu-chien	趙祖堅
Bao-an	保安	Chao Tzu-chü	趙子舉
Beiguan	北管	Chao Yü-shih	趙與時
chai	齋	Chao-ch'ing	昭清
Chai-mao	寨帽	Chao-hsien	昭仙
Chan T'ai-ch'u	詹太初	Ch'ao-hsien (abbey)	朝仙
Ch'an	襌	*ch'ao-jan*	超然
Chang Chi-hsien	張繼先	*ch'ao t'ien*	朝天
Chang Hsi-i	張希逸	Che (river)	浙
Chang Hsiao-hsiang	張孝祥	Che-hsi	浙西
Chang Pang-ch'ang	張邦昌	Che-tsung	哲宗
Chang Shih	張栻	Che-tung	浙東
Chang Te-lung	張德隆	Ch'e Kung	車公
Chang Yen	張顏	*chen* (hold down)	鎮
Chang Yen-fa	張炎發	Chen hsing t'u	真星圖
Chang Yü-ch'u	張宇初	*chen-jen*	真人
Chang Yü-hu	張于湖	Chen Rongsheng	陳榮盛
Chang Yuan-feng	張緣峰	Chen-tsung	真宗
Chang Yuan-shu	章元樞	Chen-yuan	貞元
Chang Yuan-ting	張元定	Ch'en	陳
Ch'ang-an	長安	Ch'en-chou	陳州
Ch'ang-sha	長沙	Ch'en-liu	陳留
chao (make clear)	昭	Ch'en P'eng-fei	陳鵬飛
chao (decree)	詔	Ch'en Tsao	陳早
Chao Po-t'i	趙伯禔	Ch'en Ts'un-hsin	陳存心

GLOSSARY

Ch'en Tung	陳東	chiao chu	教主
Ch'en T'ung-tsu	陳同祖	Ch'iao-hsien	橋仙
Ch'en Tzu-shih	陳子宬	Chieh Ch'i-ssu	揭傒斯
Ch'en Yuan-ch'eng	陳元承	Chien-ch'ang	建昌
Ch'en Yuan-chin	陳元晉	Chien-ch'ang Chün	建昌軍
Ch'en Yuan-ying	陳元應	chien chi	劍脊
Cheng	鄭	chien-chiao	監醮
Cheng-ho	政和	chien-chu	箋注
Cheng Huang	城隍	chien ch'un	劍春
Cheng-i	正一	Chien-ho	監河
Cheng Mao	鄭愻	Chien-k'ang	建康
Cheng Sung	鄭松	Chien-te	建德
Ch'eng Chü-fu	程鉅夫	Ch'ien Ping	錢丙
ch'eng-huang shen	城隍神	Ch'ien Tang	錢謙
Ch'eng-tu-fu	成都府	Ch'ien-tao	乾道
Cheung	張	Ch'ien-te	乾德
chi	脊	chih (rule)	治
Chi-chou	吉州	chih (office)	職
chi-ch'ou	己丑	chih i	至意
chi-hai	己亥	Chih-hui shang-p'in	
Chi-shui	吉水	ta-chieh	智慧上品大戒
ch'i	氣	Chih-wan	至晚
Ch'i (prefecture)	齊	Chih-yuan	至元
Ch'i (Prince of)	蘄	chin (present day)	今
Ch'i-chen	祈真	chin (submit)	進
Ch'i-fu	七富	Chin (state)	晉
ch'i i	奇異	Chin (Jurchen)	金
ch'i-lao	耆老	Chin-ch'i	金溪
Ch'i-li (mountain)	七里	Chin-hua	金華
Chia	賈	Chin-ling	金陵
chia-hua	家話	chin-shih	進士
Chia-hui	嘉惠	ch'in ch'ung chih shih i	欽崇之實意
chia shang	加尚	Ch'in-feng	秦風
Chia-ting	嘉定	Ch'in Kuei	秦桂
Chia Tsai	賈載	Ch'in-tsung	欽宗
chia-wu	甲午	ching	旌
chia-yü	家語	Ching-hsi	京西
Chiang-chou	江州	Ching-hsiang	淨薌
chiang chün	將軍	ching hui	淨穢
chiang han	將旱	Ching-k'ang	靖康
Chiang-hsi	江西	ching shou	淨手
Chiang-huai	江淮	ching shui	淨水
Chiang-nan	江南	Ching-ting	景定
Chiang Shu-yü	蔣叔輿	Ching-tung	京東
Chiang-tung	江東	Ching-yun	景雲
ch'iang ming	強名	ch'ing (feelings)	情
chiao	醮	ch'ing (measure)	頃

Ch'ing (prefecture)	青	Ch'üan-chou	泉州
Ch'ing (dynasty)	清	*chün* (army)	軍
Ch'ing-ch'eng (Mt.)	青城	*chün* (commandery)	郡
Ch'ing-ch'i	清溪	*chün* (lord)	君
Ch'ing-chiang	清江	Chün (Mt.)	軍
Ch'ing-tu	清都	*chün chiang*	軍將
Ch'ing-yuan	慶元	*chün-chieh-tu*	軍節度
Ch'ing-yun	青雲	Chün-shan miao	軍山廟
chiu	醮	*chün-shih*	軍事
chiu chuan huan	九轉還	*cun shen*	村神
chiu chuan huan tan	九轉還丹	*dou*	斗
chiu chuan tan	九轉丹	*erh* (particle)	而
chiu-pen	舊本	*erh* (you)	爾
chiu-t'ien shih-che	九天使者	*fa-kuan*	法官
Chiu-yao ko	九曜閣	*fa-shih*	法師
Ch'iu Hu	丘祐	Fan	范
Ch'iu Shou-ching	丘守靜	Fan Ling	粉嶺
chou (boat)	舟	*fang-han*	方函
chou (prefecture)	州	fann-kon	幡竿
Chou (dynasty)	周	*fei-chang*	飛章
Chou Meng-jo	周夢若	*fei-chang pai-piao*	飛章拜表
Chou Pi-ta	周必大	Feng-ch'eng	奉城
chu	注	Feng-hua	奉化
Chu Chih-ch'ing	朱智卿	Feng I-weng	馮翼翁
Chu Chung-su	朱仲素	Feng-t'ai (mountain)	鳳臺
Chu Hsi	朱熹	Feng-tu	酆都
Chu Huan	朱渙	*fu* (prefecture)	府
Chu-ling	朱陵	*fu* (talisman)	符
chu miao	諸廟	Fu-chien	福建
Ch'u	楚	Fu-ch'iu	浮丘
Ch'u Kun-liang	邱坤良	Fu-ch'iu Po	浮丘伯
ch'uan (boat)	船	Fu-chou	撫州
ch'un	春	Fu-chou (Fu-chien)	福州
Ch'un-hsi	淳熙	Fu²-chou	富州
Ch'un-hua	淳化	Fu Hsuan	傅選
Chung-chien	忠簡	Fujian	福建
Chung-hua	中華	Fu-jung (mountain)	芙蓉
ch'ung	沖	*fu-ti*	福地
Ch'ung-chi	沖寂	Fu-sheng (monastery)	福勝
Ch'ung-hsien	崇仙	Fu T'ien-hsin	符天信
ch'ung-hsu t'ung-miao		Hai-k'ang	海康
shih-ch'en	沖虛通妙侍宸	Hai-nan	海南
Ch'ung-jen	崇仁	Han (dynasty)	漢
Ch'ung-ning	崇寧	Han (Prince of Ch'i)	韓
Ch'ung-yu	沖佑	Han Yü	韓愈
Chü-hsien	聚仙	Hang-chou	杭州
Chü-jung	句容	*he ch'i*	賀啟

GLOSSARY

he piao 賀表
he shu 賀疏
Ho 何
Ho I 何異
Ho-pei 河北
Ho-tung 河東
hou 侯
Hou-kuan 侯官
Hsi-i 希逸
Hsi-ning 熙寧
Hsia-hao 下邽
Hsia Tzu-ying 夏子嬰
hsiang (image) 相
Hsiang (mountain) 相
Hsiang-ch'eng 香城
Hsiang-fu 祥符
hsiang jen 鄉人
Hsiang Yü 項羽
hsiao chi 校籍
Hsiao Tzu-yun 蕭子雲
Hsiao Yü-hsuan 蕭雨軒
Hsieh 謝
Hsieh I 謝逸
Hsieh K'o 謝薖
Hsieh Ling-yun 謝靈雲
Hsieh O 謝諤
hsien (immortal) 仙
hsien (display) 顯
Hsien-ch'un 咸淳
hsien feng 仙風
Hsien-lin 仙林
hsien-shui 仙水
hsien-t'ien 先天
Hsien-yen 仙嚴
Hsien-yu 仙遊
hsien-yuan 仙員
hsin 信
Hsin (river) 信
hsin chih 信之
Hsin-chou 信州
Hsin Hsing 新興
Hsin-hua 新華
Hsin-kan 新淦
hsin-mao 辛卯
hsing 杏
Hsing-lo 興樂
Hsing-tzu 星子

hsing-tz'u 行祠
Hsiung 熊
Hsiung Chiang 熊將
Hsiung Chih-ch'ang 熊之常
Hsiung P'u 熊浦
Hsiung Shan-jen 熊山人
Hsiung T'ien-ch'ang 熊天常
Hsu (Perfected Lord) 徐
Hsu (Lady) 許
Hsu Cheng 徐正
Hsu Ching-yang 許旌陽
Hsu Hsun-ch'üan 胥遁權
Hsu Sun 許遜
Hsu Tzu-shih 徐子石
Hsu Tz'u-hsueh 徐次學
Hsu Yun-sheng 許雲昇
Hsuan-chou 宣州
Hsuan-ho 宣和
Hsuan-yuan 玄元
Hsueh Hsuan-ch'ing 薛玄卿
Hsun Po-tzu 荀伯子
Hu 胡
Hu-chou 湖州
Hu Ch'üan 胡銓
Hu-pei 湖北
Hu Shou-chen 胡守真
Hu Tao-hsuan 胡道玄
Hua- 華
Hua-kai 華蓋
Hua-kai shan 華蓋山
Huai (river) 淮
Huai-chin 懷金
Huai-nan 淮南
Huai-tung 淮東
Huang (surname) 黃
Huang (river) 黃
Huang Chen 黃震
Huang-ch'ing 皇慶
Huang Chung 黃裏
Huang Fu 黃符
Huang Jen-jung 黃仁榮
Huang Lü-chung 黃履中
Huang Mi-chien 黃彌堅
Huang Shih-yung 黃世永
Huang Ssu-hu 黃思護
Huang Tsung-i 黃宗一
Huang-t'ung 凰桐

GLOSSARY

Huang Wen-ch'ang	黃文昌	Kao Tzu-yü	高子羽
Huang Wen-sheng	黃文晟	Kao-yu	高郵
Huang Yang	黃仰	*ke ch'ui liu mien*	各垂旒冕
Huang Yao	黃瑤	ken-siao	見笑
Huang Yuan-shou	黃元受	ken-tiao	見朝
Huang Yueh	黃鉞	*keng-shen*	庚申
huang-kuan	黃冠	Keng Yen-hsi	耿延禧
hui-shou	會首	Kiang-hsi	江西
Hui-ti	惠帝	Koon Yam	觀音
Hui-tsung	徽宗	*kuan*	觀
Hung-chou	洪州	*kuan-hsi*	關係
Hung Hsun	洪巡	*kuan shu*	盥嗽
Hung Kua	洪适	Kuan-yin	觀音
Hung Mai	洪邁	Kuang-ch'ang	廣長
Hung Ying-hsien	洪應賢	Kuang-hsi	廣西
i (employ)	役	Kuang-tung	廣東
I (forester)	益	Kuei-ch'i	貴溪
I (river)	宜	*kuei-mao*	癸卯
I An-ning	易安寧	K'un-lun	崑崙
I-chien chih	夷堅志	*kung*	公
i-ch'ou	乙丑	*kung-pu*	功布
I-huang	宜黃	*kung p'u san ch'ien*	
i-jen	異人	*hang*	功蒲三千行
i pen	一本	*K'ung Tzu chia-yü*	孔子家語
i pen yun	一本云	*kuo* (state)	國
I To-fu	易多福	Kuo	郭
i wei jan	以為然	Kuo Chün	郭峻
Jao Chieh	饒節	Kuo Ju-ching	郭汝敬
Jao-chou	饒州	Kuo Ju-hsien	郭汝賢
Jao Tung-t'ien	饒洞天	Lam Tsuen	林村
jen-ch'en	壬辰	Lao-chün	老君
jen-ch'ing	人情	*lao-ta*	老大
Jen Tao-yuan	任道元	Lao Tzu	老子
Jiangxi	江西	Lei-chou	雷州
ju (you)	汝	Li	李
Ju (river)	汝	*li*	理
Ju-ching	汝敬	*li* (distance measure)	里
Ju-hsien	汝賢	*li* (plum)	李
jui hsiang	瑞相	Li Chao-i	李昭義
Jung-chou	容州	Li-chou	藜州
K'ai-feng	開封	Li Chung-fu	李仲甫
K'ai-huang	開皇	Li Chung-te	李仲德
K'ai-pao	開寶	Li Ch'ung-yuan	李沖元
K'ai-yuan	開元	Li Hsiu	李修
Kan (river)	贛	Li Hu	李胡
kan-ch'ing	感情	Li Kung-yen	李公諺
Kao-tsung	高宗	Li Liu	李劉

Li Po-ku	李博古
Li T'ao	李燾
Li-tsung	理宗
Li Tui	李兌
Li Tzu-chen	李子真
Li Yen-hua	李彥華
Li Yen-yuan	李晏元
Li Yuan-fang	李元方
Liang (dynasty)	梁
Liang-che	兩浙
Liang-ch'i	梁谿
Liang Kun	梁緄
Liao (dynasty)	遼
Liao (surname)	廖
Lieh-hsien chuan	列仙傳
lieh sheng	列聖
Lin (village)	林
Lin-an	臨安
Lin-ch'uan	臨川
Lin-chiang	臨江
Lin-chiang Chün	臨江軍
Lin Hsiao-yao	林逍遙
Lin-ju	臨汝
Lin Ling-su	林靈素
Ling (king)	靈
Ling-hsing	靈興
Ling-ku	靈谷
Ling-pao	靈寶
Lin Te-ch'i	林特起
Liu	劉
Liu Ch'en-weng	劉辰翁
Liu Hsiang	劉向
Liu Hsiang (editor)	劉祥
Liu Hsin-shu	劉信叔
Liu Hsun	劉壎
Liu Kung-ch'en	劉公臣
Liu P'ing-hui	劉平暉
Liu Sung	劉宋
Liu Tzu-hsu	劉自虛
Liu Yuan-tsai	劉元載
Lo (mountain)	羅
Lo (surname)	羅
Lo-an	樂安
Lo Chang	羅璋
Lo Ch'un-po	羅春伯
Lo-fu (mountain)	羅浮
Lo Hsu-chou	羅虛舟
Lo Kung-yuan	羅公遠
Lo Pin	羅彬
Lo-p'ing	樂平
Lo Tien	羅點
Lo Tou-nan	羅斗南
Lo Tuan-ying	羅端英
Lo Wu-i	羅無逸
Lo Yeh	羅燁
Lu	路
Lu Chiu-yuan	陸九淵
Lu Hsiu-ching	陸修靜
Lu-ling	廬陵
Lu-shan	廬山
luan	鸞
Luan	樂
Luan Pa	樂巴
Luan Shu-yuan	樂叔元
Lung-hsing Fu	隆興府
Lung-hu (mountain)	龍虎
lung t'ou an chiu ch'iu	龍投按舊湫
Lung-yueh-t'ou	龍躍頭
Lü	呂
lü	律
Lü Pen-chung	呂本中
Lü Tung-pin	呂洞賓
Ma (mountain)	麻
Ma-ku (mountain)	麻姑
Ma Tsu (Ma-tsu)	媽祖
Mao (Lord)	茅
Mao-shan	茅山
mei (plum)	梅
Mei	梅
Mei Fu	梅福
Mei Hsuan	梅鋗
Mi-ming	彌明
miao chi	妙濟
ming	命
Ming (dynasty)	明
Ming-chen k'o	明真科
Ming-chou	明州
Ming-kung shu-p'an ch'ing-ming chi	明公書判清明集
mo tsou	默奏
mou	畝
Naitō Torajirō	內藤虎二郎
Nan-ch'ang	南昌

GLOSSARY

Nan-chen	南真	Po-wen	博文
Nan-ch'eng	南城	P'u Ju-lin	蒲汝霖
Nan-feng	南豐	*sa-sao*	灑掃
Nanjing	南京	Sa Shou-chien	薩守堅
Nan-k'ang	南康	*saam-ts'ing*	三清
Nan-k'ang Chün	南康軍	*sai*	賽
Nankuenshen	南鯤鯓	*sai-kong*	師公
Nan-ling	南陵	*sai-kong-kut*	師公骨
Nan-ts'un	南村	San Chieh Kung	三結公
Nan-yang	南陽	*san-ch'ing*	三清
Nieh T'ien-hsi	聶天錫	*san lu*	三廬
nien-p'u	年譜	San-yuan p'in	三元品
Ou-yang Ch'e	歐陽澈	San-yuan p'in-chieh	三元品戒
Ou-yang Hsiu	歐陽修	Shan-hsiu	善修
Ou-yang Te-ming	歐陽德明	Shan-tung	山東
pa	把	Shang-ch'ing	上清
Pa	巴	*Shang-ch'ing t'ien-hsin cheng-fa*	上清天心正法
Pa-ling	巴陵		
Pa-shan	巴山	Shang-hsien	上仙
Pai Yü-ch'an	白玉蟾	Shang Jih-hsuan	商日宣
pao	報	Shang-kuan Miao-chi	上官妙濟
pao-chia	保甲	*shang lun*	尚論
pao hsien	褒顯	*shang ti*	上帝
Pao-kai	寶蓋	*shang t'ien you ming*	上天有命
Pao-yu	寶祐	Shao-hsing	紹興
pei-chi ch'ü-hsieh yuan	北極驅邪院	Shao-ting	紹定
Pei-feng	北酆	Shao-wu	紹武
Peimen	北門	*she*	社
Pei-ti fu	北帝符	*she jen mu*	射人目
Pei-ti fu-wen	北帝符文	*shen*	神
P'ei	沛	Shen T'ing-jui	沈庭瑞
pen	本	*shen-chiang*	神將
pen-shan	本山	*shen-hsiao*	神霄
pen-shih	本師	*shen-p'eng*	神棚
Penglai	蓬萊	*shen-ping*	神兵
p'eng	棚	Sheng-yuan	昇元
P'eng-ch'eng	彭城	*shih* (show)	示
P'eng-lai	蓬萊	Shih-hsien	石仙
Pi-chia	筆架	*shih-ta-fu*	士大夫
Pi-fu	辟富	Shih Te-yü	師得遇
Pi Tsao	畢造	Shih-yung	世永
Pien-chou	汴州	*shizhu*	施主
Ping-chien	冰澗	*shu*	疏
ping-ma chien-ya	兵馬監押	Shu-chou	舒州
ping-tzu	丙子	Shu-yuan	叔元
P'ing Ching-tsung	平敬宗	*shuang-ling*	霜翎
Po-t'ang	伯堂	Shui Kuan	水官

Shun-ti	順帝	Te-ch'ing	德清
Ssu-wen	肆文	Te-ch'ing Chün	德慶軍
su hsi	素習	Te-ch'ing Chün-	
su hsien	宿仙	chieh-tu	德慶軍節度
su ku	宿骨	Te-hsiu	德修
sui	雖	Te-shao	德紹
Sui (dynasty)	隨	Te-shen	德深
Sun Shih-tao	孫士道	Te-yuan	德遠
Sun Ti	孫覿	Teng	鄧
Sung (dynasty)	宋	Teng-chou	鄧州
Sung An-kuo	宋安國	Teng Shih	鄧寔
Sung hsing-t'ung	宋刑統	Teng Tzu-yang	鄧子揚
Sung hui-yao	宋會要	Teng Yu-kung	鄧有功
Sung-shan	嵩山	Ti Kuan	地官
Ta-ch'ien	大乾	*ti shen*	地神
Ta-fu	大浮	*ti-so*	帝所
Ta-hua	大華	*tieh*	牒
Ta-kuan	大觀	*tien* (palace)	殿
Ta-liang	大梁	T'ien Hou	天后
Ta-mao	大茅	T'ien-ch'i	天齊
ta-shih-wang	大士王	T'ien-ch'ing	天慶
ta-tsiu	大醮	*T'ien-hsin cheng-fa*	天心正法
Ta Wu Chang	大無常	T'ien-hua	天華
taai-sz	大士	*t'ien kao*	天高
taai-sz-wong	大士王	T'ien Kuan	天官
Tainan	臺南	T'ien Kung	天公
T'ai (Mt.)	泰	*T'ien-shih*	天師
T'ai-ho	太和	Tin Hau	天后
T'ai-k'ang	太康	*T'in-sz*	天師
T'ai-p'ing	太平	Ting Chin	丁謹
t'ai-shang	太上	*ting-ssu*	丁巳
Tanaka Issei	天中一正	T'ing-ssu	廷嗣
T'an Tzu-hsiao	譚子宵	*t'o tsan*	脫懺
T'an Wu-lei	譚五雷	Tou-su	道士
tang	當	*t'ou tsan*	投懺
T'ang (dynasty)	唐	*tsai-ts'ung*	再從
T'ang Chao	唐肇	Ts'ai Ching	蔡京
T'ang Yuan-ling	唐元陵	*tsan*	讚
Tao-hsien	道仙	*tsan shu*	讚書
tao-hsueh	道學	*ts'an luan chia hao*	驂鸞駕鶴
tao-ku	道骨	Ts'ang-chou	滄洲
tao-shih	道士	*tsao hua*	造化
Tao Te Ching	道德經	*tsao-wu*	造物
Tao-tz'u	道祠	Ts'ao (mountain)	曹
tao-yuan	道緣	Ts'ao-p'ing	曹坪
Te-ch'iang	德強	Tseng	曾

GLOSSARY

Tseng Chao	曾肇	Tzu-hsin	子昕
Tseng Chi-li	曾季貍	*tzu-hsuan tung*	紫玄洞
Tseng Feng	曾丰	Tzu-wen	子文
Tseng Kung	曾鞏	Tz'u-hsi	慈溪
tseng mei hao shih	增美號謚	*wang*	王
tseng p'i	增賁	Wang	王
Tseng Pu	曾布	Wang An-shih	王安石
Tseng Tsai	曾宰	*wang-chiao*	王醮
Tseng Yen-t'ung	曾彥通	Wang Fa-chin	王法進
Tso chuan	左傳	Wang Fang-p'ing	王方平
Tsou Fen	鄒賁	Wang Hsi-chih	王羲之
Tsou Kai	鄒陔	Wang Hsiang-chih	王象之
Tsou T'ao	鄒陶	Wang-hsien	望仙
Tsou Tsung-mo	鄒宗謨	Wang K'o-ming	王克明
Tsou Ts'ung-chou	鄒從周	Wang Ku	王古
tsu-ti	族弟	Wang Kuei	王珪
Ts'ui	崔	Wang Pao	王褒
ts'ui (shade)	翠	Wang T'ing-jui	汪廷瑞
ts'ui (collect)	萃	Wang Tsao	汪早
Tsung-chen pi-yao	總真必要	Wang-tzu Chin	王子晉
ts'ung-hsiung	從兄	Wang Wen-ch'ing	王文卿
tu (ford)	渡	Wang Ying-ch'en	汪應辰
tu (ordain)	度	Wang Yeh	王埜
tu (salvation)	度	*wang-yeh*	王爺
Tu Hsien-hsing	杜仙興	*wei* (seat)	位
Tu Kao	杜杲	*wei* (sheriff)	尉
Tu To	杜鐸	Wei (kingdom)	魏
Tu Ti	土地	Wei Liao-weng	魏了翁
Tu Wu	杜蕪	Wei-ming	偉明
Tu-jen ching	度人經	Wei Su	危素
T'u-nan shu	圖南書	*wei yü ch'ing*	慰輿情
T'u Ta-hsiang	涂大向	Wen (rite-master)	文
t'u-ti	土地	Wen (marshal)	溫
t'u-ti kung	土地公	Wen-chou	溫州
Tuan-p'ing	端平	Wu	吳
Tudi Gong	土地公	Wu Ch'ao-tsung	吳朝宗
t'ui-hsin ling	退心嶺	Wu Ch'eng (author)	吳澄
Tung Shen-shih	董侁師	Wu Ch'eng	
Tung-t'ing	洞庭	(character in story)	吳城
t'ung-chih-lang	通知郎	Wu Ch'ih	吳墀
T'ung-chih lüeh	通志略	Wu Ching	吳經
T'ung-ch'uan-fu	潼川府	Wu-chou	婺州
tzu ch'an chih wu	自產之物	*wu-chu*	巫祝
Tzu-chi	紫極	Wu Hang	吳沆
Tzu-chou	梓州	Wu Hsieh	吳澥
Tzu-hsiao	紫宵	*wu-hsu*	戊戌

GLOSSARY

Wu Hsun	吳塤	Yü Chi	虞集
Wu I	吳異	*Yü-ch'ih tai-t'ien*	
Wu-i	武夷	*hsun-hsiu*	玉敕代天巡狩
Wu I-o	吳一鶚	Yü-hua	玉華
Wu Jui	吳芮	Yü-kan	餘干
Wu Kuang	吳洸	*yü shih hsun chih*	
Wu Mien	吳沔	*Hua-kai*	於是尋至華蓋
Wu Shan-fu	吳善甫	*Yü-ssu*	玉笥
Wu Shih-liang	武師亮	*Yü-ti chi-sheng*	輿地紀勝
Wu T'ao	吳濤	Yü-t'ing	玉廳
Wu Te-hsiu	吳德修	Yü-wen Ts'ui-chung	宇文粹中
Wu Tsung	吳	*yuan* (destiny)	緣
Wu Yu-lin	吳有鄰	*yuan* (vow)	願
Wu-yuan	務源	Yuan (dynasty)	元
yang	陽	Yuan (prince)	元
Yang-chou	楊州	Yuan Chiang	元絳
Yang-tzu	揚子	Yuan-feng	緣峰
Yeh	葉	Yuan-fu	元符
Yeh Fa-shan	葉法善	Yuan-fu Wan-ning	元符萬寧
yen	驗	Yuan-k'ang	元康
Yen (Marquis)	閻	Yuan Miao-tsung	元妙宗
Yen Chen-ch'ing	顏真卿	Yuan-pao	元寶
Yen-chou	嚴州	Yuan-shou	元受
Yen-hsien	彥先	Yuan-shu	元樞
Yen Hung-i	閻弘毅	Yuan-ti	元帝
Yen Lu-kung	顏魯公	Yuan T'ing-chih	袁庭植
Yen Shu	晏殊	Yuan-tso	元祚
Yen Ya-t'ui-erh	鄢牙推兒	*yuan-wai-mao*	員外帽
Yen-yu	延祐	*yueh*	約
Yi (forester)	益	Yueh (state)	越
yin	陰	Yueh (surname)	樂
Yin (county)	鄞	*yueh hu*	樂戶
Yin-chen	隱簽	Yueh-shan	約山
yin-ssu	淫祀	Yueh Shih	樂史
yin-yang	陰陽	Yun-lin	雲林
yu-ching	游境	Yung-ch'ung	永崇
Yu Tao-shou	游道首	Yung-feng	永豐
Yü (River)	盱	Yung-hsing (abbey)	永興
Yü	虞	Yung-hsing-chün	永興軍
Yü-chang	預章	Zhong Kui	鐘魁

Index

A-Ch'üan, 35
Abbey of the Reclusive Perfected, 83, 85, 294n21
Abridged Code (Lu Hsiu-ching), 318n48
Ahern, Emily Martin, 209, 255–56, 257, 266
Altar of the Ascent, 48
Altar of the Five Mounts, 300n88
Altar of the Putting on of Robes, 299n74
Altar of the Three Pure, 26, 47, 288n4
altars, in Offering ceremonies, 233
Amitabha (Buddha), 20
ancestor worship, 18, 250. *See also* kinship
Andersen, Poul, 205, 272–74, 275, 276, 277, 284n2
Annales, 9
anti-reformers, New Laws and, 105
apparitions, 18, 284n33
appointment edicts, versus enfeoffment, 186–88
Army Mountain god, 103, 130, 131, 132, 144–45. *See also* Mt. Chün (Army Mountain)
Ascend-to-Immortality Abbey, 54
auspicious sites, or special places, 49–57, 168–69. *See also* entries under "Mt."
authority: bureaucratic model and, 150–51; enfeoffment as State, 184; Four Immortals and, 138; gods as metaphor for, 3, 13–14, 141–42; of Jao Tung-t'ien, 31;

kinship and, 3; models of divine, 4, 10, 31; parental, 166; of practitioners, 39, 150; proper and improper gods and, 37, 138; in *Sacrificial Statutes*, 286n41; of special place, 49–57; Taoist practitioners and, 150–51, 206–7, 236; Three Immortals and, 71–72, 116, 123–24, 130; transition, 3; Two Immortals and, 133; in *Verities of the Three Perfected Lords Fu-ch'iu, Wang, and Kuo of Hua-kai Mountain*, 57
"automobile" saints/gods, 128, 168, 309n34

Bacon, Francis, 14, 283n27
Barth, Fredrik, 6–7, 9, 209–10, 319n3, 323n99
Battle Plain, 54
Bee King story, 189–90
belief, theories of, 12–13. *See also* religion
Biographies of Immortals (*Lieh hsien chuan*) (Liu Hsiang), 60
"Biography of (Lin) Ling-su" (Chao Tao-i), 311n3
Birnbaum, Raoul, 284n33
Black Turtle Ridge, 153
Bloody Tree Hollow, 299n78
Bokenkamp, Steven, 286–87n59
Bol, Peter, 129
Boltz, Judith: on authorship and dates of *Verities of the Three Lords*, 277, 279; on

349

Boltz, Judith *(continued)*
  Household Talk, 148; on Northern Sung, 27; on secular and divine office, 189; on Shu-chou name change, 326n13; on Teng Yu-kung issue and dates, 271–72, 274, 275, 284nn1,2,4
bone, symbolism in Chinese kinship and descent systems, 164, 313n33. *See also* Way-bone
Book of Odes, 250
Bow Mount, 54
Bridged-the-Immortals Abbey, 54
Buddhism: abolition of, 120, 197, 212; ghost-eater god relationship to, 321n70; Investigation Commissioner cult and, 247; Kuan-yin and Taoist Offerings, 232; popular gods and, 18, 19–20; temple consecrations and, 322n83
bureaucratic model. *See also* Hung Mai; *I-chien chih (Record of the Listener)* (Hung Mai): authority and, 150–51; Celestial Heart sect and, 30–36, 57, 148–54, 263; characteristics of, 4, 171–72, 267, 314n1; classical gods, 142–44; despotic signifier and, 321n70; elite and, 161–62; enfeoffments and, 145–46, 181–88, 322n75; ethnographers on, 252–60; extraordinary man concept versus, 4, 162–67; Five Thunders practice and, 148–52; frameworks and, 251–52; god worship and, 195–97, 252–55, 259, 316nn29,30; hell concept of, 264, 291n38; hierarchy in, 257; Hung Mai stories and, 69–71, 197, 235, 316nn29,30,32,33; Jade Emperor in, 31, 33, 149, 150, 151, 152, 164, 173, 242; local gods and lack of, 155, 161–62; local officials and Taoist, 171, 189–95, 216–18; nested hierarchy concept and, 261–62; Offering ceremonies and, 215, 216–18, 222, 235, 236, 243–44; religious vocabulary and, 257; souls in, 18; teacher/student motif and, 166; Three Immortals cult and (*see* Three Immortals cult); usage of, conditions for, 267; variations in perspectives on, 8–9; in *Veritable Record of the Two Perfected Lords,* 57, 59–60, 123, 290–91n38, 304n135; in *Verities of the Three Perfected Lords Fu-ch'iu, Wang, and Kuo of Hua-kai Mountain,* 57–58, 63–64, 133
Bureau for Expelling Perverse Forces, 31

Cavern of Pure Perfection, 163, 164
Cavern of Purple Tenuity (*tzu-hsuan tung*), 93, 299n75
Celestial Heart sect, 4, 18, 24. *See also Correct Rites of Celestial Heart from Shang-ch'ing* (Teng Yu-kung); *Spirit Code: A Numinous Text from the Marrow of Shang-ch'ing* (Teng Yu-kung); bureaucratic model and, 30–36, 57, 148–54, 263; divine hierarchy in, 31, 38–39, 292n60; gods of, 38–39, 42–44; local cults and, 36–42, 190, 286nn41,51; locality and, 40, 42, 169; masters/practitioners of, 29–38, 40, 41, 44–45, 151–52, 202–3; revelations and texts, 26–29, 36; rites of, 28–36, 285n16; secular practitioners in, 190–93; State responsibilities and, 190; Taoism and, 42–46; texts of, 27, 29–30; Three Immortals cult versus, 36, 39–40, 47–48, 56–57, 69–70
Celestial Lord of the Limpid Waves, 149
Ceremonial Forms for the Performance and Completion of the Unsurpassed Grand Retreat of the Yellow Register (Wu-Shang huang-lu ta-chai li-ch'eng i) (Chiang Shu-yü), 42–43, 215
Cerutti, Simona, 282n8
Chan T'ai-ch'u, 99–101, 277, 278, 302nn122,123
Chang Chi-hsien, 273
Chang Hsiao-hsiang, 135, 187
Chang Pang-ch'ang, 206
Chang Te-lung, 199
Chang Yen, 106, 302n119
Chang Yen-fa, 301n101
Chang Yuan-feng, 301n101
Chang Yuan-shu: on Altar of the Five Mounts, 300n88; authorship of last four chapters of *Verities of the Three Lords,* 277–80; on carved images, 304n140; on Ch'i-chen Abbey, 78–79; on "Clean Water," 300n83; dating of material of, 301n101; dream of Two Immortals, 133; on immortal geese, 299n80; on "Immortal Medicines" and "Omen Stoves," 300n86; miracle stories of, 60, 62–65, 98, 99, 123; naming of self by, 290n36, 291n43; Northern Sung miracle stories of, 106–7; preface of, 128–29; *Verities of Mt. Hua-kai* of, 49, 99, 112, 113, 127–28, 277, 290n35, 292n59
Chang Yuan-ting, 301n101

Chang Yü-ch'u, 85
Chao-ch'ing Abbey, 90, 93, 111, 117, 319n23
Chao Po-t'i, 28
Chao Po-wu, 28
Chao Tao-i, 152–53, 157, 158, 159, 161, 162
Chao T'o, 310n42
Chao Tsu-chien, 34–35, 44
Chao Tzu-chü, 28, 42, 191–92
Chao Yü-shih, 311n3
Ch'ao-hsien Abbey, 80, 91–92
ch'ao t'ien (have audience with Heaven), 289n21
chen ("leading peak"), concept of, 307n3
Chen Rongsheng, 216
Chen-tsung (emperor), 27, 31
Ch'en family, 110, 118
Ch'en P'eng-fei, 88–89
Ch'en Po-yang, 118
Ch'en Tsao, 69
Ch'en T'ung-tsu, 110
Ch'en Yuan-ch'eng, 193–94, 195
Ch'en Yuan-chin, 88–89, 96, 106, 110, 305n148, 306n150
Ch'en Yuan-ying, 280
Cheng Mao, 137
Cheng Sung, 296n44
Ch'eng Chü-fu, 154–55, 161
Chessboard Rock, 79
Che-tsung (emperor), 184
ch'i (material force), 13
Ch'i-chen (Pray to the Perfected) Abbey, 77, 78–79
Ch'i-li Mountain, 55–56
Chia, Ms., 107–8, 291n38
Chia-hui Abbey, 92
Chiang-nan Hua-kai shan chih (Hsu Yun-sheng), 303–4n135
Chiang Shu-yü, 42–43
Ch'iao-hsien Abbey, 103, 273, 275–76
Chieh Ch'i-ssu, 92
Ch'ien Ping, 35, 36
Ch'ien Tang, 189–90
Ch'ien-te period, 293n8
Chih-hui shang-p'iu ta chieh. See *Major Precepts of the Upper Chapter of Wisdom*
Chikusa Masaaki, 306–7n164
Chin dynasty, 293n8
Chin Yün-chung, 272
Ch'in Kuei, 193

Ch'in-tsung (emperor), 121
Ching Ch'i-p'eng, 298n59
Ching-yun (Bright Clouds) Abbey, 77–78
ch'ing (sentiment), 264–65
Ch'ing-ch'i Abbey, 91
Ch'iu Hu, 85
Ch'iu Shou-ching, 115
Chou dynasty, 59
Chou Meng-jo, 87–88, 111, 125–26, 132, 143, 169
Chou Pi-ta, 86, 87, 89
Chou Tsao, 310n42
Christian, William, 67
Chu Chih-ch'ing, 153
Chu Chung-su, 166, 272
Chu Hsi, 141, 145, 294n21
Chu Huan, 106, 126, 169
Ch'u Kunliang, 237
Chuang Tzu, 298n66
Ch'ung-hsien [Kuan] Abbey, 101–5, 273, 275–76, 314n10
Ch'ung t'ung-miao shih-ch'en Wang hsien-sheng chia-hua. See *Household Talk of the Void-Soaring, Mystery Penetrating Imperial Attendant, Master Wang*
Chün Mountain Shrine, 85. *See also* Army Mountain god; Mt. Chün
city god, 38, 227
civil service examinations, 283n28, 315n16. *See also* degree holders
Classic of the Yellow Court, 294n23
"Clean Water" gully, 300n83
clothing, in Offering rituals, 238
Cohen, Myron, 222
Comprehensive Mirror of the Successive Generations of Perfected Transcendents and Those Who Embody the Way (Li-shih chen-hsien t'iao t'ung-chien) (Chao Tao-i), 152–53
Correct Rites of Celestial Heart from Shang-ch'ing (Shang-ch'ing t'ien-hsin cheng-fa) (Teng Yu-kung): authorship of, 271–77; on Celestial Heart master, 44; content of, 28, 29–30; dating of, 273, 275–76; on Four Immortals, 142; on Jao Tung-t'ien in preface, 166; late Northern Sung date of, 27; on Offerings, 45; preface to, 39; talismans and god of locality, 38; Three Perfected Lords in preface of, 39; on transmission of the Way, 167
Correct Rites of Celestial Heart (T'ien-hsin cheng-fa), 26

352   INDEX

courtesy names, 118, 168, 298n64, 305–6n150
cranes, 2, 282n2, 288n6, 299n72
cults, local: Celestial Heart sect and, 36–42, 190, 286nn41,51; elite and, 220, 221–22, 226, 236, 240, 242–43; hierarchy of gods and (*see* gods: hierarchy of); Offerings and, 220, 234–35, 239–40; State and, 103–5, 143, 145–46, 207, 247; State gods and, 20, 101–5, 120–21, 139, 153, 207, 247; Taoism as framework in, 211–12, 237–38, 240; Three Immortals and, 4, 72–73, 130–37; of Three Lords, 2; *Verities of the Three Perfected Lords* on, 72–73, 135
culture, religion and, 5–7, 8, 10–11, 209

D'Andrade, Roy, 7, 9, 209, 282n8, 319n3
Davis, Ned, 318n48
Dean, Kenneth, 214, 251; on community, 320n46; on "despotic signifier," 321n75; on frequency of Offerings, 213; on in-temple Offerings attendees, 222; on Taoism as local cult framework, 211–12, 236, 237–40; on *Tu-jen ching* on scripture, 313n42
DeGlopper, Donald, 264–65
degree holders, as symbol of locality, 107, 119, 242, 243–44, 305n149
demons, local gods as, 219, 299n78
Dipper, pacing, 30, 54, 57, 192, 193, 281n1, 293n10
Divine Empyrean sect (*shen-hsiao*), 27–28, 120–21, 144, 146, 173
divine officials, Chinese gods as. *See* bureaucratic model
Dragon Casting Pond, 299n77
Dragon Spring Mountain, 292n60
Drum-Court for Reporting Grievances, 149
Duara, Prasenjit, 325n13
Dubisch, Jill, 67
Durkheim, Emile, 10

Eastern Marchmount, 291n38
Ebrey, Patricia, 210, 317n42
ecumenism, 236
elite (*shih-ta-fu*), 2, 105, 145. *See also* poetry; bureaucratic model and, 161–62; Ch'ung-jen, 134; Divine Empyrean sect and, 120–21; Four Immortals cult and, 134–37; Fu-chou, 141; kinship interrelationships among, 118–19, 122–23, 130, 294n21, 298n65, 305n145, 306nn150,158; locality and Immortals, 130–31, 169–70; in miracle stories, 106–10, 131; Offerings and, 220, 221–22, 226, 236, 240, 242–43; personal model and, 130; political executions impact on, 119–20; rise of Fu-chou, 17, 111; State and Fu-chou, 116–21, 122, 144, 146; symbolic resistance to State and, 245–46; terminology for, 307n8; Three Immortals cult and secular, 21, 85, 90, 112, 116–17, 124–25, 130; Three Immortals during Yuan dynasty and, 96–97; *Verities of the Three Perfected Lords* and, 112
enfeoffments: appointment edicts versus, 186–88; bureaucratic model and, 322n75; of Four Immortals, 116, 134, 142, 145; graded system of, 314n8; language of communication in, 185–86; numbers of, 303n133; State and local gods, 20, 101–5, 145–46, 181–88, 325n11; as State authority, 184; of Three Immortals, 116, 144, 184–86, 303n135
extraordinary man concept, versus bureaucratic model, 4, 162–67

False Learning faction, 122
Fan An, 38
Faure, David: description of New Territories Offerings, 223–25; dual religions in Offerings, 249, 320n53; on frequency of Offerings, 213; on ghost-eater god, 321n70; on lay organizers of Offerings, 240–41; on local gods, 229; on vows for Offerings, 226
Feng I-weng, 92
Feuchtwang, Stephen, 222; on gods as metaphor for state, 3; on lay organizers of Offerings, 240, 251–52; on local gods, 254, 316n31, 325n11; on Offerings and local cults, 220; on Offerings and politics, 221–22
Fire Master, personage of, 28–29, 149, 150, 159, 164, 165, 313n34
Five Pecks of Rice movement, 202
Five Thunders practice: bureaucratic model and details of, 148–52; in Fu-chou, 286n53; locality and Immortals in, 169;

INDEX   353

masters of, 28–29, 38, 173; Wang Wen-ch'ing as master of, 147
Four Immortals cult, 22; authority and, 138; elite and, 134–37; enfeoffments of, 116, 134, 142, 145; Fu-ch'iu (Lord) and, 135; Huang Chen and, 114, 138, 142–43; inscription for, 142–43; State and, 135–36; Three Immortals cult in relation to, 73, 115–16; *Verities* on, 60, 135
Freedman, Maurice, 8
Freeman, Susan Tax, 326n16
Fried, Morton, 264
Fu-ch'iu, Lord: accounts of, 89, 160; ascent of, 133; choice of Mt. Hua-kai, 53; early life of, 49; enfeoffments and, 184–85, 303n135; Four Immortals cult and, 135; nature and significance of, 59–60, 61; as one of Three Lords, 2, 115; origin myth and, 1; in poetry, 93–94; Tea-Brewing Hollow and, 299n81; as teacher of Two Perfecteds, 121, 130; titles of, 297n50; Two Perfected Lords' ascent and, 57–58; in *Veritable Record of the Two Perfected Lords*, 73
Fu-ch'iu's Altar, 54
Fu Hsuan, 28
Fu T'ien-hsin, 167, 272, 273

Gaborieau, Marc, 67
Gallin, Bernard, 252, 253
Gazetteer of Mt. Lung-hu, 176
Geertz, Clifford, 5–6, 10–11, 282nn8,11
General Views of a Dweller in Reclusion (Yin-chü Hung-i) (Liu Hsun), 86–87
"gentleman of the Way" (*tao-shih*), 44, 45, 287n64. *See also* Taoism
ghost-eater god, 321n70
gift exchanges, 265–66
gods. *See also names of specific gods, deities, and Immortals*: authority and, 3, 4, 13–14, 37, 138, 141–42; automobile, 128, 168, 309n34; bureaucratic model and worship of, 195–97, 252–55, 259, 316nn29,30; categories of, 196–97; Celestial heart sect and, 38–39, 42–44; classical model of, 143–44; definitions of, 13, 18–19, 126; as demons, 219, 299n78; enfeoffment of (*see* enfeoffments); hierarchy of, 218–19, 224, 258–59, 286n45, 292n60, 320n54,

322n76, 325n11; household-god relationships, 253–54; humans worshipped as, 154–62; Immortals or Perfected versus, 39; local, 211, 219, 229, 254–55, 316n31, 318n48, 325n11; local, bureaucratic model and, 155, 161–62; local, in Taoist Offering rites, 227, 228, 229; local, State and, 101–5, 120–21, 139, 153, 207; Offering ceremonies (*see* Offering ceremonies); as officials, 3, 267; ordinary people and (*see* ordinary (lay) people: gods); personal model and (*see* personal model: gods and); representations of, 268; State and (*see* bureaucratic model; State); as symbols, 13–14; Taoist pantheon of, 210–11, 230, 247–49; Taoist rites and non-Taoist, 248–49; titles and prefixes of, 181, 188, 297nn49,50, 302n126; variety of, 18–19, 20; vows and, 67–69
Golden Boat, 299n79
Golden Fowl Grotto, 299n76
Gregory, Peter, 210, 317n42

Hall of Rejoicing at Rain, 89, 90
Hall of the Three Pure, 80
Han dynasty, 59
Han Shu, 309–10n42. *See also History of Former Han*
Han Yü, 294n24
Hansen, Valerie, 21, 103, 196, 198, 303n133
Hartwell, Robert, 307nn8,9
he shu, 290n37
healing, as focus of Taoist sects, 27–28, 29, 30, 38
Heavenly Master sect, 176
Heaven's Great August Emperor, 296n46
Hei-sha (Black Killer), 272
hell, bureaucratic concept of, 264, 291n38
hell/death stories, 290–91n38, 316n32
Hemp Lady, 289n34
Hemp Spring, 140, 310n59
History of Former Han, 60, 135, 309n42
History of Later Han, 136
Ho Chung, 298n59
Ho family, 118
Ho I, 95–96, 106, 132, 134, 300n83, 301n91
Hong Kong New Territories, 223–31
Hopi, 283n21
household-god relationships, 253–54

Household Talk of the Void-Soaring, Mystery Penetrating Imperial Attendant, Master Wang (Ch'ung-hsu t'ung-miao shih-ch'en Wang hsien-sheng chia-hua) (Wang Wen-ch'ing), 148–51, 157, 159, 161, 311–12n4
Hsi-ning period, 100
Hsiang-fu Abbey, 80
Hsiang Yü, 131
Hsiao-tsung (emperor), 276
Hsiao Tzu-yun, 78
Hsiao Yü-kan, 160
Hsieh I, 97
Hsieh K'o, 97
Hsieh Ling-yun, 83
Hsieh O, 92
hsin (belief), theories of, 12–13
Hsing-lo Abbey, 96, 301n100
Hsiung Chiang, 107
Hsiung Chih-ch'ang, 107, 305n145
Hsiung family, 118
Hsiung P'u: as degree holder, 107, 119, 305n149; Hua-kai cult devotion and, 108, 111, 118, 120; kinship relationships of, 305n145
Hsiung Shan-jen, 153
Hsiung T'ien-ch'ang, 305n145
Hsu, Francis, 228–29, 231, 241, 244–45, 250
Hsuan-wu, 272
Hsuan-yuan Abbey, 58
Hsu Cheng, 276
Hsu Hsun-ch'üan, 87
Hsu Sun, 247
Hsu Tzu-shih, 88
Hsu Tz'u-hsueh, 160
Hsu Yun-sheng, 303n135
Hsueh Hsuan-ch'ing, 160
Hsun Po-tzu, 294n22
Hu Shou-chen, 134, 310n43
Hu Tao-hsuan, 160
Hua-kai cult. See Mt. Hua-kai, Three Lords cult
Hua-kai shan Fu-ch'iu Wang Kuo sen chen-chün shih shih. See *Verities of the Three Perfected Lords Fu-ch'iu, Wang, and Kuo of Hua-kai Mountain*
Huang Chen: background of, 307n1; Four Immortals and, 114, 134; on Immortals and locality, 169; Lo family and, 109; on Luan Pa and "improper worship," 136–37; Mt. Hua-kai Immortals and, 115, 116; "Praying for Rain and Escorting to Two Shrines," 310–11n59; Three Immortals cult and, 137–44
Huang Ch'ung, 109
Huang Fu, 295n28
Huang Jen-hung, 187
Huang Lü-chung, 85–86, 87, 130, 295n28
Huang Mi-chien, 279, 280
Huang Wen-ch'ang, 295n28
Huang Wen-sheng, 295n28
Huang Yang, 295n28
Huang Yao, 152
Huang Yueh, 85, 86, 87, 89, 295n27
Hui-tsung (emperor), 147; Divine Empyrean Taoism and, 27, 120; enfeoffment of Lord Fu-ch'iu, 184–85; enfeoffments under, 103; Taoists and, 20, 27, 173, 197, 276, 312n4; Wang Wen-ch'ing and, 152, 156
Hung Ching-kao, 37
Hung Kua, 37
Hung Mai: belief portrayed in stories of, 12–13; bureaucratic elements in stories of, 67–71, 197, 235, 316–17n34, 316nn29,30,32,33; Celestial Heart masters in stories of, 34, 37–38, 44–45, 151–52; god stories of, 315–16n28, 316n29; judgment stories of, 68–70, 71, 287n68; locality and stories of, 40, 189–95, 286n45; on Mt. Chün, 85–86, 295n27; Offerings in stories of, 212–13, 214; official name changes and, 326–27n13; possession stories of, 34–36, 38, 286n44; purgatory stories of, 316n29; religion in stories of, 18; on Ta Ch'ien god, 128, 315n16; Taoism and market in stories of, 198–99; on Wu I, 306n150

I An-ning, 85
I-chien chih. See *Record of the Listener*
I-hsing Abbey, 288–89n14
I To-fu, 92
Immortal Geese Pond, 299n80
immortality elixir, 132, 293n11
Immortal Lord White Dragon of the Sages' Well, 90
"Immortal Medicines," 300n86
Immortals. *See also* Four Immortals cult; Three Immortals cult; *names of specific Immortals*: ascension of, 53–54, 57–58,

129, 133, 282n2, 286n50, 308n26; definition of, 126, 142, 143, 165, 168
Immortals breath *(hsien feng)*, 163, 164
Immortals' Woods Abbey, 54
Immortal Women's Peak, 54
Imperial Metaphor (Feuchtwang), 325n11
improper worship *(yin-ssu)*, 36–37, 136–37, 138
inscriptions: Chen Yuan-chin, 306n150; epitaph, 296n38; Feng I-feng, 92; for Four Immortals, 142–43; funeral, 295n28; Hsu Cheng, 88; Huang Chen, 136–37, 142–43; Li Chung-yuan, 121; Liu Ch'en-weng, 91–92; Pai Yü-ch'an, 89–90, 312n20; Tseng Chao, 130; Tseng Feng, 300n87; Wang An-shih, 80–81; for Wang Wen-ch'ing, 157–58, 160–61; Wu Ch'eng, 90–91, 296nn43,44, 305n150; Yen Chen-ch'ing, 2, 49–50, 98, 104, 121–22, 123, 304n135; Yü Chi, 157–58, 160–61, 306n158; Yueh Shih, 79
Investigation Commissioner of the Nine Heavens *(chiu-t'ien shih-che)*, 247

Jade Emperor, in bureaucratic model, 31, 33, 149, 150, 151, 152, 164, 173, 242
Jade Pavilion, 54
Jao Chieh, 97
Jao Tung-t'ien, 36, 40; advice and transformation, 129; ascent of, 47–48; authority of, 31; biography of, 278; dates of, 284n1; lineage of, 272; revelation to, 26–27; *Spirit Code* on, 273; teacher of, 166; Three Immortals and, 99; *Veritable Record of the Two Perfected Lords* on, 274
Jen Tao-yuan, 45
"jeweled fringe," 298n68
Jochim, Christian, 324n125
Johnson, David, 249, 250
Jordan, David, 253, 254
Journal of a Return to Lu-ling (Kuei Lu-ling chi) (Chou Pi-ta), 86
judgment stories, 68–70, 71, 287n68
Jurchen people, 16, 120

Kao-tsung (emperor), 117
Kao Tzu-hsu, 160
Katz, Paul, 249, 322–23n88, 325n13

Khitan people, 16
King Ling, 59
kinship: authority and, 3; bone symbolism in Chinese, 164, 313n33; *ch'ing* and, 265; elite, 118–19, 122–23, 130, 294n21, 298n65, 305n145, 306nn150,158; god worship and, 254, 317nn35,36; Three Immortals worship and, 118–19, 122–23, 272; of Two Perfected Lords, 61–62; Wu family and, 306n150; Yü Chi, poetry, and, 96–97, 110; Yueh Shih, poetry, and, 293n12
Kleeman, Terry, 211
kuan-hsi, 265
Kuan-yin, 232, 267, 321n70
Kuei Lu-ling chi. See *Journal of a Return to Lu-ling*
kung-pu (merit cloth/flag), 299n71
K'ung Tzu chia-yü ("Household Talk of Master Kung"), 311–12n4
Kuo, Lord: ascent of, 129, 308n26; authority and, 133; enfeoffments of, 184, 303n135; journey motif in accounts about, 49, 50, 89; kinship relationships of, 61; miracles of, 24; Offerings to, 68, 213; Tea-Brewing Hollow and, 299n81; Tiger-Track Rock and, 299n72
Kuo Chün, 100, 103, 104, 302n122
Kuo Ju-ching, 91
Kuo Ju-hsien, 91

Lagerwey, John: on bureaucratic aspect of Taoist written communications, 216–18; on lay organizers of Offerings, 222; on local gods, 211, 219; on Taoist Offerings rituals, 234, 321n57
Lao Tzu, 321n70
lay people. *See* ordinary (lay) people
Leach, Edmund, 11
Learning of the Way *(tao-hsueh)*, 17, 20, 122, 145, 203. *See also* Neo-Confucianism
Lepetit, Bernard, 9–10
li (principle), 264–65
Li Chung-yuan, 60, 121, 303n133
Li family, 96, 118, 134–35
Li Hsiu, 134, 310n43
Li Hu, 134, 310n43
Li Jui, 186–87
Li Kung-yen, 279
Li Liu, 134
Li hsien chuan. See *Biographies of Immortals*

Li Po-ku, 134
Li-shih chen-hsien t'iao t'ung-chien. See *Comprehensive Mirror of the Successive Generations of Perfected Transcendents and Those Who Embody the Way*
Li T'ao, 134
Li-tsung (emperor), 185
Li Yeh-hua, 118
Li Yen-hua, 119, 120, 134
Li Yen-yuan, 74, 298nn69,70
Li Yuan-fang, 186
Li Yun-ssu, 134
Liang Kun, 34–36, 199
Lin Hsiao-yao, 168
Lin-ju Academy, 141
Lin Ling-su, 27, 120, 173–74, 311n3, 312n4
Lin T'e-ch'i, 199
Ling-pao scriptures, 42, 286–87n59
Liu Ch'en-weng, 91–92
Liu Hsiang, 60, 106, 274, 277–78, 279, 280
Liu Hsin-shu, 194
Liu Hsun, 86–87, 128, 131, 168–69, 312n19
Liu Yuan-tsai, 79
Lo Ch'un-po. *See* Lo Tien
Lo family, 108–9, 118
Lo Hsu-chou, 160
Lo Kung-yuan, 93–94, 298n65
Lo Pin, 108–9, 109, 212–13
Lo Tien: kinship relationships and Fu-chou elite, 118, 298n65; on Lord Fu-ch'iu, 60; in miracle stories, 109; poetry on Hua-kai Immortals, 93–94, 96, 106, 135
Lo Tou-nan, 109–10
Lo Wu-i, 109
Lo Yeh, 109
Lord Goose's Clay, 299n80
Losing Heart Ridge, 299–300n82
Lu Chiu-yuan (Lu Hsiang-shan), 17, 141, 144
Lu Hsiu-ching, 318n48
Lu Yuan-su, 272
luan-birds, 2, 93, 282n2, 288n6, 299n72
Luan Pa, 93–94, 135, 136–37, 142, 298n64
Lü (empress), 59, 60
Lü Pen-chung, 294n21
Lü Tung-pin, 193–94, 195

Ma-ku, 289n34
Ma-tsu (T'ien Hsu), 227, 228, 240
Major Precepts of the Upper Chapter of Wisdom (Chih-hui shang-p'in ta chieh), 287n59

market, Taoism and, 197–205, 269, 317–18n47, 318n48, 322n83
Martin, Emily. *See* Ahern, Emily Martin
McNeill, William, 14
meaning, systems of, 208–9
Meaning of the Spring and Autumn Annals (Wang T'ing-ssu), 61, 123
Mei Fu, 100, 113, 134, 135–36, 142, 302n123, 310n44
Mei Hsuan, 81, 131
Mei Peak, 134
Ming-chen-k'o. See *Ordinances of the Luminous Perfected*
Ming dynasty, 27, 49, 84
Ming-kung shu-p'an ch'ing-ming chi, 303n128
Mintz, Sidney, 15
miracle stories: of Chang Yuan-shu, 60, 62–65, 98, 99, 123; elite in, 106–10, 131; poetry and, 100; Three Immortals and, 62, 132, 133, 263; in *Veritable Record of the Two Perfected Lords,* 60, 62–65, 98, 99–101, 123, 289n35; in *Verities of the Three Perfected Lords,* 105, 106–10, 133, 209, 250–51, 278, 298n62
Mohists, 171
Mongols, 16
Mother of Thunder, 164, 166
mountains, of Fu-chou, 52. *See also names of specific mountains*
Mt. Chin-hua, 76
Mt. Ch'ing-ch'eng, 160
Mt. Chung-hua, 289n14
Mt. Chün (Army Mountain): description and history of, 81–82, 83; early elite worship of local cult, 130–31; fading of god of, 144–45; Hung Mai on, 295n27; Three Immortals cult and, 85–87; Three Immortals displacement of god of, 111, 132; Wang Wen-ch'ing and, 147, 164
Mt. Feng-t'ai, 76
Mt. Hsiang, 114, 115, 134, 136, 137, 142, 310n59. *See also* Mt. Pa
Mt. Hsien-yu, 93, 297nn54,55
Mt. Hua-kai: alternative names of, 77; Celestial Heart revelations at, 26–27, 36; Ch'ung-hsien Abbey incident, 101–5; "Clean Water" gully, 300n83; dating by descriptions of, 276–77, 296n46; early Southern Sung accounts of, 88–92; miraculous herbs and plants at, 327n25; name and meaning of, 281–82n1; non-

Celestial Heart revelations at, 47–48; origin myths about, 1–2; pilgrimages to, 22–23, 89; poetry associated with, 79–80, 300n85, 312n20; as special place, 49–57, 168; "Tower for Viewing the Immortals," 88; Two Lords discovery of, 50–51, 53, 125–26; *Veritable Record of the Two Perfected Lords* on, 51, 54; *Verities of the Three Perfected Lords* on, 49–51, 53. See also Three Immortals cult

Mt. Huang-t'ung, 88

Mt. Lin-ch'uan, 292n5

Mt. Ling-ku (Numinous Gorge), 80–81, 83, 84, 92, 111, 115, 130, 305n149

Mt. Lo, 93–94

Mt. Lo-fu, 175

Mt. Lung-hu, 183

Mt. Ma, 90

Mt. Ma-ku, 50, 54, 98, 140, 289n34

Mt. Mao, 44, 176, 182

Mt. Pa, 22, 60, 93–94, 136, 137, 292–93n5, 292n60. See also Mt. Hsiang

Mt. Pao-kai, 76, 77. See also Mt. Hua-kai

Mt. Pi-chia (Brush Rack), 23, 89, 296n39

Mt. Ta-fu, 206

Mt. T'ai ("Eastern Mount"), 26, 31, 32–33, 196, 267

Mt. Wang-hsien, 76–77

Mt. Wu-t'ai, 284n33

Mt. Yü-ssu, 50, 51, 55, 98

Naitō Torajirō, 14

names, changes in official, 326–27n13

Needham, Joseph, 15

Neo-Confucianism, influence of, 13, 17, 19, 20–21, 129, 137, 142, 143, 250. See also Learning of the Way

nepotism, principles associated with, 259

Neskar, Ellen, 141

nested hierarchy concept, 261–62

New Laws, 104–5, 145, 146

New Territories, Hong Kong, 223–31

Nickerson, Peter, 314n1, 318n48

Nieh T'ien-his, 160

"nine revolutions" elixir, 132, 293n11

Nine-Yang Palace for Overseeing the Perfected, 152

Ning-tsung (emperor), 276

Northern Bourne Bureau for Expelling Perverse Forces (*pei-chi ch'ü-hsieh yuan*), 31

Northern Sung: appointment edict from, 186–87; Boltz on (*see* Boltz, Judith); description of, 16; elite and Three Immortals cult, 125; elite in, 2, 145; miracle stories of, 106–7; origins of Taoist practitioners in capital, 177; origins of Taoist practitioners not in capital, 178; Taoist practitioners and locality in, 175–76; written sources on Three Immortals, 27, 79–82, 97, 98, 99–101, 105–6, 106–7, 271–77, 278, 284nn1,2,4, 289n35

Offering ceremonies, 43; accounts of, 87–88, 90 (*see also* Dean, Kenneth; Faure, David; Feuchtwang, Stephen; Lagerwey, John; Sangren, Steven; Schipper, Kristofer); altars in, 233; Buddhism and, 232; bureaucratic model and, 215, 216–18, 222, 235, 236, 243–44; clothing for, 238; *Correct Rites* on, 45; drama performances in, 234–36, 237–38, 241; frameworks for, 211–12, 237–38, 240, 241–44, 250–51; frequency of, 213; functions of, 214–15; god processions in, 234–36, 258; in Hong Kong New Territories, 223–31; in-temple attendees, 222; lay participants in, 222; Lin Village Alliance, 227; local cults and, 220, 234–35, 239–40; local gods and, 227, 228, 229; for Lord Kuo, 68, 213; ordination and, 45; organizing committees for, 221–22, 240–44, 251–52; outside temples, 231–36; personal model and, 71; purpose of, 207, 214; reasons for, 207–8, 213–14; rituals of, 219–20, 221, 223–26, 233–34, 239–40, 321n57; spirit mediums in, 235–36; State and, 222–23; stories in *I-chien chih*, 212–13, 214; in Taiwan, 216–23, 239, 240, 250; Taoist liturgy and, 220, 223–25, 237–39, 244, 246, 249; Taoist notions of authority in, 206–7; "Taoist-on-top" pattern in, 220, 225; Taoist rituals alongside local, 227–28; Teng lineage, 228; Twelve Royal Lords, 242–43, 251, 267, 323n96; *Verities of the Three Perfected Lords* on, 72, 206, 212–13, 226; vows for, 65–67, 226, 291n49; written communications to gods in, 215, 216–18; Yellow Register Offering, 45, 169

Offering of the Kings (Twelve Royal Lords). *See* Twelve Royal Lords Offering
Offering of the Lin Village Alliance, 227
Offering of the Teng lineage, 228
"Omen Stoves," 300n86
Ordinances of the Luminous Perfected (Ming-chen k'o), 287n59
ordinary (lay) people: bureaucratic model and, 267–68; gods, direct versus indirect contact with, 19, 23–24, 199–201, 206, 291n49, 317n42; gods and, 43, 154–62, 155, 196, 252–53, 257–58, 316n31; gods' titles and, 188; Offerings and, 210, 221–22, 240–44, 250, 251–52; ritual ignorance and, 244–45, 323n99; spirit mediums and, 201–2, 235–36, 253; symbolic resistance to State and, 246; during Tang-Sung transition, 15–16, 318n48; Two Immortals' advice to, 129
ordination, Taoism and, 44, 45, 113, 197, 306–7n164
Ou-yang Ch'e, 97, 117–20, 144, 308n17
Ou-yang Hsiu, 186
Ou-yang hsiu-chuan chi, 308n17

Pai Yü-ch'an, 23, 89, 154, 175, 296n39, 312n20
Palace of Upper Purity, 174
Pao-kai, 281n1
Patriarch of the Clear Stream, 239
Pavilion of the Multitude of Immortals, 89
Pease, Jonathan, 294n17
pei-chi ch'ü-hsieh yuan. *See* Northern Bourne Bureau for Expelling Perverse Forces
Pei-ti fu, 273, 274
P'ei Sheng-chung, 300n87
penal code, Sung dynasty, 33–34, 285n26, 287n59
personal model: characteristics of, 4–5, 265–66; *chiao* and, 319–20n31; "child-parent" concept and, 255–56; elite and, 130; extraordinary man concept, versus bureaucratic model, 4, 162–67; frameworks and, 251–52, 262–63; gods and, 43, 94, 252–53, 255–56; Hung Mai stories and, 71, 317n35; Mei Fu and, 310n44; Offering ceremonies and, 71; in Taoist divine world, 166, 267, 319–20n31; teacher/student motif and, 166–67; Three Immortals miracle stories and, 62–65, 94, 263; usage of, conditions for, 267; vows and, 265; Wang Wen-ch'ing and, 158–59
Pi Tsao, 199
pilgrimages, 22–23, 84, 324n2
"pin of office" *(tsan)*, 301n93
Pin-t'ui lu (Chao Yü-shih), 311n3
P'ing Ching-tsung, 153, 166
plague gods, 231, 244, 249, 323n88
"Platform for Rebirth in Heaven," 30
Poems of Ling-ku (Wang An-shih), 80–81
poetry: *ch'ing* in, 264; elite Yuan dynasty, 96–97; Han Yü and, 294–95n24; kinship and, 96–97, 110, 293n12; local, 93; Lo Tien, 93–94, 96, 106, 135; miracle stories and, 100; Mt. Hua-kai in, 79–80, 300n85, 312n20; Mt. Ling-ku in, 83–84; to rain and cloud god, 82; Sun Ti, 297nn54,55; Three Immortals in, 92–97, 106, 135, 312n20; Tseng Chi-li, 83–84, 89, 115, 264, 294n22; Wang An-shih, 97; Wang Wen-ch'ing in, 154, 157; Yü Chi, 298n59; Yueh Shih and, 293n12
possession stories, 34–36, 38, 286n44
prayer: Huang Chen and, 138–40; "Praying for Rain and Escorting the Two Shrines," 310–11n59; Three Immortals and, 23–24
"Praying for Rain and Escorting the Two Shrines" (Huang Chen), 310–11n59
"Praying for Rain to the Perfected Lord of Hemp Spring" (Huan Chen), 140–41
Precepts of the Three Primes (San-yuan p'in), 13
Precepts of the Three Primordials (San-yuan p'in-chieh), 287n59
Presentation of the Memorial, 321n57
priests, names for, 313n33. *See also* Taoism: professional religious class in
P'u Ju-lin, 155
Pure land preachers, 20. *See also* Buddhism
purgatory stories, 316n29

reborn bone *(su ku)*, 165
reborn Immortals, 165
Record of Lin-ch'uan (Hsun Po-tzu), 294n22
Record of the Imperial Domains in the T'ai-p'ing Era (T'ai-ping huan-yü chi) (Yueh Shih), 77–78, 80, 81, 86, 104, 111, 292n5
Record of the Listener (I-chien chih) (Hung Mai): bureaucratic elements in stories in, 67–71, 197, 235, 316–17n34, 316nn29,30,32,33; Celestial Heart

masters in stories of, 34, 37–38, 44–45, 151–52; content of, 12–13, 18; god stories in, 315–16n28, 316n29; hell/death stories in, 290–91n38, 316n32; judgment stories in, 68–70, 71, 287n68; locality and stories in, 40, 189–95, 286n45; Offerings in stories in, 212–13, 214; official name changes and, 326–27n13; possession stories in, 34–36, 38, 286n44; purgatory stories in, 316n29; religion in stories in, 18; Ta-Ch'ien god in, 128, 315n16; Taoism and market in stories of, 198–99; Wu family in, 306n150
Record of the Three Perfected (Li Chung-yuan), 303n135
reductionism, 198
Reiter, Florian, 246–47, 277, 279, 323nn104,105
religion. *See also* gods; *names of specific cults, gods, Immortals, and sects*: culture and, 5–7, 8, 10–11, 209; dual, 249, 320n53; as purchased good, 198; Sung, description of, 18–21
Religion of the Yellow Emperor movement, 257, 324n125
Retreat ceremony, 43
Ripe Spring, 151
"rite master" (*fa-shih*), 44
Ritual of Declaring Penitence to Heaven and Earth of the Pure Retreat of Ling-pao, 247
rituals, in Taoism. *See* Offering ceremonies; Taoism
Rosenberg, Harold, 8
Rothkrug, Lionel, 309n34

Sa Shou-chien, 160
Sacrifice (*sai*) ritual, 249–50
Sacrificial Statutes, 37, 115, 286n41
saints, worship and, 128, 168, 268–69, 309n34, 326n16
San-yuan p'in. *See Precepts of the Three Primes*
San-yuan p'in-chieh. *See Precepts of the Three Primordials*
Sanchis, Pierre, 67
Sangren, Steven, 3, 214, 261, 324n2; on *chiao*, 213; on gods as bureaucrats, 259; on Offerings ritual, 220; on personal model in Sung *chiao*, 319–20n31; on rationalizers, 318–19n2; on stove god and fire, 324n128

The Scenery of the Empire Recorded (Yü-ti chi-sheng) (Wang Hsiang-chih), 76–77
Schafer, Edward, 281n1
Schipper, Kristofer, 45, 214, 216, 246, 267, 323n106; on divisions in modern Taoism, 44, 239, 241–43, 244, 247–49; on frequency of Offerings, 213; Hymes translation issues with, 287nn67,68; on lay participants in Taoist Offerings ritual, 222; on local gods, 254–55; T'ang-Sung transition and local gods/Taoism, 318n48; on Taoist Offerings ritual, 219; on Twelve Lords in Ming dynasty texts, 323n96
Secret Essentials of the Most High on Assembling the Perfected for Relief of the State and Deliverance of the People (T'ai-shang tsung-chen pi-yao) (Yuan Miao-tsung), 27, 33, 37, 44, 271, 272
Seidel, Anna, 42
self-mortification rituals, 235
Shang-ch'ing Ku-sui ling-wen kuei-lü. *See Spirit Code: A Numinous Text from the Marrow of Shang-ch'ing*
Shang-ch'ing t'ien-hsin cheng-fa. *See Correct Rites of Celestial Heart from Shang-ch'ing*
Shang-hsien Abbey, 101–5, 302n127
Shang Jih-hsuan, 199
Shang-kuan Miao-chi, 159
she, 286n45
Shen-hsiao Taoism, 312n4
Shen T'ing-jui, 304n135. *See also Veritable Record of the Two Perfected Lords* (Shen T'ing-jui); biography of, 99, 277, 278; bureaucratic model elements in texts of, 57; commentaries in texts of, 49, 274, 288n8; on Mt. Hua-kai after Two Immortals' ascent, 54; Northern Sung information in texts of, 97; on Shang-hsien Abbey, 104; teacher search motif of, 51, 53
Shen-tsung (emperor), 303n135
Shih Te-yü, 135
Shrine of Beneficent Response, 312n19
Shu-chou, 326n13
Six Dynasties, 172
Skorupski, John, 11, 13
Smith, Robert J., 8
"sojourning gentlemen," 141, 313–14n47
Southern Perfected *(Nan-chen)* Abbey, 92

Southern Sung: appointment edict from, 187; dating of documents from, 272; description of, 16, 17; early evidence of Three Immortals worship in, 85–88; elite in (*see* elite); origins of Taoist practitioners in capital, 179; origins of Taoist practitioners not in capital, 180; Taoist practitioners and locality in, 175–76; texts of, 56; written sources on Three Immortals, 271, 278 (*see also specific written sources*)
Spain, 326n16
Spirit Code: A Numinous Text from the Marrow of Shang-ch'ing (Shang-ch'ing ku-sui ling-wen kui-lü) (Teng Yu-kung), 27; authorship and dating of, 271–77; on Celestial Heart code, 33–34, 37, 286n41; on Celestial Heart masters, 44; contrasts with other texts, 287n59; dating of, 272–73, 276
spirit mediums, reasons for, 201–2, 235–36, 253, 317n45
spirit officers (*shen-chiang*), 31, 149
spirits, penal code and, 33–34, 287n59
spirit troops (*shen-ping*), 31, 48
Spirit Turtle Ridge, 147, 157, 160
Spiro, Melford, 283n21
State: Celestial Heart sect and responsibilities of, 190; court and Taoism, 173–81; enfeoffment of gods (*see* enfeoffments: State and local gods); Four Immortals and, 135–36; Fu-chou elite and, 116–21; gods as metaphor for, 3, 4, 13–14, 141–42, 257, 259; gods of, 20, 138–39, 247, 286n41; local cults and, 103–5, 143, 145–46, 207, 247; local officials and, 188–95; Offerings ritual and, 222–23; Ou-yang Ch'e case and, 117–20; symbolic resistance to, 245–46; Three Immortals cult and, 73–75, 101–5, 144; Two Perfected Lords and, 73–75
Stein, Rolf A., 42, 73
Stone Cavern of Mt. Chün, 153
Stove God, 258–60, 324n128
Strickmann, Michael, 27, 210, 286–87n59
Su Shih, 105
Sun Ti, 22, 92–93, 297nn54,55
Sung An-kuo, 194
Sung China: general description of, 14–18; penal code in, 285n26; religious variety in, 18–21

Sung hsing-t'ung, 285n26
Sung hui-yao, 102, 103, 302n127
Survey of Taoist Literature, Tenth to Seventeenth Centuries (Boltz), 271–72
Sutton, Donald, 234–36
Sword's Edge Ridge, 65, 300n85
symbols, gods as, 13–14. *See also* gods

Table of the Three Realms, 219, 220, 229
Ta-ch'ien god (God of Beneficent Response), 100, 128, 168, 181, 312n19, 315n16
T'ai-ho period, 293n8
T'ai-k'ang Teng lineage offering, 228
T'ai-p'ing huan-yü chi. See *Record of the Imperial Domains in the T'ai-p'ing Era*
T'ai-shang tsung-chen pi-yao. See *Secret Essentials of the Most High on Assembling the Perfected for Relief of the State and Deliverance of the People*
Taiwan, 45, 166, 216–23, 239, 240, 250, 255
talismans (*fu*), 30, 38, 193, 273–74, 285n16
Tanaka Issei, 226–28, 238, 241, 320–21n55
T'an Tzu-hsiao, 26, 48
T'an Wu-chen, 160
T'ang Chao, 90
T'ang dynasty, 284n33, 299n77
Tang-Sung transition, 15–16, 318n48
T'ang Yuan-ling, 298n59
Tao-hsien, 90
Tao-hsueh. *See* Learning of the Way
Taoism: authority and practitioners in, 150–51, 206–7, 236; Buddhism and (*see* Buddhism); bureaucratic model use in, 171, 189–95, 216–18 (*see also* bureaucratic model); Celestial Heart sect and, 42–46; changes in, 171–72; divisions in modern, 44, 239, 241–43, 244, 247–49; as framework for local cults, 211–12, 237–38, 240; healing as focus of, 27–28, 29, 30, 38; Hui-tsung and, 20, 27, 173, 197, 276, 312n4; lay participants in (*see* ordinary (lay) people); market and, 197–205, 269, 317–18n47, 318n48, 322n83; non-Taoist gods and rites of, 248–49; Offerings rituals, 223–25, 237–39, 244, 246, 249 (*see also* Offering ceremonies); ordination and, 44, 45, 113, 197, 306–7n164; origins of Mt. Lung-hu Taoists, 183; origins of Mt. Mao Taoists, 182; pantheon of, 210–11, 230,

247–49; personal model in, 166, 267, 319–20n31; professional religious class in, 67, 113, 148–55, 208–9, 215–16, 244–45, 287n64, 313n33, 317n46; purchase of ordinations in, 197; ritual and liturgy in, 219, 321n57, 322nn83,86 (*see also* Offering ceremonies); single-systems-of-meanings argument and, 208–9; State court and, 173–81; State enfeoffments and, 181–88; State local officials and, 189–95; symbolic resistance to, 245–46; Three Immortals cult and, 167–70 (*see also* Three Immortals cult); translocal network of practitioners of, 175–76, 177, 179, 180, 202–4; vegetarianism and, 322n79; Western scholars on pantheon of, 210–11. *See also* Divine Empyrean sect *(shen-hsiao)*

tao-ku. *See* Way-bone
tao-shih. *See* "gentleman of the Way"
Tao Te Ching, 294n23
Tea-Brewing Hollow, 299n81
teacher/student motif: in accounts of Wang Wen-ch'ing, 159–60, 163, 164–65; personal versus bureaucratic, 166–67; in Three Immortals cult, 51, 53, 58–59, 121, 122, 124, 130
Te-ch'ing Chün, 326n13
Te-hsiu. *See* Wu Mien
Teng Ch'ih-ju, 298n59
Teng Ssu-huan, 142
Teng Tzu-yang, 135
Teng Yu-kung, 36, 42; as author of *Correct Rites* and *Spirit Code*, 271–77; Boltz on dates of, 271–72, 284n2; Celestial Heart code and, 33–34; on Celestial Heart masters, 44; on Jao Tung-t-'ien and transmission of rites, 166; on Jao Tung-t-'ien's discovery of texts, 40; parallels with Yuan Miao-tsung, 284n3; preface to *Correct Rites* on Three Immortals, 39; texts of, 27 (see also *Correct Rites of Celestial Heart from Shang-ch'ing* (Teng Yu-kung); *Spirit Code: A Numinous Text from the Marrow of Shang-ch'ing* (Teng Yu-kung)); text submitted to emperor, 286n55
Ten Kingdoms, 49
Three Halls god, 36
Three Immortals cult, 4. *See also* Mt. Hua-Kai; abbeys and, 77–80 (*see also* names of specific abbeys); authority and, 71–72, 116,

123–24, 130; beliefs and practices associated with, 21–24; bureaucracy and, 168; Celestial Heart sect and, 36, 39–40, 47–48, 56–57, 69–70; dating of beginning of, 85, 98–99; enfeoffment and, 116, 144, 184–85, 303n135; Four Immortals cult in relation to, 73, 115–16; Huang Chen and, 137–44; Hung Mai cook story of, 13, 69, 296n33; journey motif in, 49, 50–51, 53, 54–56, 89, 124, 127; kinship and, 118–19, 122–23, 272; local cults and, 4, 72–73, 130–37; locality and, 21, 54, 56, 124, 168–69; miracle stories and, 62, 132, 133, 263; mountains associated with, 80–82, 85–87; Northern Sung on (*see* Northern Sung: written sources on Three Immortals); Offerings and (*see* Offering ceremonies); opponents of, 137–44; in parallel narratives, 111–12; personal relationships to, 62–65, 94, 263; in poetry, 92–97, 106, 135, 312n20; prayer and direct intercession of, 23–24; punishment and, 68–70; reason for secular elite adoption of, 116–17; secular elite and, 21, 85, 90, 96–97, 112, 116–17, 124–25, 130; single system of meanings and, 208; Southern Sung on, 85–88, 271, 278 (*see also specific written sources*); spread of, 91; State and, 73–75, 101–5, 144; Taoists and, 167–70; teacher/student motif in, 51, 53, 58–59, 121, 122, 124, 130; texts of (see *Verities of the Three Perfected Lords Fu-ch'iu, Wang, and Kuo of Hua-kai Mountain*); thunder and lightning deities and, 301n89; titles of, 297nn49,50; vows and, 67–69
Three Lords cult, 17–18
Three Perfected Lords cult, 31, 39
Three Pure, 39–40, 113, 207, 269, 276, 288n4, 322n76
Three Radiants, 29, 31
Three Sages, 200, 317n44
Three Worthies, 200, 317n44
T'ien-hsin cheng-fa. *See Correct Rites of Celestial Heart*
T'ien Hou (Ma Tsu), 227, 228, 240
Tiger-Track Rock, 299n72
titles, of gods, 181, 188, 297nn49,50, 302n126
"Tower for Viewing the Immortals," 88

Tower of the Flocking Kingfishers, 89
"transformation by refinement," 30
Tseng Chao, 81–82, 83, 86, 87, 130, 131
Tseng Chi-li, 86, 87, 92, 111, 305n149;
    kinship relationships of, 130, 294n21;
    poetry of, 83–84, 89, 115, 264, 294n22;
    preface of, 83, 85
Tseng Feng, 88, 300n87
Tseng Kung, 97
Tseng Pu, 81, 83, 85, 86, 103, 120, 130, 295n28
Tseng Tsai, 294n21
Tso Chuan, 142
Tsou Fen, 166–67
Tsou Pen, 272
Tu Hsien-hsing, 79
Tu Kao, 168, 313n47
Tu-jen ching, 313n42
Tu To, 313n47
Tu Tzu-hsin, 169
t'u-ti kung. See Tudi Gong
Tudi Gong *(t'u-ti kung)*, 254. *See also* gods, local
T'ung-chih lueh, 273
Turner, Victor, 8
Twelve Immortals of West Mountain, 60
Twelve Royal Lords Offering, 242–43, 251, 267, 323n96
Two Perfected Lords, 130. *See also* Kuo, Lord; Three Immortals cult; Wang, Lord; ascent of, 53–54, 57–58, 95, 129, 282n2, 308n26; enfeoffment of, 184; kinship of, 61–62; origin myths of, 1–2; sites associated with, 87–88; State and, 73–75. *See also* Three Perfected Lords cult
Tzu-hsiao Abbey, 91

Unities and Diversities in Chinese Religion (Weller), 324n124

vegetarianism, Taoism and, 322n79
The Veritable Record of Ta-ch'ien (Liu Hsun), 128, 168–69
Veritable Record of the Two Perfected Lords (Shen T'ing-jui): bureaucratic model in, 57, 59–60, 123, 290–91n38, 304n135; versus commentary in, 288n8; dating of, 98–99, 274; on Jao Tung-t'ien, 274; journey motif in, 51, 53, 54; miracle stories in, 60, 62–65, 98, 99–101, 123, 289n35; on Mt. Hua-Kai, 49–51, 53; primary commentary in, 54–55, 56, 58–59, 97, 133, 279, 288n14; secondary commentary in, 56, 97, 279, 289n14
Verities of Mt. Hua-kai (Chang Yuan-shu), 49, 99, 112, 113, 127–28, 277, 290n35, 292n59
Verities of the Three Perfected Lords Fu-ch'iu, Wang, and Kuo of Hua-kai Mountain (Hua-kai shan Fu-ch'iu Wang Kuo san chen-chün shih-shih) (Shen T'ing-jui): authority relationships in, 57; authorship of, 277–80; bureaucratic imagery in, 57–58, 63–64, 133; on Ch'i-chen Abbey, 78–79; Ch'ung-hsien Abbey incident in, 101–5; dating of, 60, 274, 277–80, 302nn106,115,119; differences from Celestial Heart texts, 47–48, 56–57; elite and, 112; on Four Immortals, 60, 135; on Fu-ch'iu, 60–61; on Hsiang-fu Abbey, 80; journey motif in, 89; on lives of the Two Lords, 49–51; on local cults, 72–73, 135; miracle stories in, 105, 106–10, 133, 209, 250–51, 278, 298n62; on Offerings, 72, 206, 212–13, 226; single system of meanings and, 208
vows: for Offering ceremonies, 65–67, 226, 291n49; parallels in, 268–69; personal model and, 265; secular practices and, 67–69

Wang, Lord: ascent of, 129, 308n26; authority and, 133; enfeoffments of, 184, 303n135; journey motif in accounts about, 49, 50, 89; kinship relationships of, 61; Tea-Brewing Hollow and, 299n81; Tiger-Track Rock and, 299n72
Wang An-shih, 302n126; appointment edict by, 186–87; as Fu-chou man, 17; inscriptions of, 80–81; as Northern Sung reformer, 16, 103, 145; poetry and Hua-kai cult, 97
Wang Fa-chin, 247
Wang Fang-p'ing, 50, 61, 122, 289n34
Wang Hsiang-chih, 76–77
Wang Hsi-chih, 294n23
Wang K'o-ming, 106, 274, 277–78, 279, 280
Wang Ku, 314n8
Wang Kuei, 302n126
Wang Po, 59

Wang T'ing-jui, 192
Wang T'ing-ssu, 61
Wang-tzu Chin, 59, 60, 297n50
Wang Tzu-hua (Fire Master). *See* Fire Master (Wang Tzu-hua)
Wang Wen-ch'ing: accounts of death of, 153–54; accounts of life of, 147, 152, 156–57, 161, 162–63; Chao reference and dating of, 311n3; commemorative essay on, 155–57; court role of, 173, 174–75; Divine Empyrean sect and, 120; as extraordinary man, 162–63; as Fire Master, 28–29; inscriptions for, 157–58, 160–61; as local god, 154–62; on practitioner skills, 165; Ta Ch'ien and locality, 168; in Taoist hierarchy, 312n4; as Taoist practitioner, 148–54; teacher/student motif in accounts of, 159–60, 163, 164–65
Wang Yang-ch'en, 295n27
Wang Yeh, 168
Water Margin, 234
Way-bone (*tao-ku*), 163, 164, 165. *See also* bone
Way-man Mao, 278
Way of Filial Piety, 247
Way-rites, 155
Wei kingdom, 293n8
Wei Liao-weng, 120
Wei Su, 96, 97, 298n59
Weller, Robert, 3, 261, 267; on gods and government officials, 257; views compared to Hymes's, 262, 324nn4,124; on personal relations model, 166
Wen, Marshall, 249
Wilson, Stephen, 269
Wolf, Arthur, 3, 8, 252, 258, 259, 263
Writings on Exhaling Wind and Rain, 163
Wu Ch'ao-tsung, 117
Wu Ch'eng (Southern Sung participant in Three Immortals cult), 302n115; kinship relations of and elite, 306n150; in miracle stories, 108
Wu Ch'eng (Yuan author): inscriptions of, 90–91, 296nn43,44, 305n150; on spread of Hua-kai cult, 92, 111, 291n38
Wu Ch'ih, 305n148, 305nn148,150
Wu family, 118, 297n55, 305nn146,150
Wu Hang, 107, 108, 117, 118
Wu Hao, 306n150

Wu Hsieh, 118
Wu Hsun, 305n150, 306n150
Wu I, 96, 106, 298n60, 301n100, 305n150
Wu Jui, 81, 131, 309–10n42
Wu Kuang, 118
Wu Mien, 108, 117, 119, 305n150
Wu Shan-fu, 107, 305n146
Wu-shang huang-lu ta-chai li-ch'eng i. *See Ceremonial Forms for the Performance and Completion of the Unsurpassed Grand Retreat of the Yellow Register*
Wu Shih-liang, 200–201
Wu T'ao, 117
Wu Te-hsiu, 118
Wu Tsung, 107, 305n150
Wu Yu-lin, 107, 305n146

Yan, Yunxiang, 265–66
Yeh Fa-shan, 135, 142, 163
Yellow Caps (*huang-kuan*), 45, 160, 213, 215
Yellow Emperor, 281n1
Yellow Register Offering, 45, 169
Yellow Register Retreat, 44, 218, 246
Yen Chen-ch'ing, 140; on ascent of Two Lords, 53–54; inscription of, 2, 49–50, 98, 104, 121–22, 123, 304n135
Yen Shu, 97
Yen Ssu-i, 118
Yen-hsien, 206, 213
Yin-chen Abbey, 115
Yin-chü t'ung-i. *See General Views of a Dweller in Reclusion*
yin-ssu. *See* improper worship
Yu Tao-shou, 166, 272
Yü, Ms., 110
Yü Chi: commemorative essay on Wang Wen-ch'ing, 155–57; on Four Immortals, 134, 135–36; inscription on Wang Wen-ch'ing, 157–58, 160–61; inscriptions of, 157–58, 160–61, 306n158; on Mt. Hsiang name change, 137; poetry and, 298n59; poetry and kinship of, 96–97, 110
Yuan Chiang, 302n126
Yuan Miao-tsung, 36; as Celestial Heart master, 40; parallels to Teng Yu-kung, 284n3; *Secret Essentials* of, 27, 33, 271, 272, 284n1; on talismans, 273–74
Yuan of Ch'u (prince), 60
Yuan-pao Abbey, 296n33

Yuan T'ing-chih, 148, 153, 163, 164, 165
Yuan dynasty, 90, 96–97, 297n49
Yuan-ti of Chin, 61, 123
Yuan-ti of Wei, 308n26
Yueh Fei, 119
Yueh Shih, 77–81, 97, 104, 292n5

Yung-chung Abbey, 288n14
Yung-hsing Abbey, 89
Yü-ti chi-sheng. See *The Scenery of the Empire Recorded*
Yü-t'ing Abbey, 301n101
Yü-wen Ts'ui-chung, 174

www.ingramcontent.com/pod-product-compliance
Lightning Source LLC
Chambersburg PA
CBHW031959220426
43664CB00005B/78